Lecture Notes in Computer Science 7349

Commenced Publication in 1973
Founding and Former Series Editors:
Gerhard Goos, Juris Hartmanis, and Jan van Leeuwen

Editorial Board

David Hutchison
  Lancaster University, UK
Takeo Kanade
  Carnegie Mellon University, Pittsburgh, PA, USA
Josef Kittler
  University of Surrey, Guildford, UK
Jon M. Kleinberg
  Cornell University, Ithaca, NY, USA
Alfred Kobsa
  University of California, Irvine, CA, USA
Friedemann Mattern
  ETH Zurich, Switzerland
John C. Mitchell
  Stanford University, CA, USA
Moni Naor
  Weizmann Institute of Science, Rehovot, Israel
Oscar Nierstrasz
  University of Bern, Switzerland
C. Pandu Rangan
  Indian Institute of Technology, Madras, India
Bernhard Steffen
  TU Dortmund University, Germany
Madhu Sudan
  Microsoft Research, Cambridge, MA, USA
Demetri Terzopoulos
  University of California, Los Angeles, CA, USA
Doug Tygar
  University of California, Berkeley, CA, USA
Gerhard Weikum
  Max Planck Institute for Informatics, Saarbruecken, Germany

Antonio Vallecillo   Juha-Pekka Tolvanen
Ekkart Kindler   Harald Störrle
Dimitris Kolovos (Eds.)

Modelling Foundations and Applications

8th European Conference, ECMFA 2012
Kgs. Lyngby, Denmark, July 2-5, 2012
Proceedings

Springer

Volume Editors

Antonio Vallecillo
Universidad de Málaga, ETSI Informática
Campus de Teatinos, Bulevar Louis Pasteur 35, 29071 Málaga, Spain
E-mail: av@lcc.uma.es

Juha-Pekka Tolvanen
MetaCase
Ylistönmäentie 31, 40500 Jyväskylä, Finland
E-mail: jpt@metacase.com

Ekkart Kindler
Harald Störrle
Technical University of Denmark
Department of Informatics and Mathematical Modelling
Richard Petersens Plads, 2800 Kgs. Lyngby, Denmark
E-mail: {eki, hsto}@imm.dtu.dk

Dimitris Kolovos
University of York, Department of Computer Science
Deramore Lane, York, YO10 5GH, United Kingdom
E-mail: d.kolovos@cs.york.ac.uk

ISSN 0302-9743   e-ISSN 1611-3349
ISBN 978-3-642-31490-2   e-ISBN 978-3-642-31491-9
DOI 10.1007/978-3-642-31491-9
Springer Heidelberg Dordrecht London New York

Library of Congress Control Number: 2012940653

CR Subject Classification (1998): D.2.1-2, D.2.4-5, D.2.7, D.2.11, D.2, D.3, F.3, K.6

LNCS Sublibrary: SL 2 – Programming and Software Engineering

© Springer-Verlag Berlin Heidelberg 2012
This work is subject to copyright. All rights are reserved, whether the whole or part of the material is concerned, specifically the rights of translation, reprinting, re-use of illustrations, recitation, broadcasting, reproduction on microfilms or in any other way, and storage in data banks. Duplication of this publication or parts thereof is permitted only under the provisions of the German Copyright Law of September 9, 1965, in its current version, and permission for use must always be obtained from Springer. Violations are liable to prosecution under the German Copyright Law.
The use of general descriptive names, registered names, trademarks, etc. in this publication does not imply, even in the absence of a specific statement, that such names are exempt from the relevant protective laws and regulations and therefore free for general use.

Typesetting: Camera-ready by author, data conversion by Scientific Publishing Services, Chennai, India

Printed on acid-free paper

Springer is part of Springer Science+Business Media (www.springer.com)

Preface

The 2012 European Conference on Modelling Foundations and Applications (ECMFA 2012) was held at the Technical University of Denmark (DTU), Kgs. Lyngby, Denmark, during July 2–5, 2012.

ECMFA is the key European conference aiming at advancing the techniques and furthering the underlying knowledge related to model-driven engineering. Model-driven engineering (MDE) is a software development approach based on the use of models for the specification, design, analysis, synthesis, deployment, testing and maintenance of complex software systems, aiming to produce high-quality systems at lower costs. In the past seven years, ECMFA has provided an ideal venue for interaction among researchers interested in MDE both from academia and industry. The eighth edition of the conference covered major advances in foundational research and industrial applications of MDE.

In 2012, the Program Committee received 106 abstracts, which finally materialized into 81 full paper submissions. From these, 20 Foundations track papers and 10 Applications track papers were accepted for presentation at the conference and publication in these proceedings. This indicates the level of competition that occurred during the selection process. The submission and the reviewing processes were administered by EasyChair, which greatly facilitated these tasks. Papers on all aspects of MDE were received, including topics such as architectural modeling and product lines, code generation, domain-specific modeling, metamodeling, model analysis and verification, model management, model transformation and simulation. The breadth of topics and the high quality of the results presented in these accepted papers demonstrate the maturity and vibrancy of the field.

The ECMFA 2012 keynote speakers were Henrik Lönn, from VOLVO Technology in Sweden, and Ed Seidewitz, from Model Driven Solutions in the USA. Abstracts of their talks are included in these proceedings. We thank them very much for accepting our invitation and for their enlightening talks.

We are grateful to our Program Committee members for providing their expertise and quality and timely reviews. Their helpful and constructive feedback to all authors is most appreciated. We thank the ECMFA Conference Steering Committee for their advice and help. We also thank our sponsors, both keynote speakers and all authors who submitted papers to ECMFA 2012. Alfred Hofmann and the Springer team were really helpful with the publication of this volume.

July 2012

Antonio Vallecillo
Juha-Pekka Tolvanen
Ekkart Kindler
Harald Störrle
Dimitris Kolovos

Organization

Program Committee

Jan Øyvind Aagedal	Norse Solutions
Vasco Amaral	FCT, Universidade Nova de Lisboa, Portugal
Terry Bailey	Vicinay Cadenas, S.A.
Stephen Barrett	Concordia University, Canada
Mariano Belaunde	Orange R&D
Reda Bendraou	INRIA Bretagne Atlantique Rennes, France
Jorn Bettin	SoftMetaWare
Xavier Blanc	Bordeaux 1 University, France
Behzad Bordbar	University of Birmingham, UK
Marco Brambilla	Politecnico di Milano, Italy
Jordi Cabot	INRIA-École des Mines de Nantes, France
Tony Clark	Middlesex University, UK
Benoit Combemale	IRIT CNRS
Diarmuid Corcoran	Ericsson AB
Zhen Ru Dai	University of Applied Science Hamburg, Germany
Juan Antonio De La Puente	Universidad Politécnica de Madrid, Spain
Zinovy Diskin	University of Waterloo, Canada
Gregor Engels	University of Paderborn, Germany
Anne Etien	University of Lille and INRIA Lille Nord-Europe, France
Stephan Flake	Orga Systems GmbH, Germany
Robert France	Colorado State University, USA
Mathias Fritzsche	SAP Research CEC Belfast, UK
Jesus Garcia-Molina	Universidad de Murcia, Spain
Sebastien Gerard	CEA, LIST
Marie-Pierre Gervais	LIP6 and Université de Paris 10 Nanterre, France
Martin Gogolla	University of Bremen, Germany
Jeff Gray	University of Alabama, USA
Esther Guerra	Universidad Autónoma de Madrid, Spain
Michael R. Hansen	Technical University of Denmark, Denmark
Reiko Heckel	University of Leicester, UK
Markus Heller	SAP Research Karlsruhe, SAP AG, Germany
Andreas Hoffmann	Fraunhofer, Germany
Teemu Kanstrén	VTT
Gabor Karsai	Vanderbilt University, USA

Thomas Kuehne   Victoria University of Wellington, New Zealand
Jochen Kuester   IBM Research
Vinay Kulkarni   Tata Research Development and Design Centre,
                          India
Ivan Kurtev   University of Twente, The Netherlands
Roberto Erik Lopez-Herrejon Institute for Systems Engineering and
                          Automation, Johannes Kepler University,
                          Austria
Dragan Milicev   University of Belgrade, Serbia
Parastoo Mohagheghi   SINTEF, Norway
Birger Møller-Pedersen University of Oslo, Norway
Tor Neple   Norse Solutions AS
Alfonso Pierantonio   University of L'Aquila, Italy
Ivan Porres   Åbo Akademi University, Finland
Olli-Pekka Puolitaival F-Secure Corporation
Arend Rensink   University of Twente, The Netherlands
Laurent Rioux   THALES R&T
Tom Ritter   Fraunhofer FOKUS, Germany
Louis Rose   The University of York, UK
Julia Rubin   IBM Research at Haifa, Israel
Bernhard Rumpe   RWTH Aachen University, Germany
Andrey Sadovykh   Softeam
Houari Sahraoui   DIRO, Université de Montréal, Canada
Bernhard Schaetz   TU München, Germany
Douglas Schmidt   Vanderbilt University
Andy Schürr   TU Darmstadt, Germany
Bran Selic   Malina Software Corp.
Renuka Sindhgatta   IBM Research - India
John Slaby   Raytheon Company
Jim Steel   The University of Queensland, Australia
Alin Stefanescu   University of Pitesti, Romania
Gabriele Taentzer   Philipps-Universität Marburg, Germany
Francois Terrier   CEA, LIST
Juha-Pekka Tolvanen   Metacase
Salvador Trujillo   IKERLAN Research Centre
Andreas Ulrich   Siemens AG
Antonio Vallecillo   University of Malaga, Spain
Ragnhild Van Der Straeten Vrije Universiteit Brussel, Belgium
Pieter Van Gorp   Eindhoven University of Technology,
                          The Netherlands
Marten J. Van Sinderen University of Twente, The Netherlands
Hans Vangheluwe   McGill University
Daniel Varro   Budapest University of Technology and
                          Economics, Hungary
Cristina Vicente-Chicote Technical University of Cartagena, Spain

Markus Voelter   Independent
Michael Von Der Beeck   BMW Group
Edward Willink   Eclipse Modeling Project
Manuel Wimmer   Business Informatics Group, Vienna University
                                of Technology, Austria
Tao Yue   Carleton University and Simula Research
                                Laboratory
Gefei Zhang   arvato systems
Olaf Zimmermann   IBM Research GmbH
Steffen Zschaler   King's College London, UK

Additional Reviewers

Abbors, Fredrik   De Mol, Maarten   Lauder, Marius
Al-Lail, Mustafa   Di Ruscio, Davide   Liu, Qichao
Ali, Shaukat   Duddy, Keith   Look, Markus
Almeida, Marcos   El Kouhen, Amine   Mallet, Frédéric
Anjorin, Anthony   Eramo, Romina   Monperrus, Martin
Aranega, Vincent   Espinazo-Pagán, Javier   Noyrit, Florian
Bajwa, Imran   Fatemi, Hassan   Pedro, Luís
Bapodra, Mayur   Fazal-Baqaie, Masud   Planas, Elena
Barat, Souvik   Fritzsche, Mathias   Radermacher, Ansgar
Barroca, Bruno   Gerth, Christian   Rath, Istvan
Baudry, Benoit   Haber, Arne   Rossini, Alessandro
Blouin, Arnaud   Hamann, Lars   Saller, Karsten
Brucker, Achim D.   Hesari, Shokoofeh   Sanchez, Oscar
Brunelière, Hugo   Horst, Andreas   Soltenborn, Christian
Burgueño, Loli   Horváth, Ákos   Strüber, Daniel
Büttner, Fabian   Ingles-Romero, Juan F.   Sun, Wuliang
Cadavid, Juan   Iovino, Ludovico   Truscan, Dragos
Cichos, Harald   Izsó, Benedek   Wouters, Laurent
Criado, Javier   Jalali, Arash   Wozniak, Ernest
Cuccuru, Arnaud   Jnidi, Rim   Ziane, Mikal
Dang, Duc-Hanh   Khan, Tamim
De Lara, Juan   Kuhlmann, Mirco

Table of Contents

Executable UML: From Multi-domain to Multi-core 1
  Ed Seidewitz

Models Meeting Automotive Design Challenges 2
  Henrik Lönn

A Commutative Model Composition Operator to Support Software
Adaptation.. 4
  Sébastien Mosser, Mireille Blay-Fornarino, and Laurence Duchien

Comparative Study of Model-Based and Multi-Domain System
Engineering Approaches for Industrial Settings 20
  *Anjelika Votintseva, Petra Witschel, Nikolaus Regnat, and
  Philipp Emanuel Stelzig*

Strengthening SAT-Based Validation of UML/OCL Models
by Representing Collections as Relations 32
  Mirco Kuhlmann and Martin Gogolla

Model Interchange Testing: A Process and a Case Study 49
  Maged Elaasar and Yvan Labiche

An Internal Domain-Specific Language for Constructing OPC UA
Queries and Event Filters 62
  Thomas Goldschmidt and Wolfgang Mahnke

Combining UML Sequence and State Machine Diagrams for Data-Flow
Based Integration Testing 74
  Lionel Briand, Yvan Labiche, and Yanhua Liu

Model Transformations for Migrating Legacy Models: An Industrial
Case Study... 90
  *Gehan M.K. Selim, Shige Wang, James R. Cordy, and
  Juergen Dingel*

Derived Features for EMF by Integrating Advanced Model Queries 102
  István Ráth, Ábel Hegedüs, and Dániel Varró

A Lightweight Approach for Managing XML Documents with MDE
Languages 118
  *Dimitrios S. Kolovos, Louis M. Rose, James Williams,
  Nicholas Matragkas, and Richard F. Paige*

Bridging the Gap between Requirements and Aspect State Machines to
Support Non-functional Testing: Industrial Case Studies 133
  Tao Yue and Shaukat Ali

Badger: A Regression Planner to Resolve Design Model
Inconsistencies.. 146
  Jorge Pinna Puissant, Ragnhild Van Der Straeten, and Tom Mens

Aspect-Oriented Modeling of Mutual Exclusion in UML State
Machines 162
  Gefei Zhang

TexMo: A Multi-language Development Environment 178
  Rolf-Helge Pfeiffer and Andrzej Wąsowski

On-the-Fly Emendation of Multi-level Models 194
  Colin Atkinson, Ralph Gerbig, and Bastian Kennel

Specifying Refinement Relations in Vertical Model Transformations 210
  Jan Rieke and Oliver Sudmann

Model-Based Automated and Guided Configuration of Embedded
Software Systems 226
  *Razieh Behjati, Shiva Nejati, Tao Yue, Arnaud Gotlieb, and
  Lionel Briand*

Lightweight String Reasoning for OCL.............................. 244
  Fabian Büttner and Jordi Cabot

Domain-Specific Textual Meta-Modelling Languages for Model Driven
Engineering 259
  Juan de Lara and Esther Guerra

Metamodel Based Methodology for Dynamic Component Systems 275
  Gabor Batori, Zoltan Theisz, and Domonkos Asztalos

Bidirectional Model Transformation with Precedence Triple Graph
Grammars 287
  Marius Lauder, Anthony Anjorin, Gergely Varró, and Andy Schürr

A Timed Automata-Based Method to Analyze EAST-ADL Timing
Constraint Specifications.. 303
  Tahir Naseer Qureshi, De-Jiu Chen, and Martin Törngren

Code Generation Nirvana 319
  Petr Smolik and Pavel Vitkovsky

A Plug-in Based Approach for UML Model Simulation................ 328
  *Alek Radjenovic, Richard F. Paige, Louis M. Rose,
  Jim Woodcock, and Steve King*

MADES: A Tool Chain for Automated Verification of UML Models of
Embedded Systems... 340
    Alek Radjenovic, Nicholas Matragkas, Richard F. Paige,
    Matteo Rossi, Alfredo Motta, Luciano Baresi, and
    Dimitrios S. Kolovos

Time Properties Verification Framework for UML-MARTE Safety
Critical Real-Time Systems 352
    Ning Ge and Marc Pantel

Unification of Compiled and Interpreter-Based Pattern Matching
Techniques 368
    Gergely Varró, Anthony Anjorin, and Andy Schürr

OCL-Based Runtime Monitoring of Applications with Protocol State
Machines 384
    Lars Hamann, Oliver Hofrichter, and Martin Gogolla

On Model Subtyping 400
    Clément Guy, Benoît Combemale, Steven Derrien,
    Jim R.H. Steel, and Jean-Marc Jézéquel

BOB the Builder: A Fast and Friendly Model-to-PetriNet
Transformer 416
    Ulrich Winkler, Mathias Fritzsche, Wasif Gilani, and Alan Marshall

Solving Acquisition Problems Using Model-Driven Engineering 428
    Frank R. Burton, Richard F. Paige, Louis M. Rose,
    Dimitrios S. Kolovos, Simon Poulding, and Simon Smith

Author Index 445

Executable UML:
From Multi-domain to Multi-core

Ed Seidewitz

Vice President, Model Driven Architecture Services a Model Driven Solutions
(a division of Data Access Technologies, Inc.), United States
ed-s@modeldriven.com

Abstract. Modeling problem domains independently of technology domains is the basis for software that is adaptable to both changing business requirements and advancing technical platforms. Moreover, implementation-independent executable models allow problem-domain validation to be built right into agile conversations with customers. These validated models can then be compiled to a target implementation platform of choice.

But, unlike traditional programming, executable modeling abstracts behavior from the problem domain, rather than abstracting from hardware computational paradigms. In particular, executable models naturally embrace concurrency, because problem domain behavior is concurrent. And, as we move into an era of multiple cores, dealing with concurrency is rapidly moving from a peripheral to a central issue in mainstream programming.

Our programming languages today, on the other hand, are too platform specific, still based too much on, and abstracting too little from, traditional sequential, von Neumann hardware architectures. What we need is a way to model problem domains that can then be compiled to the highly concurrent multi-core platforms around the corner as easily as the traditional platforms of yesterday. This is exactly what executable modeling offers.

Work over the last few years has now provided new standards for precise execution semantics for a subset of UML and an associated action language. Taking advantage of these new standards, executable UML holds out the promise of addressing some fundamental issues for the next generation of programming - from multi-domain to multi-core.

Models Meeting Automotive Design Challenges

Henrik Lönn

Systems and Architecture, Department of Mechatronics & Software
Volvo Technology, Gothenburg, Sweden
henrik.lonn@volvo.com

Abstract. Automotive systems are increasingly complex and critical. Their development accounts for a considerable share of the budget, both in terms of cost and time. The development process is complex, involving multiple development teams in varying disciplines, roles, departments, companies and locations, each using their own tools and notations.

One contribution to meeting these challenges is to use a common ontology that integrates information according to recognized patterns, an Architecture Description Language. The purpose of EAST-ADL is to capture engineering information related to automotive electrical/electronic (E/E) system development, from early phase to final implementation. The system implementation is represented using AUTOSAR, i.e. EAST-ADL is complementary to AUTOSAR, adding information beyond the software architecture to serve engineering work already in early phases.

The EAST-ADL model has a core part representing the E/E system, which interfaces to an Environment model for near and far environment. Extensions for cross-cutting concerns or evolving modelling concepts annotate the core elements with these additional aspects. One of the Extensions concerns dependability and captures information related to safety. Another extension captures system timing using events, event chains and timing constraints.

The EAST-ADL system model is organized in 4 abstraction levels, see Figure 1, from the *Vehicle Levels* abstract and solution-independent feature models over the *Analysis Levels* hardware independent functional models and the *Design Levels* hardware-allocated functional architecture to the *Implementation Level* AUTOSAR software and hardware architecture.

Based on an agreed modelling approach such as AUTOSAR and EAST-ADL, research and development on modelling technology, tools and methodology for automotive EE system development can continue more efficiently. Such results will allow the multitude of company specific approaches to be leveraged and gradually replaced by off-the shelf solutions.

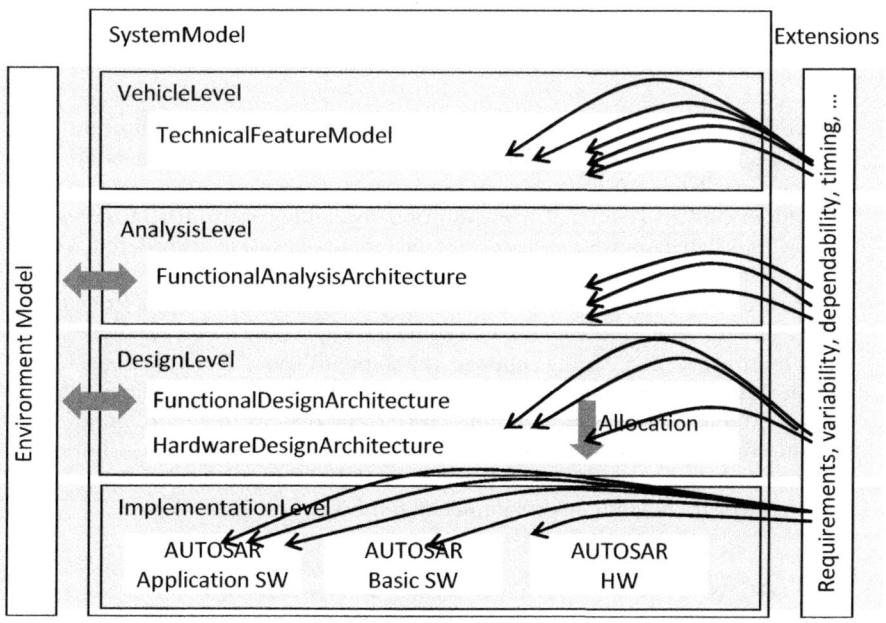

Fig. 1. EAST-ADL organization - core, plant and extensions

A Commutative Model Composition Operator to Support Software Adaptation[*]

Sébastien Mosser[1], Mireille Blay–Fornarino[2], and Laurence Duchien[3]

[1] SINTEF IKT, Oslo, Norway
sebastien.mosser@sintef.no
[2] I3S – UMR CNRS 7271 (formerly 6070), University Nice
Sophia–Antipolis, France
blay@polytech.unice.fr
[3] INRIA Lille–Nord Europe, LIFL – UMR CNRS 8022,
University of Lille 1, France
laurence.duchien@inria.fr

Abstract. The *adaptive software* paradigm supports the definition of software systems that are continuously adapted at run–time. An adaptation activates multiple features in the system, according to the current execution context (*e.g.*, CPU consumption, available bandwidth). However, the underlying approaches used to implement adaptation are ordered, *i.e.*, the order in which a set of features are turned on or off matters. Assuming feature definition as etched in stone, the identification of the *right* sequence is a difficult and time–consuming problem. We propose here a composition operator that intrinsically supports the commutativity of adaptations. Using this operator, one can minimize the number of ordered compositions in a system. It relies on an action–based approach, as this representation can support preexisting composition operators as well as our contribution in an uniform way. This approach is validated on the Service–Oriented Architecture domain, and is implemented using first–order logic.

1 Introduction

The *"adaptability"* of a software is defined through its capability to react to changes and consequently to adapt itself to new environments [24]. Adaptation is now considered as a first–class problem [19], and software must be developed with the ability of being adapted during their whole life–cycle, to properly support the emergence of new technologies and the obsolescence of legacy ones. Adaptation mechanisms strongly rely on composition operators to support the introduction (or removal) of new features inside adaptive systems [15]. For example, the detection of a sudden drop in network bandwidth turns on a cache feature, and thus triggers the composition of cache artifacts (*i.e.*, model elements)

---

[*] This work is partially funded by the EU Commission through the REMICS project (contract number 257793), the SINTEF strategic project MODERATES, the French Ministry of Higher Education and Research, Nord–Pas de Calais Regional Council and FEDER through the Contrat de Projets Etat Region Campus Intelligence Ambiante (CPER–CIA) 2007-2013.

with the existing system. Existing approaches used to support such compositions rely on order–dependent operators, *e.g.*, aspect weaving [12] or functional composition [1]. Thus, the order in which features are turned on or off matters.

This order–dependency triggers several issues in the context of adaptive systems, as the designer has to explicitly control this order. The model elements associated to a feature F are composed with the existing system s as soon as the adaptation engine identifies a situation that requires F to be present in s. An immediate problem is the adaptation of unforeseen elements introduced by other features which lead to unexpected results (so-called *fragile point-cut* problem in the aspect-oriented literature [9]). Thus, the implementation of such feature assets is difficult: it must take into account the implementation of all the other feature assets to be sure that its composition produces the expected system.

In this paper, **we propose a new composition operator (called *parallel*, and denoted as $\parallel$) that allows designers to minimise the number of ordered compositions** (and the associated issues, *e.g.*, non–deterministic result if two compositions cannot commute). Using this operator, it is possible to reify that several features are turned on independently of each others, ensuring commutativity at the composition level, by construction. Such a property helps to tame the complexity of feature definition, guarantees the determinism of the computed result and also ensures the consistency of the composed system, whatever the order of composition used at the implementation level is.

2 Motivations and Challenges

Motivations. The starting point of this study is the modelling of a *Car Crash Crisis Management System* (CCCMS), started in 2010. This case study was designed as a prototypical usage of aspect–oriented modelling techniques [13], involving multiple concerns that had to be composed in a non–trivial way with respect to the requirements document. During the elaboration of our response to this case study [21], we encountered several situation where multiple and different concerns had to be composed on the same element in the original model. Actually, this situation happened 40 times in this case study, and up to 5 concerns were composed on these *shared join points* (SJP). Thus, up to $5! = 120$ combinations can be used if we consider these compositions as sequential. More critically, these sequences do not lead to the same result, as some of them cannot commute safely! The designer has to identify which order has to be used for each SJP.

The second step that triggers our research of a new operator to support composition is the study of dynamic adaptation in the context of business processes. Where the models handled by the CCCMS were "simply" design models (*i.e.*, static), we describe in [22] a process used to support the dynamic adaptation and un-adaptation of running business processes. According to a *"models@run.time"* point of view, the adaptation of a running system is assimilated to the composition of new model elements with the model associated to the running system, and the propagation of the adapted model at the run-time level. But contrarily to the CCCMS, in this case, there is no human-in-the-loop to control the order of compositions. Based on *Complex–Event Processing* (CEP) techniques, the adaptation engine automatically triggers

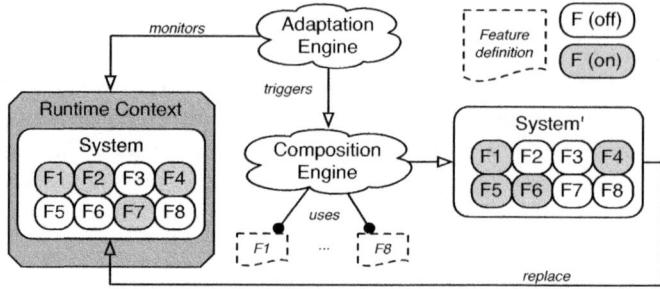

Fig. 1. Intrinsic relation between *adaptation* and *composition*

the needed composition, without any human intervention, as depicted in FIG. 1. We consider here a system s as the result of the composition of a set of features (here $s = \{F_1, F_2, F_4, F_7\}$). The adaptation engine monitors at run-time the execution context, and according to changes in this context, identify the new set of feature needed in the system ($s' = \{F_1, F_4, F_5, F_6\}$). It triggers the composition engine to properly compose all these features in order to build the adapted system s'. Then, the old system is replaced by the newly composed one, and the adaptation loop continue. As a consequence, the potential non-determinism of the composition process is a critical issue. The adaptation engine identifies a set of features needed in the system (*e.g.*, a cache, a local database, a low-energy consumption wifi driver) according to the current context, and if the composed system depends on the way these features are composed (*i.e.*, their order), the result of the adaptation process in not predictable. As a matter of fact, additional knowledge has to be *a-priori* stored in the adaptation engine to patch the composition directive generated by the CEP engine. This knowledge introduces ordering constraints needed to enact a correct sequence of compositions.

Running example. To illustrate our proposition, and for the sake of concision, we restrict the problem to its essence and use a simple model m to represent the system to be adapted. The associated class–diagram is depicted in FIG. 2(a). This model initially contains two classes C_1 and C_2. We also consider the two following adaptations:

S: This adaptation introduces a class SC in the given model, and adds an inheritance relation between all the top-level[1] classes and SC. It is a simplification of the modifications needed to introduce an *Observable* pattern into a model.
A: This adaptation introduces a class AC in the given model, and adds an aggregation relation between all the top-level classes and AC. This adaptation can be used to add a persistence manager at the higher level of abstraction and then supports instance persistence through polymorphism.

---

[1] A *top–level* class is defined here as a class that does not inherits from another one, *i.e.*, at the top-level of the inheritance hierarchy.

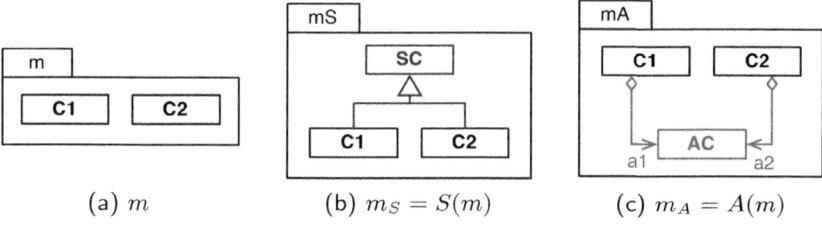

Fig. 2. Feature composition: $F(\mu)$

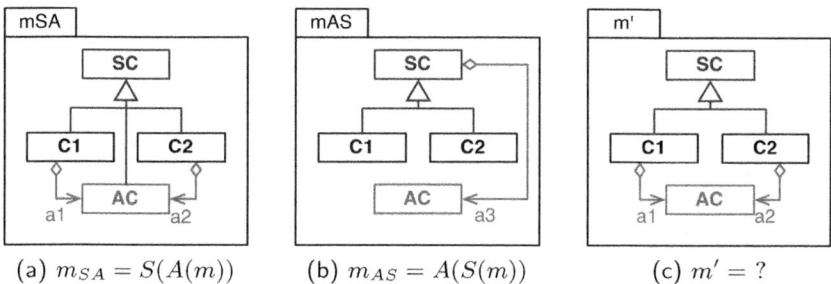

Fig. 3. Sequential composition ($S \bullet A \neq A \bullet S$)

Such adaptations represent *de facto* new features to be introduced (*i.e.*, composed) in the model. Batory et al. [2] use modern mathematics to model features and their introduction: *(i)* programs are constants, and *(ii)* features are functions that produce a program when applied to a program. Thus, we consider here a program tantamount a model, and we denote as $F(\mu)$ the fact that the model elements associated to the feature F are composed with the model μ (*i.e.*, F is a model transformation). We depict in FIG. 2(b) and FIG. 2(c) the two previously described features, separately composed with m.

According to this representation, the explicit ordering of feature introduction is modelled through functional composition: $(F \bullet G)(\mu) = F(G(\mu))$. In sequential composition, the commutativity of features depends on their internal definitions. As A and S both *(i)* modify all the available top-level classes and *(ii)* introduce a new one, their sequential composition cannot commute, as represented in FIG. 3(a) and FIG. 3(b). This issue highlights the fact that $\bullet$ is not commutative by essence: the order of the composition impacts the obtained model. As a consequence, this compositional model cannot be used to produce the model depicted in FIG. 3(c) without changing the implementation of A or S.

Challenges. An obvious solution is to consider that the features should not use quantified definitions (*i.e.*, avoid constructions like "for all top level classes do ...") but instantiated definitions instead (*i.e.*, use only constructions like "for C_1 and C_2, do ..."). Unfortunately, this approach scale with difficulty (in the CCCMS case study, a feature had to be applied at 27 different places), and does

not allow one to reuse a feature from a system to another one (usually, these
selectors are implemented as XPath expression to dynamically identify model
elements). Thus, to produce the model m', where A and S are introduced independently of each others, we need to define an explicitly unordered composition
operator, denoted as $||$. This operator is complementary to the $\bullet$ one, as it ensures commutativity of features composition when such a property is needed.
Several challenges need to be faced to define $||$:

$\mathcal{C}_1$: *Adaptation re-usability.* To support the reuse of an adaptation, a designer must be able to define an adaptation independently of the concrete models element defined in the targeted system (*e.g.*, using quantifiers, "for all ...").

$\mathcal{C}_2$: *Adequacy with "usual" composition operator such as aspects weaving or features composition.* The key idea is not to reinvent the wheel. We aim to propose a new operator that complements the others when an ordering is not explicitly needed.

$\mathcal{C}_3$: *Adaptation Isolation & Determinism.* If at the requirements level two features are not expressed as joint (*i.e.*, there is no explicit ordering dependencies between them), the composition operator must be able to reflect this decision and consequently ensure a deterministic result.

$\mathcal{C}_4$: *Inconsistency detection.* Through usual composition operator, both $S \bullet A$ and $A \bullet S$ lead to consistent (but different) models after composition. The composition operator must be able to identify inconsistencies that can be introduced during the process, if any.

The contribution of this paper aims to tackle these challenges, through the definition of a *parallel* composition operator, denoted as $||$. We assume that the features used to implement adaptations are based on property selection (*e.g.*, "for all model elements like *this*, do *that*"), as this writing style supports feature re-usability into multiple systems ($\mathcal{C}_1$). On the one hand, if a designer knows the composition order associated to a given set of features, he/she can use existing composition operators to implement the composition ($\mathcal{C}_2$). On the other hand, when such an order is not explicit, the application of a feature F must not impact the application of feature F', for all input models ($\mathcal{C}_3$). Nevertheless, as such isolated composition may lead to inconsistencies, we provide an automated mechanism to identify inconsistencies in the composed result ($\mathcal{C}_4$).

3 An Action–Based Approach

Inspired by cutting–edges researches on the modelling research field (*e.g.*, PRAXIS), we use an action–based approach to represents models. According to this paradigm, *"Every model can be expressed as a sequence of elementary construction operations. The sequence of operations that produces a model is composed of the operations performed to define each model element."* [4]. This section formalises the action–orientation used to support the definition of both $||$ and $\bullet$ (formally defined in SEC. 4).

Formalising Actions. The PRAXIS method [4] defines four operations to model models, allowing one to *(i)* create a model element, *(ii)* delete a model element, *(iii)* set a property in a model element (setProperty) and finally *(iv)* set a reference from a model element to another one (setReference). We propose here a generalisation of the approach where the expressiveness is dedicated to the handling of attributed graphs. Consequently, we are not restricted to class-based models, and this definition works for any type of artifact that can be represented by a graph (the validation example relies on behavioural model initially modelled as business processes). That is, we consider a model as a set of model elements (*i.e.*, nodes), interconnected through relations (*i.e.*, edges). Sets are intrinsically unordered, and do not contain duplicates. Using first–order logic as underlying foundations, we define the following closed terms (*i.e.*, actions) to interact with a given model:

- $add_n(N, Kind)$: introduces a node N in the model. $Kind$ specializes the node (*e.g.*, a class, a UML annotation).
- $add_e(N, N', Kind)$: defines an edge from N to N' in the model. $Kind$ specializes the reified relation (*e.g.*, inheritance, aggregation).
- $del_e(N, N', Kind)$: deletes the edge from N to N', according to its $Kind$ (as several relations of different kinds may exist between two nodes).
- $del_n(N)$: deletes the node N in the model.

Models as Action Sets. We define a model as a tuple of four action sets (EQ. 1). A model $\mu \in \mathcal{M}$ is composed by *(i)* a set of node additions A_n, *(ii)* a set of edges additions A_e, *(iii)* a set of edge deletions D_e and finally *(iv)* a set of node deletions D_n. In our example, node kinds are restricted to $\{Cl\}$ (for "class"), and relation kinds are defined in $\{Ag, In\}$ (respectively "aggregation" and "inheritance"). For example, considering each class as a node, the model depicted in FIG. 2(a) is reified in EQ. 2.

$$\mu = (A_n, A_r, D_r, D_n) \in \mathcal{M} \tag{1}$$
$$m = (\{add_n(C_1, Cl), add_n(C_2, Cl)\}, \emptyset, \emptyset, \emptyset) \tag{2}$$

The union of two models is used to combine several models into a single one. It is defined as the distribution[2] of the usual set union operator into each contained set:

$$\mu = (A_n, A_e, D_e, D_n) \cup (A'_n, A'_e, D'_e, D'_n) = (A_n \cup A'_n, A_e \cup A'_e, D_e \cup D'_e, D_n \cup D'_n)$$

Relations with action sequences. We do not use plain action sequence representation to avoid permutations issues. Using such a representation, two different action sequences (s_0, s_1) that lead to the same model are considered as non–equal, where our set–driven representation (μ) ensures unicity:

$$s_0 = [add_n(a, Cl), add_n(b, class)], s_1 = [add_n(b, Cl), add_n(a, Cl)], s_0 \neq s_1$$
$$\mu = (\{add_n(a, Cl), add_n(b, Cl)\}, \emptyset, \emptyset, \emptyset)$$

---

[2] One can notice that such a distribution can also be used to implement others model combination operator (*e.g.*, intersection, difference).

The underlying idea is that a sequence of actions always respects the following steps: it *(i)* adds nodes, *(ii)* adds edges between these nodes, *(iii)* deletes existing edges and finally *(iv)* deletes isolated nodes. In a given step, the internal ordering does not matter (adding x before y is not relevant with regard to the final model). Thus, one can see our representation as a canonical form of an action sequence mandatory to build a given model: the division into four subsets supports this partial ordering.

Consistency. Using this representation, model consistency is ensured according to several logical rules. As the detection of inconsistencies in models is a dedicated research field [3], we always assume in this paper that the handled models are *consistent*. For a given model $\mu = (A_n, A_r, D_r, D_n)$, this property is ensured according to the following rules:

P_1: *"Related elements existence"*. An action that adds a relation between two elements (here classes) C and C' assumes that these two classes are added with the associated actions in A_n (EQ. 3).

P_2: *"Deletion of existing relations"*. An action that deletes a relation between two elements C and C' with a given $Kind$ assumes that this relation is added in A_e (EQ. 4).

P_3: *"Deletion of isolated elements"*. An action that deletes an element C assumes that all relations involving C are deleted in D_e (EQ. 5).

$$add_e(C, C', \_) \in A_e \Rightarrow add_n(C, Cl) \in A_n \wedge add_n(C', Cl) \in A_n \quad (3)$$

$$del_e(C, C', k) \in D_e \Rightarrow add_e(C, C', k) \in A_e \quad (4)$$

$$del_n(C) \in D_n \Rightarrow \begin{cases} \forall add_e(C, X, K_{cx}) \in A_e, \exists del_e(C, X, K_{cx}) \in D_e \\ \wedge \; \forall add_e(Y, C, K_{yc}) \in A_e, \exists del_e(Y, C, K_{yc}) \in D_e \end{cases} \quad (5)$$

4 Using Actions to Support ∥ and •

In this section, we present how the model representation described in the previous section supports feature introduction, and the definition of both • and ∥ operators.

Using Actions to Introduce Features. Using a functional approach, base models are considered as *constants* (*e.g.*, $\mu \in \mathcal{M}$), and features are defined as *functions* that map an input model μ into an enriched model μ'. Thus, introducing a feature F into a model μ means to use the latter as the input of the former: $\mu' = F(\mu)$. In our approach, we propose to consider F as a two steps function: *(i)* the copy of the input model μ into the output one and *(ii)* the generation of the actions necessary to modify μ and then produce the expected model as output, denoted as $\Delta_F(\mu)$. Our action–based representation of models allows the designer to represent these elements in an endogenous way, as both μ and $\Delta_F(\mu)$ are modelled as sets of actions. Thus, we obtain μ' as the following: $\mu' = F(\mu) = \mu \cup \Delta_F(\mu)$.

For example, we consider here the feature S described in the previous section. Assuming a function named *top* that returns the set of top-level classes discovered in its input, one can implement Δ_S as the following: for an input model μ, it *(i)* adds the SC class and then *(ii)* generates the addition of an inheritance relation between all top-level classes and SC.

$$\Delta_S : \mathcal{M} \to \mathcal{M}$$
$$\mu \mapsto (\{add_c(SC, Cl)\}, \{add_e(X, SC, In) | X \in top(\mu)\}, \emptyset, \emptyset)$$

Thus, the introduction of S in m (FIG. 2(b)) is modelled as the following:

$$m = (\{add_n(C_1, Cl), add_n(C_2, Cl)\}, \emptyset, \emptyset, \emptyset)$$
$$\Delta_S(m) = (\{add_c(SC, Cl)\}, \{add_e(C_1, SC, In), add_e(C_2, SC, In)\}, \emptyset, \emptyset)$$
$$m_S = S(m) = m \cup \Delta_S(m)$$
$$= (\{add_c(SC, Cl), add_n(C_1, Cl), add_n(C_2, Cl)\},$$
$$\{add_e(C_1, SC, In), add_e(C_2, SC, In)\}, \emptyset, \emptyset)$$

As said in the consistency paragraph, we assume to work with consistent models and features. Thus, the introduction of a feature into a model always leads to a *consistent* model: let μ a consistent model, and F a given feature. Even if $\Delta_F(\mu)$ may be inconsistent (*e.g.*, deleting a class that is added in μ and not in $\Delta_F(\mu)$, violating P_3), the result of its union with m is therefore consistent.

4.1 Sequential Composition: •

Using F and G as two features, and μ a model, we define the functional composition operator • as the following:

$$G(\mu) = \mu \cup \Delta_G(\mu)$$
$$(F \bullet G)(\mu) = F(G(\mu)) = G(\mu) \cup \Delta_F(G(\mu)) = \underbrace{\mu \cup \Delta_G(\mu)}_{G(\mu)} \cup \Delta_F(\underbrace{\mu \cup \Delta_G(\mu)}_{G(\mu)})$$

The operator holds the following properties, and thus behaves as the "usual" operator:

– Identity: Let Id be the identity feature[3], and F a given feature. $F = F \bullet Id$.
– Idempotence: Let F be a feature. In the general case, $F(F(\mu)) \neq F(\mu)$
– Commutativity: this property cannot be ensured in the general case, and its implementation–dependent. It can be ensured if and only if the two functions F and G are orthogonal. In the general case, $F \bullet G(\mu) \neq G \bullet F(\mu)$.

Running example. We now consider Δ_A, the function used to implements the previously defined A feature:

$$\Delta_A : \mathcal{M} \to \mathcal{M}$$
$$\mu \mapsto (\{add_n(AC, class)\}, \{add_e(X, AC, Ag(\_)) | X \in top(\mu)\}, \emptyset, \emptyset)$$

---
[3] $\forall \mu \in \mathcal{M}, \Delta_{Id}(\mu) = (\emptyset, \emptyset, \emptyset, \emptyset) \Rightarrow Id(\mu) = \mu$.

With this function and the previously defined one Δ_S, one can build the model m_{SA} depicted in Fig. 3(a), which represents $(S \bullet A)(m)$.

$$\Delta_A(m) = (\{add_n(AC, Cl)\}, \{add_e(C_1, AC, Ag(a_1)), add_e(C_2, AC, Ag(a_2))\}, \emptyset, \emptyset)$$
$$m_A = A(m) = m \cup \Delta_A(m)$$
$$= (\{add_n(AC, Cl), add_n(C_1, Cl), add_n(C_2, Cl)\},$$
$$\{add_e(C_1, AC, Ag(a_1)), add_e(C_2, AC, Ag(a_2))\}, \emptyset, \emptyset)$$
$$top(m_A) = \{AC, C_1, C_2\}$$
$$\Delta_S(m_a) = (\{add_n(SC, Cl)\},$$
$$\{add_e(C_1, SC, In), add_e(C_2, SC, In), add_e(AC, SC, In)\}, \emptyset, \emptyset)$$
$$m_{SA} = S(A(m)) = m \cup \Delta_A(m) \cup \Delta_S(m \cup \Delta_A(m)) = m_A \cup \Delta_S(m_A)$$
$$= (\{add_n(AC, Cl), add_n(C_1, Cl), add_n(C_2, Cl), add_n(SC, Cl)\},$$
$$\{add_e(C_1, AC, Ag(a_1)), add_e(C_2, AC, Ag(a_2)),$$
$$add_e(C_1, SC, In), add_e(C_2, SC, In), add_e(AC, SC, In)\}, \emptyset, \emptyset)$$

4.2 Parallel Composition: ||

Using F and G as two features, and μ a model, we define the parallel composition operator || as the following:

$$F(\mu) = \mu \cup \Delta_F(\mu), \ G(\mu) = \mu \cup \Delta_G(\mu)$$
$$(F||G)(\mu) = F(\mu) \cup G(\mu) = \mu \cup \Delta_F(\mu) \cup \Delta_G(\mu)$$

As the || operator is defined over set union, it holds the following properties:

– Identity: considering Id as the identify feature and F as a given feature, $(F||Id)(\mu) = \mu \cup \Delta_F(\mu) \cup (\emptyset, \emptyset, \emptyset, \emptyset) = F(\mu)$.
– Idempotence: let F be a given feature. $F||F(\mu) = F(\mu) \cup F(\mu) = F(\mu)$.
– Commutativity: the operator relies on set union, which is commutative. $(F||G)(\mu) = (G||F)(\mu) = \mu \cup \Delta_F(\mu) \cup \Delta_G(\mu)$.

When applied to the previous example, one can build the model m' depicted in Fig. 3(c) as the following:

$$m' = (A||S)(m) = m \cup \Delta_A(m) \cup \Delta_S(m)$$
$$= (\{add_n(AC, Cl), add_n(C_1, Cl), add_n(C_2, Cl), add_n(SC, Cl)\},$$
$$\{add_e(C_1, AC, Ag(a_1)), add_e(C_2, AC, Ag(a_2)),$$
$$add_e(C_1, SC, In), add_e(C_2, SC, In)\}, \emptyset, \emptyset)$$

4.3 Impact on Model Consistency

The previously described definition of feature composition assumes their consistency: for a given model μ and any feature F, the composition of F with μ always leads to a consistent model (*i.e.*, a model that respects the P_i constraints).

•: the sequential composition operator is consistent by construction: it simply chains the compositions.
||: the parallel composition operator works on a different basis (*i.e.*, model union), and then may lead to inconsistent models.

Let F and G two consistent features. For a given model μ, we ensure by construction that both $F(\mu)$ and $G(\mu)$ are also consistent. But their parallel composition $\mu' = F(\mu) \cup G(\mu)$ may be inconsistent, according to the following rules:

P_1: *"Related elements existence"*. This property is violated if and only if a feature adds a relation that involves an element deleted by another feature.
P_2: *"Deletion of existing relations"*. This property can be violated if and only if a feature F deletes a relations added in another feature F'. Such a situation also implies a violation of P_1 (F' defines a relation between unknown elements).
P_3: *"Deletion of isolated elements"*. This property is violated since a feature deletes an element used by the other one in a newly added relation (see P_1).

In fact, the computation of an inconsistent resulting model (*after* the composition) identifies an issue in the features: they cannot be composed in parallel as is, as one relies on the other. It is then a typical use case for a sequential composition (•). It tackles challenge C_4, as such erroneous situation can be automatically detected (*e.g.*, through the satisfaction of a logical predicate).

5 Implementation and Validation

In this section, we describe how the approach is implemented in a logical language, and emphasize the need for using the || operator in the context of a complex case study.

5.1 Implementation

We provide a reference implementation of the approach[4]. This framework supports the definition of features as Prolog predicates, and includes a *Domain–Specific Language* (DSL) to express compositions. This language is domain independant, as it relies on the action sequences previously defined, reifying models as attributed graphs. The engine compiles compositions expressed through the DSL into logical predicates (using ANTLR[5]), and supports their execution in a Prolog interpreter (SWI-Prolog[6]). At run-time, SWI-Prolog provides the JPL framework, which implements a bidirectional Java/Prolog bridge. Thus, the engine can be connected to any tool reachable through the Java language, *e.g.*, the *Eclipse Modeling Framework* (EMF). The implementation of the running example used in this paper is available in the code repository[7].

---
[4] http://www.gcoke.org
[5] http://www.antlr.org/ (version 3.3)
[6] http://www.swi-prolog.org/ (version 5.10.4)
[7] http://code.google.com/p/gcoke/source/browse/trunk/lines/ase_xp/

Listing 1.1. Ordered composition (•): $m_{sa} \neq m_{as}$

```
composition ordered(m) {
  a(model: m)    => (output: m_a);
  s(model: m_a)  => (output: m_sa);
} => (m_sa);
```

Listing 1.2. Parallel composition ($||$): $m' = (A||S)(m) = (S||A)(m)$

```
composition parallel(m) {
  s(model: m) => (output: m_p);
  a(model: m) => (output: m_p);
} => (m_p);
```

Using the engine, one can express compositions using the DSL. We represent in LST. 1.1 how the framework supports ordered compositions (•). A composition is named (here ordered), and consumes models (here m) to produces new ones (here m_sa). The way such models are produced is represented as a set of composition directives: line 2 implements the application of the feature a using m as input model, and storing its output into m_a. A directive is triggered as soon as all its input artifacts are available (*i.e.*, existing or computed by another directive). The parallel composition operator is implemented as the absence of order between directives (LST. 1.2, next page). In a composition named parallel, we only declare that s and a use the model m as input, and store their result in m_prime (lines 2 and 3). In front of such a declaration, the engine computes each set of actions independently, and will perform the union of the generated actions sequences before executing it. If an inconsistency is detected (which is not the case here), an error is raised to the designer.

5.2 Validation

We focus here on the CCCMS case study, as it is the largest one we used to validate the $||$ operator. The case study was designed by Kienzle *et al.* [13] as a reference framework to compare different aspect–oriented modelling approaches. This example is a *real-life* example, involving thousands of model elements according to real-life business processes. In this context, the considered models to be composed reify business processes, *i.e.*, behavioural models. The business processes involved in the CCCMS[8] are modelled as graphs, where nodes are activities and relations implement a partial order between these activities. The case study defines hundreds of activities scheduled by thousands of relations, which makes the example suitable for "real–life" complexity. We instantiated two variants of the requirements: *(i)* a system that only fits the *business* requirements and *(ii)* a system that includes several *non–functional* (NF) concerns. The final system

---

[8] http://www.adore-design.org/doku/examples/cccms/start

(including NF concerns) defines 146 compositions. As stated in the motivations of this paper, we identified up to 40 shared join points in this study ($\sim 27\%$). On these points, up to 5 concerns had to be composed, leading to 120 potential sequences of composition. This situation triggers a humongous amount of verifications to be checked on the composed system, which is modelled as a set of dense graphs (hundreds of nodes, thousands of relations). Thus, the execution of checkers to verify the consistency of the composed system costs a lot of resource and CPU–time, as the verifications rely on the systematic check of each path defined in a given graph (subject to combinatorial explosion).

While designing the CCCMS, instead of systematically using the • operator and manage all the complexity by hand, we used the || operator to support the compositional approach. The requirement document stated that the features were supposed to be orthogonal, and as a consequence the || operator perfectly implements this intention. The inconsistency detection mechanism (applied on action sequence instead of large graphs) was then used to identify the situations where an order should be defined. Results are summarised in TAB. 5.2.

- The business version uses 24 features and defines 28 composition directives to build the complete system. It can then be considered as a large simplification of the expected system. In this version, only 2 composition directives where identified as conflicting, and actually had to be explicitly ordered (*i.e.*, implements a • composition). All the other compositions can be computed independently. This point illustrates that from a business point of view, the absence of ordering is really important. Applying these features as an ordered sequence can produce unexpected results, like the ones shown in FIG. 3. Through sequential composition, designers would had to *(i)* check the composed system to verify that the obtained result does not contain such feature interactions and/or *(ii)* avoid the usage of quantifiers to anticipate such situations.
- The introduction of NF concerns includes in our case five additional features, dealing with security, persistence and statistical logging. In this configuration, we use 146 composition directives to build the complete system (business + NF). Up to 73% of these directives were unordered in this case study. The others requires an order to meet the requirement specifications. For example, we had to introduce security features after all the others to secure the complete process. It is important to notice that this need was not explicitly documented in the requirements, but accurately detected by the inconsistency detection mechanism. This point highlights the complementarity of the sequential and parallel composition operators.

Table 1. Composition directives used in the CCCMS

System	#Composition	#Ordered	#Parallel
Business	28	2 (7%)	26 (93%)
Business + NF	146	39 (27%)	107 (73%)

6 Related Works

Modern mathematics were proposed as a support of feature–oriented software development [2]. This algebraic representation allows the usage of equation optimisers to rewrite the compositions in an efficient way [16]. It is possible to reify the interaction of a feature and another one [17] using mathematical derivative function. Another lead is to use commuting diagrams [14] to explore the different composition orders. The way features are composed together can be constrained through the usage of *design constraint rules*, expressed as attributed grammars [18]. A "valid" composition is consequently identified as a word recognised by the design constraint grammar (identifying conflicting features upstream). The contribution of this paper complements these works, as it also reify compositions as mathematical expressions. The major difference with these works is the definition of a commutative and idempotent composition operator.

The opposite approach of the one described in this paper is to analyse the set of available features and to automatically identify the needed composition order, as implemented by the CAPUCINE framework [25]. Using CAPUCINE, a *Feature Diagram* (FD [8]) is used to express the business variability of a given system. Using an aspect–oriented modelling approach, features are bound to assets that implement aspect models: a fragment of model to be added (*i.e.*, advice) and a selector used to identify where this fragment should be added (*i.e.*, point-cut). CAPUCINE analyses the given elements according to two directions: from the FD to the models and *(i)* from the models to the FD. On the one hand, the latter analyses the set of selectors against the set of model fragments, and identifies hidden dependencies between features that were not expressed in the FD. On the other hand, the former verifies for each constraints expressed in the FD (*e.g.*, "F requires F'") if the implementation follows it (*i.e.*, the selector defined in F matches elements defined in the fragment of model associated to F'). These analysis are complementary to the parallel composition operator, as one can use it to automatically discriminate the features that requires a sequential (•) composition and the features that rely on the parallel operator (||). Thus, it is possible to *(i)* detect hidden ordering with CAPUCINE and *(ii) ensure* that others features are composed in isolation.

Another lead to ensure commutative composition is followed by the model transformation community [5]. In this work, the key idea is to analyse the set of model elements impacted (*e.g.*, read, modified, deleted) by a given transformation τ, and then reason about these different sets to check if two transformations may commute. This reasoning capabilities are formalised using set theory, and dedicated to model–transformation. Such an analysis ensures the consistency of models after a parallel composition. Thus, this approach complements ours: *a posteriori* inconsistency detection can be avoided at run-time if commutativity safety can be proved. However, our composition operator *ensures* the parallel application of a set of features, by construction, whatever their definition.

Model weaving can also be considered as a way to support adaptation. This paradigm relies on aspect weaving at the model level. In this context, it is possible to use optimisation techniques to select the best model to be woven with the current one [26]. But intrinsically, these approaches implements an aspect weaving algorithm, which is by nature not commutative. Our approach is thus complementary to these ones, as one can implement our || operator in such a framework and then support unordered composition.

More specifically, the MATA approach [27] supports the weaving of models aspects using a graph–based approach. This approach supports powerful conflict detection mechanisms, used to support the "safe" composition of models [23]. The underlying formal model associated to this detection is based on critical pair analysis [7]. Initially defined for term rewriting systems and then generalised to graph rewriting systems, critical pairs formalise the identification of a minimal example associated to a potentially conflicting situation. This notion supports the development of rule–based systems, identifying conflicting situations such as "the rule r will delete an element matched by the rule r'" or "the rule r generates a structure which is prohibited according to the existing preconditions". This work is complementary with the one presented in this paper, as it can be used to handle inconsistencies in a more detailed way.

7 Conclusions and Perspectives

In this paper, we introduced a new composition operator (denoted as ||), that enables the parallel composition of existing features. Using an action–based approach, we formally defined this new operator and the existing ones (*e.g.*, sequential), as well as its prototypical implementation using a logical language. We identified four challenges, accurately tackled by the approach. The operator supports feature re-usability ($\mathcal{C}_1$), and complements the existing ones (to be used when an order is needed, $\mathcal{C}_2$). It also ensures determinism in the composition ($\mathcal{C}_3$), as the composition order does not matter when || is used. Finally, inconsistency detection mechanisms are provided to ensure the safety of the parallel composition ($\mathcal{C}_4$). The operator was validated in the context of SOA business processes, illustrating how it scales in front of large systems.

Immediate perspectives of this work are to apply the operator to multiple application domains. We plan to focus on the two following research fields, which highly rely on compositions to support their adaptation: *(i)* Cloud–computing and *(ii)* Internet of Things. For the former, it is known that the design of efficient distributed systems is a tedious task. The use of composition algorithms to support their adaptation according to a step-wise approach tames such a complexity, and ensure properties in the composed result (difficult to be checked by humans). In the context of the REMICS[9] project, we are dealing with the migration of legacy systems into cloud-based application. In this context, the need for adaptation is double: *(i)* models of legacy applications have to be adapted *w.r.t* models of clouds to enact a cloud version of the application, and *(ii)* at run-time, run-time models have to be adapted to accurately use the power of the cloud (*e.g.*, "elasticity", which refers to an unlimited resource provisioning capability). The Internet of Things domains is driven by the multiplication of embedded

---

[9] http://remics.eu/, EU FP7, STREP.

devices (*e.g.*, sensors, smartphone, PDA, tablet PC). Intrinsically, the Internet of Things aims to compose multiple devices into an autonomic entity, able to reconfigure itself at run-time [6], according to changes in its environment (*e.g.*, a more accurate display device is discovered, and the application is reconfigured to broadcast the main content to this new device) [20]. These two application domains will support large-scale experimentation of the || operator, based on real case studies provided by industrial partners.

References

1. Batory, D., Sarvela, J.N., Rauschmayer, A.: Scaling Step-Wise Refinement. IEEE Transactions on Software Engineering 30, 2004 (2004)
2. Batory, D.S.: Using Modern Mathematics as an FOSD Modeling Language. In: Smaragdakis, Y., Siek, J.G. (eds.) GPCE, pp. 35–44. ACM (2008)
3. Blanc, X., Mougenot, A., Mounier, I., Mens, T.: Incremental Detection of Model Inconsistencies Based on Model Operations. In: van Eck, P., Gordijn, J., Wieringa, R. (eds.) CAiSE 2009. LNCS, vol. 5565, pp. 32–46. Springer, Heidelberg (2009)
4. Blanc, X., Mounier, I., Mougenot, A., Mens, T.: Detecting Model Inconsistency through Operation-Based Model Construction. In: Schäfer, W., Dwyer, M.B., Gruhn, V. (eds.) ICSE, pp. 511–520. ACM (2008)
5. Etien, A., Muller, A., Legrand, T., Blanc, X.: Combining Independent Model Transformations. In: Shin, S.Y., Ossowski, S., Schumacher, M., Palakal, M.J., Hung, C.C. (eds.) SAC, pp. 2237–2243. ACM (2010)
6. Fleurey, F., Morin, B., Solberg, A.: A Model-driven Approach to Develop Adaptive Firmwares. In: Giese, H., Cheng, B.H.C. (eds.) SEAMS, pp. 168–177. ACM (2011)
7. Heckel, R., Küster, J.M., Taentzer, G.: Confluence of Typed Attributed Graph Transformation Systems. In: Corradini, A., Ehrig, H., Kreowski, H.-J., Rozenberg, G. (eds.) ICGT 2002. LNCS, vol. 2505, pp. 161–176. Springer, Heidelberg (2002)
8. Kang, K.C., Cohen, S.G., Hess, J.A., Novak, W.E., Peterson, A.S.: Feature-Oriented Domain Analysis (FODA) - Feasibility Study. Tech. rep., The Software Engineering Institute (1990), http://www.sei.cmu.edu/reports/90tr021.pdf
9. Kastner, C., Apel, S., Batory, D.: A Case Study Implementing Features Using AspectJ. In: Proceedings of the 11th Int. Software Product Line Conference, pp. 223–232. IEEE Computer Society, Washington, DC (2007)
10. Katz, S., Mezini, M., Kienzle, J. (eds.): Transactions on Aspect-Oriented Software Development VII - A Common Case Study for Aspect-Oriented Modeling. LNCS, vol. 6210. Springer, Heidelberg (2010)
11. Katz, S., Ossher, H., France, R., Jézéquel, J.-M. (eds.): Transactions on Aspect-Oriented Software Development VI, Special Issue on Aspects and Model-Driven Engineering. LNCS, vol. 5560. Springer, Heidelberg (2009)
12. Kiczales, G., Hilsdale, E., Hugunin, J., Kersten, M., Palm, J., Griswold, W.G.: An Overview of AspectJ. In: Lee, S.H. (ed.) ECOOP 2001. LNCS, vol. 2072, pp. 327–353. Springer, Heidelberg (2001)
13. Kienzle, J., Guelfi, N., Mustafiz, S.: Crisis Management Systems: A Case Study for Aspect-Oriented Modeling. In: T. Aspect-Oriented Soft. Dev. [10], pp. 1–22
14. Kim, C.H.P., Kästner, C., Batory, D.: On the Modularity of Feature Interactions. In: Procs of the 7th Int. Conf. on Generative Programming and Component Engineering, pp. 23–34. ACM, New York (2008)

15. Kniesel, G.: Type-Safe Delegation for Run-Time Component Adaptation. In: Guerraoui, R. (ed.) ECOOP 1999. LNCS, vol. 1628, pp. 351–366. Springer, Heidelberg (1999), doi:10.1007/3-540-48743-3_16
16. Liu, J., Batory, D.: Automatic Remodularization and Optimized Synthesis of Product-Families. In: Karsai, G., Visser, E. (eds.) GPCE 2004. LNCS, vol. 3286, pp. 379–395. Springer, Heidelberg (2004)
17. Liu, J., Batory, D.S., Nedunuri, S.: Modeling Interactions in Feature Oriented Software Designs. In: Reiff-Marganiec, S., Ryan, M. (eds.) FIW, pp. 178–197. IOS Press (2005)
18. McAllester, D.: Variational Attribute Grammars for Computer Aided Design (Release 3.0). Tech. rep. MIT (1994)
19. McKinley, P.K., Sadjadi, S.M., Kasten, E.P., Cheng, B.H.C.: Composing Adaptive Software. Computer 37, 56–64 (2004)
20. Morin, B., Barais, O., Jezequel, J.M., Fleurey, F., Solberg, A.: Models@ Run.time to Support Dynamic Adaptation. Computer 42(10), 44–51 (2009)
21. Mosser, S., Blay-Fornarino, M., France, R.: Workflow Design Using Fragment Composition – Crisis Management System Design through ADORE. In: T. Aspect-Oriented Software Development [10], pp. 200–233
22. Mosser, S., Hermosillo, G., Le Meur, A.F., Seinturier, L., Duchien, L.: Undoing Event-Driven Adaptation of Business Processes. In: 8th International Conference on Services Computing (SCC 2011), pp. 1–8. IEEE, Washington DC (2011)
23. Mussbacher, G., Whittle, J., Amyot, D.: Semantic-Based Interaction Detection in Aspect-Oriented Scenarios. In: RE, pp. 203–212. IEEE Computer Society (2009)
24. Oreizy, P., Medvidovic, N., Taylor, R.N.: Runtime Software Adaptation: Framework, Approaches, and Styles. In: Companion of the 30th Int. Conf. on Software Engineering, ICSE Companion 2008, pp. 899–910. ACM, New York (2008)
25. Parra, C., Cleve, A., Blanc, X., Duchien, L.: Feature-Based Composition of Software Architectures. In: Babar, M.A., Gorton, I. (eds.) ECSA 2010. LNCS, vol. 6285, pp. 230–245. Springer, Heidelberg (2010)
26. White, J., Gray, J., Schmidt, D.C.: Constraint-Based Model Weaving. In: T. Aspect-Oriented Software Development VI [11], pp. 153–190
27. Whittle, J., Jayaraman, P.K., Elkhodary, A.M., Moreira, A., Araújo, J.: MATA: A Unified Approach for Composing UML Aspect Models Based on Graph Transformation. In: T. Aspect-Oriented Software Development VI [11], pp. 191–237

Comparative Study of Model-Based and Multi-Domain System Engineering Approaches for Industrial Settings

Anjelika Votintseva, Petra Witschel, Nikolaus Regnat, and Philipp Emanuel Stelzig

Siemens AG, Otto-Hahn-Ring 6, Munich, Germany
{anjelika.votintseva,petra.witschel,
nikolaus.regnat,philipp.stelzig}@siemens.com

Abstract. A typical approach for the development of multi-domain systems often carries the risk of high non-conformance costs and time-consuming re-engineering due to the lack of interoperability between different domains. In its research project "Mechatronic Design", the Siemens AG develops an integrated, model-based and simulation-focused process to perform a frontloading engineering approach for multi-domain systems.

The paper presents two use cases from this project as two implementation approaches to system modeling and simulation being synchronized at early design phases. Both use cases utilize the standardized system modeling language SysML and the multi-domain simulation language Modelica. One use case evaluates the standardized OMG SysML4Modelica profile for transformation between SysML and Modelica. The other use case uses a Modelica independent and proprietary profile aiming at more flexible usage. For both approaches, advantages and disadvantages are identified and compared. Depending on the project objectives, the general suitability of the approaches is also judged.

Keywords: model-based system engineering, simulation, multi-domain systems, SysML, Modelica, comparative study, industrial use cases.

1 Introduction

Model-based systems engineering (MBSE) is the formalized application of modeling to support system requirements, design, analysis, verification and validation activities beginning in the conceptual design phase and continuing throughout development and later life cycle phases [1]. It is especially challenging to manage the development of multi-domain systems. In the present context, by multi-domain systems we understand those involving both multiple technical disciplines (like mechanics, electrics, software) and different engineering methods (e.g. in this context, architecture description, system simulation). MBSE enables an integrated process to develop constituent parts of such systems in an integrated way. In addition to descriptive models, using executable models allows system architects to run simulations. Within the internal company-wide research project of Siemens AG called "Lighthouse Project Mechatronic Design" (LHP MDE), an integrated, model-based and simulation-focused process is under development to perform a frontloading engineering approach for multi-domain products.

Our paper exemplifies how system modeling and system simulation can be used and synchronized at early design phases for concept evaluation and functional design. With the design of an electrical car (eCar) and the development of medical equipment (Artis Floorstand), two use cases of LHP MDE are examined in more details, where different development groups follow different approaches. For description of the system model, in the both use cases the standardized system description language SysML [2] has been used which is based on the unified modeling language UML [3]. SysML is currently becoming an industrial standard in the domain of system modeling as it allows consistent structuring of complex systems with easily understandable graphical visualization. The quantitative analysis has in both cases been performed with the Modelica language [4]. Modelica is very suitable for multi-domain simulations, as it allows to model – in an object-oriented way – any system that can be described by differential algebraic equations. It is possible to create Modelica models graphically and textually, what makes it particularly well-suited for automatic transformations. SysML and Modelica are increasingly used in different projects at Siemens AG.

Research is already performed to combine UML-based system description with Modelica-based simulation. In [5] a UML Profile called ModelicaML is presented which enables integrated modeling and simulation of system requirements and design. Another profile named SysML4Modelica [6] concentrates on the combination between SysML and Modelica. Problems in developing complex multi-domain systems are tackled in further works. For example, Model Integrated Mechatronics (MIM) [7] is an architecture that promotes model integration for different kinds of artifacts allowing concurrent engineering of mechanical, electronic and software components. It simplifies the integrated development process by using the construct of Mechatronic Components. The Functional (Digital) Mockup [8] approach is synergistic design synchronization, model execution and analysis, providing a tight integration of mechanics with electronics and software and a smooth integration of dependability predictions during the early development phases.

This paper is structured as follows. In Section 2, the two application areas eCar and Artis Floorstand are introduced together with their development processes. Section 3 contains implementation details. The comparison of the proposed approaches is performed in Section 4. Section 5 concludes and gives an outlook for future works.

2 Application Areas and Proposed Development Processes

This section provides an overview of the selected use cases – eCar and Artis Floorstand. The development processes proposed within these use cases are outlined together with exemplary workflows justifying the chosen ways of tool integration.

2.1 Use Case eCar

The use case eCar is related to the development of a hypothetical electrical vehicle [9]. In our sample model we concentrate on the level of functional architecture and abstract logical design to show how architectural decisions at early development stages can be analyzed and compared. As an example of an early decision, we consider the question if a concept with one or two electric motors is more advantageous. In one concept, a single electrical motor, connected via a mechanical differential to the front wheels of the vehicle, is used. In the other concept, two independent motors are individually attached to the front wheels. This choice of concepts visualized in Fig. 1 (left-hand) has impact on a variety of non-functional requirements like efficiency, battery range, drive comfort and costs. One focus of our works was the evaluation of battery consumption under control of a new SW component, an adaptive cruise control (ACC). The car in front was assumed to drive according to the New European Drive Cycle (NEDC) shown in Fig. 1 (right-hand). This example demonstrates the integration of software and environment models in modern multi-domain systems.

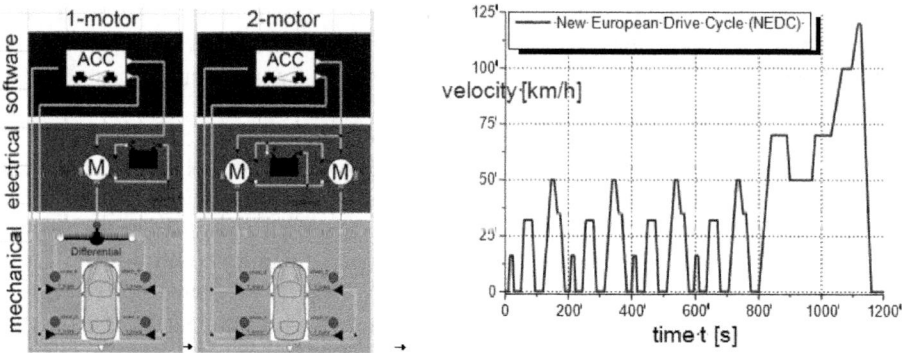

Fig. 1. Abstract models for the sample multi-domain system eCar and an input drive cycle

In this use case, the standardized SysML4Modelica profile [6] was evaluated. The specification of the profile describes how to represent elements of Modelica within SysML. Using this approach, a system architect can select an appropriate level of detail, which is then transformed automatically into Modelica.

Development Process
A typical eCar development process contains such phases as requirements, functional architecture, logical architecture, physical and software design, integration and testing activities. A generic system model can be configured into different product configurations containing instances of physical elements and software implementations, as well as other product parameters. After a product configuration is specified within SysML, some parts of the model required for the further analysis are decorated with the domain-specific stereotypes and tags (in this case from the SysML4Modelica profile). This can be applied to whole components or just to some model elements (blocks or their properties). After that, Modelica simulation models are generated automatically for different product configurations. Components from software design are inserted into UML projects where they are developed further. Selected results from the domain-specific analysis are transferred back to the system model, e.g. as product parameters or component properties.

Exemplary Workflow

In the use case eCar, we have assumed a workflow starting from SysML, where the different kinds and levels of the system architecture are developed and different kinds of analysis are managed (e.g., validation activities are specified and mapped to tools, dependencies are defined between artifacts).

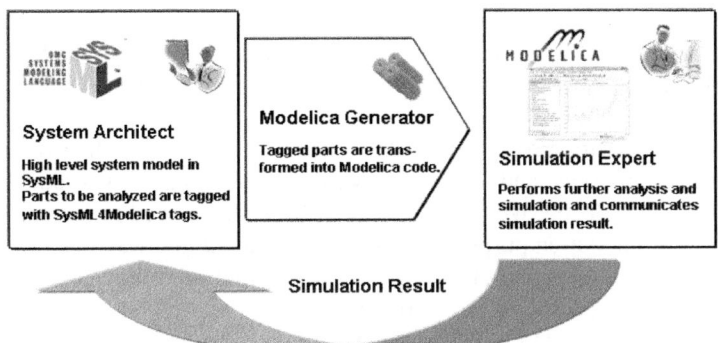

Fig. 2. Exemplary system engineering workflow with feedback in the use case eCar

In the use case eCar, a system architect performs the following steps (see Fig. 2):

1. develop a high level architecture in SysML,
2. add details to the components,
3. select a part of the system to be analyzed with additional tools by marking these elements with specific stereotypes (SysML4Modelica),
4. (automatically) transform this part of the system to the target language and pass the resulting model to the simulation experts for the further analysis.

The simulation experts then delivers the results of the analysis back to the system architect, who updates the system with the parameters from the simulation results.

2.2 Use Case Artis Floorstand

The use case Artis Floorstand refers to a particular configuration from the Artis product family of C-arm systems produced by Siemens Healthcare which are most notably used in angiography as carriers for imaging devices. A characteristic feature of these systems is that the mechanical structure is mainly fixed and further development often concentrates on improving the performance or studying other non-functional aspects. Typical challenges arising in the development are e.g. reaching higher rotation speed (e.g. from 20°/s to 45°/s) to allow a faster imaging process and reduce patient exposure to radiation, or better positioning accuracy (e.g. a maximum tolerance of ±2° for rotational movements instead of ±5°) for higher imaging quality. To this end, the influence of certain design decisions has to be analyzed as early as possible. For instance, how big are the resulting torques when accelerating the C-arm to higher rotation speeds? Can these torques be generated by the electric motors used so far? What is the benefit of more costly, yet more precise gears? How does smaller clearance or higher stiffness in the gears affect positioning accuracy? During the early development stages all architectural decisions need to consider such non-functional aspects and therefore a tradeoff analysis has to be made, with multi-body simulations being most suitable for a first quantitative analysis.

Traditionally, parts of this development process were based on textual system specifications. However, with increasing system complexity, this approach was found to be unsatisfactory. Thus, the main aim of our work was to show the benefit of SysML models against pure textual specifications and evaluate how these SysML models can be used for early system simulations to support design decisions with a high-level tradeoff analysis.

For multi-body simulation aspects Modelica was used but as the evaluation of different simulation tools and languages was still ongoing it was decided that the SysML4Modelica profile will not be applied. Instead, we tried to include information needed for the simulation purposes in the SysML model in a way that allows a simple export into the simulation tool of choice. Most importantly however, we found that information being specific to any particular physical or mathematical model or simulation environment would clutter the SysML model with information that is of no use for the system architect. Also, the system architect cannot be expected to be an expert in physical or mathematical modeling.

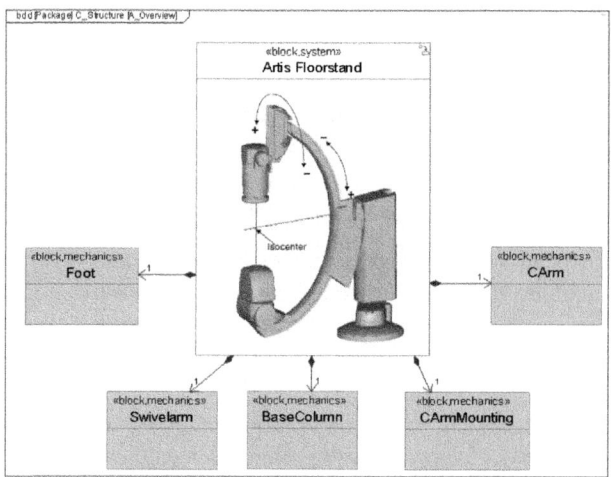

Fig. 3. High-level SysML representation for Artis Floorstand

Development Process
The selected development process for this use case contains the phases: requirements, identification of key hazards, description of the system functionalities and structure, and finally system simulation to verify the requirements. As part of the system structure definition, different views (mechanical, electrical, etc.) are created.

For this use case with a higher level of complexity in the system specifications, it appears more suitable to transfer only a "skeleton" of a simulation model to the simulation expert out of the system model. This skeleton should reflect the system's physical structure, and be connected to the essential design parameters stored in the SysML model. The simulation expert extends the skeleton to a complete simulation model, exploiting his expertise in physical and mathematical modeling, to cope with the simulation requirements.

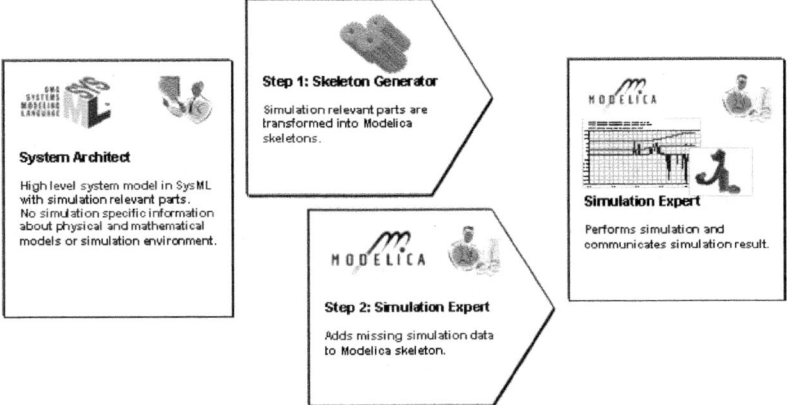

Fig. 4. Exemplary workflow "From SysML to simulation" in the use case of Artis Floorstand

Exemplary Workflow

A system architect of this use case performs the following steps (shown in Fig. 4):

1. develop the high-level architecture in SysML,
2. add simulation relevant data and mark them using dedicated stereotypes,
3. (automatically) create a Modelica skeleton model for the respective SysML components, as well as their connections.

This relieves the simulation expert from the burden of getting the simulation relevant information from a text based document or by interviewing the system architect. The simulation expert then proceeds as follows:

1. open the Modelica skeleton model (he got from the system architect),
2. add missing data to the skeleton, e.g. by editing the connect-equations and connectors,
3. perform the simulation with the essential design parameters being taken from the SysML model,
4. communicate the simulation results and findings to the system architect.

Given the completed simulation model, the system architect then has the possibility to study the system performance under variations of the essential design parameters (trade-off simulations) over which the Modelica model remains coupled to the SysML model. In particular, this can be done autonomously by the simulation expert.

3 Implementation Details

This section presents details how the development processes are realized in the different use cases. Aspects of system modeling over different development cycles are regarded in more details. Benefits from reuse and refinement of models of different abstraction levels are discussed.

3.1 Use Case eCar

In the eCar use case, during the first stage of system development, a low-fidelity model of the system interfaces is constructed. In this stage, the models focus on the analysis of basic information and energy flow. As interfaces are defined in SysML, system simulations are continuously used to evaluate if the interfaces contain all relevant information and reflect the natural technical variables used by the domain experts to design the components. As the design process continues, individual component models are iteratively enriched by more details. In the late stages of a multi-domain development process, the system simulation is used for testing of hardware components. SysML information is used as a central hub for keeping the various component and test revisions synchronized with the system simulation. In this example, physical design refers to mechanical and electronic components modeled with a Modelica tool. Software design addresses software architecture developed with a UML tool.

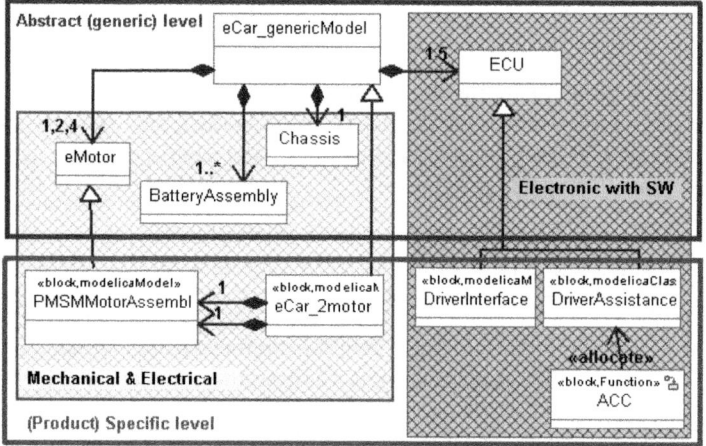

Fig. 5. Introducing a new function (ACC) into existing architecture

Fig. 5 shows an abstract representation of a part of the logical architecture with a sample software component for the ACC function intended to be mapped to one of the electronic control units (ECUs). It also shows some examples for variants of physical constituents of an electrical car and their ECUs as well as variants of software algorithms and drive cycles (inputs for ACC sensors) specified via the generalization relation. To configure specific products, one of the variants for each constituent is selected and connections between these specialized blocks are defined within the SysML internal block diagrams. A variant PMSMMotorAssembly of an electromotor, BatteryAssembly and Chassis from the physical design, as well as product configurations for 1-motor and 2-motor and all their elements (blocks, connectors etc.) are marked with SysML4Modelica stereotypes. These elements are translated automatically into Modelica models. The ECU with ACC software is connected to "physical parts" as an instance of the abstract interface block (ACC) containing the reference to the output of the functionality evaluation for a specific drive cycle. Fig. 1 (left-hand) shows the simulation models generated out of the product configurations in SysML.

3.2 Use Case Artis Floorstand

A major insight of the use case Artis Floorstand is that different levels of abstraction of simulation models should be kept well separated from the system description. If the system description is refined, also the simulation models have to be refined accordingly. In the approach of this use case, the reuse of physical and mathematical models depends on the nature of the refinement. If the system architect refines the SysML model in the sense that block diagrams are added or deleted, reuse of the physical and mathematical models added to the Modelica skeleton by the simulation expert is ensured through the use of preserved areas in the generated Modelica code skeleton.

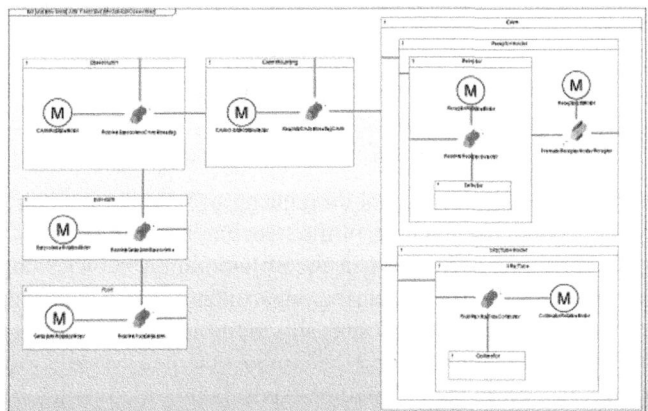

Fig. 6. SysML Internal Block diagram showing mechanical connections

Moreover, physical and mathematical models added by the simulation expert can be reused for subsequent studies if stored appropriately (e.g. in libraries). Otherwise, the reuse of simulation models has to be judged by the simulation expert. Especially in the case when the structure of the SysML model is changed (e.g., a block is divided into several parts), it is not clear whether the corresponding physical and mathematical models are still compatible with the new system structure. A major advantage of the strict separation of system description and physical and mathematical modeling is that the simulation expert has all the freedom to exploit his expertise, while consistency with the system description is ensured by automatically generated

Modelica skeletons. The same goes for the essential design parameters that are included in the system description. However, the simulation expert has to use these parameters manually, which is acceptable as long as the number of such parameters is small.

The following elements store the simulation relevant data within the SysML model:

- Internal block diagrams were used to model specific views of the system like the mechanical view (shown in Fig. 6).
- Block properties not only for models of the system parts but also as specific mechanical joints (e.g. revolute or prismatic). Also dedicated stereotypes and icons were used to make such elements distinguishable on diagrams.
- Mechanical connections modeled via associations marked with a dedicated stereotype «mechanics» which also included specific color setting to make them easily visible on diagrams.
- Attributes for block properties added to store additional information (e.g. weight, size) for system parts.

All these elements and diagrams are of interest to the system architect but are also relevant for simulation purposes; they are used to generate Modelica skeletons but could also be easily used as input for any other simulation language.

4 Comparison of the Proposed Approaches

In this section, advantages and shortcomings of the proposed approaches as well as challenges regarding their suitability in industrial settings are discussed. The following benefits are found to be common for the both approaches.

- SysML models allow for consistent structuring of complex technical systems and an easy-to-understand visualization of the structure and behavior.
- Major improvements are observed in the collaboration between the requirements engineering and the system engineering departments. This stems from the fact that requirements may be connected more easily to the components or subsystems.
- The generation of Modelica code (skeletons) out of a SysML model is another major improvement since the simulation expert is provided with a consistent structure of the system and no longer has to infer the structure himself.

This makes the collaboration between developers of different phases formal and with less or no communication errors.

The differences of the approaches are described in the following subsection and summarized in Table 1.

4.1 Advantages and Disadvantages of both Approaches

The approach used in the use case eCar is seen to have advantages concerning information distribution and collocation thanks to a SysML-based overall system description structured into development phases, levels of abstraction/details, and considered aspects/analysis. Especially, the possibility of early evaluation of the system design through the combination of SysML animation and Modelica simulation in a frontloading approach saves development costs and time. However the synchronization between SysML and Modelica seems to be very challenging, because the current version of the SysML4Modelica profile allows transforming the complete Modelica models into SysML. This level of detail in the SysML4Modelica profile is not relevant for the high-level system architecture. It cannot be assumed that a system architect has the detailed knowledge of the semantics (and usage) of Modelica specific elements, nor of physical or mathematical modeling. In the case when the SysML model is intended to play the role of a container of the complete information, this will make the system description too complex and difficult to manage.

The reasonable usage of the standardized transformation SysML4Modelica is that each system architect is free to choose the level of details for the intended transformation, which he wants and is able to capture in the system description. It is not required that he uses the complete SysML4Modelica profile. Similarly, in this way the transformation is not restricted to a limited set of predefined interfaces, but can be refined at any time of the development.

An essential drawback of this approach is that the synchronization interfaces between SysML and Modelica, while defined with the help of stereotypes in SysML, are not distinguishable within Modelica anymore. This makes the automation of the feedback step (when results of the simulation are fed into the system description) challenging and still not standardized. The "feedback"-interfaces must be distinguishable within Modelica models to avoid that the whole Modelica model is mapped to the SysML model. Another drawback of this approach can be the limitations for the simulation experts when the generated simulation models need to be modified while keeping them compliant with the original model in SysML. Moreover this standardized profile can only be used only with Modelica-based simulation environment.

To showcase the approach of Artis Floorstand, a prototype model transformation script was implemented that allowed generation of Modelica skeletons based on specifically stereotyped SysML elements. This was justified by the request that the system descriptions shall not be contaminated with simulation-specific data, owing to the fact that the roles of system architect and simulation expert are normally assigned to two different people or departments. A big advantage of the approach is therefore that the persons working on the architecture or the simulation only need to know their own language (e.g. SysML or Modelica) and respective tools but not both. The simulation expert retains the full flexibility in setting up physical and mathematical models for the system, both of different levels of abstraction and different levels of detail, while the SysML model is not overloaded with simulation-specific data. In addition, consistency between the structure of the SysML-based system description and the simulation models is ensured through the automatic generation of Modelica code skeletons. Another collaborative benefit is that a system architect can reuse the simulation models established by the simulation expert independently from the expert's support for trade-off analyses.

One drawback of the concept is the effort needed to identify the necessary information that is relevant to connect it to the simulation (most notably Modelica connector classes). This task would remain highly project specific, but also strongly tied to the simulation that should be performed. The concept may therefore only be feasible for projects or problem classes where the simulation goal is clearly identified as both the SysML model as well as the transformation rules needs to be tailored to fit this goal.

Table 1 summarizes the comparison of the considered approaches.

Table 1. Assessment of comparison aspects for the two approaches

Aspects for comparison	Approaches used in	
	eCar	Artis Floorstand
Complexity within SysML representation	probably high	always low
Completeness of generated simulation models	complete is possible	only code frames
Flexibility of changing simulation models	low	high
Selection of the interfaces to simulation	flexible	fixed
Flexible selection of simulation tools	fixed language	possible
Synchronization efforts between formalisms	high	low
Usability	may be complex	easy
Area of application	universal	project specific

4.2 Challenges in Industrial Practice

The both procedures for the use cases described above carries specific challenges especially in an industrial setting:

- It has to be decided which information should be modeled within the system description language and the simulation model. A system architect must be able to identify the goal of the simulation at different development phases and specify simulation relevant attributes in a non intrusive way. Thus, a trade-off between the following aspects is the most challenging:
  - A system architect should not be challenged with loads of simulation specific elements within his SysML model.
  - The SysML model needs to contain enough data that allows the generation of a meaningful simulation model.
- As most multi-domain systems are designed in increasingly large teams, interfaces are often set up at early design stages, and later can be modified corresponding to new requirements or other changes in the environment. This implies rework on the existing models. On the other hand the cooperation between different stakeholders must be as easy as possible to provide a fast reply to the external changes.
- The multi-domain design community is more and more following iterative design processes with a need of iteration results (e.g. from the component level) to be fed back to the system description. Therefore, the model transformation tools need to have two-way capabilities also handling conflicts during synchronization.

5 Conclusion and Outlook

In this paper two multi-domain systems engineering approaches, integrating model-based system description and simulation, have been compared. Each of the two approaches shows advantages that justify its application in the specific project setting but also reveals some weaknesses that have to be minimized. As a result of this case study we see the following focus for the future work. The challenges of synchronization between SysML and Modelica need to be explored in more detail. The possibility for the automatic updates of the system models with the results of the simulation should be investigated. And we plan to evaluate the usage of the SysML4Modelica profile in other use cases with the aim to identify the extent to which simulation details can be effectively managed within the SysML model.

References

1. International Council on Systems Engineering (INCOSE): Systems Engineering Vision 2020, Document No. INCOSE-TP-2004-004-02, Version 2.03 (2007), http://www.incose.org/ProductsPubs/pdf/SEVision2020_20071003_v2_03.pdf
2. Object Management Group: OMG Systems Modeling Language (OMG SysML), V.1.2, OMG formal specification formal/2010-06-02 (June 2010), http://www.sysml.org/docs/specs/OMGSysML-v1.2-10-06-02.pdf
3. Object Management Group: Unified Modeling Language: Superstructure, V.2.3, formal/2010-05-05 (2010), http://www.omg.org/spec/UML/2.3/
4. Fritzson, P.A.: Principles of object-oriented modeling and simulation with Modelica 2.1. John Wiley & Sons, Inc. (2004)
5. Schamai, W., Fritzson, P.: Paredis, C., Pop, P.: Towards Unified System Modeling and Simulation with ModelicaML: Modeling of Executable Behavior Using Graphical Notations. In: Proc. of the 7th Modelica Conference, Como, Italy, September 20-22 (2009)
6. Paredis, C., et al.: An Overview of the SysML-Modelica Transformation Specification. In: Proc. of the 20th Anniversary INCOSE Int. Symp., Chicago, IL, July 12-15 (2010)
7. Thramboulidis, K.: Model Integrated Mechatronics – Towards a new paradigm in the development of manufacturing systems. IEEE Transactions on Industrial Informatics 1(1) (2005)
8. Enge-Rosenblatt, O., et al.: Functional Digital Mock-Up and the Functional Mock-up Interface – Two Complementary Approaches for a Comprehensive Investigation of Heterogeneous Systems. In: Proc. of the 8th Int. Modelica Conference (2011)
9. Votintseva, A., Witschel, P., Goedecke, A.: Analysis of a Complex System for Electrical Mobility Using a Model-Based Engineering Approach Focusing on Simulation. Procedia Computer Science 6, 57–62 (2011)

Strengthening SAT-Based Validation of UML/OCL Models by Representing Collections as Relations

Mirco Kuhlmann and Martin Gogolla

University of Bremen, Computer Science Department
Database Systems Group, D-28334 Bremen
{mk,gogolla}@informatik.uni-bremen.de

Abstract. Collections, i. e., sets, bags, ordered sets and sequences, play a central role in UML and OCL models. Essential OCL operations like role navigation, object selection by stating properties and the first order logic universal and existential quantifiers base upon or result in collections. In this paper, we show a uniform representation of flat and nested, but typed OCL collections as well as strings in form of flat, untyped relations, i. e., sets of tuples, respecting the OCL particularities for nesting, undefinedness and emptiness. Transforming collections and strings into relations is particularly needed in the context of automatic model validation on the basis of a UML and OCL model transformation into relational logic.

1 Introduction

Models are a central means to master complex systems. Thus, for developing systems, building precise models is a main concern. Naturally, the examination of the validity of complex systems must be supported via tracing and checking model properties.

We employ the Unified Modeling Language (UML) and its accompanying textual constraint and query language OCL (Object Constraint Language) for the description of models. For automatically analyzing and validating models, we utilize *relational logic*. Relational logic is efficiently implemented in Alloy [11] and its interface Kodkod [19] which transforms relational models into boolean satisfiability (SAT) problems. As a consequence, our task consists in transforming our source languages UML and OCL as well as the considered model properties into structures and formulas of the target language relational logic. This way, we enable SAT-based validation of UML/OCL models. We have started to implement the transformation from UML/OCL to relational logic in a so-called model validator [13] which has been integrated into our UML-based Specification Environment (USE) [8].

In this paper, we focus on a vital aspect of UML/OCL models, namely the handling of OCL collection kinds (set, bag, ordered set, and sequence)[1] and

---

[1] One collection kind (e. g., set) can be manifested in different concrete collection types (e. g., Set(Integer) and Set(Bag(String))).

strings. OCL collections and collection operations play a central role in the language. They are crucial for building precise UML/OCL models which can be successfully analyzed and checked. For instance, the evaluation of existentially and universally quantified formulas is based upon collections of values like in Person.allInstances->exists(p|p.age<18). Another naturally used operation is role navigation which results in collection values, e.g., when the allowed states of a structural model given in form of a class diagram have to be restricted and the restriction involves two classes and an association navigation path between the classes, the association path will be evaluated in OCL through a collection expression. The following example ensures a minimum salary by collecting the employees of all companies using navigation: Company.allInstances.employee->forAll(e| e.salary>3000).

The example model shown as a UML class diagram in Fig. 1 emphasizes the use of strings and different types of collections. A university is located in a specific state encoded by a two character string, e.g., 'DK' or 'US'. A person may have several postal and e-mail addresses and may be enrolled in a university. While postal addresses are always unordered (Set(String)), the e-mail addresses of a person can be prioritized by using an ordered set of addresses, or be retained without any prioritization by using a set. The abstract type Collection(String) allows for determining the concrete type (OrderedSet(String) or Set(String)) at runtime.

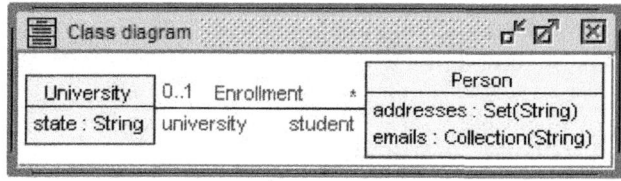

Fig. 1. Example UML Class Diagram with String and Collection Type Attributes

The following example OCL invariant further constrains the model. It requires each person who is a student at a university to have a postal address in the same state the university is located. For this purpose, it checks whether the string representing the university's location also occurs at any position in at least one postal address string of the student.

```
context Person inv AccessibleStudents:
  self.university.isDefined implies
    self.addresses->exists(a|
      Set{1..a.size}->exists(i|a.substring(i,i+1)=self.university.state))
```

However, when comparing UML and OCL, our source languages for describing models, and relational logic, our direct target language utilized for automatic model validation, we observe an impedance mismatch: (a) OCL offers four collection kinds whereas relational logic and its implementation Alloy directly support only relations, i.e., sets of flat tuples; *"other structures (such as lists and sequences) are not built into Alloy the way sets and relations are*" (see p. 158 in [11]) (b) OCL is a typed language whereas plain relational logic is untyped. This means that the OCL type system has to be represented in relational logic and the missing collection kinds have to be encoded as sets. (c) The lack of *"higher-order relations"* implies that *"collections of collections"* which often occur in UML/OCL models are not directly supported in Alloy [1]. Consequently, the challenge is to respect all involved OCL particularities in the translation which means that nested collections as well as OCL type rules, the undefined value, and empty collections deserve special attention.

We present a uniform transformation which respects all language inherent differences between UML/OCL collections and flat relations of relational logic. Furthermore, we enable the representation of structured string values in relational logic. A comprehensive representation of UML/OCL collections and strings in relational logic is the premise for the translation of collection and string operations and, hence, a comprehensive approach to automatic UML/OCL model validation utilizing Kodkod and SAT solving. However, there is currently no other SAT-based approach which supports models like the example depicted in Fig. 1 or the related OCL constraint.

The rest of this paper is structured as follows. Section 2 associates the content of this paper with the SAT-based model validation context. The central Sect. 3 will show how OCL collections and strings are represented as relations. First, we introduce the approach considering exemplary transformations. Then, we illustrate the underlying transformation algorithms. After a discussion of performance implications in Sect. 4 and related work Sect. 5, we conclude with Sect. 6.

2 Model Validation via SAT Solving: Context

Our validation approach bases upon checking model properties by inspecting the properties of model instances (snapshots), e.g., the existence or non-existence of specific snapshots allows conclusions about the model itself. As shown in Fig. 2, the USE *model validator* allows developers to automatically analyze properties of their UML/OCL models by translating them into relational structures, i.e., bounded relations and relational formulas, which can be handled by the model finder Kodkod. In addition to a model, the properties under consideration, usually given in form of OCL expressions, as well as user-configurations with respect to the search space are transformed and handed over to Kodkod.

Kodkod in turn employs SAT solvers to find a solution, i.e., proper instantiations of specified relations, fulfilling the given formulas. Found SAT instances are therefore translated back into instances of the specified relations. In the end, the model validator transforms the relational instances into instances of the UML/OCL model and visually presents the found solution in form of an object diagram to the developer.

Since UML/OCL collections and strings values play a central role in precisely specified models, corresponding validation approaches must support the four collection kinds and their peculiarities as well as strings in order to provide a

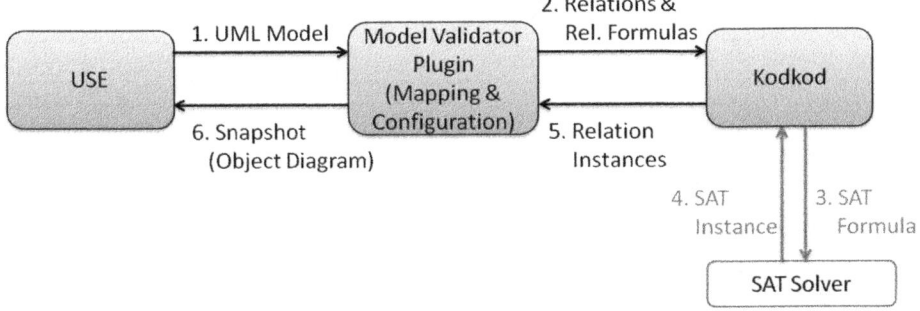

Fig. 2. Transformation process involving the USE model validator

comprehensive validation platform. The transformation algorithm discussed in this paper has been implemented in the model validator enabling the definition of meaningful OCL constraints on the one hand, and user-defined properties which are to be inspected on the other hand.

3 Transforming Collections and Strings into Relations

Relational logic describes formulas whose evaluation is based on flat relations with different arities, i. e., sets of tuples with atomic components, since relational logic forbids nested relations. Beside boolean and integer operations, relational logic naturally supports set operations like union and set comprehension. A central operation is the relational join for accessing specific components (i. e., columns) of tuples and for connecting tuples of different relations.

Relations generally have the same properties as OCL sets which are unordered and do not allow duplicate elements.[2] Thus, there is a straightforward way to translating non-nested sets into unary relations, e. g., Set{2,1,3} can be represented by the relation [[3],[1],[2]]. On the other hand, the following characteristics of OCL collections must be respected:

- Bags and sequences require the support of duplicate elements.
- Ordered sets and sequences require the support of ordered elements.
- All collection kinds require the support of nested collections.

A universally applicable transformation must cover all of these properties.

3.1 The Basic Idea

In this subsection we consider the first two named properties (support of duplicate and ordered elements), nested collections, and strings as well as the handling of undefined and empty values in greater detail. The comparability of collection and string values must be preserved by their relational representation. This essential aspect is discussed at the end of this subsection.

---

[2] Henceforth, the term 'set' refers to an OCL set.

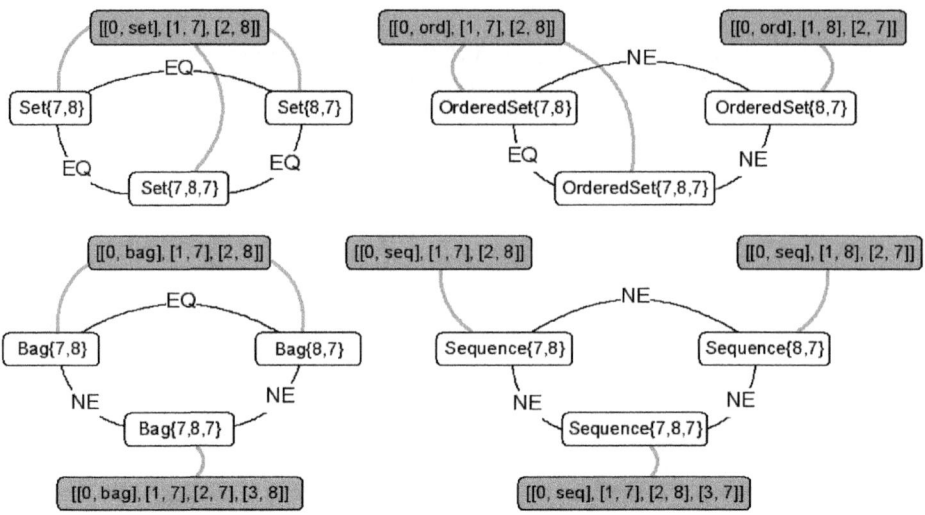

Fig. 3. Distinction of OCL collections and the corresponding translation into relations

Handling of Flat Collections. In Fig. 3 we illustrate the properties of the four OCL collection kinds based on three concrete literals, in each case. The OCL literals – depicted in white boxes – involve duplicate elements and elements in a particular order. Two literals are equal (EQ), i.e., they represent the same value, or are not equal (NE). For instance, while Bag{7,8} equals Bag{8,7}, the collection value OrderedSet{7,8} does not equal OrderedSet{8,7}.

Collection literals describing the same value should naturally yield the same (identifying) relational representation which are shown in grey boxes and by grey connecting lines. The translation assigns an index $1 \leq i \leq n$ to each element of a collection with n elements, determining an explicit element position. See, for example, the relational representation of the value Sequence{7,8,7}. The corresponding relational representation relates the index 1 to the first element (7), index 2 to the second element (8) and index 3 to the last element (7).

The depicted, grey relations reveal four distinctive features of the transformation which do not directly result from the collection properties, but from explicit design decisions:

- The elements of a set or bag are indexed in the respective relational representation, although sets and bags are intrinsically unordered and sets do not include duplicate elements.
- m duplicates of element e in a bag occur m times in the respective relational representation.[3]
- The elements of sets and bags are sorted in the resulting relations based on the natural order of integer values. For example, considering the literals Set{7,8} and Set{8,7}, the integer value 7 always precedes the value 8 in the relational representation of both sets.

---
[3] An alternative would be tuples counting element occurrences (e.g., [e,m]).

– The special index 0 indicates a typing tuple that determines the collection kind a relation represents (set, bag, ord, seq).

The first two features (an order for sets resp. bags and retention of explicit duplicates) directly follow from our intention to define a uniform transformation with no exceptional cases and resulting case distinctions, clearly simplifying (a) the representation of nested collections, and (b) the translation of OCL collection operations into relational logic. The last two aspects (sorting elements and explicit typing) allow us to compare OCL collection values in relational logic through an explicit sorting of their elements, as we will discuss at the end of this subsection.

Handling of Nested Collections and Strings. In the case of nested collections, the elements of a collection are in turn collections. In order to encapsulate the individual collections, i.e., to determine which value belongs to which collection, there must be an additional indicator. Following our uniform translation, a natural way to representing collection type elements is the use of a new index column, as shown in the following example:

```
Set{7}              --> [[ 0,set    ],     the relation represents a set
                    [  1,7      ]]     the first element is 7
Set{8,9}            --> [[ 0,set    ],     the relation represents a set
                    [  1,8      ],     the first element is 8
                    [  2,9      ]]     the second element is 9
Sequence{Set{7},
         Set{8,9}}  --> [[0,seq,seq],    the relation represents a sequence[4]
                    [1,0,set   ],     the first element is a set
                    [1,1,7     ],     the first element of the set is 7
                    [2,0,set   ],     the second element is a set
                    [2,1,8     ],     the first element of the set is 8
                    [2,2,9     ]]     the second element of the set is 9
```

The support of OCL collections also allows for representing string values. While strings may be seen as atomic values (e.g., 'Ada' --> [[Ada]]), it is often necessary to consider a string as a value with an inner structure. Thus, because there is a need in OCL for manipulating and querying strings, they are treated like sequences of characters and are identified by a respective string typing tuple (e.g., 'Ada' --> [[0,str],[1,A],[2,d],[3,a]]). A set of strings can thus be seen as sequences of values nested in a set:

```
Set{'Ada','Bob'} --> [[0,set,set],
                     [1,0,str], [1,1,A], [1,2,d], [1,3,a],
                     [2,0,str], [2,1,B], [2,2,o], [2,3,b]]
```

---

[4] Since all tuples of a relation must have the same arity, we use the collection kind indicator (e.g., seq) to fill typing tuples until they yield the required number of components. Multiple indicators in one typing tuple, thus, have no special meaning.

In OCL, sets, bags, sequences and ordered sets are specializations of *Collection*, and all basic types are subtypes of *OclAny*. Thus, for example, we can create collections including elements of type Collection(OclAny):

```
Set{Sequence{5,6,5},Set{'Ada',7,'Bob',8}} =
Set{Set{7,8,'Ada','Bob'},Sequence{5,6,5}} -->
[[0,set,set,set],
 [1,0,set,set],
 [1,1,1,7],
 [1,2,1,8],
 [1,3,0,str],[1,3,1,A],[1,3,2,d],[1,3,3,a],
 [1,4,0,str],[1,4,1,B],[1,4,2,o],[1,4,3,b],
 [2,0,seq,seq],
 [2,1,1,5],
 [2,2,1,6],
 [2,3,1,5]]
```

If string and non-string basic types are mixed, the non-string basic type values are brought into the complex string representation by handling them as if they were strings of length one with an absent typing tuple, e. g., the integer value 7 is represented as [1,7] instead of [7].

The translation result of the previous example is a relation that represents a set including collections of sequences. Each additional nesting level adds a further index column to the relation. The fourth column determines the character or integer value. The third column determines the position of the characters in a string. The second column determines the position of a string within a collection. The first column determines the position of the collection in the outer set.

For instance, the tuple [1,3,2,d] determines 'd' to be the second character of the third element ('Ada') in the first element (Set{7,8,'Ada','Bob'}) of Set{Set{7,8,'Ada','Bob'},Sequence{5,6,5}}.

Undefined and Empty Collections. Empty collections are naturally represented by the absence of further tuples besides the typing tuple. Undefined (un) collections on the other hand yield a characteristic relational representation. This representation allows us to identify at which nesting level an undefined value occurs (c. f. the three different levels in the following example). Furthermore, undefined values are not accompanied by typing tuples, since the information which concrete type an undefined value represents is irrelevant.

```
Set{Undefined, Set{}, Set{Undefined, Set{}, Set{Undefined}}} -->
[[0,set,set,set],    the relation represents a set
 [1,un,un,un],       the first element is an undefined collection
 [2,0,set,set],      the second element is an empty set
 [3,0,set,set],      the third element is a set
 [3,1,un,un],        its first element is an undefined collection
 [3,2,0,set],        its second element is an empty set
 [3,3,0,set],        its third element is a set
 [3,3,1,un]]         which includes an undefined value
```

Making Ordered Relations Comparable. In Fig. 3 we depicted the equality and inequality of specific collection literals. Since sets and bags are intrinsically unordered, we obtain the properties: Set{7,8}=Set{8,7} and Bag{7,8}= Bag{8,7}. Accordingly, an equality check regarding the relational representation of both sets and both bags, respectively, must evaluate to true. We can achieve a general valid comparability at the relational level (a) by sorting the elements of the relational representations of sets and bags on demand (e. g., in the case of an equality check, or the casting operation Set::asSequence()), or (b) by sorting the elements already during the creation process. We applied the latter strategy which results in a unique representation of equal collection values through direct sorting:

Set{7,8} --> [[0,set],[1,7],[2,8]] <-- Set{8,7} and
Bag{7,8} --> [[0,bag],[1,7],[2,8]] <-- Bag{8,7}

SAT-based validation implies bounded search spaces, i. e., at the UML level, a limited set of covered model instances. Hence, the set of participating values (boolean, integer, enumeration, character, or object type)[5] is finite. This allows us to create a total order on all available values and to define a sorting algorithm with respect to the precedence of these values. Within the previous example of nested collections with mixed basic type values, the literals Set{7,8,'Ada','Bob'} and Set{'Ada',7,'Bob',8} yield the same relational representation after sorting the elements (integer precedes string). The example shows three further properties of the sorting algorithm:

- The sorting of sets and bags has a recursive nature, i. e., sorting is applied at each nesting level. Before an outer set or bag can be sorted, its elements must have been sorted.
- Sequences, ordered sets and strings are never sorted, since the order of their elements (or characters, respectively) is significant (e. g., Sequence{5,6,5}<> Sequence{5,5,6}). If they, however, include set or bag valued elements, these sets and bags have to be sorted (e. g., Sequence{Set{8,7},Set{2,1}}= Sequence{Set{7,8},Set{1,2}}).
- Beside basic values, also strings and collections obtain an explicit precedence, based on the collection kind, number of elements (or characters, respectively), and precedence of their elements (or characters), e. g., 'Bo' < 'Ada', 'Ada' < 'Bob', Set{7} < Bag{7}, Set{7} < Set{1,2}, and Set{1,2} < Set{7,8}.

The need for typing tuples directly follows from the need for comparability. Since the values Bag{7,8} --> [[0,bag],[1,7],[2,8]] and Set{7,8} --> [[0,set],[1,7],[2,8]] are not equal, a relational representation without typing tuples would lead to an invalid conclusion for equality:

Set{7,8} --> [[1,7],[2,8]] <-- Bag{7,8} ≠

---

[5] The character type includes the alphabetic characters which are needed to create string values. The basic predefined type Real is currently not supported.

3.2 Realization of the Transformation Algorithms

In this section, we explain the details of translating UML/OCL collections into relations by considering the relevant transformation algorithms. Since the algorithm for constructing strings at the relational level is a special case of the creation of flat sequences, we focus on the general handling of collections.

First, we consider the core algorithm describing the creation of collection values. Then, we go into details of sorting collections which is needed in the context of sets and bags.

The Collection Creation Algorithm. The algorithm for creating UML/OCL collections in their relational representation includes two main aspects: (a) Each given element which should be included into the collection and is already available in a relational representation is incrementally indexed and added to the resulting relation. Duplicate elements are discarded if the resulting relation should represent a set or ordered set. (b) Relations representing sets or bags are sorted in the end. In this case, the following sorting algorithms become relevant. For details see Algorithm 1 in the appendix.

The Collection Sorting Algorithms. The central sorting algorithm includes the main activities for sorting relations representing sets or bags. It takes all possible pairs of elements existing in the given relation and determines which element precedes the other. The number of predecessors an element possesses then determines its new position in the sorted relation. The element without predecessors obtains the first position (index 1), and an element with x predecessors becomes the $x+1$th element in the sorted relation. For details see Algorithm 2 in the appendix.

The precedence of two complex, collection-valued elements is determined by a further algorithm which respects the following precedence rules: undefined collections precede sets, sets precede sequences, sequences precede bags, bags precede ordered sets; in the case of collections of the same kind, the number of elements within these collections becomes relevant; if the numbers are identical, the precedence of the elements within the two considered collections must be recursively determined. For details see Algorithm 3 in the appendix.

The recursive calculation of element precedences may end at different levels of nested values. For example, consider the following pairs of collections:

A: Set{Set{Set{7}}}, Bag{Set{Set{7}}}
B: Set{Set{Set{7}}}, Set{Set{Bag{7}}}
C: Set{Set{Set{7}}}, Set{Set{Set{8}}}

In each case the left side precedes the right side. While in pair A the precedence can be directly determined (sets precede bags), pair B demands a nested (recursive) comparison until the elements Set{7} and Bag{7} at the second nesting level are reached. In the case of pair C, the final level of recursion is reached, i.e., the level at which only simple values occur (7 and 8).

As mentioned before, each validation task given to the USE model validator describes a *finite* user-defined *universe* of simple values (i.e., boolean, integer, enumeration, character, or object type). As a consequence, the precedence of these simple values can always be specified via a total order relation.[6] Given such a total order relation and two simple values, the precedence of both values can directly be calculated. For details see Algorithm 4 in the appendix.

4 Discussion

A bounded search space of the model validator (resp. Kodkod) requires bounded relations and thus bounded collection representations. Kodkod considers the set of all available (user-defined) simple values as a universe of atoms. Relations are bounded to a set of possible tuples by determining a set of possible atoms (a domain) for each column of the relation tuples. For instance, a relation that represents the type Set(Set(Boolean)) yields tuples of the form:

[$index_1$, $index_2$, $value$], with
$index_1 \in Domain_1 = \{0, 1, ..., x, \text{un}\}$, where x is a user defined maximum number,
$index_2 \in Domain_2 = \{0, 1, ..., x, \text{un}, \text{set}\}$, and
$value \in Domain_3 = \{\text{true}, \text{false}, \text{un}, \text{set}\}$.

There are $|Domain_1| * |Domain_2| * |Domain_3|$ possible tuples which can be included by an instance of the considered relation. As we have explained before, each nesting level of collections adds one additional column to the respective relation, increasing its arity by one. A nesting depth of n implies a relation of arity $n+2$ (or $n+3$ if strings are involved). Consequently, each additional nesting level considerably increases the search space and correspondingly reduces the SAT solving performance. Furthermore, Kodkod limits the maximum arity of involved relations und thus the maximum nesting depth: $|universe|^{max\_arity} < 2^{31} - 1$. Future work will comprise the optimization of the search space by bounding the possible tuples to OCL collection specific patterns.

There is also potential for optimization with respect our representation of OCL collections as flat relations. However, our aim is to present a universally defined and applicable approach in this paper. A concrete implementation can naturally realize several optimizations like discarding typing tuples, if the collection types can be statically determined, i.e., *Collection* is not involved, or using a simple representation of OCL sets and strings in form of unary relations, if only non-nested collections and no complex string values are needed. That is, while our approach supports all OCL collections structures, it can be thinned out as required.

In order to inspect the performance implications in the context of a complete implementation of our approach, let us consider the class diagram shown in Fig. 4

---

[6] In the case of values which do no yield a natural order, the model validator explicitly induces one, e.g., the order of objects is determined by the order the corresponding object identifiers are declared within the model validator, independent of the classes they instantiate.

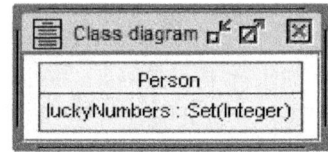

Fig. 4. UML Class with a Set-valued Attribute

which models persons with a set of lucky numbers, as well as the following OCL invariant which demands that people have unique sets of lucky numbers. Please note that in our approach for transforming UML and OCL models into relational models, classes are translated into unary relations, holding atoms which represent object identifiers. Attributes are translated into relations connecting object identifiers with attribute values, plus relational constraints ensuring attribute values of the specified type. In the case of collection-valued attributes, an object is related to each individual tuple of the corresponding collection value. An example instance of the attribute relation Person_luckyNumbers is shown at the end of this section.

```
context p:Person
  inv uniqueLuckyNumbersSets:
    Person.allInstances->forAll(p1,p2|
      p1.luckyNumbers=p2.luckyNumbers implies p1=p2)
```

```
--> (sketch of a translation into relational logic)
(all p1:Person, p2:Person |
  p1.Person_luckyNumbers=p2.Person_luckyNumbers => p1=p2)
```

First, we use the model validator to automatically translate this UML and OCL model into a relational model, and initiate a search for valid instances in the context of 4, 8, and 12 person objects. Then, we repeat this procedure for nested attribute types. Table 1 reveals the corresponding search times. The second column yields the results for a simple set representation using unary relations, e.g., Set{7,8} --> [[7],[8]] instead of the complex representation discussed in this paper, e.g., Set{7,8} --> [[0,set],[1,7],[2,8]].

Table 1. Comparison of SAT Solving Performance regarding different Nesting Levels

#Persons	Set(Int) (simple)	Set(Int)	Set(Set(Int))	Set(Set(Set(Int)))
4	62 ms	437 ms	2200 ms	14955 ms
8	109 ms	764 ms	5132 ms	62540 ms
12	140 ms	1326 ms	16497 ms	140522 ms

In the context of type Set(Set(Integer)) and 4 required person objects, we, for example, obtain the following class and attribute relation instances as a result which are automatically transformed by the model validator into the object diagram shown in Fig. 5.

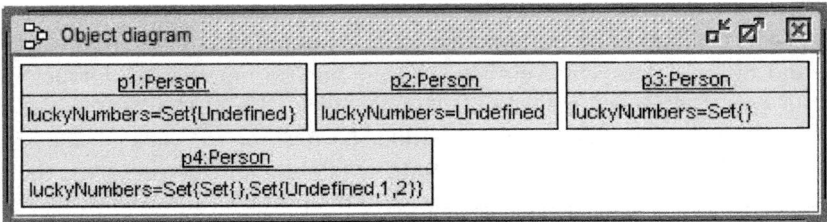

Fig. 5. Solution in the context of 4 Objects and Type Set(Set(Integer))

```
Person=[[p1],[p2],[p3],[p4]]
Person_luckyNumbers=[
  [p1,0,set,set,set],[p1,1,un,un,un],
  [p2,un,un,un,un],
  [p3,0,set,set,set],
  [p4,0,set,set,set],
    [p4,1,0,set,set],
    [p4,2,0,set,set],[p4,2,1,un,un],[p4,2,2,1,1],[p4,2,3,1,2]]
```

5 Related Work

Our paper has connections to many related works. The collection kinds set, bag and list (sequence) are considered in the context of functional programming in [10,23] whereas our approach is designed for object-oriented design and modeling. The Object Query Language OQL [7] uses three (set, bag, list) of the four OCL collections in the same way as they are employed in OCL but without defining a formal semantics. [16] makes a proposal to complete the OCL collections in a lattice-like style leading to union and intersection types. The work concentrates on the OCL collection kind set.

General type and container constructors similar to sets or bags are considered for database design using ER modeling in [9]. [4] represents the OCL standard collections with an extended OCL metamodel allowing for practical tool support with the aim of code generation. [6] studies fundamental properties of OCL collections in order to establish a new generalization hierarchy and focusses of the relationship between sets and ordered sets. [22] proposes a unified description of OCL collection types and OCL basic data types. [14] translates OCL into Maude and represents OCL collections by introducing new algebraic sorts without considering the complete OCL type system. A mapping of non-nested OCL collections and strings into bit-vector logic is done in [17]. In [5] the authors describe a staged encoding of OCL strings that performs reasoning on string equalities and string lengths before fully instantiating the string.

Our approach is based on relational logic which is implemented in the powerful Alloy system described in [11]. Alloy supports non-nested sets and sequences modeled as functions mapping integer (indices) to the sequence elements. The

UML2Alloy approach presented in [1] tackles the translation of UML and OCL concepts into Alloy. The authors sketch the possibility to describe sequences, bags and ordered sets via Alloy structures, but do not discuss further details like the preservation of collection comparability. While the representation of nested collections in Alloy is not possible, because of the lack of higher-order relations and restrictions with respect to available Alloy structures, the Alloy interface Kodkod [19] which we utilize in our approach allows users to handle plain relations with arbitrary contents.

Alloy and Kodkod are used for many purposes. [3] translates conceptual models described in OntoUML for validation purposes into Alloy. In [12] modeling languages and their formal semantics, in [21] enterprise architecture models based on ontologies are specified and analyzed with Alloy. Kodkod has been utilized for executing declarative specifications in case of runtime exceptions in Java programs [15], reasoning about memory models [20], or generating counterexamples for Isabelle/HOL a proof assistant for higher-order logic (Nitpick) [2]. [18] use Kodkod for checking the consistency of models described with basic UML concepts.

6 Conclusion

We have discussed a uniform representation of strings and nested, typed collections in form of flat, untyped sets respecting the OCL particularities for nesting, undefinedness and emptiness. Collections are a central modeling feature in UML and OCL for model inspection and model validation and verification. We have successfully implemented this approach in our model validator and applied it in several middle-sized examples.

As future work, we want to check the approach with larger case studies. In particular, we have to check whether efficiency improvement may be made by factoring out type information from the collection instances. A small benchmark for checking collection and string values could be developed. With respect to OCL, one might propose an OCL simplification based on the experience with the difficult handling of undefinedness in order to shorten the gap between the source and target languages.

Furthermore, the concepts for sorting collections at the relational level which we have discussed in this paper can be reused for standardizing corresponding OCL *sort* operations. Such operations could deterministically lead from unordered collections to sorted collections, e. g.,

```
Set{1,2,3}->sort = OrderedSet{1,2,3} = Set{2,3,1}->sort,
Bag{1,2,2,3}->sort = Sequence{1,2,2,3} = Bag{2,1,2,3}->sort, and
Set{OrderedSet{2,1}, OrderedSet{1,2}}->sort =
OrderedSet{OrderedSet{1,2}, OrderedSet{2,1}}.
```

However, also ordered collections (which are not necessarily sorted) need sometimes to be sorted, so that we propose using this sort operation for all four collection kinds.

References

1. Anastasakis, K., Bordbar, B., Georg, G., Ray, I.: On challenges of model transformation from UML to Alloy. SoSyM 9(1), 69–86 (2010)
2. Blanchette, J.C., Nipkow, T.: Nitpick: A Counterexample Generator for Higher-Order Logic Based on a Relational Model Finder. In: Kaufmann, M., Paulson, L.C. (eds.) ITP 2010. LNCS, vol. 6172, pp. 131–146. Springer, Heidelberg (2010)
3. Braga, B.F.B., Almeida, J.P.A., Guizzardi, G., Benevides, A.B.: Transforming OntoUML into Alloy: towards conceptual model validation using a lightweight formal method. ISSE 6(1-2), 55–63 (2010)
4. Bräuer, M., Demuth, B.: Model-Level Integration of the OCL Standard Library Using a Pivot Model with Generics Support. ECEASST 9 (2008)
5. Büttner, F., Cabot, J.: Lightweight String Reasoning for OCL. In: Vallecillo, A., et al. (eds.) ECMFA 2012. LNCS, vol. 7349, pp. 240–254. Springer, Heidelberg (2012)
6. Büttner, F., Gogolla, M., Hamann, L., Kuhlmann, M., Lindow, A.: On Better Understanding OCL Collections or An OCL Ordered Set Is Not an OCL Set. In: Ghosh, S. (ed.) MODELS 2009. LNCS, vol. 6002, pp. 276–290. Springer, Heidelberg (2010)
7. Cattell, R.G.G., Barry, D.K.: The Object Data Standard: ODMG 3.0. Morgan Kaufmann (2000)
8. Gogolla, M., Büttner, F., Richters, M.: USE: A UML-Based Specification Environment for Validating UML and OCL. Science of Computer Programming 69, 27–34 (2007)
9. Hartmann, S., Link, S.: Collection Type Constructors in Entity-Relationship Modeling. In: Parent, C., Schewe, K.-D., Storey, V.C., Thalheim, B. (eds.) ER 2007. LNCS, vol. 4801, pp. 307–322. Springer, Heidelberg (2007)
10. Hoogendijk, P.F., Backhouse, R.C.: Relational Programming Laws in the Tree, List, Bag, Set Hierarchy. Sci. Comput. Program. 22(1-2), 67–105 (1994)
11. Jackson, D.: Software Abstractions: Logic, Language, and Analysis. MIT Press (2006)
12. Kelsen, P., Ma, Q.: A Lightweight Approach for Defining the Formal Semantics of a Modeling Language. In: Czarnecki, K., Ober, I., Bruel, J.-M., Uhl, A., Völter, M. (eds.) MODELS 2008. LNCS, vol. 5301, pp. 690–704. Springer, Heidelberg (2008)
13. Kuhlmann, M., Hamann, L., Gogolla, M.: Extensive Validation of OCL Models by Integrating SAT Solving into USE. In: Bishop, J., Vallecillo, A. (eds.) TOOLS 2011. LNCS, vol. 6705, pp. 290–306. Springer, Heidelberg (2011)
14. Roldan, M., Duran, F.: Dynamic Validation of OCL Constraints with mOdCL. ECEASST 44 (2011)
15. Samimi, H., Aung, E.D., Millstein, T.: Falling Back on Executable Specifications. In: D'Hondt, T. (ed.) ECOOP 2010. LNCS, vol. 6183, pp. 552–576. Springer, Heidelberg (2010)
16. Schürr, A.: A New Type Checking Approach for OCL Version 2.0? In: Clark, A., Warmer, J. (eds.) Object Modeling with the OCL. LNCS, vol. 2263, pp. 21–41. Springer, Heidelberg (2002)
17. Soeken, M., Wille, R., Drechsler, R.: Encoding OCL Data Types for SAT-Based Verification of UML/OCL Models. In: Gogolla, M., Wolff, B. (eds.) TAP 2011. LNCS, vol. 6706, pp. 152–170. Springer, Heidelberg (2011)
18. Van Der Straeten, R., Pinna Puissant, J., Mens, T.: Assessing the Kodkod Model Finder for Resolving Model Inconsistencies. In: France, R.B., Kuester, J.M., Bordbar, B., Paige, R.F. (eds.) ECMFA 2011. LNCS, vol. 6698, pp. 69–84. Springer, Heidelberg (2011)

19. Torlak, E., Jackson, D.: Kodkod: A Relational Model Finder. In: Grumberg, O., Huth, M. (eds.) TACAS 2007. LNCS, vol. 4424, pp. 632–647. Springer, Heidelberg (2007)
20. Torlak, E., Vaziri, M., Dolby, J.: MemSAT: checking axiomatic specifications of memory models. SIGPLAN Not. 45, 341–350 (2010), http://doi.acm.org/10.1145/1809028.1806635
21. Wegmann, A., Le, L.-S., Hussami, L., Beyer, D.: A Tool for Verified Design using Alloy for Specification and CrocoPat for Verification. In: Jackson, D., Zave, P. (eds.) Proc. First Alloy Workshop (2006)
22. Willink, E.D.: Modeling the OCL Standard Library. ECEASST 44 (2011)
23. Wong, L.: Polymorphic Queries Across Sets, Bags, and Lists. SIGPLAN Notices 30(4), 39–44 (1995)

A Collection Creation and Sorting Algorithms

The presented algorithms abstract from complex language characteristics of relational logic and are designed to clarify the overall activities for creating and sorting UML/OCL collections at the relational level.

collectionCreation(colKind, ...elements)
input: *the required collection kind* (colKind $\in$ {set,bag,ord,seq}),
      a list of elements *already available in relational representation*
output: *a collection of kind* colKind *including the properly ordered elements*
  newCol $\leftarrow$ []
  index $\leftarrow$ 1
  for each e **in** elements **do**
    if colKind *is* bag *or* sequence *or* e *does not already exist in* newCol **then**
      indexed_e $\leftarrow$ *add* index *as first component to each tuple of* e
      newCol $\leftarrow$ newCol $\cup$ indexed_e
      index $\leftarrow$ index + 1
    end
  end
  newCol $\leftarrow$ newCol $\cup$ *typing tuple*
  if newCol *is* set *or* bag **then**
    return complexSort(newCol)
  else
    return newCol
  end

Algorithm 1: Creating relations for representing UML/OCL collections

complexSort(col)
input: *an unsorted relation* col *representing a set or bag*
output: *a relation with sorted elements*
  predecessorMap $\leftarrow$ *empty map*
  for each e_1, e_2 *in* col **do**
    if complexPredecessor(e_1,e_2) = e_1
      or (complexPredecessor(e_1,e_2) = Undefined
        and original e_1 *position* < *original* e_2 *position*) **then**
      predecessorMap.add(e_1,e_2)
    end
  end
  positionMap $\leftarrow$ *empty map*
  for each e **in** col **do**
    positionMap.add(e, |predecessorMap(e)|+1)
    modified_e $\leftarrow$ e *with topmost index replaced by* positionMap(e)
    col $\leftarrow$ col *with* e *replaced by* modified_e
  end
  return col

Algorithm 2: Sorting relations representing sets or bags

complexPredecessor(e_1, e_2)
input: *two complex elements*
output: *the preceding element*
  if e_1 *is a singleton, i. e., a relation including just a simple value* **then**
    return simplePredecessor(e_1, e_2)
  else
    if e_1 *is undefined and* e_2 *is undefined* **then** *return* Undefined **end**
    if e_1 *is undefined and* e_2 *is not undefined* **then return** e_1 **end**
    if e_1 *is not undefined and* e_2 *is undefined* **then return** e_2 **end**
    if e_1 *is a set and* e_2 *is not a set* **then return** e_1 **end**
    if e_1 *is not a set and* e_2 *is a set* **then return** e_2 **end**
    if e_1 *is a sequence and* e_2 *is not a sequence* **then return** e_1 **end**
    if e_1 *is not a sequence and* e_2 *is a sequence* **then return** e_2 **end**
    if e_1 *is a bag and* e_2 *is not a bag* **then return** e_1 **end**
    if e_1 *is not a bag and* e_2 *is a bag* **then return** e_2 **end**
    if e_1 *has less elements than* e_2 **then return** e_1 **end**
    if e_2 *has less elements than* e_1 **then return** e_2 **end**
    relevantElement ← null
    for each *position* i *in* e_1 *und* e_2 **do**
      e_1_elem ← *element at position* i *of* e_1
      e_2_elem ← *element at position* i *of* e_2
      if complexPredecessor(e_1_elem, e_2_elem) = Undefined **then**
        continue
      else
        if complexPredecessor(e_1_elem, e_2_elem) = e_1_elem **then**
          return e_1
        else
          return e_2
end end end end
return Undefined

Algorithm 3: Determining the precedence of elements

simplePredecessor(TO, e_1, e_2)
input: *a binary relation* TO *specifying a total order for all simple values*
    so that if [x,y] ∈ TO, x *is the direct predecessor of* y,
    two simple elements
output: *the preceding element*
  if $e_1 = e_2$ **then**
    return Undefined
  else if [e_1,e_2] ∈ closure(TO) **then**
    return e_1
  else
    return e_2
  end

Algorithm 4: Determining the precedence of simple values

Model Interchange Testing: A Process and a Case Study

Maged Elaasar[1] and Yvan Labiche[2]

[1] IBM Canada Ltd, Rational Software, Ottawa Lab
770 Palladium Dr., Kanata, ON. K2V 1C8, Canada
melaasar@ca.ibm.com
[2] Carleton University, Department of Systems and Computer Engineering
1125 Colonel By Drive, Ottawa, ON K1S5B6, Canada
labiche@sce.carleton.ca

Abstract. Modeling standards by the Object Management Group (OMG) enable the interchange of models between tools. In practice, the success of such interchange has been severely limited due to ambiguities and inconsistencies in the standards and lack of rigorous testing of tools' interchange capabilities. This motivated a number of OMG members, including tool vendors and users, to form a Model Interchange Working Group (MIWG) to test and improve model interchange between tools. In this paper, we report on the activities of the MIWG, presenting its testing process and highlighting its design decisions and challenges. We also report on a case study where the MIWG has used its process to test the interchange of UML and SysML models. We make observations, present statistics and discuss lessons learned. We conclude that the MIWG has indeed defined a rigorous, effective and semi-automated process for model interchange testing, which has resulted in more reliable interchange of models between participating tools.

Keywords: Model, Interchange, MOF, UML, SysML, XMI, OCL.

1 Introduction

Model Driven Architecture (MDA) [1] is an approach to the development of systems advocated by the Object Management Group (OMG). MDA encourages the specification of system functionality as models. A model organizes information based on a metamodel. A metamodel describes the concepts and relationships of a modeling language, like UML [2] and BPMN [3]. A metamodel is itself organized based on a modeling language called MOF [4]. The OMG standardizes many modeling languages, including the aforementioned. One of the main challenges of the OMG has been representing models in a machine-independent format that allows their interchange between modeling tools. This led to the definition of XMI [5], a standard for representing MOF-based models in XML.

Many modeling tools have implemented XMI since its introduction. However, the success of XMI as an interchange format has been severely limited (Section 6) for two main reasons. First, XMI defines a set of complex mapping rules between MOF and XML (e.g., properties whose values are the default values are not serialized) that have not been consistently implemented by tools. Second, in an attempt to be flexible, XMI provides a number of mapping options (e.g., a property may be serialized as an XML element or an XML attribute.), making it harder for tools that implement different options to interchange models.

However, other important reasons for the limited success of model interchange has in fact little to do with XMI itself. First, modeling language specifications do not clearly define how their diagrammatic notation maps to their metamodel. This often leads to tools representing models (typically defined through diagrams) differently using the metamodel. Second, for logistical and/or competitive reasons, tool vendors are not necessarily motivated to improve their model interchange support.

This dismal state of model interchange had long motivated the OMG to seek a solution. An early attempt to define a test suite for interoperability certification was not successful due to lack of support and resources. More recently, a number of OMG members formed a Model Interchange Working Group (MIWG) with the goal of testing and improving interoperability between tools. The group had more success due to the following reasons: (i) market pressure from large users who use multiple tools (e.g., the US Department of Defense—DoD); (ii) involvement of major tool vendors who could instigate change; (iii) involvement of experts as neutral parties to interpret and fix the standards; (iv) available resources and technology to automate some of the testing activities; (v) agreement among the parties involved to carry out the testing activities in private and to control the publicity of the results so as to be able to share proprietary information.

In this paper, we report and reflect on the activities of the MIWG. In particular, we present a rigorous model interchange testing process defined by the MIWG. The process allows the definition and execution of test cases (creating models, exporting them, then importing them) using participating tools. We discuss the process's design decisions, challenges and tool support. In addition, we report on a case study where the process was used to test model interchange between tools supporting two standard modeling languages, namely UML and SysML [6] (a profile of UML). We describe the executed test cases and highlight interesting results and lessons learned.

The rest of this paper is structured as follows: Section 2 describes the entire model interchange testing process; strategies that were used to improve the scalability of the testing process are described in Section 3; Section 4 reports on a case study involving the interchange testing of UML and SysML models; a discussion of the results and outstanding issues is provided in Section 5; Section 6 highlights related work. Finally, conclusions and future work are discussed in Section 7.

2 Model Interchange Testing Process

The first task of the MIWG was to define a process for model interchange testing between tools of a given modeling language. The focus was on testing the interchange of models, which are instances of MOF-based metamodels, hence interchangeable with XMI. Out of scope was the interchange of the diagrammatic notation, which is still defined informally with text and pictures (a problem that the OMG is trying to address with the new Diagram Definition specification [7]).

The MIWG testing process, depicted in Figure 1 with a UML activity diagram, involves defining and executing a number of model interchange test cases. Each test case is designed to test an area of a modeling language. The area under test could be large (e.g., UML Sequence Diagrams) or small (e.g., specific types of Actions in UML Activity Diagrams). Test case execution entails defining a reference model, exporting it from one tool and importing it into another. The incremental testing process involves four roles (represented by the activity diagram's swim lanes in Figure 1). These roles can be played by one or more of the parties who participate in the process. As indicated in the diagram, the roles are *MIWG*, which defines test cases, *producer* and *consumer* who use their tools to export/import models, thereby executing test cases, and *implementer* who resolves issues detected by the process. Each role and the activities it performs are further discussed below.

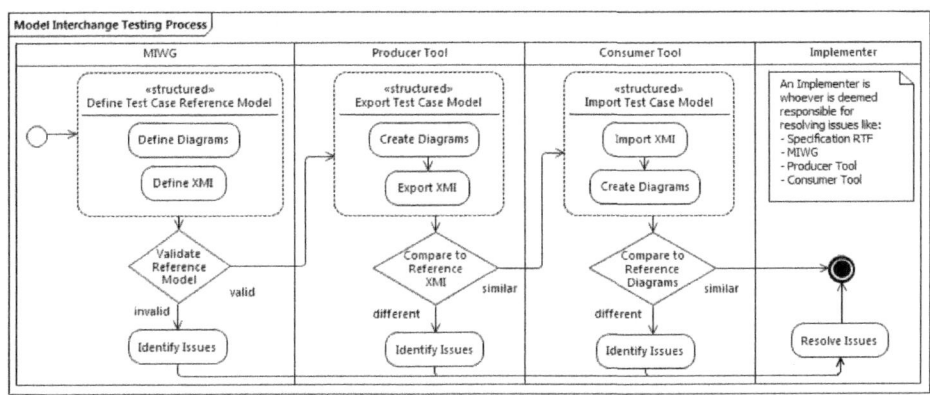

Fig. 1. The MIWG testing process (for one test case)

The process is initiated by the MIWG defining test cases that cover areas of a modeling language for which the MIWG feels it important that tools provide accurate interchange. Then, for each test case, a small exemplary reference model that covers the tested area is created. A reference model, typically defined by an expert who is familiar with the syntax of the related area, is specified with one or more diagram images representing the concrete syntax of the model, and an XMI file representing the abstract syntax of the model. Since it would be tedious to produce these artifacts manually, one of the participating tools is used to produce drafts. If necessary, the MIWG may edit these drafts manually using a simple text or image editor. As a byproduct of this activity, the MIWG sets guidelines for test case definition to avoid ambiguities (e.g., a missing visibility symbol in a UML diagram means an element's visibility is not set vs. being notationally elided). These guidelines are documented either on the diagrams (as notes) or on the MIWG's wiki [8] (when applicable to several diagrams). A reference model is only declared ready after having been validated by the MIWG. Identified issues are resolved by an implementer who can either be the MIWG (for issues with test cases) or a relevant standard's revision task force (RTF) (for issues with that standard). Notice that the reference model serves as a test oracle [14], which is an artifact that determines the expected representation of a model exported from a producer tool when a test case is executed.

Once its reference model is ready, execution of a test case starts. The first step is for each participating vendor (referred to as a producer in Figure 1) to manually recreate (as opposed to import) the reference model using capabilities of his/her tool. If the tool does not support some of or all the areas being tested, the producer can provide documentation about those limitations, along with any possible workarounds. Then, the producer exports the model as XMI and the diagrams as images. After that, the producer compares the exported XMI to the reference one, identifies issues and analyzes them. Depending on the root causes of the issues, they get resolved by an implementer who can be the producer (for differences with the reference model), the MIWG or a relevant standard RTF.

Once the exported artifacts by a producer are available, each of the other participants (referred to as a consumer in Figure 1) proceeds to the importing step. In this step, a consumer creates a model by importing the exported XMI of the producer then recreating similar diagrams by dragging imported model elements onto them. Notice that diagrams are either not included in the XMI exports or included in a proprietary format within XMI:extension tags, and therefore not necessarily imported by the consumer tool, thus the need to manually creating the diagrams. If the consumer tool does not support some of the areas being tested, it can provide documentation about those limitations, along with any possible workarounds. After that, the consumer exports the diagrams as images for comparison with the reference images. Although not required by the process, exporting the imported model to XMI for comparison with the reference XMI can be done. During the comparison, issues are identified, analyzed, and eventually resolved by an implementer who can be the consumer (for issues related to importing the XMI file or differences with the reference diagrams not caused by the producer), the producer, the MIWG, or a relevant standard RTF.

Based on the description of the MIWG testing process given above, and assuming N tools are involved and T test case specifications (i.e., reference models) are created, we note that the process involves N exports for each of the T test cases, followed by N-1 imports for each export. This gives the process a linear scalability of [T.N] on export, but a polynomial scalability of [T.N.(N-1)] on import. We also note that the process is parameterized by the following parameters: the standards being tested, the participant tools and the test cases. Since some or all of these parameters may be subject to revision during a testing period, partly to address identified issues, the testing process may need to be re-executed multiple times, hindering scalability. Finally, we note that some of the activities of the process, like issue identification and analysis, are done manually, which makes them tedious and error-prone. In the following section, we discuss how the MIWG improved the scalability of its process.

3 Improving Scalability of the Testing Process

Although the MIWG testing process (as defined in Section 2) was found to be reasonably effective (Section 4) in resolving the most egregious problems of model interchange (e.g., inconsistent XMI support), its execution required excessive effort. The polynomial scalability on import (a tedious activity that includes manually creating and comparing diagrams) was prohibitive. The consensus of the group was that testing N-1 imports per export may no longer be necessary once the main roadblocks of model interchange were resolved. Instead, the group agreed that validating the exported models by comparing them to the reference models, along with testing the import of the reference models only, may suffice going forward.

The activity diagram in Figure 2 shows the revised MIWG testing process. Notice that after validation of the reference model by the MIWG, both producers and consumers can proceed with their activities and that the import activity involves only the reference model (not the exports by the other N-1 producers). As a result, the process goes from N-1 to 1 import per consumer, giving the revised process a linear scalability of [T.N] on import. However, the process may reveal issues where exports deviate from reference models regardless of whether consumer tools can handle the deviation. Therefore, the revised process provides weaker, less direct evidence that tools can interchange models. In contrast, using the original process, all N participants might incorrectly, though consistently, export and import a model and therefore no interchange problem would be exposed among those participants.

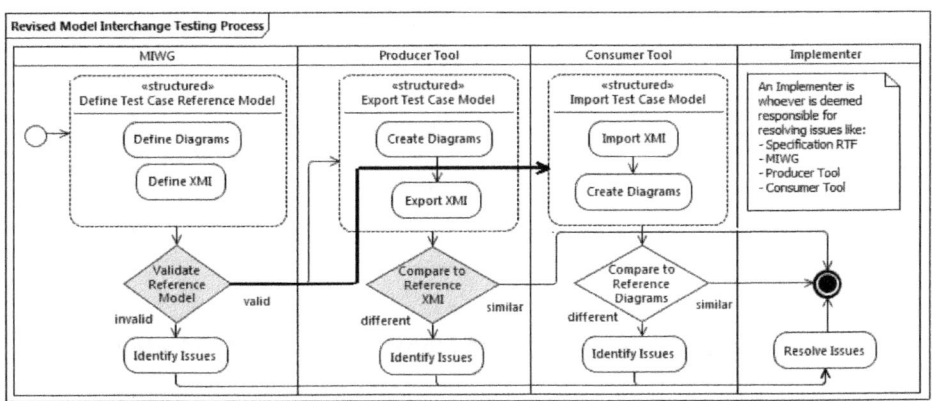

Fig. 2. The revised MIWG testing process (for one test case)

Another change in the revised process, highlighted by grey diamonds in Figure 2, is automating the validation of XMI files and their comparison to the reference XMI. The MIWG developed a web-based tool called the Validator [9] (hosted by the US National Institute of Standards and Technology) to automate this task. The tool (Figure 3) allows uploading an exported XMI file and comparing it to the corresponding reference XMI. The result is a detailed report outlining: (a) compliance issues with the relevant metamodel (found by checking type, multiplicity, and OCL constraints) and XMI (found by checking the XMI rules) and (b) differences with the reference model (found by structurally comparing the two models).

In fact, comparing the two models was initially attempted at the text level by converting both files to Canonical XMI [11], a dialect of XMI contributed by the MIWG. Recall from Section 1 that XMI has many options, increasing both its flexibility and complexity. The Canonical dialect of XMI eliminates these options by fixing their values (e.g., a root XMI element is always required, all properties must be specified as XML elements except those in the XMI namespace, like xmi:id, and uuids are mandatory). Once in that dialect, files could be compared side by side to show text deltas. However, comparison by this method reports low level deltas (e.g., line x has changed) that are hard to analyze. Consequently, the group switched to structural comparison, where models are treated as graphs of elements and compared hierarchically. The elements in both graphs are matched by their type, qualified names and/or other characteristics. This method reports higher level deltas (e.g. attribute x has a different value) that are much easier to understand and analyze.

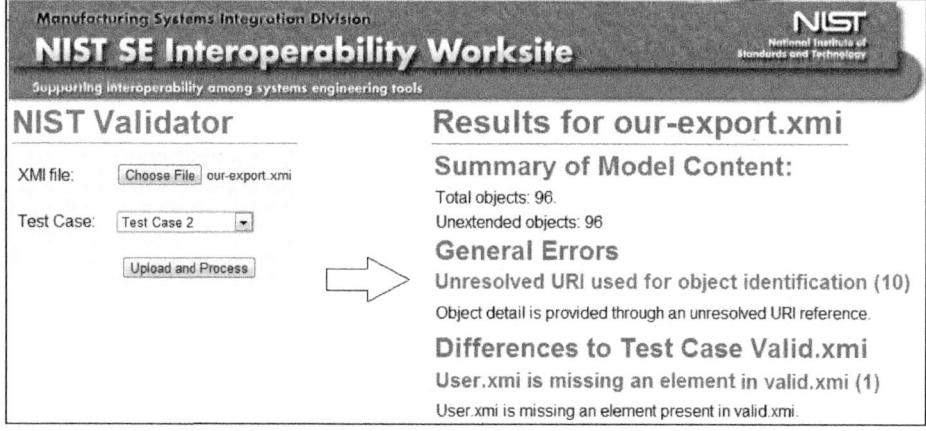

Fig. 3. The Validator Tool: the our-export.xmi file was uploaded and tested against test case 2 (left); validation results (excerpt) are reported (right)

4 Case Study: Interchange of UML and SysML Models

The MIWG validated its testing process by interchanging UML 2.3 and SysML 1.2 models using XMI 2.1. The goal was to assess whether the process was effective in testing and improving interoperability between participating tools through the identification and resolution of model interchange issues. We describe the setup and execution of this case study. We also report on and analyze its results.

4.1 Case Study Setup

The MIWG chose UML and SysML (a profile of UML) mainly because of market pressure from influential users (like DoD). Moreover, both languages are large, complex and popular making them good candidates for testing model interchange and validating the testing process. Table 1 shows the tools that participated in this case study, along with their vendors and latest tested versions.

The case study involved defining a test suite consisting of 16 test cases, summarized in Table 2. Twelve of these were for UML and five were for SysML (TC12 pertained to both UML and SysML). Notice that SysML tests alone would not have sufficed since not all of UML is used by SysML. Most test cases were defined with multiple diagrams. They were also designed to be small in size (to permit easy checking) yet maximize coverage of their language areas. The interested reader is referred to [8] for more details on the test cases and their actual coverage of UML and SysML model elements.

For each test case, the MIWG chose a tool with which to define a reference model. The chosen tool was typically one that supported most (if not all) of the required notation and XMI syntax for the test case. However, for practical reasons, the choice of the tool was more often motivated by the fair distribution of workload between the MIWG members. The gaps in support and the (notation and XMI) imperfections were overcome with manual edits using an image or a text editor. The effort required to produce the reference model varied with the complexity of the test case and the group's level of expertise with the relevant areas of the specifications. It mainly involved manual inspection of the diagrams and the XMI and checking their validity against the specifications. In some cases, this was partially automated with the model validation features of some tools. As the group gained experience, defining valid reference models became easier.

In addition, during reference model definition, some information in the XMI was found to be not representable in the notation (e.g., the visibility of UML classes or which library of primitive types was used). In this case, notes were added to the diagrams to document them. (A note was used rather than a UML comment since the latter would appear in the XMI.) In some cases, the MIWG documented guidelines that applied to all test cases of the case study on its wiki [8].

Table 1. The tools participating in the case study

Vendor	Tool	Version
Atego	Artisan® Studio	7.2m
IBM	RSx	8.0.3
IBM/Sodius	IBM Rhapsody	7.6.x
No Magic	MagicDraw	17.0
SOFTEAM	Modelio	2.4.19
Sparx Systems	Enterprise Architect	9.1

Table 2. Test cases of UML and SysML

UML Test Cases		SysML Test Cases
TC1-Simple Class Model	TC7-State Machines	TC10-Blocks
TC2-Advanced Class Model	TC8-Use Cases	TC 11-Requirements
TC3-Profile Definition & App.	TC9-Interactions	TC12a-Activity Swim Lanes
TC4-Simple Activity Model	TC12b-Activity Swim Lanes	TC14-Parametrics
TC5-Advanced Activity Model	TC13-Instance Specifications	TC16-Allocations
TC6-Composite Structure	TC15-Structured Activity Nodes	

4.2 Case Study Execution

The case study was carried out over the course of 30 months and in two separate phases. In the first phase, which spanned the first 21 months, the MIWG executed the original testing process as defined in Section 2. Based on 16 test cases and 6 participating tools, a total of 96 (16x6) exports and 480 (16x6x5) imports were run, at least once each. Some had to be rerun multiple times as standards, test cases and/or tools were being revised. This alerted the group to the process's scalability problems. Hence, in the second phase, which spanned the next 9 months, the MIWG decided to switch to the revised process as defined in Section 3. In contrast to the first phase, a total of 192 (16x2x6) imports had to be run only in this phase.

4.3 Case Study Results

Before discussing the results, it is important to note that no tool-specific results will be disclosed, in accordance to an agreement among the MIWG members. In fact, the MIWG originally tried to keep a tool capability matrix but that quickly proved problematic because it was (i) commercially sensitive and (ii) hard to maintain, especially since tools continuously undergo revision that may positively or negatively impact their model interchange support. Instead, the MIWG agreed to give the general public the ability to assess tools on their own at any time. Specifically, the MIWG made the exported test case models from each tool available [8]. These models can be compared to the reference models using the Validator tool [9], which was used during the revised process in this case study. These assessments may be used for evaluating the interchange capabilities/limitations of a particular tool, as part of a tool selection process, or to set expectations for the use of a tool in a project.

In the remainder of this section, we report on the overall results of this case study. During the first phase, the exported and imported models were validated and compared to the reference models manually by the participants. This helped uncover major issues, especially with the tools' support of the UML metamodel and SysML profile, which hindered the successful interchange of models. For example, it showed that tools represented models with similar diagrams differently using the metamodel and/or profile. It also showed that tools were not consistently using the official URLs. Some effort was spent at the beginning to address these issues to unblock interchange.

Additionally, it was observed that some tools exported extra model elements (e.g., container elements) that were not required by test cases. Although legal according to the UML/SysML standard, such elements were sometimes not expected by consumer tools. Similarly, some producer tools exported non-standard information (e.g., diagrams) in the XMI files. This was legal when such information was enclosed in XMI: extension elements to allow a consumer tool to ignore it. The MIWG proposed that producer tools use the XMI:exporter tag to specify their tool name. This can help consumer tools recognize and optionally process these extensions if they can.

Furthermore, we observed that the case study achieved good test coverage of UML and SysML standards (59% of UML metaclasses and 55% of SysML stereotypes). However, we also observed that tools were not consistent in their support of some areas of the standards. This could be attributed to ambiguities in these standards and/or to bugs in the tools. For example, tools did not have consistent default values for the multiplicity of a UML typed element or for the visibility of a UML packageable element. The MIWG clarified to vendors that the former should be *1..1* and the latter should be *public*. Another example was the names of SysML stereotypes that were sometimes different in XMI from those shown in the graphical notation when applied to UML elements.

During the second phase of the case study, consumers manually analyzed and reported on their imports of reference models. On the other hand, producers reported on their exports using the Validator tool, which allowed them to: (a) analyze their conformance to the (XMI, MOF and modeling language) standards and (b) compare them to the reference models. Figure 4 shows the results of the conformance analysis. The lines represent the average number of (all occurrences of all) issues/bugs reported by tools for their first (dashed line) and their last (solid line) export of each test case (on average vendors exported each test case 3-4 times due to bug fixes and/or changes in reference models). The average number of issues across all test cases was 65 at the start and 52 at the end (a drop of 20%). However, the number increased for some test cases (e.g., 9) due to ambiguities in related areas of UML (e.g., sequence diagrams) that made most tools inconsistent with it. Best results were achieved for Class and Instance diagrams (test cases 1, 2 and 11) and SysML requirements (test case 13).

On the other hand, when comparing the exported models to the reference ones (Figure 5), we observe that the average number of differences across all test cases was 26 at the start and 24 at the end (a drop of 8%). (The lines in Figure 5 represent the average number of differences reported by tools for each test case.) However, we note that differences did not always decrease (e.g., test case 4, 10 and 15). While this might be due to human error while recreating the reference models (e.g., naming elements differently), it could also be a symptom of the complexity of some areas of the standards (e.g., advanced activities), which causes implementation difficulties.

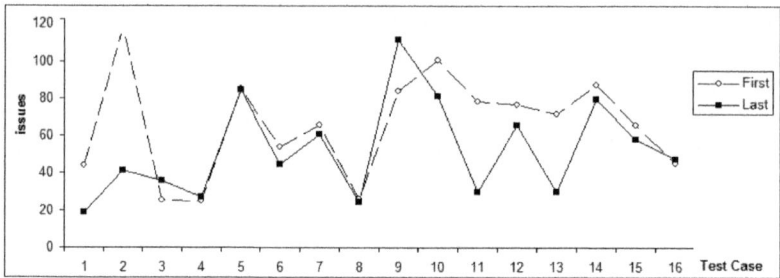

Fig. 4. Issues related to conformance to standards before and after case study

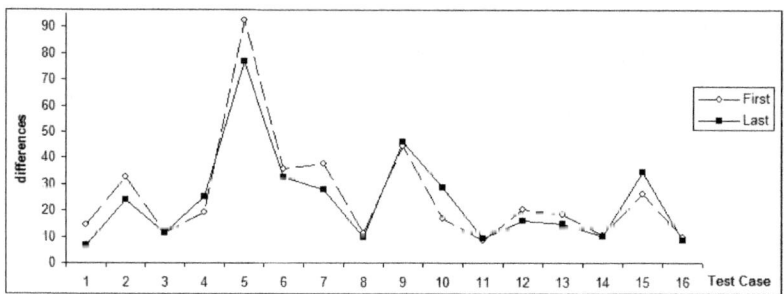

Fig. 5. Differences to reference models before and after case study

5 Discussion

The case study, presented in Section 4, shows that the MIWG testing process is effective for assessing model interchange between tools. It also shows that tool vendors can work together to improve model interchange. Versions of participating UML and SysML tools, available now on the market, are more interoperable than they were when the MIWG initiated its work, although there is certainly room for further improvement. Interoperability can directly benefit users as it may significantly improve quality and productivity and increase the investment in models.

The MIWG finds that XMI is an adequate model interchange mechanism. Nonetheless, the group admits that XMI 2.1 is a complex standard, though much of the complexity has been reduced in XMI 2.4 with the definition of Canonical XMI, as a result of this case study. The group also finds that most of the remaining interchange issues relate to either ambiguities/inconsistencies in the UML/SysML standards or bugs in the tools' support of these standards, rather than with the tools' XMI support. For example, a handful of issues have been logged against UML sequence diagrams that the standard does not fully define how they map to the UML metamodel. Another issue is against SysML, where one of the UML constraints (on property *Property::partWithPort*) does not apply in the context of SysML.

One of the challenges of model interchange that has surfaced in this case study is that tools differ in the versions of the standards they support. For example, while most participating tools have moved to UML 2.3, some have not, while others have moved to 2.4 already. Those that did not move still managed to participate by manually editing their models. However, the authors[1] recommend that the testing process only moves to a newer version of a standard when a significant number of participating tools have moved to it. The authors also recommend that standards remain backward compatible in their minor revisions to motivate vendors to adopt them quicker.

Regarding the MIWG process, the authors note that the revised process is still quite labor intensive. Specifically, it requires expertise in defining and validating the reference models. Fortunately, once those models are defined, they can be reused by new tools. The process also requires the MIWG to manually analyze issues reported by the Validator tool to identify root causes. Furthermore, by not importing the exported models directly, the revised process provides a weaker proof of interchange. It may also expose bugs in producer tools that could have been tolerated by importer tools in the original less scalable process. Therefore, the authors recommend that the original process still be initially executed, at least once per test case, before switching to the more scalable revised process. Finally, the process focuses on testing the syntactical interchange of models only. It does not include testing the semantics, which relate to how models are used (e.g., executed).

6   Related Works

Although everyone who is working, or has worked, in a MDA context has anecdotal evidence that there are issues with model interchange, there has been very little published work that systematically studies those issues.

Alanen et al. [14] performed a simple case study whereby they created a simple class diagram (not focusing on specific features of the modeling language) using six different UML modeling tools. They then exported the diagram to XMI and manually compared, using a text editor, the six generated XMI files. They observed some discrepancies in the files and concluded (like the MIWG) that one of the main issues when practicing model interchange was the different versions of XMI and UML standards supported by tools. They advocated the need for a compliance test suite for checking XMI compatibility, which is an outcome of the MIWG work.

Persson et al. studied XMI compatibility between six commercial and three open source modeling tools [15], using one model (class diagram). They showed that XMI-based model interchange between UML modeling tools was weakly supported in practice. In a different publication [16], they experimented with two industrial size models, one commercial tool for creating the models and three open source tools to interchange with. The experimental procedure was the following, for each of the two models: (1) create the model using the commercial tool; (2) export the model to XMI and check conformance to the XMI standard using available automated XML checkers; (3) import the XMI using each of the three open source software tools (some imports failed even after changing the input XMI file to something expected by the tool) and visually check the diagram obtained; (4) export from the open source software, possibly fixing the generated XMI file; (5) import (back) into the

---

[1] Some comments made by the authors of this paper are not necessarily the ones of the MIWG.

commercial tool; and (6) visually compare the obtained diagram with the one they started the process with. They reported that manually fixing the XMI files was necessary so they conformed to the XMI standard, and sometimes fixes were insufficient to successfully complete the process. They concluded that model interchange based on XMI was not mature enough to be used in an industrial setting. They conducted a similar study in 2006 [17], using a different set of producer/consumer tools and a much simpler class diagram model (without focusing on important features of the language), and confirmed the limitations of the export/import, although they noticed an improvement when using the new XMI 2.0.

More recently, Eichelberger et al. [18] report on a comprehensive survey of the compliance of current modeling tools to the UML standard, focusing on a large set (476) of UML modeling features. With respect to XMI, they studied the structural compliance of exported XMI files to the XMI standard. They report that only four out of 68 tools have an acceptable level of compliance. With respect to XMI, they report that 47% of the tools do not pass the structural XMI validity test, 3% (i.e., two) tools, pass the XMI validity test, while the remaining 50% offer no XMI at all. They did not however try to import the XMI files into other tools.

In summary, some have attempted to study model interchange with XMI before. They differ from the process we discuss in this paper in one or more of the following ways: (i) They did not specifically and systematically define targeted reference models (they instead used available models); (ii) They did not necessarily systematically investigate pairs of producer/consumer tools; (iii) They did not involve the vendors of the producer/consumer tools to investigate and fix the root causes of encountered issues; (iv) They did not try to automate parts of the process.

7 Conclusion and Future Work

Modeling standards enable automated exchange of modeling information among tools. Due to errors and ambiguities with those standards and the lack of rigorous testing between tools, the full benefit of model interchange could not be realized. The MIWG has defined and validated a rigorous incremental model interchange testing process. The process has been fine tuned to scale with the number of participating tools. It has also been used in a case study to assess UML and SysML model interchange between six tools. A suite of 16 test cases has been defined and executed. The case study has led to improving interoperability between these tools as well as these tools' conformance to the standards (by 20%). The MIWG has also made the process public and partially repeatable to allow interested communities to assess the interchange capabilities and limitations of participating tools for their purposes.

Going forward, the MIWG plans to test other model interchange situations, like importing XMI files conforming to older versions of the standards or importing fragmented models with cross references. Another area of future work is round trip (export-import-change-export-import) testing. Yet another area is testing diagram interchange (when language-specific diagram definition standards become available and implemented). Finally, newer versions of UML/SysML/XMI specifications will be tested, in addition to other standards (e.g., UPDM [12] and SoaML [13] profiles).

Acknowledgements. The authors would like to thank the entire MIWG team for the great work this paper reports on. The authors would also like to particularly acknowledge the following MIWG members: Peter Denno (NIST) and Pete Rivett (Adaptive), for reviewing this paper.

References

1. Model Driven Architecture, http://en.wikipedia.org/wiki/Model-driven_architecture
2. Unified Modeling Language, Superstructure v2.4.1., http://www.omg.org/spec/UML/2.4.1
3. Business Process Model and Notation v2.0., http://www.omg.org/spec/BPMN/2.0/
4. Meta Object Facility Core v2.4.1., http://www.omg.org/spec/MOF/2.4.1/
5. MOF 2 XMI Mapping v2.4.1., http://www.omg.org/spec/XMI/2.4.1/
6. Systems Modeling Language, v1.2., http://www.omg.org/spec/SysML/1.2/
7. Diagram Definition v1.0 FTF Beta 2., http://www.omg.org/spec/DD/1.0/Beta2/
8. MIWG Wiki, http://www.omgwiki.org/model-interchange
9. NIST Validator, http://syseng.nist.gov/se-interop/sysml/validator
10. OMG Object Constraint Language v.2.3.1., http://www.omg.org/spec/OCL/2.3.1/
11. Canonical XMI, FTF Beta 1, http://www.omg.org/cgi-bin/doc?ptc/12-01-01
12. Unified Profile for DoDAF and MODAF v2.0., http://www.omg.org/spec/UPDM/2.0/
13. Service Oriented Architecture Modeling Lang. v1.0., http://www.omg.org/spec/SoaML/1.0/
14. Alanen, M., Porres, I.: Model Interchange Using OMG Standards. In: Proc. of the 31st EUROMICRO Conf. on Soft. Eng. and Advanced Apps., pp. 450–459 (September 2005)
15. Persson, A., Gustavsson, H., Lings, B., Lundell, B., Mattsson, A., Ärlig, U.: OSS tools in a heterogeneous environment for embedded systems modelling: an analysis of adoptions of XMI. In: Proc. of the 5th Workshop on Open Source Software Engineering (May 2005)
16. Persson, A., Gustavsson, H., Lings, B., Lundell, B., Mattsson, A., Ärlig, U.: Adopting Open Source Development Tools in a Commercial Production Environment—Are we Locked-in? In: Proc. of 10th EMMSAD (June 2005)
17. Lundell, B., Lings, B., Persson, A., Mattsson, A.: UML Model Interchange in Heterogeneous Tool Environments: An Analysis of Adoptions of XMI 2. In: Wang, J., Whittle, J., Harel, D., Reggio, G. (eds.) MoDELS 2006. LNCS, vol. 4199, pp. 619–630. Springer, Heidelberg (2006)
18. Eichelberger, H., Eldogan, Y., Schmid, K.: A Comprehensive Survey of UML Compliance in Current Modelling Tools. In: SE 2009. LNI, vol. 143, pp. 39–50 (2009)

An Internal Domain-Specific Language for Constructing OPC UA Queries and Event Filters

Thomas Goldschmidt and Wolfgang Mahnke

ABB Corporate Research Germany,
Industrial Software Systems Program
{thomas.goldschmidt,wolfgang.mahnke}@de.abb.com

Abstract. The OPC Unified Architecture (OPC UA) is becoming more and more important for industrial automation products. The development of OPC UA components is currently supported by the use of SDKs for OPC UA. However, these SDKs provide only low level support for creating OPC UA based applications. This leads to higher development efforts. The domain-specific metamodel defined by OPC UA defines serves as a good basis for creating domain-specific languages on a higher abstraction level. This has the potential of reducing development efforts. In this paper, we focus on the event filter and query part of OPC UA. Current SDKs only provide interfaces for constructing an object tree for these queries and event filters programmatically. Creating and maintaining these object structures is tedious and error prone. Therefore, we introduce an internal DSL approach for constructing OPC UA queries and event filters based on the OPC UA information model and the Language Integrated Queries (LINQ) feature available in .Net.

1 Introduction

The OPC Unified Architecture (OPC UA) is becoming more and more important for industrial automation products. It is a central component to modern industrial applications. Classic OPC (OLE for Process Contol) defined an industry-wide adopted set of standards for accessing and distributing data in industrial systems. With the more recent OPC UA, new facilities like a unified address space model, service oriented interfaces and an extensible metamodel have been introduced. This allows OPC UA to be used from small embedded systems, industrial controllers, Distributed Control Systems (DCS) up to Manufacturing Execution Systems (MES) and Enterprise Resource Planning (ERP) systems.

The development of OPC UA components is currently supported by the use of special software development kits (SDKs) for OPC UA. These SDKs provide means for developing code that deals with the creation and navigation in the OPC UA information model, registration of monitors for value changes and calling of defined methods as well as connection and session handling. However, one of the largest drawbacks of working directly with these SDKs is that they often focus on dealing with technical interfaces rather than providing an easier programming model for developers. The OPC specification already proposes that higher level languages such as a graphical information modeling language [1] may be used to efficiently develop OPC UA applications. However, apart from the already mentioned graphical modeling of information models including code generation from it [2,3,4] no DSL support is provided by currently available OPC UA SDKs. More specifically, there is currently no support for defining OPC UA queries and event filters on a higher level of abstraction. Developers have to create them using object structures programmatically. This code, that accesses elements from the address space, has to deal with node identifiers or browse names that are mostly passed as string variables. During design time it is therefore not checked if the specific nodes and/or variables that code accesses actually exist in the used address space. Furthermore, the code is very lengthy and not clearly structured. This leads to error prone implementations and thus additional test effort while developing these OPC UA components.

In our previous work [5] we analyzed the different use cases in OPC UA development which may be improved by developing and using a DSL for them. One of the use cases where we identified the largest impact at a relatively low additional development effort was the creation of DSL for query and event filter creation. Therefore, we decided to build an internal DSL for this use case. Internal DSLs [6] are based on the syntax of a host language and add additional language constructs to that language which are in a compile step mapped towards structures of the host language. The advantage of such internal DSL is that existing IDEs can be reused without extensions and programmers do not need to learn a new syntax. A language feature of C#/.Net that is designed to be used in such a way is the Language Integrated Queries (LINQ) [7] feature. It provides a concrete syntax that is similar to SQL and uses a closure mechanism underneath. A query specified in LINQ is internally translated into an expression tree based on such a closure.

The contribution of this paper is an internal domain-specific language that facilitates LINQ to specify OPC UA queries and event filters. We provide a mapping specification of LINQ constructs to those used on OPC UA queries and event filters. Based on a generated object model of the target information model developers get code completion and error recognition for their specified queries. Furthermore, we demonstrate how the LINQtoOPCUA generator, which we developed, facilitates LINQ expression trees to instantiate the abstract syntax objects of OPC UA queries and event filters.

The remainder of this paper is structured as follows. A short introduction to OPC UA including its event filters and queries is given in Section 2. The query/event filter DSL that we designed is introduced in Section 3. A critical discussion of our DSL is presented in Section 4. Section 5 concludes this paper and outlines future work.

2 OPC Unified Architecture

OPC UA provides a secure, reliable, high-performing communication infrastructure to exchange different types of data in industrial automation. That includes current data like measurements (e.g. from a temperature sensor) and setpoints (e.g. for defining the desired level of a tank), events (e.g. device lost connection) and alarms for abnormal conditions (e.g. a boiler reached a critical level). In addition, it provides the history of current data (e.g. the temperature trend the last day or the last ten years) and of events (what events of a certain type occurred the last five days). In order to provide semantic with the data, also meta data is exchanged in terms of an information model. In Figure 1 depicts an example of an OPC UA address space.

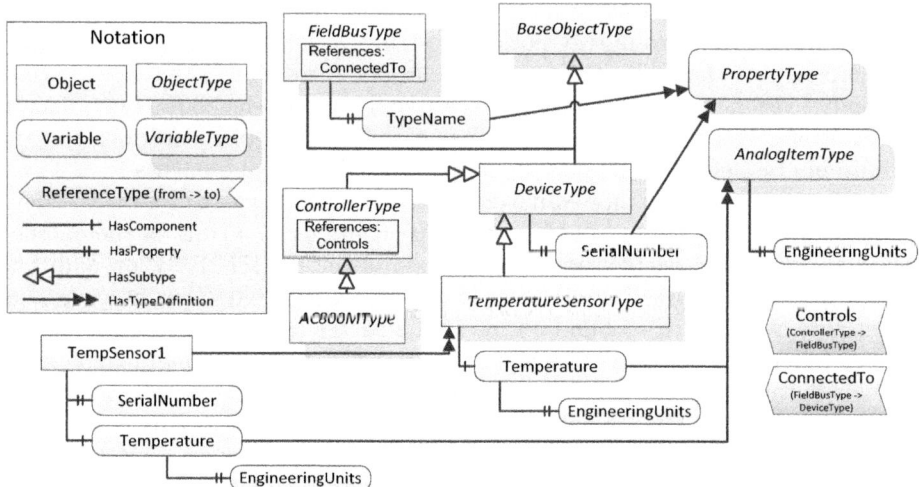

Fig. 1. Example of an Address Space in OPC UA

On the right hand of Figure 1 the type system is shown, with object types in a type hierarchy. For example, the *DeviceType* is an abstract object type representing all kinds of devices. It defines a variable called *SerialNumber*. A subtype *TemperatureSensorType* adds the *Temperature* variable, including the *EngineeringUnits*. Variables are typed as well, like the *Temperature* of type *AnalogItemType* defined by the OPC Foundation. This type adds a property to the variable containing the *EngineeringUnits*. On the left hand an instance of the *TemperatureSensorType*, *TempSensor1*, is shown. The instances contain the concrete values, like the temperature measured by *TempSensor1*.

OPC UA is based on a client server model where the client asks for data and the server delivers the data. The client has the option to read and write the data, but also to subscribe to data changes or event notifications. In addition, the client can browse the address space of the server and read the meta data information. For large and complex address spaces the client also has the capability to query the address space for information, for example asking for all temperature sensors that are currently measuring a temperature larger than 25 °C.

Clients can subscribe to events by subscribing to objects marked as event notifiers, which already provides some filtering based on how the objects are structured in the address space. In addition, they can specify an event filter to define the event fields they want to receive as well as define the events they are interested in. To provide information about the structure of events supported by the server, the server provides an event type hierarchy. It uses the concept of abstract object types to define the event type hierarchy and variables to define the fields of events. In case of alarms concrete object types are used, as alarms can be represented in the address space in order to configure alarms, for example specifying the limit for an alarm. Figure 2 shows an example of an event type hierarchy. The *BaseEventType* is defined by the OPC UA specification [1], and the *DeviceStatusType* is a subtype providing the *HealthStatus* of a device. Clients can, for example, define an event filter for the *HealthStatus* reaching a critical level.

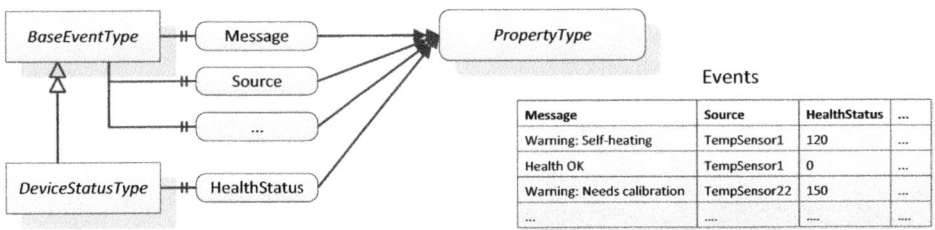

Fig. 2. Example of an Event Type Hierarchy in OPC UA

2.1 Event Filter Creation

Event filters in OPC UA are used in the creation of event subscriptions to define which kinds of events are relevant for a certain subscription. The specification [8] only defines the service interface used for registering such filters. Current OPC UA SDKs implement this service and provide a class which resembles the abstract syntax tree of the expressions. The specification informatively provides examples for concrete syntaxes (graphical, table-based or text based) for event filters. As OPC servers can be relatively thin and should not bother with extensive expression parsing, the OPC Foundation intentionally used the abstract syntax on the interface for these filters. However, users should not directly deal with the abstract syntax, but should use a nicely designed concrete syntax for defining these filters. Currently none of the SDKs implements a concrete syntax for event filters.

2.2 Query Creation

Similar to the event filtering mechanism the OPC UA specification defines query services on an abstract interface level. Concrete syntaxes are informatively proposed, but there is currently no implementation of any of these syntaxes by existing SDKs.

In contrast to the event filters, for which handlers are already implemented in the SDK and OPC UA stack, queries are mostly routed down to the server implementation. On this layer the abstract syntax should then be mapped down to whatever query mechanism the underlying data source uses. This could for example be an SQL like language. In this case this use case is also relevant for server implementations.

2.3 Queries and Event Filters Metamodel

The OPC UA specification [8] already proposes that there should be a concrete syntax for event filters and queries. Both languages provide query like constructs, such as *select* and *where* clauses. OPC UA SDKs provide means for programmatically creating select, when and where clauses. However, writing the code that creates them causes a lot of overhead as each single select, where clause and all operands have to be instantiated and parametrized and then plugged together.

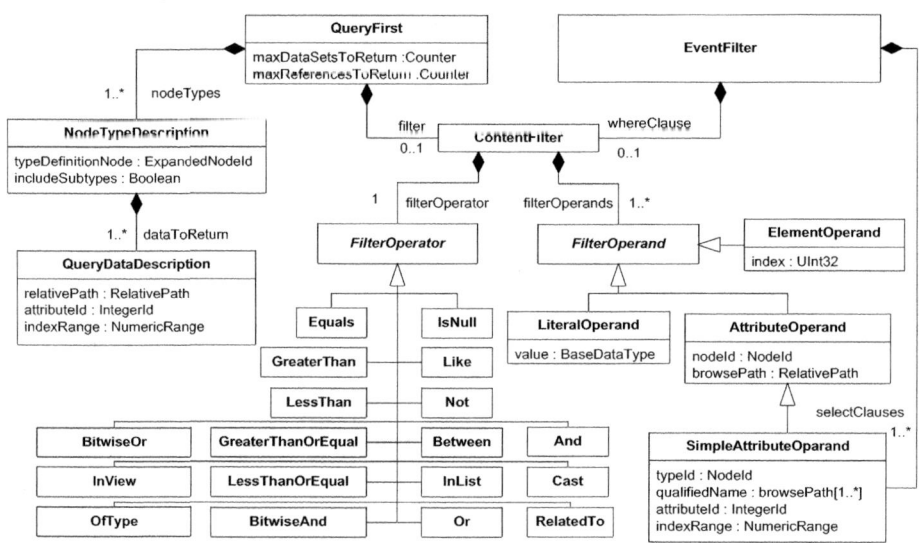

Fig. 3. Metamodel of the OPC UA queries and event filtes services

Figure 3 depicts a metamodel which we derived from the specification of the queries and event filter services given in [8]. SDKs implement this metamodel as classes of an abstract syntax. These classes are then instantiated and plugged together to create queries and event filters. Listing 1 gives an example constructing an event filter based on these classes using the OPC Foundation .Net SDK. Node identifiers and property names have to be provided as string parameters and the object tree is also constructed manually. The OPC UA specification defines that such constructs have to be validated and sanity-checked by servers that receive them at runtime. However, there is currently no way of checking their validity already at the time of development.

Listing 1. Example code that creates an OPC UA event filter that selects the message, the source and the health status of all events of type *DeviceStatusType* that have a *HealthStatus* greater than 100.

```
EventFilter eventFilter = new EventFilter();

SimpleAttributeOperand selectClause0 = new SimpleAttributeOperand();
Opc.Ua.QualifiedNameCollection browsePath;

// Select Event Field Message
selectClause0.AttributeId = Attributes.Value;
selectClause0.TypeId = DeviceStatus.NodeId;
Opc.Ua.QualifiedName propName = new Opc.Ua.QualifiedName("Message", 0);
browsePath = new QualifiedNameCollection();
browsePath.Add(propName);
selectClause0.BrowsePath = browsePath;

// Select Event Field Source
SimpleAttributeOperand selectClause1 = new SimpleAttributeOperand
    { AttributeId = Attributes.Value,
        TypeId = DeviceStatus.NodeId };
propName = new Opc.Ua.QualifiedName("Source", 0);
browsePath = new QualifiedNameCollection();
browsePath.Add(propName);
selectClause1.BrowsePath = browsePath;

// Select Event Field HealthStatus
SimpleAttributeOperand selectClause2 = new SimpleAttributeOperand
    { AttributeId = Attributes.Value,
        TypeDefinitionId = DeviceStatus.NodeId };
propName = new Opc.Ua.QualifiedName("HealthStatus", 1);
browsePath = new QualifiedNameCollection {propName};
selectClause2.BrowsePath = browsePath;

ContentFilter cf = new ContentFilter();

ContentFilterElement cfe = new ContentFilterElement {
    FilterOperator = FilterOperator.GreaterThan};
propName = new Opc.Ua.QualifiedName("HealthStatus", 1);
SimpleAttributeOperand op1 = new SimpleAttributeOperand(
    DeviceStatus.NodeId, propName);
LiteralOperand op2 = new LiteralOperand(100u);
cfe.SetOperands(new List<FilterOperand> { op1, op2 });
cf.Elements.Add(cfe);

// Add to filter
eventFilter.SelectClauses.Add(selectClause0);
eventFilter.SelectClauses.Add(selectClause1);
eventFilter.SelectClauses.Add(selectClause2);
eventFilter.WhereClause = cf;
```

3 The Query/Event Filter DSL

OPC UA client applications are often written using C#/.Net. C# provides a feature called "language integrated queries" (LINQ). LINQ provides a concrete, SQL-like syntax that is directly integrated into C#. It is intended to be mapped to specific query languages such as SQL depending on the target purpose. To achieve this, LINQ includes means for accessing the expression trees of these queries directly from the code. This enables us to create a mapping from LINQ to OPC UA event filters / queries.

For the design of the DSL we tried to keep as close as possible to the semantics of the original LINQ while achieving a complete coverage of features provided by OPC UA. Our approach assumes that there is are node classes available for the part of the address space for which queries are specified. These node classes can easily be generated using the tools available from the OPC Foundation [4], CommServer [2] or Unified Automation [3]. The generator takes a XML based description of the address space as input and generates the appropriate classes for the Object Types, Reference Types, etc. Alternatively the classes can be developed manually. For a manual implementation it is important that there is a clear mapping between the developed classes and the NodeIds defined in the address space. Based on the generated or manually developed classes and the corresponding mapping, we translate the classes used in the LINQ expressions to NodeIds. The NodeIds are then used in the event filter and query elements that are then passed to the OPC UA stack.

The architecture of our mapping approach is depicted in Figure 4. The (generated) address space classes serve as in input data source for the LINQ processor. Based on these classes it is possible to formulate queries in an SQL-like manner. At compile time, the LINQ expression parser creates a LINQ expression tree [9] from this query code. This tree can be accessed at runtime. From this runtime representation the LINQToOPCUA generator instantiates the appropriate classes from OPC UA which resemble the event filter or query.

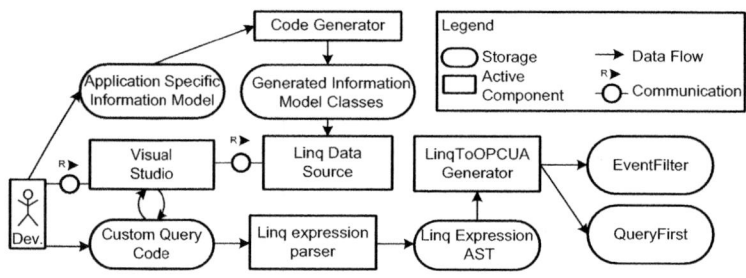

Fig. 4. Architecture of the LINQ for OPCUA prototype

Event filters and queries reuse the same elements such as ContentFilters and SimpleAttributeOperands as illustrated in Figure 3. However, the structure of a query differs from the one of an event filter. Still we were able to use the same syntax based on LINQ for both use cases as shown in the following subsections.

3.1 Event Filter

As shown in Figure 3 an event filter consists of two major parts, *where* clauses and *select* clauses. The former are *ContentFilter* elements that are common with the ones used in queries (see Section 3.3). The latter are specific to event filters

An Internal DSL for Constructing OPC UA Queries and Event Filters   69

and contain *SimpleAttributeOperands*. Used in this context, the *SimpleAttributeOperands* refer to attributes of the filtered *EventType*. For example, a custom event type *DeviceStatusType* may specify, in addition to generic event attributes such as *Message* and *Source*, an additional custom attribute *HealthStatus*. These attributes may then be selected in the select clauses of an event filter to be included in the message returned by the subscription.

We map these OPC UA select clauses to the select clause available in LINQ. In this select clause we construct an anonymous type (using *new* { ... }). The members of this type can now be formed by properties from the event type class. This class is given by an initial, typed result list that is specified in the *from .. in .. part* of the LINQ query. Listing 2 gives an example for such a query. The basic result list *query* specifies to filter for the *DeviceStatusType*. Based on the usage of that class in *from cEvent in query* the *select* part references the attributes *Message*, *Source* and *HealthStatus* of *DeviceStatusType*. The *where* clause part is handled as described in Section 3.3.

Listing 2. LinqToOpcua example showing the creation of an event filter. This statement corresponds to the about 30 lines of code shown in Listing 1 without using the DSL.

```
var query = new List<DeviceStatus> { };
Expression<Func<IEnumerable<object>>> linqExp = () =>
from cEvent in query where cEvent.HealthStatus > 100
  select new { cEvent.Message, cEvent.Source, cEvent.HealthStatus };
EventFilter eventFilter = getEventFilter(linqExp);
```

The LINQToOPCUA generator uses the LINQ expression tree as input. Using a tree walker approach it traverses the expression tree and instantiates the appropriate OPC UA objects. The objects for the *select* clause are created when traversing a *MethodCallExpression* referring to the *Select* method. Then, for each *MemberExpression* within this clause it instantiates a *SimpleAttributeOperand*. The *NodeId* for the operand is looked up based on the class used for the expression's source. For the example given in Listing 2 this is the *DeviceStatusType* as this is the type of the *cEvent* variable used in the select clause.

3.2 Query

In contrast to event filters the query service (*QueryFirst*) does not use *SimpleAttributeOperands* as select clause. It rather uses so called *QueryDataDescriptions* that are connected to *NodeTypeDescriptions*. The latter is comparable to the *from* clause of SQL. Therefore, a natural match to map this to LINQ is the corresponding *from ... in ...* construct in LINQ. Thus, for each of these constructs one entry in the *nodeTypes* collection is added.

Listing 3 shows an example OPC UA query using LINQ based on the information model described in Figure 1. The *NodeTypeDescriptions* derived from this query are: The type of *controllers*, which is *ControllerType*, the type of the *Controls* reference, which is *FieldBusType* and the type of *ConnectedTo* which is of type *DeviceType*. We defaulted the *includingSubtypes* attribute of the *NodeType-Descriptions* to *true* as we considered this the major use case. For specifying the omission of subtypes we use the *NoSubTypes()* method as shown with *controllers* list.

Listing 3. LinqToOpcua example showing the creation of a query

```
/// Example 3: Get ControllerType.SerialNumber, FieldBusType.TypeName,
/// DeviceType.SerialNumber where a controller controls a field bus and the field bus
/// has a connected device and the field bus has a TypeName = 'PB' or 'FF' and
/// the temperature sensor's engineering unit is ''Kelvin'' and the temperature
/// is greater than 256.
var controllers = new List<Controller> { };

Expression<Func<IEnumerable<object>>> linqExp = () =>
from controller in NoSubTypes(controllers)
from fieldbus in (controller.Controls)
from devices in fieldbus.ConnectedTo
where (fieldbus.TypeName == "PB" && fieldbus.TypeName == "FF") &&
    device is TemparatureSensor &&
    ((TemparatureSensor)device).Temparature.EngineeringUnit == "Kelvin" &&
    ((TemparatureSensor)device).Temparature.Value > 256
select new { controller.SerialNumber, FieldBusType.TypeName, DeviceType.SerialNumber };
```

The elements to be returned from a query are specified by the *dataToReturn* reference pointing to a list of *QueryDataDescriptions*. We map this list to the *select* clause of the LINQ query. Its *relativePath* is directly derived from the C# *MemberExpressions*. In the query example (Listing 3) these are *ControllerType:SerialNumber*, *FieldBusType:TypeName* and *DeviceType:SerialNumber*.

Note that we default the *attributeId* to *value* as we consider this is the most frequent use case. If other attributes shall be returned by the query (like *NodeId*, *EventNotifier, etc.*) we provide additional methods for specifying this (e.g., *NodeId(controller.SerialNumber)*). The *filter* clause of a query is handled the same way as the *where* clause in event filters.

3.3 Content Filter

We map *ContentFilters* to *where* clauses in LINQ. In the LINQ expression tree they occur as *MethodCallExpression ("Where")* expressions. *ContentFilter* elements consist of two types of elements, one *FilterOperator* and one or more *FilterOperands*. Most of the operands are also available in C# in a similar way. Therefore, we define a mapping from these operators to the OPC UA operators as shown in Table 1. For some of the operators there is no suitable counterpart in C#. For these operators we provide methods taking the appropriate parameters (e.g., `InView()`).

The operands of a *ContentFilter* a defined by the operands of the respective C# expression. We create *LiteralOperand* for literal expressions like ("FF" or 256) and *SimpleAttributeOperands* for *MemberExpressions* respectively. The *nodeId* of the involved elements available from the (generated) node classes and can therefore easily be extracted from the involved objects during translation.

Table 1. Operator Mapping from LINQ to OPC UA

LINQ Construct	LINQ syntax	OPC UA Event Filter Construct
ExpressionType.AndAlso	&&	FilterOperator.And
ExpressionType.OrElse	||	FilterOperator.Or
ExpressionType.Or	|	FilterOperator.BitwiseOr
ExpressionType.And	&	FilterOperator.BitwiseAnd
ExpressionType.Convert	(Type)obj	FilterOperator.Cast
ExpressionType.Equal	==	FilterOperator.Equals
ExpressionType.GreaterThan	>	FilterOperator.GreaterThan
ExpressionType.GreaterThanOrEqual	>=	FilterOperator.GreaterThanOrEqual
ExpressionType.LessThan	<	FilterOperator.LessThan
ExpressionType.LessThanOrEqual	<=	FilterOperator.LessThanOrEqual
MethodCallExpression ("Like")	Like(op1,op2)	FilterOperator.Like
ExpressionType.Not	~/!	FilterOperator.Not
ExpressionType.TypeIs	is	FilterOperator.OfType
MethodCallExpression ("Between")	Between(op1,op2,op3)	FilterOperator.Between
MethodCallExpression ("InList")	InList(op1,op2[])	FilterOperator.InList
MethodCallExpression ("InView")	InView(op1,view)	FilterOperator.InView
ExpressionType.NotEqual	!= null	FilterOperator.IsNull

3.4 FilterOperator.RelatedTo

A special operator not defined in the mapping given in Table 1 is the *RelatedTo* operator. The OPC UA specification [8] defined this operator as follows:

> TRUE if the target Node is of type Operand[0] and is related to a NodeId of the type defined in Operand[1] by the Reference type defined in Operand [2]. Operand[0] or Operand[1] can also point to an element Reference where the referred to element is another RelatedTo operator. This allows chaining of relationships (e.g. A is related to B is related to C). [...]

This concept is similar to *join* operations in SQL. However, LINQ queries can already be based on a *connected* object model where direct references between objects are modeled as properties of the respective classes. Therefore, a join operation can be specified in a much more concise manner. For example, joining two sets of objects *ControllerType* and *FieldBusType* results in the following LINQ expression: *from controller in controllers from fieldbus in controller.Controls*. This will result in a join of controllers with their related fieldbusses.

Instead of explicitly writing all *RelatedTo* filters required for an OPC UA query we derive them from the *from* clauses of the LINQ query automatically. For example, given the *from* clause specified in Listing 3 we can derive the following nested *RelatedTo* filter: *RelatedTo(ControllerType, RelatedTo(FieldBusType, DeviceType, ConnectedTo), Controls)*. As the *form* clause then is used for the specification of *NodeTypeDescriptions* as well as *RelatedTo* clauses we get a concise, easy to read LINQ query including both parts.

OPC UA allows to filter for specific sub types within *RelatedTo* filters. For example, a filter might specify *RelatedTo(FieldBusType, TemperatureSensorType, ConnectedTo)* where *TemperatureSensorType* is a subtype of *DeviceType*. To achieve this kind of filtering an additional expression in the *where* clause is required. For the mentioned example, we would need to add the following: *device is TemperatureSensorType*.

4 Discussion

In order to evaluate our DSL we analyzed it w.r.t. its applicability and usability. We defined the following research questions to help us with this assessment.

Is the DSL development approach powerful enough to enable the development of a complex DSL? Being a query language, LINQ can be mapped to other languages the like. OPC UA event filters and queries are a perfect match for this mapping. DSLs for other purposes would much likely be developed using a different concrete syntax.

How complex is the creation of the DSL using the approach? Through the LINQ expression trees which are available directly from the LINQ statement via reflection, a DSL can be created by implementing a visitor pattern which can be created with little effort. The effort for implementing and testing the visitor was about 3 days.

Can developers effectively use the created DSL? As the syntax of LINQ is pretty close to SQL which is a well-known query language, most developers will be able to immediately use the DSL without too much learning overhead. Especially due to code completion and static type checking in LINQ queries, developers can quickly learn the usage of the DSL compared approaches using a purely string based query language. We evaluated our DSL by going through all query examples described in the specification [8] and developing the corresponding LINQ queries. As a result all of the examples could be expressed with our language. OPC UA allows to have its information models extended by new properties and references not only on type level but also on instance level. Therefore, there may be references for which no code was generated from the information model, yet. To use our DSL also in these cases we provide helper methods that generically access references and properties of within an address space as shown in Listing 4. Of course, some big advantages, i.e., the type safety and code completion features of our DSL are not available in this scenario.

Is the development with the DSL more efficient than creating lower level code? Even though an additional component, i.e., the LINQtoOPCUA generator needs to be maintained, efficiency should be higher than developing queries in lower level code. Especially, as the reduction in amount of lines of code is about an order of magnitude. The queries described as reference in the specification [8] could be expressed using LINQ with 3 to 10 lines of code.

Does it make sense to have this DSL for OPC UA? The OPC UA specification already proposes to use some kind of DSL for this use case. Using the LINQ-based solution provides a lightweight solution for it. Being an internal DSL that is well integrated into the IDE, consisting only of a few additional mapping classes, the effort for creating and maintain this DSL amortizes quickly. Thus, projects using the Event Filter or Query mechanisms benefit from the use of this DSL.

Listing 4. LinqToOpcua generic access

```
from controller in controllers
from fieldbus in NavigateReference(Controller, "Controls")
from device in NavigateReference(fieldbus, "ConnectedTo")
select new {ControllerSN = GetProperty(controller, "SerialNumber"),
    FieldbusName = GetProperty(fieldbus, "TypeName"),
    DeviceSN = GetProperty(device, "SerialNumber") };
```

5 Conclusions and Future Work

In this paper, we presented a DSL for developing OPC UA event filters and queries based on (generated) information model classes and LINQ. We facilitate the existence of information model classes which exist for OPC UA object types, their properties and references to base LINQ queries on them. Having the information model accessible on code level allows for type safe definition of LINQ queries. Using a such queries and the corresponding information model as input we can instantiate the appropriate classes given by OPC UA SDKs. Furthermore, as LINQ is a part of the standard .Net programming model many developers are already familiar to its syntax. Having a defined mapping to OPC UA allows them to reuse their knowledge in the automation domain.

Future work will deal with introducing the LINQToOPCUA DSL in current OPC UA development projects within ABB. Based on the experience gained in these projects we will be able to improve the DSL and assess its usability and impact on developer efficiency.

References

1. OPC Foundation: OPC UA Specification: Part 3 - Address Space Model (2010), http://opcfoundation.org/UA/Part3
2. CommServer: OPC UA Address Space Model Designer (2011), http://www.commsvr.com
3. Unified Automation GmbH: UaModeler (2011), http://www.unified-automation.com
4. OPC Foundation: OPC UA SDK 1.01 (2011), http://www.opcfoundation.org
5. Goldschmidt, T., Mahnke, W.: Evaluating domain-specific languages for the development of OPC UA based applications. In: 7th Vienna International Conference on Mathematical Modelling (MATHMOD)Special Session Modelling and Model Transformation in Automation Technologies (2012)
6. Fowler, M.: Domain-Specific Languages. Addison-Wesley Professional (2010)
7. Marguerie, F., Eichert, S., Wooley, J.: LINQ in action. Manning Publications Co., Greenwich (2008)
8. OPC Foundation: OPC UA Specification: Part 4 - Services (2010), http://opcfoundation.org/UA/Part4
9. Torgersen, M.: Querying in C#: how language integrated query (LINQ) works. In: Companion to the 22nd ACM SIGPLAN Conference on Object-Oriented Programming Systems and Applications Companion, OOPSLA 2007, pp. 852–853. ACM, New York (2007)

Combining UML Sequence and State Machine Diagrams for Data-Flow Based Integration Testing

Lionel Briand[1], Yvan Labiche[2], and Yanhua Liu[2]

[1] Centre for Security, Reliability, and Trust (SnT), University of Luxembourg, Luxembourg
lionel.briand@uni.lu
[2] Carleton University, SQUALL Lab, 1125 Colonel By Drive, Ottawa, ON, K1S5B6, Canada
{labiche,yliu}@sce.carleton.ca

Abstract. UML interaction diagrams are used during integration testing. However, this will typically not find all integration faults as some incorrect behaviors are only exhibited in certain states of the collaborating classes during interactions. State machine diagrams are typically used to model the behavior of state-dependent objects. This paper presents a technique to enhance interaction testing by accounting for state-based behavior as well as data-flow information. UML sequence and state machine diagrams are combined into a control-flow graph to then generate integration test cases, adapting well-known coupling-based, data-flow testing criteria. In order to assess our technique, we developed a prototype tool and applied it on a small case study. The results suggest that the proposed technique is more cost-effective than the most closely related approach reported in the literature, which only relies on control flow analysis.

Keywords: UML 2, Interaction diagram, State machine, Data flow, Coupling, Integration testing.

1 Introduction

In an object-oriented system, objects collaborate to provide functionalities. Even when classes have been unit tested thoroughly, unexpected failures may arise when they collaborate, leading to the identification of integration faults. Class integration testing focuses on class interactions to ensure functional correctness.

The Unified Modeling Language (UML) has become the de-facto standard for analysis and design of object-oriented software systems [1]. A number of papers (e.g., [2-7]) have proposed test case generation strategies from different UML design artifacts: interaction diagrams (sequence or communication diagrams) have been used to test class integration [2], interaction diagrams along with state machine diagrams have been used for state-based integration testing [3, 5, 7], and state machine diagrams have been used to perform unit testing [4].

The interactions among different instances can be specified using UML sequence diagrams, which are therefore suitable diagrams for integration testing [2]. However, testing interactions among classes based solely on those diagrams is not enough to find all integration faults as some incorrect behaviours are only exhibited in certain states of the collaborating objects during an interaction. This has somewhat been confirmed [8] since experimental results show that test suites derived from sequence diagrams and test suites derived from state machines find complementary sets of faults. Others showed that combining sequence and state information leads to detecting faults in the implementation of guard conditions and that such faults would not necessarily be found by solely using sequence diagrams [7]. Thus, one of our objectives is to generate class integration test cases from a combination of sequence and state machine diagrams, as suggested by others [9], so as to fully exercise the state-based behavior of interacting objects to uncover state-dependent interaction faults.

Note that a system under test may have several sequence diagrams to model its use cases. Our approach will not take all sequence diagrams as inputs. Instead, we only focus on one use case / sequence diagram at a time (e.g., one could start with the most critical ones). Additionally, our approach relies on model elements such as messages, guards, triggers, and actions that have remained unchanged in all versions of UML 2 to date. Unless necessary, we therefore do not indicate any specific version of UML 2 and simply refer to UML in the remainder of the paper.

Adequacy criteria are used to avoid exhaustive testing, which is often impractical (if even feasible), while gaining sufficient confidence in the system under test. One of our objectives is to offer a set of adequacy criteria for our test model built by combining sequence and state machine diagrams. Previous research, both theoretical and empirical, has revealed that data- and control-flow strategies may be complementary. Since previous test case generation strategies, comparable to ours, rely on control-flow criteria, we define data-flow criteria for our test model.

The rest of the paper is organized as follows. Section 2 discusses related work. We then propose a comprehensive methodology to combine UML sequence and state machine diagrams in one test model to conduct coupling-based, data-flow analysis. A set of mapping rules from a UML sequence diagram and state machine diagrams to the test model are formalized by using OCL (Section 3): rules match messages in sequence diagrams to state machine transitions, integrating state machine information into a control flow graph derived from a sequence diagram. Data flow information is analyzed based on the input models, operation signatures and operation contracts, and coupling data-flow criteria are applied to derive test cases (Section 4). A prototype tool has been developed to semi-automate the methodology. A case study is reported in section 5, where we study the cost-effectiveness of our approach and compare it to a previously published one. Conclusions and future work are outlined in section 0.

2 Related Work

There is a plethora of testing techniques based on one or more of the most used UML diagrams: class, activity, sequence, state machine diagrams. For instance, a quick search (conducted in March 2011) on Inspec and Engineering Village databases for papers published between 2007 and 2011 with keywords "testing", "UML", and "sequence diagram" (to be searched in titles, abstracts and keywords) resulted in a list of more than 36 unique publications. It is not our intent here to discuss them all, or even list them all, since most of them do not relate closely to our objective: How can we account for the fact that messages in sequence diagrams can be received by objects in different states? Furthermore, none of these papers attempts to apply data-flow criteria. We rather focus below on the few published approaches that attempt to combine sequence and state machine diagrams [3, 7, 10-16].

One approach is to combine the class, sequence and state machine diagrams to create a test model, a form of control flow graph with data-flow information [7]. Data-flow information pertains to variable assignments from sequence diagrams (i.e., arguments passed to messages, return values used to set variables) and post-conditions of operations triggered by messages. In the combination process, a sequence diagram becomes a control flow graph, that is extended thanks to state machine diagrams (the ones of the classes whose instances are used in the sequence diagram) as follows: if a message in a sequence diagram fires at least one transition in a state machine, the extended control flow graph contains as many nodes/messages as transitions that can potentially be fired, thereby specifying the alternative behaviours that can be triggered. Only control flow criteria (i.e., node, edge, path coverage) are then used to derive test sequences: the data flow information is not used for test case selection; data flow information is used to identify test inputs. A similar combination procedure is described by Ali et al. [3] though from UML 1.x statecharts and collaboration diagrams. No data-flow criterion is used to select test cases. Other similar combinations have been proposed [12, 13], sometimes extending Ali et. al. procedure. Again, only control flow criteria are used to select test cases. Instead of sequence diagrams, some authors combine statecharts and activity diagrams (e.g., [14, 15]). The combination procedures are similar to the ones previously mentioned, and only control flow criteria are used. Sokenou suggests that for each sequence of messages identified in a sequence diagram, an initialization sequence be identified from statecharts [16]. This requires, similarly to the approaches discussed so far, that we identify in which states messages in sequence diagrams can be triggered and received.

The main differences between these works and our work are twofold: we create a different control flow graph test model, and use data-flow test criteria, which they do not. With respect to the latter difference, although previous test models sometimes contain data-flow information [7] (though to a lesser extent as they do not identify uses and definitions of variables for instance), data-flow information is not used to build test sequences (i.e., using data-flow adequacy criteria). Rather it is used to help find test inputs for test sequences derived from control-flow criteria. With respect to the construction of the test models, our approach is different in one or more of the following ways: we support the UML 2 notation to a larger extent (e.g., not all previous approaches support asynchronous messages or "par" combined fragments); we believe our solution is more flexible since we make fewer assumptions with respect to the consistency between the sequence and the state machine diagrams (e.g., some previous works assume that the sequence of messages received by a lifeline is a legal sequence of transitions in the state machine describing the behaviour of the lifeline's object, whereas we acknowledge their could be some inconsistencies between the two depending on the level of details the designer put in the diagrams); our test model accurately represents nested calls (it is not possible in previous test models to identify which message triggers which other messages—calls are flattened, similarly to [17]). This latter difference about the test model is very important since without information on nested calls, it is impossible to apply criteria specifically targeting interactions between callers and callees.

Another related work [10] relies on AUML sequence and state machine diagrams—AUML is at the same time an extension of UML for specifying agents and testing interactions between them, and a subset of the UML notation. The authors transform those diagrams into a Maude (formal) model, which is used as test model. There is, however, no combination of the sequence and state machine diagrams since the Maude's rewriting rules are only derived from the state machines describing the behaviour of the communicating agents.

Sequence diagrams are also used as test objectives to trigger sequences of transitions in state machines [6, 11, 18-20]. In essence, the authors rely on existing, user-defined (control-flow) test objectives specified as sequence diagrams whereas we intend to (semi-)automatically identify (data-flow) test objectives.

Other related work extends the information provided in sequence diagrams with possible polymorphic messages, i.e., messages that can potentially trigger polymorphic calls [21], instead of state information. This work is complementary to ours and we will study the possibility of combining both approaches in our future work.

Earlier most cited works in the domain include test case generation from UML 1.x collaboration diagrams [2], from communicating finite state machines [5], from communicating UML 1.x statecharts [22]. Our work differs as we combine sequence and state machine diagrams into one test model and use data-flow testing criteria.

3 Message/Event/Action Control Flow Graph (MEACFG)

We transform a sequence diagram and state machine diagrams (of the classes involved in the sequence diagram) into a control flow graph—our test model—which we model as an activity diagram. We describe the construction of our test model in two steps, for illustration purposes only (i.e., our tool generates the test model in one step): we represent the control flow relationship among the messages of the UML sequence diagram (section 3.1) and add state information from state machine diagrams, matching messages in sequence diagrams to state machine transitions (section 3.2). The figures in this section and in section 4 illustrate different, un-related abstract examples, instead of one running example, as this allows us to present the main aspects of our approach in a condensed way: a (real) running example illustrating the same aspects would involve much larger diagrams that would not fit in a conference paper. Section 4 describes the use of the test model to generate test cases.

3.1 From a UML Sequence Diagram to a Control Flow Graph

A message control flow graph (MCFG) represents a UML sequence diagram using the UML activity diagram notation. Executable nodes in the MCFG for a sequence diagram correspond to messages in the sequence diagram, while control nodes show the sequence of execution of messages and object nodes show data-flow. In the following, UML metaclasses are written in courier font.

MCFG nodes are of three types: control nodes, executable nodes, and object nodes. A control node can be one of the following: initial node, final node, fork node, join node, decision node, and merge node. Each MCFG has a single initial node and final node. An executable node in the MCFG is an Action node, which may be a StructuredActivityNode or a CallOperationAction (specializations of Action), corresponding to a message in the sequence diagram that either triggers other messages or not, respectively. A structured activity node contains several executable nodes, control nodes, and object nodes, which indicates a call hierarchy among messages in the sequence diagram. Each structured activity node has its own initial and final nodes. CallOperationActions and StructuredActivityNodes can have pre- and postconditions. An ObjectNode is used in an Activity to indicate object flow. In the MCFG, object nodes are used to specify input and output parameters for each operation shown in the sequence diagram and show object flow between actions (class Pin). An ActivityPartition records the target of a message/call whereas we can get the source of a message/call from its nesting node in the MCFG. If a node corresponding to a message is nested in a structured activity node, then the structured activity node is the source of the message.

We assume the ExecutionSpecification (a.k.a. activation bar in UML 1.x) is specified on the lifeline of the sequence diagram. This is to ensure that we can unambiguously identify messages that trigger each other. For instance, Fig. 1 (a) does not have execution specifications and is ambiguous as it can correspond to either figure (b) or (c): in figure (a), one does not know whether message m4 is invoked by m1 or m3. Since some CASE tools, such as IBM RSA, support ExecutionSpecification, we consider this a reasonable assumption.

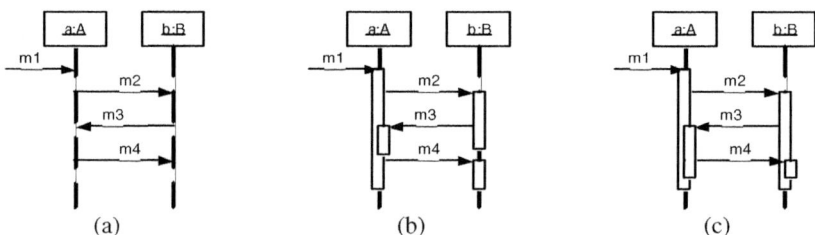

Fig. 1. Usefulness of execution specifications

The construction of a MCFG for a sequence diagram is detailed below where we show how each important UML sequence diagram construct is transformed into a MCFG construct. To facilitate the discussion, we use the example of Fig. 2: sequence diagram (left) and corresponding MCFG (right); where node m1 (MCFG) denotes message m1 (sequence diagram), pre- and post-conditions of the operation invoked by message m1 are constraints associated with node m1, and g1 is a guard condition. Stereotypes conform to UML notations [23]: a StructuredActivityNode has a <<Structured>> stereotype; the pre- and post-conditions of a node (obtained from the class diagram) have <<localPrecondition>> and <<local-Postcondition>> stereotypes; nodes inside a LoopNode have <<LoopSetup>>, <<LoopTest>>, and <<LoopBody>> stereotypes for each section of a LoopNode, respectively. Additional examples illustrating the transformation can be found in [24].

Each **synchronous message** that does not trigger any other message is transformed into a CallOperationAction. A synchronous message that triggers other messages is transformed into a StructuredActivityNode, containing activity nodes corresponding to the messages it triggers. In Fig. 2, m1 invokes m2 and therefore m1 is transformed into a StructuredActivityNode that contains an ActivityNode representing m2: more specifically m1 contains a loop since m2 appears in a loop combined fragment (loops are discussed below). Structured activity node m1 has two input pins, for the two parameters of message m1 in the sequence diagram.

UML defines different message sorts, two basic forms of which are operation calls and signals. If a message is an operation call, the pre- and post-condition of the message are those of the operation. If a message is a signal, i.e., the specification of an asynchronous communication between objects, it is realized by an operation, usually called the signal handler. There are two ways to specify the handler of a signal. One is to declare an operation with stereotype <<signal>>, which has the same name as the signal, in the class or interface to indicate the receipt of the signal. In this case, the pre- and post-conditions of a signal are those of the signal handler operation. Another way is to use a signal as a trigger of a transition in the receiver's state machine. The actions on the transition are the handlers of the signal. In this case, the signal is just a trigger to invoke the handlers and its pre- and post-conditions are empty.

If a message does not have a sender lifeline or is sent by an actor, we specify a node contained by the activity corresponding to that sequence diagram. If a message is sent several times to the same object, we create several nodes in the MCFG.

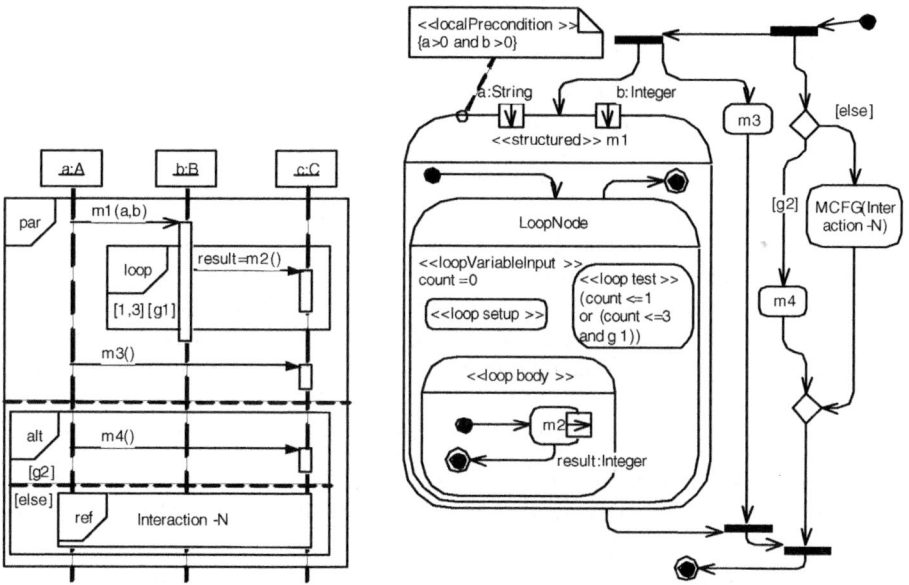

Fig. 2. A sequence diagram and its corresponding MCFG

par combined fragments and **asynchronous messages** denote concurrent executions, which we specify with fork and join nodes. In Fig. 2, the sequence diagram is made of a par combined fragment (to divide the sequence of messages m1 and m3 from the alternative combined fragment containing m4). Additionally, in the first part of the par combined fragment, message m1 is asynchronous. This results in two fork nodes and two join nodes in the activity diagram. It is important to note that, referring to Fig. 2, although the sequence diagram does not specify when the asynchronous call m3 will eventually finish (and return), the corresponding MCFG does indicate that m3 will not finish after m1. The behaviour specified in the MCFG therefore does not necessarily correspond to what was initially intended in the sequence diagram. We made this decision anyway since we needed to specify a behaviour that is possibly coherent with the sequence diagram. Plus, without additional information about m1 and m3 (e.g., expected execution times) it is not possible to specify exactly the same behaviour as in the sequence diagram: we do not know where to place the merge node for the asynchronous message. As a result, some data flow information may not be accurate: either false positive or false negative. Only additional case studies will tell us the extent of the impact of our decision. Future work could look into using the MARTE profile when specifying the sequence diagram to obtain a more consistent MCFG.

A **loop combined fragment** is specified with a LoopNode, and its setup, test, and body sections [1, 23], specified inside the structured activity node with different stereotypes (Fig. 2). The loop body is a structured activity node containing nodes for the messages inside the loop combined fragment. Nothing in a loop combined fragment really corresponds to a loop setup, which is therefore empty. The test section is a Boolean expression evaluated before or after the body section, depending on the value of attribute isTestedFirst of the loop node object [23]. Since a loop combined fragment is a 'while' loop, attribute isTestFirst is set to true for each loop node in the MCFG. In a loop combined fragment, the guard may include a lower and an upper number of iterations as well as a Boolean expression. After the minimum number of iterations has executed, if either the Boolean expression is false or the maximum number of iterations is reached[1], then the loop terminates [23]. In Fig. 2, [1, 3] denotes the minimum and maximum number of iterations, and [g1] indicates the Boolean expression to be satisfied. To model such a complex condition in the MCFG, we add a variable, named count with stereotype <<loopVariableInput>> [1], to the loop node to count the number of iterations (**Fig. 2**). Although not shown in **Fig. 2**, all paths inside the body section of the loop node finish with an activity node incrementing variable count. Then, we can write the test section of the loop node as follows[2]:

   count <= minimum or
   (count <= maximum and Boolean_expression_in_loop_combined_fragment).

An **alt combined fragment** denotes alternative flows of messages, each flow being specified in an interaction operand. This is rendered in our MCFG with a decision

---

[1] If there is only one number, the loop executes a fixed number of times. If there is no minimum and maximum numbers, the loop lower and upper bounds are considered to be 0 and infinity, and the Boolean expression solely determines the number of iterations.

[2] This general form can be modified if the loop combined fragment has only a min and max number of iterations, only a fixed number of iterations, or only a Boolean expression.

node with as many outgoing edges as interaction operands, and a merge node for merging the different flows. Each outgoing edge of the first decision node has a guard, the one of the corresponding interaction operand. An `opt` **combined fragment** is a specific case that specifies only one interaction operand.

A `break` **combined fragment** specifies a behaviour triggered only under a specific condition and otherwise skipped. When the condition is true, and the corresponding behaviour finishes, the flow jumps to the end of the enclosing interaction fragment (some behaviour of the enclosing interaction fragment is skipped). So a `break` combined fragment is represented as a decision node with two outgoing edges: one skipping the conditional behaviour and one flowing to the conditional behaviour. The flow after the conditional behaviour does not merge the skipping flow (as in an `opt`). Instead, it merges a control node that corresponds to the end of the enclosing interaction fragment. This can be one of the following: (1) a decision (merge) node if the enclosing interaction fragment is an `alt` or an `opt` combined fragment; (2) a join node if the enclosing interaction fragment is a `par` combined fragment; (3) a node right after a loop node, if the enclosing interaction fragment is a `loop` combined fragment; (4) the final node of the activity diagram, if none of the above applies.

An `InteractionUse` **interaction fragment** refers to an interaction, i.e., another sequence diagram. This is modeled in our MCFG as a `CallBehaviorAction` named after the `InteractionUse` name (Fig. 2). This `CallBehaviorAction` can have input and output pins if the `InteractionUse` has actual parameters.

There are other types of combined fragments, namely `critical`, `neg`, `assert`, `strict`, `seq`, `ignore` and `consider`. These are considered to be less used by modelers and we do not account for them. Future work will look into that issue.

Messages in a sequence diagram may have parameters and return values. This is modeled in our MCFG as `InputPins` and `OutputPins` of nodes (either `CallOperationAction` or `StructuredActivityNode`) corresponding to messages. For an `in` parameter, an `InputPin` is added to the node, with appropriate type obtained from the class diagram. For an `out` parameter or a return value, an `OutputPin` is added to the node. If a parameter is an `inout` parameter, we add both an `InputPin` and an `OutputPin`. These pins are useful for identifying definitions and uses of variables in the MCFG. In Fig. 2, parameters a and b of message m1 are modeled as two input pins with corresponding types, shown at the boundary of the structured activity node m1. Similarly, the return value of message m2 is modeled as an output pin of node m2, which indicates that m2 delivers a value back to m1.

The MCFG also contains notes describing pre- and post-conditions of operations, obtained from the class diagram: one example is illustrated in Fig. 2 for node m1.

A sequence diagram may show recursive calls, which are not handled in our MCFG generation. However, we consider that the behaviour models we are dealing with are not at the level of detail where recursion would appear. Indeed, we consider recursion to be a low-level design decision (algorithm) whereas we are using analysis and high-level design models as input.

3.2 Adding State Information

A message in a sequence diagram can trigger transitions in some state machines. Adding state information to the MCFG is to identify, as accurately as possible, the transitions in state machines that may be fired by messages.

In UML one can add a StateInvariant on a Lifeline to specify conditions that hold before or after a message or sequence of messages. If such information is available, we can precisely identify which transition(s) in the state machine of the target object of the message(s) is actually triggered by the message. If the actions resulting from firing a transition are not shown in the sequence diagram (i.e., the message firing the transition should trigger messages corresponding to actions), this information can be added to the MCFG (i.e., nested node). The obtained MEACFG combines the behaviours specified in a sequence diagram and state machines.

If state invariants are not specified on lifelines, we proceed as follows. For each MCFG node n, that corresponds to message m, if the behaviour of the receiver of m is not specified by a state machine, then we do not modify the MCFG. Should the opposite occur, we look at the state machine, and identify transitions that m triggers. (Note that we only support explicit triggers and do not handle completion events in the state machine.) Then, we add to the MCFG the behaviour(s) specified in the state machine when m triggers those transitions. Three different situations can occur:

Case 1: Node n is a CallOperationAction instance, i.e., m does not invoke any interclass message. (We assume that intra-class messages may have been omitted to simplify the sequence diagram, but that interclass messages should always be specified.) The transitions fired by m should not have any (interclass) operations or signals as actions (consistency between the diagrams). However, it is possible that the transitions have intra-class operations or signals as actions. What the message is doing to the object may be specified in the state machine but not in the sequence diagram. Therefore, the transitions that m can trigger are those without any action or those with intra-class operations or signals as actions.

Case 2: Node n is a StructuredActivityNode instance (except loop nodes), i.e., m invokes other messages, and the messages triggered by m should match some sequences of transition actions in the state machine of the recipient of m (consistency between the diagrams). The transitions that m can fire are those with actions matching the messages triggered by m.

Case 3: No matching is possible. In this case, we consider there is an inconsistency between the diagrams, which has to be resolved by the user.

Fig. 3 illustrates cases 1 and 2 for the same state machine (left). In Fig. (a), MCFG node m1 is an action node representing message m1 in the sequence diagram. Since m1 doesn't invoke any inter-class message, both transitions t1 (no resultant action) and t2 (the resultant action is an intra-class operation) in the state machine correspond to the sequence diagram (assuming action a1() is an intra-class action, whereas m2() and m3() are not). In Fig. (b), m1 is a structured activity node corresponding to message m1 in the sequence diagram: m1 invokes messages m2 and m3. Therefore, transition t3 in the state machine is the behaviour triggered by m1 in this sequence diagram as messages invoked by m1 match the sequence of actions (m2 and m3) on t3.

Once we have identified transition(s) matching a message m, state, guard condition, and additional action information on the transitions are added to the MCFG, producing the MEACFG. If there is only one identified transition, the source state and target state of the transition are transformed into Boolean expressions that are associated with the incoming and outgoing edges of the executable node n in the MEACFG respectively. This is the case of Fig. 3 (b), and the procedure above leads to Fig. 4 (b). The format of the Boolean expressions is [objectName.state = stateName] where objectName is derived from the lifeline of the sequence diagram, and stateName is obtained from the state machine diagram of the object. If a class has a state attribute, we use it in the Boolean expression directly. Otherwise, a state attribute is added to the class implicitly for generating test cases and deriving test oracle.

If there are actions on the transition, m invokes operations. Thus, n is a structured activity node, and contains nodes specifying invoked actions. The first action on the transition is connected to the outgoing edge of the initial node in n, and the outgoing edge of the last action is connected to the flow final node. Actions connect to each other according to their written order on the transition.

If there is more than one identified transition that message m can fire, a decision node is added to specify alternative paths resulting from several fired transitions. Each path corresponds to one of those transitions. For each transition, and therefore for each outgoing edge from the decision node, the approach described above is applied. The paths then merge into another decision node. This is illustrated in Fig. 4 (a) that is derived from Fig. 3 (a): the alternatives indicate that what happens in the MCFG node m1 in Fig. 3 (a) depends on whether the state of the object is S1 (m1 is triggered as part of transition t1 and the new state is S2) or S2 (m1 is triggered as part of transition t2, which triggers a1, and the new state is S3).

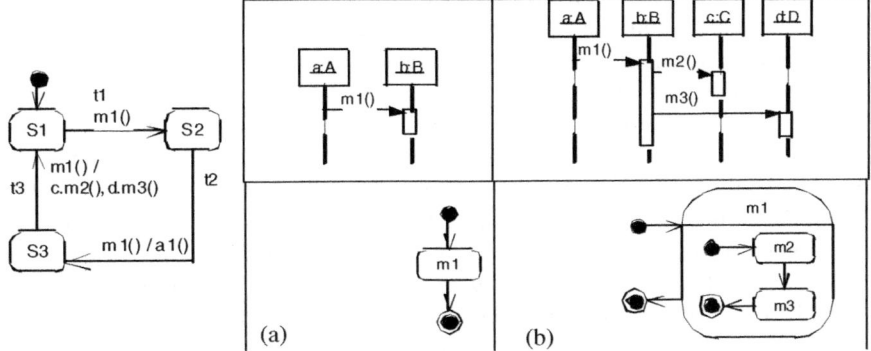

Fig. 3. Illustrating the recovery of state information

4 Coupling-Based Testing of Class Interactions

The MEACFG test model is more complete than previous attempts (i.e., a larger portion of the UML standard is accounted for), as discussed in section 2. With this test model, one can use control-flow adequacy criteria as in previous works, but also data-flow criteria as discussed below.

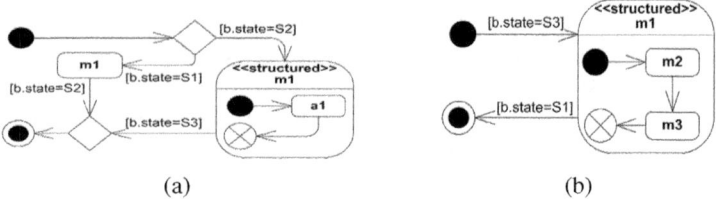

Fig. 4. MEACFG: MCFG plus state information

Coupling-based data-flow criteria for integration testing of procedural software [25] have been adapted to class integration testing [26]. We adapt them to model-based integration testing, and use them to generate integration test cases. In a nutshell, the criteria [25, 26] are to exercise paths between the last definitions of variables before calls to and returns from the called operation, and the first uses of variables after calls to and returns from the called operation. Due to space constraints we refer the reader to [24-26] for more details on these criteria. What matters and requires a detailed discussion is how we identify definitions and uses of variables in a MEACFG, which we discuss below and illustrate with Fig. 5: (a) sequence diagram and (b) corresponding MEACFG (definitions and uses are indicated on the side of the diagram, for illustration purposes only). (The corresponding class diagram is not shown.)

A MEACFG is a control flow graph showing sequences of executions of operations (nodes) and calls between these operations (structured activity nodes). A structured activity node (e.g., node m1) is a caller message/operation and its nested nodes (e.g., node m3) are called messages/operations: each pair (n1, n2) in the MEACFG where n1 is a structured activity node and n2 is a node (either structured activity or not) representing a message denotes a call, n2 being the call site, i.e., the place in the control flow indicating the call; for instance pairs (m1, m2), (m1, m3) and (m1, m4) represent the three calls m1 makes, m2, m3, and m4 denoting call sites.

As discussed earlier, actual parameters, mapping formal ones, and return values become pins. For instance, actual parameter pf1 of operation m1, maps to formal Integer parameter pa1, and becomes an input pin to structured activity node m1. With respect to data-flow, input pins denote uses whereas output pins denote definitions.

All the formal parameters of a caller message are specified as being defined in the initial node of the corresponding structured activity node, e.g., formal parameter pa1 is defined in the initial node of structured activity node m1. Additionally, any local variable in a structured activity node is considered to be defined in the initial node of that structured activity node, e.g., 1P, and at for m1. We consider a variable to be local when it is not an attribute or reference that can be accessed (directly or through a navigation) from the context object executing the corresponding (enclosing) operation/message. The return value of a structured activity node, if there is one, is also specified as being defined at the initial node of the structured activity node, e.g. ret for node m1. These ensure that if our analysis does not detect any definition of such variables/parameters between the initial node of the structured activity node and a call site (where one of the variables would be passed as an actual parameter) we have at least one coupling-definition involving the use of that variable at the call site. This is a conservative heuristic to ensure that uses of variables/parameters are exercised by the testing criteria. This may however result in coupling-definitions that do not exist, e.g., if there is a definition between the initial node of the structured activity node and the call site that we cannot detect, the coupling-definition we identify with our heuristic is not the right one. Only case studies will tell us the extent of false-positives. Such a heuristic is necessary since we decided to work only from models, which are, in essence, abstractions.

This data flow information is solely retrieved from operation signatures (from the class diagram). Additional data flow information is identified from guard conditions (e.g., `alt` and `loop` combined fragments), state invariants, and operation contracts. Guard conditions such as g1 and g2 in Fig. 5, if expressed in OCL, can be analyzed automatically to identify the variables, formal parameters, attributes, links they manipulate, and which translate into uses on edges in the MEACFG. For the analysis of OCL expressions, we rely on a previous work [4] where the authors defined a set of rules to systematically analyze OCL expressions and identify definitions and uses of model elements (attributes, links, collections, ...). Possible types of uses and definitions have been formally specified using OCL expressions, based on the MEACFG metamodel, which can be found in [24] along with illustrating examples.

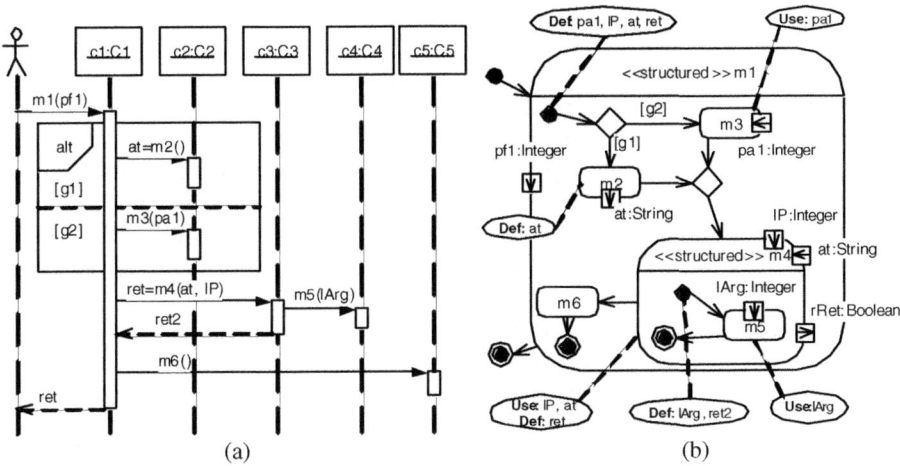

Fig. 5. Illustrating data flow in MEACFG

For the MEACFG, annotated with data-flow information as discussed above, coupling-based testing criteria [25, 26], and a graph algorithm to identify test objectives for these criteria (typically definition-clear paths) and then test paths (i.e., complete paths, from start node to end node, in the MEACFG), can be readily applied. Given such test objectives and test paths, our approach relies on manual identification of test inputs to make test paths executable. In the future we will investigate a solution to automatically identify such test inputs [7, 27]. What we presented above applies directly to the notion of parameter coupling, i.e., when two operations interact through parameters. Other types of coupling [25], e.g., shared variable coupling (which in our context can translate into attribute coupling), can be accounted for in a similar way.

5 Case Study

To conduct our case study we implemented our approach as an Eclipse plugin using IBM Rational Software Architect (RSA). It is based on EMF (to model the MEACFG) and RSA's model-to-model transform engine (to create a MEACFG from a sequence diagram and related state machine diagrams). More details about the tool architecture are available in [24].

To validate our approach, we compared it with SCOTEM [3], as our approach is closely related to it. In doing so we want to investigate whether using data-flow criteria (our approach) improves fault detection over control-flow criteria (SCOTEM). Indeed, the SCOTEM approach supports four control-flow testing criteria to generate test paths: Single-Path, Transition, n-Path, and Path testing criteria. Another comparison that could be investigated is with [7] though, as described above, this approach covers a smaller subset of the UML notation and relies on additional assumptions about the modeling methodology. We defer this comparison to future work.

We therefore use the same case study system as the one used to evaluate SCOTEM: the Arithmetic Tutor (AT) system. To determine the effectiveness of our approach, we seeded faults into the code, using mutation operators, as has been done in numerous similar experiments and showed to be an adequate way of comparing testing techniques [28]. We used the same mutant programs as in the SCOTEM case study since (1) these mutants were carefully selected to be varied (in terms of operators and locations in the source code) and lead to interaction faults, and (2) this will allow us to precisely compare the effectiveness of the two approaches. We refer the reader to [3, 24] for more details on this aspect. Overall, 49 mutants were generated by using 12 mutation operators.

The AT case study teaches a variety of arithmetic operations to students and provides self-evaluation of learning activities. It can be run in two modes: training and assessment. In the training mode, the AT system provides complete, step-wise gradual explanations for arithmetic operations. Students can choose any type and complexity of arithmetic operations to learn. In the assessment mode, the AT system randomly generates a set of operations to evaluate the arithmetic skills of a student, and the complexity of generated problems is dynamically adjusted according to the student performance. The detailed performance for each session is logged and the history record of the student is updated at the end of each session.

The AT system that we consider, and that was used in [3], is an incomplete design and implementation, which is a simple version of the assessment mode that generates basic arithmetic operations only, such as addition, subtraction, multiplication, and division. The problems are generated randomly by the AT system (complexity of generated problems are not taken into account in our case study). The AT case study is implemented in Java, and contains nine classes (including 42 methods, 339 LOC): five of them are specified with state machines (with more than one state). The UML sequence and state machine diagrams are available in [24], where the constructed MEACFG (with data flow information) can also be found.

Since different test suites for the different criteria could result in different mutation scores, to provide a meaningful evaluation and also facilitate the comparison with the SCOTEM approach, we adopted the SCOTEM strategy and chose 10 randomly selected adequate test suites for each testing criterion and calculated the minimum, average, and maximum mutation scores for each of them. For each criterion, the 10 adequate test suites have the same test paths (in the MEACFG). What differ are the test inputs to execute the paths.

Test suites generated for the Coupling-Defs criterion have six paths, which detected 45 to 49 mutants. The mutation score of a Coupling-Defs adequate test suite was 98% on average. Call-Sites, Coupling-Uses, and Coupling-Paths criteria generated 18, 18, and 27 test paths, respectively, and adequate test suites were all able to detect all mutants, which is probably due to the fact that the case study is simple.

A qualitative investigation of alive mutants when using Coupling-Defs showed that the mutation operators modified conditional statements. These correspond to guards in MEACFG edges, and since Coupling-Defs does not necessarily cover those edges, the corresponding adequate test suites may miss the mutants.

A comparison between SCOTEM and our approach is summarized in Table 1. The table reports on the different criteria supported by the two approaches, the number of paths (i.e., test cases) the criteria require, and the mutation score achieved (on average over 10 adequate test suites).

Table 1. SCOTEM vs. our approach

SCOTEM			MEACFG		
Criteria	Number of Test paths	Mutant scores on average	Criteria	Number of Test paths	Mutant scores on average
Single-Path	1	75%	Coupling-Defs	6	98%
Transition	3	91%	Call Sites	18	100%
n-Path (n=82)	82	95%	Coupling-Uses	18	100%
Path	162	100%	Coupling-Paths	27	100%

Single-Path and Transition criteria (SCOTEM), with one and three tests respectively, can only detect less than 91% mutants, and n-Path only kills 95% of the mutants with many more tests (82). However, Coupling-Defs (MEACFG) kills 98% mutants with six test paths only. When applying Call Sites, Coupling-Uses and Coupling-Paths criteria (MEACFG), we only need 18 to 27 test paths to kill all the mutants. However, to achieve 100% mutation score following the SCOTEM approach, one needs to execute all the 162 paths, which is much more expensive and may turn out to be impossible for a larger system. We analyzed mutants that remain alive when following the SCOTEM approach, and we noticed that they are state-related faults: an object is in a wrong state before receiving a message, or the states of the sending and receiving objects of a message contradict the specification of the message. Given that the data-flow criteria specifically focus on definition and uses of variables and some of the variables specified in the MEACFG are specifically modeling changes of states (e.g., in conditions), it is not surprising that data-flow adequate test suites have more chances (with fewer tests) to find those faults. The results of this case study show that coupling data-flow criteria are effective for selecting test paths from the MEACFG to detect state faults. Though the case study used is admittedly simple, it nevertheless shows a significant improvement over SCOTEM, which was our objective.

6 Conclusion

Testing interactions among classes based on UML interaction diagrams may not find all integration faults as some incorrect behaviors may only be exhibited in certain states of the collaborating classes during an interaction. Additionally, data-flow testing criteria are known, in general, to complement control-flow ones. Hence, this paper has presented a comprehensive approach to conduct state-based integration testing based on coupling data-flow testing criteria. The approach consists in combining information from a UML 2 sequence diagram and state machine diagrams (of the classes whose instances are involved in the sequence diagram) and then generating a control flow graph (a UML activity diagram). It does so while supporting a large portion of the UML 2 sequence and state machine notations. This graph is annotated with data-flow information, also derived from the UML model (operation signatures, message and transition guards, operation contracts), and is used as a test model to derive test cases according to well known coupling-based, data-flow testing criteria.

The approach has been implemented in a tool and used in a case study to compare it with the closely related SCOTEM approach. Results show that accounting for state and coupling-based, data-flow information when deriving tests from sequence diagrams is more cost-effective at finding faults than simply relying on control-flow information (SCOTEM).

Several venues for future work can be identified. Among them we can mention experimenting with our approach using case study systems of varying complexities, comparing the cost and effectiveness of the different criteria, comparing it with SCOTEM, and comparing our approach with other approaches (e.g., [7]).

References

[1] Pender, T.: UML Bible. Wiley (2003)
[2] Abdurazik, A., Offutt, J.: Using UML Collaboration Diagrams for Static Checking and Test Generation. In: Evans, A., Caskurlu, B., Selic, B. (eds.) UML 2000. LNCS, vol. 1939, pp. 383–395. Springer, Heidelberg (2000)
[3] Ali, S., Briand, L.C., Rehman, M.J., Asghar, H., Zafar, Z., Nadeem, A.: A State-based Approach to Integration Testing based on UML Models. IST 49(11-12), 1087–1106 (2007)
[4] Briand, L.C., Labiche, Y., Lin, Q.: Improving the Coverage Criteria of UML State Machines Using Data Flow Analysis. STVR 20(3), 177–207 (2010)
[5] Gallagher, L., Offutt, A.J., Cincotta, A.: Integration testing of object-oriented components using finite state machines. STVR 16(4), 215–266 (2006)
[6] Pelliccione, P., Muccini, H., Bucchiarone, A., Facchini, F.: TeStor: Deriving Test Sequences from Model-based Specifications. In: ACM CBSE, pp. 267–282 (2005)

[7] Bandyopadhyay, A., Ghosh, S.: Test input generation using UML sequence and state machines models. In: IEEE ICST, pp. 121–130 (2009)
[8] Kansomkeat, S., Offutt, J., Abdurazik, A., Baldini, A.: A comparative evaluation of tests generated from different UML diagrams. In: ACIS SNPD, pp. 867–872 (2008)
[9] Wu, Y., Chen, M.-H., Offutt, A.J.: UML-Based Integration Testing for Component-Based Software. In: Erdogmus, H., Weng, T. (eds.) ICCBSS 2003. LNCS, vol. 2580, pp. 251–260. Springer, Heidelberg (2003)
[10] Mokhati, F., Badri, M., Badri, L., Hamidane, F., Bouazdia, S.: "Automated testing sequences generation from AUML diagrams: a formal verification of agents' interaction protocols". IJAOSE 2(4), 422–448 (2008)
[11] Pickin, S., Jard, C., Jeron, T., Jezequel, J.-M., Le Traon, Y.: Test synthesis from UML models of distributed software. IEEE TSE 33(4), 252–268 (2007)
[12] Sarma, M., Mall, R.: Automatic generation of test specifications for coverage of system state transitions. IST 51(2), 418–432 (2009)
[13] Wu, C.-S., Chang, W.-C., Kim, S., Huang, C.-H.: Generating State-based Polymorphic Interaction Graph from UML Diagrams for Object Oriented Testing. In: IAENG IMECS, pp. 726–731 (2011)
[14] Barisas, D., Bareiša, E.: A Software Testing Approach Based on Behavioral UML Models. ITC 38(2), 119–124 (2009)
[15] Swain, S.K., Mohapatra, D.P., Mall, R.: Test Case Generation Based on State and Activity Models. JOT 9(5), 1–27 (2010)
[16] Sokenou, D.: Generating Test Sequences from UML Sequence Diagrams and State Diagrams. In: GI Jahrestagung, pp. 236–240 (2006)
[17] Garousi, V., Briand, L.C., Labiche, Y.: Control Flow Analysis of UML 2.0 Sequence Diagrams. In: ECMFA, pp. 160–174 (2005)
[18] Ledru, Y., du Bousquet, L., Bontron, P., Maury, O., Oriat, C., Potet, M.-L.: Test Purposes: Adapting the Notion of Specification to Testing. In: IEEE ASE, pp. 127–134 (2001)
[19] Li, L., Zhongsheng, Q., He, T.: Test purpose-based test generation for Web applications. In: IEEE NDT, pp. 238–243 (2009)
[20] En-Nouaary, A., Liu, G.: Timed test cases generation based on test purposes expressed as message sequence charts. In: IEEE ICTTA, pp. 585–586 (2004)
[21] Zeng, Y., Chen, L.-P., Chai, Y.-X., Zhou, X.: UML-based approach to generate polymorphic testing sequence and its implementation. In: WRI WCSE, pp. 251–255 (2009)
[22] Hartmann, J., Imoberdorf, C., Meisinger, M.: UML-Based Integration Testing. In: ACM ISSTA, pp. 60–70 (2000)
[23] OMG, UML 2.0 Superstructure Specification, Object Management Group, Final Adopted Specification ptc/03-08-02 (2003)
[24] Liu, Y.: Combining UML 2.0 sequence and state machine diagrams for control- and data-flow based integration testing, M.A.Sc. thesis, Carleton University (2009)
[25] Jin, Z., Offutt, A.J.: Coupling-based Criteria for Integration Testing. STVR 8(3), 133–154 (1998)
[26] Briand, L.C., Labiche, Y., Wang, Y.: A comprehensive and systematic methodology for client-server class integration testing. In: IEEE ISSRE, pp. 14–25 (2003)
[27] Ali, S., Iqbal, M.Z., Arcuri, A., Briand, L.C.: A Search-based OCL Constraint Solver for Model-based Test Data Generation. In: IEEE QSIC (2011)
[28] Andrews, J.H., Briand, L.C., Labiche, Y., Namin, A.S.: Using Mutation Analysis for Assessing and Comparing Testing Coverage Criteria. IEEE TSE 32(8), 608–624 (2006)

Model Transformations for Migrating Legacy Models: An Industrial Case Study

Gehan M.K. Selim[1], Shige Wang[2], James R. Cordy[1], and Juergen Dingel[1]

[1] School of Computing, Queen's University, Kingston, Ontario, Canada, K7L3N6
[2] Electrical and Controls Integration Lab, General Motors Research & Development, Warren, Michigan, USA, 48090
{gehan,cordy,dingel}@cs.queensu.ca, shige.wang@gm.com

Abstract. Many companies in the automotive industry have adopted MDD in their vehicle control software development. As a major automotive company, General Motors has been using a custom-built, domain-specific modeling language, implemented as an internal proprietary metamodel, to meet the modeling needs in its control software development. As AUTOSAR (AUTomotive Open System ARchitecture) is being developed as a standard to ease the process of integrating components provided by different suppliers and manufacturers, there is a growing demand to migrate these GM-specific, legacy models to AUTOSAR models. Given that AUTOSAR defines its own metamodel for various system artifacts in automotive software development, we explore using model transformations to address the challenges in migrating GM legacy models to their AUTOSAR equivalents. As a case study, we have built a model transformation using the MDWorkbench tool and the Atlas Transformation Language (ATL). This paper reports on the case study, makes observations based on our experience to assist in the development of similar types of transformations, and provides recommendations for further research.

Keywords: Model Driven Development (MDD), model transformations, AUTOSAR, transformation languages and tools, automotive control software.

1 Introduction

MDD is a relatively new software development methodology that uses models for software specification and communication. In MDD, software development is a sequence of model transformations where abstract models are successively converted into detailed models, and eventually into code. Model transformations are implemented using a model transformation language, which can be declarative, imperative, or hybrid. While a declarative language yields a compact specification, an imperative language is more capable of specifying complex transformations.

As one of the early MDD adopters in industry, General Motors (GM) has created a domain-specific modeling language, implemented as an internal proprietary metamodel, for Vehicle Control Software (VCS) development. The metamodel defines modeling constructs for vehicle control software development, including schedules and interfaces. VCS models conforming to this metamodel have been used in several vehicle production domains at GM, such as body control and monitoring.

Recently, AUTOSAR (the AUTomotive Open System ARchitecture) [2] has been developed as an industry standard to facilitate integration of software components from different manufacturers and suppliers and enable exchangeability and interoperability among them. AUTOSAR defines its own metamodel with a well-defined layered architecture and interfaces. Since converging to AUTOSAR is a strategic direction for future modeling activities, transforming GM legacy models to their equivalent AUTOSAR models becomes essential. Model transformation is a key enabling technology to achieve this convergence objective.

Despite the existence of studies in MDD industry adoption [19][23], no transformation is reported to have migrated legacy models in the automotive industry. To test the practicality of using transformations for migrating industrial legacy models, we have implemented a transformation of GM legacy models to AUTOSAR models.

The rest of this paper is organized as follows. Section 2 discusses the process context in which our transformation is implemented. Section 3 describes the source and target metamodels of the transformation. Section 4 details the transformation development. Section 5 discusses our experiences and issues that require further research. Section 6 provides a summary, a comparison to related work and future work.

2 VCS Development, Models and Model Transformations

Applying transformation requires understanding of the development process, which provides a context for the transformation. The VCS development process is described as a V-diagram (Fig. 1). The stages on the left-hand side of the V-diagram are design and implementation activities, and the stages of the right-hand are integration and validation activities. The design starts from system requirements models, which are decomposed into hardware and software subsystem requirements models. The subsystem requirements models then are assigned to engineering groups for refinement into design models and then implemented by hardware and software components. These implemented components are integrated into Electronic Control Units (ECUs), configured for a designated vehicle product. The components are then tested at various levels against their models on the same level on the left-hand side of the V-diagram.

Different types of models in different formalisms are manipulated in the VCS development process. For example, control models use differential equations and timing-variation functions; software models use dataflow diagrams or class diagrams; and architecture models use annotated block diagrams. Selected modeling tools (e.g., Simulink, Rhapsody) and languages (e.g., UML, AADL) are used for modeling.

The transformations used in the VCS development process can be *horizontal or vertical transformations*. Horizontal transformations manipulate models at the same abstraction level but possibly in different formalisms, e.g. transforming a Matlab Stateflow state machine into a UML state machine. Such transformations are normally used to verify integration of subsystems to realize a system function. The source and target modeling languages may have different syntax, but must share similar semantics. Vertical transformations manipulate models at different abstraction levels, e.g. generating a deployment model from software and hardware architecture models. Vertical transformations are usually more complex than horizontal transformations due to the different semantics of the source and target models.

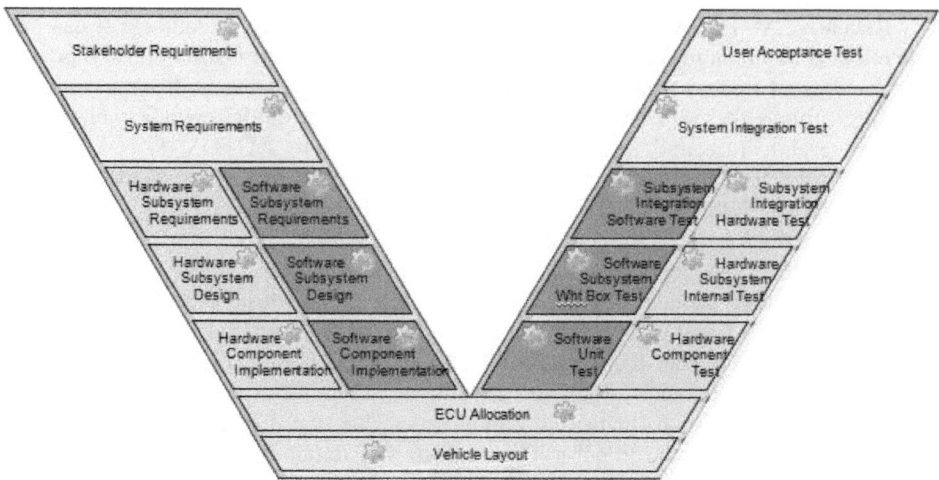

Fig. 1. V-Diagram for the VCS development process

3 Source and Target Metamodels

In this study, our models are those generated and used at the software subsystem design stage in the VCS development process. The source metamodel is an internal, proprietary GM metamodel which we will refer to as the GM metamodel. The target metamodel is the AUTOSAR System Template [2]. To simplify the exercise without losing generality, a subset of the two metamodels is manipulated in the transformation. Specifically, we focus on the modeling elements related to the software components' deployment and interactions, as discussed below.

3.1 The GM Metamodel

Fig. 2 illustrates the meta-types in the GM metamodel[1] that represent the physical nodes, deployed software components and their interactions. The *PhysicalNode* type specifies a physical node on which software is deployed. A *PhysicalNode* may contain multiple *Partition* instances, each of which defines a processing unit or a memory

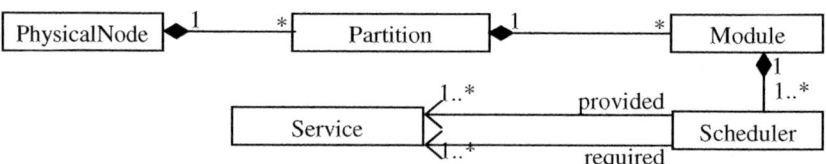

Fig. 2. The subset of the GM metamodel used in our transformation

---

[1] The metamodel has been altered for reasons of confidentiality. However, the relevant aspects required for the purpose of this paper have all been preserved.

partition on which software is deployed. Multiple *Module* instances can be deployed on a single *Partition*. The *Module* type is the atomic, reusable element in a product line and can contain multiple *Scheduler* instances. The *Scheduler* type is the basic unit for software scheduling and manages services provided or required by behavior-encapsulating entities. Thus, each *Scheduler* may provide or require many *Services*.

3.2 The AUTOSAR Metamodel

The AUTOSAR metamodel is defined as a set of templates, each of which is a collection of classes used to specify an AUTOSAR artifact. The *System* template [3] is used to capture the configuration of a system or an Electronic Component Unit (ECU). An ECU is a physical unit on which software is deployed. When used for the configuration of an ECU, the template is referred to as the *ECU Extract*. Fig. 3. shows the metatypes in the ECU Extract that capture software deployment on an ECU.

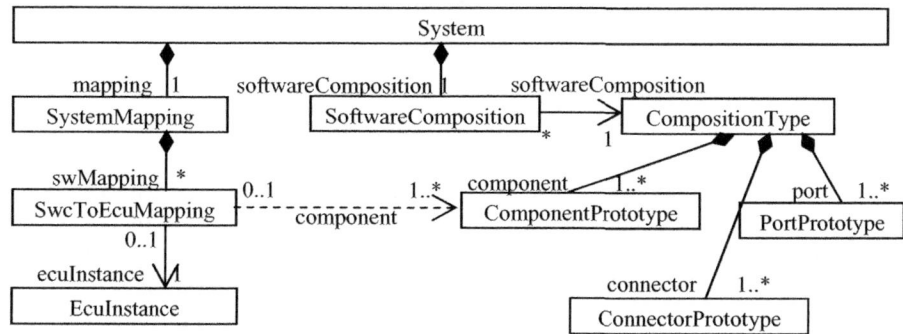

Fig. 3. The AUTOSAR System Template containing relevant types used by our transformation

The ECU extract contains the *System* type which aggregates *SoftwareComposition* and *SystemMapping* elements. The *SoftwareComposition* type points to the *CompositionType* type which eliminates any nested software components in a *SoftwareComposition* instance. The *SoftwareComposition* type models the architecture of the software components deployed on an ECU, their ports, and the ports' connectors. Software components are modeled using the *ComponentPrototype* type; ports are modeled using the *PPortPrototype* type or *RPortPrototype* type for providing or requiring services; connectors are modeled using the *ConnectorPrototype* type.

The *SystemMapping* type binds the software components to ECUs and the data elements to signals and frames. The *SystemMapping* type aggregates the *SwcToEcuMapping* type, which maps *ComponentPrototype* elements to an *EcuInstance*. According to AUTOSAR, only one *SwcToEcuMapping* instance should be created for every processing unit or memory partition in an ECU.

4 GM-to-AUTOSAR Model Transformation

We implement a GM-to-AUTOSAR model transformation to demonstrate the practicality of adopting transformations in the automotive industry. We rationalize our choice of the tool and language and we summarize the pragmatics of the chosen language. We then discuss the transformation rules and implementation details. Our transformation takes as inputs the source GM metamodel, the target AUTOSAR system template, and an input GM model. The output is an AUTOSAR model.

4.1 Selecting Model Transformation Tool and Language

Several tools and their accompanying languages have been considered for implementing the transformation including IBM Rational Asset Manager (RAM) [13], the RulesComposer add-on for IBM Rhapsody [14], and MDWorkbench [18].

After investigating the candidate tools, we concluded that IBM RAM and Rules Composer are not suitable for this transformation. RAM is a repository-based tool that offers APIs to create relationships between repository assets (e.g. models). The APIs can manipulate a model as a whole, not the individual model elements. As fine-grained manipulations are essential for our transformation, the support provided by RAM is not sufficient. RulesComposer is a rule-based model-to-text generator. Rules are specified as templates composed of static text and placeholders. When executed, the static text is copied into the output, and the placeholders are extracted from the input models. When defining rules, one must ensure that the template generates well-formed XMI files. Thus, defining the template is time-consuming and error-prone. Moreover, the rule templates can be very verbose, and thus, difficult to maintain.

MDWorkbench is an Eclipse-based tool for developing model-to-model transformations using the Atlas Transformation Language (ATL) [1] or the Model Query Language (MQL) [18]. ATL has declarative and imperative constructs, while MQL has imperative constructs only. MDWorkbench can manipulate models conforming to the metamodels registered in the tool (e.g. AUTOSAR) using rules defined in ATL and MQL. Thus, we choose MDWorkbench to implement the transformation. ATL was chosen rather than MQL because ATL provides flexibility to mix-and-match declarative and imperative constructs in the same rule definition.

4.2 ATL Pragmatics

In ATL, a model transformation is defined as a set of rules and helpers. Rules specify the creation of output model elements. Helpers are used to modularize a transformation. ATL defines four types of rules and two types of declarative helpers.

Rule Types. The four types of rules are matched rules, lazy rules, unique lazy rules, and called rules. A matched rule specifies how a source pattern is transformed to a target pattern. Matched rules are executed in the order of their specification and are automatically executed once for each matching pattern. A lazy rule is a rule that is executed only when called for a matching pattern and can be called multiple times for any match in the input model. A unique lazy rule is a rule that is executed only when called and can be called at most once for any match in the input model. A called rule is a parameterized rule that is executed only when called and creates an element in the output model without matching any source patterns. The four kinds of rules have an optional imperative code block to specify complicated functionality.

Matched rules are suitable for automatic detection of all pattern matches in the input model and creation of their corresponding target patterns; lazy rules and unique lazy rules are suitable for selective pattern matching, with consideration of the number of times these rules should be run; and called rules are suitable for creating output model elements that do not match any input model elements.

Helper Types. The two types of helpers are functional helpers and attribute helpers. A functional helper is a parametric function that is evaluated each time it is called. An attribute helper is a non-parametric function that is evaluated only in the first call. An attribute helper is more efficient to implement a non-parametric functionality. Otherwise, a functional helper can implement a parametric functionality.

4.3 Model Transformation Design and Development

Our transformation rules were crafted in consultation with domain experts at GM to realize the required mappings between the metamodels. For reasons of confidentiality, we present a simplified version of the actual rules. Let *M* be the input GM model and *M'* the to-be-generated output AUTOSAR model. The rules are defined as follows:

1. For every element *physNode* of the *PhysicalNode* type in M, generate an element *sys* of the *System* type, an element *swcompos* of the *SoftwareComposition* type, a containment relation (*sys, swcompos*), an element *composType* of the *CompositionType* type, a relation (*swcompos, composType*), an element *sysmap* of the *SystemMapping* type, a containment relation (*sys, sysmap*) and an element *ecuInst* of the *EcuInstance* type in M';
2. For every element *partition* of the *Partition* type in M, generate an element *swc2ecumap* of the *SwcToEcuMapping* type and a containment relation (*sysmap, swc2ecumap*) in M';
3. For every containment relation (*physNode, partition*) in M, generate a relation (*swc2ecumap, ecuInst*) in M';
4. For every element *mod* of the *Module* type in M, generate an element *comp* of the *ComponentPrototype* type in M';
5. For every containment relation (*partition, mod*) in M, generate a containment relation (*composType, comp*) and a relation (*sw2ecumap, comp*) in M';
6. For every relation (*sched, svc*) of the *provided* type between a *sched* element of the *Scheduler* type and a *svc* element of the *Service* type with a containment relation *(mod, sched)*, generate a *pPort* element of the *PPortPrototype* type and a containment relation (*composType , pPort*) in M';
7. For every relation (*sched, svc*) of the *required* type between a *sched* element of the *Scheduler* type and a *svc* element of the *Service* type with a containment relation *(mod, sched)*, generate a *rPort* element of the *RPortPrototype* type and a containment relation (*composType, rPort*) in M'.

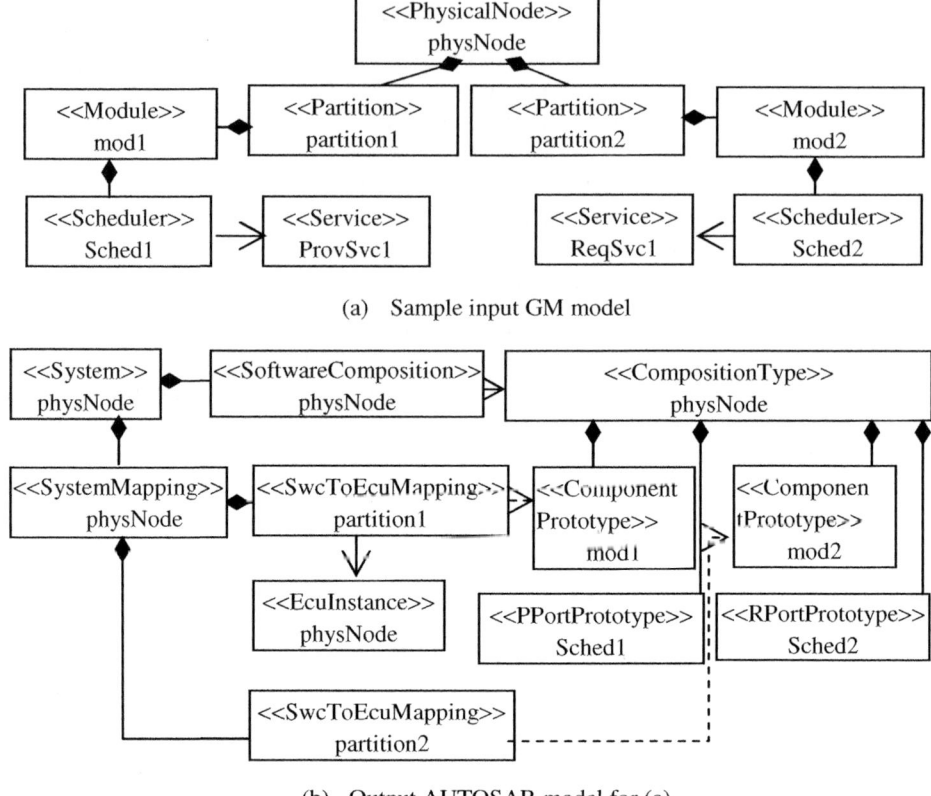

Fig. 4. (a) Sample GM input model and (b) its corresponding AUTOSAR output model

Fig. 4 demonstrates the required transformation from a sample GM model (Fig. 4 (a)) to its expected output AUTOSAR model (Fig. 4(b)) based on the above mentioned rules. The *PhysicalNode* element is mapped to a *System* element, an *EcuInstance* element, a *SystemMapping* element, a *SoftwareComposition* element, and a *CompositionType* element (Rule 1). The *Partition* elements are mapped to the *SwcToEcuMapping* elements (Rule 2), each of which is associated with the generated *EcuInstance* element (Rule 3). The *Module* elements are mapped to the *ComponentPrototype* elements aggregated by a *CompositionType* element and referred to by their corresponding *SwcToEcuMapping* elements (Rules 4-5). The *Scheduler* element aggregating a provided *Service* is mapped to a *PPortPrototype* element (Rule 6). The other *Scheduler* element is mapped in a similar manner (Rule 7).

The transformation development follows an iterative, incremental process. First, a simple GM model is created in the MDWorkbench model editor. Then, a transformation is implemented to transform the input GM model into an AUTOSAR model. The AUTOSAR model is then validated and if the transformation is correct, the process is repeated with additional types in the input model and additional transformation rules. If the output model contains errors, the transformation is analyzed and fixed.

Validation is performed manually. For an input GM model, an expected output AUTOSAR model is created in the MDWorkbench Model Editor. The transformation's output model is compared with the manually-created model. Equivalence of the models implies a correct transformation.

4.4 The Transformation Implementation Using ATL

The GM-to-AUTOSAR transformation contains two ATL matched rules and 9 functional helpers implementing the 7 rules in Section 4.3. We also define 6 attribute helpers to access the model attribute values. Table 1 lists the matched rules and functional helpers and their implemented rules in Section 4.3.

Table 1. Matched rules and functional helpers and the implemented rules

Matched Rule (MR)/ Functional Helper (FH)	Corresponding Rules: Section 4.3
MR1: createComponent	4
MR2: initSysTemplate	1
FH1: initEcuInst	1
FH2: createSwc2EcuMappings FH3: initSingleSwc2EcuMapping	2-3
FH4: addComponents	5
FH5: getAllPPortsInEcu FH6: createPPort	6
FH7: getAllRPortsInEcu FH8: createRPort	7
FH9: getAllSWCinEcu	5

The matched rule `createComponent` maps *Module* elements to *ComponentPrototype* elements. The matched rule `initSysTemp` maps a *PhysicalNode* element to a *System* element, a *SystemMapping* element, a *SoftwareComposition* element and a *CompositionType* element by calling the 9 functional helpers to implement rules 1-3 and 5-7. The helper `initECUInst` initializes an *EcuInstance* element. The helper `initSingleSwc2EcuMapping` initializes a *SwcToEcuMapping* instance. The helper `createSwc2EcuMappings` creates a list of *Swc2EcuMapping* elements corresponding to all the *Partition* elements in the input model. The helper `getAllSwcInEcu` creates the containment relation between the *CompositionType* elements and the *ComponentPrototype* elements. The helper `addComponents` creates the relation between the *SwcToEcuMapping* elements and their corresponding *ComponentPrototype* elements. The helper `getAllPPortsInEcu` creates a *PPortPrototype* element using the helper `createPPort` for *Schedulers* with at least one provided *Service*. Similar helpers generate *RPortPrototype* elements.

The ATL predefined function `resolveTemp` connects the *ComponentPrototype* elements created by the `createComponent` matched rule to the *CompositionType* elements created by the `initSysTemp` matched rule.

Implementing the transformation revealed some insights on using MDWorkbench and ATL in industrial applications. Both the GM and the AUTOSAR metamodels are complex in structure. To process models conforming to complex metamodels, ATL provides flexibility of using declarative and imperative constructs to implement complex transformations. Moreover, since the output models have many relationships among model elements, decisions on where an element should be created in the transformation such that it will be accessible for the downstream transformation are required. One such example is the relation between the *SoftwareComposition* element and the *ComponentPrototype* element. The transformation can be either specified as one rule or modularized as many rules. Although modularization requires that the order of the rules be consistent with their dependencies, ATL mitigates this drawback through the `resolveTemp` function which allows a rule to reference the elements that are yet to be generated by other rules regardless of their specification order. However, the `resolveTemp` function makes the transformation less readable and difficult to debug, so the function should be used only when necessary.

For validation, sample GM models were created in the MDWorkbench Model Editor, including the model in Fig. 4(a), and were used for evaluation. The output models were verified as described in Section 4.3. The transformation was found to produce the expected output models. Sample GM models were used for validation instead of actual GM models since many of the actual GM models did not conform to the GM metamodel, which represents a major challenge for adopting MDD in industrial environments.

5 Discussion

Based on our case study, we present open issues requiring further investigation for successful adoption of model transformations in the automotive industry. Recommendations for MDD tool and language development are also discussed.

5.1 Interoperability of MDD Tools

One of the major challenges encountered in our study was the lack of interoperability between commercial tools for developing transformations. Specifying the model transformation using ATL was not straightforward due to the formats of the manipulated metamodels. ATL can only manipulate MOF [21] or Ecore [23] metamodels, which the GM metamodel in Rhapsody native format is not compatible with. This required the conversion of the GM metamodel to a compatible format.

MDWorkbench has a Rhapsody connector that allows importing the GM metamodel into MDWorkbench and converting it to Ecore format. To avoid the issue of dual license from different vendors with different licensing policies with such an approach, we addressed the problem using XMI. An Ecore metamodel is essentially an XMI file and Rhapsody has an XMI toolkit to export Rhapsody metamodels to XMI files. Exporting the GM metamodel using the XMI toolkit generated an XMI file that does not conform to the Ecore meta-metamodel. To create an Ecore version, we import the

XMI into RulesComposer as a metamodel, which creates an Ecore metamodel and an Eclipse plugin project. Exporting the project from RulesComposer to MDWorkbench as a plugin generates a registered GM Ecore metamodel.

Blanc et al. [5] decomposed the interoperability problem into two concerns: the compatibility of the exchanged models, and the definition of an exchange mechanism. Their study proposed an architecture to address these two concerns. Implementing transformations between tools manipulating models that conform to different metamodels was proposed in [6], [4]. Kolovos et al. [15] proposed a framework that supports composing model management tasks with software development tasks in coherent workflows. Although these solutions have been integrated into IDEs, they are not fully automated in applications. MDD tools and transformation languages deserve further research to support easy integration and interoperability with each other.

5.2 Optimization in Model Transformations

Our transformation mapped GM models representing a deployment of the software components on physical nodes to their equivalent AUTOSAR models. The transformation exercised one mapping between the two metamodels and generated an AUTOSAR model reflecting the deployment configuration. From the deployment perspective, there are other design options that may yield a more desirable deployment in the output AUTOSAR model with respect to some utility function.

Solutions exist to support optimization during the transformation. Schätz et al. [22] proposed a formalized approach to explore the design space using rule-based transformations. Intermediate models were represented using a relational formalization and rules were represented using predicates. Drago et al. [9] proposed the QVT-Rational framework to explore design options which optimize quality metrics. First, a domain expert specifies the metamodels to be manipulated, the quality metrics of interest, the quality-prediction tool chain and the method for design feedback generation. Then, a designer specifies desirable values for quality metrics and asks QVT-Rational for design solutions. Tools that target industry use need to support scalable design-space exploration to aid developers in exploring design options of the generated model.

5.3 Dealing with Semantic Differences between Metamodels

Identifying which target metamodel elements best represent a given source metamodel element can be a difficult task. Reasons include: (1) the precise semantics of a metamodel may not have been documented sufficiently and only be fully known to metamodel developers themselves; consultation of these developers may be time consuming or even impossible. (2) The lack of support in metamodel evolution often means that the metamodels contain redundancies or inconsistencies. (3) The mapping of source to target elements is dependent on the transformation's purpose, because it determines to what extent aspects of model semantics can be removed (e.g., for abstraction), preserved (e.g., for refactorings) or refined (e.g., for code generation).

To facilitate transformation development, techniques to (1)enforce documenting metamodel semantics, (2) suggest mappings between metamodels using similarity matching or "learning" [17], [20], and (3) validate transformations are of high interest.

6 Conclusions and Future Work

In this study, we present a solution to migrating legacy VCS design models using model transformations in the automotive industry. The study has two major goals: (1) exploring the practicality of using model transformations in an industrial context to map between industrial metamodels and (2) benefitting GM by supporting automated convergence to AUTOSAR. The implemented transformation converts domain-specific GM models to their equivalent AUTOSAR models. We discussed the transformation context in the development process. Based on our experiences, we discuss which tool and language are appropriate for implementing the transformation, the challenges encountered and open issues that need further investigation.

Research studies on adopting MDD in industry have been published [19], [23], but a few investigated adopting transformations in industry. Daghsen et al. [8] transformed AUTOSAR timing models to classical scheduling models to perform timing analysis. Giese et al. [12] used triple graph grammars to synchronize between SysML system engineering models and AUTOSAR software engineering models. Our study differs from other studies in that the two manipulated metamodels are complex, industrial metamodels, which allows us to draw realistic conclusions regarding the practicality of adopting transformations in industry. Our study considers the entire transformation development process, from tool and language selection to transformation creation and validation. Future work includes extending the transformation to the full GM metamodel and using white-box or black-box testing [11], [16] for validation.

Acknowledgements. This work is supported in part by NSERC, as part of the NECSIS Automotive Partnership with General Motors, IBM Canada and Malina Software Corp.

References

[1] Atlas Transformation Language – ATL, http://eclipse.org/atl/
[2] AUTOSAR Consortium. AUTOSAR, http://AUTOSAR.org/
[3] AUTOSAR Consortium. AUTOSAR System Template,
   http://AUTOSAR.org/index.php?p=3&up=1&uup=3&uuup=3&uuuup=0&uuuuup=0/AUTOSAR_TPS_SystemTemplate.pdf
[4] Bezivin, J., Brunelière, H., Jouault, F., Kurtev, I.: Model engineering support for tool interoperability. In: Workshop in Software Model Engineering (WiSME), Montego Bay, Jamaica (2005)
[5] Blanc, X., Gervais, M.-P., Sriplakich, P.: Model Bus: Towards the Interoperability of Modelling Tools. In: Aßmann, U., Aksit, M., Rensink, A. (eds.) MDAFA 2003. LNCS, vol. 3599, pp. 17–32. Springer, Heidelberg (2005)
[6] Brunelière, H., Cabot, J., Clasen, C., Jouault, F., Bézivin, J.: Towards Model Driven Tool Interoperability: Bridging Eclipse and Microsoft Modeling Tools. In: Kühne, T., Selic, B., Gervais, M.-P., Terrier, F. (eds.) ECMFA 2010. LNCS, vol. 6138, pp. 32–47. Springer, Heidelberg (2010)

[7] Cottenier, T., Berg, A., Elrad, T.: The Motorola WEAVR:Model weaving in a large industrial context. In: Aspect-Oriented Software Development (AOSD), Vancouver, Canada (2007)
[8] Daghsen, A., Chaaban, K., Saudrais, S., Leserf, P.: Applying holistic distributed scheduling to AUTOSAR Mmethodology. In: Embedded Real-Time Software & Systems (ERTSS), Toulouse, France (2010)
[9] Drago, M.L., Ghezzi, C., Mirandola, R.: Towards Quality Driven Exploration of Model Transformation Spaces. In: Whittle, J., Clark, T., Kühne, T. (eds.) MODELS 2011. LNCS, vol. 6981, pp. 2–16. Springer, Heidelberg (2011)
[10] Eclipse Modelling Framework (EMF), http://wiki.eclipse.org/EMF
[11] Fleurey, F., Baudry, B., Muller, P.-A., Le Traon, Y.: Qualifying input test data for model transformations. Software System Modelling (SoSyM) 8(2), 185–203 (2007)
[12] Giese, H., Hildebrandt, S., Neumann, S.: Model Synchronization at Work: Keeping SysML and AUTOSAR Models Consistent. In: Engels, G., Lewerentz, C., Schäfer, W., Schürr, A., Westfechtel, B. (eds.) Nagl Festschrift. LNCS, vol. 5765, pp. 555–579. Springer, Heidelberg (2010)
[13] IBM Corporation. IBM Rational Asset Manager (RAM), http://www01.ibm.com/software/rational/products/ram/
[14] IBM Corporation. IBM Rational Rhapsody, http://www.ibm.com/developerworks/downloads/r/rhapsodydeveloper/index.html
[15] Kolovos, D., Paige, R., Polack, F.: A framework for composing modular and interoperable model management tasks. In: Model Driven Tool & Process Integration (MDTPI), Berlin, Germany (2008)
[16] Küster, J., Abd-El-Razik, M.: Validation of model transformations - First experiences using a white box approach. In: Model Development, Validation & Verification (MoDeVa), Genova, Italy, pp. 62–77 (2006)
[17] Mandelin, D., Kimelman, D., Yellin, D.: A Bayesian approach to diagram matching with application to architectural models. In: Intl. Conf. on Software Engineering (ICSE), Shanghai, China, pp. 222–231 (2006)
[18] Sodius. MDWorkbench, http://www.mdworkbench.com/
[19] Mohagheghi, P., Dehlen, V.: Where Is the Proof? - A Review of Experiences from Applying MDE in Industry. In: Schieferdecker, I., Hartman, A. (eds.) ECMDA-FA 2008. LNCS, vol. 5095, pp. 432–443. Springer, Heidelberg (2008)
[20] Nejati, S., Sabetzadeh, M., Chechik, M., Easterbrook, S., Zave, P.: Matching and merging of Statechart specifications. In: Intl. Conf. on Software Engineering (ICSE), Minneapolis, USA, pp. 54–64 (2007)
[21] Object Management Group (OMG): Meta Object Facility (MOF) Specification — Version 1.4 (April 2002)
[22] Schätz, B., Hölzl, F., Lundkvist, T.: Design-space exploration through constraint-based Mmodel transformation. In: Engineering of Computer Based Systems (ECBS), Oxford, UK, pp. 173–182 (2010)
[23] Steinberg, D., Budinsky, F., Paternostro, M., Merks, E.: Chapter 5 Ecore Modeling Concepts. In: Eclipse Modeling Framework, 2nd edn. Addison-Wesley Professional (2009)
[24] Teppola, S., Parviainen, P., Takalo, J.: Challenges in the deployment of model driven development. In: Intl. Conf. on Software Engineering Advances (ICSEA), Porto, Portugal, pp. 15–20 (2009)

Derived Features for EMF
by Integrating Advanced Model Queries*

István Ráth, Ábel Hegedüs, and Dániel Varró

Budapest University of Technology and Economics,
Department of Measurement and Information Systems,
1117 Budapest, Magyar tudósok krt. 2
{rath,hegedusa,varro}@mit.bme.hu

Abstract. When designing complex domain-specific languages, metamodels are frequently enriched with *derived features* that correspond to attribute values or references (edges) representing computed information in the model. In the popular Eclipse Modeling Framework, these are typically implemented as imperative Java code.

In the paper, we propose to integrate the EMF-INCQUERY model query framework to the Ecore metamodeling infrastructure in order to facilitate the efficient and automated (re-)computation of derived attributes and references over EMF models. Such an integration allows to define derived features using an expressive graph-based model query language [1], and offers high performance and scalability thanks to the incremental evaluation technique of EMF-INCQUERY [2]. In addition, our approach offers to automate two typical associated challenges of EMF tools: (1) values of derived features are immediately recalculated upon model changes and (2) notifications are sent automatically to other EMF model elements to report changes in derived features.

1 Introduction

The design of complex domain-specific languages (e.g. in the automotive or avionics domains) frequently necessitate the use of advanced metamodeling techniques. Metamodels are complemented with *well-formedness constraints*, which enable the validation of the consistency of instance models with respect to such constraints, thus allowing to spot design flaws early in the development process. *Derived features*, which correspond to attribute values or references (edges) that represent computed information in the model, also proved to be useful in complex metamodeling scenarios. For instance, they frequently serve as auxiliary (helper) functions when implementing model simulators, and they also allow to compact the storage of the model.

In the popular Eclipse Modeling Framework (EMF), these derived features are most often implemented as user-defined algoritms computed by imperative

---
* This work was partially supported by the CERTIMOT (ERC_HU-09-01-2010-0003) project, the grant TÁMOP (4.2.2.B-10/1–2010-0009) and the János Bolyai Scholarship.

Java code. Unfortunately, (1) most existing techniques re-calculate values of derived features in EMF models on-demand (i.e. when corresponding getters are called), which hinders integration into user interfaces where changes in the values of derived features should immediately be reflected. Furthermore, (2) it is challenging to properly implement notification propagation between (a chain of) derived features upon value changes, which is necessary when components or model elements are required to depend upon a derived feature. Finally, (3) as the calculation of derived features is always started from scratch (not taking previous computations and changes into account), it is also challenging to implement complex queries in Java in a way that does not severely impact the overall performance.

The advanced model query framework EMF-INCQUERY has proved to be efficient in the incremental re-validation of well-formedness constraints over large models [2] scaling up to millions of elements[1]. Its expressive, declarative graph-based query language offers high level of reuse in queries [1]. In the paper, we propose to seamlessly integrate the EMF-INCQUERY framework to the Ecore metamodeling infrastructure, in order to facilitate the efficient and automated computation of derived attributes and references over EMF models.

Our proposed approach, which is fully implemented and documented[2], offers to automate the entire workflow of developing derived features in EMF. In the approach, (1) derived features are defined using an expressive graph-based model query language and are calculated by an algorithm that (2) listens to all *incoming notifications* that impact on the computation, (2) issues *outgoing notifications* when the value of the derived feature changes, (3) keeps an *up-to-date cache* that is refreshed based on incoming notifications and used for computing outgoing notification. Finally, (4) since outgoing notifications may cause incoming notifications, the algorithm also *stabilizes such notification loops*.

In the rest of the paper, Section 2 provides a brief overview on derived features in EMF models. Then, we propose to use a graph based model query language to define derived features for EMF in Section 3. Section 4 provides a detailed architecture and core algorithms to synthesize notifications for derived features based upon incremental query evaluation. Additional issues for seamless integration to the EMF infrastructure are discussed in Section 5. Finally, Section 6 overviews related work and Section 7 concludes our paper.

2 Derived Features in EMF

Derived features in EMF models represent information that can be calculated from other model elements and typically represent an aggregate view of the model. Essentially, we distinguish between *derived attributes* and *derived references* (representing "virtual" connections between model elements). In our example, both are represented graphically by the **derived** stereotype in Figure 1.

---

[1] The current paper does not include performance specific contributions to the EMF-INCQUERY framework, we kindly refer the reader to http://viatra.inf.mit.bme.hu/performance for additional details.

[2] http://viatra.inf.mit.bme.hu/incquery/examples/derivedfeatures

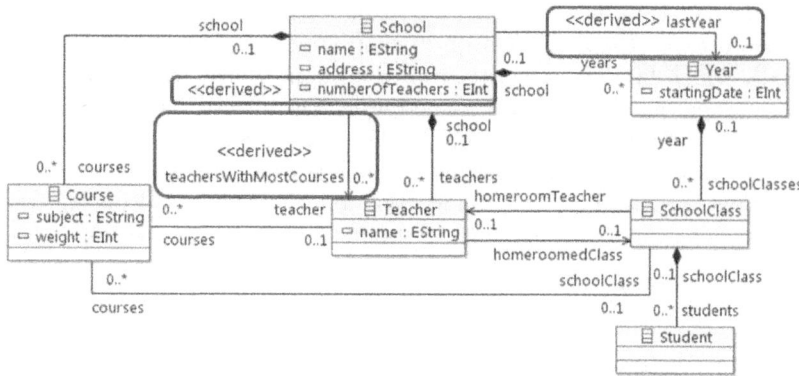

Fig. 1. The metamodel of the Schools domain

In the current paper, we illustrate our approach on a simple demonstration domain of Schools (encoded in EMF's Ecore language as illustrated in Figure 1) that manage Courses involving Teachers, and enroll their students assigned to Years and SchoolClasses. The metamodel contains simple EAttributes (like e.g. name of a Teacher or the startingDate of the school Year) and regular EReferences such as the school of a Teacher. More importantly for the sake of this paper, it also contains three *derived features*:

- numberOfTeachers is a derived attribute of School representing a counter for the total number of Teachers belonging to the School as represented by the corresponding school EReference;
- lastYear is a derived reference from School to Year, and points to the last academic Year stored in the model, which can be calculated from the startingDate of all Years;
- teachersWithMostCourses represent the busiest teachers of the School, i.e. those who teach the most courses.

Derived features in EMF are not maintained explicitly in instance models, but calculated on-demand by hand-written code. These calculations are frequently supported by ad-hoc Java implementations integrated directly into the EMF model representation, which significantly reduces the portability and compatibility of the metamodel.

Unfortunately, developers may encounter additional key challenges when aiming to use derived features in EMF models:

- **Performance.** Depending on the complexity of the semantics of derived features, their evaluation may impose a *severe performance impact* (since complex calculations and extensive model traversal may be necessary for execution). Note that this scalability issue is especially important when derived feature values need to be re-evaluated many times and will affect all other software layers using the model code, including the user interface, model transformations, well-formedness validators etc.

– **Notifications.** Due to the *difficulty of propagating notifications* for derived features, derived features are typically re-evaluated on demand. This may also manifest as model changes not (properly) triggering user interface updates. Note that EMF defines the notifications for derived features as well, however, it is the programmer's responsibility to create notifications. Since the values of derived features are usually not cached, proper notifications including the old values (e.g. setting a single value or removing from a list) are hard to implement. Furthermore, notifications of one derived feature may cause new notifications, leading to notification loops, the programmer must ensure that these are stabilized in order to avoid infinite loops.

Our proposal, namely, the integration of an advanced model query framework EMF-INCQUERY provides a solution for all of these challenges using a high-level graph-based query language for defining derived value calculations. As the performance characteristics of the EMF-INCQUERY engine have been shown to be agnostic of query complexity and model size [2], derived features of complex semantics and inter-dependencies can be used without severe evaluation performance degradation. Additionally the update propagation mechanism of EMF-INCQUERY (using *delta monitors* [3]) will be connected to the EMF Notification layer so that the application software components are automatically kept up-to-date about the value changes of derived features.

3 Definition of Derived Features as Model Queries

We now propose to use the graph pattern based model query language of EMF-INCQUERY as the specification language for derived features of EMF models. Therefore a brief introduction to this query language is provided first, followed by a detailed description on how this general purpose query language is adapted to specify derived features.

3.1 Model Queries by Graph Patterns: An Overview

Graph patterns [4] are an expressive formalism used for various purposes in model-driven development, such as defining declarative model transformation rules, capturing general-purpose model queries including model validation constraints, or defining the behavioral semantics of dynamic domain-specific languages. A graph pattern (GP) represents conditions (or constraints) that have to be fulfilled by a part of the instance model. A basic graph pattern consists of *structural constraints* prescribing the existence of nodes and edges of a given type, as well as *expressions* to define *attribute constraints*. A *negative application condition* (NAC) defines cases when the original pattern is *not* valid (even if all other constraints are met), in the form of a negative sub-pattern. A match of a graph pattern is a group of model elements that have the exact same configuration as the pattern, satisfying all the constraints (except for NACs, which must not be satisfied). The complete query language of the EMF-INCQUERY framework is described in [1], while several examples will be given below.

3.2 Derived Features as Model Queries

Sample derived features First, we demonstrate on an example how the graph pattern teachersWithMostCourses(S,T) (Figure 2) can be used to express the calculation of the derived EReference teachersWithMostCourses (connecting *School* and *Teacher* in Figure 1), that is, to identify those teachers who have the maximum number of *Course* instances assigned (through the *Teachers.courses* reference).

```
1  pattern teacherWithMostCourses(S, T)=
2  {
3    School.teachers(S,T);
4    neg pattern moreCourses(S,T) = {
5      Teacher.courses(T,C) # N;
6      School.teachers(S,T2);
7      Teacher.courses(T2,C2) # M;
8      check(M > N);
9    }
10 }
```

Fig. 2. Model query to define teachersWithMostCourses in graphical and textual syntax

This model query formulated as a graph pattern has two parameters: S and T, denoting the source and the target end of the derived EReference. The query defines the designated set of teachers by combining a NAC and cardinality constraints. It expresses that a teacher T belongs to this set if and only if there is no other teacher $T2$ whose number of courses M (calculated by counting the number of elements connected along the *courses* reference) would be larger than the number of courses N (counted as before) of teacher T. The right side of Figure 2 shows the corresponding textual syntax.

Model queries for derived features numberOfTeachers and lastYear are defined similarly in Figure 3. The definition of the latter contains some additional interesting language elements.

- The modifier **shareable** prescribes that different (but type consistent) pattern variables are allowed to be bound to the same model elements (e.g. $D1$ and $D2$ can be bound to the same date element).
- Y =/= Y2 checks that the two model elements bound to variables Y and $Y2$ are different.
- Using the **find** keyword, graph patterns are allowed to reuse other graph patterns. Therefore, if a derived feature is defined as a model query by a corresponding graph pattern, this derived feature can be reused in other queries, and thus, in other derived features. In fact, we will discuss in Section 5 that even legacy derived features (defined by Java code) can participate in such usage with appropriate notification mechanisms.

Derived features can be defined as model queries using the graph pattern based language of EMF-INCQUERY if the following three well-formedness rules are met by corresponding query definitions:

```
1  pattern numberOfTeachers(S,N)=
2  {
3    School.teachers(S,T) # N;
4  }
```

```
1   pattern lastYear(S,Y)= {
2     find years(S,Y);
3     neg shareable pattern laterYear(S,Y)= {
4       find years(S,Y);
5       find startingDateOfYear(Y,D1);
6       find years(S,Y2);
7       find startingDateOfYear(Y2,D2);
8       check(D1 < D2);
9       Y =/= Y2;
10  } }
```

Fig. 3. Model queries for numberOfTeachers and lastYear

1. *Each graph pattern should have exactly two parameters.* In case of derived attributes, the first parameter denotes the corresponding EClass of the attribute, while the second parameter denotes the value of the parameter itself (see numberOfTeachers). In case of derived references, the first parameter denotes the source (i.e. the container EClass) while the second parameter denotes the target of the EReference.
2. *First parameter: always input.* General model queries allow the same pattern to be used with either input or output parameters (i.e. parameter bindings can be carried out at execution time), in case of derived features, the first parameter (referring to the container) should always be an input parameter, which is a bound to a type-compliant contextual EMF object (e.g. S is bound in all three graph patterns above). This restriction is conceptually equivalent to the context element of an OCL constraint.
3. *Restrictions on result set.* In case of a derived features with explicit lower and upper bounds (e.g. 1..* or 0..1), the result set of the model query should comply with these restrictions. While upper bounds can be enforced by omitting results, the violation of lower bound is logged only as warnings.

In the actual query language, rules 1 and 2 are can be satisfied either by using exactly two query parameters, or by using *pattern annotations* for multi-parameter queries that explicitly specify which of the parameters is the context and which one will correspond to the target (or value). Furthermore, the adherence to all three rules are checked at editing time by a built-in query language validator in the EMF-INCQUERY tooling. In summary, the modular nature of the EMF-INCQUERY language aims to allow the language engineer to construct a library of cross-referencing queries without copy-paste reuse.

4 From Incremental Query Evaluation to Notifications for Derived Features

In this section, we outline how the incremental query features of the EMF-INCQUERY framework are integrated to notification-based applications in transparent way, by mapping changes of the results sets to notification objects for derived features. We present an architectural overview and an algorithm to carry out this mapping.

4.1 Incremental Evaluation of Queries

The key to efficient evaluation and change notification for derived features is the incremental graph pattern matching infrastructure of the EMF-INCQUERY framework (introduced in [3]). The internal architecture is shown in Figure 4.

The input for the incremental graph pattern matching process is the EMF instance model and its notification API. Callback functions can be registered through this API for instance model elements that receive notification objects (e.g. ADD, REMOVE, SET etc.) when an elementary manipulation operation is carried out.

Based on a query specification, EMF-INCQUERY constructs a Rete rule evaluation network [3] that processes the contents of the instance model to produce the query result at its output node. Query results are then post-processed by *auto-generated query components* to provide a type-safe access layer for easy integration into applications. This Rete network remains in operation as long as the query is needed: it continues to receive elementary change notifications

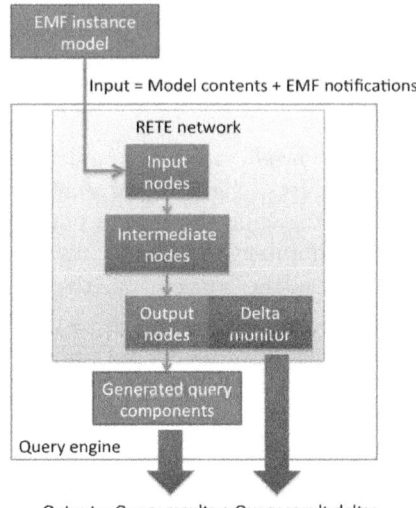

Fig. 4. The EMF-INCQUERY architecture

and propagates them to produce *query result deltas* through its *delta monitor* facility, which are used to incrementally update the query result. These deltas can also be processed externally, which is a key feature for the integration of derived features (Section 4.2).

By this approach, the query results (i.e. the match sets of graph patterns) are continuously maintained as an in-memory cache, and can be retrieved directly. Even though this imposes a slight performance overhead on model manipulation, and a memory cost proportional to the cache size (approx. the size of match sets), EMF-INCQUERY can evaluate very complex queries over large instance models very efficiently. These special performance characteristics [2] address the scalability challenge (Section 2) as long as enough memory is available, as they allow EMF-INCQUERY-based derived features to be evaluated incrementally, even for complex queries over large instance models.

4.2 Integration Architecture

To support derived features, the outputs of the EMF-INCQUERY engine are to be integrated into the EMF model access layer at two points: (1) *query results* are provided in the getter functions of derived features, and (2) *query result deltas* are processed to generate EMF Notification objects that are passed through the standard EMF API so that application code can process them transparently. The overall architecture of our approach is shown in Figure 5.

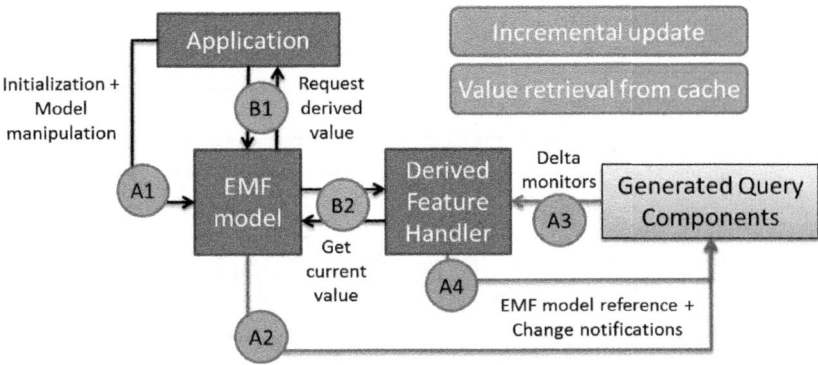

Fig. 5. Overview of the integration architecture

The application accesses both the model and the query results through the standard EMF model access layer – hence, no modification of application source code is necessary. In the background, as a novel component type, *derived feature handlers* are attached to the EMF model plugin that integrate the generated query components (pattern matchers). This approach follows the official EMF guidelines of implementing derived features and is identical to how ad-hoc Java code, or OCL expression evaluators are integrated.

When an EMF application intends to read a derived feature (B1), the current value is provided by the corresponding derived feature handler (B2) by simply retrieving the value from the cache of the related query. When the application modifies the EMF model (A1), this change is propagated to the generated query components of EMF-INCQUERY along notifications (A2), which may update the delta monitors of the derived features (A3). Changes of derived features may in turn trigger further changes in the results sets of other derived features (A4).

Illustrative example. Figure 6 illustrates a detailed elaboration EMF-INCQUERY feature handlers, which process elementary model manipulation notifications to update, and generate notifications for derived features. The figure corresponds to a case where the user created a new Teacher for a School through the Editor which is essentially a School.getTeachers().add(teacher) method call on the Model. During the add method, the School EObject sends an ADD notification to the Notification Manager, which will notify the EMF-INCQUERY Query Engine about the model modification. The Query Engine updates the match sets of each query and registers the match events in the Deltamonitor. Once it's finished with updating the Rete network, it invokes the callback method of each IncqueryFeatureHandler. Each handler has a Deltamonitor from which it retrieves the found and lost match events since the last callback to processes them. During the processing, the handler may send notifications of its own that are propagated to listeners. Anytime the derived feature value is retrieved from the model (e.g. getNumberOfTeachers), the handler is accessed for the current value of the feature, which is returned directly.

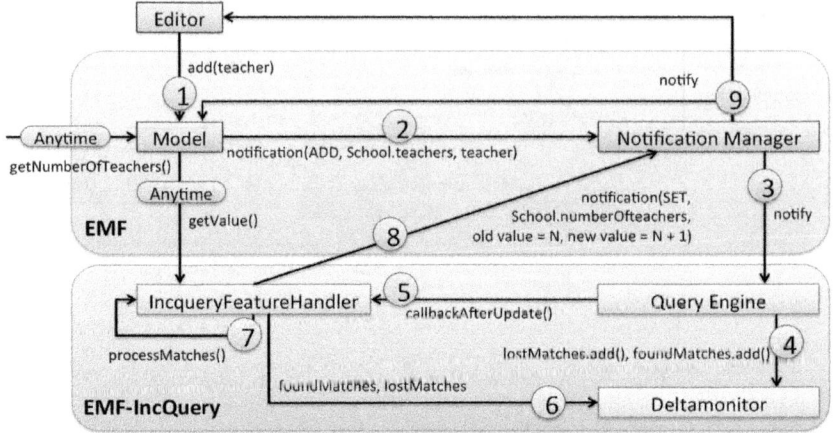

Fig. 6. Elaboration of the execution

4.3 From Changes of Match Sets to Notifications

We now explain the notification processing and propagation procedure in algorithmic detail. For the sake of simplicity, we introduce an auxiliary discriminator variable $Kind$ whose value represents three distinct cases:

- SINGLE and MANY correspond to derived references of target multiplicity 1 and *, respectively (lastYear and teachersWithMostCourses in Figure 3);
- COUNTER corresponds to the simplified case where a value of the derived attribute is defined as the match set size of a query (see numberOfTeachers in Figure 3).
- More complex derived feature kinds with an arbitrary, deterministic iteration algorithm can also be handled by the approach.

The main part of our derived feature handler algorithm is an event loop that is called by the EMF-INCQUERY query engine each time the underlying Rete network is updated as a result of some model manipulation (see Algorithm 1).

The algorithm is initialized with the following input variables (line 1): (1) the EObject *Source* whose derived feature is handled; (2) the derived *Feature*; (3) the *DeltaMonitor* for the query matcher; and (4) the previously mentioned discriminator value $Kind$. Each handler stores an internal value for the feature, initialized in line 2 depending on $Kind$. Finally, the handler uses two global variables: pU for storing partial events and the set N of unsent notifications.

Algorithm 1. Main event loop

```
 1: let S ← Source, F ← Feature, DM ← DeltaMonitor, k ← Kind    ▷ Input variables
 2: let (k = SINGLE)?iV ← null : (k = COUNTER)?iV ← 0 : iV ← ∅   ▷ Internal value init
 3: let pU ← null, N ← ∅                                         ▷ Global variables
 4: function EVENTLOOP
 5:     let pU ← null
 6:     let found ← PROCESSFOUNDMATCHES(DM.matchFoundEvents)      ▷ Processing found events
 7:     let DM.matchFoundEvents ← DM.matchFoundEvents \ found     ▷ Removing events
 8:     let lost ← PROCESSLOSTMATCHES(DM.matchLostEvents)         ▷ Processing lost events
 9:     let DM.matchLostevents ← DM.matchLostevents \ lost        ▷ Removing events
10:     if partialUpdate ≠ null then    ▷ Stored value not yet used, handle partial match event
11:         let N ← N ∩ notification(SET, null, pU)
12:         let iV ← pU                                           ▷ Updating value
13:     end if
14:     while N ≠ ∅ do                                            ▷ Notification sending loop
15:         let n ← N[0]
16:         let N ← N \ n
17:         S.eNotify(n)                                          ▷ Sending notification through source
18:     end while
19: end function
```

Algorithm 2. Processing match-found events

```
 1: function PROCESFOUNDMATCHES(events)
 2:     let P ← ∅
 3:     for all e ∈ events do
 4:         if e.source = S then
 5:             let target ← e.target                             ▷ Extracting feature target from event
 6:             if k = COUNTER then
 7:                 let N ← N ∩ notification(SET, iV, iV + 1)
 8:                 let iV ← iV + 1                               ▷ Updating value of repeating algorithm
 9:             else if k = SINGLE then
10:                 let pU ← target                               ▷ Storing value for later processing
11:             else if k = MANY then
12:                 let N ← N ∩ notification(ADD, null, target)
13:                 let iV ← iV ∩ target                          ▷ Updating value
14:             end if
15:         end if
16:         let P ← P ∩ e
17:     end for
18:     return P
19: end function
```

The event loop starts from line 4, it first resets the partial event store, then processes matches found since the last execution of the loop (line 6). These events are supplied by the delta monitor of the query and removed after processing is finished. Similarly, the matches lost since the last execution are also processed (line 8) and removed after. When a derived feature with SINGLE kind is used and only a match-found event occurs without a match-lost event, an additional processing step is required to handle the partial event (line 11). This occurs when the query did not lose any matches since the last event loop, but a new match is found. This translates to a notification representing the setting of the feature value from $null$ to pU (line 12). Finally, if there are any unsent notifications (line 14), the first notification n in the list N is sent through the $Source$ EObject. By separating the notification sending from the calculation of the derived feature value, the notification loop is stabilized, since new notifications caused by n are simply added to the list N, which will be depleted after all, if causal circularity between the definitions of derived features is avoided.

Algorithm 3. Processing match-lost events

```
 1: function PROCESSLOSTMATCHES(events)
 2:     let P ← ∅
 3:     for all e ∈ events do
 4:         if e.source = S then
 5:             let target ← e.target              ▷ Extracting feature target from event
 6:             if k = COUNTER then
 7:                 let N ← N ∩ notification(SET, iV, iV − 1)
 8:                 let iV ← iV − 1               ▷ Updating value of repeating algorithm
 9:             else if k = SINGLE then
10:                 let N ← N ∩ notification(SET, target, pU)   ▷ Using stored value
11:                 let iV ← target                             ▷ Updating value
12:                 let pU ← null                               ▷ Resetting stored value
13:             else if k = MANY then
14:                 let N ← N ∩ notification(REMOVE, target, null)
15:                 let iV ← iV \ target                        ▷ Updating value
16:             end if
17:         end if
18:         let P ← P ∩ e
19:     end for
20:     return P
21: end function
```

New matches. The handling of match-found events is detailed in Algorithm 2. The PROCESSFOUNDMATCHES function iterates through the match-found events (line 3), and extracts the target object from the event (line 5), if the source EObject of the event equals *Source*. Depending on the *Kind* of the feature, a notification is created and the internal value is updated (line 7 for COUNTER and line 12 for MANY). For SINGLE kind features, the target object is stored for later usage (line 10). Finally, the list of processed events is returned.

Lost matches. The handling of match-lost events is similar to the processing of match-found events, see Algorithm 3. The PROCESSLOSTMATCHES function iterates through the match-lost events (line 3), and extracts the target object from the event (line 5), if the source EObject of the event equals *Source*. Depending on the *Kind* of the feature, a notification is created and the internal value is updated (line 7 for COUNTER and line 14 for MANY). For SINGLE kind features, the stored value of *pU* is used for creating the notification (line 10). Finally, the list of processed events is returned at the end of the function.

Summary. In summary, the combined pattern matching and notification processing process ensures that EMF-INCQUERY-based derived features behave exactly as normal features of EMF instance models. This addresses the final, integration-related challenge of Section 2), by ensuring that user interfaces, model validators etc. can safely depend on such derived features, without on-demand querying.

5 Integration Issues with EMF Tooling

5.1 Integration with Ecore

In the prototype implementation of our proposal, we integrated our approach to the EMF Tooling by a code generator that supports the automatic generation of integration code for our components (EMF-INCQUERY *derived feature handlers*). The input of the code generator is a simple generator model (referencing the EMF genmodel for the domain) that crosslinks derived features with EMF-INCQUERY query specifications (which are stored as EMF models thanks to the Xtext2-based tooling).

```
teachersWithMostCoursesHandler = IncqueryFeatureHelper.createHandler(
        this,
        SchoolIncqDerivedPackage.Literals.SCHOOL__TEACHERS_WITH_MOST_COURSES,
        TeacherWithMostCoursesMatcher.FACTORY,
        "School",
        "Teacher",
        FeatureKind.MANY_REFERENCE);
* @generated NOT
*/
public EList<Teacher> getTeachersWithMostCourses() {
    if(teachersWithMostCoursesHandler != null) {
        Collection<Object> temp = teachersWithMostCoursesHandler.getManyReferenceValue();
        return new UnmodifiableEList<Teacher>(this,
                SchoolIncqDerivedPackage.Literals.SCHOOL__TEACHERS_WITH_MOST_COURSES,
                temp.size(), temp.toArray());
    } else {
        return new UnmodifiableEList<Teacher>(this,
                SchoolIncqDerivedPackage.Literals.SCHOOL__TEACHERS_WITH_MOST_COURSES,
                0, null);
    }
}
```

Fig. 7. Sample generated code for derived feature handler instantiation and getter

The generated integration code (Figure 7) consists of (a) the instantiation of derived feature handlers (in the constructor of EObjects), which ensures that their lifecycle is tied to the hosts, to enable their garbage collection together with the instance model itself; (b) getter implementations that delegate calls to the appropriate function of the feature handler object, and wrap the result in unmodifiable ELists to ensure that any attempt to write to derived features will result in a runtime exception.

5.2 Integration with Legacy Java Code for Derived Features

In practice, a complete refactoring of an EMF-based tool to exclusively use EMF-INCQUERY-based derived features might not be realistic. Hence, we implemented an additional *derived feature adapter* (Figure 8) as a lightweight add-on component for EMF model plugins, which can be used to augment existing derived feature implementations (regardless of whether Java or OCL is used).

The basic concept motivated by a suggestion in the Eclipse FAQ[3] is analogous to the previous discussion. The language engineer can add a few lines of Java code

---
[3] http://wiki.eclipse.org/EMF/Recipes#Recipe:_Derived_Attribute_Notifier

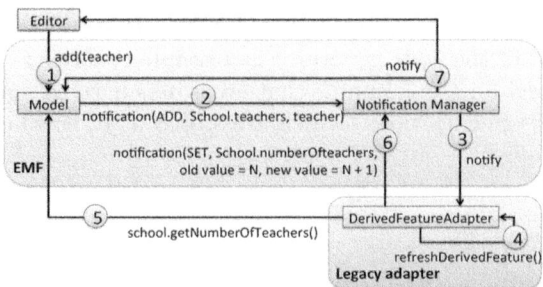

Fig. 8. Derived feature handlers

to the generated EMF model plugin: these derived feature adapters attach listeners (through the EMF Notification API) to the (explicitly specified) features a derived feature depends on, and receive notifications when model changes are registered (steps 1-2-3 in Figure 8). These notification objects are then processed and converted into new notification objects for the derived feature, propagating through the manager to application code (steps 4-5-6-7 in Figure 8).

This approach has additional key advantages: (1) notification support can be added – with a small implementation effort – to "legacy" derived features, without having to re-write them in EMF-INCQUERY; (2) queries specified in EMF-INCQUERY (whether for derived features, or on-the-fly validation purposes, or within model transformations) can reference derived features seamlessly.

6 Related Work

Model queries over EMF. There are several technologies for providing declarative model queries over EMF, e.g. EMF Model Query 2 [5] and EMF Search [6]. Other graph pattern based techniques like [7,8] have been successfully applied in an EMF context. But none of these support incremental evaluation, therefore they cannot be used for integrating derived features in the way we proposed.

OCL evaluation approaches. OCL [9] is a standardized navigation-based query language, applicable over a range of modeling formalisms. Taking advantage of the expressive features and wide-spread adoption of OCL, the project Eclipse OCL provides a powerful query interface that evaluates OCL expressions over EMF models. However, backwards navigation along references in EMF can still have low performance [2], which may influence the performance of OCL evaluation without additional support.

Aiming at incremental evaluation, the impact analysis (IA) approach for OCL constraints [10] is functionally similar to our approach (but conceptually different in terms of underlying incremental algorithm) in using change notifications to identify constraints that should be re-evaluated, although it does not cache partial matches. An added feature of our approach is to automatically provide notifications for derived features (which could be – but currently is not – implemented for OCL tools). As future work, we aim to compare IA and our approach and even combine the benefits of our current implementation with the benefits of existing OCL-based solutions.

Cabot et al. [11] present an approach for incremental runtime validation of OCL constraints and uses promising optimizations, however, it works only on boolean constraints, and as such it is less expressive than our technique.

An interesting model validator over UML models [12] incrementally re-evaluates constraint instances whenever they are affected by changes, however the approach is only applicable in environments where read-only access to the model can be easily recorded, unlike EMF. Additionally, the approach is tailored for model validation, general-purpose model querying is not viable.

Balsters [13] presents an approach for defining database views in UML models as derived classes using OCL. The derived classes in this case are the result set of queries, which is similar to the match sets provided by EMF-INCQUERY. Note, that while the OCL approach does not offer incrementality, an EMF-INCQUERY based approach would.

Derived features. There are several approaches that make extensive use of derived features or provide additional support for their usage.

The PROGRES language [14] allows the rule-based programming of graph rewriting systems. It uses derived attributes for encoding node properties concerning aspects of dynamic semantics. The language includes support for defining how these derived attributes are calculated, and also uses functional attribute dependencies that would allow similar implementation as described in Section 5. However, PROGRES has not been adapted to EMF up to our best knowledge. The FUJABA [15] tool suite also supports derived edges by path expressions in a non-incremental way.

In [16] Diskin describes a theoretical model synchronization framework that uses derived references for propagating changes between corresponding models. The derived attributes defined in the framework are queries, similarly to our approach, although algebraic and not incrementally updated.

Scheidgen [17] presents a MOF tool that allows the definition of derived features using OCL. It handles derived attributes and operations as custom code provided by the user and redirects calls using reflection, thus incrementality is not supported.

JastEMF [18] is a semantics-integrated metamodeling approach for EMF. It uses derived features as side-effect free operations (i.e. queries) and refers to them as the static semantics of the model. Therefore, our query-based approach could be integrated with JastEMF without problems.

ConceptBase.cc [19] is a database system for metamodeling and method engineering. It allows the definition of active rules that react to events and can update the database or call external routines. Using this functionality, it would be possible to create derived features in models that are updated incrementally based on the data stored in the ConceptBase.cc database. On the other hand, this framework has not been applied in an EMF context.

In a previous tool paper of ours [20], we give an architectural overview of the entire EMF-INCQUERY tool where derived features are listed as one of the new features of the tool. The current paper provides all the technical details on using incremental queries for derived features in EMF.

7 Conclusion

We proposed to seamlessly integrate the EMF-INCQUERY framework to the EMF infrastructure in order to facilitate the efficient and automated computation of derived attributes and references over EMF models by advanced model queries. Our approach (1) allows to define derived features using an expressive graph-based model query language, (2) offers high performance and scalability thanks to the incremental evaluation technique of EMF-INCQUERY [2], and (3) automatically provides notifications to and from derived features which has to be implemented manually in an EMF application.

Future work. Our current research directions include the application of query-based derived features for handling soft interconnections in EMF models and for managing virtual EMF objects derived from query result sets. Furthermore, the EMF-INCQUERY framework is under active development, with derived feature support being only one of its many capabilities.

Acknowledgements. We would like to thank E.D. Willink for his suggestions on improving the paper and the anonymous reviewers for their helpful comments.

References

1. Bergmann, G., Ujhelyi, Z., Ráth, I., Varró, D.: A Graph Query Language for EMF Models. In: Cabot, J., Visser, E. (eds.) ICMT 2011. LNCS, vol. 6707, pp. 167–182. Springer, Heidelberg (2011)
2. Bergmann, G., Horváth, Á., Ráth, I., Varró, D., Balogh, A., Balogh, Z., Ökrös, A.: Incremental Evaluation of Model Queries over EMF Models. In: Petriu, D.C., Rouquette, N., Haugen, Ø. (eds.) MODELS 2010. LNCS, vol. 6394, pp. 76–90. Springer, Heidelberg (2010)
3. Ráth, I., Bergmann, G., Ökrös, A., Varró, D.: Live Model Transformations Driven by Incremental Pattern Matching. In: Vallecillo, A., Gray, J., Pierantonio, A. (eds.) ICMT 2008. LNCS, vol. 5063, pp. 107–121. Springer, Heidelberg (2008)
4. Varró, D., Balogh, A.: The Model Transformation Language of the VIATRA2 Framework. Science of Computer Programming 68(3), 214–234 (2007)
5. The Eclipse Project: EMF Model Query 2, http://wiki.eclipse.org/EMF/Query2
6. The Eclipse Project: EMFT Search,
   http://www.eclipse.org/modeling/emft/?project=search
7. Biermann, E., Ermel, C., Taentzer, G.: Precise Semantics of EMF Model Transformations by Graph Transformation. In: Czarnecki, K., Ober, I., Bruel, J.-M., Uhl, A., Völter, M. (eds.) MODELS 2008. LNCS, vol. 5301, pp. 53–67. Springer, Heidelberg (2008)

8. Giese, H., Hildebrandt, S., Seibel, A.: Improved flexibility and scalability by interpreting story diagrams. In: Proceedings of GT-VMT 2009, vol. 18. ECEASST (2009)
9. The Object Management Group: Object Constraint Language, v2.3.1. (January 2012), http://www.omg.org/spec/OCL/2.3.1/
10. Uhl, A., Goldschmidt, T., Holzleitner, M.: Using an OCL impact analysis algorithm for view-based textual modelling. ECEASST 44 (2011)
11. Cabot, J., Teniente, E.: Incremental integrity checking of UML/OCL conceptual schemas. J. Syst. Softw. 82(9), 1459–1478 (2009)
12. Groher, I., Reder, A., Egyed, A.: Incremental Consistency Checking of Dynamic Constraints. In: Rosenblum, D.S., Taentzer, G. (eds.) FASE 2010. LNCS, vol. 6013, pp. 203–217. Springer, Heidelberg (2010)
13. Balsters, H.: Modelling Database Views with Derived Classes in the UML/OCL-framework. In: Stevens, P., Whittle, J., Booch, G. (eds.) UML 2003. LNCS, vol. 2863, pp. 295–309. Springer, Heidelberg (2003)
14. Schürr, A.: Introduction to PROGRESS, an Attribute Graph Grammar Based Specification Language. In: Nagl, M. (ed.) Graph-Theoretic Concepts in Computer Science. LNCS, vol. 411, pp. 151–165. Springer, Heidelberg (1990)
15. Nickel, U., Niere, J., Zündorf, A.: The FUJABA environment. In: Proc. ICSE 2000, pp. 742–745 (2000)
16. Diskin, Z.: Model Synchronization: Mappings, Tiles, and Categories. In: Fernandes, J.M., Lämmel, R., Visser, J., Saraiva, J. (eds.) GTTSE 2009. LNCS, vol. 6491, pp. 92–165. Springer, Heidelberg (2011)
17. Scheidgen, M.: On implementing MOF 2.0 new features for modelling language abstractions (2005)
18. Bürger, C., Karol, S., Wende, C., Aßmann, U.: Reference Attribute Grammars for Metamodel Semantics. In: Malloy, B., Staab, S., van den Brand, M. (eds.) SLE 2010. LNCS, vol. 6563, pp. 22–41. Springer, Heidelberg (2011)
19. Jeusfeld, M.A., Jarke, M., Mylopoulos, J.: Metamodeling for Method Engineering. The MIT Press (2009)
20. Bergmann, G., Hegedüs, Á., Horváth, Á., Ráth, I., Ujhelyi, Z., Varró, D.: Integrating Efficient Model Queries in State-of-the-Art EMF Tools. In: Furia, C.A., Nanz, S. (eds.) TOOLS 2012. LNCS, vol. 7304, pp. 1–8. Springer, Heidelberg (2012)

A Lightweight Approach for Managing XML Documents with MDE Languages

Dimitrios S. Kolovos, Louis M. Rose,
James Williams, Nicholas Matragkas, and Richard F. Paige

Department of Computer Science, University of York,
Derramore Lane, Heslington, York, YO10 5GH, UK
{dkolovos,louis,jw,nikos,paige}@cs.york.ac.uk

Abstract. The majority of contemporary model management languages that support MDE tasks (such as model transformation, validation and code generation) require models to be captured using metamodelling architectures such as Ecore and MOF. In practice, a limited subset of modelling tools – with the exception of some UML tools – build atop such architectures. For many modelling languages and tools outside of the UML/Ecore/MOF family, plain XML is a widely used model storage and exchange format. In this paper, we argue for the importance of integrating XML-based models in the MDE process. We identify the challenges involved in integrating XML-based models into MDE processes, and we present a technical solution that addresses these challenges, which enables developers to perform a wide range of model management tasks on models captured in XML.

1 Introduction

Model Driven Engineering (MDE) focuses on elevating machine-processable *models* to first-class artefacts of the software development process. MDE is technology-agnostic in the sense that it does not prescribe a specific architecture or framework atop which models should be captured, or a particular format in which they should be stored. Therefore, in principle, any structured machine-processable document can play the role of a model in an MDE process.

The majority of recent research on MDE has focused on 3-level metamodelling architectures where models conform to metamodels which are defined in terms of architecture / framework-specific metamodelling languages such as MOF [1] or Ecore [2]. As a result, most contemporary model management languages that support tasks such as model transformation, code generation, model validation etc., require models to be captured atop such architectures. In practice however, very few modelling tools actually use MOF/Ecore to manage and store their models; XML appears to be the most commonly used model persistence format [3].

Although XML is clearly inferior for MDE purposes to elaborate object-oriented metamodelling architectures from a technical perspective, due to its popularity and simplicity, it has the potential of lowering the entry barrier and playing the role of a stepping stone for the wider adoption of automated model management and MDE. In an effort to make model management languages and MDE techniques more accessible to XML-literate developers, in this paper we propose a lightweight approach for providing first-class support for managing XML documents within Epsilon [4], a mature and well-established family of model management languages. By first-class in this context, we mean support for XML documents in their native standard W3C DOM[1] representation, and not through an implicit or a behind-the-scene injection to a proprietary representation (e.g. as instances of an Ecore-based XML metamodel) that Epsilon already provides support for.

The remainder of the paper is organised as follows. In Section 2 we discuss the importance of XML for MDE and highlight the need for providing first-class support for XML documents in model management languages. In Section 3 we discuss how we implemented such support in the context of Epsilon and in Section 4 we present a case study that illustrates using languages of the Epsilon platform to perform model management tasks on XML documents. In Section 5 we discuss related work and in Section 6 we conclude and provide directions for further work on this subject.

2 Background and Motivation

XML is ubiquitous in the world of software: a vast number of off-the-shelf tools either use XML as a native format for storing structured data they manage, or provide import/export capabilities from/to XML. Also, literally hundreds of modelling languages have been defined atop XML [3] such as the Systems Biology Markup Language (SBML)[2], the Financial products Markup Language[3] and exchange formats such as the Graph Exchange Language[4]. This is consistent with the experience obtained through our interaction with industrial collaborators, which also indicates that XML is particularly popular as a native representation format for bespoke modelling tools developed in-house.

Compared to contemporary metamodelling architectures such as EMF and MOF, plain XML is technically inferior as it only supports capturing tree-structured metadata and does not provide support for types. XML Schema remedies these limitations by adding support – among other – for formalising cross-references between XML elements, and for defining complex and primitive types but is still geared more towards the concrete representation rather than towards the abstract syntax of the metadata it models.

Despite its technical limitations, we argue that plain XML has the potential to lower the entrance barrier for developers that have not been previously exposed to MDE; it can be used to enable developers to capture primitive *models* that contain domain-specific information of interest and start managing them in an

---

[1] http://www.w3.org/DOM/
[2] http://sbml.org/
[3] http://www.fpml.org/
[4] http://www.gupro.de/GXL/

automated manner with MDE languages, without requiring them to first become familiar with metamodelling architectures such as EMF and MOF. In the sequel, and if automated model management (e.g. code generation, model transformation, validation) appears to be delivering results, a transition to a contemporary metamodelling architecture that addresses the limitations of XML is the next logical step.

In the following sections we demonstrate an approach for contributing first-class support for managing plain XML documents to the Epsilon family of MDE languages. Our aim with this work is to render MDE languages useful and attractive to developers that are experienced with XML but not with metamodelling architectures, thus providing means that lower the entrance barrier to MDE.

2.1 Epsilon

Epsilon [4] is a mature and well-established family of interoperable languages for model management. Languages in Epsilon can be used to manage models of diverse metamodels and technologies. At the core of Epsilon is the Epsilon Object Language (EOL) [5], an OCL-based imperative language that provides features such as model modification, multiple model access, conventional programming constructs (variables, loops, branches etc.), user interaction, profiling, and support for transactions. Although EOL can be used as a general-purpose model management language, its primary aim is to be reused in task-specific languages. Thus, a number of task-specific languages have been implemented atop EOL, including those for model transformation (ETL), model comparison (ECL), model merging (EML), model validation (EVL), model refactoring (EWL) and model-to-text transformation (EGL).

With regard to the types of models supported, Epsilon provides the Epsilon Model Connectivity (EMC) layer that offers a uniform interface for interacting with models of different modelling technologies. Currently, EMC drivers have been implemented to support EMF [2] (XMI 2.x), MDR [6] (XMI 1.x) and Z [7] specifications in LaTeX using CZT [8] Also, to enable users to compose complex workflows that involve a number of individual model management tasks, Epsilon provides ANT [9] tasks and an inter-task communication framework discussed in detail in [10].

3 Managing XML Documents in Epsilon

In this section we illustrate how we have implemented first-class support for managing XML documents in all the languages provided by Epsilon to perform tasks such as model transformation, validation, comparison, refactoring, merging and code generation.

3.1 The Epsilon Model Connectivity Layer

The Epsilon Model Connectivity (EMC), shown in Figure 1, is an abstraction layer for managing models in Epsilon. Via EMC, the model management

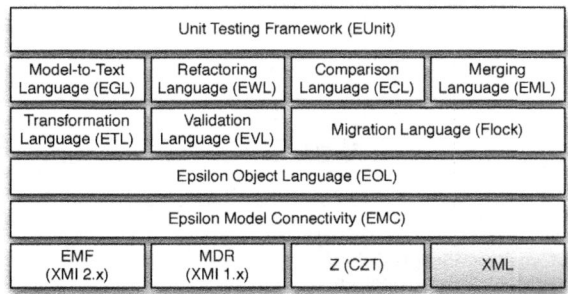

Fig. 1. Overview of the architecture of Epsilon

languages of Epsilon can query and modify models of varying modelling technologies without needing to be aware of the low-level details of each technology.

EMC enables developers to implement *drivers* – essentially classes that implement the IModel interface of Figure 2 – to support diverse modelling technologies. This work illustrates the design and implementation of an additional driver (on top of the existing drivers for managing EMF, MDR and Z models) for interacting with schema-less XML documents.

In addition to abstracting over the technical details of specific modelling technologies, EMC facilitates the concurrent management of models expressed with different technologies. For instance, Epsilon can be used to transform an EMF-based model into an MDR-based model, to perform inter-model validation between a Z model and an EMF model, or to develop a code generator that consumes information from an EMF-based and an XML model at the same time.

3.2 The Plain XML EMC Driver

To support management of XML documents with languages of the Epsilon family, a new driver has been implemented atop EMC. The XML driver uses the standard W3C DOM Java implementation as the underlying representation for XML documents and this, combined with the ability of Epsilon languages to invoke Java operations enables developers to access the complete standard DOM API[5] in their model management programs.

By contrast to drivers for 3-tier architectures such as EMF/MOF, in this driver, in the absence of a metamodel or a schema, the developer needs to assist Epsilon in navigating the XML model and performing type coercion / casting. Therefore, the plain XML driver (shaded box in Figure 1) uses predefined naming conventions to allow developers to programmatically access and modify XML documents in an elegant and concise way. It is worth noting that providing support for XML documents in Epsilon did not require any other changes beyond

---

[5] http://www.w3.org/DOM/

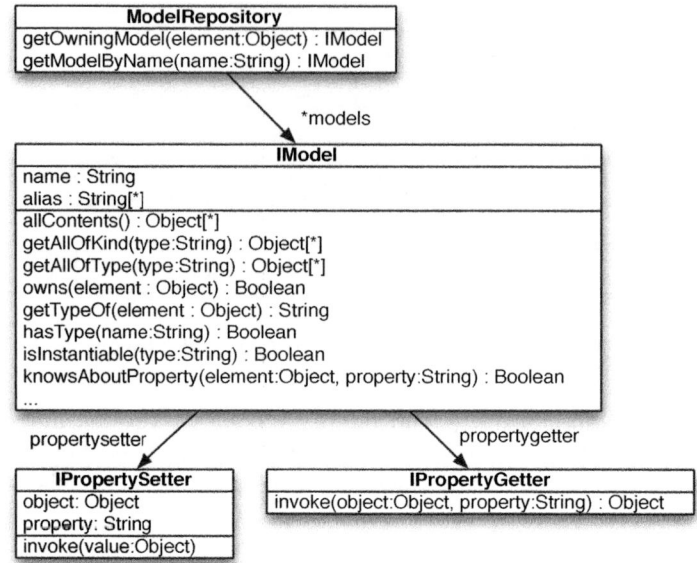

Fig. 2. The Model Connectivity Layer of Epsilon

the addition of the XML driver. This section outlines the supported conventions using the document of Listing 1.1 as a running example.

```xml
<?xml version="1.0" encoding="UTF-8" standalone="no"?>
<library>
  <book title="Eclipse Modeling Framework" pages="744">
    <author>Dave Steinberg</author>
    <author>Frank Budinsky</author>
    <author>Marcelo Paternostro</author>
    <author>Ed Merks</author>
    <published>2009</published>
  </book>
  <book title="Eclipse Modeling Project: A Domain-Specific
      Language (DSL) Toolkit" pages="736">
    <author>Richard Gronback</author>
    <published>2009</published>
  </book>
  <book title="Official Eclipse 3.0 FAQs" pages="432">
    <author>John Arthorne</author>
    <author>Chris Laffra</author>
    <published>2004</published>
  </book>
</library>
```

Listing 1.1. Example XML document

Accessing Elements by Tag Name. The t_ prefix before the name of the tag is used to represent a type, instances of which are all the elements with that tag. For instance, t_book.all can be used to retrieve all elements tagged as <book> in the document, t_author.all to retrieve all <author> elements etc. Also, if b is an element with a <book> tag, then b.isTypeOf(t_book) shall return true.

```
1  // Get all <book> elements
2  var books = t_book.all;
3
4  // Get a random book
5  var b = books.random();
6
7  // Check if b is a book
8  // Prints 'true'
9  b.isTypeOf(t_book).println();
10
11 // Check if b is a library
12 // Prints 'false'
13 b.isTypeOf(t_library).println();
```

Listing 1.2. Accessing elements by tag name

Getting and Setting Attribute Values of Elements. An attribute name, prefixed by a_, can be used as a property of the element object. For example, if b is the first book of the XML document of Listing 1.1, b.a_title will return EMF Eclipse Modeling Framework. Attribute properties are readable and writable.

In this example, b.a_pages will return 744 as a string. For 744 to be returned as an integer, the i_ prefix should be used instead (i.e. b.i_pages. The driver also supports the following prefixes: b_ for boolean, s_ for string (alias of a_) and r_ for real values.

```
1  // Print all the titles of the books in the library
2  for (b in t_book.all) {
3    b.a_title.println();
4  }
5
6  // Print the total number of pages of all books
7  var total = 0;
8  for (b in t_book.all) {
9    total = total + b.i_pages;
10 }
11 total.print();
12
13 // ... the same using collect() and sum()
14 // instead of a for loop
15 t_book.all.collect(b|b.i_pages).sum();
```

Listing 1.3. Getting and setting attribute values

Getting/Setting the Text of an Element. The .text property can be used to read/write the value of the textual content of an element.

```
1  for (author in t_author.all) {
2    author.text.println();
3  }
```

Listing 1.4. Getting and setting the text of an element

Accessing the Parent of an Element. The .parentNode read-only property can be used to retrieve the parent node of an element.

```
1  // Get a random book
2  var b = t_book.all.random();
3
4  // Print the tag of its parent node
5  // Prints 'library'
6  b.parentNode.tagName.println();
```

Listing 1.5. Getting the parent of an element

Retrieving the Children of an Element. The .children read-only property can be used to retrieve all the child-nodes of an element.

```
1  // Get the <library> element
2  var lib = t_library.all.first();
3
4  // Iterate through its children
5  for (b in lib.children) {
6    // Print the title of each child
7    b.a_title.println();
8  }
```

Listing 1.6. Getting the children of an element

Getting Child Elements with a Specific Tag Name. Using what has been discussed so far, this can be achieved using a combination of the .children property and the select/selectOne() EOL operations. However, the driver also supports e_ and c_-prefixed shorthand properties for accessing one or a collection of elements with the specified name respectively. e_ and c_ properties are read-only.

```
1  // Get a random book
2  var b = t_book.all.random();
3
4  // Get its <author> children using the
5  // .children property
6  var authors = b.children.select(a|a.tagName = "author");
7
8  // Do the same using the shorthand
```

```
9   authors = b.c_author;
10
11  // Get its <published> child and print
12  // its text using the
13  // .children property
14  b.children.selectOne(p|p.tagName = "published").text.
        println();
15
16  // Do the same using the shorthand
17  // (e_ instead of c_ this time as
18  // we only want one element,
19  // not a collection of them)
20  b.e_published.text.println();
```

Listing 1.7. Getting children with a specific tag name

Creating New Elements. The standard new operator can be used to create new elements in the XML document.

```
1   // Check how many <books> are in the library
2   // Prints '3'
3   t_book.all.size().println();
4
5   // Creates a new book element
6   var b = new t_book;
7
8   // Check again
9   // Prints '4'
10  t_book.all.size().println();
```

Listing 1.8. Creating new elements

Add a Child to an Existing Element. The .appendChild(child) operation can be used to add a child-node to an element. If the node to be added is already a child of another node, it is first detached from its previous parent.

```
1   // Create a new book
2   var b = new t_book;
3
4   // Get the library element
5   var lib = t_library.all.first();
6
7   // Add the book to the library
8   lib.appendChild(b);
```

Listing 1.9. Adding a child to an existing element

Setting the Root Element of an XML Document. The .root property of the model can be used to set the root element of an XML document.

```
1   XMLDoc.root = new t_library;
```
Listing 1.10. Setting the root element of an XML document

The XML driver also supports (optional) caching so that expensive operations such as collecting all elements with a particular tag do not need to be performed repetitively.

3.3 Alternative Design Choices

As discussed above, the plain XML driver presented in this section makes use of particular naming conventions – such as the t_, and c_ prefixes – to specify XML model element types, to distinguish between child elements and attribute values, to specify the expected result type when retrieving children of an element by name (single element vs. collection of elements), and to perform type-casting of the values of attributes. Given that Epsilon is dynamically typed, the prefixes could have been eliminated in an alternative design, but this would have introduced several inconveniences, which are now discussed.

Ordinarily, Epsilon throws a runtime error when trying to use undefined variables or types of model element that do not exist. These runtime errors provide valuable information to users, alerting them to problems with their programs. Schema-less models, such as plain XML models, do not provide type information. Without the t_ prefix for XML model element types, the EOL interpreter would become unable to distinguish between undefined variables and XML model element types. Consequently, undefined variables would have to be treated as XML model element types, and the user would not be alerted to the potential error in their program. In addition, had we not used c_ and e_ to distinguish between single and multiple children, all child element navigations would need to return a collection of elements. Also, explicitly specifying attribute value type-casting using the i_, r_, b_ prefixes avoids unintended type casts.

In our view, employing these prefixes makes up to an extent for the lack of a formal metamodel and makes code easier – albeit slightly more verbose – to write and maintain.

4 Case Study

In this section we present a case study that demonstrates how the XML driver that was presented in the previous section can be used to validate and transform the XML-based OO model of Listing 1.11 to a respective EMF-based UML model. This case study has been intentionally kept simple for brevity reasons.

```
1   <?xml version="1.0"?>
2   <model>
3       <class name="Customer">
4           <property name="name" type="String"/>
5           <property name="address" type="Address"/>
6       </class>
```

```
7      <class name="Invoice">
8         <property name="serialNumber" type="String"/>
9         <property name="customer" type="Customer"/>
10        <property name="items" type="InvoiceItem" many="true"
             />
11     </class>
12     <class name="InvoiceItem">
13        <property name="quantity" type="Integer"/>
14        <property name="product" type="Product"/>
15     </class>
16     <class name="Product">
17        <property name="name" type="String"/>
18        <property name="unitPrice" type="Float"/>
19     </class>
20     <class name="Address">
21        <property name="number" type="String"/>
22        <property name="postCode" type="String"/>
23     </class>
24     <datatype name="String"/>
25     <datatype name="Integer"/>
26     <datatype name="Float"/>
27  </model>
```

Listing 1.11. OO model captured using XML

Listing 1.12 illustrates a constraint expressed using the Epsilon Validation Language (EVL) which checks that the type of each property in the XML model of Listing 1.11 corresponds to a defined type (class or datatype). Line 2 defines that the constraint applies to all elements tagged as property and line 5 checks that there is an element tagged as datatype or class whose name matches the value of the type attribute of the property. If such an element is not found, in lines 7-9 a diagnostic message is produced.

```
1   import "util.eol";
2   context t_property {
3      constraint TypeMustBeDefined {
4
5         check : typeForName(self.a_type).isDefined()
6
7         message : "Property " + self.a_name + " of class " +
8            self.parentNode.a_name + " is of unknown type: " +
9            self.a_type
10     }
11  }
```

Listing 1.12. XML validation constraint expressed in EVL

Listing 1.13 illustrates a model-to-model transformation expressed using the Epsilon Transformation Language (ETL) that transforms the XML model of Listing 1.11 to an EMF-based UML model. The transformation consists of 4 rules which transform elements tagged as model, class, property and datatype to respective Models, Classes, Properties and DataTypes in the target UML model. This transformation illustrates how EMC enables programs in all Epsilon languages to manage models that conform to different technologies concurrently.

```
import "util.eol";

rule t_model2Model
    transform s : XML!t_model
    to t : UML!Model {

    t.packagedElement.addAll(s.children.equivalent());
}

rule t_class2Class
    transform s : XML!t_class
    to t : UML!Class {

    t.name = s.a_name;
    t.ownedAttribute.addAll(s.children.equivalent().
        select(e|e.isTypeOf(UML!Property)));
}

rule t_property2Property
    transform s : XML!t_property
    to t : UML!Property {

    t.name = s.a_name;
    var type = typeForName(s.a_type);
    t.type = type.equivalent();

    if (s.b_many) { t.upper = -1; }

    if (not type.isTypeOf(XML!t_datatype)) {
        var association = new UML!Association;
        association.ownedEnds.add(t);
        var opposite = new UML!Property;
        opposite.type = s.parentNode.equivalent();
        association.ownedEnds.add(opposite);
        UML!Model.all.first().packagedElement.
            add(association);
    }

}

rule t_datatype2DataType
    transform s : XML!t_datatype
    to t : UML!DataType {

```

```
45      t.name = s.a_name;
46
47  }
```

Listing 1.13. XML to UML transformation expressed in ETL

```
1  operation typeForName(type : String) {
2      return allTypes().selectOne(t|t.a_name = type);
3  }
4
5  operation allTypes() : Sequence {
6      return XML!t_class.all.includingAll(XML!t_datatype.all);
7  }
```

Listing 1.14. Utility methods (util.eol) used in Listings 1.13 and 1.12

5 Related Work

The importance of XML has been recognised by the developers of the Eclipse Modelling Framework (EMF) and as a result EMF provides support for managing schema-based XML documents. To support schema-based XML documents, EMF provides a built-in transformation that can produce an Ecore metamodel from an XML schema, a parser that can parse XML files that conform to an XSD into in-memory models that conform to the respective Ecore metamodel, and a serialiser that can then persist in-memory models back to XML. While Ecore and XSD share many common features such as being able to define complex structures (e.g. through EClasses in Ecore and Complex Types in XSD), inheritance, references with cardinality etc. they also differ in some respects. For instance, XSD can define anonymous complex types while Ecore cannot define anonymous EClasses, EMF models can contain multiple root objects while XML documents can only have one root node, Ecore does not have equivalent constructs for the XSD <choice> element or the mixed feature, etc. In an effort to compensate for these differences, the XSD to Ecore transformation employs conventions that, while necessary, can lead to non-straightforward Ecore metamodels.

For example, the XML Schema of listing 1.15 is transformed into the Ecore metamodel illustrated in Figure 3. In the Ecore metamodel the reader can observe the ItemType and ItemType1 EClasses which have been generated by the anonymous complex types in lines 8 and 21 of the XSD. Also, in order for a developer to access the text content of an item element, they need to query the mixed feature of ItemType (or ItemType1) – which is not straightforward for a developer with no EMF expertise.

```
1  <?xml version="1.0" encoding="UTF-8" standalone="no"?>
2  <xs:schema xmlns:xs="http://www.w3.org/2001/XMLSchema">
3
4      <xs:element name="invoice">
```

```
5   <xs:complexType>
6     <xs:sequence>
7       <xs:element name="item">
8         <xs:complexType mixed="true">
9           <xs:sequence>
10            <xs:element name="unitPrice" type="xs:float"
                 />
11          </xs:sequence>
12        </xs:complexType>
13      </xs:element>
14    </xs:sequence>
15  </xs:complexType>
16 </xs:element>
17 <xs:element name="order">
18   <xs:complexType>
19     <xs:sequence>
20       <xs:element name="item">
21         <xs:complexType mixed="true">
22           <xs:sequence>
23             <xs:element name="quantity" type="xs:int"/>
24           </xs:sequence>
25         </xs:complexType>
26       </xs:element>
27     </xs:sequence>
28   </xs:complexType>
29 </xs:element>
30 </xs:schema>
```

Listing 1.15. Example XML Schema

The Atlas Transformation Language (ATL) provides support for schema-less XML documents through an injection transformation that converts an XML document to a respective EMF model that conforms to a simple Ecore-based XML metamodel, and an extraction transformation that does the reverse. As such, the syntax for managing XML documents in ATL is particularly verbose as illustrated by Listings 1.16 and 1.17.

```
1  XML!t_book.all.first().a_title.println();
```

Listing 1.16. EOL statement that prints the title of the first book

```
1  XML!Element.allInstances()->select(e|e.name = 'book')->
       first()
2  .children->select(c|c.oclIsTypeOf(XML!Attribute)
3      and c.name = 'title')->first().value.println();
```

Listing 1.17. Equivalent ATL statement that prints the title of the first book

Xlinkit [11] is a tool for checking consistency issues in distributed documents. Using Xlinkit, developers can specify cross-document constraints that can be automatically evaluated to reveal inconsistencies. For the specification of

```
▼ ⬢ Invoice
    ▶ ExtendedMetaData
    ▼ 目 DocumentRoot
        ▶ ExtendedMetaData
        ▶ mixed : EFeatureMapEntry
        ▶ xMLNSPrefixMap : EStringToStringMapEntry
        ▶ xSISchemaLocation : EStringToStringMapEntry
        ▶ invoice : InvoiceType
        ▶ order : OrderType
    ▶ 目 InvoiceType
    ▼ 目 ItemType
        ▶ ExtendedMetaData
        ▶ mixed : EFeatureMapEntry
        ▶ quantity : Int
    ▶ 目 ItemType1
    ▶ 目 OrderType
```

Fig. 3. Ecore metamodel generated from the XML Schema of Listing 1.15

constraints, Xlinkit defines an XML-based language that uses XPath [12] for document navigation. Listing 1.18 demonstrates an exemplar Xlinkit constraint that applies on a UML and a Java model and states that for each class in the UML model, a class with the same name must exist in the Java model. In our view, the main shortcoming of this approach is that the concrete syntax of the expression language is based on XML and that, as illustrated in Listing 1.18, results in lengthy and challenging to read and maintain specifications.

```
1  <globalset id="classes"
2    xpath="//Foundation.Core.Class[@xmi.id]"/>
3  <globalset id="javaclasses" xpath="/java/class"/>
4  <consistencyrule id="r1">
5   <forall var="c" in="classes">
6    <exists var="j" in="javaclasses">
7     <equal
8       op1="c/Foundation.Core.ModelElement.name/text()"
9       op2="j/@name"/>
10    </exists>
11   </forall>
12  </consistencyrule>
```

Listing 1.18. Example Xlinkit constraint

6 Conclusions and Further Work

In this paper we have highlighted the importance of XML in the context of MDE; in particular we have discussed the role of XML both as a legacy format in which a significant amount of data is already encoded, and as a means of lowering the entrance barrier for newcomers in MDE. Following that we illustrated a technical solution for adding first-class support for XML to the Epsilon MDE platform so that plain XML documents can be used in a wide range of MDE tasks such as model validation, transformation, comparison, merging and code generation as they are and without needing to first transform them to models that conform to metamodelling architectures such as MOF or EMF.

Although in this paper we have illustrated a solution for adding support for managing XML documents to a particular family of model management languages, it is worth noting that this approach is also directly applicable to other model management languages (such as ATL[13] or MOFScript[14]) that provide a layer of indirection between the language run-time and the concrete modelling technologies they support.

Acknowledgements. The work in this paper was supported by the European Commission via the MADES and INESS projects, co-funded under the 7th Framework programme (grants #218575 (INESS), #248864 (MADES)).

References

1. Object Management Group. Meta Object Facility (MOF) 2.0 Core Specification, http://www.omg.org/cgi-bin/doc?ptc/03-10-04
2. Steinberg, D., Budinsky, F., Paternostro, M., Merks, E.: EMF: Eclipse Modelling Framework. 2nd edn. Eclipse Series. Addison-Wesley Professional (December 2008)
3. CoverPages. XML Applications and Initiatives (June 2005), http://xml.coverpages.org/xmlApplications.html
4. Eclipse Foundation. Epsilon Modeling GMT component, http://www.eclipse.org/gmt/epsilon
5. Kolovos, D.S., Paige, R.F., Polack, F.A.C.: The Epsilon Object Language (EOL). In: Rensink, A., Warmer, J. (eds.) ECMDA-FA 2006. LNCS, vol. 4066, pp. 128–142. Springer, Heidelberg (2006)
6. Sun Microsystems. Meta Data Repository, http://mdr.netbeans.org
7. Woodcock, J., Davies, J.: Using Z: Specification, Refinement, and Proof. Prentice-Hall (March 1996)
8. Community Z Tools, http://czt.sourceforge.net
9. The Apache Ant Project, http://ant.apache.org
10. Kolovos, D.S., Paige, R.F., Polack, F.A.C.: A Framework for Composing Modular and Interoperable Model Management Tasks. In: Proc. Workshop on Model Driven Tool and Process Integration (MDTPI), ECMDA, Berlin, Germany (June 2008)
11. Nentwich, C., Capra, L., Emmerich, W., Finkelstein, A.: xlinkit: A Consistency Checking and Smart Link Generation Service. ACM Transactions on Internet Technology 2(2), 151–185 (2002)
12. W3C. XML Path Language (XPath), Official Web-Site, http://www.w3.org/TR/xpath
13. Jouault, F., Kurtev, I.: Transforming Models with ATL. In: Bruel, J.-M. (ed.) MoDELS 2005. LNCS, vol. 3844, pp. 128–138. Springer, Heidelberg (2006)
14. Oldevik, J.: MOFScript User Guide, http://www.eclipse.org/gmt/mofscript/doc/MOFScript-User-Guide.pdf

Bridging the Gap between Requirements and Aspect State Machines to Support Non-functional Testing: Industrial Case Studies

Tao Yue and Shaukat Ali

Certus Software V&V Center, Simula Research Laboratory
P.O. Box 134, 1325, Lysaker, Norway
{tao,shaukat}@simula.no

Abstract. Requirements are often structured and documented as use cases while UML state machine diagrams often describe the behavior of a system. State machines capture rich and detailed behavior of a system, which can serve as a basis for many automated activities such as automated test case and code generation. The former is of interest in this paper. Non-functional behavior can be modeled using standard UML state machines, but usually results in complex state machines. To cope with such complexity, Aspect-Oriented Modeling (AOM) is often recommended. AspectSM is a UML profile defined to model crosscutting behavior on UML state machines called as aspect state machines with the focus of supporting model-based test case generation for non-functional behavior. Hence, an automatic transition from use cases to aspect state machines would provide significant, practical help for testing system requirements. In this paper, we propose an approach to automatically generate aspect state machines from use cases for the purpose of non-functional testing. Our approach is implemented in a tool, which we used for two industrial case studies. Results show that high quality aspect state machines can be generated, which can be manually refined at a reasonable cost to support testing.

Keywords: Use Case Modeling, UML, Aspect State Machine, Model-Based Testing (MBT), State-based Testing.

1 Introduction

Model-based testing (MBT) has attracted much attention in both industry and academia, as indicated by a large number of MBT tools produced in recent years [1]. MBT however relies on complete and precise models for executable test case generation. Developing such models has always been a challenge, especially for large-scale industrial systems, and entails a thorough domain understanding and solid modeling expertise. Oftentimes, developing such models is difficult for Software Quality Assurance teams as they are often not sufficiently acquainted with modeling. On the other hand, these teams are comparatively much more familiar with writing textual use cases and the application domain.

    This paper is part of an automated methodology (aToucan [2, 3]) to assist the development of high-level models from use case models (UCMods). The aToucan tool relies on a number of existing technologies and is built as an Eclipse plug-in. aToucan involves three steps. 1) Requirements engineers manually define use cases complying with a use case modeling approach, Restricted Use Case Modeling (RUCM) [4, 5], which relies on a use case template and a set of restriction rules for textual Use Case Specifications (UCSs) to reduce the imprecision and incompleteness inherent to UCSs. We have conducted two controlled experiments with human subjects [5] to evaluate RUCM and results indicate that RUCM, though it enforces a template and restriction rules, has enough expressive power, is easy to use, and helps improve the understandability of use cases. 2) aToucan reads these textual UCSs to identify Part-Of-Speech (POS) and grammatical relation dependencies of sentences, and then records that information into an instance of UCMeta (our intermediate metamodel). UCMeta complies with the restrictions and use case template of RUCM, is currently composed of 108 metaclasses, and is implemented as an Ecore model, using Eclipse EMF [6]. During this transformation, the Stanford Parser [7] is used as a Natural Language (NL) parser in aToucan. 3) Transform the instance of UCMeta into UML models. The generation of UML models relies on Kermeta [8]. Due to space limitation, the detailed description of aToucan is given in [2] and we omit it from this paper.

We have proposed an approach [9], as part of the aToucan framework, to automatically generate standard, system-level UML state machines from use case models. The focus of this work is however on generating aspect state machines in AspectSM, a UML profile which was defined to model crosscutting behavior on UML state machines with the focus of supporting model-based non-functional testing [10]. AspectSM has been evaluated both empirically (through controlled experiments, e.g., [11-13]) and practically (via real industrial case studies, e.g., [10]) to be applicable. These models are subsequently refined such that executable test cases can be generated using our MBT tool, TRansformation-based tool for Uml-baSed Testing (TRUST) [14]. The TRUST tool has been successfully applied to two industrial case studies for model-based functional and non-functional testing [14]. In this paper, we performed two industrial case studies: a video conference system from Cisco Systems Inc, Norway [15] and a subsea oil production system from FMC Technologies [16] were performed, to evaluate UML state machines and aspect state machines modeling non-functional behaviors generated by aToucan. The generated state machines were evaluated by domain experts, who assessed them to mostly conform to the existing, manually developed state machines.

The rest of the paper is organized as follows. In Section 2, we briefly discuss RUCM, AspectSM and the running example being used to exemplify the transformation. The transformation approach is discussed in Section 3. The industrial case studies are discussed in Section 4. The related work is presented in Section 5 and Section 6 concludes the paper.

2 Background

In this section, we briefly, due to space limitation, review the use case modeling approach RUCM (Section 2.2) and AspectSM (Section 2.3). A running example will be presented in Section 2.1 to exemplify RUCM and the transformations.

2.1 Running Example

The running example is a simplified subsystem (called Saturn) of a communication system (Video Conferencing System (VCS)) developed by Cisco Systems Inc, Norway [15], which is a leading global provider of telepresence, high-definition video conferencing and mobile video products and services. This subsystem is the industrial case study used to evaluate this work (Section 4).

The core functionality of a VCS is sending and receiving multimedia streams. The use case diagram capturing main use cases of the simplified subsystem Saturn is given in Figure 1. Saturn deals with establishing video conferencing calls, disconnecting calls, and starting/stopping presentations. It can also receive requests for establishing calls, disconnecting calls, and starting/stopping presentations from other video conferencing systems (Endpoints) participating in a videoconference. The endpoints communicating with Saturn are modeled as secondary actors in the use case diagram.

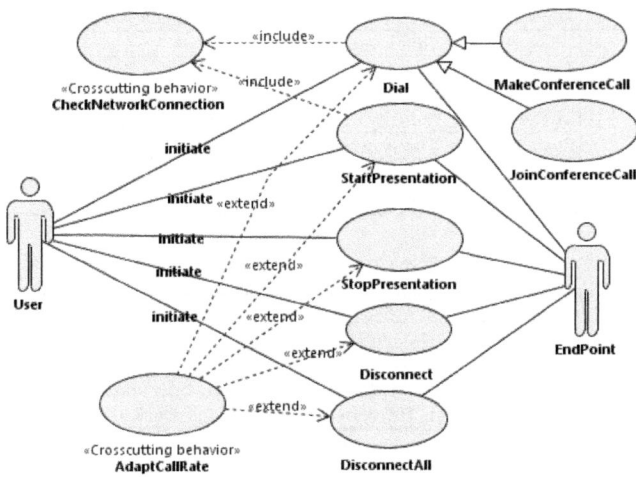

Fig. 1. Use case diagram of Saturn

2.2 RUCM

RUCM encompasses a use case template and 26 well-defined restriction rules [4]. Rules are classified into two groups: restrictions on the use of NL, and rules enforcing the use of specific keywords for specifying control structures. The goal of RUCM is to reduce ambiguity and facilitate automated analysis. Two controlled experiments evaluated RUCM in terms of its ease of application and the quality of the analysis models derived by trained individuals [4, 5]. Results showed that RUCM is overall easy to apply and that it results in significant improvements over the use of a standard use case template (without restrictions to the use of NL), in terms of the quality of derived class and sequence diagrams. UCSs documented with RUCM of use cases AdaptCallRate and CheckNetworkConnection (Figure 1) are presented in Table 1 and Table 2. UCSs of the other use cases in Figure 1 are provided in [9] for a reference.

2.3 AspectSM

Using the AspectSM profile [10], we model crosscutting behaviors as a UML state machine with stereotypes, which is called as aspect state machine and hence reduce modeling effort when compared to modeling crosscutting directly on UML state machines. The readability of models is then improved as crosscutting behavior that tends to be redundant when modeled directly is clearly separated out and expressed once. This profile was developed by augmenting many of the concepts in existing UML state machine profiles for AOM in order to achieve the specific goal of supporting automated, model-based non-functional testing. Due to the space limitation, we didn't provide stereotypes and their attributes in this paper, however, their details can be found in [10].

Table 1. Use case AdaptCallRate

Use Case Name	AdaptCallRate
Brief Description	The system adjusts the call rate based on the quality of services of the network.
Precondition	Network connection is established.
Primary Actor	Timer
Basic Flow	1) The system VALIDATES THAT the network is experiencing packet loss.
	2) The system gradually decreases conference call rate to the minimum call rate
	Postcondition: The system is in a degraded mode.
Specific Alt. Flow (RFS Basic flow 1)	1) The system gradually increases conference call rate up to the maximum call rate.
	Postcondition: The system is in the normal operation mode.

Table 2. Use case CheckNetworkConnection

Use Case Name	CheckNetworkConnection
Brief Description	The system checks the network connection.
Precondition	The system is idle.
Basic flow	1) The system VALIDATES THAT Network connection is OK.
	Postcondition: The network connection is checked.
Specific Alt. Flow (RFS Basic flow 1)	1) The system sends a failure message to User. 2) ABORT.
	Postcondition: The system is idle.

3 Approach

The transformation from the textual UCMod to the instance of UCMeta is not discussed in this paper, but provided in [2] for a reference. In this section, we however only focus on the transformation from instances of UCMeta to the base and aspect state machines. We present detailed transformation rules in Section 3.1. The steps required for transforming generated state machines into the state machines that can be used for automated test case generation are presented in Section 3.2.

3.1 Transformation

Before generating aspect state machines, we should first identify crosscutting behaviors. Two heuristics should be followed to identify crosscutting behavior use cases (CUSs) in the use case model. First, if a use case is included more than once or extends more than one use cases, it is a candidate CUS. A user later on can always manually identify crosscutting behavior. The rest of the section describes how to generate the base state machine and after that, how to generate aspect state machine(s) for identified crosscutting behaviors.

3.1.1 Generating Base State Machine

The transformation from an instance of UCMeta to a base state machine involves three rules, summarized in Table 3. These rules are adapted from [9], where we described the transition to standard UML state machines. The difference between generating a base state machine in the context of aspect-oriented modeling and a standard UML state machine is that when generating the base state machine, identified crosscutting behaviors should not be specified in the base state machine, as they are modeled as aspect state machines. Subscripts on rule numbers (Column 1, Table 3) indicate the type of the rule: "c" and "a" denote composite and atomic rules, respectively; a composite rule is decomposed, whereas an atomic rule is not. The automatically generated base state machine diagram for the use case model presented in Section 2.1 is provided in Figure 2.

Table 3. Summary of transformation rules for generating the base state machine for the system

Rule #		Description
1_a		a) Generate an instance of UML StateMachine, as the base state machine, for the use case model. The name of the state machine should be the name of the system (e.g., 'Saturn') plus 'base state machine'. b) Generate the initial state (instance of Pseudostate with PseudostateKind = initial) for the state machine. c) Generate an instance of State, named as 'start', representing the start state of the state machine. d) Generate an instance of Transition. Its trigger is named as 'construct'. This transition connects the initial state to the start state.
2_c		Invoke rules 2.1-2.4 to process each use case of the use case model that is considered as not specifying crosscutting behaviors.
2.1_a		Generate an instance of State for the precondition of the use case, as long as such a state has not been generated, which is possible because two use cases might have the same preconditions.
2.2_a		Generate an instance of State for the postcondition of the basic flow of the use case, as long as such a state has not been generated.
2.3_a		If the use case does not include any other use case, then connect the state corresponding to the precondition to the state representing the postcondition of the basic flow of the use case with the transition whose trigger is the name of use case. Otherwise, invoke rule 3.
2.4_c		Process the postcondition of each alternative flow of the use case.
	$2.4.1_a$	Generate an instance of State for the postcondition of each alternative flow.
	$2.4.2_a$	Connect the state corresponding to the precondition of the basic flow to the states corresponding to the postconditions of the alternative flows with transitions whose triggers are the name of use case.
3_c		Process Include relationships between use cases. Notice that use cases capturing identified crosscutting behaviors are not processed with the following rules, as separate rules will be applied to generate aspect state machines for them (Section 3.1.2).
3.1_a		Connect the precondition of the included use case to the postcondition of the flow of events where the included use case is included in the including use case through a transition. Connect the precondition of the included use case to the postconditions of the alternative flows of the included use case.
3.2_a		If there is a sequence of included use cases in the including use case, then link all the preconditions of the included use cases sequentially, and then link the precondition of the last use case to the postcondition of the including use case through transitions.

Rule 1 generates an instance of UML StateMachine for a UCMod, which can then be visualized as a state machine diagram, the initial state (an instance of Pseudostate), the start state (an instance of State), and the transition (an instance of Transition) from the initial state to the start state.

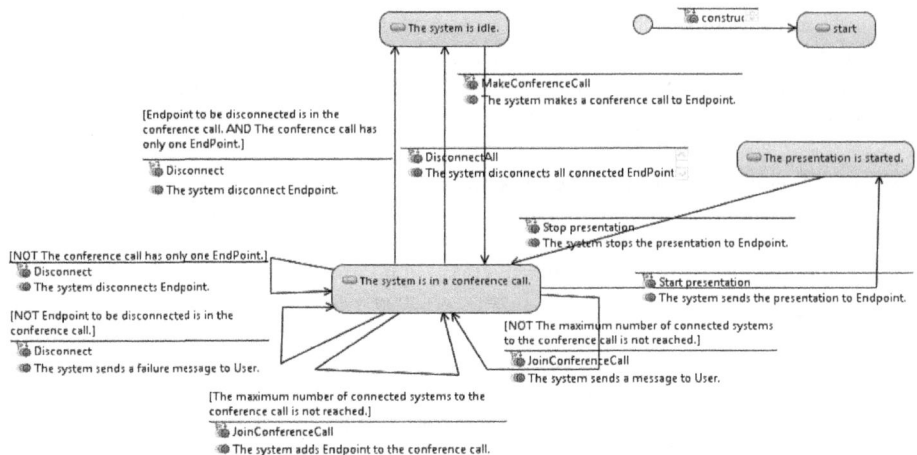

Fig. 2. Generated base state machine

Composite rule 2 invokes rules 2.1-2.4 to process each use case of the UCMod. Notice that we generate a single, system level base state machine for the whole UCMod. We generate an instance of `state` for the precondition (Rule 2.1) and each postcondition (Rule 2.2), but making sure that no duplicate state is generated. Since the precondition of a use case indicates what must happen before the use case can start and the postconditions of the use case specify what must be satisfied after the use case completes, we define Rule 2.3 to generate a transition between the state derived from the precondition and the state derived from the postcondition of the basic flow. Rule 2.4 processes the postcondition of each alternative flow of the use case. Notice that RUCM enforces that each flow of events (both basic flow and alternative flows) of a UCS contains its own postcondition. This characteristic of RUCM makes the transformation (Rule 2.4) systematic. When generating transitions, how to determine the guard condition, trigger, and effect is described in [9], due to space limitation. Rule 3 processes each include relationship of the UCMod.

3.1.2 Generating Aspect State Machines

In this section, we describe the transformation for generating aspect state machines. Generated aspect state machines for two CUSs in Figure 1 are shown in Figure 3 and Figure 4, respectively. Notice that the base state machine has to be generated before the rules are applied to generate any aspect state machine. We generate an aspect state machine with stereotypes from AspectSM for each identified crosscutting behavior.

Rule 1 generates an instance of UML `StateMachine`, stereotyped with <<Aspect>>, which can then be visualized as a state machine diagram. Stereotype <<Aspect>> has two attributes: `name` and `baseStateMachine`, which represent the name of the aspect and the base state machine, on which the aspect is applied ([10]). The `name` of <<Aspect>> is the name of the included use case (extending use case) and the `baseStateMachine` should refer to the base state machine. Notice that we generate a single base state machine for the system. Therefore, the multiplicity of attribute `baseStateMachine` of <<Aspect>> is always 1. For example, both the name of the aspect state machine and the name of <<Aspect>> are 'AdaptCallRate' when generating the aspect state machine for use case AdaptCallRate, and the aspect state machine refers to its base state machine (Figure 2), though this information is not shown in Figure 3. **Rule 2** generates the initial state (an instance of Pseudostate).

Rule 3 generates a state stereotyped with AspectSM stereotype <<Pointcut>>. A *pointcut* in AspectSM selects one or more joinpoints with similar properties, where advices can be applied [10]. Six attributes are defined for stereotype <<Pointcut>> in AspectSM: name, type, selectionConstraint, beforeAdvice, afterAdvice, and aroundAdvice. The name of the pointcut state and <<Pointcut>> is generated as string "SelectStates X', where X can be any number uniquely identifying a state in the aspect state machine. Notice that it is possible to have more than one state stereotyped with <<Pointcut>>. For example, as shown in Figure 3, the pointcut state SelectedStates1 is generated for use case AdaptCallRate. Two pointcut states SelectedStates1 and SelectedStates2 are generated for use case CheckNetworkConnection.

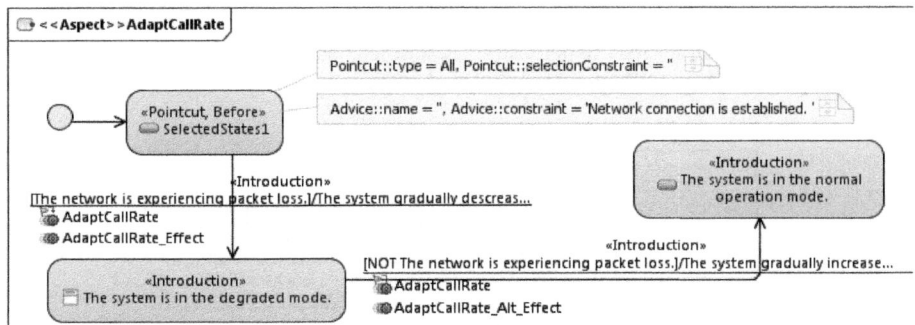

Fig. 3. Generated aspect state machine for use case AdaptCallRate

The type and selectionConstraint of the pointcut should be determined by the following three rules:

- If the CUS extends all the use cases or is included by all the use cases in the base state machine, then the type of the pointcut is 'All', and the selectionConstraint should be equal to empty. As shown in Figure 3, state SelectedStates1 selects all the states in the base state machine through the <<Pointcut>> attribute type, since use case AdaptCallRate extends all the use cases except the other crosscutting use case CheckNetworkCondition. There is no point to assign a value to selectionConstraints as all the use cases are selected.
- If the CUS extends a subset of the use cases or is included by a subset of the use cases in the base state machine, then the type is 'Subset', and the selectionConstraint should be a list of the names of the states generated for the preconditions and postconditions of the use cases either including or being extended by the CUS in the base state machine. For example, as shown in Figure 4, state SelectedStates1 selects a subset of the states in the base state machine: The system is in a conference call. and The presentation

is started. and The system is idle. (Figure 2). The reason of selecting these three states from the base state machine is that they were generated for either the preconditions or the postconditions of use cases MakeConferenceCall, JoinConferenceCall, and StartPresentation, which all include use case CheckNetworkConnection (Figure 1).
- If the CUS extends one use case or is included by one use case in the base state machine, then the type of the pointcut is 'One', and the selectionConstraint of the pointcut should be the states generated for the precondition and postconditions of the use case either including or being extended by the CUS in the base state machine.

Though there are three types of advices in AspectSM, in our transformation only beforeAdvice is used to introduce the precondition of the CUS as additional state invariants, through stereotype <<Before>>, to the selected states of the base state machine. As shown in Figure 3 and Figure 4, beforeAdvice is introduced to the state invariants of the selected states through state SelectedStates1. Notice that AspectSM has three types of advice (i.e., Before, After and Around). In our context, we only use Before, but we could have used After, which can bring the same semantics to the generated aspect state machines, as we discussed in our previous work [10] where AspectSM is discussed in details.

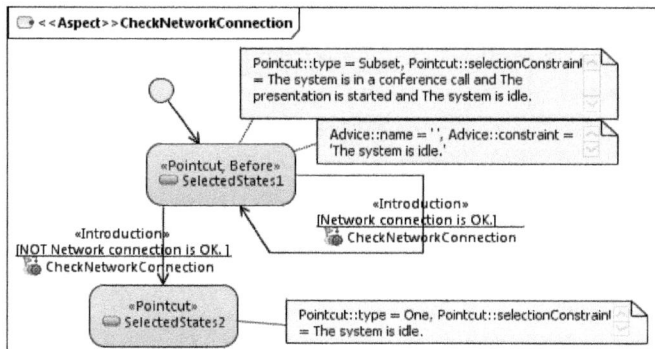

Fig. 4. Generated aspect state machine for use case CheckNetworkConnection

Rule 4 generates the transition (an instance of Transition) from the initial state to the pointcut state. **Rule 5** handles the postcondition of the basic flow of the CUS. There are two situations for applying this rule:
- If the CUS is an extending use case, generate a state for the postcondition, as long as such a state has not been generated in the base state machine. This newly generated state should be stereotyped with AspectSM stereotype <<Introduction>> showing that this state will be introduced in the base state machine. Otherwise, a pointcut state should be generated to point to the existing state in the base state machine. Rule 3 should be followed to generate values for the attributes of stereotype <<Pointcut>>. For example, as shown in Figure 3, state The system is in a degraded mode. is generated,

corresponding to the postcondition of the basic flow of use case AdaptCallRate (Table 1). Also generate a transition stereotyped with <<Introduction>> to connect the pointcut state either to the newly generated state or the pointcut state pointing to the existing state in the base state machine (Rule 5). The trigger of the transition should be the name of the CUS. The guard is the conjunction of all the conditions of the condition sentences in the basic flow of the use case. The effect of the transition should be the last step of the basic flow. For example, in Figure 3, a transition between SelectedStates1 and The system is in the degraded mode. is generated with trigger AdaptCallRate, guard The system is experiencing packet loss., and effect The system gradually decreases conference call rate to the minimum call rate.
- If the CUS is an included use case, a self-transition stereotyped with <<Introduction>> is generated for the pointcut state (Rule 3). The trigger of the transition should be the name of the included use case. The guard is the conjunction of all the conditions of the condition sentences in the basic flow of the CUS. The effect of the transition should be the last step of the basic flow. For example, as shown in Figure 4, a self-transition for SelectedStates1 is generated, with trigger CheckNetworkConnection and guard Network connection is OK. Notice that when the last step of the basic flow of the use case is a condition check sentence (containing keyword VALIDATES THAT), we don't generate an effect for the transition. This is because condition check sentences are considered as representing system internal interactions [5].

Rule 6 handles alternative flows of the CUSs in a similar fashion as for base state machine (Rule 2.4, Table 3). The difference is that, when a new state is generated for the postcondition of an alternative flow, stereotype <<Introduction>> should be always applied; when an existing state is identified in the base state machine for the postcondition, then a pointcut state should be generated in the aspect state machine and it should point to the existing state in the state machine through attribute selectionConstraint of <<Pointcut>>. For example, as shown in Figure 4, a transition is generated between SelectedStates1 and SelectedStates2 as state The system is idle. has been generate as a state in the base state machine (Figure 2). In Figure 3, a state The system is in the normal operation mode. is generated and a transition between states SelectedStates1 and The system is in the normal operation mode.

Rule 7 handles the situation when a CUS includes other use cases and these use cases are only connected to the CUS. In such case, Rule 2.3 and Rule 3 in Table 3, used for generating the base state machine, should be applied. As for Rule 7, the difference is that whenever a new state or transition is generated, stereotype <<Introduction>> should be applied and whenever an existing state is identified in base state machine, a poincut state should be generated.

3.2 Transition to State Machines for Automated Test Generation

The following steps should be followed to refine the generated base and aspect state machines so that they can be used as an input to automatically generate test cases.

1. The generated base and aspect state machines have to be manually refined by a user. More specifically, in the generated state machines, missing transitions and states should be added, extra states and transitions should be removed, and incorrect ones should be modified. For the generated aspect state machines, the user additionally has to refine elements related to AspectSM.
2. Add state invariants using the Object Constraint Language (OCL) [17] for each state of the generated state machines based on the actual state variables of a system.
3. Map all the triggers of all the state machine diagrams to the actual API calls of the SUT so that the API of the system can be invoked while executing test cases generated from the state machines.
4. Last, it is also required to replace textual guard conditions of the generated state machines with corresponding OCL constraints, based on the state variables and/or input parameters of the triggers associated with the guards.

4 Industrial Case Studies

Our goal here is to assess 1) whether the tool does generate system-level state machine diagrams based on UCMods, 2) whether our transformation rules are semantically complete, 3) whether our transformation rules lead to state machine diagrams that are syntactically correct, and 4) whether the automatically generated state machine diagrams can be refined by test engineers to support MBT with a reasonable effort. Regarding point 3, syntactic correctness means that a generated state machine diagram conforms to the UML 2.2 state machines notations. Regarding point 2, semantic correctness means that a generated state machine diagram correctly represents its UCMod; all the constructs that are related to the transformation in the UCMod are correctly transformed by following the transformation rules and no redundant model elements are generated.

Regarding the first three evaluation points, two large-scale, network-based and distributed systems, respectively from the communication domain and the maritime and energy sectors are used to evaluate our approach. One is a Video Conference System (VCS) and the other is a Subsea Oil Production System (SOPS).

VCS contains four endpoints, which are of the same functionalities. These functionalities are modeled as the same set of use cases. Each endpoint has 10 use cases; in total the whole system contains 40 use cases. The core functionality of the system manages the sending and receiving of multimedia streams. Audio and video signals are sent through separate channels and there is also a possibility of transmitting presentations in parallel with audio and video. Presentations can be sent by only one conference participant at a time and all others receive it. Each of the VCS endpoint is operated by a human actor. A timer is needed to periodically initiate the adaption of call rate. Eight crosscutting concerns (e.g., *Standby*, *Do Not Disturb*, *Noise Cancellation*) were specified and transformed into aspect state machines using our approach.

SOPSs are large-scale, integrated, distributed, and highly configurable systems of systems for managing exploitation of oil and gas production fields, with various field layouts ranging from single satellite wells to large multiple sites (more than 50 wells).

SOPS has four different types of systems, three of which are located above the sea level and the other is located in subsea. These systems have distinct functionalities and are connected through different types of communication media. Due to the reason that we had no access to all the requirements of these systems, we were not able to specify the UCSs of all the systems. Only 12 out of 65 representative use cases were specified. We modeled the following six crosscutting concerns (e.g., Operation Mode Exchange, Runtime Configuration, Data Update Mechanism Switch) using RUCM and they are transformed into aspect state machines using our approach.

In total, 14 aspect state machines were generated and we carefully examined them, and we could verify that the generated state machines were syntactically correct and mostly but not entirely semantically complete. Due to space limitation and confidential issues, we are not able to provide more detailed information about these two industrial case studies.

5   Related Work

We conducted a systematic literature review [18] on transformations of textual requirements into analysis models, represented as class, sequence, state machine, and activity diagrams. A carefully designed paper selection procedure in scientific journals and conferences from 1996 to 2008 and Software Engineering textbooks identified 20 primary studies (16 approaches). The method proposed here is based on the results of this review, with a focus on automatically deriving state machine diagrams from UCMods.

A series of methods is proposed in [19] (one of the primary studies of our systematic review [18]) to precisely capture requirements and then manually transform requirements into a conceptual model composed of object models (e.g., class diagrams), dynamic models (i.e., state machines and sequence diagrams), and functional diagrams. The approach does not purport to provide a solution for transforming requirements into analysis models. Instead, it proposes a set of techniques for users to precisely specify requirements and conceptual models, and also proposes a process to guide the users in deriving the conceptual models from the requirements. No transformation method is reported in the paper.

Somé [20], another primary study of our systematic review, proposes an approach to generate finite state machines from use cases in restricted Natural Language (NL). The approach requires the existence of a domain model. The domain model serves two purposes: a lexicon for the NL analysis of use cases, and the structural basis of the state transition graphs being generated. The domain model acts as the lexicon for NL analysis of the use cases, because the model elements of the domain model are used to document the use cases. For example, actors of the use cases refer to the classes of the domain model. Interactions between the system and the actors are defined as one type of use case operations (also including branching statements, use case inclusion statements) which correspond to class operations in the domain model. An algorithm is described in the paper to explain how to automatically transform the use cases plus the domain model into state machines. A working example is used to explain the approach. No case study is presented to evaluate the approach.

In summary, none of the existing approaches is able to fully and automatically generate either standard UML state machine diagrams or aspect state machines from requirements, which is what we are proposing in the paper.

6 Conclusion

The success of Model-based testing (MBT) relies on developing complete and precise input models. Especially to support modeling system non-functional behavior such as robustness and security, which is typically crosscutting functional behavior and thus modeling such behavior directly with functional behavior is not scalable since it leads to redundant and cluttered models. To cope with this issue, usually Aspect-oriented Modeling (AOM) is recommended to model crosscutting behavior. In this paper, we focused on a UML 2.0 profile (AspectSM), which supports comprehensive aspect modeling for UML 2.0 state machines (aspect state machines) and enables automated non-functional testing. As with other Aspect-Oriented Modeling (AOM) approaches, AspectSM can potentially offer several benefits such as: enhanced modularization, easier evolution of models, increased reusability, reduced modeling effort, and improved readability [11-13]. Developing such aspect state machines from scratch is a challenging task, especially when testers are not acquainted with modeling. To assist the initial modeling required for MBT, we propose an approach to transform use case specifications into UML state machines and aspect state machines.

A precise and rigorous use case modeling approach (RUCM) was proposed in [4] and was used in this paper, as part of aToucan [2, 3, 9], to automatically generate UML and aspect state machines from use cases. We evaluated our approach on two industrial case studies and we assessed the quality of generated base and aspect state machines and found them largely consistent. Our industry partners benefited not only from the executable test cases, but also from the system specification expressed as UML and aspect state machines and precise requirements expressed with RUCM. All these activities took no more than few hours, including documenting the use case model and refining the generated base and aspect state machines.

References

1. Shafique, M., Labiche, Y.: A Systematic Review of Model Based Testing Tool Support. Carleton University. Technical Report SCE-10-04
2. Yue, T., Briand, L.C., Labiche, Y.: Automatically Deriving a UML Analysis Model from a Use Case Model. Simula Research Laboratory. Technical Report 2010-15 (2010)
3. Yue, T., Briand, L.C., Labiche, Y.: An Automated Approach to Transform Use Cases into Activity Diagrams. In: Kühne, T., Selic, B., Gervais, M.-P., Terrier, F. (eds.) ECMFA 2010. LNCS, vol. 6138, pp. 337–353. Springer, Heidelberg (2010)
4. Yue, T., Briand, L.C., Labiche, Y.: A Use Case Modeling Approach to Facilitate the Transition towards Analysis Models: Concepts and Empirical Evaluation. In: Schürr, A., Selic, B. (eds.) MODELS 2009. LNCS, vol. 5795, pp. 484–498. Springer, Heidelberg (2009)

5. Yue, T., Briand, L., Labiche, Y.: Facilitating the Transition from Use Case Models to Analysis Models: Approach and Experiments. Accepted for publication in Transactions on Software Engineering and Methodology, TOSEM (2011)
6. Eclipse Modeling Framework (EMF), http://www.eclipse.org/modeling/emf/
7. The Stanford Natural Language Processing Group. The Stanford Parser version 1.6
8. Triskell team, http://www.kermeta.org/
9. Yue, T., Ali, S., Briand, L.: Automated Transition from Use Cases to UML State Machines to Support State-Based Testing. In: France, R.B., Kuester, J.M., Bordbar, B., Paige, R.F. (eds.) ECMFA 2011. LNCS, vol. 6698, pp. 115–131. Springer, Heidelberg (2011)
10. Ali, S., Briand, L., Hemmati, H.: Modeling Robustness Behavior Using Aspect-Oriented Modeling to Support Robustness Testing of Industrial Systems. Accepted for publication in the Journal of Software and Systems Modeling (2011)
11. Ali, S., Yue, T., Briand, L.: Empirically Evaluating the Impact of Applying Aspect State Machines on Modeling Quality and Effort. Simula Research Laboratory. Technical Report 2011-06 (2011)
12. Ali, S., Yue, T., Briand, L.: Does Aspect-Oriented Modeling Help Improve the Readability of UML State Machines? Simula Research Laboratory. Technical Report 2010-11 (2011)
13. Ali, S., Yue, T.: Comprehensively Evaluating Conformance Error Rates of Applying Aspect State Machines for Robustness Testing. In: ACM International Conference on Aspect-Oriented Software Development (AOSD)
14. Ali, S., Hemmati, H., Holt, N.E., Arisholm, E., Briand, L.C.: Model Transformations as a Strategy to Automate Model-Based Testing - A Tool and Industrial Case Studies. Simula Research Laboratory. Technical Report (2010-01) (2010)
15. Cisco Norway (Tandberg), http://www.tandberg.no/
16. FMC Technologies, http://www.fmctechnologies.com/
17. OMG: OCL 2.0 Specification. Final Adopted Specification
18. Yue, T., Briand, L.C., Labiche, Y.: A systematic review of transformation approaches between user requirements and analysis models. Requirements Engineering 16 (2011)
19. Insfrán, E., Pastor, O., Wieringa, R.: Requirements Engineering-Based Conceptual Modelling. In: Requirements Engineering, pp. 61–72
20. Some, S.S.: An approach for the synthesis of state transition graphs from use cases, pp. 456–462. CSREA Press

Badger: A Regression Planner to Resolve Design Model Inconsistencies

Jorge Pinna Puissant[1], Ragnhild Van Der Straeten[2,3], and Tom Mens[1]

[1] University of Mons, 20 Place du Parc, Mons, Belgium
{jorge.pinnapuissant,tom.mens}@umons.ac.be
[2] Vrije Universiteit Brussel, Brussel, Belgium
rvdstrae@vub.ac.be
[3] Université Libre de Bruxelles, Brussel, Belgium

Abstract. One of the main challenges in model-driven software engineering is to deal with design model inconsistencies. Automated techniques to detect and resolve these inconsistencies are essential. We propose to use the artificial intelligence technique of automated planning for the purpose of resolving software model inconsistencies. We implemented a regression planner in Prolog and validated it on the resolution of different types of structural inconsistencies for generated models of varying sizes. We discuss the scalability results of the approach obtained through several stress-tests and discuss the limitations of our approach.

Keywords: automated planning, inconsistency resolution, model, scalability.

1 Introduction

One of the main challenges in *model-driven software engineering (MDE)* is to deal with evolving models, and to provide automated mechanisms to support this evolution [23]. A particular point of attention is to manage inconsistencies in software models [20]. Such model inconsistencies are inevitable, because a software system's description is composed of a wide variety of diverse models, some of which are developed and maintained in parallel. Our research does not focus on the activity of model inconsistency *detection*, that has become well-established. Instead, we address the *resolution* of model inconsistencies. In particular, we focus on more automated ways to resolve a selection of previously identified model inconsistencies through the generation of so-called *resolution plans*.

To do this, we use the technique of *automated planning* [19] originating from the field of artificial intelligence. This technique allows the generation of possible resolution plans through an automated planner without the need of manually writing resolution rules. In [18] we used the progression planner called *FF* [7,8]. Using this planner in the context of inconsistency resolution suffers from various scalability problems and lack of expressiveness, making the approach unusable in practice. To address the aforementioned limitations we present here a new planner called *Badger*[1], a *regression planner* implemented in Prolog.

---

[1] The name *Badger* comes from the *honey badger*, an animal that is able to run backwards.

This paper is structured as follows. Section 2 introduces the problem of model inconsistency resolution and presents a motivating example. Section 3 introduces automated planning. Section 4 explains the automated planner *Badger* that we implemented for resolving model inconsistencies. Its scalability to large models is assessed in Section 5. Section 6 discusses the threats to validity, Section 7 presents the related work and Section 8 concludes this paper.

2 Model Inconsistency Resolution

A wide variety of modeling languages, domain-independent as well as domain-specific, exists. As a consequence, there are many different kinds of, often interrelated, models that can suffer from many types of inconsistencies. In this paper the Unified Modeling Language (UML) is used to express design models because it is the de-facto general-purpose modeling language [17]. Its visual notation consists of a set of different diagram types, such as class diagrams, sequence diagrams and statecharts, each expressing certain aspects of a software system. These diagrams are interrelated and inconsistencies in and between them can arise easily.

In this article, we will restrict ourselves to the subset of the UML metamodel for class diagrams shown in Figure 1[2]. Table 1 lists a set of 13 structural model inconsistency types we will consider based on the elements occurring in this metamodel and on the well-formedness constraints of the UML 2.3 metamodel expressed in OCL [2, 6, 17, 22, 25]). Each entry in Table 1 consists of an id followed by the metamodel element on which the constraint is specified in the UML specification. Next, a short description of the inconsistency type is given, followed by the page number of the UML Superstructure document [17] where the inconsistency type can be found.

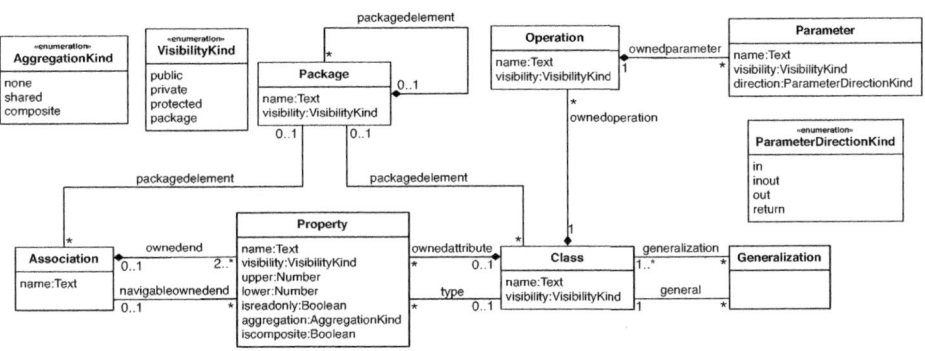

Fig. 1. Simplified fragment of the UML metamodel for class diagrams

---

[2] Because our approach relies on a metamodel independent representation, it can be used with other structural models as well.

Table 1. List of considered structural model inconsistency types

id	model element	description of the inconsistency type (see [17])
I_1	Association	Only binary associations can be aggregations (p. 39)
I_2	Element	Elements that must be owned must have an owner (p. 65)
I_3	Named Element	If a NamedElement is not owned by a Namespace, it does not have a visibility (p. 101)
I_4	Multiplicity Element	A multiplicity must define at least one valid cardinality that is greater than zero. (p. 97)
I_5	Multiplicity Element	The lower bound must be a non-negative integer literal (p. 97)
I_6	Multiplicity Element	The upper bound must be greater than or equal to the lower bound (p. 97)
I_7	Classifier	The general classifiers are the classifiers referenced by the generalization relationships (p. 54)
I_8	Classifier	Generalization hierarchies must be directed and acyclic. A classifier can not be both a transitively general and transitively specific classifier of the same classifier (p. 54)
I_9	Classifier	A classifier may only specialize classifiers of a valid type (p. 54)
I_{10}	Property	A multiplicity on an aggregate end of a composite aggregation must not have an upper bound greater than 1 (p. 127)
I_{11}	Property	Only a navigable property can be marked as readOnly (p. 128)
I_{12}	Property	The value of isComposite is true only if aggregation is composite (p. 128)
I_{13}	Operation	An operation can have at most one return parameter (p. 107)

Consider as a motivating example the simple class diagram shown in Figure 2. The diagram contains two structural inconsistency occurrences, one of type "I_{10}: Multiplicity composition constraint" and one of type "I_{13}: Operation return constraint" (see Table 1). The occurrence of I_{10} arises because the composite association (represented by a black diamond) between classes Car and Wheel has an upper multiplicity greater than 1 (namely 2) at the composite end, which is in contradiction with the fact that a part in the composition cannot be shared between multiple components. An occurrence of I_{13} occurs when an operation in a class returns more than one parameter. The operation getDiameter():float,integer of class Wheel has two return parameters.

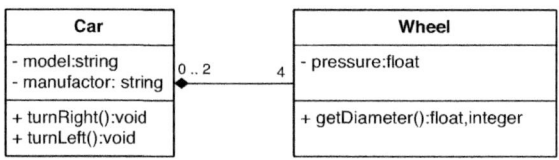

Fig. 2. Class diagram with 2 inconsistency occurrences

Each inconsistency occurrence can be resolved by several resolutions. For example, changing the upper multiplicity from 2 to 1 can resolve the occurrence of I_{10}, while replacing the composite association by a regular association resolves the inconsistency occurrence as well. The occurrence of I_{13} can be resolved by removing one of both return parameters or by changing one of the return parameters into an input parameter.

3   Automated Planning

Our aim is to tackle the problem of inconsistency resolution by generating possible resolutions without the need of manually writing resolution rules or writing any procedures that generate possible resolutions. The approach needs to enable the resolution of multiple inconsistency occurrences at once and to perform the resolution in a reasonable time. In addition, the approach needs to be generic, i.e., it needs to be easy to apply it to different modeling languages. In [24] we explored the usage of model finders for this purpose. In this article, we use *Automated Planning* instead.

Automated planning aims to generate plans, i.e., sequences of actions that lead from an initial state to a state meeting a specific predefined goal. Each planning approach consists of a *representation language* to describe the *problem domain*, a *problem*, an *algorithm* describing the mechanism to solve the problem, and a sequence of *generated plans* produced as output of the algorithm.

The *problem domain* (e.g., model inconsistency resolution) is expressed as a *set of possible actions* (e.g., to change a model). A *possible action* specifies a *valid* way to go from one state to another. The action is composed of a *precondition* that specifies the conditions that must hold in order for the action to be applicable, and an *effect* that specifies the changes to be made to the current state.

The *problem* that needs to be solved in the problem domain (e.g., an inconsistent model such as the one in Figure 2) is expressed by an *initial state* and a *desired goal*. The initial state represents the current state of the world (the inconsistent model). The desired goal is a partially specified state that describes the world that we would like to obtain (a consistent model).

A *generated plan* is a sequence of actions, generated automatically by the planning algorithm, to transform the initial state into a state that satisfies the desired goal.

Many *algorithms* exist to solve planning problems. A first approach consists in translating the problem and its domain into a satisfiability problem, and using a model checker or SAT solver to find a solution [9]. A second way consists in using a state space search algorithm. The state space can be traversed through *progression* planning or *regression* planning. Progression planning performs a forward search that starts in the initial state and tries to find a sequence of actions that reaches a goal state. Regression planning starts from the goal state and searches backwards to find a sequence of actions that reaches the initial state.

4   Badger

We have chosen to implement a regression planner, because it depends on the size of the desired goal and works only with relevant actions. A relevant action is an action that contributes to the achievement of the goal. The search space of a regression planner will be significantly smaller than the one of a progression planner, as the latter depends mainly on the size of the initial state and does not exclude irrelevant actions.

We implemented the planner algorithm in Prolog, since Prolog's built-in backtracking mechanism allows the planner to easily generate multiple resolution plans among which the user can choose the most suitable one.

4.1 Problem and Problem Domain

The **initial state** is expressed as a conjunction of logic literals that represents the input model. We specify the models using Praxis [2], a language that represents models and model changes as sequences of elementary model operations (`create`, `addProperty`, `addReference`, `delNode`, `remProperty`, `remReference`). Praxis comes with a suite of Eclipse plugins: a plugin to reason about ECore and XMI models; a plugin to generate class diagram models of varying sizes [15]; and a model inconsistency detection engine [2]. As an example, the class *Car* of the class diagram model of Figure 2 is represented as follows[3]:

```
create(c1, class).
addProperty(c1, name, 'Car').
create(att1, property).
addProperty(att1, name,'model').
addReference(att1, type,string).
addReference(c1, ownedattribute, att1).
create(att2, property).
addProperty(att2, name,'manufactor').
addReference(att2, type,string).
addReference(c1, ownedattribute, att2).
create(op1, operation).
addProperty(op1, name,'turnRight').
addReference(c1, ownedoperation,op1).
create(op2, operation).
addProperty(op2, name,'turnLeft').
addReference(c1, ownedoperation,op2).
```

This way of representing models offers several advantages. The elementary model operations are metamodel independent, i.e., they can be used together with any kind of structural metamodel. The second parameter of each model operation refers to an element of the metamodel (e.g., `class`, `ownedattribute`, `parameter`, `ownedoperation`).

The **desired goal** is a partially specified state that represents the objective to be reached, namely the absence of model inconsistencies, as a negation of inconsistency occurrences. An inconsistency occurrence is detected if it matches the pattern defined by the inconsistency type. Table 2 presents all logic operators that are allowed to specify the desired goal, inspired by the list of common constructs found in inconsistency types [5, 16, 21]. Our approach does the strict

---
[3] In principle, each of the listed model operations should also have a timestamp that we have left out for the sake of readability.

minimum to accomplish this goal. For example, if the user wants to solve the inconsistency "the lower multiplicity must be greater than 0", *Badger* will proposes 1 as solution to avoid an infinite number of possibilities.

Table 2. Logic Operators. Although the operators value comparison, property comparison and counting are only shown with the > function, the other comparison functions can be used as well : $<, \geq, \leq, =, \neq$

Name		
Negative literal	Syntax	not(P)
	Semantics	$\neg P$
	Example	not(lastAddProperty(ae2,iscomposite,'true'))
Conjunction	Syntax	[P, Q]
	Semantics	$P \wedge Q$
	Example	[lastAddProperty(c1,name,'Vehicle'), lastAddProperty(c2,name,'Aircraft')]
Disjunction	Syntax	or [P, Q]
	Semantics	$P \vee Q$
	Example	or [lastAddProperty(c1,name,'Vehicle'), lastAddProperty(c1,name,'Aircraft')]
Universal quantification	Syntax	forall(P,Q)
	Semantics	$\forall x (P(x) \Rightarrow Q(x))$
	Example	forall(lastCreate(X,class), lastAddProperty(X,name,Y))
Existential quantification	Syntax	exists(P)
	Semantics	$\exists x P(x)$
	Example	exists(lastCreate(X,class))
Value comparison	Syntax	compare(P,>,v)
	Semantics	$\forall n \in \mathbb{N}(P(n) \wedge v \in \mathbb{N} \wedge n > v)$
	Example	compare(lastAddProperty(ae1,lower_mult,X),>,0)
Property Comparison	Syntax	compare(P,>,Q)
	Semantics	$\forall n, m (P(n) \wedge Q(m) \wedge n > m)$
	Example	compare(lastAddProperty(ae1,upper_mult,X),>, lastAddProperty(ae1,lower_mult,Y))
Counting	Syntax	count(P,>,v)
	Semantics	$(|\{x|P(x)\}| > v \wedge v \in \mathbb{N})$
	Example	count(lastAddReference(assID,member,X),>,2)
Transitive Navigability	Syntax	nav(From, Kind, To)
	Semantics	$(Kind(From, To) \Rightarrow nav(From, Kind, To)) \vee$ $\exists c (nav(From, Kind, c) \wedge nav(c, Kind, To) \Rightarrow nav(From, Kind, To))$
	Example	nav(c1,generalization,c9)

As an example, the desired goal to resolve an inconsistency occurrence of type I_{10} is specified below as a negation of this inconsistency occurrence, using the logic operators of Table 2. It disallows the upper bound of the multiplicity on the aggregate end of a composite aggregation to be greater than 1.

```
or [not(lastAddProperty(prop1,aggregation,'composite')),
    not(compare(lastAddProperty(prop1,upper,X),>,1))]
```

The use of prefix `last` in model operation `lastAddProperty` is needed to point to those operations in the model that are not followed by other operations canceling their effects [2]. Using the negation of the inconsistency occurrences in the desired goal will only be able to resolve inconsistency occurrences that have already been identified previously. For this detection, we can rely on the detection approach proposed by [2].

A **possible action** specifies a *valid* way to go from one state to another. The action is composed of a *precondition* (pre) that specifies the conditions that must hold in order for the action to be applicable, and an *effect* (eff) that specifies which Praxis model operations will be added to the current state. The validity of an action (can) is verified by using a *metamodel* that imposes constraints on the model. The metamodel needed to validate the set of actions is specified as a set of logic facts in Prolog: fact mme represents the metamodel elements; mme_property represents the properties of the specified metamodel element and the kind of value that is used (*e.g.*, text, boolean, int); mme_reference represents the relationships between two metamodel elements, and the name that this relationship has. The metamodel used in this paper corresponds to the one shown in Figure 1.

The logic rules below specify the possible action setProperty. The pre rule states that the old property must exist before it can be changed. The can rule is used to verify that the new value is correctly typed and that is different from the old value. The eff rule expresses the two model operations changing the value of a property.

```
pre(setProperty(Id,MME,Property,OldValue,NewValue),
    [lastAddProperty(Id,Property,OldValue)]).

can(setProperty(Id,MME,Property,OldValue,NewValue)) :-
    mme_property(MME,Property,Type),
    call(Type,NewValue),
    NewValue \== OldValue.

eff(setProperty(Id,Property,OldValue,NewValue),
    [remProperty(Id,Property,OldValue),
     addProperty(Id,Property,NewValue)]).
```

4.2 The Algorithm

The *algorithm* used by *Badger* is based on the ones explained in [3]. *Badger* uses a *recursive best-first search (RBFS)* to recursively generate a state space and search for a solution in that state space. *RBFS* is a *best-first search* that explores the state space by expanding the most promising node. To do this the algorithm needs 3 functions: a *successor function*, an *evaluation function* and a *solution function*. The *successor function* generates the child nodes of a particular node, and is used to generate the state space. It strongly depends on the problem to be solved. The *evaluation function* f evaluates the child nodes to find the most promising one. It is defined as the sum of a *heuristic function* h and a *cost function* g: $f(n) = h(n) + g(n)$ where $h(n)$ is the minimal estimation of the cost to reach a solution from the node n, and $g(n)$ is the actual cost of the path to reach n. The *solution function* checks if a particular node is one of the solutions. These 3 functions are independent of the search algorithm, which means that we can also use other best-first search algorithms (e.g. A*, iterative-deepening A*, memory-bounded A*). We have chosen to use *RBFS* because it only keeps the current search path and the sibling nodes along this path, making its space complexity linear in the depth of the search tree.

The *heuristic function* used by *Badger* is a known planner heuristic that *ignores the preconditions*. Every action becomes applicable in every state, and a single literal of the desired goal can be achieved in one step. Remember that the desired goal is a conjunction/disjunction of logic literals that represents one or more negations of inconsistency occurrences. This implies that the heuristic can be defined as the number of unsatisfied literals in the desired goal. The cost function used by *Badger* is the user-specified cost of applying each action. These costs affect the order in which the plans are generated. The user can, for example, give more importance to actions that add and modify model elements than to actions that delete model elements.

The *solution function* used by *Badger* checks if there are no more unsatisfied literals in the desired goal.

The *successor function* is the most complex one and is at the heart of the planning algorithm and proceeds as follows: (i) select a logic operator from the desired goal and generate a literal that satisfies this operator; (ii) analyse the effect (the `eff` rule) of each action to find one that achieves this literal; (iii) validate (the `can` rule) if the selected action can be executed; (iv) protect the already satisfied literals by checking if the execution of the selected action does not undo a previously satisfied literal; (v) regress goals through actions by adding the preconditions of the action (the `pre` rule) as new literals in the goal and by removing the satisfied literals from the goal.

4.3 Generated Plans

The *generated plans* produce a sequence of actions that transform the initial, inconsistent model into a model that does not have any of the inconsistency occurrences specified in the desired goal. Moreover, the generated resolution plans do not lead to ill-formed models (that do not conform to their metamodel) as long as all metamodel constraints are given as part of the problem specification.

Two complete resolution plans, each containing only two actions, that solve the inconsistency occurrences of the motivating example are given below:

```
1. setProperty(pro1,upper,2,1)
2. setProperty(par1,direction,'return','in')
```

```
1. setProperty(pro1,aggregation,'composite','none')
2. delNode(par1, parameter)
```

If we unfold the *effects* of each action from a resolution plan, we obtain a sequence of elementary Praxis model operations, that can be applied directly to transform the inconsistent model into a consistent one. For the first plan above, this sequence of operations looks as follows:

```
1. remProperty(pro1,upper,2)
2. addProperty(pro1,upper,1)
```

3. remProperty(par1,direction,'return')
4. addProperty(par1,direction,'in')

The number of actions proposed to resolve an inconsistency occurrence involving the modification of a reference in the desired goal depends on the size of the initial state (*i.e.*, it depends on the number of model elements). This negatively affects the performance of the algorithm and the number of generated resolution plans. To avoid generating many resolution plans that each refer to a concrete model element (e.g., one of the many classes in a class diagram), we introduced the notion of *temporal elements* as an abstraction of such a set of concrete model elements. A temporal element is represented as a tuple (+other,X,Y) where X is the model element type (e.g. class) and Y is the set of model elements of this type that cannot be used as part of the proposed resolution. Once the resolution plan is generated, the user can replace the temporal element by a concrete element that does not belong to Y, to avoid re-introducing the same inconsistency occurrence.

In order to assess whether *Badger* generates meaningful resolution plans, we manually verified all plans (between 3 and 10) generated for 5 very small class diagram models. The plans corresponded to what we expected, though we did not always agree with the order in which the plans were generated. By modifying the *cost function* $g(n)$, however, we can easily adapt the order according to the user's preferences. As will be discussed in section 6, carrying out a controlled user study with *Badger* to determine the most suitable order of the generated resolution plans is left as future work. In the next section, we report on the scalability of *Badger* for resolving structural model inconsistencies.

5 Scalability Study

Due to the unavailability of a sufficiently large sample of realistic UML models, we make use of an existing model generator that was proposed, mathematically grounded and validated in [15]. This model generator enables us to study the impact of the size of the models on the approach. It also enables us to apply our approach to a large set of models with a wide range of different sizes.

We used the model generator to create 941 models with model sizes ranging from 21 to 10849 model elements (i.e., elements obtained using the Praxis elementary operation create). Obviously, the generated models also contain references (from 21 to 11504) and properties (from 40 to 22903), obtained using the elementary operations addProperty and addReference, respectively.

These experiments were carried on a 64-bit computer with 2.53GHz Intel Core 2 Duo processor and 4Gb RAM. We used the 64-bit version of SWI-Prolog 6.0.2, running on the Ubuntu 11.04 operating system. All timing results obtained were averaged over 10 different runs to account for performance variations.

5.1 Experimental Results

In a first experiment, we have run *Badger* on all generated models and computed the timing results for generating a single resolution plan. We analysed the relation between the number of model elements and the time (in seconds) needed to resolve only one inconsistency occurrence of a particular type. In order to compare the timing results for different inconsistency types, we repeated the experiment for each of the 13 considered inconsistency types shown in Table 1.

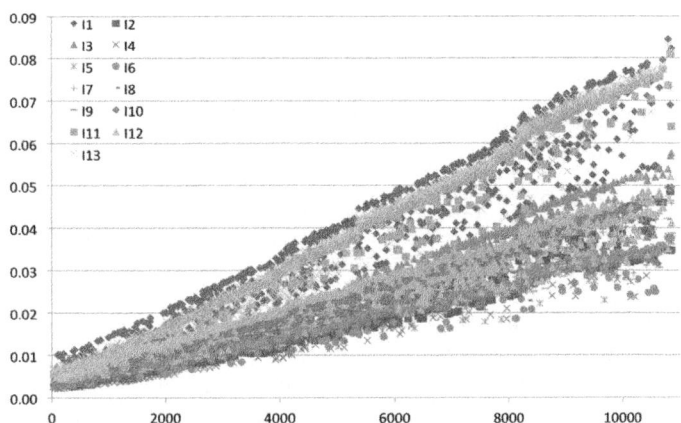

Fig. 3. Comparison of execution time (y-axis, expressed in seconds) per model size (x-axis, expressed as number of model elements) for resolving a single inconsistency occurrence in 941 different models. Different colours and symbols represent different inconsistency types.

The results of the experiment are visualised in Figure 3. The time needed to resolve occurrences of a particular inconsistency type mainly depends on the size of the model and on the number of logic literals in the desired goal. For example, I_{13} requires 4 literals and takes on average 4.2 times longer than I_5 that only uses 1 literal.

We fitted four different types of parametric regression models with 2 parameters to the data: a linear model, a logarithmic model, a power model and an exponential model. The goodness of fit of each type of model was verified using the coefficient of determination R^2. Its value is always between 0 and 1, and a value close to 1 corresponds to a good fit. Table 3 shows the obtained R^2 values. In order to easily distinguish the best regression models, values higher than 0.90 are indicated in *italics*, while values higher than 0.95 are indicated in **boldface**. In addition, per inconsistency type the regression models with the highest R^2 value are marked with (*).

By analysing Table 3 we observe that the logarithmic regression models provide the worst results. In contrast to the three other considered types of regression models, its R^2 values are always lower than 0.8. For these reasons, we exclude this type of regression model from the remainder of the analysis of our results. Based on the R^2 values the linear models appear to be the best in all cases (with an $R^2 > 0.95$ in 10 out of 13 cases). A visual interpretation also confirms that the linear models are the best match. The exponential and power models are also very good fits, with R^2 values that are always close to or above 0.9.

Table 3. R^2 values of four different parametric regression models used to fit the timing results

	Linear $y = a + b\ x$	Log $y = a + b\ \ln(x)$	Power $y = a\ x^b$	Exponential $y = a\ e^{b\ x}$
I_1	0.935 (*)	0.741	0.891	0.892
I_2	0.930 (*)	0.668	0.872	0.927
I_3	**0.950** (*)	0.687	0.888	0.910
I_4	**0.981** (*)	0.789	0.934	0.902
I_5	**0.987** (*)	0.767	0.933	0.923
I_6	**0.975** (*)	0.764	0.918	0.926
I_7	**0.975** (*)	0.737	0.898	0.943
I_8	**0.965** (*)	0.686	0.843	0.935
I_9	**0.975** (*)	0.736	0.894	0.941
I_{10}	**0.975** (*)	0.778	0.936	0.907
I_{11}	**0.981** (*)	0.752	0.929	0.908
I_{12}	0.942 (*)	0.754	0.906	0.905
I_{13}	**0.977** (*)	0.718	0.888	0.923

In a second experiment, we studied how the generation of resolution plans with *Badger* scales up when resolving multiple inconsistencies *of different types* together. For each considered model, we resolved together one occurrence of each of the 13 inconsistency types. Because not all models have at least one occurrence of inconsistency type I_8, during our analysis we distinguished between models containing 12 inconsistency occurrences (excluding I_8) and models containing 13 occurrences.

Figure 4 (top part) presents the results of this experiment. The resolution time only increases slightly as the model size increases. None of the fitted regression models provide an R^2 value higher than 0.25. The execution time is lower for 12 inconsistency occurrences (mean = 0.268, median = 0.265) than for 13 occurrences (mean = 0.341, median = 0.336). Another factor that determines the execution time is the number of actions in the resolution plan. For resolving 12 inconsistency occurrences, we require between 8 and 11 actions (median =10), while for 13 occurrences we need between 9 and 12 actions (median = 11). In addition, the resolution time increases as the number of actions increases, as shown in the box plots of Figure 4 (bottom part).

In a third experiment, we studied how the generation of a resolution plan with *Badger* scales up if we want to resolve multiple inconsistency occurrences *of the same type* together. To test this, we generated a very large model containing more than 10,000 elements and a large number of inconsistency occurrences of each type. We excluded inconsistency type I_8 because the generated model did not contain enough occurrences of this type. For each of the remaining 12 inconsistency types we computed the time required to resolve an increasing number of occurrences (ranging from a single one to 70). Figure 5 visualizes the results. Given the rapid increase of execution time as the number of inconsistency occurrences increases, we fitted quadratic models (second degree polynomial), power models and exponential models to the data. The *adjusted* R^2 (to account for a different number of parameters in the regression models) was very high for the 3 types of models. The quadratic models had the best fit, with an *adjusted* $R^2 > 0.95$ in all cases, followed by the exponential models (> 0.92 in all cases,

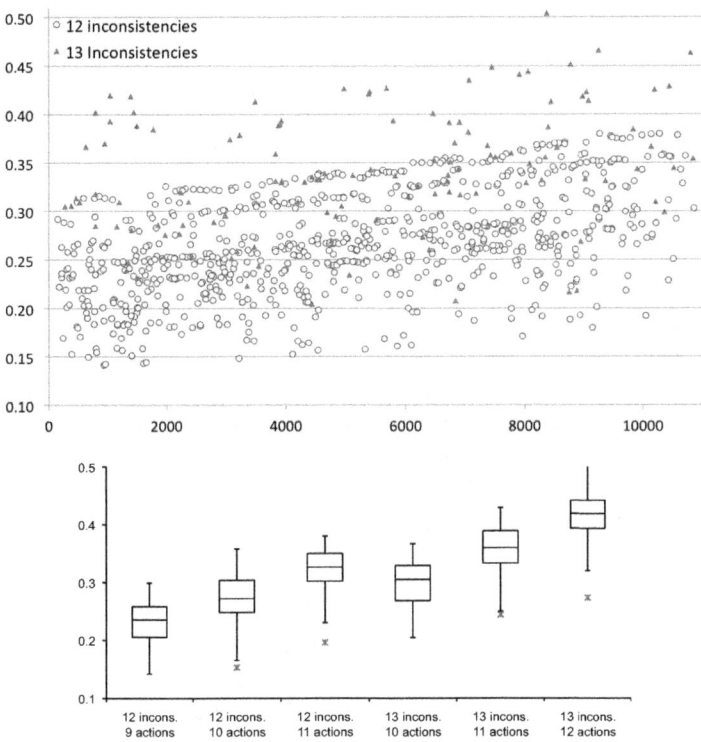

Fig. 4. Top: Time comparison (y-axis, in seconds) per model size (x-axis, in number of model elements) for resolving multiple inconsistencies of different types in 941 different models. **Bottom:** Boxplots showing effect of number of actions on execution time.

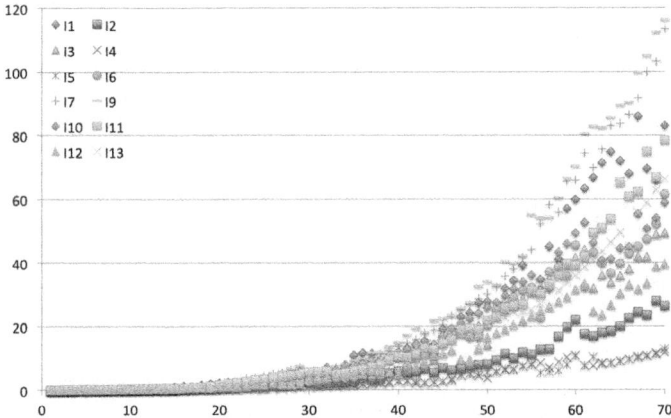

Fig. 5. Execution time (y-axis, in seconds) per number of inconsistency occurrences of the same type (x-axis) for resolving multiple inconsistency occurrences in a very large model. Different colours and symbols represents different inconsistency types.

and > 0.95 in 5 out of 12 cases). The different growth rates observed in Figure 5 reflect the complexity of the inconsistency type to be resolved. For example, the inconsistency types whose resolution only requires the change of property values take less time than those that need changes to references between model elements, because of the additional multiplicity constraints required for the latter.

6 Threats to Validity

Our approach has only been stress-tested on class diagram models. However, the fact that we rely on a metamodel independent representation (using sequences of Praxis elementary model operations) makes it straightforward to apply it to other types of structural models as well. We considered only a limited set of inconsistency types, but tried to include a variety of different expressions and elementary model operations. It remains an open question whether and how the approach can be generalised to non-structural inconsistencies and models.

The regression planner we implemented for doing our experiments may still contain some bugs we are not aware of. To carry out our experiments, we relied on an external model generator [15]. This may cause a bias as the generated models may not look like "real" models. This bias is limited since the model generator relies on the Boltzmann random sampling method that generates, in a scalable way, uniform samplings of any given size.

Our planner generates all possible resolution plans one after another, thanks to Prolog's backtracking mechanism. In this article we only evaluated the scalability for generating a single plan on a wide variety of models containing a wide range of different inconsistencies. In order to make the approach useful in practice, the resolution that the user actually prefers should be one of the first generated resolution plans. The order in which resolution plans are generated can be modified easily by modifying the cost function of the planner algorithm, as explained in section 4. In addition, entire resolution plans can be omitted by attaching an infinite weight to certain actions. Assessing what would be the most suitable parameters for the cost function in practice requires a controlled user study, which is left as future work.

7 Related Work

Several approaches have been proposed to resolve model inconsistencies. In our previous work [14] we specified resolution rules manually, which is an error-prone process. Automatic generation of inconsistency resolution actions aims to resolve this problem. Nentwich *et al.* [16] achieve this by generating resolution actions automatically from the inconsistency types. The execution of these actions, however, only resolves one inconsistency occurrence at a time. As recognised by the authors, this causes problems when inconsistency occurrences and their resolutions are interdependent. Mens *et al.* [13] propose a formal approach based on graph transformation to analyse these interdependencies.

Xiong et al. [25] define a language to specify inconsistency rules and the possibilities to resolve the inconsistencies. This requires inconsistency rules to be annotated with resolution information. Almeida da Silva et al. [1] propose an approach to generate resolution plans for inconsistent models, by extending inconsistency detection rules with information about the causes of the inconsistency, and by using manually written functions that generate resolution actions. In both approaches inconsistency detection rules are polluted with resolution information.

Instead of explicitly defining or generating resolution rules, a set of models satisfying a set of consistency rules can be generated and presented to the user. Egyed et al. [6] define such an approach for resolving inconsistency occurrences in UML models. Given an inconsistency occurrence and using choice generation functions, their approach generates possible resolution choices, i.e., possible consistent models. The choice generation functions depend on the modeling language, i.e., they take into account the syntax of the modeling language, but they only consider the impact of one consistency rule at a time. Furthermore these choice generation functions need to be implemented manually.

In [24] we use *Kodkod*, a SAT-based constraint solver using relational logic, for automatically generating consistent models. While the approach guarantees correctness and completeness (within the considered lower and upper bounds of the relations defined in the problem), a major limitation is its poor performance and lack of scalability.

Küster and Ryndina [11] introduce the concept of side-effect expressions to determine whether or not a resolution introduces a new inconsistency occurrence. They attach a cost to each inconsistency type to compare alternative resolutions for the same inconsistencies. Other authors also use the automatic resolution to solve different kinds of software engineering problems. For example, Jose et al. [10] present an algorithm based on a reduction to the maximal satisfiability problem, to automatically locate a set of potential cause of error in C programs. Demsky and Rinard [4] present an approach to automatically detect and resolve errors in data structures. Mani et al. [12] collect runtime information for the failing transformation in a model transformation program, and compute repair actions for the input model.

8 Conclusion

In this article we used automated planning, a logic-based approach originating from artificial intelligence, for the purpose of model inconsistency resolution. We are not aware of any other work having used this technique for this purpose.

We implemented a regression planner in Prolog. It requires as input a model and a set of inconsistency occurrences. In contrast to other inconsistency resolution approaches, the planner does not require the user to specify resolution rules manually or to specify information about the causes of the inconsistency. To specify models in a metamodel-independent way, and to be able to reuse an existing model generator, we relied on the Praxis language [2].

We have stress-tested our approach on 941 automatically generated UML class diagram models of varying sizes using a set of 13 structural inconsistency types based on OCL constraints found in the UML metamodel specification. Our approach for resolving inconsistency occurrences appears to be linear in the size of the model, and scales up to models containing more than 10000 model elements. The execution time also increases as the number of actions in the resolution plan increases. With respect to the number of inconsistency occurrences, the approach is quadratic in time. However, controlled user studies are still needed to adapt the cost function and evaluate the preferred order of the generated resolution plans.

Acknowledgments. This work has been partially supported by (i) the F.R.S. - FNRS through FRFC project 2.4515.09 "Research Center on Software Adaptability"; (ii) research project AUWB-08/12-UMH "Model-Driven Software Evolution", an *Action de Recherche Concertée* financed by the *Ministère de la Communauté française - Direction générale de l'Enseignement non obligatoire et de la Recherche scientifique, Belgium*; (iii) the Interuniversity Attraction Poles Programme – Belgian State – Belgian Science Policy.

References

1. Almeida da Silva, M.A., Mougenot, A., Blanc, X., Bendraou, R.: Towards Automated Inconsistency Handling in Design Models. In: Pernici, B. (ed.) CAiSE 2010. LNCS, vol. 6051, pp. 348–362. Springer, Heidelberg (2010)
2. Blanc, X., Mougenot, A., Mounier, I., Mens, T.: Detecting model inconsistency through operation-based model construction. In: Proc. Int'l Conf. Software Engineering, vol. 1, pp. 511–520 (2008)
3. Bratko, I.: Prolog programming for artificial intelligence. Addison-Wesley (2001)
4. Demsky, B., Rinard, M.C.: Automatic detection and repair of errors in data structures. In: Int'l Conf. on Object Oriented Programming, Systems, Languages and Applications, pp. 78–95. ACM (2003)
5. Egyed, A.: Automatically detecting and tracking inconsistencies in software design models. IEEE Trans. Software Eng. 37(2), 188–204 (2011)
6. Egyed, A., Letier, E., Finkelstein, A.: Generating and evaluating choices for fixing inconsistencies in UML design models. In: Proc. Int'l Conf. Automated Software Engineering, pp. 99–108. IEEE (2008)
7. Hoffmann, J.: FF: The Fast-Forward Planning System. The AI Magazine (2001)
8. Hoffmann, J., Nebel, B.: The FF Planning System: Fast plan generation through heuristic search. Journal of Artificial Intelligence Research 14, 253–302 (2001)
9. Jiménez Celorrio, S.: Planning and Learning under Uncertainty. PhD thesis, Universidad Carlos III de Madrid (2010)
10. Jose, M., Majumdar, R.: Cause clue clauses: error localization using maximum satisfiability. In: Proc. Conf. on Programming Language Design and Implementation, pp. 437–446. ACM (2011)
11. Küster, J.M., Ryndina, K.: Improving Inconsistency Resolution with Side-Effect Evaluation and Costs. In: Engels, G., Opdyke, B., Schmidt, D.C., Weil, F. (eds.) MODELS 2007. LNCS, vol. 4735, pp. 136–150. Springer, Heidelberg (2007)

12. Mani, S., Sinha, V.S., Dhoolia, P., Sinha, S.: Automated support for repairing input-model faults. In: Int'l Conf. on Automated Software Engineering, pp. 195–204. ACM (2010)
13. Mens, T., Van Der Straeten, R.: Incremental Resolution of Model Inconsistencies. In: Fiadeiro, J.L., Schobbens, P.-Y. (eds.) WADT 2006. LNCS, vol. 4409, pp. 111–126. Springer, Heidelberg (2007), doi:10.1007/978-3-540-71998-4_7
14. Mens, T., Van Der Straeten, R., D'Hondt, M.: Detecting and Resolving Model Inconsistencies Using Transformation Dependency Analysis. In: Wang, J., Whittle, J., Harel, D., Reggio, G. (eds.) MoDELS 2006. LNCS, vol. 4199, pp. 200–214. Springer, Heidelberg (2006)
15. Mougenot, A., Darrasse, A., Blanc, X., Soria, M.: Uniform Random Generation of Huge Metamodel Instances. In: Paige, R.F., Hartman, A., Rensink, A. (eds.) ECMDA-FA 2009. LNCS, vol. 5562, pp. 130–145. Springer, Heidelberg (2009)
16. Nentwich, C., Emmerich, W., Finkelstein, A.: Consistency management with repair actions. In: Proc. 25th Int'l Conf. Software Engineering, pp. 455–464. IEEE Computer Society (May 2003)
17. Object Management Group. Unified Modeling Language: Superstructure version 2.3. formal/2010-05-05 (May 2010)
18. Pinna Puissant, J., Mens, T., Van Der Straeten, R.: Resolving model inconsistencies with automated planning. In: 3rd Workshop on Living with Inconsistencies in Software Development. CEUR Workshop Proceeding (September 2010)
19. Russell, S., Norvig, P.: Artificial Intelligence: A Modern Approach, 3rd edn. Prentice-Hall (2010)
20. Spanoudakis, G., Zisman, A.: Inconsistency management in software engineering: Survey and open research issues. In: Handbook of Software Engineering and Knowledge Engineering, pp. 329–380. World Scientific (2001)
21. Van Der Straeten, R.: Inconsistency management in model-driven engineering: an approach using description logics. PhD thesis, Vrije Universiteit Brussel (2005)
22. Van Der Straeten, R., Mens, T., Simmonds, J., Jonckers, V.: Using Description Logic to Maintain Consistency between UML Models. In: Stevens, P., Whittle, J., Booch, G. (eds.) UML 2003. LNCS, vol. 2863, pp. 326–340. Springer, Heidelberg (2003)
23. Van Der Straeten, R., Mens, T., Van Baelen, S.: Challenges in Model-Driven Software Engineering. In: Chaudron, M.R.V. (ed.) MODELS 2008. LNCS, vol. 5421, pp. 35–47. Springer, Heidelberg (2009)
24. Van Der Straeten, R., Pinna Puissant, J., Mens, T.: Assessing the Kodkod Model Finder for Resolving Model Inconsistencies. In: France, R.B., Kuester, J.M., Bordbar, B., Paige, R.F. (eds.) ECMFA 2011. LNCS, vol. 6698, pp. 69–84. Springer, Heidelberg (2011)
25. Xiong, Y., Hu, Z., Zhao, H., Song, H., Takeichi, M., Mei, H.: Supporting automatic model inconsistency fixing. In: Proc. ESEC/FSE 2009, pp. 315–324. ACM (2009)

//
Aspect-Oriented Modeling of Mutual Exclusion in UML State Machines

Gefei Zhang*

arvato systems Technologies GmbH
gefeizhang@acm.org

Abstract. Mutual exclusion is a very common requirement in parallel systems. Yet its modeling is a tedious task in UML state machines, one of the most popular languages for behavior modeling. We present HiLA, an aspect-oriented extension of UML state machines, to address this problem. In HiLA, mutual exclusion can be modeled in a highly modular and declarative way. That is, the logic of mutual exclusion is modeled at a dedicated place rather than by model elements scattered all over the state machine, and the modeler only needs to specify which states to mutually exclude rather than how to exclude them.

1 Introduction

UML state machines [9] are widely used for modeling software behavior. They are considered as simple and intuitive, and even deemed to be "the most popular modeling language for reactive components" [3]. Actually, UML state machines also exhibit some modularity problems. In particular, modeling synchronization of parallel regions, e.g. mutual exclusion of states, is often a tedious task using plain UML. The synchronization logic has to be specified imperatively, the involved model elements are often scattered all over the model, thus the resulting state machine is hard to read and prone to error, for an example see [13]. Due to the popularity of UML state machines as well as the importance of parallelism and synchronization, it is desirable to enhance UML state machines by language constructs which allow mutual exclusion to be modeled in a modularized and intelligible way.

Given the cross-region nature of parallelism, Aspect-Oriented Modeling is a promising paradigm for modeling region synchronization in UML state machines. The language of High-Level Aspects (HiLA, [11]) is an aspect-oriented UML extension, which improves the modularity of state machines considerably. Compared with other approaches of aspect-oriented state machines, such as [1,2,7,8], the distinguishing feature of HiLA is that HiLA aspects are *semantic*. That is, HiLA aspects are defined as modification of the *behavior* of the base machine rather than its (abstract) *syntax*. This way, the modeler only needs to specify *what* to do instead of *how* to do it.

---

* Sponsored by Ludwig-Maximilians-Universität München and the EU project ASCENS, 257414.

The semantic approach of HiLA is also valuable for modeling region synchronization. In previous work [11,13], we showed how HiLA supports highly modular modeling of *passive waiting*, i.e., the region about to enter a critical state passively waiting for the "blocking" state (in another region) to be left *ordinarily*, as designed in the base machine. In this paper, we extend HiLA to cover another kind of mutual exclusion, which we call *active commanding*, where the blocking state is deactivated immediately, so that the waiting region can enter its critical state at once. Both strategies have realistic use cases, see e.g. [13,14] In both cases, using HiLA reduces the complexity of mutual-exclusion modeling considerably.

The rest of this paper is organized as follows: in the following Sect. 2 we give an overview of syntax and semantics of UML state machines, and show why the support for mutual-exclusion modeling provided by plain UML is insufficient. A brief overview of HiLA is given in Sect. 3.1, before in Sect. 3.2 the HiLA solution of modeling mutual exclusion is presented. Our implementation of HiLA aspects (weaving) is outlined in Sect. 4. Finally, we discuss some related work and draw conclusions.

2 UML State Machines

A UML state machine provides a model for the behavior of an object or component. Figure 1 shows a state machine modeling (in a highly simplified manner) the behavior of a player during a part of a game.[1] The player—a magician—starts in a state where she has to chose a NewLevel. Upon completion of the preparations she is transferred into the Play state which contains two concurrent regions, modeling two different *concerns* of the magician's intelligence. The upper region describes her possible movements: in each level the player initially starts in an entrance hall (Hall), from there she can move to a room in which magic crystals are stored (CrystalRoom) and on to a room containing a Ladder. From this room the player can either move back to the hall or, after fighting with some computer figure and winning, exit the level.

The lower region specifies the magician's possible behaviors. She may be Idle, gathering power for the next fight, Spelling a hex, or Fighting. She may escape from the fight and try to spell another hex, or, if she wins the fight in the Ladder room, wins the level and move on to another level. Any time while Playing, she can leave the game and quit.

2.1 Syntax and Informal Semantics

We briefly review the syntax and semantics of UML state machines according to the UML specification [9] by means of Fig. 1. A UML state machine consists of *regions* which contain *vertices* and *transitions* between vertices. A vertex is either a *state*, which may show hierarchically contained regions; or a *pseudo state* regulating how transitions are compound in execution. Transitions are triggered by

---
[1] This example is inspired by [15].

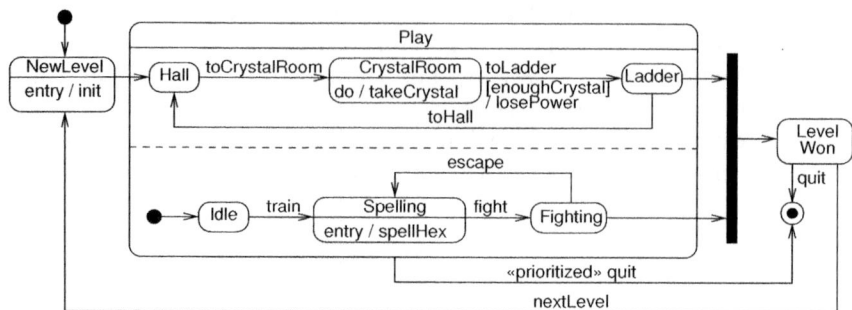

Fig. 1. Example: UML state machine

events and describe, by leaving and entering states, the possible state changes of the state machine. The events are drawn from an *event pool* associated with the state machine, which receives events from its own or from different state machines.

A state is *simple*, if it contains no regions (such as NewLevel in Fig. 1); a state is *composite*, if it contains at least one region; a composite state is said to be *orthogonal* if it contains more than one region, visually separated by dashed lines (such as Play). A region may also contain state and other vertices. A state, if not on the top-level itself, must be contained in exactly one region. A composite state and all the states directly or recursively contained in it thus build a tree.

Each state may[2] show an *entry* behavior (like spellHex in Spelling) and an *exit* behavior (not shown here), which are executed on activating and deactivating the state, respectively; a state may also show a *do activity* (like in CrystalRoom), which is executed while the state machine sojourns in this state. Transitions are triggered by events (toCrystalRoom, fight), show guards (enoughCrystal), and specify effects to be executed when a transition is fired (losePower). Completion transitions (e.g., the transition leaving NewLevel) are triggered by an implicit *completion event* emitted when a state completes all its internal activities. Events may be *deferred* (not shown here), that is, put back into the event pool if they are not to be handled currently. By executing a transition its source state is left and its target state entered; transitions may also be declared to be *internal* (not shown), thus skipping the activation-deactivation scheme. An *initial* pseudo state, depicted as a filled circle, represents the starting point for the execution of a region. A *final* state, depicted as a circle with a filled circle inside, represents the completion of its containing region; if all top-level regions of a state machine are completed then the state machine terminates. Transitions to and from different regions of an orthogonal composite state can be synchronized by *fork* (not shown here) and *join* pseudo states, presented as bars. For simplicity, we omit the other pseudo state kinds (entry and exit points, shallow and deep history, junction, choice, and terminate).

---

[2] In the following, we require that each state does have an entry and an exit action, which, however, may be NOP, doing nothing.

At run time, states get activated and deactivated as a consequence of transitions being fired. The active states at a stable step in the execution of the state machine form the active *state configuration*. Active state configurations are hierarchical: when a composite state is active, then exactly one state in each of its regions is also active; when a substate of a composite state is active, so is the containing state too. The execution of the state machine can be viewed as different active state configurations getting active or inactive upon the state machine receiving events. Note that for any given region, at most one direct substate of the region can be active at any given time, because a state configuration can contain at most one direct substate of the region.

For example, an execution trace, given in terms of active state configurations, of the state machine in Fig. 1 might be (NewLevel), (Play, Hall, Idle), (Play, Hall, Spelling), (Play, Hall, Fighting), (LevelWon), followed by the final state, which terminates the execution.

Note that events received by a state machine are stored in an *event pool*. The UML Specification [9] does not enforce any order to dispatch the events. The concrete dispatching strategy is deliberately delegated to the concrete implementation. Events may be prioritized, though a standard notation for priorities is not defined. In HILA, we assume the concrete implementation to be able to handle two priorities: high and normal, and notate high-priority events with stereotype «prioritized». For example, in Fig. 1, when an event quit is received, and state Play is active, then the event is handled immediately (and the game is over), even though there may be other events waiting in the pool.

2.2 Mutual Exclusion in UML State Machines

Mutual exclusion is a very common feature in parallel systems. Yet it is fairly difficult to model in plain UML.

To prevent two states (from two different regions, see above) from being simultaneously active, we can actually distinguish two strategies: passive waiting and active commanding. Suppose states s_1 and s_2 are to be mutually excluded, the containing region being r_1 and r_2, $r_1 \neq r_2$, respectively. Suppose s_1 is active, and, if not for the mutual exclusion requirement, the current event would now cause a transition to be fired and, as a consequence, s_2 would be activated. Now we can actually apply two strategies to achieve mutual exclusion:

– In passive waiting, region r_2 would wait passively for s_1 to become inactive. Mutual exclusion is achieved by delaying an ordinary transition of the original state machine. The waiting region has no influence on the time it has to wait.
– In active commanding, an additional event (not available in the original state machine) is sent, so that s_1 will immediately and be left, and s_2 is activated right thereafter. This strategy activates s_2 as soon as possible, interrupting whatever s_1 may be undertaking.

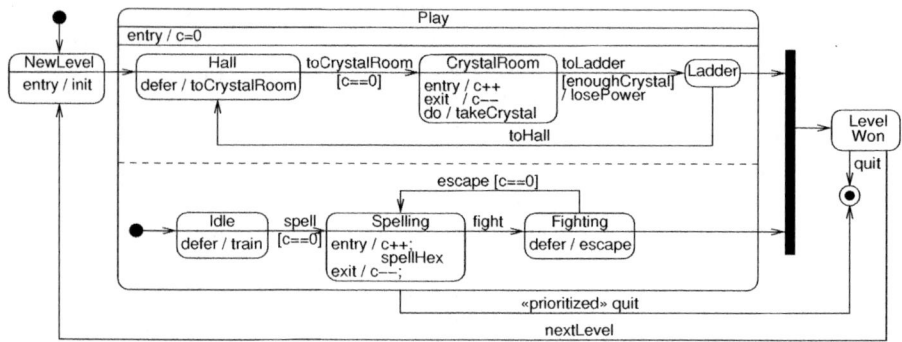

Fig. 2. Mutual exclusion in plain UML: passive waiting

Both strategies have realistic use cases, see e.g. [13,14]. Unfortunately, both are hard to model using plain UML.

As an example, assume for the above example a mutual-exclusion rule that requires the magician not to spell a hex in the crystal room. That is, in Fig. 1, the states CrystalRoom and Spelling must not be simultaneously active. A possible implementation of passive waiting to achieve the mutual exclusion is modeled in Fig. 2. A variable c is introduced and used to control the access to the two critical states: it is initialized as 0 in the entry action of Play, increased whenever CrystalRoom or Spelling is activated, and decreased whenever one of the two states is deactivated. The three transitions that activate the two states (from Hall to CrystalRoom, from Idle to Spelling, and from Fighting to Spelling), are extended by a guard, such that they are only fired when c equals 0, which means that the other critical state is currently inactive and the mutual exclusion rule is satisfied. A subtle point is that we have to declare the events toCrystalRoom, spell, and escape to be deferrable in the states Hall, Idle, and Fighting respectively. In this way the transitions are only postponed if the other critical state is active, and will be automatically resumed without requiring the events to be sent again. Otherwise the events would be lost in case exactly one of the critical states were active, since the event would then be taken from the event pool without firing a transition. Overall, the model elements we introduced make one region passively wait until some state in another region is left.

The other strategy, active commanding, is modeled in Fig. 3. In addition to variable c and the related entry and exit actions introduced above, new junctions, states and prioritized signals are also necessary. In the upper region, the (compound) transition from Hall to CrystalRoom is only enabled if c equals to 0, which means that the other critical state, Spelling, is inactive hence activating CrystalRoom would not break the mutual-exclusion rule. On the other hand, if c is not 0, i.e. Spelling is active, then Wait1 is activated. Within its entry action, a signal stopS is sent to the state machine itself and, due to the high priority (indicated by stereotype «prioritized»), handled immediately. Since Spelling is active, the transition to Idle is fired, which means Spelling now becomes inactive. The transition sends then an event cntn1, which is also handled immediately in

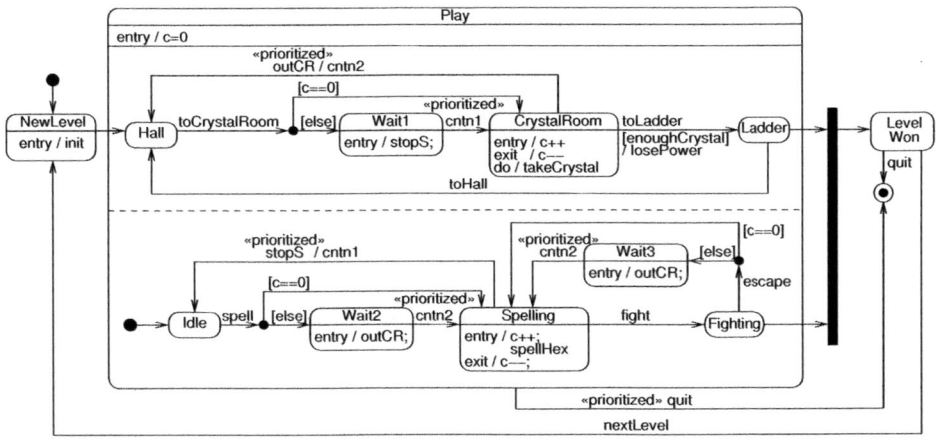

Fig. 3. Mutual exclusion in plain UML: active commanding

the upper region, where the transition from Wait1 to CrystalRoom is fired. Now CrystalRoom is active. The active state configuration consists of Play, CrystalRoom, and Idle. The function of Wait2 and Wait3 is similar. Overall, the Wait* states, the case distinctions, and the additional, prioritized events build up a mechanism for transitions in one region to send events which can actively influence the behavior of another region.

In both cases, it is obviously unsatisfactory that modeling even such a simple mutual exclusion rule requires modification of many model elements, scattered all over the state machine. The modification of the behavior is even in such a relatively simple example hard to understand. Furthermore, it is easy to introduce errors which are hard to find. Such modeling makes maintenance difficult, the models are complex and prone to errors.

3 Modeling Mutual Exclusion with HiLA

As a possible solution of UML state machines' modularity problems, the language High-Level Aspects (HiLA, [11,16]) was defined as an aspect-oriented extension for UML state machines. HiLA provides high-level constructs for declarative, as opposed to imperative, behavior modeling.

3.1 HiLA in a Nutshell

The concrete syntax of a HiLA aspect is shown in Fig. 4 and explained in the following. Syntactically, a HiLA aspect is a UML template containing at least a name, a pointcut and an advice. The template parameters allow easy customization, so that aspects for functionalities such as logging, transactions or mutual exclusions can easily be reused in many places.

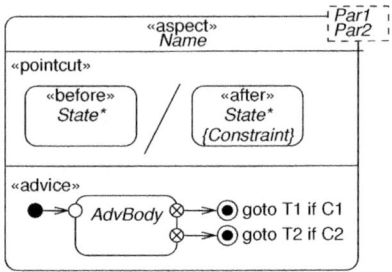

Fig. 4. HiLA: concrete syntax

An aspect is applied to a UML state machine, which is called the *base machine*. An aspect defines some additional or alternative behavior of the base machine at some points in time during the base machine's execution. The behavior is defined in the *advice* of the aspect; the points in time to execute the advice are defined in the *pointcut*. The advice (stereotype «advice» in Fig. 4) also has the form of a state machine, except that 1) transitions may carry out a special kind of action and 2) the final states may carry a label. The "body" of the advice, i.e. the part without the initial vertex, the final states, and the connecting transitions, models the behavior to carry out.

The special actions are called *commanding actions*. A commanding action has the form @X goto Y, and means that if state X (in the base machine) is active, then it should be deactivated, and state Y (in the base machine) should be activated. A label consists of a state, which should be activated when the advice is finished and the execution of the base machine should be resumed. We refer to this state as the *resumption state* of the final state. The label may optionally be guarded by a *resumption constraint*, which is indicated by the keyword if and has the form (like|nlike) StateName* where StateName is the set of the qualified names of the base machine's states. like S is true iff after the resumption all states contained in S will be active, otherwise nlike S is true.

The pointcut («pointcut») specifies the "interesting" points in time when the advice is executed. The points in time may be 1) when a certain state of the base machine is just about to become active or 2) a set of states has just been left. The semantics of a pointcut can be regarded as a selection function of the base machine's transitions: a pointcut «before» s selects all transitions in the base machine whose firing makes state s active, and a pointcut «after» S selects those transitions whose firing deactivates S.

Overall, an aspect is a graphical model element stating that at the points in time specified by the pointcut the advice should be executed, and after the execution of the advice the base machine should resume execution by activating the state given by the label of the advice's final state, when the conditions given there are satisfied. For «before» and «after» pointcuts, this "point in time" is always the firing of a transition; we say that this transition is *advised* by the advice.

3.2 Modeling Mutual Exclusion with HiLA

Since states to mutually exclude are always in different, parallel regions, mutual exclusion is actually a special case of cross-region communication. HiLA provides elegant solutions for modeling cross-region communication in general and mutual exclusion in particular. For the very common feature of mutual exclusion, reusable templates for its modeling are defined.

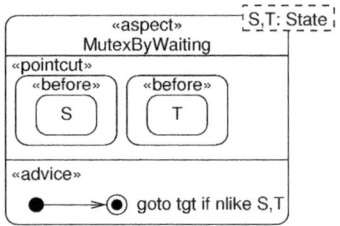

Fig. 5. HiLA template modeling mutual exclusion by passive waiting

Passive Waiting. The basic idea of aspect-oriented modeling of passive waiting is to define an aspect to interrupt the execution of the transition that would otherwise break the mutual-exclusion requirement, and to delay the resumption from the aspect until the other critical state is inactive again.

In HiLA, passive waiting is modeled by (instances of) the template shown in Fig. 5. The template takes two State parameters, S and T. The pointcut is a shortcut of "«before» S or «before» T", and specifies all the points in time when either S or T is just about to get active. In such moments the advice is executed, which contains an empty body and simply conducts the base machine to resume the advised transition (by going to its target), when after the resumption the states S and T would not be both active (condition nlike S, T). Compared with the UML solution, the imperative details of mutual exclusion are now transparent for the modeler, the modeling is non-intrusive, the semantics of the aspect (template) is much easier to understand hence less error-prone. Instantiating the template by binding S to Enchanted and T to CrystalRoom elegantly prevents our magician from entering the crystal room while being enchanted and also from becoming enchanted while in the CrystalRoom.

Active Commanding. Active commanding not only modifies the behavior of the region that has to wait, but the blocking state (contained in another region) is also deactivated immediately. In HiLA, we use a commanding action (see Sect. 3.1) to achieve this behavior.

Figure 6(a) shows an aspect template for modeling mutual exclusion by active commanding. Before state S or T becomes active, the advice is executed, in which state S is told to move to X and T to move to Y. Note that this actually means "before S becomes active tell T to move to Y" (because in this moment S cannot be active, and the @S event will be simply discarded) and "before T becomes active tell S to move to X". Instantiating the template by binding S to

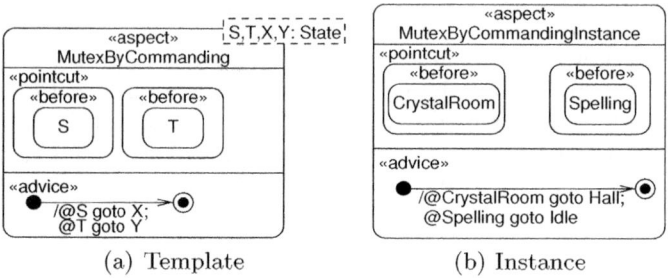

Fig. 6. HiLA: mutual exclusion by active commanding

CrystalRoom, T to Fighting, X to CrystalRoom, and Y to Spelling yields the concrete aspect shown in Fig. 6(b), which models the active-commanding implementation of mutual exclusion in our example. Again, compared with the UML solution, the HiLA solution is higher-level and much more easier to construct and to comprehend.

4 Weaving

Weaving is the process of transformation the base machine to incorporate the behavior modeled in aspects. In the following, we show the weaving techniques to implement the execution resumption from aspect to base machine and to implement commanding actions. These techniques are essential for the implementation of mutual-exclusion aspects. Note however, the techniques were designed for very general HiLA aspects, of which mutual-exclusion aspects are just special cases. See also [15] for other techniques used in the weaving process of HiLA, such as tracking the last active state configuration (used in implementing «after» aspects) or removing pseudo-states (used to handle with syntax variations of UML state machines).

In the following, we first present a simple transformation of the base machine to allow us to track active states during the base machine's execution. We then describe in Sect. 4.2 how an aspect is woven if it is the only aspect advising a given transition. Even on this simplistic stage, correct implementation of execution resumption and commanding events necessitates some elaborate techniques. Then, in Sect. 4.3, we expand the basic-weaving techniques to cover weaving of multiple aspects as well.

Notation. Given an aspect α, we refer to the set of the advice's top-level final states as $\mathcal{F}(\alpha)$. We assume that the final states contained in $\mathcal{F}(\alpha)$ are numbered. For each $f \in \mathcal{F}(\alpha)$, $\mathsf{num}(f)$ returns its number, $\mathsf{cond}(f)$ returns its resumption condition, and $\mathsf{label}(f)$ returns its label. Given a number $\mathsf{num}(f)$, we write $F(\mathsf{num}(f))$ to get f. Given a transition t, we refer to its source, target, guard, and action as $\mathsf{src}(t)$, $\mathsf{tgt}(t)$, $\mathsf{guard}(t)$, and $\mathsf{eft}(t)$, respectively.

4.1 Tracking Active States

In plain UML, the information of which states are currently active is not provided by any built-in language construct. On the other hand, this information is essential for the implementation of HiLA aspects modeling cross-region communication. We therefore extend the entry and exit action of each state in the base machine before actual weaving. The purpose of the extension is to store for each state in a variable if it is currently active or not. That is, for each state s in the base machine, we define a boolean variable a_s, which is initialized to be false, and set it to be true and false in the entry and exit action of s, respectively. This way, a_s is true iff s is active. This idea is shown in Fig. 7.

Fig. 7. Transformation for tracking active states

With this transformation, it is very easy to determine for a given set of states if all states contained in it are active. We ignore in this paper the details, and simply use impl(cond(f)) to notate the correct implementation of checking if the resumption condition of a final state is satisfied.

4.2 Weaving a Single Aspect

In HiLA, aspects are woven as a composite state containing (an implementation of) the advice. The composite state is inserted into each transition advised by the aspect.

Basic Idea. The basic idea of weaving a «before» aspect[3] is shown in Alg. 1. For each transition τ of the base machine, we assume it is advised by at most one aspect, which we call α. We first remove τ from the base machine, and replace it by the model elements we are going to insert. We insert a new state Asp into the base machine, insert an implementation of the advice into (the only region of) Asp (line 5), and set the completion event, which we notate as *, as deferrable (line 6). The "implementation" is a copy of the advice, except that commanding actions need a more involved implementation, see below. We also insert a junction j, and connect it with Asp by a transition. For each $f \in \mathcal{F}(\alpha)$, we still have to resolve its label since labels are not defined in UML. To this end, we extend the effect of the transition t leading to f by an action to store num(f) in a variable gt (line 10), insert a transition t'' from j to the label state of f (line 11), and guard (line 12) this transition so that it is only enabled when gt is equal to the number of f (which means f was the final state where the execution of the advice terminated) and the resumption condition is satisfied.

---

[3] In this work it suffices to consider only «before» aspects, because only these are needed to model mutual exclusion. In the case of «after» aspects, state Asp is slightly more involved, see [15].

Algorithm 1. Weaving a single aspect to transition

Require: each transition advised by at most one aspect
1: **for** each transition τ **do**
2:    **if** τ advised by aspect α **then**
3:       removeTransition(τ)
4:       Asp $\leftarrow$ insertState
5:       insertAdvice(α, Asp)
6:       setDefer(Asp, *)
7:       $j \leftarrow$ insertJunction; $t' \leftarrow$ insertTransition(Asp, j);
8:       **for** $f \in \mathcal{F}(\mathsf{Asp})$ **do**
9:          $t \leftarrow$ transition σ, such that $\mathsf{tgt}(\sigma) = f$
10:         eft(t) $\leftarrow$ eft(t) $\cdot$ '$gt \leftarrow$ num(f)'   ▷ store the number of final state
11:         $t'' \leftarrow$ insertTransition(j, label(f))
12:         guard(t'') $\leftarrow$ '$gt =$ num(f) $\wedge$ impl(cond(f))'
13:       **end for**
14:    **end if**
15: **end for**

As an example, Fig. 8(b) shows the result of weaving the very general aspect (we assume the pointcut to be a «before» pointcut, though) given in Fig. 4 to a transition as given in Fig. 8(a). At run time, after the execution of *AdvBody*, the transition to one of the final states inside Asp is fired, and the final state is activated. Then, depending on the value of gt, the transition from Asp to T1, T2 or Y is activated in the right moment, i.e., when the resumption condition is also satisfied.

Commanding Actions. In HiLA, the advice of an aspect may contain commanding actions. Basically, the "command" is implemented by an event sent to the base machine itself, to be handled by the addressee. To ensure that the event is handled immediately, we need to prioritize the handling of the event.

Commanding actions may be carried out by transitions within the advice. Recall that we insert an implementation of the advice into (a region) of the state Asp (Alg. 1, line 5). Actually the implementation is simply a copy of the advice, except that transitions sending commanding events need a more involved implementation, as will be explained in the following.

We require that the transition executing an commanding action have a state as its target. Note that we do not lose generosity due to this requirement, since all pseudo-states as transition targets can be eliminated by a semantic-preserving normalization process, see [11, Ch. 5]. Recall that a commanding action has the form @X goto Y, and that it causes state X to go to Y (both defined in the base machine) immediately. We refer to the source vertex of the transition as V, which may or may not be a state, and refer to the target state as S, see Fig. 9(a), where we assumed V is also a state.

While weaving, this transition is not simply copied into the state Asp, but transformed as follows: we insert into the region containing V and S a junction j, a state Waiting and connection transitions. Note trigger cntn of the transition

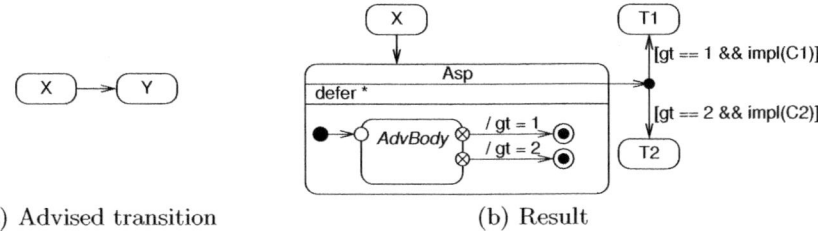

(a) Advised transition (b) Result

Fig. 8. Weaving a single «before» aspect

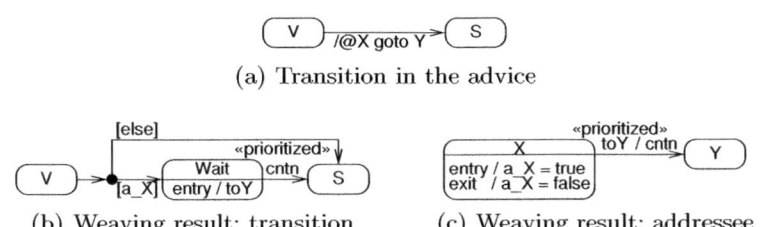

(a) Transition in the advice

(b) Weaving result: transition (c) Weaving result: addressee

Fig. 9. Weaving: commanding action

from Wait to S has a high priority. Additionally, in the region containing X and Y, a transition t from X to Y is also inserted. The trigger of transition t is an event toY, which has high priority and will be handled as soon as received.

At run time, when the transition leaving V is fired, one of the two following cases applies: if X is active (i.e. if a_X is true), then state Wait is activated, and, within its entry action, the signal toY is sent. Since X is active, and toY has a high priority, the transiton to Y is handled immediately, which means X becomes inactive, a signal cntn is sent, and Y gets active. Back in the upper region, Wait is active, cntn has a high priority, therefore the transition to T is fired, and the execution of the advice is finished. On the other hand, if X is not active when t_1 is fired, then Y is simply activated, just "as usual", and the mutual-exclusion requirement is not violated.

Applying the above algorithms to our example, weaving an instance of Fig. 5 with S bound to CrystalRoom and T bound to Spelling to the base machine given in Fig. 1 yields a result that is very similar to Fig. 2, and weaving Fig. 6(b) to the base machine yields a result very similar to Fig. 3. Since the weaving techniques are designed for general HiLA aspects, the weaving result of very simple advice may exhibit some overhead. We consider optimization to be an interesting piece of future work.

4.3 Multiple Aspects

Obviously, only in trivial systems it applies (as assumed above) that a transition is advised by at most one aspect. In any realistic system, multiple aspects may be interacting, i.e. advising the same transition. In such cases, it is essential for the weaving algorithm to help determine or even reconcile potential conflicts.

Algorithm 2. Weaving multiple aspects

```
 1:                                  ▷ General case: multiple aspects advising one transition
 2: for each transition τ do
 3:    A ← {α | α advising τ}
 4:    if A ≠ ∅ then
 5:       removeTransition(τ)
 6:       Asp ← insertState
 7:       setDefer(Asp, *)
 8:       j ← insertJunction; t' ← insertTransition(Asp, j);
 9:       for each α advising τ do
10:          insertAdvice(α, Asp);
11:          for f ∈ F(Asp) do
12:             t ← transition σ, such that tgt(σ) = f
13:             eft(t) ← eft(t) · 'gt(α) ← num(f)'    ▷ store the number of final state
14:          end for
15:       end for
16:       F ← ⋃_{α∈A} F(α)
17:       for g ∈ ⋃_{f∈F} label(f) do
18:          t'' ← insertTransition(j, g)
19:          guard(t'') ← ' ⋀_{α∈A} F(gt(α)) = g ∧ impl(cond(F'(gt(α))))'
20:       end for
21:       Err ← insertState
22:       t_e ← insertTransition; guard(t_e) ← 'else'
23:    end if
24: end for
```

Resumption. When a transition is advised by multiple aspects, it is important to ensure that all aspects (i.e. their advice) are executed, and that the aspects specify the same resumption state to go to after the execution. If they specify different resumption states, it is a conflict. To this end, we extend the algorithm presented in Sect. 4.2 to Alg. 2. For each advising aspect, we insert an implementation of its advice into a region of Asp (line 10). Therefore, Asp is in general an orthogonal state, containing a multitude of regions, to be executed in parallel at run time. Instead of inserting a transition from junction j to label(f) for each final state f (Alg. 1, line 7), we now insert a transition to each state g such that g is the resumption state of some final state of the advice of any of the aspects (line 18). The guard of the transition ensures that the transition is enabled iff in each the region, the actual resumption state is really the target of the transition (line 19).[4] Otherwise, if different resumption states are specified by different aspects, this is a conflict situation. In this situation, state Exception is activated, inserted to the base machine by in lines 21 and 22.

Commanding Actions. The idea of weaving commanding actions shown in Sect. 4.2 also works for multiple aspects. If a state is addressee of multiple commanding actions, then multiple transitions will be introduced. It is important,

---

[4] Recall that $F(gt(α))$ returns the $gt(α)$-th final state of (the advice of) aspect $α$.

though, to generate different event names for the different transitions. This way, conflicting is eliminated.

5 Related Work

HiLA is a semantic approach, i.e., HiLA aspects define modifications of the semantics of the base machine. Therefore, the semantics of an aspect can be described in a purely behavioral manner. The modeler only needs to specify what to do (in this paper: what to mutually exclude), and no longer has to specify how do to it in imperative details, since the details are hidden behind the weaving algorithms and thus transparent to the modeler. In comparison, prevalent approaches of incorporating aspect-orientation into UML state machines, such as [1,2,7,8], are mainly syntactic. Aspects typically define transformations of the (abstract syntax) of the base model. It is therefore the modeler's job to define aspects (modifications of the syntax of the base machine) such that the overall behavior of the modified base machine is the desired one.

The semantics of such syntactic aspects are usually defined by by graph transformation systems, such as Attributed Graph Grammar (AGG, [10]). Consistency checks are supported by a confluence check of the underlying graph transformation, see e.g. [7]. Due to the syntactic character of the aspects, this check is also syntactic: there may be false alarms if different weaving orders lead to syntactically different but semantically equivalent results. In contrast, in our approach described above, the error state is only entered when the resumption variables are really conflicting.

The pointcut language JPDD [6] also allows the modeler to define "stateful" pointcuts. Compared with HiLA, a weaving process is not defined. State-based aspects in reactive systems are also supported by the Motorola WEAVR tool [17]. Their aspects can be applied to the modeling approach Rational TAU[5], which supports flat, "transition-centric" state machines. In comparison, HiLA is also applicable to UML state machines, that in general include concurrency. Ge et al. [5] give an overview of an aspect system for UML state machines. They do not give enough details for a thorough comparison, but it appears that the HiLA language is significantly stronger the theirs, and that the issues presented in this paper are not addressed by their solution.

To the author's knowledge, declarative modeling of mutual exclusion is not directly supported by the above approaches.

6 Conclusions and Future Work

We have presented how HiLA, an aspect-oriented extension of UML, can be applied to model mutual exclusion in UML state machines, as well as weaving techniques used to implement mutual-exclusion aspects. Using HiLA, both passive waiting and active commanding can be modeled highly modularly and

---
[5] http://ibm.com/software/awdtools/tau/

declaratively. That is, mutual-exclusion is modeled at a dedicated place rather than by model elements scattered all over the state machine, and the modeler only has to specify which states to mutually exclude rather than how to do it. Moreover, our implementation minimizes potential conflicts between aspects by weaving interacting aspects into parallel regions of a composite state.

Currently we are working on an extension of the tool Hugo/HiLA [11] to automate the weaving process of commanding aspects. Future work includes investigation of how HiLA can help model interactive user interfaces [12] more modularly, as well as techniques of factorizing aspects out of plain UML state machines.

References

1. Ali, S., Briand, L.C., Arcuri, A., Walawege, S.: An Industrial Application of Robustness Testing Using Aspect-Oriented Modeling, UML/MARTE, and Search Algorithms. In: Whittle, J., Clark, T., Kühne, T. (eds.) MODELS 2011. LNCS, vol. 6981, pp. 108–122. Springer, Heidelberg (2011)
2. Clarke, S., Baniassad, E.: Aspect-Oriented Analysis and Design: the Theme Approach. Addison-Wesley (2005)
3. Drusinsky, D.: Modeling and Verification Using UML Statecharts. Elsevier (2006)
4. Engels, G., Opdyke, B., Schmidt, D.C., Weil, F. (eds.): MODELS 2007. LNCS, vol. 4735. Springer, Heidelberg (2007)
5. Ge, J.-W., Xiao, J., Fang, Y.-Q., Wang, G.-D.: Incorporating Aspects into UML State Machine. In: Proc. Advanced Computer Theory and Engineering (ICACTE 2010). IEEE (2010)
6. Hanenberg, S., Stein, D., Unland, R.: From Aspect-Oriented Design to Aspect-Oriented Programs: Tool-Supported Translation of JPDDs into Code. In: Barry, B.M., de Moor, O. (eds.) Proc 6th Int. Conf. Aspect-Oriented Software Development (AOSD 2007), pp. 49–62. ACM (2007)
7. Jayaraman, P.K., Whittle, J., Elkhodary, A.M., Gomaa, H.: Model Composition in Product Lines and Feature Interaction Detection Using Critical Pair Analysis. In: Engels et al. [4], pp. 151–165
8. Mahoney, M., Bader, A., Elrad, T., Aldawud, O.: Using Aspects to Abstract and Modularize Statecharts. In: Proc. 5th Int. Wsh. Aspect-Oriented Modeling, Lisboa (2004)
9. OMG, Unified Modeling Languague Superstructure, Version 2.4.1. Specification, Object Management Group (2011),
 http://www.omg.org/spec/UML/2.4.1/Superstructure/
10. Taentzer, G.: AGG: A Graph Transformation Environment for Modeling and Validation of Software. In: Pfaltz, J.L., Nagl, M., Böhlen, B. (eds.) AGTIVE 2003. LNCS, vol. 3062, pp. 446–453. Springer, Heidelberg (2004)
11. Zhang, G.: Aspect-Oriented State Machines. PhD thesis, Ludwig-Maximilians-Universität München (2010)
12. Zhang, G.: Aspect-Oriented UI Modeling with State Machines. In: Van den Bergh, J., Sauer, S., Breiner, K., Hußmann, H., Meixner, G., Pleuss, A. (eds.) Proc. 5th Int. Wsh. Model-Driven Development of Advanced User Interfaces (MDDAUI 2010), pp. 45–48 (2010)

13. Zhang, G., Hölzl, M.: HiLA: High-Level Aspects for UML State Machines. In: Ghosh, S. (ed.) MODELS 2009. LNCS, vol. 6002, pp. 104–118. Springer, Heidelberg (2010)
14. Zhang, G., Hölzl, M.: Improving the Modularity of Web-Application Models with Aspects (submitted, 2012)
15. Zhang, G., Hölzl, M.: Weaving Semantic Aspects in HiLA. In: Hirschfeld, R., Tanter, É., Sullivan, K.J., Gabriel, R.P. (eds.) Proc. 11th Int. Conf. Aspect-Oriented Software Development (AOSD 2012), pp. 263–274. ACM (2012)
16. Zhang, G., Hölzl, M., Knapp, A.: Enhancing UML State Machines with Aspects. In: Engels et al. [4], pp. 529–543
17. Zhang, J., Cottenier, T., van den Berg, A., Gray, J.: Aspect Composition in the Motorola Aspect-Oriented Modeling Weaver. Journal of Object Technology 6(7), 89–108 (2007)

TexMo: A Multi-language Development Environment

Rolf-Helge Pfeiffer and Andrzej Wąsowski

IT University of Copenhagen, Denmark
{ropf,wasowski}@itu.dk

Abstract. Contemporary software systems contain a large number of artifacts expressed in multiple languages, ranging from domain-specific languages to general purpose languages. These artifacts are interrelated to form software systems. Existing development environments insufficiently support handling relations between artifacts in multiple languages.

This paper presents a taxonomy for multi-language development environments, organized according to language representation, representation of relations between languages, and types of these relations. Additionally, we present TexMo, a prototype of a multi-language development environment, which uses an explicit relation model and implements visualization, static checking, navigation, and refactoring of cross-language relations. We evaluate TexMo by applying it to development of a web-application, JTrac, and provide preliminary evidence of its feasibility by running user tests and interviews.

1 Introduction

Maintenance and enhancement of software systems is expensive and time consuming. Between 85% to 90% of project budgets go to legacy system operation and maintenance [6]. Lientz et. al. [19] state that 75% to 80% of system and programming resources are used for enhancement and maintenance, where alone understanding of the system stands for 50% to 90% percent of these costs [25].

Contemporary software systems are implemented using multiple languages. For example, PHP developers regularly use 1 to 2 languages besides PHP [1]. The situation is even more complex in large enterprise systems. The code base of OFBiz, an industrial quality open-source ERP system contains more than 30 languages including General Purpose Languages (GPL), several XML-based Domain-Specific Languages (DSL), config files, property files, and build scripts. ADempiere, another industrial quality ERP system, uses 19 languages. ECommerce systems Magento and X-Cart utilize more than 10 languages each.[1] Systems utilizing the model-driven development paradigm additionally rely on multiple languages for model management, e.g., meta-modelling (UML, Ecore, etc.) model transformation (QVT ATL, etc.), code generation (Acceleo, XPand, etc.), and model validation (OCL, etc.).[2]

---
[1] See ofbiz.apache.org, adempiere.com, magentocommerce.com, x-cart.com
[2] See uml.org, eclipse.org/modeling/emf, omg.org/spec/QVT, eclipse.org/atl, eclipse.org/acceleo, wiki.eclipse.org/Xpand, omg.org/spec/OCL respectively.

TexMo: A Multi-language Development Environment

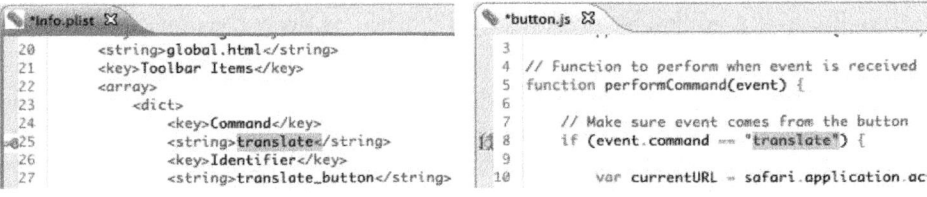

(a) Declaration of the *translate* command attached to a button.

(b) JavaScript code that is executed whenever the button is pressed.

Fig. 1. Declaration of a command and its use

We call software systems using multiple languages, *Multi-Language Software Systems (MLSS)*. Obviously, the majority of modern software systems are MLSSs.

Development artifacts in MLSS can be models, source code, property files, etc. To simplify presentation, we refer to all these as *mograms* [18]. Mograms in MLSS are often heavily interrelated. For example, OFBiz contains many hundreds of relations across its languages [23,13]. Unfortunately, relations across language boundaries are fragile. They are broken easily, as development environments neither visualize nor statically check them.

Consider the following scenario. For simplicity of presentation we use a small example. Our work, though, is not tight to a particular selection of languages, or the particular example system.

Example Scenario. Bob develops a *Safari* web browser *extension*. The extension contributes a button to Safari's menu bar. Pressing the button translates the current web-page to English using *Google translate* and presents it in a new tab. Browser extensions are usually built using HTML, CSS and JavaScript. Bob's extension consists of three source code files: *Info.plist*, *button.js*, and *global.html*.

Plist files serve as an interface for the extension. They tell Safari what the extension contributes to the UI. In Bob's extension, the *Plist* file contains the declaration of a `translate` command attached to a toolbar button (Fig. 1a). *JavaScript* code contains logic attached to buttons, menus, etc. Bob's *button.js* forwards the current URL to Google's translation service whenever the corresponding button is pressed (Fig. 1b). Every extension contains a *global.html* file, which is never displayed. It contains code which is loaded at browser start-up or when the extension is enabled. It is used to provide code for extension buttons, menus, etc. Bob's *global.html* file (not shown here) contains only a single script tag pointing to *button.js*.

In Fig. 1a the `translate` command for the button is defined. Fig. 1b shows how the translate command is used in *button.js* in a string literal. This is an example of a *string-based reference* to *Info.plist*. Such string-based references are common in development of MLSSs.

Now, imagine Bob renaming the command in *Info.plist* from `translate` to its Danish equivalent `oversæt`. Obviously, the browser plugin will not work anymore since the JavaScript code in *button.js* is referring to a non-existing command. Symmetrically, the reference is broken whenever the "translate" string literal is modified in the button.js file, without the corresponding update to Info.plist. □

Existing Integrated Development Environments (IDE) do not directly support development of MLSSs. IDEs do not visualize cross-language relations (markers left to line numbers and gray highlighting in Fig. 1). Neither do they check statically for consistency of cross-language relations, or provide refactorings across mograms in multiple languages. We are out to change this and enhance IDEs into *Multi-Language Development Environments (MLDE)*.

This paper introduces a taxonomy of design choices for MLDEs (Sec. 2). The purpose of this taxonomy is twofold. First, it serves as requirements list for implementing MLDEs, and second it allows for classification of such. We argue for the validity of our taxonomy by a survey of related literature and tools.

As the second main contribution, the paper presents TexMo (Sec. 3), an MLDE prototype supporting textual GPLs and DSLs. It implements actions for *visualization* of, *static checking* of, *navigation* along, and *refactoring* of interlanguage relations, and facilities to declare inter-language relations. Additionally, TexMo provides standard editor mechanisms such as syntax highlighting. We position TexMo in our taxonomy and evaluate it by applying it to development of an MLSS and user tests followed by interviews.

2 Taxonomy of Multi-language Development Environments

Popular IDEs like Eclipse or NetBeans implement separate editors for every language they support. A typical IDE provides separate Java, HTML, and XML editors, even though these editors are used to build systems mixing all these languages. Representing languages separately allows for an easy and modular extension of IDEs to support new programming languages. Usually, IDEs keep an *Abstract Syntax Tree (AST)* in memory and automatically synchronize it with modifications applied to concrete syntax. IDE editors exploit the AST to facilitate source code navigation and refactorings, ranging from basic renamings to elaborate code transformations such as *method pull ups*.

Inter-language relations are a major problem in development of MLSS [23,13,12]. Since they are mostly implicit, they hinder modification and evolution of MLSS. An MLDE is an IDE that addresses this challenge by not only integrating tools into a uniform working experience, as IDEs do, but also by integrating languages with each other. MLDEs support across language boundaries the mechanisms implemented by IDEs for every language separately.

We surveyed IDEs, programming editors[3], and literature to understand the kind of development support they provide. We realized that 4 features, that

---

[3] IDEs: Eclipse, NetBeans, IntelliJ Idea, MonoDevelop, XCode. Editors: MacVim, Emacs, jEdit, TextWrangler, TextMate, Sublime Text 2, Fraise, Smultron, Tincta, Kod, gedit, Ninja IDE. (See project websites at: www.itu.dk/~ropf/download/list.txt)

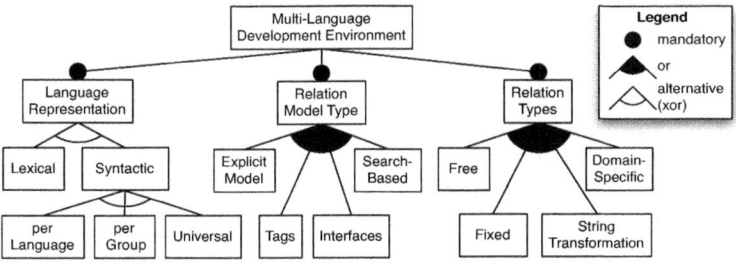

Fig. 2. Taxonomy for multi-language development environments

visualization, *navigation*, *static checking*, and *refactoring* are implemented by all IDEs and by some programming editors. Thus, in order to support developers best, MLSS need to consider delivering these features across language boundaries as their essential requirements:

1. *Visualization.* An MLDE has to highlight and/or visualize inter-language references. Visualizations can range from basic markers, as for instance in the style of Fig. 1 to elaborate visualization mechanisms such as treemaps [7].
2. *Navigation.* An MLDE has to allow navigating along inter-language relations. In Fig. 1, the developer can request to automatically open *button.js* and jump to line 8, when editing *Info.plist*. All surveyed IDEs allow to navigate source code. Further, IDEs allow for source code to documentation navigation, a basic multi-language navigation.
3. *Static Checking.* An MLDE has to statically check the integrity of inter-language relations. As soon as a developer breaks a relation, the error is indicated to show that the system will not run error free. All surveyed IDEs provide static checking by visualizing errors and warnings.
4. *Refactoring.* An MLDE has to implement refactorings, which allow easy fixing of broken inter-language relations. Different IDEs implement a different amount of refactorings per language. Particularly, rename refactorings seem to be widely used in current IDEs [21,31].

To address these requirements one needs to make three main design decisions: **a)** *How to represent different programming languages?* **b)** *How to inter-relate them with each other?* **c)** *Using which kind of relations?*

Systematizing the answers to these questions led us to a domain model characterizing MLDEs. We present this model in Fig. 2 using the feature modeling notation [5,16]. An MLDE always represents mograms based on the their language (*Language Representation*). Furthermore, an MLDE has to represent inter-language relations (*Relation Model Type*). This feature is essential for augmenting an IDE to an MLDE. Finally, an MLDE associates types to inter-language relations (*Relation Types*). An IDE first becomes an MLDE if it supports inter-language relations, i.e., as it implements an instance of this model.

The following subsections detail and exemplify the fundamental MLDE characteristics of our taxonomy. References to the surveyed literature are inlined.

2.1 Language Representation Types

We consider two main types of language representation, lexical and syntactic language representation. The former always works on an artifact directly without constructing a more elaborate representation, whereas the latter is always based on a richer data-structure representing mograms in a certain language. Syntactic language representation can represent mograms per language, per language group, or universally.

Lexical Representation. Most text editors, such as EMacs, Vim, and jEdit, implement lexical representation. Mograms are loaded into a buffer in a language agnostic manner. Syntax highlighting is implemented solely based on matching tokens. Due to lack of sufficient information about the edited mogram such editors provide limited support for static checking, code navigation, and refactoring.

Syntactic Representation. Per Language. Typical IDEs represent mograms in any given language using a separate AST, or a similar richer data structure capturing a mogram's structure; for instance Eclipse, NetBeans, etc. Unlike lexical representation, a structured, typed representation allows for implementation of static checking and navigation within and between mograms of a single language but not across languages. The advantage using per language representation, compared to per language group and universal representation, is that IDEs are easily extensible to support new languages.

Using models to represent source code is getting more and more popular[4]. This is facilitated by emergence of language workbenches such as EMFText, XText, Spoofax, etc.[5] The MoDisco [4] project, a model-driven framework for software modernization and evolution, represents Java, JSP, and XML source code as EMF models, where each language is represented by its own distinct model. These models are a high-level description of an analyzed system and are used for transformation into a new representation. The same principle of abstracting a programming language into an EMF model representation is implemented in JaMoPP [11]. Similarly, JavaML [3] uses XML for a structural representation of Java source code. On the other hand, SmartEMF [12] translates XML-based DSLs to EMF models and maps them to a Prolog knowledge base. The EMF models realize a per language representation. Similarly, we represent OFBiz' DSLs and Java using EMF models to handle inter-component and inter-language relations [23].

Syntactic Representation. Per Language Group. A single model can represent multiple languages sharing commonalities. Some languages are mixed or embedded into each other, e.g., SQL embedded in C++. Some languages extend others, e.g., AspectJ extends Java. Furthermore, languages are often used together, such as JavaScript, HTML, XML, and CSS in web development. Using

---

[4] Language workbenches mostly use modeling technology to represent ASTs. Therefore, we use the terms AST and model synonymously in this paper.

[5] See www.languageworkbenches.net for the annual language workbench competition.

a per language group representation allows increased reuse in implementation of navigation, static checks and refactoring in MLDEs, because support for each language does not need to be implemented separately.

For example, the IntelliJ IDEA IDE (jetbrains.com/idea), supports code completion for SQL statements embedded as strings in Java code. X-Develop [28,27] implements an extensible model for language group representation to provide refactoring across languages. AspectJ's compiler generates an AST for Java as well as for AspectJ aspects simultaneously. Similarly, the WebDSL famework represents mograms in its collection of DSLs for web development in a single AST [8]. *Meta*, a language family definition language, allows the grouping of languages by characteristics, e.g., object-oriented languages in *Meta(oopl)* [14]. The Prolog knowledge base in [12] can be considered as a language group representation for OFBiz' DSLs, used to check for inter-language constraints.

Syntactic Representation. Universal. Universal representations use a single model to capture the structure of mograms in any language. They can represent any version of any language, even of languages not invented yet. Universal representations use simple but generic concepts to represent key language concepts, such as blocks and identifiers or objects and associations. A universal representation allows the implementation of navigation, static checking, and refactoring only once for all languages. Except for TexMo, presented in Sec. 3, we are not aware of any IDE implementing a universal language representation.

The per group and the universal representations are generalizations of the per language representation. Both represent multiple languages in one model. Generally, there are two opposing abstraction mechanisms: *type abstraction* and *word abstraction* [29]. Type abstraction is a unifying abstraction, whereas word abstraction is a simplifying abstraction.

For example, both Java and C# method declarations can include modifiers, but the set of the actual modifiers is language specific. The synchronized modifier in Java has no equivalent in C#. Under the type abstraction, Java and C# method declarations can be described by a *Method Declaration* type and an enumeration containing the modifiers. In contrast, under the word abstraction, Java and C# method declarations would be described by a common simple *Method Declaration* type that neglects the modifiers. Obviously, in the type abstraction Java and C# method modifiers are distinguishable, whereas in the more generic word abstraction this information is lost.

Type abstraction is preferable for per group representations. Word abstraction is preferred for universal representations. The choice of abstraction influences the specificity of the representation, affecting the tools. Word abstractions are more generic than type abstractions. For instance, more cross-language refactorings are possible with the per group representation, while the refactorings in the systems relying on the universal representation automatically apply to a wider class of languages.

2.2 Relation Model Types

Software systems are implemented using multiple mograms. At the compilation stage, and often only at runtime, a complete system is composed by relating all the mograms together. Each mogram can refer to, or is referenced by, other mograms. An MLDE should maintain information about these relations. We observe four different techniques to express cross-language relations:

Explicit model. For example, *mega-models* [15], *trace models* [22,9], *relation models* [23], or *macromodels* [24]. All these are models linking distributed mograms together.

Tags. Hypertext systems, particularly HTML code links substructures or other artifacts with each other by tags. Tags define anchors and links within an artifact [10]. Hypertext systems interpret artifacts, anchors, and links. first after interpretation a link is established.

Interfaces. Interfaces are anchors decoupled from artifacts. An interface contains information about a development artifact's contents and corresponding locations. For example, OSGi manifest files or model and meta-model interfaces describe component and artifact relations [13].

Search-based. There is no persistent representation of relations at all. Possible relation targets are established after evaluating a search query. Search-based relations are usually used to navigate in unknown data. For example, in [30] relations across documents in different applications are visualized on user request by searching the contents of all displayed documents.

2.3 Relation Types

Here we elaborate on relations between mograms in different languages. Since we consider only textual languages all the following relation types relate strings.

Free relations are relations between arbitrary strings. They rely solely on human interpretation. For example, natural language text in documentation can be linked to source code blocks highlighting that certain requirements are implemented or that a programmer should read some documentation. Steinberger et. al. describe a visualization tool allowing to interrelate information across domains, even across concrete syntaxes [26]. Their tool visualizes relations between diagrams and data.

Fixed relations: Relations between equal strings are fixed relations. Fixed relations occur frequently in practice. For example, the relation between an HTML anchor declaration and its link is established by equality of a tag's argument names. Figure 1 shows an example of a fixed relation across language boundaries.

Waldner et. al. discuss visualization across applications and documents [30]. Their tool visualizes relations between occurrences of a search term matched in different documents.

String-transformation relations are relations between similar strings, or functionally related strings. For example, a Hibernate configuration file (XML) describes how Java classes are persisted into a relational database. The Hibernate framework requires that a field specified in the XML file has a corresponding get and set method in the Java class. A string fieldName in a Hibernate configuration file requires a getter with name getFieldName in the corresponding Java class. Depending on the direction, a string-transformation relation either attaches or removes get and capitalizes or decapitalizes fieldName.

Domain-Specific Relations (DSRs) are relations with semantics specific to a given domain or project. DSRs are always typed. Additionally, DSRs can be free, fixed or string-transformation relations. For example, a requirements document can require a certain implementation artifact, expressing that a certain requirement is implemented. At the same time, some Java code can require a properties file, meaning that the code will only produce expected results as soon as certain properties are in place. We consider any relation type hierarchy domain-specific, e.g., trace link classification [22].

The first three relation types, free, fixed, and string-transformation relations are untyped. They are more generic than DSRs, since they only rely on physical properties of relation ends. Fixed, string-transformation, and domain-specific relations can be checked automatically, which allows to implement tools supporting MLSS development, such as error visualization and error resolution.

3 TexMo as an MLDE Prototype

TexMo[6] addresses the requirements listed in Sec. 2 and it implements an instance of our MLDE taxonomy. TexMo uses a *key-reference* metaphor to express relations. In the example of Fig. 1, the command *declaration* takes the role of a *key* (Fig. 1a) and its uses are *reference* (Fig. 1b). TexMo relations are always many-to-one relations between *references* and *keys*. We summarize how TexMo meets the requirements presented in Sec. 2:

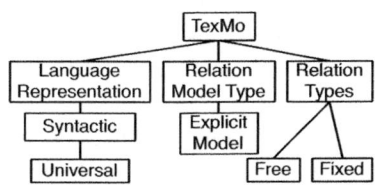

Fig. 3. The feature model instance describing TexMo in our taxonomy of MLDEs

1. *Visualization.* TexMo highlights keys and references using gray boxes, see line 25 in Fig. 1a and line 8 Fig. 1b. Keys are labeled with a key icon and references are labeled by a book icon; see Fig. 1 left to line numbers. Inspecting markers reveals detailed information, e.g., how many references in which files refer to a key, see Fig. 4b.

---

[6] TexMo's source code including the text model and the relation model is available online at: www.itu.dk/~ropf/download/texmo.zip

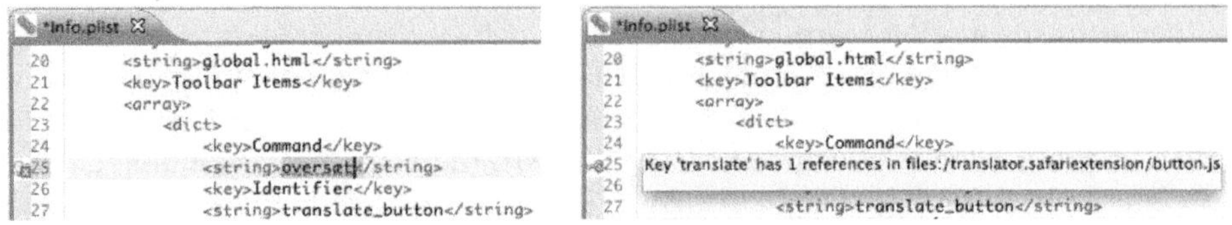

(a) A broken relation between command declaration and its use, see Fig. 1b.

(b) Detailed relation information attached to a key marker.

Fig. 4. Visualization and information for inter-language relations

2. *Navigation.* Users can navigate from any reference to the referred key and from a key to any of its references. Navigation actions are called via the context menu.
3. *Static checking.* Fixed relations in TexMo's relation model (RM) are statically checked. Broken relations, i.e., fixed relations with different string literals as key and reference, are underlined red and labeled by a standard error indicator in the active editor, see Fig. 4a.
4. *Refactoring.* Broken relations can be fixed automatically using quick fixes. TexMo's quick fixes are key centric rename refactorings. Applying a quick fix to a key renames all references to the content of the key. Contrary, applying a quick fix to a reference renames this single reference to the content of the corresponding key.

On top of these multi-language development support mechanisms, TexMo provides syntax highlighting for 75 languages. GPLs like Java, C#, and Ruby, as well as DSLs like HTML, Postscript, etc. are supported. Standard editor mechanisms like undo/redo are implemented, too.

Universal Language Representation. The Text Model. TexMo implements a universal language representation since such an MLDE is easily applicable for development of any MLSS.

All textual languages share a common coarse-grained structure. The text model (Fig. 5), an AST of any textual language, describes blocks containing paragraphs, which are separated by new lines and which contain blocks of words. Words consist of characters and are separated by white-spaces. The only model elements containing characters are word-parts, separators, white-spaces, and line-breaks. Blocks, paragraphs, and word blocks describe the structure of a mogram. Separators are non-letters within a word, e.g., '/','.', etc., allowing represent of typical programming language tokens as single words.

TexMo treats any mogram as an instance of a textual DSL conforming to Fig. 5. For example, a snippet of JavaScript code if(event.command == , line 8 in Fig. 1b, looks like: Block(Paragraph[WordBlock(Word[WordPart("if"), SeperatorPart(content:"("), WordPart("event"), SeperatorPart("."), WordPart("command"), WhiteSpace(" ")]), ...]) (using Spoofax [17] AST notation).

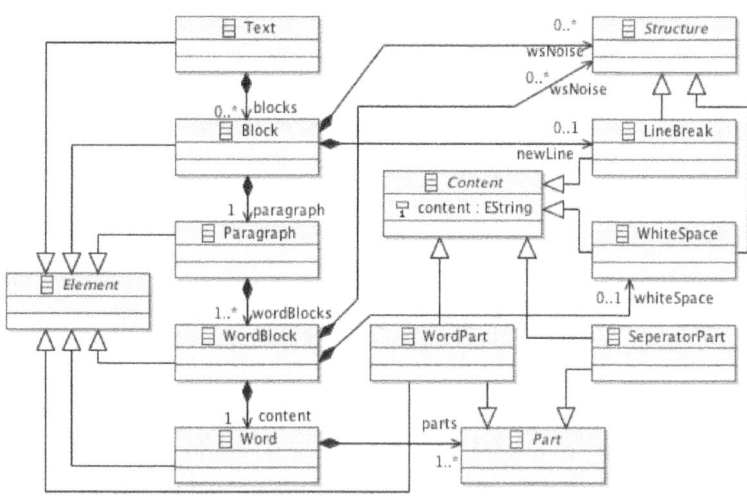

Fig. 5. The open universal model for language representation

An Explicit Relation Model. TexMo uses an instance of the Relation Model (RM) presented in Fig. 6 to keep track of relations between multi-language mogram code. Our RM allows for relations between mogram contents (ElementKey and ElementReference), between mogram contents and files (Artifacts) or components (Components), and between files and components. This allows for example to express relations in case mogram code requires another file, which occurs frequently, e.g., in HTML code.

The RM instance is kept as a textual artifact. The textual concrete syntax is not shown here, since the RM is not intended for human inspection. TexMo automatically updates the RM instance whenever developers modify interrelated mograms. That is, TexMo supports evolution of MLSS. Currently, the RM is created manually. TexMo provides context menu actions to establish relations between keys and references. Future versions of TexMo will integrate pattern based mining mechanism [23,9] to supersede manual RM creation.

Relation Types. TexMo's RM currently implements fixed and explanatory relations. Explanatory relations are free relations in our taxonomy. Keys and references of fixed relations contain the same string literal. Figure 1 shows a fixed relation and Fig. 4 shows a broken fixed relation. Explanatory relations allow to connect arbitrary text blocks with each other, for example documentation information to implementation code.

4 Evaluation

In this section we discuss TexMo's applicability. First, we evaluate TexMo's language representation mechanism, i.e., its representation of mograms as text

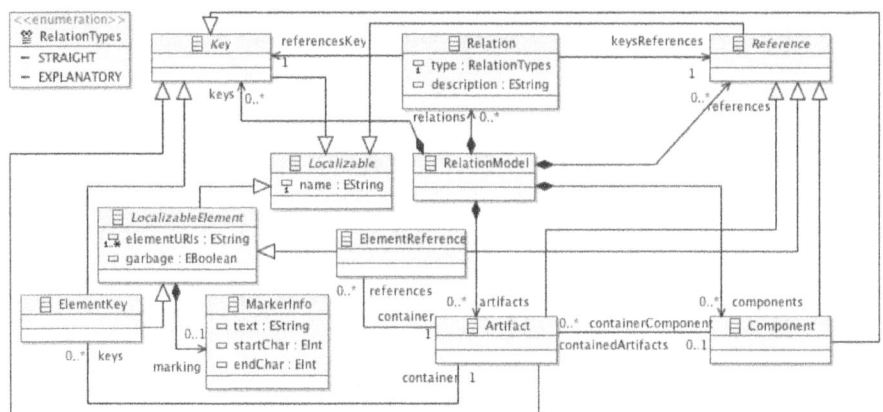

Fig. 6. TexMo's explicit relation model

models. Second, we provide preliminary evidence on the feasibility of TexMo by testing user acceptance. Furthermore, we discuss applicability of TexMo's relation model with respect to keeping inter-language relations while testers are using TexMo.

The subject used for this evaluation is the open-source web-based bug-tracking system, JTrac. JTrac's code base consists of 374 files. The majority of files, 291, contain source code in Java (141), HTML (65), property files (32), XML (16), JavaScript (8), and 29 other source code files such as Shell scripts, etc. Similar to many web-applications, JTrac implements the model-view-controller (MVC) pattern. This is achieved using popular frameworks: Hibernate (`hibernate.org`) for OR-Mapping and Wicket (`cwiki.apache.org/WICKET/`) to couple views and controller code. The remaining 83 files are images and a single jar file. We did not consider these files in our evaluation since they do not contain information in a human processable, textual syntax. Clearly, JTrac is an MLSS.

4.1 Universal Language Representation

To evaluate TexMo's universal language representation, we manually opened all 291 mograms with the TexMo editor to check if a correct text model can be established. By correct we mean that any character and string in a source code artifact has a corresponding model element in the text model, which in turn allows the RM to interrelate mograms in different languages. The files used are available at: `www.itu.dk/~ropf/download/jtrac_experiment.zip`.

We concluded that all 291 source code files can be opened with the TexMo editor. For all files a correct text model has been established.

4.2 User Test

To test user acceptance, we let 11 testers perform three typical development tasks. The testers included 4 professional developers, 3 PhD students, and 4 undergraduate students, with median 3 years of working experience as software developers.

Using only a short tutorial, which explains TexMo's features the testers had to work on the JTrac system. First, they had to find and remove a previously injected error, a broken fixed relation. Second, they had to rename a reference and fix the now broken relation. Third, they had to replace a code block, which removes two keys. We captured the screen contents and observed each tester. After task completion, each tester filled out a questionnaire. Questions asked for work experience, proficiency in development of MLSS using Java, HTML, and XML. Additionally, two open questions on the purpose of the test and on the usefulness of TexMo where asked. After the completion of questionnaires we had a short, open discussion about TexMo where we took notes on tester's opinions.

We conclude that the testers understand and use MLDE concepts. Seven testers applied inter-language navigation to better understand the source code, i.e., to inspect keys and references whenever an error was reported. Furthermore, another seven used rename refactorings to securely evolve cross-language relations in JTrac. All testers were able to find all errors and to fix them. In the following we quote a selection of the testers arguing about usefulness of TexMo (we avoid quoting complete statements for the sake of brevity). Their statements indicate that visualization, static checking, navigation and refactoring across language boundaries are useful and that such features are missing in existing IDEs.

Q: *"Do you think TexMo could be beneficial in software development? Why?"*
A_1: *"TexMo's concepts are really convincing. I would like to have a tool like this at work."*
A_2: *"Liked the references part and the checking. Usually, if you change the keys/references you get errors at runtime [which is] kind of late in the process."*
A_3: *"[TexMo] improves debugging time by keeping track of changes on source code written in different programming languages that are strongly related. I do not know any tool like this."*
A_4: *"I see [TexMo] useful, especially when many people work on the same project, and, of course, in case the projects gets big."*
A_5: *"I did development with Spring and a tool like TexMo would solve a lot of problems while coding."*
A_6: *"In large applications it is difficult to perform renaming or refactoring tasks without automated tracking of references. ... If there would be such a reference mechanism between JavaScript and C#, it would save us a lot of work."*
A_7: *"[TexMo] solves [a] common problem experienced when software project involves multiple languages."*

Robustness of the Relation Model. To run the user test and to demonstrate that the RM can express inter-language relations in an MLSS, we established a RM relating 9 artifacts containing 51 keys, 87 references, via 87 fixed relations with each other. The RM relates code in Java, HTML, and properties files with each other. We did not aim for a *complete* RM, since we focus on demonstrating TexMo's general applicability. After the testers had finished their development tasks, we inspected the RMs manually to verify that they still correctly interrelate keys and references.

We conclude that TexMo's RM is robust to modifications of the MLSS. After modification operations, all relations in the RM correctly relate keys and references across language boundaries.

A common concern of the testers related to replacing a code block containing multiple keys with a new code block, where TexMo complains about a number of created dangling references in corresponding files. We did not implement a feature to automatically infer possible keys out of the newly inserted code, since we consider this process impossible to automate completely.

4.3 Threats to Validity

The code base of JTrac might be to small to allow to generalize that any textual mogram in any language can be represented using TexMo's text model. However, we think that nearly 300 source code files in 15 languages gives a rather strong indication. The RM used for the user tests might be to small and incomplete. We were not interested in creating a complete RM, but only concerned about its general applicability.

To avoid direct influence on the testers in an oral interview, we used a written questionnaire. All quotes in the paper are taken from this written data.

5 Related Work

Strein et. al. argue that contemporary IDEs do not allow for analysis and refactoring of MLSS and thus are not suitable for development of such. They present X-Develop an MLDE implementing an extensible meta-model [28] used for a syntactic per language group representation. The key difference between X-Develop and TexMo is the language representation. TexMo's universal language representation allows for its application in development of any MLSS regardless of the used languages. Similarly, the IntelliJ IDEA IDE implements some multi-language development support mechanisms. It provides multi-language refactorings across some exclusive languages, e.g., HTML and CSS. Unlike in TexMo, these inter-language mechanisms are specific to particular languages since IntelliJ IDEA relies on a per language representation.

Some development frameworks provide tools to enhance IDEs. Our evaluation case, JTrac relies on the web framework Wicket. *QWickie* (code.google.com/p/qwickie), an Eclipse plugin, implements navigation and renaming support between inter-related HTML and Java files containing Wicket code. The drawback of framework-specific tools is their limited applicability. QWickie cannot be used for development with other frameworks mixing HTML and Java files.

Chimera [2] provides hypertext functionality for heterogeneous *Software Development Environments (SDE)*. Different programs like text editors, PDF viewers and browsers form an SDE. These programs are viewers through which developers work on different artifacts. Chimera allows for the definition of anchors on views. Anchors can be interrelated via links into a hyperweb. TexMo is similar in that models of mograms can be regarded as views where each model element can serve as an anchor for a relation. Chimera is not dynamic. It does not automatically evolve anchors while mograms are modified. Subsequent to modifications, Chimera users need to manually reestablish anchors and adapt the links to it. Contrary, TexMo automatically evolves the RM synchronously to modifications applied to mograms. Only after deleting code blocks containing keys, users need to manually update the dangling references.

Meyers [20] discusses integrating tools in multi-view development systems. One can consider language integration as a particular flavor of tool integration. Meyers describes basic tool integration on file system level, where each tool keeps a separate internal data representation. This corresponds to the per language representation in our taxonomy. Meyers' *canonical* representation for tool integration corresponds to our universal language representation. Our work extends Meyers work by identifying a per language group representation.

6 Conclusion and Future Work

We have presented a taxonomy of multi-language development environments, and TexMo, an MLDE prototype implementing a universal language representation, an explicit relation model supporting free and fixed relations. The taxonomy is established by surveying related literature and tools. We have also argued that implementation of TexMo meets is design objectives and evaluated adequacy of its design. By itself TexMo demonstrates that design of useful MLDEs is feasible and welcomed. We reported very positive early user experiences.

To gather further experience, we plan to extend TexMo with string-transformation and domain-specific relations and compare it to an MLDE using a per language representation. We realized that it is costly to keep an explicit RM updated while developers work on a system, especially the larger a RM grows. Therefore, we will experiment with a search-based relation model. This will also overcome the vulnerability of an explicit RM to changes applied to mograms outside the control of the MLDE.

Note, TexMo's RM does not only allow the interrelation of mograms of different languages but also of mograms in a single language. We do not focus on this fact in this paper. However, this ability can be used to enhance and customize static checks and visualizations beyond those provided by current IDEs without extending compilers and other tools.

While working with TexMo we realized that a universal language representation is favorable if an MLDE has to be quickly applied to a wide variety of systems with respect to the variety of used languages. Furthermore, there is a trade-off between the language representation mechanism and the richness of the tools an MLDE can provide. Basic support, like visualization, highlighting, navigation and rename refactorings, can be easily developed on any language representation, with very wild applicability if the universal representation is used. More complex refactorings require a per group or a per language representation.

In future we plan to build support to automatically infer inter-language relations. Fixed and string-transformation relations can be automatically established by searching for equal or similar strings. This process is not trivial as soon as a language provides for example scoping. Then inferring inter-language relations has to additionally consider language specific scoping rules. Inferring domain-specific relations has to rely on additional knowledge provided by developers, for example as patterns [23], which explicitly encode domain knowledge. Inferring free relations is probably not completely automatable but relying on heuristics and search engines could result in appropriate inter-language relation candidates.

Acknowledgements. We thank Kasper Østerbye, Peter Sestoft and David Christiansen for discussion and feedback on models for representation of language groups and for feedback on the TexMo prototype. EMFText developers have provided technical support during TexMo's development. Chris Grindstaff has developed the Color Editor (gstaff.org/colorEditor), parts of which were reused for TexMo's syntax highlighting. Last but not least, we also thank all the testers participating in the experiment.

References

1. Zend Technologies Ltd.: Taking the Pulse of the Developer Community, http://static.zend.com/topics/zend-developer-pulse-survey-report-0112-EN.pdf (February 2012)
2. Anderson, K.M., Taylor, R.N., Whitehead Jr., E.J.: Chimera: Hypermedia for Heterogeneous Software Development Enviroments. ACM Trans. Inf. Syst. 18 (July 2000)
3. Badros, G.J.: JavaML: A Markup Language for Java Source Code. Comput. Netw. 33 (June 2000)
4. Bruneliere, H., Cabot, J., Jouault, F., Madiot, F.: MoDisco: A Generic and Extensible Framework for Model Driven Reverse Engineering. In: Proc. of the IEEE/ACM International Conference on Automated Software Engineering (2010)
5. Czarnecki, K., Eisenecker, U.W.: Generative Programming: Methods, Tools, and Applications (2000)
6. Erlikh, L.: Leveraging Legacy System Dollars for E-Business. IT Professional 2 (May 2000)
7. de Figueiredo Carneiro, G., Mendonça, M.G., Magnavita, R.C.: An experimental platform to characterize software comprehension activities supported by visualization. In: ICSE Companion (2009)
8. Groenewegen, D.M., Hemel, Z., Visser, E.: Separation of Concerns and Linguistic Integration in WebDSL. IEEE Software 27(5) (2010)
9. Guerra, E., de Lara, J., Kolovos, D.S., Paige, R.F.: Inter-modelling: From Theory to Practice. In: Petriu, D.C., Rouquette, N., Haugen, Ø. (eds.) MODELS 2010, Part I. LNCS, vol. 6394, pp. 376–391. Springer, Heidelberg (2010)
10. Halasz, F.G., Schwartz, M.D.: The Dexter Hypertext Reference Model. Commun. ACM 37(2) (1994)
11. Heidenreich, F., Johannes, J., Seifert, M., Wende, C.: Closing the Gap between Modelling and Java. In: van den Brand, M., Gašević, D., Gray, J. (eds.) SLE 2009. LNCS, vol. 5969, pp. 374–383. Springer, Heidelberg (2010)
12. Hessellund, A.: SmartEMF: Guidance in Modeling Tools. In: Companion to the 22nd ACM SIGPLAN Conference on Object-Oriented Programming Systems and Applications Companion (2007)

13. Hessellund, A., Wąsowski, A.: Interfaces and Metainterfaces for Models and Metamodels. In: Czarnecki, K., Ober, I., Bruel, J.-M., Uhl, A., Völter, M. (eds.) MODELS 2008. LNCS, vol. 5301, pp. 401–415. Springer, Heidelberg (2008)
14. Holst, W.: Meta: A Universal Meta-Language for Augmenting and Unifying Language Families, Featuring Meta(oopl) for Object-Oriented Programming Languages. In: Companion to the 20th annual ACM SIGPLAN Conference on Object-Oriented Programming, Systems, Languages, and Applications (2005)
15. Jouault, F., Vanhooff, B., Bruneliere, H., Doux, G., Berbers, Y., Bezivin, J.: Inter-DSL Coordination Support by Combining Megamodeling and Model Weaving. In: Proceedings of the 2010 ACM Symposium on Applied Computing (2010)
16. Kang, K.C., Cohen, S.G., Hess, J.A., Novak, W.E., Peterson, A.S.: Feature-Oriented Domain Analysis (FODA) Feasibility Study. Tech. rep., Carnegie-Mellon University Software Engineering Institute (1990)
17. Kats, L.C.L., Visser, E.: The Spoofax Language Workbench: Rules for Declarative Specification of Languages and IDEs. In: OOPSLA (2010)
18. Kleppe, A.: Software Language Engineering: Creating Domain-Specific Languages Using Metamodels (2008)
19. Lientz, B.P., Swanson, E.B., Tompkins, G.E.: Characteristics of Application Software Maintenance. Commun. ACM 21 (June 1978)
20. Meyers, S.: Difficulties in Integrating Multiview Development Systems. IEEE Softw. 8 (1991)
21. Murphy-Hill, E., Parnin, C., Black, A.P.: How we refactor, and how we know it. In: Proc. of the 31st International Conference on Software Engineering (2009)
22. Paige, R.F., Drivalos, N., Kolovos, D.S., Fernandes, K.J., Power, C., Olsen, G.K., Zschaler, S.: Rigorous Identification and Encoding of Trace-Links in Model-Driven Engineering. Softw. Syst. Model. 10 (October 2011)
23. Pfeiffer, R.-H., Wąsowski, A.: Taming the Confusion of Languages. In: France, R.B., Kuester, J.M., Bordbar, B., Paige, R.F. (eds.) ECMFA 2011. LNCS, vol. 6698, pp. 312–328. Springer, Heidelberg (2011)
24. Salay, R., Mylopoulos, J., Easterbrook, S.: Using Macromodels to Manage Collections of Related Models. In: van Eck, P., Gordijn, J., Wieringa, R. (eds.) CAiSE 2009. LNCS, vol. 5565, pp. 141–155. Springer, Heidelberg (2009)
25. Standish, T.A.: An Essay on Software Reuse. IEEE Trans. Software Eng. (1984)
26. Steinberger, M., Waldner, M., Streit, M., Lex, A., Schmalstieg, D.: Context-Preserving Visual Links. IEEE Transactions on Visualization and Computer Graphics (InfoVis 2011) 17(12) (2011)
27. Strein, D., Kratz, H., Lowe, W.: Cross-Language Program Analysis and Refactoring. In: Proc. of the 6th IEEE International Workshop on Source Code Analysis and Manipulation (2006)
28. Strein, D., Lincke, R., Lundberg, J., Löwe, W.: An Extensible Meta-Model for Program Analysis. IEEE Trans. Softw. Eng. 33 (September 2007)
29. Wagner, S., Deissenboeck, F.: Abstractness, Specificity, and Complexity in Software Design. In: Proc. of the 2nd International Workshop on the Role of Abstraction in Software Engineering (2008)
30. Waldner, M., Puff, W., Lex, A., Streit, M., Schmalstieg, D.: Visual Links Across Applications. In: Proc. of Graphics Interface (2010)
31. Xing, Z., Stroulia, E.: Refactoring practice: How it is and how it should be supported — an Eclipse case study. In: Proc. of the 22nd IEEE International Conference on Software Maintenance (2006)

On-the-Fly Emendation of Multi-level Models

Colin Atkinson, Ralph Gerbig*, and Bastian Kennel

University of Mannheim, Mannheim, Germany
{atkinson,gerbig,kennel}@informatik.uni-mannheim.de

Abstract. One of the main advantages of multi-level modeling environments over traditional modeling environments is that all ontological classification levels are treated in a uniform way and are all equally available for immediate, on-the-fly modification. However, such flexibility is a two-edged sword, since a minor change in a (meta-) ontological level can have a dramatic impact on other parts of the ontology (i.e. collection of ontological levels) - requiring a large number of "knock-on" changes to keep the overall ontology correct. To effectively exploit the modeling flexibility offered by multi-level modeling environments therefore, modelers need semi-automated support for emending ontologies to keep them consistent in the face of changes. In this paper we describe a model emendation architecture and illustrate how it can help modelers maintain the correctness of an ontology.

Keywords: multi-level emendation, orthogonal classification architecture, ontological classification, linguistic classification.

1 Introduction

Although meta-modeling is now a widely practiced activity in software engineering, and meta-models play a pivotal role in advanced model-driven development projects, most contemporary modeling environments still place unnecessary limitations on the way meta-models can be defined, evolved and applied. This is because most environments are still based on the idea of applying a two-level physical platform to a logical multi-level modeling hierarchy in a fixed and unchangeable way. Traditional modeling environments apply the physical platform to the M_2 and M_1 levels of the OMG model hierarchy so that the M_2 level is the frozen type level (i.e. hardwired into the platform) and the M_1 level is the editable instance data. Meta-modeling environments (such as language engineering environments) apply the platform to the M_3 and M_2 levels so that M_3 is the frozen type level and the M_2 level is the evolvable instance data. This approach is fine as long as users are content to work within the single evolvable level supported by a tool, but it requires complex transformations and recompilations to be performed as soon as they wish to make the results of their work applicable

---

* Ralph Gerbig was supported by Deutsche Forschungsgemeinschaft (DFG) as part of SPP 1496 "Reliably Secure Software Systems".

to lower logical levels not supported by the tool. These transformations and recompilations required to "deploy" a model are not only cumbersome and time consuming, they are also error prone. To support such scenarios tools like Edapt [4] in the EMF universe exist.

Multi-level modeling aims to overcome this problem by making all logical classification levels editable and evolvable as linguistic instance data in a uniform and level-agnostic way. It is still based on a two-level physical platform, but the frozen type model (the linguistic model) is specially designed to support multiple logical (a.k.a ontological) levels at the linguistic instance level below. This so called Orthogonal Classification Architecture (OCA) therefore supports two distinct forms of classification, organized in two orthogonal dimensions - linguistic classification which is supported directly by the underlying physical platform and ontological classification which is supported within the evolvable linguistic level. By arranging for all end user modeling and meta-modeling services (e.g. DSL definition and application capabilities) to be supported within the ontological levels all modeling capabilities at all classification levels become equally accessible, editable and evolvable as instance data within the tool.

This so called "real-time" (meta-)modeling capability provides tremendous flexibility and evolvability advantages for model-driven development, and makes it easier to use models at run-time to drive the execution of systems in an adaptable and knowledge-driven way. However, it also creates tremendous problems for modelers to keep a model up-to-date whenever changes are made, and to ensure that an ontology (the collection of ontological data across all the ontological levels) remains consistent. Since the number of ontological levels is unlimited, a change to a model element in one ontological level (i.e. a model) could have an impact on a large number of elements over an unlimited number of lower and higher ontological levels. The effective use of this extra flexibility is therefore contingent on the multi-level modeling environment providing dynamic, real-time (i.e. on-the-fly) support for propagating the effects of a change to the affected parts of the ontology. Sometimes this may be performed automatically, but in most cases the tool needs to obtain further input from modelers about the intended effects of changes.

In terms of today's software engineering environments, this capability most closely resembles the idea of refactoring that is used to improve the quality of software engineering artifacts [5]. Refactoring involves the enactment of various kinds of enhancements to a software artifact to change it into a new form. It has traditionally been applied to code or architecture artifacts but there is increasing awareness of the value of applying it at the level of models [12,3] and ontologies [9,7]. However, refactoring as recognized in traditional software engineering environments differs from the on-the-fly changes required in multi-level modeling environments in one important and fundamental aspect - the former are performed with the specific goal of retaining the original meaning of the artifact concerned, while the latter are performed with the specific goal of changing the meaning of a currently invalid ontology to make it valid again. We therefore use the term "emendation" rather than "refactoring" to characterize the process of evolving a multi-level model, on the fly, to restore it to a state of validity since this precisely captures the intent and nature of the process. Emendation is defined as "an alteration designed to correct or improve" in the Miriam-Webster English dictionary [10]. We believe this therefore represents the most accurate term for describing the process of (and associated techniques for) making changes to an ontology (i.e. a set of ontological levels) in order to bring it back to a state of correctness after a user-induced change.

As well as introducing the notion and goals behind model emendation the contribution of this paper is to present an architecture for automatic emendation support and an initial prototype we have developed to support it. The remainder of this paper is structured as follows: in the next section we first introduce multi-level modeling (Section 2). In the section after that ontology consistency and the resulting requirements for an emendation service are outlined (Section 3). After identifying the ontology consistency requirements, an architecture which can support emendation of multi-level models and our prototypical implementation are presented (Section 4). Afterwards, we show how semi-automatic emendation support can help a modeler on a small example of an online pet store (Section 5). The paper then closes with a discussion of future work (Section 6) and a conclusion (Section 7).

2 Multi-level Modeling

Multi-level modeling supports the creation of ontologies containing an arbitrary number of classification levels (i.e. models) unlike traditional modeling environments like MOF or Ecore, where the number of classification (i.e. meta-) levels is fixed and limited. This is an advantage when a modeler is modeling a domain with more than two inherent classification levels. With traditional approaches a modeler can only capture two levels, the meta-model and the meta-model instance. The key to supporting multi-level modeling is the so called Orthogonal Classification Architecture (OCA) in which (the majority of) model elements have two fundamental types rather than one as illustrated in Figure 1 - an ontological type, defined by the modeled problem domain at L_1, and a linguistic one defined by the level-spanning modeling language at L_2. Traditional modeling environments mix up these two kinds of classification. For example, in Ecore the meta-level M_3 usually describes the available language constructs which are then instantiated at level M_2 and M_1 to capture the domain of interest. In contrast, in a multi-level modeling environment, linguistic and ontological (i.e. domain) classification are separated into two distinct classification dimensions as illustrated in Figure 1. Linguistic classification is indicated through vertically dotted instantiation arrows whereas ontological classification is indicated through horizontally dashed classification arrows. This orthogonality gives the architecture on which multi-level modeling bases its name [1](Orthogonal Classification Architecture). Linguistic classification does not only provide a linguistic type but also linguistic attributes (e.g. potency) called traits. Ontological attributes provided through a model element's ontological type are called attributes.

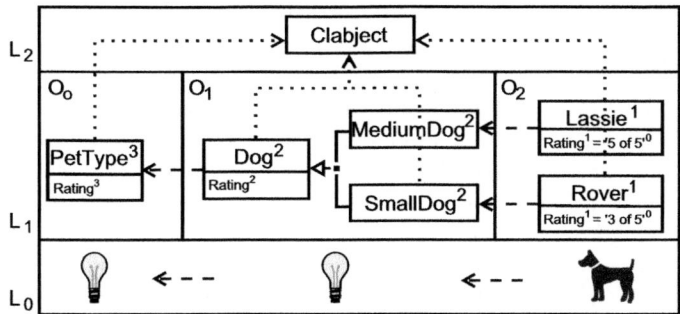

Fig. 1. The pet store web shop ontology

From the diagram in Figure 1 it is clear that model elements residing in the middle levels of ontologies, e.g. Dog, are simultaneously an instance of a type at a higher ontological level, PetType, and types for model elements on lower ontological levels, Lassie and Rover, at the same time. To capture this class/object duality of model elements the term "clabject" which is a composite of the words "class" and "object" is introduced.

Every ontological model element in L_1, the so called ontology, has an annotation in the form of a superscript. This number is the element's potency. Features (attributes and methods) and attribute values also have a potency. The notion of potency allows a clabject to be instantiated over a predefined number of ontological levels, depending on the properties of the subject of the model. Potencies can have either a non-negative integer value or ∗ value representing infinity or unlimited. If a clabject has an integer potency, p, every instance of that clabject at the lower level must have potency p-1. Thus, a clabject with potency 0 can have no instances. A clabject with ∗ potency can have instances with any integer potency or with ∗ potency. The example in Figure 1 shows the potencies of all model elements. All elements at level O_0 have a potency of 3, their instances at level O_1 have potency 2 and their instances at level O_2 have potency 1. Feature potency specifies over how many levels a feature can endure over, i.e. be passed on to instances. That is why this value is also called durability. A feature with durability 1 exists in the following level only, a feature with durability 2 in the following 2 levels and so on. The value potency (mutability) determines over how many levels an attribute can be changed. A value with mutability 0 cannot be changed on the next level while a value with mutability 1 can be changed on the next level. In terms of traditional modeling languages like UML, clabjects with potency 1 correspond to traditional types and clabjects with potency 0 correspond to traditional objects. No equivalent in the UML can be found for clabjects with potencies higher than 1.

Another major difference between multi-level modeling environments and traditional modeling technologies is that one can change all levels of a multi-level model at the same time. Changes on one level immediately effect all other levels. We usually refer to this concept as real-time (meta-)modeling. In traditional meta-modeling environments the meta-model is fixed when editing a meta-model instance (i.e. a model). Moreover, when editing a meta-model, instances of that model are usually not directly accessible. Because only two levels are ever available for modeling (usually the meta-model and model), we refer to such environments as two-level modeling environments. The limitations of such environments make it difficult for a language engineer to alter more than one level on-the-fly during model creation. When all model levels are equally available for modeling at all times new possibilities for creating, debugging and extending domain-specific modeling languages are created.

Figure 1 shows an ontology which classifies different kinds of pets and their instances. Level O_0 defines the ontological type PetType with Potency 3 which is the basis for all types of pets, e.g. dogs or cats. Having a potency of 3 enables PetType to be instantiated over the next three levels. PetType owns the attribute Rating which expresses the rating of a pet. The durability of 3 states that the rating attribute must exist on the next three levels. The mutability of the attribute is not shown because it is the same as the durability (the default). Thus the mutability of Rating is also 3. The category Dog is instantiated on O_1 as instance of PetType. Dog is further subdivided into SmallDog and MediumDog as subtypes of Dog. These ontological types from O_1 are used to create Rover and Lassie as instances at level O_2. The potency 1 of the elements on O_2 states that these can be instantiated on one more level which is not shown here. In addition to their ontological type every model element in the ontological levels also has a linguistic type, clabject, indicated through the dotted vertical instantiation arrows.

3 Ontology Consistency Semantics

The central premise when emending an ontology after a user-induced change is that the ontology was *correct* before the change occurred and shall be *correct* again afterwards. Two questions are of fundamental importance for the following discussion:

1. What does it mean for an ontology to be "correct"?
2. How can the ontology "break", i.e. which aspects of the correctness can be violated by a change?

We define two concepts for the informal meaning of correctness. First, an ontology is **consistent** if there is no information inside the ontology that contradicts another statement in the ontology. Second, an ontology is **complete** if it is consistent and all the statements inside the ontology are true. The detailed formal definition of all concepts presented in this paper can be found in [6].

The difference between consistency and completeness stems from the maturity of the ontology. If a clabject has potency two, the statement is that there are (or will be) instances of the clabjects instances. If those 2nd order instances are not present yet, the ontology is not *complete*. If there are no contradictions otherwise, it is nevertheless *consistent*. The focus of this paper is to restore ontology **consistency** by applying emendation operations.

3.1 Ontology Consistency

Building up on the informal definition of consistency above, the property of ontology consistency is split up in two parts:

REQ 1: All classification relationships have to be correct, i.e. an instance has to be an instance of its type according to multi-level classification semantics.

REQ 2: All generalization relationships have to be correct, i.e. the classified model (i.e. ontological level) has to respect the claims implied by the boolean traits of the generalization.

Classifications point from the instance to the type and generalizations are statements about the instances of the sub- and supertypes. So for the consistency of one model, the classifications of the models itself as well as the generalizations of the classifying model are relevant. If the subject model is at the top of the model stack, it has no classifications or classifying model. So the top model is always consistent by definition. Figure 2 gives an overview of the constraints.

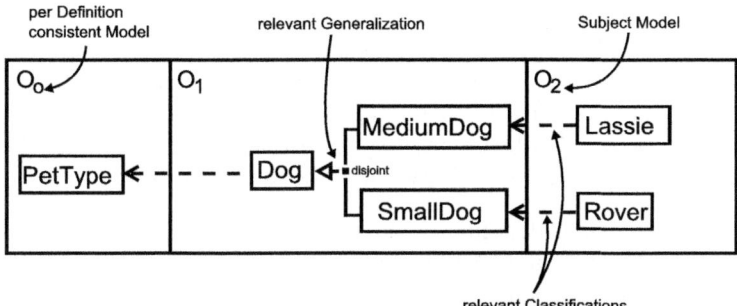

Fig. 2. Ontology consistency dependencies

3.2 Classification Correctness

The correctness of a classification requires the instance to be an instance of the type according to multi-level classification semantics. For an instance to be an instance of the type, it has to define all the properties defined by the type[1] and have a conforming potency. Conforming potency means that the potency is one lower than the type's potency. In case the type's potency is $*$ the instance's potency has to be $*$ or any positive natural number. Having all properties means that for every feature its type defines, the instance has to define a conforming feature. For every mandatory connection the type takes part in, the instance has to take part in a corresponding connection. Connection participation is mandatory if the connection has a potency greater than zero and the multiplicity of the

---

[1] The notion of instance actually has a more refined meaning, including different kinds of instances depending on whether they define more properties than needed by the type or not. See [6] for details. Strictly speaking the rules presented here are valid only for isonymic classification relationships

other end of the connection is greater than zero. Both features and connection participation are properties that can be inherited from supertypes. To conform a feature has to match the name and conform to the durability of the type's corresponding feature. If the feature is an attribute, the value potency has to conform and if the type's attribute has 0 mutability the value has to be the same. So the requirements of classification correctness can be summarized as:

REQ 1.1: The potency of the instance has to conform to the type's potency.

REQ 1.2: For every feature of the type the instance has to have a conforming feature.

REQ 1.3: For every mandatory connection the type participates in, the instance has to participate in a conforming one.

3.3 Generalization Correctness

The correctness of a generalization requires that the classified domain respects the constraints imposed by the boolean traits of the generalization. Formally, the correctness of a generalization also requires that every instance of the subtype[2] is also an instance of the supertype. This constraint is true by definition as the properties of the supertype are always a subset of the properties of the subtype. A generalization can have three boolean traits: *disjoint, complete* and *intersection*. Although their type is boolean, these traits do not need to be set, this means that a generalization can choose between three alternatives[3]:

1. it can state that it is disjoint,
2. it can state that it is not disjoint or
3. it can make no statement about disjointness.

The difference between the second and the third is that the third does not impose any constraints whereas the second states that the opposite of disjointness is true. So detailed requirements of generalizations are:

REQ 2.1: If the generalization is disjoint there must not be an instance of the supertype that is an instance of more than one of the subtypes. If the generalization is not disjoint, there has to be an instance of the supertype that is an instance of more than one of the subtypes.

REQ 2.2: If the generalization is complete, there must not be an instance of the supertype that is not an instance of any of the subtypes. If the generalization is not complete, there has to be an instance of the supertype that is not an instance of any of the subtypes.

REQ 2.3: If the generalization is an intersection, there must not be an instance of all the supertypes that is not an instance of the subtype. If the generalization is not an intersection, there has to be an instance of all the supertypes that is not an instance of the subtype.

---

[2] There may be more than one subtype, or more than one supertype.
[3] On the example of disjoint.

4 Suggested Emendation Service Architecture

The architecture for context sensitive ontology emendation support, displayed in Figure 3, consists of 3 components, the multi-level model, the emendation service and the impact analyzer. The emendation service subscribes to changes in the ontology. It is unimportant how the changes to the ontology are actually performed (e.g. via code, graphical editor, tree structure editor etc.). Once the emendation service is notified of a change to the ontology, it asks the impact analyzer to compute all model elements which are effected by this change. For impact analysis, the classification semantics and the resulting requirements presented earlier in this work are used. If the computation reveals an impact on more than the changed model element, the emendation service is triggered. This then suggests operations which can be performed to rectify the situation and asks the user to select which is the most appropriate. Alternatively the user can cancel the actions that are about to be executed by the emendation service. After configuration, the emendation service executes the emendation operations which are needed to keep the model consistent. If no impact on other than the changed model element is calculated by the impact analyzer the emendation services does not act. The architecture shows that the configuration information for the impact analyzer and the emendation service is loosely coupled and can be changed on the fly while using a multi-level modeling environment.

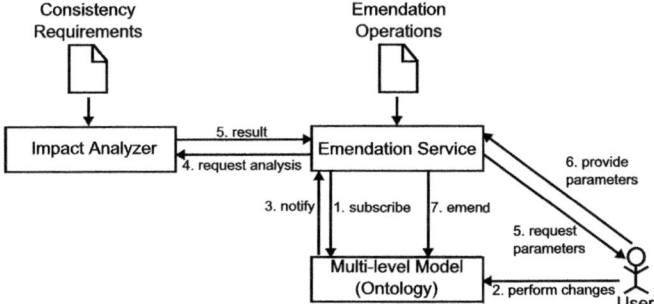

Fig. 3. The suggested emendation service architecture

Some changes to an ontology are hard to support with an automatic emendation service in an appropriate way. One of these cases is the introduction of a connection with a multiplicity with a lower bound higher than "1". In such a case all instances of the clabject at the opposite end of this connection end must have added a connection to an instance of the clabject at the connection end with the lower bound higher than "1". It is very hard to automatically guide a user through such a process because, for example, the clabjects to which the instance clabject needs to be connected may not exist at the time of the change. In such cases automated emendation is not recommended and model validation is preferred. After saving the multi-level model, all model elements with inconsistencies are marked and in some cases automatic fixes are provided for the indicated problems. However, such model validation approaches are beyond the scope of this paper.

At the time of writing, a prototype implementation of this proposed emendation architecture is implemented in the Melanie [13] multi-level modeling tool. The consistency rules and emendation operations are currently hard coded into the tool but this will be changed in future versions. Melanie provides automatic and context sensitive emendation support and a limited number of classification related emendation operations. However, the number of these operations is continually growing. Support for automatically applying recorded emendation operations to other, deployed ontologies (e.g. [9]) is not implemented at the moment. The user does not explicitly need to invoke the emendation mechanism to get assistance while editing a model. All changes to the edited ontology are permanently tracked and evaluated. As soon as a user performs an operation on a classification relationship that requires mandatory changes to more than the currently edited model element, he/she automatically receives assistance from Melanie's emendation service. A dialog or sophisticated wizard, depending on the operation, can be displayed to guide the user through the process of emendation. The collected input from the user is then used to configure the emendation service before execution. If the user does not want any assistance he can simply switch off the emendation support via the user interface. In addition to the emendation service Melanie provides basic model validation services and operations to fix errors which are invoked when a multi-level model is saved.

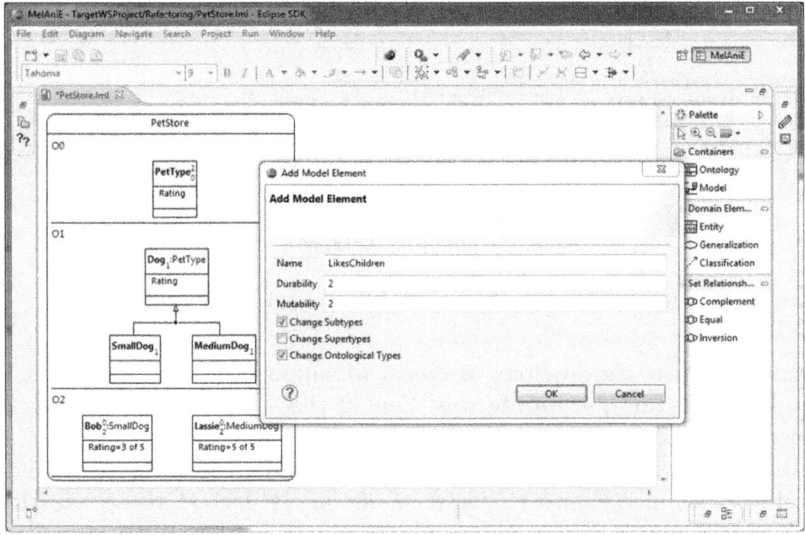

Fig. 4. Screenshot of the emendation support offered by Melanie. The attribute LikesChildren is added to MediumDog.

Figure 4 shows the dialog that a user receives, after performing an operation which effects more than the directly changed model-element. Here the user added the feature LikesChildren to the clabject MediumDog. The impact analyzer has noticed that this change can potentially effect the instances of MediumDog which is Lassie in this case. Additionally, this could also effect the superclass Dog. If the user also wants to change the clabject Dog its ontological type PetType, and the instances of SmallDog namely Rover are effected as well. Hence, the displayed dialog offers the options "Change Subtypes", "Change Supertypes", "Change Ontological Types" to configure the emendation service. In this case the user decides to not change the supertype which is indicated by the not selected "Change Supertypes" option in the "Add Model Element" dialog. After selecting "OK" the emendation operations are performed. If the user selects "Cancel" and explicitly states by doing so that no action is desired, the emendation service will perform no action. The example shown here is quite simple. More extensive support in the form of wizards guiding a user through a multi-staged emendation process can be provided if appropriate.

5 Case Study: Emendation of an Online Pet Store

In this section we show how multi-level model emendation services can help a modeler keep an online pet store [2] correct in the face of ongoing changes. The chapter is organized according to refactoring operation categories proposed by Opdyke [11]: "Creating a Program Entity", "Deleting a Program Entity", "Changing a Program Entity" and "Moving a Member Variable". The following list of emendation operations is not exhaustive but rather a starting point illustrating the need and use of emendation operations. However, the operations in the following subsections where chosen to cover the most common operations which are executed on an ontology during evolution. Figure 5 shows the pet store ontology described in the previous multi-level modeling introduction. A shop sells different PetTypes. In the beginning only Dogs are sold. These are divided into MediumDog and SmallDog with two instances - Lassie and Rover. This ontology builds the basis for the web store because all content of the web store is generated out of this ontology. Therefore, changing the ontology changes the content in the web store. Throughout the case study changes in the pet store's environment need to be reflected in the ontology. After a short explanation of the reason for the change, the nature of the applied abstract change

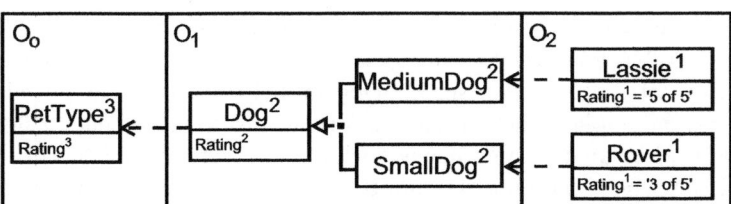

Fig. 5. The initial pet store ontology

operation (highlighted in italics) applied is described, the violated requirements are enumerated and the automated steps suggested by the emendation service are elaborated.

5.1 Adding New Pets and LikesChildren Attribute - Creating a Program Entity

The web store decides to sell dogs as well as cats. Thus on O_1 Cat is instantiated from PetType and two subclasses HairyCat and GroomedCat are added. From these two subclasses Max and Moritz are instantiated. *Adding a new clabjects* does not violate any ontology consistency rules as the new model elements do not participate in a classification relationship or effect any model elements participating in a classification relationship. *Adding new clabjects through instantiation* does not effect the classification relationship between a type and the new instance as all rules for classification are automatically satisfied by the instantiation operation. Thus, the impact analyzer calculates no impact on the changed ontology and does not invoke the semi-automated emendation support. However, the process of instantiating an instance from a type can be interpreted as an emendation operation itself, because a new model element together with a classification relationship are created and setup to automatically fulfill all sub-requirements of REQ1.

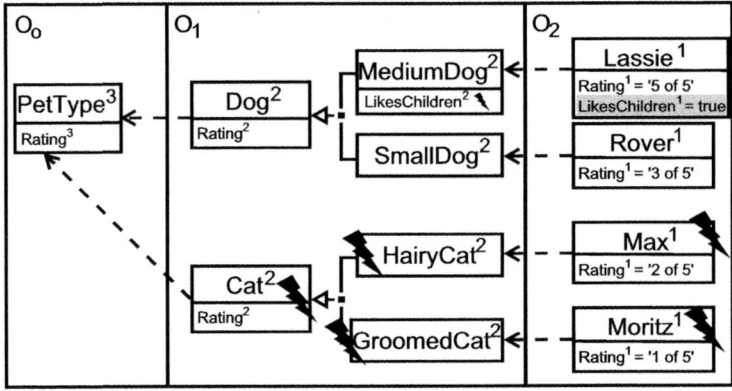

Fig. 6. The pet store ontology after adding cats and the LikesChildren attribute

Furthermore, some customers reported that it is useful to know if a MediumDog is suitable for parents. Hence, the pet store owner decides to add the LikesChildren attribute to the MediumDog model element. The *introduction of new features* can violate the classification relationship consistency rule REQ1.2 which states that an instance needs to have one conforming feature for each feature of the type. Changing the number of features, whether by adding or removing them, breaks this requirement for the clabject in the role as instance and type. The clabject's types need to have the feature added so that the clabject has one conforming feature for each feature of the type and the instances need to have the new feature added for the same reason. In this case the impact analyzer detects a violation between MediumDog and Lassie because MediumDog now owns the feature LikesChildren which is not owned by Lassie. The user is automatically assisted in fixing this by adding the attribute to all instances of MediumDog. MediumDog is not involved in any other classification relationships, either as type or instance so no further changes are needed. Figure 6 shows the resulting ontology with cats and the LikesChildren attribute added.

5.2 Changing the Potency of PetType, LikesChildren and Rating - Changing a Program Entity

Later the pet store decides that no instances of model elements at level O_2 are needed. Hence, the potency of PetType is changed from 3 to 2 to fix the number of available model levels to three. A *change to the potency of a clabject* violates REQ1.1 which defines that an instance's potency has to conform to the potency of its type. Such a change means the model element's potency does not conform to the type's potency anymore and the instance's potency does not conform to the model element's anymore. The impact analyzer detects this change to the potency of PetType and calculates that a change to the potency violates the classification relationships it takes part in. Thus, it offers to change the potency of all model elements which are instances of PetType - Dog, Cat, MediumDog, SmallDog, HairyCat, GroomedCat, Lassie, Rover, Max, Moritz.

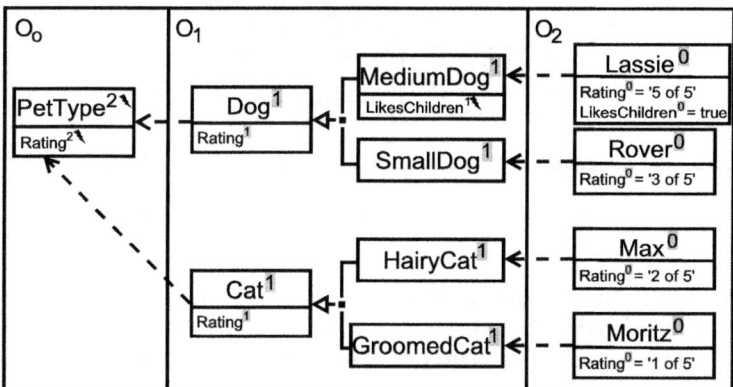

Fig. 7. The Ontology after changing the potency of PetType, Rating and LikesChildren

Additionally the pet store owner decides to also change the durabilities of Rating and LikesChildren. *Changing traits of a feature* violates REQ1.2 in relation to name, durability, mutability and value because these are used to define the conformance of features. By changing one of these the number of conforming features between a model element and its types and instances changes. This can be fixed by changing all features that conformed before the change so that these still conform after the change. The potencies are recalculated and changed as shown in Figure 7.

5.3 Deleting Rating and HairyCat - Deleting a Program Entity

After having added cats to the pet store, the owner notices that these are very poorly rated by users which is not good for his business. This leads to the decision to remove the Rating attribute from the pet store. To do so the attribute is removed from the PetType model element in the store's ontology. *Deleting a feature* can violate the classification relationship requirement REQ1.2 as the number of features changes. The clabject now has fewer features than its type and the instances have more than the changed clabject. Again this is detected by the impact analyzer which calculates that the consistency rules for all instances of PetType are violated. To restore consistency after the change to the ontology, the emendation service offers to automatically remove the attribute from Dog, Cat, Lassie, Max and Moritz.

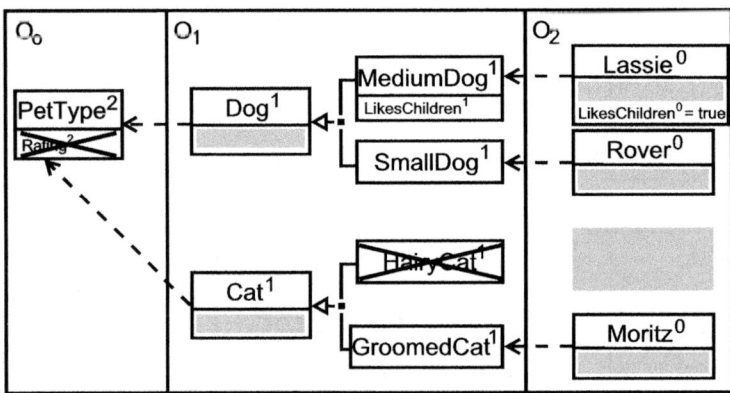

Fig. 8. The pet store ontology after removing the Rating attribute

To avoid the danger of accidents during the approaching New Years Eve the pet store owner decides to temporarily remove hairy cats from the web store. This leads to the removal of HairyCat. *Deleting a clabject* does not violate any classification requirements as long as it does not provide attributes to instances by taking part in an inheritance relation ship. This would lead to a violation of REQ1.2 which could for instance be fixed by deleting the feature provided through the clabject to the instances. In this case HairyCat does not provide any attributes through inheritance thus no emendation operation for preserving classification semantics need to be enacted. However, the emendation service could notice the deletion of HairyCat and offer to also delete its instances to save the modeler the manual editing effort. Figure 8 shows the new ontology without the Rating attribute, the HairyCat clabject and its instance Max.

5.4 Moving LikesChildren - Moving a Member Variable

After various complaints about incidents between cats bought in the pet store and children of customers, the pet store owner sees the need to also capture whether cats are suitable for children. Hence the already existing attribute LikesChildren is moved from MediumDog to PetType. A *move operation of a feature or clabject* is a delete operation on the source and an add operation at the target. Thus the previous presented emendation operations for creation and deletion of a program entity can be applied as the same requirements for classification relationships are violated. The impact analyzer detects the violations introduced through the delete and add operation and notifies the emendation service that all instances of PetType violate at least one of the classification relationship consistency requirements. To fix this, the emendation service offers to add the attribute LikesChildren to Dog, Cat, Rover, Max and Moritz. The resulting ontology is shown in Figure 9.

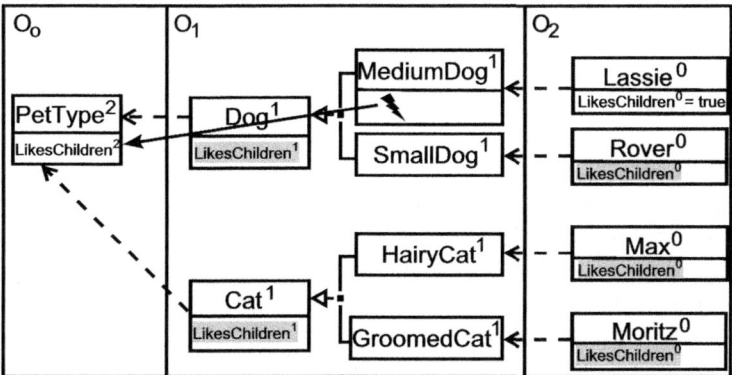

Fig. 9. The pet store ontology after moving the LikesChildren attribute and Lassie clabject

6 Future Work

This paper has presented an overview of our initial realization of the idea of on-the-fly emendation support for multi-level models. A method to flexibly configure the emendation service and impact analyzer needs to be developed. Furthermore, a study on how to most effectively support modelers during the change of a model is required. It is important to provide modelers with as much support as possible but not in a way that the automated emendation service decreases their efficiency.

When considering the evolution of a model the question of how to transport these changes to other models arises. We believe the multi-level modeling approach described in this paper comes closer to the notion of "mogram" defined by Kleppe [8] than any other meta-modeling approach available today. In short, a mogram is a software program written using a modeling language instead of a programming language. This claim is based on the fact that our multi-level models are completely self contained DSL-based packages of information which can exist side by side in the same execution environment. The traditional modeling approach with a centralized meta-model requires models to be "deployed" to a central model repository and reconfigured before they can be interpreted. In our approach a DSL can be used in a multi-level model environment without configuration or deployment of any separate meta-model. This is similar to starting e.g. a Java program in the Java Virtual Machine. In this case no prior setup of the VM is needed and different versions of a program can run side by side. In this sense multi-level models are closer to mograms than traditional two-level models. However, treating every model as a closed piece of software also has a disadvantage. All models basing on the same version of a language can differ from each other as they do not have a central and fixed meta-model. Thus a mechanism to transport the refactoring operations to other deployed multi-level models is needed. We are currently investigating the recording of refactoring changes and automatic application to other multi-level models.

7 Conclusions

The paper presents initial investigations into the provision of on-the-fly emendation support for multi-level models (i.e. ontologies) based on the orthogonal classification architecture. In contrast to today's model refactoring technologies which only support the changing of meta-models and the subsequent application of these changes to model instances the approach presented here modifies all levels of a model simultaneously. A second novelty of the approach is that a model, whilst being edited, is continuously monitored for changes so that emendation support operations can be proactively suggested by the emendation service. In contrast, traditional model refactoring approaches require modelers to explicitly request refactoring support. These changes are then recorded and transported to other model instances. To do so current approaches need to generate a cumbersome model transformation which updates the dependent model levels in a subsequent, decoupled refactoring step. In conclusion, we hope these initial investigations into on-the-fly emendation will provide the foundation for a much more sophisticated automated emendation support that can make the vision of truly real-time meta-modeling become a reality.

References

1. Atkinson, C., Gutheil, M., Kennel, B.: A Flexible Infrastructure for Multilevel Language Engineering. IEEE Transactions on Software Engineering (2009)
2. Basler, M., Brydon, S., Nourie, D., Singh, I.: Introducing the Java Pet Store 2.0 Application (2007),
 http://java.sun.com/developer/technicalArticles/J2EE/petstore/

3. Brosch, P., Seidl, M., Wieland, K., Wimmer, M., Langer, P.: The operation recorder: specifying model refactorings by-example. In: OOPSLA Companion, pp. 791–792 (2009)
4. Eclipse Foundation: Edapt (2012), http://www.eclipse.org/edapt/
5. Fowler, M.: Refactoring: Improving the Design of Existing Code. Addison-Wesley, Boston (1999)
6. Kennel, B.: A Unified Framework for Multi-Level Modeling. Ph.D. thesis, University Mannheim (2012)
7. Klein, M., Noy, N.F.: A component-based framework for ontology evolution. In: Workshop on Ontologies and Distributed Systems at IJCAI 2003 (2003)
8. Kleppe, A.: Software Language Engineering: Creating Domain-specific Languages Using Metamodels. Addison-Wesley (2009)
9. Maynard, D., Peters, W., Sabou, M., dÁquin, M.: Change management for metadata evolution. In: International Workshop on Ontology Dynamics (IWOD) ESWC 2007 Workshop (2007)
10. Miriam-Webster: Definition of Emendation (2012), http://www.merriam-webster.com/dictionary/emendation
11. Opdyke, W.F.: Refactoring object-oriented frameworks. Ph.D. thesis, Champaign, IL, USA, uMI Order No. GAX93-05645 (1992)
12. Reimann, J., Seifert, M., Aßmann, U.: Role-Based Generic Model Refactoring. In: Petriu, D.C., Rouquette, N., Haugen, Ø. (eds.) MODELS 2010, Part II. LNCS, vol. 6395, pp. 78–92. Springer, Heidelberg (2010)
13. University of Mannheim - Software Engineering Group: MelaniE - Multi-level modeling and ontology engineering Environment (2012), http://www.eclipselabs.org/p/melanie

Specifying Refinement Relations in Vertical Model Transformations[*]

Jan Rieke[**] and Oliver Sudmann

University of Paderborn, Heinz Nixdorf Institute,
Zukunftsmeile 1, 33102 Paderborn, Germany
{jrieke,oliversu}@uni-paderborn.de

Abstract. In typical model-driven development processes, models on different abstraction levels are used to describe different aspects. When developing a mechatronic system, an abstract system model is used to describe everything that is relevant to more than one of the disciplines involved in the development. The discipline-specific implementation is then carried out using different concrete discipline-specific models.

During the development, changes in these discipline-specific models may affect the abstract system model and other disciplines' models. Thus, these changes must be propagated to ensure the overall consistency. Bidirectional model transformation and synchronization techniques aim at automatically resolving such inconsistencies.

However, most changes are discipline-specific refinements that do not affect other disciplines. Therefore, vertical model transformations also have to take into account that these refinements must not be propagated. Current model transformation techniques, however, do not provide sufficient means to specify and detect whether a change is just a refinement.

In this paper, we propose a way to formally define such refinements. These definitions are then used by the model transformation engine to automatically synchronize models of different abstraction levels.

Keywords: Vertical Model Synchronization, Triple Graph Grammars (TGG), Refinement/Abstraction, Mechatronic System Design.

1 Introduction

The development of mechatronic systems, from modern household appliances to transportation systems, requires the close collaboration of multiple disciplines, such as mechanical engineering, electrical engineering, control engineering, and software engineering. First, an abstract, discipline-spanning *system model* is created by an interdisciplinary team of engineers. Next, this system model is transformed into different concrete, *discipline-specific models*, which engineers from

---

[*] This work was developed in the course of the Collaborative Research Center 614 – Self-optimizing Concepts and Structures in Mechanical Engineering – University of Paderborn, funded by the Deutsche Forschungsgemeinschaft.
[**] Supported by the International Graduate School Dynamic Intelligent Systems.

each discipline now alter to implement the system. As changes to a discipline-specific model may affect the discipline-spanning system model and other disciplines' models, avoiding inconsistencies is crucial.

To automatically synchronize the different models used during the development, a concept is needed to bidirectionally propagate changes between the different models. If, for instance, one discipline-specific model is significantly changed, these changes must be propagated to the system model, and from there to the other discipline-specific models. Bidirectional model-to-model transformation techniques are a promising approach for such scenarios.

However, not all changes affect the overall consistency. If an engineer performs a change to their discipline-specific model, such a change may either be a *discipline-specific refinement*, which must not be propagated to other models, or a *discipline-spanning relevant change*, which also affects the system model and other disciplines' models. This is due to the differing levels of abstraction between the system model and the discipline-specific models: For one abstract model, there exist several consistent concrete models. In other words, in a consistency mapping from a system model to a discipline-specific model, discipline-specific refinements are all changes that can be performed on the discipline-specific model so that it still corresponds to the system model. Thus, such a mapping from an abstract model to a more concrete model is a 1-to-n mapping.

In a conceptual view, we have an abstract language A (the system model's meta-model) and a concrete language B (the discipline-specific meta-model).[1] To transform a word $a \in A$ to a word $b \in B$, we use an initial transformation function $I \subseteq (A \to B)$. However, as B is more concrete than A, a consistency relation R contains more elements than I and is not a function: $I \subseteq R \subseteq (A \times B)$. An operation $op \in (B \to B)$ is a consistency-preserving refinement iff $\forall a \in A, b \in B : (a,b) \in R \Rightarrow (a, op(b)) \in R$, i.e., both the concrete model before and after the operation map to the same abstract model.

Therefore, when defining such a vertical[2] model transformation, we also have to consider non-functional consistency relations. Existing model transformation approaches (e.g., [16,7,11]), however, do not provide sufficient support for that, because they mostly work for functional relations only. Even if the transformation language allows specifying non-functional mappings, it is not well supported by the synchronization algorithm. Furthermore, it is time-consuming and error-prone to define all possible refinements directly in the consistency relation by hand, and doing so makes the consistency relation difficult to maintain.

Thus, we suggest an inductive approach: We take the functional transformation relation I as a fixed input, manually define a set of consistency-preserving refinement operations, and combine both to compute the consistency relation R. In practical scenarios, such an approach is more flexible, because the

---

[1] We use "language" and "meta-model" (as well as "word" and "model") interchangeably here. For a more formal comparison of both concepts, see Amelunxen and Schürr [1].
[2] Horizontal transformations map between models of the same abstraction level, vertical transformations map between models of different abstraction levels [15].

consistency-preserving refinement operations can be defined by discipline experts who do not need to know the transformation language. Only the initial, functional transformation I is defined by a transformation engineer.

To sum up, our approach works as follows. First, we formally define an initial transformation function I, and discipline-specific refinements in terms of in-place model transformation rules. Each of these so-called *refinement rules* describes a change to a model that is considered to be a refinement operation. Second, we apply these refinement rules on the initial, functional transformation relation I, generating an altered consistency relation R that also covers these refinement operations. To perform model synchronization with such non-functional consistency relations, we present an improved synchronization algorithm based on Triple Graph Grammars (TGGs) [17], a rule-based formalism for declaratively specifying relations between models.

The paper is structured as follows. The running example is presented in Sec. 2. Furthermore, we give details about the development of mechatronic systems and the models and tools in use. In Sec. 3, we describe the foundations of the model synchronization technique we use. In Sec. 4, we introduce the language to define refinements and explain how to derive the consistency relation R. The required extensions to the model synchronization algorithm are described in Sec. 5. Finally, we discuss related work in Sec. 6 and conclude the paper in Sec. 7.

2 Running Example

As an example, we consider the *RailCab* research project[3]. Its vision is that, in the future, the schedule-based railway traffic will be replaced by small, autonomous RailCabs, which transport passengers and goods on demand, being more energy efficient by dynamically forming convoys.

When developing a mechatronic system, a team of engineers from all involved disciplines (mechanical engineering, electrical engineering, control engineering, and software engineering) starts developing an abstract system model. Here, an interdisciplinary specification language called CONSENS [5] is used.

Fig. 1 shows parts of the RailCab's *active structure*, which is part of the system model and shows of which elements the system consists and how these system elements interact. RailCabs can communicate with each other using the Communication Module, allowing negotiating the formation of convoys. When forming a convoy, all following RailCabs have to change the control strategy for the velocity to avoid collisions: Instead of using the Velocity Controller that uses a reference speed v^*_{RailCab} and the actual speed v_{RailCab} to calculate the acceleration force F^*, RailCabs now use the Distance Controller that uses a reference distance d^* and the actual distance d to the preceding RailCab as input [12].

A state diagram in the system model specifies the communication protocol to negotiate convoys (Fig. 2). When a RailCab in noConvoy state receives a createConvoy message from another RailCab approaching from behind, it switches to the convoyLeader state in at most 500 ms. Vice versa, a RailCab may form a

---

[3] Neue Bahntechnik Paderborn/RailCab: http://www-nbp.uni-paderborn.de/

Specifying Refinement Relations in Vertical Model Transformations 213

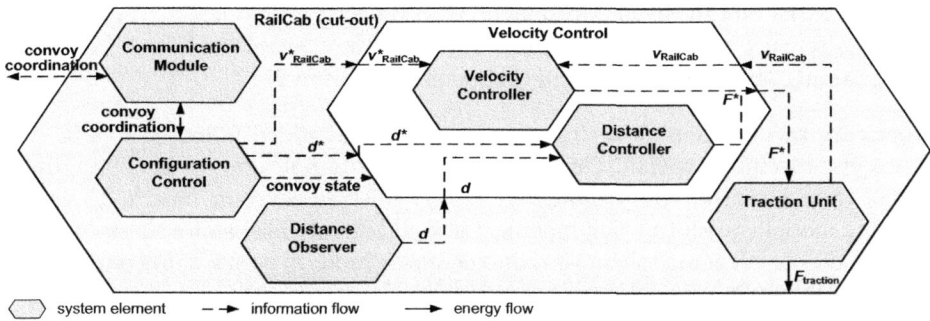

Fig. 1. Parts of the active structure of the RailCab system

convoy with a RailCab in front by sending a createConvoy message and switching to convoyFollower. Convoys may be canceled by a breakConvoy message.

The different disciplines use this system model as the basis for their discipline-specific refinements and implementation. During the development, however, inconsistencies between the system model and the different discipline-specific models may arise. Consider the following process as an example.

1. The discipline-specific models are generated from the system model by different *initial* model transformations. Initial MATLAB/Simulink and Stateflow models are derived for the control engineering. Software engineers use MechatronicUML models [10] for defining the structure and behavior for the discrete parts of the software, especially the communication behavior.
2. The disciplines' engineers start refining their models. E.g., the control engineer defines how to switch between the two control strategies. Due to safety and comfort reasons, sudden steps in the acceleration force F^* must be avoided. Thus, this reconfiguration of controllers requires some time. Therefore, so-called fading states are introduced in the control engineering models in which the actual reconfiguration takes place. This change does not affect other disciplines. Therefore, it must not be propagated to the system model.
3. The software engineer identifies a weakness within the original behavior: The convoy negotiation protocol does not allow the leader RailCab to reject a convoy proposal for safety reasons, e.g., when transporting dangerous cargo. Thus, the behavior in the software model is extended by modifying the corresponding state diagram, now allowing the rejection of convoys.

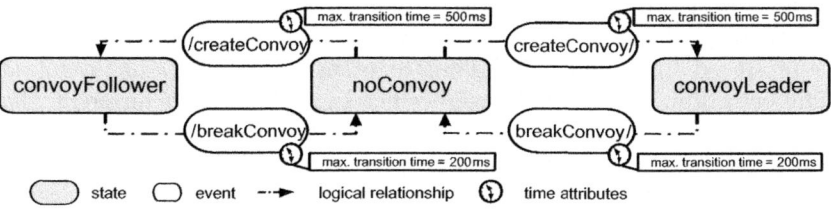

Fig. 2. State diagram describing the convoy communication behavior of the RailCab

4. Next, this modification is propagated to the system model.
5. Finally, this modification is propagated to the control engineering models, retaining the discipline-specific refinements of step 2.

There are two challenges in this process. First, the added fading states in step 2 are just discipline-specific refinements, as they do not affect other disciplines. Thus, they must not be propagated to the abstract system model. However, existing model transformation techniques would simply propagate these changes, as they do not recognize them as refinements. Second, in step 5 some parts of the control engineering model have to be modified according to the changes in the system model. However, the changed state diagram of the system model cannot be simply copied to the control engineering model, as this target model has already undergone some changes in the meantime which must not be overwritten (the addition of fading states in step 2). The challenge is to update the model in a way that these discipline-specific refinements are not destroyed or become invalid, but are reasonably integrated with the changes from the system model.

Fig. 3 shows in detail how the different behavioral models evolve during this development process (the MechatronicUML model and the transformation to it are not important for the comprehension of this paper and have been removed for presentation purposes). First, discipline-specific models are generated from the system model using Triple Graph Grammar transformations (step 1, also marked with ① in Fig. 3). For software engineering, a MechatronicUML model is generated, which contains a Real-Time Statechart that specifies the behavior for the convoy management (① left). For control engineering, we generate initial MATLAB/Simulink and Stateflow models, e.g., a Stateflow chart for the convoy management (① right). As the meta-modeling concepts for state-based behavior are similar in the CONSENS language and the Stateflow language, this transformation is straightforward.

Before we explain the rest of this process in Sect. 4 and 5, we give an introduction to Triple Graph Grammars, the model transformation language we use to define the mapping to the disciplines' models.

3 Foundations of Triple Graph Grammars

Bidirectional model transformation techniques are a promising approach for automatically synchronizing the different models during the development. Here, we use a concept called *Triple Graph Grammars* (TGGs) [17]. TGGs are a rule-based formalism that allows us to specify how corresponding graphs or models can be produced "in parallel" by linking together two graph grammar rules from two different graph grammars. More specifically, a TGG rule is formed by inserting a third graph grammar rule to produce the so-called *correspondence* graph that links the nodes of the other two graphs. Thus, a TGG is a graph grammar that defines a language of corresponding graph triples. TGGs can be interpreted for different transformation and synchronization scenarios. Before we describe these scenarios, let us consider the structure of TGG rules.

Specifying Refinement Relations in Vertical Model Transformations 215

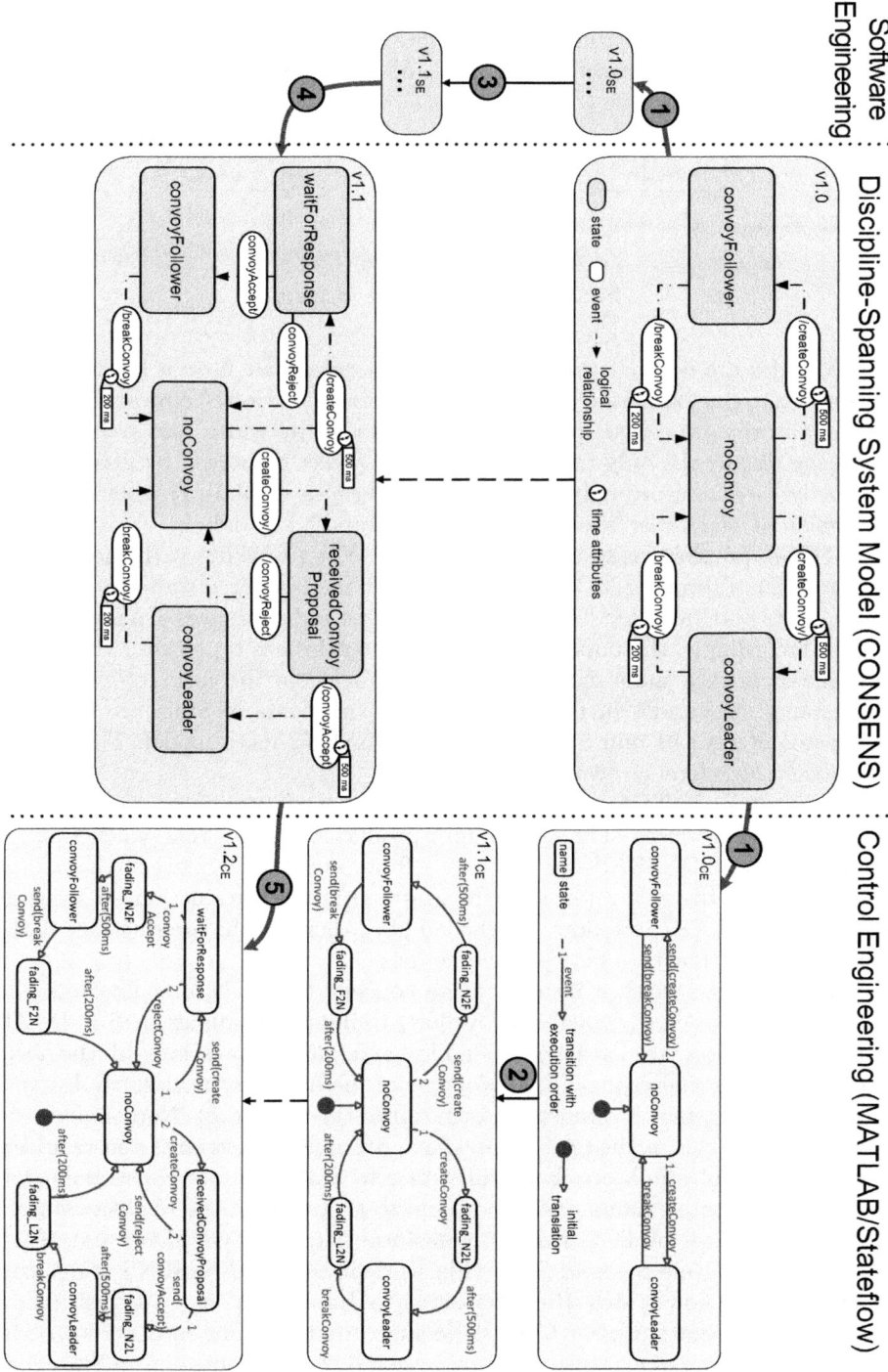

Fig. 3. Evolution of the different models during the development process

3.1 Triple Graph Grammar Rules

Fig. 4 illustrates a TGG rule, State to State, which is taken from a TGG that defines the mapping between CONSENS and MATLAB/Stateflow.

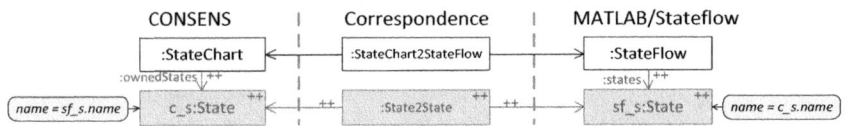

Fig. 4. TGG Rule State to State

TGG rules are non-deleting graph grammar rules that have a left-hand side (lhs) and a right-hand side (rhs) graph pattern. The nodes appearing on the lhs and the rhs are called *context nodes*, displayed by white boxes. The nodes appearing on the rhs only are called *produced nodes*, displayed by green boxes, labeled by "++". Accordingly, there are *context edges*, displayed by black arrows, and *produced edges*, displayed by green arrows and "++" labels.

In TGGs, graphs are *typed* and *attributed*. When working with models and meta-models in terms of MOF, this means that the host or *instance* model contains objects and links that are instances of classes and references of a given meta-model. Accordingly, the nodes and edges in the rules are typed over the classes and references in a meta-model. Nodes are labeled in the form "*Name:Type*". For instance, the nodes in the left column of rule State to State are typed by the classes StateChart and State from the CONSENS meta-model. The edge is typed over the reference ownedStates.

The columns of a TGG rule describe model patterns of different meta-models and are called *domains*. The left-column production states that when there is a StateChart in CONSENS, we can add a State and a link between them. The right column of the rule represents the graph grammar production for creating States in MATLAB/Stateflow. In the middle, there is the production of the correspondence structure between the models.

Our TGG rules further introduce the concept of *attribute constraints* and *application conditions* (depicted by yellow, rounded rectangles in Fig. 4). Attribute constraints are attached to nodes and have expressions of the form $\langle prop \rangle = \langle expr \rangle$, where $\langle prop \rangle$ is a property of the node's type class, and $\langle expr \rangle$ is an OCL expression that must conform to the type of $\langle prop \rangle$. Node names can be used as variables in the OCL expression. Attribute constraints constrain the attribute value of an object. E.g., rule State to State has two constraints that express that a state's name has to be equal to the name of the opposite state.

We defined a set of TGG rules to transform between CONSENS and MATLAB/Stateflow. Rule State to State (Fig. 4) defines how CONSENS states correspond to Stateflow states. Rule Transition to Transition (Fig. 5) describes how transitions between states in CONSENS map to transitions in Stateflow. The maximum duration of a transition is represented by an annotation in Stateflow.

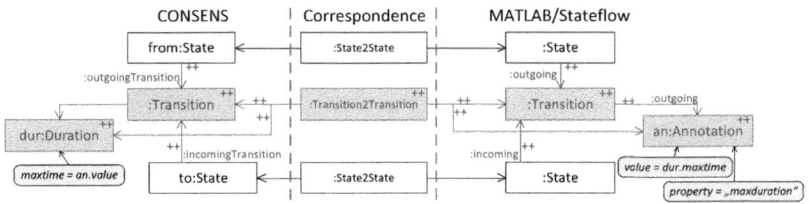

Fig. 5. TGG Rule Transition to Transition

3.2 Application Scenarios

A TGG defines a language of corresponding graph (or model) triples. However, we want to use TGGs for a model-to-model transformation. To do so, we can interpret TGGs for different *application scenarios*. One scenario, called *forward transformation*, is to create one "target" graph corresponding to a given "source" graph. In this case, to apply a TGG rule, it is *interpreted* as follows: First, the context pattern of the rule is matched to *bound* model elements, which are objects and links that were previously matched by another rule application. Second, the source produced pattern is matched to yet *unbound* parts in the source model. If a matching respecting these conditions is found, the produced target and correspondence patterns are created. Doing so, the final transformation result is a valid graph/model triple that is an element of the language defined by the TGG. The *backward* direction works accordingly, reversing the notion of source and target. We refer to Greenyer and Kindler [8] for further details on TGGs and the binding semantics.

Our TGG engine interprets attribute constraints (of the form $\langle prop \rangle = \langle expr \rangle$) as assignments in the target domain. If a TGG rule shall support both transformations directions, assignments must be specified for both directions.

In a situation where a triple of corresponding models is given and a change occurs in one domain model, this change can be propagated by *incrementally updating* only the affected parts of the model. This is also called *model synchronization*, and in general works in two steps: First, for every changed or deleted element in the source model, we check whether the rule application that translated this element is still valid. If it is not valid any more, the rule application is revoked by deleting the produced elements in the target model and removing the bindings of the source produced elements. Second, for every source model element that is not bound yet (i.e., elements that were added or whose bindings have been removed in the first step), we try to apply new rules as in a regular forward transformation. This is necessary to ensure that the synchronization result is again a valid graph/model triple. The backward direction works accordingly.

4 Defining Refinements

In step 2 of the process, the control engineers implement the controllers using MATLAB/Simulink and Stateflow. Especially, they modify the Stateflow model by incorporating additional states which describe the fading behavior when switching between the controller configurations (② in Fig. 3). Such a change is considered a discipline-specific refinement, as it does not affect other disciplines. Therefore, it must neither be propagated to the discipline-spanning system model nor to the other disciplines. However, when using existing model transformation techniques, these additional states would be nevertheless propagated back to the system model: When synchronizing the models, the TGG Rule State to State (see Fig. 4) is applicable for the new intermediate states. The TGG rule Transition to Transition is also applicable for the new transitions.

A transformation engine can deal with hierarchical refinements (like adding sub-states or subcomponents) by simply ignoring everything "below" an existing element. We described in our previous work [6] how this can be achieved using *relevance annotations* to mark elements subject to the transformation. However, for complex, non-hierarchical refinements as described above, this is not sufficient. Thus, we need another means to specify refinements. We propose that discipline experts define a set of *refinement rules* that describe which kinds of changes to a discipline-specific model are regarded as discipline-specific refinements. Generally, a refinement rule formally describes a refinement by a precondition (left-hand side) and a replacement (right-hand side).

Fig. 6 shows a refinement rule in concrete syntax which defines that adding an intermediate state is a discipline-specific refinement. It describes that a transition may be replaced by a combination of a transition, a state and another transition. In addition, it is specified by a constraint that the new state and transitions must not violate the maximum duration of the original transition. Furthermore, no other incoming or outgoing transitions are allowed for the intermediate state.

This refinement rule covers the addition of the fading states. Using this rule, we can add this refinement to the consistency relation R, so the model synchronization can detect that adding the fading states is a refinement. However, as described later, it is important to store the information that a refinement took place, i.e., that the transition createConvoy/ in the system model (v1.0 in Fig. 3) now corresponds to the transition-state-transition combination in the control engineering model (v1.1$_{CE}$).

Basically, a refinement rule is a graph transformation rule. When choosing the language to define refinements, we sought to cover as many refinements as possible on the one hand and, on the other hand, not making the language

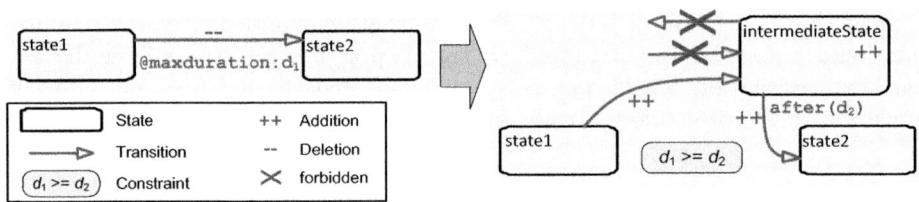

Fig. 6. Refinement rule (concrete syntax) for adding intermediate states in the Stateflow control engineering model

too complex to make analyses impractical. We identified several different refinements from different disciplines (e.g., fault-tolerance patterns like triple modular redundancy, functional partitioning of components, load balancing) which can be described in terms of such graph transformation rules. However, it remains to be investigated further whether we may need a more sophisticated language for other refinements which we have not identified, yet.

Our goal was that these refinement rules should be integrated into the consistency relation R, so that the model transformation engine itself can deal with refinements without fundamental changes to the synchronization algorithm. In this way, formal properties of TGGs like correctness or completeness are still valid and we do not have to heavily modify the existing synchronization tool. We therefore add the information from the refinement rules to the TGG rule set that defined the initial transformation I, creating an altered TGG rule set for the consistency relation R.

The basic idea is to check where refinement rules match in the original TGG rules in the target domain. Whenever a refinement rule's precondition can be found in a TGG rule, we create a copy of that TGG rule and apply the refinement rule in this TGG rule copy. In this way, we derive new TGG rules which map the same source pattern to the refined target pattern. Consider the refinement rule from Fig. 6. This refinement rule's precondition (left-hand side) matches in the target domain of the TGG rule Transition to Transition (Fig. 5). We now copy that TGG rule and apply the refinement rule onto its target domain. That means that we delete every node and edge from the TGG rule which match deleted elements in the refinement rule, and create new nodes and edges for everything that is created by the refinement rule. Furthermore, we create constraints in the new TGG rule for constraints in the refinement rules. Fig. 7 shows the resulting refined TGG rule. This new TGG rule now matches whenever a refinement according to the refinement rule took place in the target model. This rule matches at the respective refined model elements; thus, the models are consistent in terms of the new synchronization rule set.

Next, we describe how the improved synchronization applies this relation R and deals with subsequent incremental updates that may affect refinements.

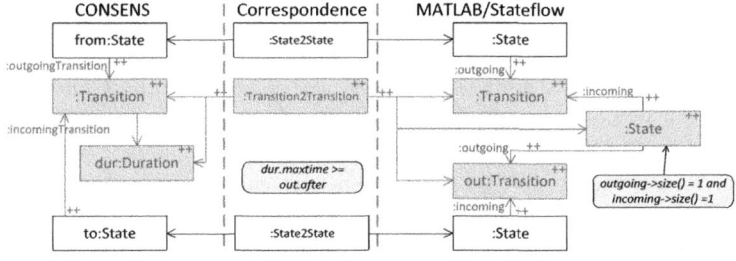

Fig. 7. TGG Rule Transition to Transition (refined, with intermediate state)

5 Model Synchronization with Refinements

Let us have a look at how the improved model synchronization algorithm deals with refinements that are introduced to the models. Fading states were added to the Stateflow model (② in Fig. 3). As the model was changed, a (backward) synchronization is triggered to propagate the change to the system model, and from there to all other affected disciplines.

As described in Sect. 3, model synchronization algorithms work in two steps: First, for everything that has been deleted (or inconsistently changed) in one model, the corresponding elements in the other model are also deleted. Second, for everything that has been added (or inconsistently changed), new corresponding elements are created. In this case, the control engineer deleted the transition from the noConvoy to the convoyLeader state and added a new fading state fading_N2L and two transitions. Thus, the synchronization would also delete the corresponding transition from the system model and then add new elements, which is what we want to avoid.

In our previous work, we proposed an improved model synchronization approach [9]. The main idea is not to delete such corresponding parts right away, but to mark them for deletion first, so they can be reused later, i.e., in subsequent rule applications. Previous model synchronization approaches would simply create new corresponding parts when new elements are transformed. Our improved synchronization tries to reuse elements marked for deletion instead: it performs a search in the set of elements marked for deletion and tries to reuse fitting elements; if they fit, they are not deleted. Only if no fitting elements that are marked for deletion can be found, new elements are created. Finally, elements marked for deletion that could not be reused are actually destroyed. For details of the improved synchronization algorithm, please refer to Greenyer et al. [9].

In this case, this improved algorithm works as follows. First, as the transition from the noConvoy to the convoyLeader state has been deleted from the Stateflow model, the corresponding transition in the system model is marked for deletion. Next, we try to apply new rules. Here, the new, refined TGG rule (Fig. 7) is applicable: It matches the transition in the system model that has been marked for deletion, and it also matches the new fading state and the new transitions in the Stateflow model. We can now apply this rule: In the CONSENS model, we reuse the transition marked for deletion, and we bind the elements of the refinement in the Stateflow model. As result, we have applied the refined TGG rule in backward direction without performing any changes to the CONSENS model just by reusing elements marked for deletion. The models are now consistent in terms of the TGG. This is exactly what we wanted to achieve: We have derived a new TGG rule which covers the refinement case described by the refinement rule. Furthermore, when later changes make the refinement invalid, e.g., when the time constraint is violated, the model transformation engine can detect this by checking the validity of the application of the refined TGG rule.

Note that we have to add precedences to the TGG rules. When propagating changes to the abstract model, we want to use these refined rules primarily, as applying the original, non-refined TGG rules would propagate the refinement to the abstract model, which we wanted to avoid. When propagating to the concrete model, we do *not* want to use the new rules, as we need a functional, deterministic transformation. Thus, we only use the initial rule set.

Let us have a look at the next steps in the development process. As explained before, the software engineers work on their model, too. They change the behavior of the software by adding the possibility to reject a convoy proposal (③ in Fig. 3). This is a discipline-spanning relevant change, as it also affects, for instance, the controller implementation in the control engineering. Thus, it is propagated back to the system model (④): The state diagram is extended by two states waitForResponse and receivedConvoyProposal and new transitions and messages (see v1.1 of the system model in Fig. 3). Instead of switching to the state convoyFollower directly after a createConvoy message is send, the follower RailCab switches to the new state waitForResponse. There, it waits for the leader RailCab to accept or to reject the convoy proposal. The leader RailCab receives the createConvoy message and changes to the new state receivedConvoyProposal, in which it decides whether it accepts or rejects the proposal. If the convoy proposal is accepted, the leader RailCab changes its state to convoyLeader and the follower RailCab changes to the state convoyFollower. If the proposal is rejected, both RailCabs return to the state noConvoy.

These changes then must be propagated to other affected disciplines. Thus, the control engineering model also has to be updated to reflect the changed communication behavior (⑤). In the example, the createConvoy/ transition was changed in the system model during the synchronization in ④. To transform this change, a naïve synchronization would first revoke the respective rule application by deleting the corresponding elements in the Stateflow model, and then try to retransform the affected elements. However, this createConvoy/ transition in the system model corresponds to a refinement introduced in v1.1$_{CE}$ (the combination of the transition createConvoy, the state fading_N2L and the transition to the convoyLeader state in the control engineering model, which are bound by the refined TGG rule). Revoking the rule would destroy the complete refinement (see Fig. 8 b)).

As such an information loss must be prevented, we again use our improved synchronization. First, we revoke rules by marking for deletion. For instance, the fading_N2L state and its incoming and outgoing transition are marked for deletion due to the revocation of the refined TGG rule. Next, we transform the new elements in the system model to the control engineering model.

In general, there may be several possibilities to reuse elements previously marked for deletion, which leads to differently updated models; all of them are consistent according to the consistency relation. The synchronization may not be able to decide automatically which is the most reasonable. In our example, the question is where the newly added states waitForResponse and receivedConvoyRequest should be added: before (Fig. 8 c)) or after the fading states (Fig. 8 d))? Of course, an expert can quickly see that d) is the correct way of updating, as the controller strategy must not be switched before every RailCab has actually

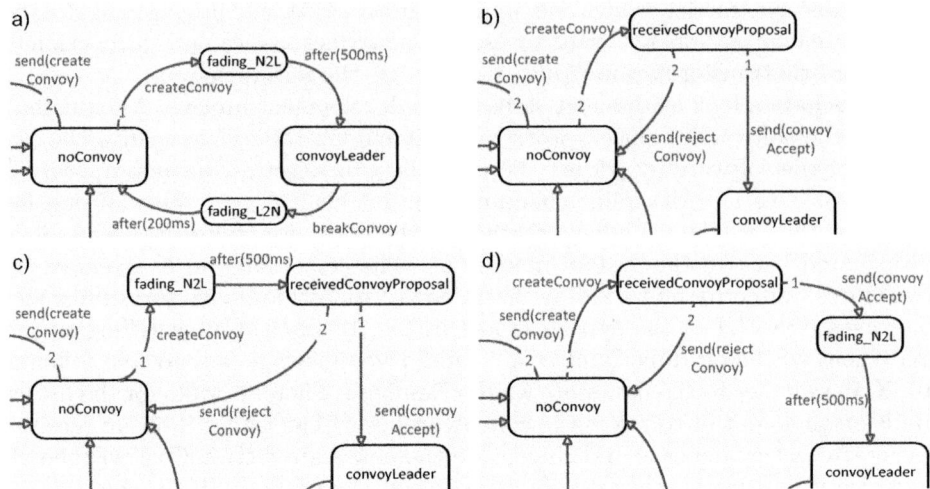

Fig. 8. Excerpts from Stateflow model: a) before updating; updated in different ways: b) lost fading state, c) "wrong" propagation of the change, d) correctly updated

approved the formation of a convoy. An automatic synchronization, however, cannot decide this.

Thus, our improved synchronization algorithm explicitly computes all reuse possibilities, rates them with respect to information loss, and asks the user in ambiguous cases which of the update possibilities is the correct one [9]. In the example, the refinement in the control engineering model that has been marked for deletion (consisting of the transition createConvoy, the state fading_N2L and the transition to the convoyLeader state) may be reusable as the corresponding control engineering part for three new transitions in the system model v1.1 (createConvoy/, /rejectConvoy, and /convoyAccept). However, the deleted refinement is not reusable as is. Some additional modifications have to be made to make it reusable in a certain case. For instance, when reusing elements marked for deletion as corresponding part for the new transition createConvoy/ (which would result in Fig. 8 c)), the target of the outgoing transition must be modified to point to the state receivedConvoyProposal.

We can sort the different update possibilities by the amount of modifications that must be made to reuse the elements: the less modifications must be made, the more likely is that this is a reasonable reuse possibility. In the example, we can reuse the refinement for the transition createConvoy/ (see Fig. 8 c)), as the source of the transition (the noConvoy state) is the same as before, but we must alter the target state. We can also reuse the refinement for the transition /convoyAccept (see Fig. 8 d)), as the target of the transition is the same (the convoyLeader state). It is, however, unreasonable to reuse the refinement for the transition /convoyReject, as neither the source nor the target state is the same as before. Thus, the expert can now decide between two reasonable reuse possibilities that are depicted in Fig. 8 c) and d).

6 Related Work

In MDA, a platform description model (PDM) is used to define the model transformation from an abstract PIM to a concrete PSM. In general, one PIM element may be mapped to more than one corresponding representation in the PSM. So-called mark models annotate the PIM and tell the model transformation which mapping to use. In contrast, our solution provides a way to capture alternative implementations using refinement rules in terms of the PSM. These alternatives are then automatically integrated into the model transformation. However, right now, we only use these refinements rules to derive model transformation rules which are not used in initial model transformations, but only match manually performed refinements. Therefore, we plan on extending our approach so that the refinement rules can be used for a) automatically deriving a mark meta-model and using a mark model to trigger alternative mappings (refinements), and b) to actively propose such possible refinements to the user.

If a refined TGG rule is applicable, its original rule will also be applicable. Here, we solve this by adding precedences. However, when having several model transformation rules applicable at the same elements in the source model, we have to determine which one to execute in general. Thus, we need to identify these conflicting rules. Therefore, we plan to include approaches like the critical-pair analysis, as described by Hermann et al. [13].

However, most solutions which implement an MDA-like process are limited to the concrete application scenario and/or models and tools. Only few publications deal with developing general solutions, e.g., to improve the usage of mark models, and only few model transformation solutions exist which deal with similar aspects as described in this paper. Körtgen [14] developed a synchronization tool for the case of a simultaneous evolution of both models. Although it does not incorporate a concept to define refinement operations, it also allows having several conflicting rules, i.e., rules that are all applicable at the same position. In a step-by-step, highly interactive process, the user may decide which alternatives should be applied. Our aim is to avoid unnecessary user interaction where that is possible. For ambiguous cases, however, we would also like to incorporate better means for user interaction into our synchronization tool.

A different approach in general is to create a single *unified modeling notation*, which includes all modeling means from all disciplines. This avoids defining model-to-model mappings, but requires a) view definitions and b) complex static semantics to ensure "internal" model consistency. Thus, the general model consistency problem remains. Several publications deal with inconsistency handling in a unified notation, e.g., Egyed et al. [4] or Atkinson et al. [2]. Although there is no fundamental conceptual drawback in using such a unified notation, our approach seems more reasonable from a practical and technical perspective in our setting, because most tools use their own model formats, anyway. Furthermore, such a unified notation is difficult to maintain. However, a more extensive discussion about this is outside the scope of this paper.

7 Conclusion and Discussion

In many model-based development processes, vertical model transformations map between models of different abstraction levels. If changes occur to a concrete model, these changes may be either relevant changes that affect the abstract model or model-specific refinements. Existing model synchronization approaches do not provide sufficient means to specify such refinement relations. In this paper, we have shown how in-place model transformation rules can be used to define refinements. We use this set of rules as input to a TGG-based synchronization approach, so that refinements can be automatically detected and will not be propagated. We have shown how this technique helps ensuring model consistency in a synchronization scenario in systems engineering.

At the moment, the refinement rules have to be defined manually, which can be a significant effort. Solutions exist which are able to identify and generalize actual model changes, e.g. Brosch et al. [3]. We plan on incorporating such approaches to (semi-)automatically derive refinement rules from examples.

We evaluated the approach using different disciplines' models from the Rail-Cab research project. We identified and successfully modeled several refinements with our approach, e.g., redundancy patterns in structural models like UML component diagrams or block-based diagrams like Matlab/Simulink, and refined behaviors in behavioral models like statecharts or activity diagrams. However, we have yet to further evaluate the suitability and the efficiency of the approach in other domains, e.g., by performing industrial case studies.

Our approach only works if a refinement rule affects only one TGG rule. If this is not the case, more sophisticated computations are necessary to derive the refined TGG rules; this is subject to future research. As this occurs especially in complex TGGs that map between models that are unsimilar in its modeling principles, our technique will currently meet its limits in such a case.

There may be more than one reasonable solution to prevent the loss of existing refinements. In such ambiguous cases, user interaction is required. As future work, we plan on investigating how this user interaction can become more intuitive and easy to use. Furthermore, by storing and analyzing previous user decisions, we may be able to further improve the automation in ambiguous cases.

References

1. Amelunxen, C., Schürr, A.: Formalising model transformation rules for UML/MOF 2. IET Software 2(3), 204–222 (2008)
2. Atkinson, C., Stoll, D., Bostan, P.: Orthographic Software Modeling: A Practical Approach to View-Based Development. In: Maciaszek, L.A., González-Pérez, C., Jablonski, S. (eds.) ENASE 2008/2009. CCIS, vol. 69, pp. 206–219. Springer, Heidelberg (2010)
3. Brosch, P., Langer, P., Seidl, M., Wieland, K., Wimmer, M., Kappel, G., Retschitzegger, W., Schwinger, W.: An Example Is Worth a Thousand Words: Composite Operation Modeling By-Example. In: Schürr, A., Selic, B. (eds.) MODELS 2009. LNCS, vol. 5795, pp. 271–285. Springer, Heidelberg (2009)

4. Egyed, A., Letier, E., Finkelstein, A.: Generating and evaluating choices for fixing inconsistencies in UML design models. In: ASE 2008, pp. 99–108 (2008)
5. Gausemeier, J., Frank, U., Donoth, J., Kahl, S.: Specification technique for the description of self-optimizing mechatronic systems. Research in Engineering Design 20(4), 201–223 (2009)
6. Gausemeier, J., Schäfer, W., Greenyer, J., Kahl, S., Pook, S., Rieke, J.: Management of cross-domain model consistency during the development of advanced mechatronic systems. In: Proc. of the 17th Int. Conf. on Engineering Design (2009)
7. Giese, H., Wagner, R.: From model transformation to incremental bidirectional model synchronization. Software and Systems Modeling 8(1) (2009)
8. Greenyer, J., Kindler, E.: Comparing relational model transformation technologies: Implementing Query/View/Transformation with Triple Graph Grammars. Software and Systems Modeling 9(1), 21–46 (2010)
9. Greenyer, J., Pook, S., Rieke, J.: Preventing Information Loss in Incremental Model Synchronization by Reusing Elements. In: France, R.B., Kuester, J.M., Bordbar, B., Paige, R.F. (eds.) ECMFA 2011. LNCS, vol. 6698, pp. 144–159. Springer, Heidelberg (2011)
10. Greenyer, J., Rieke, J., Schäfer, W., Sudmann, O.: The Mechatronic UML development process. In: Tarr, P.L., Wolf, A.L. (eds.) Engineering of Software, pp. 311–322. Springer, Heidelberg (2011)
11. Hearnden, D., Lawley, M., Raymond, K.: Incremental Model Transformation for the Evolution of Model-Driven Systems. In: Wang, J., Whittle, J., Harel, D., Reggio, G. (eds.) MoDELS 2006. LNCS, vol. 4199, pp. 321–335. Springer, Heidelberg (2006)
12. Henke, C., Tichy, M., Schneider, T., Böcker, J., Schäfer, W.: Organization and control of autonomous railway convoys. In: Proc. of the 9th Int. Symposium on Advanced Vehicle Control (2008)
13. Hermann, F., Ehrig, H., Orejas, F., Golas, U.: Formal Analysis of Functional Behaviour for Model Transformations Based on Triple Graph Grammars. In: Ehrig, H., Rensink, A., Rozenberg, G., Schürr, A. (eds.) ICGT 2010. LNCS, vol. 6372, pp. 155–170. Springer, Heidelberg (2010)
14. Körtgen, A.T.: Modellierung und Realisierung von Konsistenzsicherungswerkzeugen für simultane Dokumentenentwicklung. Ph.D. thesis, RWTH Aachen University (2009)
15. Mens, T., Van Gorp, P.: A taxonomy of model transformation. Electronic Notes in Theoretical Computer Science 152, 125–142 (2006)
16. Object Management Group (OMG): MOF Query/View/Transformation (QVT) 1.0 Specification (2008), http://www.omg.org/spec/QVT/1.0/
17. Schürr, A.: Specification of Graph Translators with Triple Graph Grammars. In: Mayr, E.W., Schmidt, G., Tinhofer, G. (eds.) WG 1994. LNCS, vol. 903, pp. 151–163. Springer, Heidelberg (1995)

Model-Based Automated and Guided Configuration of Embedded Software Systems

Razieh Behjati[1,2], Shiva Nejati[1], Tao Yue[1],
Arnaud Gotlieb[1], and Lionel Briand[1,3]

[1] Simula Research Laboratory, Lysaker, Norway
[2] University of Oslo, Oslo, Norway
[3] University of Luxembourg
{raziehb,shiva,tao,arnaud,briand}@simula.no

Abstract. Configuring Integrated Control Systems (ICSs) is largely manual, time-consuming and error-prone. In this paper, we propose a model-based configuration approach that interactively guides engineers to configure software embedded in ICSs. Our approach verifies engineers' decisions at each configuration iteration, and further, automates some of the decisions. We use a constraint solver, SICStus Prolog, to automatically infer configuration decisions and to ensure the consistency of configuration data. We evaluated our approach by applying it to a real subsea oil production system. Specifically, we rebuilt a number of existing verified product configurations of our industry partner. Our experience shows that our approach successfully enforces consistency of configurations, can automatically infer up to 50% of the configuration decisions, and reduces the complexity of making configuration decisions.

Keywords: Product configuration, Model-based software engineering, Constraint satisfaction, UML/OCL.

1 Introduction

Modern society is increasingly dependent on embedded software systems such as Integrated Control Systems (ICSs). Examples of ICSs include industrial robots, process plants, and oil and gas production platforms. Many ICS producers follow a product-line engineering approach to develop the software embedded in their systems. They typically build a generic software that needs to be configured for each product according to the product's hardware architecture [5]. For example, in the oil and gas domain, embedded software needs to be configured for various field layouts (e.g., from single satellite wells to large multiple sites), for individual devices' properties (e.g., specific sensor resolution and scale levels), and for communication protocols with hardware devices.

Software configuration in ICSs is complicated by a number of factors. Embedded software systems in ICSs have typically very large configuration spaces, and their configuration requires precise knowledge about hardware design and specification. The engineers have to manually assign values to tens of thousands of configurable parameters, while accounting for constraints and dependencies between the parameters. This results in many configuration errors. Finally, the hardware and software configuration processes are often isolated from one another. Hence, many configuration errors are detected very late and only after the integration of software and hardware.

Software configuration has been previously studied in the area of software product lines [20], where support for configuration largely concentrates on resolving high-level variabilities in feature models and their extensions [18,13,11], e.g., the variabilities specified for end-users at the requirements-level. Feature models, however, are not easily amenable to capturing all kinds of variabilities and hardware-software dependencies in embedded systems. Furthermore, existing configuration approaches either do not particularly focus on interactively guiding engineers or verifying partial configurations [19,6], or their notion of configuration and their underlying mechanism are different from ours, and hence, not directly applicable to our problem domain [16,14].

Contributions. We propose a model-based approach that helps engineers create consistent and error-free software configurations for ICSs. In our work, a large amount of the data characterizing a software configuration for a particular product is already implied by the hardware architecture of that product. Our goal is, then, to help engineers assign this data to appropriate configurable parameters while maintaining the consistency of the configuration, and reducing the potential for human errors. Specifically, our approach (1) interactively guides engineers to make configuration decisions and automates some of the decisions, and (2) iteratively verifies software and hardware configuration consistency. We evaluated our approach by applying it to a subsea oil production system. Our experiments show that our approach can provide certain types of user guidance in an efficient manner, and can automate up to 50% of configuration decisions for the subjects in our experiment, therefore helping save significant configuration effort and avoid configuration errors.

In Section 2 we motivate the work and formulate the problem by explaining the current practice in configuring ICSs. We give an overview of our model-based solution in Section 3. SimPL methodology [5] for modeling families of ICSs is briefly presented in Section 4. We present our model-based approach to the abovementioned configuration problems in Section 5. An implementation of our approach as a prototype tool is presented in Section 6. An evaluation of the approach using our prototype tool is given in Section 7. In Section 8, we analyze the related work. Finally we conclude the paper in Section 9.

2 Configuration of ICSs: Practice and Problem Definition

Figure 1 shows a simplified model of a fragment of a subsea production system produced by our industry partner. As shown in the figure, products are composed of mechanical, electrical, and software components. Our industry partner, similar to most companies producing ICSs, has a generic product that is configured to meet the needs of different customers. For example, different customers may require products with different numbers of subsea Xmas trees. A subsea

Xmas tree in a subsea oil production system provides mechanical, electrical, and software components for controlling and monitoring a subsea well.

Product configuration is an essential activity in ICS development. It involves configuration of both software and hardware components. Currently, software and hardware configuration is performed separately in two different departments within our industry partner. In the rest of this paper, whenever clear from the context, we use *configuration* to refer either to the configuration process or to the description of a configured artifact.

The software configuration is done in a top-down manner where the configuration engineer starts from the higher-level components and determines the type and the number of their constituent (sub)components. Some components are invariant across different products, and some have parameters whose values differ from one product to another. The latter group, known as *configurable components*, may need to be, further, decomposed and configured. The configuration stops once the type and the number of all the components and the values of their configurable parameters are given.

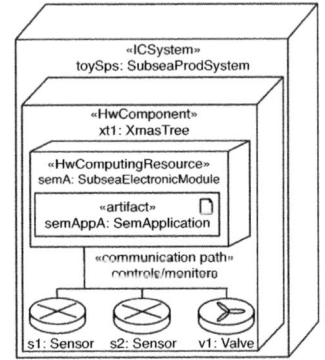

Fig. 1. A fragment of a simplified subsea production system

For example, software configuration for a family of subsea production systems starts by identifying the number and locations of SemApplication instances. Each instance is then configured according to the number, type, and other details of devices that it controls and monitors. To do this, the configuration engineer (the person who does the configuration) is typically provided with a hardware configuration plan. However, she has to manually check if the resulting software configuration conforms to the given hardware plan, and that it respects all the software consistency rules as well. In the presence of large numbers of interdependent configurable parameters this can become tedious and error-prone. In particular, due to lack of instant configuration checking, human errors such as incorrectly entered configuration data are usually discovered very late in the development life-cycle, making localizing and fixing such errors unnecessarily costly.

In short, the existing configuration support at our industry partner faces the following challenges (which seem to be generalizable to many other ICSs [5]): (1) Checking the consistency between hardware and software configurations is not automated. (2) Verification of partially-specified configurations to enable instant configuration checking is not supported. (3) Engineers are not provided with sufficient interactive guidance throughout the configuration process. In our previous work [5], we proposed a modeling methodology to properly capture and document, among other things, the software-hardware dependencies and consistency rules. In this paper, we build on our previous work to develop an automated guided configuration tool that addresses all the above-mentioned challenges.

3 Overview of Our Approach

Figure 2 shows an overview of our automated model-based configuration approach. In the first step, we build a configurable and generic model for an ICS family (the Product-line modeling step). In the second step, the Guided configuration step, we interactively guide users to generate the specification of particular products complying with the generic model built in the first step.

During the product-line modeling step, we provide domain experts with a UML/MARTE-based methodology, called SimPL [5], to manually create a product-line model describing an ICS family. The SimPL methodology enables engineers to create product line models from textual specifications and the scattered domain experts knowledge. These models can then be utilized to automate the configuration process. They include both software and hardware aspects as well as the dependencies among them. The dependencies are critical to effective configuration. Currently, most of these dependencies exist as tacit knowledge shared by a small number of domain experts, and only a fraction of them, mostly those related to software, have been implemented in the existing tool used by our industrial partner. Our domain analysis [5], however, showed that failure to capturing all the dependencies have led to critical configuration errors. We briefly describe and illustrate the SimPL methodology in Section 4.

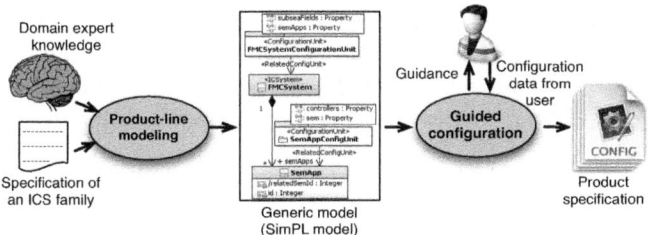

Fig. 2. An overview of our configuration approach

During the configuration step, engineers create full or partial product specifications by resolving variabilities in a product-line model. In our work, configuration is carried out iteratively, allowing engineers to create and validate partial product specifications, and interactively, guiding engineers to make decisions at each iteration. Therefore, our approach alleviates two shortcomings of the existing tool discussed in Section 2. Our configuration mechanism enables engineers to resolve variabilities in such a way that all the constraints and dependencies are preserved. At each iteration, the engineer resolves some of the variabilities by assigning values to selected configurable parameters. Our configuration engine, which is implemented using a constraint solver, automatically evaluates the engineer's decisions and informs her about the impacts of her decision on the yet-to-be-resolved variabilities, hence, guiding her to proceed with another round of configuration. In Sections 5 and 6, we describe in details how the configuration step is designed and implemented, respectively.

4 Product-Line Modeling

In the first step of our approach in Figure 2, we use the SimPL modeling methodology [5] to create a generic model of an ICS family. The SimPL methodology enables engineers to create architecture models of ICS families that encompass, among other things, information about variability points in ICS families.

The SimPL methodology organizes a product-line model into two main views: the *system design view*, and the *variability view*. The system design view presents both hardware and software entities of the system and their relationships using the UML class diagram notation [1]. Classes, in this view, represent hardware or software entities distinguished by MARTE stereotypes [2]. The dependencies and constraints not expressible in class diagrams are captured by OCL constraints [3]. The variability view, on the other hand, captures the set of system variabilities using a collection of *template* packages. Each template package represents a *configuration unit* and is related to exactly one class in the system design view. Template parameters of each template package in the variability view are related to the configurable properties of the class related to that package. Template packages and template parameters are inherent features in UML and are intended to be used for the specification of generic structures. In the reminder of this section, we first describe a small fragment of a subsea product-line model, which is used as our running example. Then, using our running example, we provide a model-based view on the essential configuration activities mentioned in Section 2.

4.1 A Subsea Product-Line Model

Figure 3 shows a fragment of the SimPL model for a subsea production system[1], SubseaProdSystem. In a subsea production system, the main computation resources are the Subsea Electronic Modules (SEMs), which provide electronics, execution platforms, and the software required for controlling subsea devices. SEMs and Devices are contained by XmasTrees. Devices controlled by each SEM are connected to the electronic boards of that SEM. The electronic boards are categorized into four different types based on their number of pins. Software deployed on a SEM, referred to as SemAPP, is responsible for controlling and monitoring the devices connected to that SEM. SemAPP is composed of a number of DeviceControllers, which is a software class responsible for communicating with, and controlling or monitoring a particular device. The system design view in Figure 3 represents the elements and the relationships we discussed above.

---

[1] This is a sanitized fragment of a subsea production case study. For a complete model, see [5].

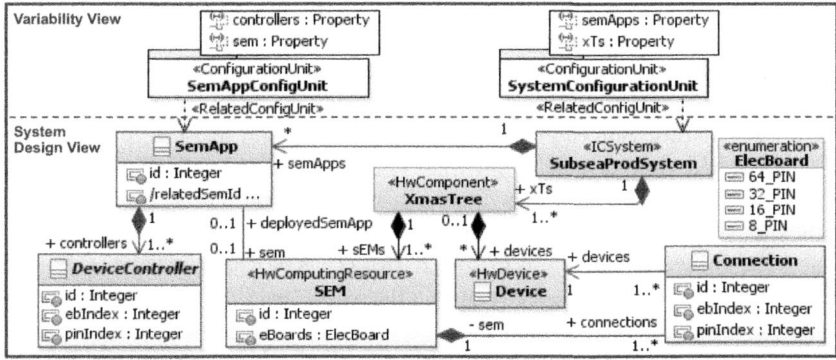

Fig. 3. A fragment of the SimPL model for the subsea production system

The variability view in the SimPL methodology is a collection of template packages. The upper part in Figure 3 shows a fragment of the variability view for the subsea production system. Due to the lack of space we have shown only two template packages in the figure. As shown in the figure, the package SystemConfigurationUnit represents the configuration unit related to the class SubseaProdSystem in the system design view. Template parameters of this package specify the configuration parameters of the subsea production system, which are: the number of XmasTrees, and SEM applications (semApps). Some of the other configurable parameters in Figure 3 are: the number and type of device controllers in a SemAPP as shown in SemAppConfigUnit using the template parameter controllers, the number of SEMs and devices in a XmasTree, etc.

As mentioned earlier, the SimPL model may include OCL constraints as well. Two example OCL constraints related to the model in Figure 3 are given below.

```
context Connection inv PinRange
self.pinIndex >= 0 and self.sem.eBoards->asSequence()->
    at(self.ebIndex+1).numOfPins > self.pinIndex

context Connection inv BoardIndRange
self.ebIndex >= 0 and self.ebIndex < self.sem.eBoards->size()
```

The first constraint states that the value of the pinIndex of each device-to-SEM connection must be valid, i.e., the pinIndex of a connection between a device and a SEM cannot exceed the number of pins of the electronic board through which the device is connected to its SEM. The second constraint specifies the valid range for the ebIndex of each device-to-SEM connection, i.e., the ebIndex of a connection between a device and a SEM cannot exceed the number of the electronic boards on its SEM.

4.2 Configuration Activities in a Model-Based Context

As mentioned in Section 2, configuration involves a sequence of two basic activities: (1) specifying the type and the number of (sub)components, and (2) determining the values for the configurable parameters of each component, while satisfying the constraints and dependencies between the parameters. We ground our configuration approach on the SimPL methodology and redefine the notion of configuration in modelling terms as follows: Given a SimPL model, configuration is creating an instance model (i.e., product specification in Figure 2) conforming to the classes, the dependencies between classes, and the OCL constraints specified in that SimPL model. Such instance model is built via two activities (1) creating instances for classes that correspond to configurable components, and (2) assigning values to the configurable parameters of those instances. For example, to configure the subsea system in Figure 3, we need to first create instances of XmasTree, SEM, Device, and SemApp, and then assign appropriate values to the configurable variables of these instances. Note that value assignment may imply instance creation as well. Specifically, a configurable parameter can represent the cardinality of an association. Assigning a value to such a parameter automatically implies creation of a number of instances to reach the specified cardinality.

5 Interactive Model-Based Guided Configuration

The outcome of the configuration step in Figure 2 is a (possibly partial) model of a product that is *consistent* with the SimPL model describing the product family to which that product belongs. In our approach, SimPL models are described using class-based models, while the product models are object-based. A product model is consistent with its related SimPL model when:

- Each object in the product model is an instance of a class in the SimPL model.
- Two objects of types C_1 and C_2 are connected only if there is an association between classes C_1 and C_2 in the SimPL model.
- The object model satisfies the OCL constraints of the SimPL model.

The above *consistency rules* are invariant throughout our configuration process, i.e., they hold at each configuration iteration even when the product model is defined partially. In this section, we first describe how our approach guides the user at each configuration iteration while ensuring that the above rules are not violated. We then demonstrate how a constraint solver can be used to maintain the consistency rules throughout the entire configuration process, and to automatically perform some of the configuration iterations.

5.1 Guided and Automated Configuration

The product configuration process is a sequence of *value-assignment* steps. At each step, a value is assigned to one *configurable parameter*. A configurable parameter can represent (1) a property in an instance of a class, (2) the size of a collection of objects in an instance of a class, or (3) the concrete type of an instance.

A *configuration* is a collection of value-assignments, from which a full or partial product model can be generated. A configuration is complete when all the configurable parameters are assigned a specific value, and is partial otherwise. Each configurable parameter has a *valid domain* that identifies the set of all values that can be assigned to that configurable parameter without violating any consistency rule. Below, we describe the guidance information that our tool provides to the user at each iteration of the configuration process.

Valid domains. At each iteration, the tool provides the user with the valid domains for all the configurable parameters. Such domains are dynamically recomputed given previous iterations. The values that the user provides should be within these valid domains, or otherwise, the user's decision is rejected and he receives an error message. For example, the valid domain for the configurable parameter pinIndex is initially 0..63. Therefore, if a user assigns to this parameter a value outside 0..63 his decision will be rejected.

Decision impacts. If the user's decision is correct, the decision is propagated through the configuration to identify its impacts on the valid domains of other configurable parameters. This may result in pruning some values from the valid domains of some configurable parameters. For example, the valid domain for the type of an eBoard in a SEM is initially {8_PIN, 16_PIN, 32_PIN, 64_PIN} (the set of all literals in the enumeration ElecBoard). If a user configures a Connection in a SEM by assigning 2 to ebIndex, and 13 to pinIndex, then according to the OCL invariant PinRange (defined above), the third eBoard in that SEM must at least have 14 pins. Therefore, such a value-assignment removes 8_PIN from the valid domain of the type of the third eBoard, resulting in the pruned valid domain {16_PIN, 32_PIN, 64_PIN}.

The impacts of the decisions are then reported to the user, in terms of reduced valid domains.

Value inference. After value-assignment propagation and pruning, the tool checks if the size of any valid domains is reduced to one. The configurable parameters with singleton valid domains are set to their only possible value. This enables automatic inferences of values for some configurable parameters, therefore, saving a number of value-assignment steps from the user. For example, in Figure 3 there is a one-to-one deployment relationship between SEM and SemApp. As a result, whenever the user creates a new instance of SEM the tool automatically creates a new instance of SemApp and correctly configures in it the cross-reference to the SEM. Inferring a value for a configurable parameter that represents the size of an object collection, is followed by automatically creating and adding to that collection the required number of objects.

5.2 Constraint Satisfaction to Provide Guidance and Automation

The main computation required for providing the aforementioned guidance and automation is the calculation of valid domains through pruning the domains of all the yet-to-be-configured parameters after each configuration iteration using the user's configuration decision.

In our approach, we use a constraint solver over finite domains to calculate the valid domains. In this approach, the configuration space of a product family forms a *constraint system* composed of a set of variables, $x_1, ..., x_n$, and a set of constraints, $\mathcal{C}$, over those variables. Variables represent the configurable parameters, and get their values from the *finite domains* $\mathcal{D}_1, ..., \mathcal{D}_n$. A finite domain is a finite collection of tags, that can be mapped to unique integers. We extract the finite domains of variables from the types of the configurable parameters, enumerations, multiplicities, and OCL constraints in the SimPL model. The constraint set $\mathcal{C}$ includes both the OCL constraints and the information, e.g., multiplicities, extracted from the class diagrams in the SimPL model. A configuration in this scheme corresponds to a (possibly partial) evaluation of the variables $x_1, ..., x_n$. Using a constraint solver the consistency of a configuration w.r.t the constraint set $\mathcal{C}$ is checked, and the valid domains, $D^*_1, ..., D^*_n$, for all the variables are calculated.

At each value-assignment step during the configuration, a value v_i is assigned to a variable x_i. This value assignment forms a new constraint $c : x_i = v_i$, which is added to the constraint set $\mathcal{C}$. The added constraint is then propagated throughout the constraint system to identify the impacts of the assigned value on other variables, and to prune and update the valid domains of those variables. This process is realized through a simple and efficient Constraint Programming technique called *constraint propagation* [15]. Constraint propagation is a monotonic and iterative process. During constraint propagation, constraints are used to filter the domains of variables by removing inconsistent values. The algorithm iterates until no more pruning is possible.

Assigning a value to a variable representing the size of a collection relates to adding items to, or removing items from the collection. Adding an item to a collection implies introducing new variables to the constraint system. Similarly, removing items from a collection implies removing variables from the constraint system. As a result, to identify the impacts of changing the size of a collection, new variables have to be added or removed during constraint propagation. This is possible as constraint propagation does not require the set of initial variables to be known a priori. However, the process is no longer monotonic in that case and may iterate forever. In our application, the number of added variables is always bounded, avoiding any non-termination problems.

In our approach, we allow users to modify the previously assigned values as long as the modification does not give rise to any conflict. Since we always keep valid domains of all the configurable parameters up-to-date, conflicts can be detected simply by checking whether the new value is still within the valid domain of the modified configurable parameter. In the following section, we further elaborate on the design of a tool implementing the configuration process presented above.

6 Prototype Tool

Figure 4 shows the architecture of the configuration engine that provides the guidance and automation mentioned in Section 5. Inputs to the engine are the generic model of the product family, and the user-provided configuration data. The configuration process starts by loading the generic model. From the loaded model, the configuration engine extracts the first set of the configurable parameters. These configurable parameters are presented to the user via the interactive user interface for collecting configuration decisions. In addition, the configuration engine generates a constraint model from the input model of the product family. This constraint model is implemented in clpfd, a library of the *SICStus Prolog* environment [8,4]. In clpfd, each configurable parameter is represented by a logic variable, to which is associated a finite set of possible values, called a finite domain. After the generic model is loaded, the configuration engineer starts an interactive configuration session for entering configuration decisions.

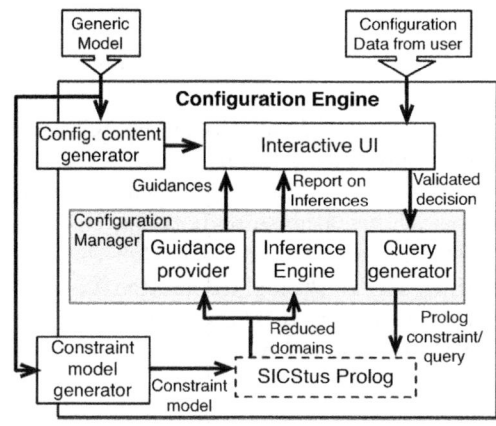

Fig. 4. Architecture of the configuration tool

The configuration engine iteratively and interactively collects configuration decisions from the user. At each iteration, the user enters the values for one or more configurable parameters. Using the domains of the configurable parameters, the consistency of the configuration decisions is checked. If the entered values are all consistent, the *Query generator* is invoked to create a new Prolog query representing a constraint system that contains all the constraints created from the collected configuration decisions. This Prolog query is then used to invoke constraint propagation in order to prune the domains. The new domains serve as inputs to the *Inference engine*, which implements the inference mechanism explained in Section 5.1 to infer values, and the *Guidance provider*, which reports the impacts of configuration choices (e.g., updated domains).

6.1 The clpfd Library of SICStus Prolog

Choosing Prolog as a host language for developing our configuration engine has several advantages. First, Prolog is a well-established declarative and high-level programming language, allowing fast prototyping for building a proof-of-concept tool, and containing all the necessary interfaces to widely-used programming languages such as Java or C++. In our tool development, we have used the jasper library that allows invoking the SICStus Prolog engine from a Java program. Second, as it embeds a finite domains constraint solver through the clpfd library, this allows us to benefit from a very efficient implementation of constraint propagation [9], and all the available constructs (e.g., combinatorial constraints) that have been proposed for handling other applications.

6.2 Mapping to clpfd

To use the finite domains constraint engine of SICStus Prolog, we need to translate an ICS product specification into clpfd. This requires: (1) translating the SimPL model characterizing the ICS family, and (2) translating the instance model representing the product.

In the first translation, we create a Prolog/clpfd program capturing the UML classes, the relationships between the classes, and the OCL constraints of the SimPL model. Our approach for this translation is very similar to a generic UML/OCL to Prolog translation given by [7]. Briefly, we map UML classes and relationships to Prolog compound terms, and every OCL (sub)expression to a Prolog *rule* whose variables correspond to the variables of the given OCL (sub)expression.

In the second translation, given an instance model, we create a SICStus Prolog query to evaluate conformance of the instance model to its related SimPL model (consisting of classes, their relationships, and OCL constraints) captured as a Prolog program as discussed above. To build such query, we map each instance in the given instance model to a Prolog list, and map every configurable parameter of that instance to an element of that list. A configurable parameter that is not yet assigned to a value becomes a variable in the list. For example, a SICStus Prolog query related to an instance model looks like check_product(Als, Ids), where Als is the list representation of all instances, and Ids is the list of the identifiers of instances. The query generator in our tool is responsible for generating these two lists from the instances created and configured by the user. Given the query check_product(Als, Ids), the constraint engine checks whether the instance model specified by Als and Ids conforms to the input SimPL model, and if so, it provides the valid domains for all the variables in Als. Note that the calculation of the valid domains terminates because Als contains a finite number of variables (as the number of the instances in the product are finite), and all variables take their values from finite domains.

7 Evaluation

To empirically evaluate our approach, we performed several experiments which are reported in this section. The experiments are designed to answer the following three main research questions:

1. What percentage of the value-assignment steps can be saved using our automated configuration approach?
2. How much do the valid domains shrink at each iteration of configuration?
3. How long does it take to propagate a user's decision and provide guidance?

Saving a number of value-assignment steps is expected to reduce the configuration effort, and reduction of the domains decreases the complexity of decision making. Therefore, answers to the first two research questions provide insights on how much configuration effort can be saved. Answering the third research question provides insights into the applicability and scalability of our technique.

To answer these questions we designed an experiment in which we rebuilt three verified configurations from our industry partner using our configuration tool. One configuration belongs to the environmental stress screening (ESS) test of the SEM hardware, which we refer to in this section as the ESS Test. The other two are the verified configurations of two complete products, which we refer to in this section as Product_1 and Product_2. Table 1 summarizes the characteristics of these configurations. We performed our experiments using the simplified generic model of the subsea product family given in Section 4. Number of objects and variables in Table 1 are calculated w.r.t that simplified model.

Table 1. Characteristics of the rebuilt configurations

	# XmasTrees	# SEMs	# Devices	# Objects	# Variables
ESS Test	1	1	111	226	343
Product_1	9	18	453	1396	2830
Product_2	14	28	854	2619	5307

We report in Sections 7.1-7.3 the evaluation and analysis that we performed on the experiments to answer the above research questions. At the end of this section, we also discuss some limitations, directions for future work, and the generalizability of our approach.

7.1 Inference Percentage

The configuration effort required for creating the configuration of a product is expected to be proportional to the number of configuration iterations and the number of value-assignment steps. Automating the latter is therefore expected to save configuration effort and minimize chances for errors. To measure the effectiveness of our approach in reducing the number of value-assignment steps, we have defined an *inference rate* which is equal to the number of inferred decisions divided by the total number of decisions:

$$inference\ rate = \frac{inferences}{manual\_decisions + inferences} \quad (1)$$

Table 2 shows the inference rates in each case.

Table 2. Inference rates

	# Manual decisions	# Inferred decisions	Inference rate (%)
ESS Test	373	16	4.11
Product_1	1459	1426	49.42
Product_2	2802	2783	49.82

Note that the inference rate for Product_1 and Product_2 is very close to 50 %. This is because of the *structural symmetry* that exists in the architecture of the system. Structural symmetry is achieved in a product when two or more components of the system have identical or similar configurations. We have modeled the structural symmetries using two OCL constraints. One specifies that each XmasTree has two SEMs (*twin SEMs*) with identical configurations (i.e., identical number and types of electronic boards and devices connected to them). The other specifies that all the XmasTrees in the system have similar configurations (e.g., all have the same number and types of devices). The first OCL constraint applies to both Product_1 and Product_2, while the second applies to Product_2 only. As a result, the inference rate for Product_2 is slightly higher than that for Product_1. Neither of the OCL constraints applies to the ESS Test, which contains only one XmasTree and one SEM. Therefore, it shows a very low inference rate. In general, the architecture of the product family, and characteristics of the product itself (e.g., structural symmetry) can largely affect the inference rate.

Our experiment shows that our approach can automatically infer a large number of consistent configuration decisions specially for products with some degree of structural symmetry. Assuming automated value-assignments have similar complexity to manual ones, our approach can save about 50% of the configuration effort of Product_1 and Product_2.

7.2 Reduction of Valid Domains

Pruned domains are the output of constraint propagation. Pruning of the domains decreases the complexity of decisions to be made. As part of our experiment, we measured how the domains shrink after each constraint propagation step. Such reduction of the domains is measured by comparing the size of each pruned domain before and after constraint propagation. This is possible and meaningful because all the domains are finite. Table 3 shows the average reduction of domains for each case. *Reduction rate* in the table is defined as the proportion of the *reduction size* (i.e., number of distinct values removed from a domain) to the initial size of the domain (i.e., the number of distinct values in a domain). In the calculations in Table 3 we have not considered domain reductions that resulted in inferences. This result shows that the domains of variables can be considerably reduced when a value is assigned to a dependent variable. Specifically, it shows that, on average, after each value-assignment step 37.98% of the values of the dependent variables are invalidated. Without such a dynamic recomputation of valid domains, there would be a higher risk for the user to make inconsistent configuration decisions. Moreover, comparing the inference rate from Table 2 and the reduction rate from Table 3 over the three cases suggests that while structural symmetry can highly affect the inference rate, it does not have a large impact on the reduction rate.

Table 3. Average shrinking of the domains

	Count*	Avg. initial domain size	Avg. reduction size	Avg. reduction rate (%)
ESS Test	732	30.557	13.803	45.17
Product_1	2564	62.125	21.367	34.39
Product_2	7557	35.97	14.205	39.49
			Avg. over all cases:	**37.98**

* total number of domains that have been pruned or reduced.
Avg.: the average over all reduced domains in the whole configuration.

7.3 Constraint Propagation Efficiency

Providing automation and guidance as part of the interactive configuration process requires the underlying computation to be sufficiently efficient for our approach to be practical.

We define the efficiency of our approach as the amount of time needed for validating and propagating the user decision. For this purpose, we have measured at each constraint propagation step the execution time, and the number of variables in the constraint system. Figure 5 shows the average time required for propagating user decisions after each value-assignment step. As shown in this figure, for products with less than 1000 variables, it takes, on average, less than one second to validate and propagate the decision. However, this time grows polynomially with the number of variables, which itself is proportional to the number of instances.

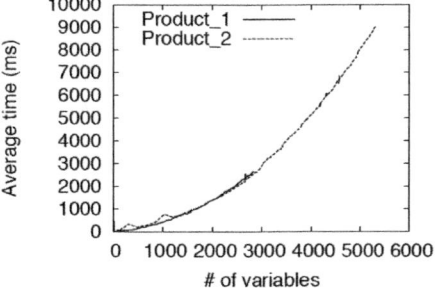

Fig. 5. Constraint propagation time grows quadratically with the number of variables (with a coefficient of determination of 0.9994)

Since in our experiment we have used a simplified model of the product family, we expect that for a complete model of the system the number of instances and the number of variables be much higher than that in this experiment. However, our experiment shows that not all of these variables are dependent on each other. To provide an insight into the level of dependency between variables, for each case, we can compute the average number of reduced domains. The average number of reduced domains is 1.8 (2564 from Table 3 divided by 1459 from Table 2) for Product_1 and, 2.7 for Product_2. In other words, on average, each variable in Product_1 (Product_2) is dependent to less than two (three) other variables. The polynomial ($O(n^2)$) growth of the execution time is, however, due to our current implementation, in which, we compute the valid domains of all variables (not only the dependent variables) by creating a new constraint propagation session after each value-assignment step. Therefore, we expect that by optimizing our implementation and incrementally adding new constraints to an existing constraint propagation session we can significantly improve the efficiency of our approach. Such an optimization requires an additional preprocessing step before creating queries and invoking the constraint solver. This needs to be investigated in more depth and is left for future research.

7.4 Discussion

Limitations and directions for future work. The inference rate and the reduction rate, in addition to be affected by the architecture of the product family, are affected by the order in which the decisions are made. An *optimal order* of applying configuration decisions can be defined as the order which can result in the maximum inference rate and reduction rate. The optimal order can be reported to the user as additional guidance. Our current implementation does not provide such a guidance and therefore the results reported in this paper are probably, a lower bound for potential configuration effort savings. It is therefore important that in the future we support the optimization of the ordering to maximize inferred decisions and the reduction of domains. Devising criteria and heuristics for finding such optimal order is one direction of our future work.

Another research question is "How useful is the guidance provided by our approach?". Answering this question requires conducting an experiment involving human subjects. This experiment is also part of future work.

Generalizability of our approach. Like any other model-based engineering approach, the effectiveness of our approach depends on the quality of the input generic models. Our configuration approach can be used to configure only the variabilities that are captured in the generic model of the product family. Similarly, the approach can validate the decisions and automatically infer decisions only based on the dependencies that are captured in the model. Our evaluation in this paper shows that the SimPL methodology and notations that we proposed in [5] enables the creation of models of the required quality.

The use of a constraint solver over finite domains limits our approach to the constraints that capture restrictions on variables with finite domains. Constraint solvers over continuous domains are available to overcome this limitation but their integration with an efficient finite domains solver is still an open research problem [10]. Moreover, as we have not encountered this type of constraint with our industry partner, we don't expect this to be a restriction in our context.

8 Related Work

Most of the existing work on constraint-based automated configuration in product-line engineering focuses on resolving variabilities specified by feature models [17] and their extensions [12]. Basic feature models cannot express complex variabilities or dependencies required for configuring embedded systems [5]. However, extended feature models that allow attributes, cardinalities, references to other features, and cloning of features are, as mentioned in [11], as expressive as UML class diagrams and can be augmented by OCL or XPath queries to describe complicated feature relationships as well.

We compare our work with the existing automated configuration and verification tools proposed for extended feature models since these are the closest to our SimPL models. FMP [11] is an Eclipse plug-in that enables creation and configuration of extended feature models. FMP can verify full or partial configurations for a subset of extended feature models, specifically those with boolean variables and without clonable features. FAMA [6] drops this limitation and can verify extended feature models with variables over finite domains. However, FAMA is more targeted towards the verification and analysis of feature models. Therefore, it does not handle validating partial configurations or help build full configurations iteratively. Finally, Mazo et. al. [19] use constraint solvers over finite domains to analyze extended feature models. This approach is the closest to ours as it can handle all the advanced constructs in extended feature models, and further enables verification of full and partial configurations.

The main limitation of all of the above approaches is that none of them supports verification and analysis of complex constraints such as those in Section 4.1. These constraints express complex relationships between individual elements or collections of elements and are instrumental in describing software/hardware dependencies and consistency rules in embedded systems. Our tool, in addition to verifying these constraints, provides interactive guidance to help engineers effectively build configurations satisfying these constraints. Finally, to the best of our knowledge, none of the above approaches have been applied to nor evaluated on real case studies.

More recently, constraint satisfaction techniques have been used to automate configuration in the presence of design or resource constraints [16,14]. The main objective is to search through the configuration space in order to find optimized configurations satisfying certain constraints. Our work, however, focuses on interactively guiding engineers to build consistent product configurations, a problem that we have shown earlier in our paper to be important in practice. We do not intend to replace human decision making during configuration. Instead, we plan to support engineers when applying their decisions in order to reduce human errors and configuration effort.

In contrast to related work in [16,14], we enable users to interact with the constraint solver during the search. This is because supporting user guidance and interactive configuration are paramount to our approach. As a result, we require a technique that is fast enough for instant interaction with users and therefore cannot rely on dynamic constraint solving, which the authors in [16] have shown to be orders of magnitude slower than the SICStus CLP(FD) library. As for DesertFD in [14], it neither provides user guidance nor enables interactive configuration.

9 Conclusion

In this paper, we presented an automated model-based configuration approach for embedded software systems. Our approach builds on generic models created in our earlier work, i.e., the SimPL models, and uses constraint solvers to interactively guide engineers in building and verifying full or partial configurations.

We evaluated our approach by applying it to a real subsea production system where we rebuilt three verified configurations of this system to evaluate three important practical factors: (1) reducing configuration effort, (2) reducing possibility of human errors, and (3) scalability. Our evaluation showed that, in our three example configurations, our approach (1) can automatically infer up to 50% of the configuration decisions, (2) can reduce the size of the valid domains of the configurable parameters by 40%, and (3) can evaluate each configuration decision in less than 9 seconds.

While our preliminary evaluations demonstrate the effectiveness of our approach, the value of our tool is likely to depend on its scalability to very large and complex configurable systems. In particular, being an interactive tool, its usability and adoption will very much depend on how fast it can provide the guidance information at each iteration. Our current analysis shows that the propagation time grows polynomially with the size of the product. But we noticed in our work that after each iteration only a very small subset of variables are affected. Therefore, if we could reuse the analysis results from the previous iterations, we could possibly improve the time it takes to analyze each round significantly.

References

1. UML Superstructure Specification, v2.3 (May 2010)
2. Marte (2012), http://www.omgmarte.org/
3. Object Constraint Language (2012), http://www.omg.org/spec/OCL/2.2/
4. Sicstus Prolog Homepage (February 2012), http://www.sics.se/sicstus/
5. Behjati, R., Yue, T., Briand, L., Selic, B.: SimPL a product-line modeling methodology for families of integrated control systems, Tech. Repo 2011-14, SRL (2011), http://simula.no/publications/Simula.simula.746
6. Benavides, D., Segura, S., Trinidad, P., Ruiz Cortés, A.: Fama: Tooling a framework for the automated analysis of feature models. In: VaMoS (2007)
7. Cabot, J., Clarisó, R., Riera, D.: Verification of uml/ocl class diagrams using constraint programming, Washington, DC, USA, pp. 73–80 (2008)
8. Carlsson, M., Mildner, P.: Sicstus prolog – the first 25 years. CoRR, abs/1011.5640 (2010)
9. Carlsson, M., Ottosson, G., Carlson, B.: An Open-Ended Finite Domain Constraint Solver. In: Hartel, P.H., Kuchen, H. (eds.) PLILP 1997. LNCS, vol. 1292, pp. 191–206. Springer, Heidelberg (1997)
10. Collavizza, H., Rueher, M., Van Hentenryck, P.: A constraint-programming framework for bounded program verification. Constraints Journal (2010)
11. Czarnecki, K., Kim, P.: Cardinality-Based Feature Modeling and Constraints: A Progress Report. In: Proceedings of the International Workshop on Software Factories at OOPSLA (2005)
12. Czarnecki, K., Helsen, S., Eisenecker, U.: Formalizing cardinality-based feature models and their specialization. In: Software Process: Improvement and Practice (2005)
13. Czarnecki, K., Pietroszek, K.: Verifying feature-based model templates against well-formedness ocl constraints. In: GPCE 2006, pp. 211–220 (2006)

14. Eames, B.K., Neema, S., Saraswat, R.: Desertfd: a finite-domain constraint based tool for design space exploration. Design Autom. for Emb. Sys. 14(2), 43–74 (2010)
15. Van Hentenryck, P., Saraswat, V.A., Deville, Y.: Design, implementation, and evaluation of the constraint language cc(fd). Selected Papers from Constraint Programming: Basics and Trends (1995)
16. Horváth, Á., Varró, D.: Dynamic constraint satisfaction problems over models. Software and Systems Modeling (November 2010)
17. Kang, K.C., Cohen, S.G., Hess, J.A., Novak, W.E., Spencer Peterson, A.: Feature-Oriented Domain Analysis (FODA) Feasibility Study. Technical Report CMU/SEI-90-TR-21 (1990)
18. Lopez-Herrejon, R.E., Egyed, A.: Detecting Inconsistencies in Multi-View Models with Variability. In: Kühne, T., Selic, B., Gervais, M.-P., Terrier, F. (eds.) ECMFA 2010. LNCS, vol. 6138, pp. 217–232. Springer, Heidelberg (2010)
19. Mazo, R., Salinesi, C., Diaz, D., Lora-Michiels, A.: Transforming attribute and clone-enabled feature models into constraint programs over finite domains. In: ENASE (2011)
20. Pohl, K., Böckle, G., van der Linden, F.J.: Software Product Line Engineering: Foundations, Principles and Techniques. Springer-Verlag New York, Inc., Secaucus (2005)

Lightweight String Reasoning for OCL

Fabian Büttner* and Jordi Cabot

AtlanMod, École des Mines de Nantes - INRIA, Nantes, France
{fabian.buettner,jordi.cabot}@inria.fr

Abstract. Models play a key role in assuring software quality in the model-driven approach. Precise models usually require the definition of OCL expressions to specify model constraints that cannot be expressed graphically. Techniques that check the satisfiability of such models and find corresponding instances of them are important in various activities, such as model-based testing and validation. Several tools to check model satisfiability have been developed but to our knowledge, none of them yet supports the analysis of OCL expressions including operations on Strings in general terms. As, in contrast, many industrial models do contain such operations, there is evidently a gap.

There has been much research on formal reasoning on strings in general, but so far the results could not be included into model finding approaches. For model finding, string reasoning only contributes a sub-problem, therefore, a string reasoning approach for model finding should not add up front too much computational complexity to the global model finding problem. We present such a lightweight approach based on constraint satisfaction problems and constraint rewriting. Our approach efficiently solves several common kinds of string constraints and it is integrated into the EMFtoCSP model finder.

Keywords: OCL, String data type, Model Finding.

1 Introduction

Model-driven Engineering (MDE) is a popular approach to the development of software based on the use of models as primary artifacts. To precisely describe the conceptual structure of a model, the Object Constraint Language (OCL) [22] has been widely accepted as a de-facto standard. In a nutshell, OCL allows to express model constraints using a first-order logic like language for objects.

Naturally, the increased precision comes along with an increased complexity of the models. This raises the need for systematic approaches to model validation, model verification, and model-based testing. Model finding (also called model instantiation) is an important problem in this context. It considers the question if a given model (including constraints) is satisfiable, and if it is satisfiable, to identify one instance of the model. While in model verification, model finders are typically used to show unsatisfiability when reasoning about implications between different constraints, the focus in model-based testing is typically on finding satisfying instances, which can be used to test a system which is based on the model.

---
* This work has been partly funded by the European Project CESAR.

The community has developed several approaches and tools for automated model finding for OCL-annotated models. To deal with the computational complexity of the problem (which is undecidable in general), most of them are based on some underlying formalism for which sophisticated decision procedures and tools exist, such as first-order logic and satisfiability modulo theory (SMT), relational logic, propositional logic, and constraint satisfaction problems (CSP).

While these approaches cover an extensive subset of OCL, to our knowledge none of them supports the String data type and its OCL operations. The primitive data types typically supported are Integer and Boolean. Given that, on the contrary, several 'real life' models actually do contain constraints over strings, there is evidently a gap that needs to be addressed. However, we need to be aware that, when compared to models that only contain Integer primitive values, adding strings to the subject of reasoning introduces another level of complexity.

There are several works that address string reasoning, some focused on checking grammar satisfiability as a stand-alone problem, others on path analysis for string-manipulating programs. However, in the context of model finding and, in particular, model-based testing, string reasoning only contributes a sub-problem to the overall search problem. Therefore, there is a trade-off between the completeness of the string reasoning procedures and the overall model finding performance.

In this paper we present a lightweight approach to integrate constraints over bounded strings into model finding using constraint rewriting and Boolean and integer constraints. It is a two-step approach that first reasons about the lengths of the strings, then infers constraints on the individual elements of the strings (their character variables). In general, our approach can be implemented in any off-the-shelf solver that supports reasoning about linear constraints. We included it in the OCL model finder EMFtoCSP [14], the successor of UMLtoCSP [7], which is based on the ECL^{i}PS^e constraint logic programming environment.

For many common constraint constellations, our approach is scalable and shows good performance, and we claim that it is suited for several practical applications that do not pose hard, non-tractable string constraints. We provide experimental results that show that models with more than a thousand strings can be found within seconds.

Paper Organization. In Sect. 2, we first discuss the state of the art for the topic. Section 3 then formally presents our approach. In Sect. 4 we discuss its limits and scalability, and present experimental results of our implementation of the approach in the tool EMFtoCSP. Section 5 concludes our contribution and identifies future work.

2 State of the Art

In this section, we describe the state of the art in model finding for OCL-annotated models in general and its translation into constraint satisfaction problems, and we put our work in the context of general formal reasoning techniques for strings.

2.1 Model Finding

The model finding (or model instantiation) problem for models with constraints can be defined as follows: Let $\mathcal{M}$ be a model defining structural elements such as classes, associations, and attributes. Let $C_\mathcal{M}$ be a set of constraints over $\mathcal{M}$. Let $I(\mathcal{M})$ denote the (possibly infinite) set of models (instances) of $\mathcal{M}$. The pair $(\mathcal{M}, C_\mathcal{M})$ is called satisfiable iff there exists a least one instance $\sigma \in I(\mathcal{M})$ such that $\sigma \models \hat{c}_i$ holds for each $c_i \in C_\mathcal{M}$, where we assume $\hat{c}_i$ to be a logical representation of c_i that can be evaluated on σ. A model that is not satisfiable is called unsatisfiable. If a model is satisfiable, one is typically interested in a satisfying instance of it, too.

Model finding is important in several tasks within the model-driven approach. It is required in the validation and testing of systems based on the model (to systematically specify test cases), validation and testing of model transformations [3,23], as well in the validation and verification of the model itself. Model finding has also been applied to verify the correctness of model transformations as transformation models (e.g., [6,5]).

The community has developed several approaches and tools for automated model finding for models with OCL constraints. To deal with the computational complexity of the problem (which is undecidable for OCL in general), most of them are based on some underlying formalism for which sophisticated decision procedures and tools exists, such as, first-order logic and SMT [9], relational logic [2,19], propositional logic [25], genetic algorithms [1], graph grammars [27] and constraint satisfaction problems [7]. All of these approaches support a more or less extensive subset of OCL (e.g., including quantifiers and collections), but, to our knowledge, the support of the String data type is very limited. [12] supports strings, but requires the user to specify an explicit procedure for the construction of potential strings and is not a black box model finding approach. [1] considers strings, but the approach, which is based on genetic algorithms, is focused on test case generation only and is (intentionally) not exhaustive. A promising approach is our view is [18], where the authors propose an encoding of OCL strings for the relational logic solver Kodkod. However, to our knowledge, this encoding still requires a constant maximum number of boolean variables, equal for all string variables (even when this length is only required for a single string).

We want to emphasize that most of the underlying formalism and solvers employed in the aforementioned approaches do support bounded bitvectors or sequences. Thus, theoretically, strings can be translated straightforwardly into these formalisms. However, unless considerably small upper bounds are imposed on string lengths, this quickly leads to extreme search spaces, with considerable effects on the runtime of the solvers and the decidability of the search problem in practice. Furthermore, this also prevents them from taking into account the String semantics on the symbolic level to reduce the search space up front.

2.2 Model Finding as a CSP

A constraint satisfaction problem (CSP) can be defined by a tuple

$$(V, C)$$

where $V = \{v_1 \in D_1, \ldots, v_m \in D_m\}$ is a set of variables v_i and their domains D_i, and C is a set of constraints over V. Where clear from the context, we will omit variable domains in the following. A constraint has the form $P(x_1, \ldots, x_n)$ where P denotes an n-ary predicate on $x_1, \ldots, x_n \in V$. An assignment β of values to variables *satisfies* a constraint $P(x_1, \ldots, x_n)$ if $P(\beta(x_1), \ldots, \beta(x_n))$ is true. If β satisfies all constraints in C, it is a *solution* to P. We say a CSP is *consistent* (or feasible) if it has a solution, and *inconsistent* (or infeasible) if it does not.

Typical constraints employed in CSPs include a combination of arithmetic expressions, mathematical comparison operators and logical operators. Common techniques for the resolution of CSPs are based on backtracking and constraint propagation. CSPs can be represented in constraint logic programming, which embeds constraints into a logic program.

Eventually, the notion of the model finding problem in MDE is similar to the notion of a CSP, but it is based on a more complex structure (the variables are objects, links, etc.). In [7] a translation of the model finding problem for OCL-annotated models into a CSP is described. Given a $\mathcal{M}$ and a set of OCL constraints $C_\mathcal{M}$, the approach defines how to infer a CSP P that is consistent iff. $\langle \mathcal{M}, C_\mathcal{M} \rangle$ is satisfiable. The solutions to P correspond to instances of $\mathcal{M}$. Technically, the derived CSP P consists of two sub-problems

$$P_\text{structure} = (\textit{Cardinalities}, \textit{CardinalityConstraints})$$

and

$$P_\text{global} = (\textit{Instance}, \textit{InstanceConstraints})$$

where the solutions of the first sub-problem are (potentially) valid sizes for the sets of objects and links. The variables of the second sub-problems include lists of objects and links. Iterating the solutions to the first sub-problem (by backtracking), these lists are instantiated (i.e., a length is assigned to them) in the second sub-problem.

In a nutshell, two kinds of constraints are employed in the second sub-problem. The first kind includes constraints over Boolean and integer arithmetic, for which constraint propagation is available in most constraint programming languages. The second kind includes specific constraints to represent, for example, navigation operations. The derivation of these constraints can be implemented, for example, using *suspended goals*.

We have implemented our String reasoning approach in EMFtoCSP [10], which is the successor of UMLtoCSP [7] and supports EMF metamodels as well as UML models. Other approaches that also express model finding in terms of constraint programming include [21,20,8].

2.3 Formal String Reasoning

Reasoning on strings has been performed in various formalisms, both for bounded and unbounded strings. Solvers for Satisfiability Modulo Theories (SMT) commonly support theories that can be used to represent strings, such as arrays and bit-vectors. Also, as a string is only a specific case of a list, any theory of lists can be applied, too. Recently, a working group for the development of a theory for strings and regular languages has been formed [4].

In addition to the theory-based approaches, several approaches reason about string using finite automata and regular expression, e.g., [17,16,13,26]. [15] incorporates regular languages into a CSP. In [28] the authors perform path analysis for String-manipulating programs using SMT, employing a two step approach similar to ours, determining an approximation of string lengths in the first step first.

In comparison to these approaches, our approach is less complex in the sense that it performs symbolic reasoning only over the lengths of strings. Due to its two-step nature, it is not suited to solve real hard (NP-hard), non-tractable string problems in reasonable time. However, it efficiently solves several less hard string problems with minimal overhead, which makes it suitable for embedding into a more general model finding procedure.

3 Lightweight String Reasoning for OCL

We now present our approach for solving OCL constraints that use the OCL data type String and its operations. Our approach can be easily integrated into existing approaches to satisfiability checking (model finding) of models and OCL constraints such as the ones presented in Sect. 2.

At its core, we formulate the problem as a CSP. We provide five constraint predicates for strings that can be used to translate OCL constraints containing string expressions. These five predicates correspond directly to five core operations of the OCL data type String, namely equality (=), size, substring, concat, and indexOf. Our five constraints predicates are resolved into constraints on integers and Booleans in two rewriting steps (described as constraint handling rules, which we introduce below). Fig. 1 depicts this process and will be explained in the following.

We assume an OCL model and its constraints have been translated into a CSP $P = (V, C)$ (e.g., as described in [7], c.f. Sect. 2.2). V includes variables of type String and C includes constraints over these variables. In the first step, we infer additional constraints on the lengths of the individual string variables. The second step then translates the string constraints into constraints on the elements of the strings (i.e., their characters). The result of this two-step process is a CSP that can be solved using off-the-shelf solvers for linear constraints.

More formally, we first employ a rewriting operation $C \leadsto C_{length}$ (described in Sect. 3.4) that extends C by additional constraints over the lengths of all string variables in V. Then, we require that a solution to the *length sub-problem* is chosen, which introduces a potential choice point in a backtracking search process. We refer to the set of constraints in which the length variables are bound to fixed lengths as $C_{length,i} \leadsto C_{inst,i}$, where i shall number the different solutions of the length sub-problem.

The second rewriting operation $C_{length,i} \leadsto C_{inst,i}$ then (a) unifies all symbolic string variables s_i with lists of individual element variables $\langle s_{i,1}, s_{i,2}, \ldots \rangle$, and (b) rewrites the semantics of the string constraints into into Boolean and integer constraints over the element variables. The solutions to $(V, C_{inst,i})$ are solutions to P. If $C_{inst,i}$ has no solution, the next valid solution $i+1$ to the length sub-problem must be selected. If there is not further solution to the length subproblem, P is *inconsistent*.

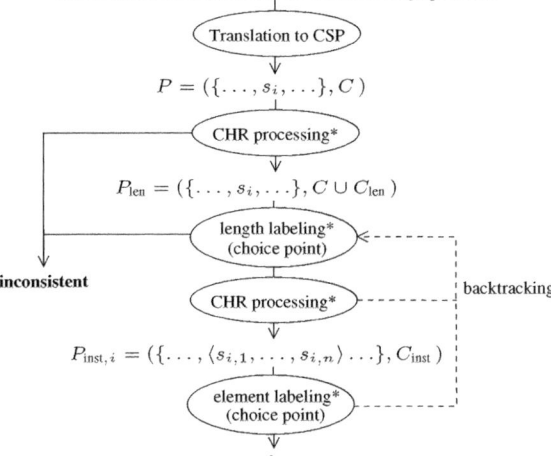

Fig. 1. The decision procedure for CSP with String constraints, including CHR processing. All processing steps (indicated with a star) are supposed to perform constraint propagation on linear and Boolean constraints.

The remaining section first describes the five OCL operations supported more precisely in Sect. 3.1. We provide our five String constraint predicates in Sect. 3.2. Sect. 3.3 gives a short primer on the constraint handling rules formalism, which we employ to define the two rewriting steps in Sections 3.4 and 3.5. We provide a complete derivation example in Sect. 3.6.

3.1 Considered OCL String Operations

The OCL specification [22] defines several operations for the data type String. In this work we consider a subset of five important core operations: the length of a string (s_1.concat(s_2)), the concatenation of two strings (s_1.concat(s_2) resp. $s_1 + s_2$), the indexed substring of a string (s_1.substring(i, j)), and the containment of a string in another one (s_1.indexOf(s_2)).

In accordance with the OCL specification, we assume the semantics of the core operations as follows: Let $\mathcal{A}$ be the set of characters, and $\mathcal{A}^*$ be the set of all strings (sequences of characters). The semantics of this core can be described by a set of interpretation functions $I(\text{size}) : \mathcal{A}^* \to \mathbb{N}$, $I(\text{concat}) : \mathcal{A}^* \times \mathcal{A}^* \to \mathcal{A}^*$, $I(=) : \mathcal{A}^* \times \mathcal{A}^* \to \mathbb{B}$, $I(\text{substring}) : \mathcal{A}^* \times \mathbb{N} \times \mathbb{N} \to \mathcal{A}^*$, and $I(\text{indexOf}) : \mathcal{A}^* \times \mathcal{A}^* \to \mathbb{N}$, as follows. $I(\text{size})(s)$ is defined to be the length of the sequence s (and can be 0). $I(=)(s_1, s_2)$ is *true* iff s_1 and s_2 have the same lengths and are equal element-wise, and *false* otherwise. $I(\text{concat})(s_1, s_2)$ is $s_1 \circ s_2$ (concatenation of sequences). $I(\text{substring})(s, i, j)$ is the subsequence from i to j, and is only defined for $1 \leq i \leq j \leq |s|$ according to the OCL specification. $I(\text{indexOf})(s_1, s_2)$ is the index of the first occurrence of s_2 in s_1 when s_1 is non-empty and 0 otherwise. In OCL, no string is a substring of the empty string (not even the empty string).

3.2 String Constraints

We define five string constraint predicates that are sufficient to express OCL constraints that use the core operations on strings as a CSP. They correspond directly to the operations (cf. Sect. 3.1). Examples for the encoding follow after this section.

Let $s, s_1, \ldots s_3$ denote string variables, and l, i, and j denote integers. The five constraints are $\text{len}(s, l)$ – the length of s is l, $\text{eq}(s_1, s_2, b)$ – s_1 and s_2 are equal iff. b is true, $\text{con}(s_1, s_2, s_3)$ – s_3 is the concatenation of s_1 and s_2, $\text{sub}(s_1, i, j, s_2)$ – s_2 is the substring of s_1 from i to j, and $\text{idx}(s_1, s_2, i)$ – the number i is either the first position at which s_2 occurs in s_1, or 0 if s_2 does not occur in s_1.

Notice that the string equality constraint has a *reified* form, which is necessary to deal with string equality in the linear and propositional reasoning. For example, the OCL constraint $s_1 = s_2$ implies $s_1 = s_3$ would be expressed as

$$P = \big(\{s_1, s_2, s_3\}, \{(b_1 \to b_2), \text{eq}(s_1, s_2, b_1), \text{eq}(s_1, s_3, b_2)\}\big)$$

where $\to$ is assumed as a predefined constraint over two Booleans.

3.3 Constraint Handling Rules

To describe the rewriting operations on constraints, we employ Constraint Handling Rules (CHR), which is a well-known formalism and has several implementations available. However, our rewriting rules can also be implemented in other ways easily. As we make only very limited use of the formalism, we only introduce a simplified form here. For a thorough presentation of the formalism we refer to [11] and [24]. In our restricted context, a constraint handling rule has one of the three syntactic forms.

$$\begin{aligned}
rulename @ c_1, \ldots, c_m &\iff c'_1, \ldots c'_n \\
rulename @ c_1, \ldots, c_m &\implies c'_1, \ldots c'_n \\
rulename @ c_1, \ldots, c_k \setminus c_{k+1}, \ldots, c_m &\implies c'_1, \ldots c'_n
\end{aligned}$$

where c_i and c'_i are constraints that typically share some variables. The common semantics of these rules is that they match a pattern of constraints $c_1, \ldots, c_m$ in the constraint store (which, in our case, is the set of constraints in the CSP). The constraints in the pattern are related by their common variables, for example, as in the pattern $c_1(s, i), c_2(s, j)$. The first kind of rules above is called a *simplification* rule. It removes the matched constraints $c_1, \ldots, c_m$ from the constraint store and replaces them by new constraints $c'_1, \ldots c'_n$. The second kind is called a *propagation* rule, which also adds $c'_1, \ldots c'_n$ to the imposed constraints, but also keeps $c_1, \ldots, c_m$ in the store. The third kind is called a *simpagation* rule and is a mixture of the former two. It keeps $c_1, \ldots, c_k$, but replaces $c_{k+1}, \ldots, c_m$ by $c'_1, \ldots c'_n$. The execution of a set of CHR rules is terminated when no more rules can be applied. For propagation rules, the CHR environment ensures that such rules are applied only once per match of their pattern.

3.4 First Rewriting Step: The Length Sub-problem

We now define the rules that infer linear additional constraints over the lengths of the string variables. This constitutes the first rewriting step in our approach (cf. Fig. 1).

Definition 1. *Length Inference Rules*

$$\text{len-dom} @ \ \text{len}(s, l) \implies 0 \leq l \leq \mathit{MaxLen}$$

$$\text{len-one} @ \ \text{len}(s, l_1) \setminus \text{len}(s, l_2) \iff l_1 = l_2$$

$$\text{eq-len} @ \ \text{eq}(s_1, s_2, r), \text{len}(s_1, l_1), \text{len}(s_2, l_2) \implies r \to l_1 = l_2$$

$$\text{con-len} @ \ \text{con}(s_1, s_2, s_3), \text{len}(s_1, l_1), \text{len}(s_2, l_2), \text{len}(s_3, l_3) \implies l_3 = l_1 + l_2$$

$$\text{sub-len} @ \ \text{sub}(s_1, i, j, s_2), \text{len}(s_1, l_1), \text{len}(s_2, l_2) \implies \begin{array}{l} l_2 = (j - i + 1), \\ 1 \leq i \leq j \leq l_1 \end{array}$$

$$\text{idx-len} @ \ \text{idx}(s_1, s_2, i), \text{len}(s_1, l_1), \text{len}(s_2, l_2) \implies \begin{array}{l} i \neq 0 \to l_1 \geq l_2, \\ l_1 = 0 \to i = 0 \end{array}$$

$$\text{eq-refl} @ \ \text{eq}(s, s, b) \iff b \leftrightarrow \text{true}$$

$$\text{eq-one} @ \ \text{eq}(s_1, s_2, b_1) \setminus \text{eq}(s_1, s_2, b_2) \implies b_1 \leftrightarrow b_2.$$

The propagation rule len-dom constrains all strings to be finite, using a maximum length *MaxLen* that can be any positive number. For example, given $\mathit{MaxLen} = 100$, the CSP $(\{s\}, \text{len}(s, l)\})$ would be rewritten to $(\{s\}, \text{len}(s, l), 0 \leq l \leq 100\})$. The simpagation rule len-one removes multiple lengths constraints for the same string and replaces them by linear constraints over the length variables. For example, $P = (\{s\}, \text{len}(s, l_1), \text{len}(s, 4), l_1 \leq 3\})$ would be rewritten to $(\{s\}, \text{len}(s, l_1), l_1 \leq 3, l_1 = 4)$ – which a linear constraint solver would detect as unsatisfiable for any l_1. The propagation rule eq-len poses conditional equality. The rules con-len, sub-len, and idx-len generate the expected constraints in the same manner. Finally, the simplification rules eq-refl and eq-one include reflexivity and *tertium non datur* into the length inference.

Please note that we included the last two rules, eq-refl and eq-one for practical reasons only, as a performance optimization (these rules add only little overhead in terms of constraint processing). They are theoretically not required, because equality of strings will be translated into pair-wise equality of their elements (see below). On the contrary, we do not include transitivity (and neither symmetry) here, in order to keep the approach lightweight, as transitivity can lead to an exponential number of equality constraints. Theoretically, $\text{eq}(s_1, s_2, \text{true})$ is of course transitive (and $\text{eq}(s_1, s_2, b)$ is symmetric), because the equality on the element variables has exactly these properties. We found, however, that turning these properties into rules produces too much overhead for the kind of (lightweight) string problems we consider.

When no more of the rules in Def. 1 can be applied (i.e., the execution of these rules has terminated), a ground assignment of all length variables has to be selected. In general, this introduces a choice point. Consider, for example, if we derived $P = (\{s_1, s_2\}, \{\text{len}(s_1, l_1), \text{len}(s_2, l_2), 1 \leq l_1 \leq 4, 1 \leq l_2 \leq 4, s_1 = s_2 - 1\})$, the choices for l_1, l_2 would be 1, 2 and 2, 3. Assuming we select 1, 2 first, we would proceed with the CSP $P = (\{s_1, s_2\}, \text{len}(s_1, 1), \text{len}(s_2, 2))$

3.5 Second Rewriting Step: Resolve String Constraints to Element Constraints

Given that a solution to the length sub-problem has been selected (i.e., all length variables have ground values), the following rule unifies all string variables with lists of element variables, where each element variable is constrained to be in the range of the alphabet $\mathcal{A}$, for which charnums is assumed to assign a corresponding set of integers from 1 to $|\mathcal{A}|$.

Definition 2. *Structural Instantiation Rule*

$$\text{len-inst} @ \; \text{len}(s, n) \iff$$
$$s = \langle x_1, \ldots, x_n \rangle, x_1 \in \text{charnums}(\mathcal{A}), \ldots, x_n \in \text{charnums}(\mathcal{A})$$

After all string variables have been instantiated using rule len-inst, all string constraints in C are finally replaced ($\iff$) by linear and Boolean constraints on the individual element variables using the following rewrite rules.

Definition 3. *Linear Representation Rules*

$$\text{eq-inst} @ \; \text{eq}(\langle x_1, \ldots, x_n \rangle, \langle y_1, \ldots, y_n \rangle, r) \iff$$
$$r \leftrightarrow \left(\bigwedge_{1 \leq i \leq n} x_i = y_i \right)$$

$$\text{con-inst} @ \; \text{con}(\langle x_1, \ldots, x_m \rangle, \langle y_1, \ldots, y_n \rangle, \langle z_1, \ldots, z_{m+n} \rangle) \iff$$
$$\left(\left(\forall_{1 \leq i \leq m} \; x_i = z_i \right), \left(\forall_{1 \leq j \leq n} \; y_j = z_{m+j} \right) \right)$$

$$\text{sub-inst} @ \; \text{sub}(\langle x_1, \ldots, x_m \rangle, i, j, \langle y_1, \ldots, y_n \rangle) \iff$$
$$\forall_{0 \leq l \leq (n-m)} \left(i = l + 1 \rightarrow \left(\bigwedge_{1 \leq k \leq n} x_{k+l} = y_k \right) \right)$$

$$\text{idx-inst} @ \; \text{idx}(\langle x_1, \ldots, x_m \rangle, \langle y_1, \ldots, y_n \rangle, i) \iff$$
$$\forall_{0 \leq l \leq (n-m)} \left(r' \leftrightarrow \left(\bigwedge_{1 \leq k \leq n} x_{k+l} = y_k \right), \right.$$
$$\left. r' \rightarrow p_l = l + 1, \neg r' \rightarrow p_l = 0 \right),$$
$$i = \text{min}^*(p_0, \ldots, p_{(n-m)})$$

where $\forall$ is used to express a set constraints and $b \leftrightarrow \bigwedge(\ldots)$ is used to represent that b is constrained to be the result of the conjunction of a set of Boolean values. r' and p_l are fresh variables and min^* is the usual minimum function on natural numbers with the exception that 0 is regarded as the largest number.

The rule eq-inst poses one Boolean constraint that r is equal to the Boolean value of the conjunction of the element-wise equality of both strings. The rule con-inst poses one equality constraint for each element of the concatenated string. The rule sub-inst poses one constraint for each possible offset l of y in x. Please notice that we can safely assume m and n to be ground values, whereas i and j can be variables. The rule does not pose further constraints on j, because j has already been expressed dependent on i by rule sub-len before (see Def. 1). Rule idx-inst is of similar nature, only that it introduces one integer variable p_l per possible offset of y in x, which is constrained to be either the position of y in x or 0. The result of i is then expressed by the (modified) minimum of these values. This minimum can be rewritten syntactically into basic linear constraints.

After the rules of Def. 3 have been applied, the resulting CSP contains only relational and arithmetic constraints on Boolean and integer values. It can be solved using off-the-shelf solvers.

3.6 Derivation Example

To illustrate the definitions so far, we now provide a complete derivation example that shows (i) how an OCL constraint is expressed in terms of our string constraints, (ii) how the length inference takes place, and (iii) how the constraints are finally resolved for a given length assignment. We consider the following OCL constraint:

$$s_1 = (s_2 + s_3).\,\text{substring}(2,3) \text{ and} (s_2 + s_3).\,\text{size}() < 10$$

It can be represented as a CSP in a straight-forward manner using the constraints previously introduced. Because constraints predicates cannot be nested, the CSP requires two additional string variables s_4, s_5 to express the results of the subexpressions $s_2 + s_3$ and $(s_2 + s_3).\,\text{substring}(2,3)$. This means that, while we are eventually interested in three strings, $s_1, s_2,$ and s_3, we have to regard five strings in the CSP. Note that a len constraint with a free length variable is included for each string. Let $MaxLen = 1000$. We assume the built-in reified Boolean resp. linear constraints $\wedge(x, y, b)$ and $<(x, y, b)$, for which the third argument is the truth value of $x \wedge y$ resp. $x < y$. The resulting CSP is

$$(\{s_1, \ldots, s_5\}, \{\,\text{len}(s_1, l_1), \text{len}(s_2, l_2), \text{len}(s_3, l_3), \text{len}(s_4, l_4), \\ \text{len}(s_5, l_5), \wedge(b_1, b_2, \text{true}), \text{eq}(s_1, s_5, b_1), \\ \text{con}(s_2, s_3, s_4), \text{sub}(s_4, 2, 3, s_5), <(l_4, 10, b_2)\}) \quad (1)$$

We assume that propagation on Boolean predicates will unify $b_1 = \text{true}$ and $b_2 = \text{true}$ from $\wedge(b_1, b_2, \text{true})$. The rewriting rules for lengths apply as follows: len-dom infers a range constraint for each string length, eq-len infers $l_1 = l_5$, con-len infers a linear constraint $l_4 = l_2 + l_3$, sub-len infers the linear constraints $l_5 = 2$ and $1 \leq i \leq j \leq l_4$. Assuming that the linear constraints propagate their bounds, the simplified resulting CSP is

$$(\{s_1, \ldots, s_5\}, \{\,\text{len}(s_1, 2), \text{len}(s_2, l_2), \text{len}(s_3, l_3), \text{len}(s_4, l_4), \\ \text{len}(s_5, 2), \text{eq}(s_1, s_5, \text{true}), \text{con}(s_2, s_3, s_4), \\ \text{sub}(s_4, 2, 3, s_5), 0 \leq l_2 < 10, 0 \leq l_3 < 10, \\ l_4 = l_2 + l_3, 3 \leq l_4 < 10\}).$$

with l_1 and l_5 being removed from the variables (as $l_1 = l_5 = 2$), At this point, no more rules are applicable until we select a solution to the length sub-problem

$$(\{l_2, \ldots l_4\}, \leq l_2 \leq 10, 0 \leq l_3 < 10, l_4 = l_2 + l_3, 3 \leq l_4 < 10\}) \quad (2)$$

We assume the assignment $\{l_1 \mapsto 2, l_2 \mapsto 2, l_3 \mapsto 3, l_4 \mapsto 3, l_5 \mapsto 2\}$ is chosen and apply rule len-inst. The CSP to solve is now

$$(\{\,s_{1,1}, s_{1,2}, s_{2,1}, s_{2,2}, s_{3,1}, s_{4,1}, s_{4,2}, s_{4,3}, s_{5,1}, s_{5,2}\}, \\ \{\,\text{eq}(s_1, s_5, \text{true}), \text{con}(s_2, s_3, s_4), \text{sub}(s_4, 1, 3, s_5), \\ \text{sub}(\langle s_{4,1}, s_{4,2}\rangle, 1, 3, \langle s_{5,1}, s_{5,2}\rangle), \\ s_{1,1}, s_{1,2}, s_{2,1}, s_{2,2}, s_{3,1}, s_{4,1}, s_{4,2}, s_{4,3}, s_{5,1}, s_{5,2} \in \text{charnums}|\mathcal{A}|\})$$

with $s_1 = \langle s_{1,1}, s_{1,2}\rangle, s_2 = \langle s_{2,1}, s_{2,2}\rangle, s_3 = \langle s_{3,1}\rangle, \langle s_{4,1}, s_{4,2}, s_{4,3}\rangle$, and $\langle s_{5,1}, s_{5,2}\rangle$.

For this example, the resolving of the rules eq-inst, con-inst, and sub-inst finally unifies several variables, leaving a CSP that is *solved* (i.e., a CSP for which every assignment of character numbers to the element variables is a solution).

$$(\{s_{1,1}, s_{1,2}, s_{2,1}, s_{2,2}, s_{3,1}\}, \{s_{1,1}, s_{1,2}, s_{2,1}, s_{2,2}, s_{3,1} \in \text{charnums}|\mathcal{A}|\})$$

All $|\mathcal{A}|^5$ solutions to this CSP are solutions to the original CSP (1) under the assignment of $\{l_2 \mapsto 2, l_3 \mapsto 1, l_4 \mapsto 3)\}$ to the length subproblem (2) with $(s_1, \langle s_{1,1}, s_{1,2} \rangle)$, $(s_2 = \langle s_{2,1}, s_{2,2} \rangle, s_3 = \langle s_{3,1} \rangle, s_4 = \langle s_{2,1}, s_{1,1}, s_{1,2} \rangle, s_5 = \langle s_{1,1}, s_{1,2} \rangle$. Naturally, in other cases not all assignments to the final CSP are solutions to the problems. In general, *search* must be performed for a solution. The impact of this search on the scalability of our approach is discussed in the next section.

4 Limits and Scalability

The rewriting rules presented in the previous section do not constitute a self-contained decision procedure. They have to be combined with a solver that is capable to reason about propositional logic and bounded integer constraints, for which decision procedures are available in various solvers. The presented constraint handling rules are terminating and confluent. This means that, in theory, every CSP on strings with bounded lengths can be solved using our approach if it can be expressed using the provided string constraint predicates and other decidable constraints. In this section, we first provide some experimental results that we gathered using our implementation of the approach, then we discuss scalability aspects in more generality.

4.1 Experimental Results

As mentioned before, we have implemented the described reasoning approach in our model finder EMFtoCSP, using the constraint handling rules support of the ECL^{i}PS^e solver. We now employ the model depicted class diagram in Fig. 2 and the following OCL constraints to illustrate performance and scalability aspects of our approach and implementation.

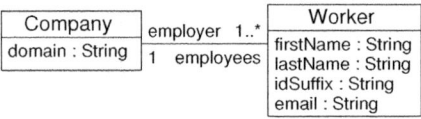

Fig. 2. Example Class Diagram annotated with OCL Constraints for its Strings

The example contains (conditional) string equality, concatenation, and and containment constraints. Due to the existential and universal quantifiers in EmailsUnique (all workers within a company must have the distinct email addresses) and OneSame (at least two workers must share first and last name), a quadratic number of of conditional equality constraints is posed. Both invariants are considerably hard in terms of computational complexity, which is why we have added them to our experiment. The constraint EmailStructured determines the structure of the email attribute in terms of concatenation.

```
context Company inv EmailsUnique:
  worker->forAll(w1,w2 | w1.email = w2.email implies w1 = w2 )
context Company inv OneSame:
  worker->exists(e1,e2 | e1 <> e2 and
                e1.firstName = e2.firstName and
                e1.lastName = e2.lastName )
context Worker inv EmailStructured:
  email = firstName + '.' + lastName + '.' +
          idSuffix + '@' + employer.domain
context Worker inv NoAt:
  firstName.indexOf('@') = 0 and
  lastName.indexOf('@') = 0
```

EMFtoCSP translates the model and its constraints into a CSP as described in Sect. 2.2. In our extended version, the OCL constraints are translated using the string constraints introduced in the previous section. Recall that the original approach consists of two sub-problems *Structure* and *Global*. In the version with string support, the length inference is included into the global sub-problem (i.e., it adds further constraints to this sub-problem). The element labeling then constitutes a new, third sub-problem *Strings*.

Table 1 show the runtimes and linear constraint propagations performed by ECL^{i}PS^e for different instance sizes of the above example. The tests were conducted on a typical office 2.2Ghz laptop running ECL^{i}PS^e 6.0 on Windows 7. All tests used a maximum string lengths of 1,000.

The table differentiates the runtimes and propagation counts for the CHR processing and the final labeling (i.e., the assignment of ground character values to the elements of all strings). For each test cases we constrained the workers to be evenly distributed among the companies. The table illustrates several aspects. First, we can see that the actual character labeling does not consume a significant amount of time once the constraint handling rules have been processed and the linear constraints have been posted.

Furthermore, we can observe that the runtimes for the cases where few companies have many workers consume the most processing time. This is due to the quadratic number of equality constraints that results from the OCL invariants EmailsUnique and OneSame. For the second row in Table 1 more than 30,000 conditional equality constraints are posed in the *Global* sub-problem. If the number of workers per company is less high, EMFtoCSP scales better, for example, when the ratio is 1:10, as in the third row.

Table 1. Experimental Results

Instance			CHR Processing		Character Labeling	
companies	workers	strings	cpu time	propagations	cpu time	propagations
1	10	41	0.1s	3,112	$\leq$ 0.1s	3,360
1	100	401	10.1s	220,192	1.1s	963,600
10	100	410	0.7s	31,120	$\leq$ 0.1s	33,600
50	100	450	0.4s	14,000	$\leq$ 0.1s	3,200
150	300	1,350	2.3s	42,000	$\leq$ 0.1s	9,600
10	300	1,210	11.7s	219,520	0.6s	440,800

4.2 General Discussion

In general, we can distinguish three categories for the solving of the CSP, where the distinction between the second and third case depends on the capabilities of he solver employed. In a nutshell, our approach works very efficiently in the first category, and less efficient in the others. We have conducted several experiments using our implementation of the approach in EMFtoCSP and the ECL^{i}PS^e solver, and found that several typical patterns of constraints encountered in models fall into the first case (and so does the previously presented example).

1. The *optimal case*: No backtracking is required, every valid length assignment yields a *solved* CSP on the string elements after applying our rewriting rules and performing constraint propagation. In this case, even very high numbers for the maximum string length (e.g., 1000) can be chosen.
2. In the *length search case*, not every valid length assignment yields a consistent CSP on the string elements, but the inconsistency of a chosen length assignment is detected by the solver without actually labeling the elements. A simple example for this case is given by the OCL constraint `s.indexOf('@') = 0 and s.indexOf('@') <> 0`, whose unsatisfiability is not recognized before instantiating the s to its element variables[1]. The ECL^{i}PS^e solver, for example, however detects that the resulting CSP (the third one in Fig. 1) is consistent without backtracking through the possible assignments of values to the element variables, leaving *MaxLen* choices for the solver before reporting inconsistency. For constraints that fall into this case, the maximum string length must be set to a reasonable small value for practical applications.
3. The *labeling trap*: In this case, the inconsistency is not detected before actually labeling the element values. To ease the labeling trap in practice, the search procedure can be split to perform a two-pass run, where the first pass tries at most one assignment to the element variables for each solution to the length problem. In the second pass, the element labeling is repeated without restrictions. This tweak to the search space traversal helps to circumnavigate the labeling trap for insufficient string lengths.

However, for most constraint patterns typically encountered in 'real live' situations, the labeling trap is not a problem. In fact, as stated before, several common constraint patterns fall even into the first category. Summarizing, we state that our approach is perfectly suited to efficiently handle lightweight string problems that have many solutions, while it is not suited to solve non-tractable string problems (which, in general, are NP-hard), that only have few solutions, and for which the employed solver runs into the labeling trap.

5 Conclusion

In the previous sections, we have presented an approach that translates OCL String constraints into a constraint satisfaction problem that can be solved using off-the-shelf solvers, and which can be integrated easily into existing model finding approaches and

---
[1] We assume the constraint is translated straightforwardly using two separate idx constraints.

tools for OCL without adding too much overhead to the underlying decision procedures. Our approach is lightweight in the sense that it efficiently finds solutions for many common OCL constraint constellations and it is suited to handle models with thousands of strings. Due to its two-step nature, we can efficiently handle strings of potentially long lengths, which otherwise would lead to search space explosion when directly encoding all strings as bitvectors of the maximum length. We therefore claim that our approach is suited for various practical ('real world') applications. It is, however, not suited to tackle hard, non-tractable string constraints that only have few solutions. These must be addressed either by one-step bit-blasting approaches or by formal regular language reasoning and theorem provers that can handle an appropriate theory.

So far we considered an important subset of OCL string operations. We expect that the remaining operations (e.g., toLowerCase, at, characters, <) can be encoded in the same manner. To our knowledge, we are the first ones that integrate reasoning on String constraints into model finding for OCL-annotated models. We have implemented our results into the EMFtoCSP (formerly UMLtoCSP) tool and provided some experimental results. While we used constraint handling rules as a formalism to define our constraint rewriting rules, our approach can be easily implemented in other ways, for example, using suspended goals in constraint logic programming.

As the next step, we will evaluate the effect of using different solvers, for our final CSPs on the element variables and compare their suitability with the constraint logic programming approach. In particular, we hope to apply our approach to the Kodkod encoding of OCL in [18], in order to directly compare the bit-blasting approach and our two-step approach. Furthermore, we will evaluate the applicability and performance of our approach using further, more extensive case studies.

References

1. Ali, S., Iqbal, M.Z.Z., Arcuri, A., Briand, L.C.: A Search-Based OCL Constraint Solver for Model-Based Test Data Generation. In: QSIC, pp. 41–50 (2011)
2. Anastasakis, K., Bordbar, B., Georg, G., Ray, I.: UML2Alloy: A Challenging Model Transformation. In: Engels, G., Opdyke, B., Schmidt, D.C., Weil, F. (eds.) MODELS 2007. LNCS, vol. 4735, pp. 436–450. Springer, Heidelberg (2007)
3. Baudry, B., Ghosh, S., Fleurey, F., France, R.B., Traon, Y.L., Mottu, J.M.: Barriers to systematic model transformation testing. Commun. ACM 53(6), 139–143 (2010)
4. Bjorner, N., Nieuwenhuis, R., Veith, H., Voronkov, A. (eds.): Decision Procedures in Soft, Hard and Bio-ware - Follow Up, vol. 1(7). Dagstuhl Reports (2011)
5. Büttner, F., Cabot, J., Gogolla, M.: On Validation of ATL Transformation Rules By Transformation Models. In: Weißleder, S., Lúcio, L., Cichos, H., Fondement, F. (eds.) Proceedings of MoDeVVa 2011. ACM Digital Library (2012), doi:10.1145/2095654.2095666
6. Cabot, J., Clarisó, R., Guerra, E., de Lara, J.: Verification and validation of declarative model-to-model transformations through invariants. Journal of Systems and Software 83(2), 283–302 (2010)
7. Cabot, J., Clarisó, R., Riera, D.: UMLtoCSP: a tool for the formal verification of UML/OCL models using constraint programming. In: Stirewalt, R.E.K., Egyed, A., Fischer, B. (eds.) Proceedings of Automated Software Engineering, ASE 2007. ACM (2007)
8. Cadoli, M., Calvanese, D., De Giacomo, G., Mancini, T.: Finite Satisfiability of UML Class Diagrams by Constraint Programming. In: Proc. of the CP 2004 Workshop on CSP Techniques with Immediate Application (2004)
9. Clavel, M., Egea, M., de Dios, M.A.G.: Checking Unsatisfiability for OCL Constraints. Electronic Communications of the EASST 24, 1–13 (2009)

10. The EMFtoCSP tool. Website,
    http://code.google.com/a/eclipselabs.org/p/emftocsp/
11. Frühwirth, T.W.: Constraint Handling Rules. In: Podelski, A. (ed.) Constraint Programming: Basics and Trends. LNCS, vol. 910, pp. 90–107. Springer, Heidelberg (1995)
12. Gogolla, M., Büttner, F., Richters, M.: USE: A UML-based specification environment for validating UML and OCL. Sci. Comput. Program. 69(1-3), 27–34 (2007)
13. Golden, K., Pang, W.: Constraint Reasoning over Strings. In: Rossi, F. (ed.) CP 2003. LNCS, vol. 2833, pp. 377–391. Springer, Heidelberg (2003)
14. González, C.A., Büttner, F., Clarisó, R., Cabot, J.: EMFtoCSP: A Tool for the Lightweight Verification of EMF Models. In: Proc. of Formal Methods in Software Engineering: Rigorous and Agile Approaches (FormSERA), Workshop at ICSE (to appear, 2012),
    http://www.formsera.org/FormSERA
15. Grahne, G., Nykänen, M., Ukkonen, E.: Reasoning about Strings in Databases. J. Comput. Syst. Sci. 59(1), 116–162 (1999)
16. Hooimeijer, P., Veanes, M.: An Evaluation of Automata Algorithms for String Analysis. In: Jhala, R., Schmidt, D. (eds.) VMCAI 2011. LNCS, vol. 6538, pp. 248–262. Springer, Heidelberg (2011)
17. Kiezun, A., Ganesh, V., Guo, P.J., Ernst, M.D., Hooimeijer, P., Ganesh, V., Guo, P.J., Ernst, M.D.: HAMPI: A solver for string constraints. In: International Symposium on Software Testing and Analysis (2009)
18. Kuhlmann, M., Gogolla, M.: Strengthening SAT-Based Validation of UML/OCL Models by Representing Collections as Relations. In: Kolovos, D. (ed.) ECMFA 2012. LNCS, vol. 7349, pp. 32–48. Springer, Heidelberg (2012)
19. Kuhlmann, M., Hamann, L., Gogolla, M.: Extensive Validation of OCL Models by Integrating SAT Solving into USE. In: Bishop, J., Vallecillo, A. (eds.) TOOLS 2011. LNCS, vol. 6705, pp. 290–306. Springer, Heidelberg (2011)
20. Malgouyres, H., Motet, G.: A UML model consistency verification approach based on metamodeling formalization. In: Proceedings of the 2006 ACM Symposium on Applied Computing, SAC 2006, pp. 1804–1809. ACM, New York (2006),
    http://doi.acm.org/10.1145/1141277.1141703
21. Maraee, A., Balaban, M.: Efficient Reasoning About Finite Satisfiability of UML Class Diagrams with Constrained Generalization Sets. In: Akehurst, D.H., Vogel, R., Paige, R.F. (eds.) ECMDA-FA. LNCS, vol. 4530, pp. 17–31. Springer, Heidelberg (2007),
    http://dl.acm.org/citation.cfm?id=1768765.1768767
22. OMG: Object Constraint Language Specification, version 2.3.1 (Document formal/2012-01-01) (2012)
23. Sen, S., Baudry, B., Mottu, J.-M.: Automatic Model Generation Strategies for Model Transformation Testing. In: Paige, R.F. (ed.) ICMT 2009. LNCS, vol. 5563, pp. 148–164. Springer, Heidelberg (2009)
24. Sneyers, J., Weert, P.V., Schrijvers, T., Koninck, L.D.: As time goes by: Constraint Handling Rules. TPLP 10(1), 1–47 (2010)
25. Soeken, M., Wille, R., Drechsler, R.: Encoding OCL Data Types for SAT-Based Verification of UML/OCL Models. In: Gogolla, M., Wolff, B. (eds.) TAP 2011. LNCS, vol. 6706, pp. 152–170. Springer, Heidelberg (2011)
26. Veanes, M., de Halleux, P., Tillmann, N.: Rex: Symbolic Regular Expression Explorer. In: ICST, pp. 498–507. IEEE Computer Society (2010)
27. Winkelmann, J., Taentzer, G., Ehrig, K., Küster, J.M.: Translation of Restricted OCL Constraints into Graph Constraints for Generating Meta Model Instances by Graph Grammars. Electr. Notes Theor. Comput. Sci. 211, 159–170 (2008)
28. Bjørner, N., Tillmann, N., Voronkov, A.: Path Feasibility Analysis for String-Manipulating Programs. In: Kowalewski, S., Philippou, A. (eds.) TACAS 2009. LNCS, vol. 5505, pp. 307–321. Springer, Heidelberg (2009), http://dblp.uni-trier.de,
    doi: http://dx.doi.org/10.1007/978-3-642-00768-2_27

Domain-Specific Textual Meta-Modelling Languages for Model Driven Engineering

Juan de Lara and Esther Guerra

Universidad Autónoma de Madrid (Spain)

Abstract. Domain-specific modelling languages are normally defined through general-purpose meta-modelling languages like the MOF. While this is satisfactory for many Model-Driven Engineering (MDE) projects, several researchers have identified the need for *domain-specific meta-modelling* (DSMM) languages providing customised meta-modelling primitives aimed at the definition of modelling languages in a specific domain, as well as the construction of meta-model families.

In this paper, we discuss the potential of *multi-level meta-modelling* for the systematic engineering of DSMM architectures. For this purpose, we present: (i) several primitives and techniques to control the meta-modelling facilities offered to the users of the DSMM languages, (ii) a flexible approach to define textual concrete syntaxes for DSMM languages, (iii) extensions to model management languages enabling the practical use of DSMM in MDE, and (iv) an implementation of these ideas in the METADEPTH tool.

Keywords: Model-Driven Engineering, Deep Languages, Domain-Specific Meta-Modelling, Textual Concrete Syntax, Multi-Level Transformations.

1 Introduction

Model-Driven Engineering (MDE) promotes an active use of models throughout the software development. These models are sometimes defined using general-purpose languages like the UML, but for restricted, well-known domains, it is also frequent the use of Domain-Specific Modelling Languages (DSMLs).

In current MDE practice, DSMLs are built by the language designer using a meta-model defined with a general-purpose meta-modelling language, like the MOF. This meta-model describes the instances that the users of the language can build in the immediate meta-level below. Thus, DSMLs usually comprise two meta-levels: the definition of the DSML and its usage. More recently, several researchers [9,16] have pointed out the utility of using domain-specific meta-modelling (DSMM) languages as a means to provide domain-specific meta-modelling primitives to customize families of similar DSMLs, e.g., for expressing traceability [16], variability [16] or to define domain-specific process modelling notations [9] and DSML profiles [13]. In this case, the language spans three meta-levels: definition of the DSMM language for a specific domain, definition of the

DSML by using the constructs provided by the DSMM language, and usage of the DSML. Unfortunately, existing approaches to DSMM are generally based on a two meta-level setting and the definition of ad-hoc "promotion" transformations between models and meta-models, which makes the adoption of DSMM cumbersome in practice. Moreover, there is no general framework for defining DSMM languages with integrated MDE support.

In this paper, we propose multi-level meta-modelling [5] as an underlying framework for DSMM, and discuss mechanisms to facilitate its adoption in MDE projects. Multi-level meta-modelling allows the definition of *deep* languages, which can be instantiated in more than one meta-level. In this way, the users of the language perform DSMM as, in each meta-level, the constructed models are instances of the upper meta-level but also meta-models w.r.t. the meta-level below. In our context, this means that a DSML is naturally defined as an instance of a DSMM language, and at the same time, it acts as a meta-model for lower meta-levels (i.e., it defines a language). Moreover, we provide: (a) means to customize the meta-modelling features that will be offered to the users of the DSMM languages, (b) a flexible way to define textual concrete syntaxes at every meta-level, and (c) model management languages able to work in a multi-level setting, enabling the use of DSMM in MDE projects (for space constraints we just show the use of model transformations). The framework is supported by METADEPTH [6], a multi-level meta-modelling tool supporting deep characterization through potency [5], and dual ontological/linguistic typing.

Paper Organization. Sec. 2 discusses related research, exposing motivations and needs in the area. Sec. 3 applies multi-level meta-modelling to DSMM and identifies some challenges: how to customise the DSMLs in a DSMM framework (Sec. 4), how to define a concrete syntax for the DSMLs (Sec. 5), and how to manipulate models in a multi-level setting (Sec. 6). Finally, Sec. 7 concludes.

2 Related Work

Several researchers have pointed out the benefits of using DSMM languages. For example, the traceability modelling language [16] (TML) is a DSMM language used to express the allowed traces and constraints between several meta-models. Its rationale is that TML users do not need the full power of EMF or MOF to construct trace meta-models, but they benefit from specific meta-modelling primitives like `Trace` and `TraceLink`. Other DSMM languages are described in [16] to express variability over DSMLs, and to extend DSMLs with interfaces for model reuse. However, no general framework for defining such DSMM languages is proposed. Instead, they use two meta-levels and define ad-hoc "promotion" transformations between models (e.g., a TML model) and meta-models (the resulting trace meta-model). These transformations are a way to emulate three meta-levels within two, hindering the construction of DSMM languages.

In [8], the authors present a language to declare component types with ports, which can be instantiated choosing a number of port instances. This DSMM language is defined in a two meta-level framework extended with capabilities to instantiate the components, emulating the existence of two meta-levels within one. The price to pay is that one has to manually encode support for the definition of class/features/data types and their instantiation, the definition and evaluation of constraints, and the emulation of inheritance within a single meta-level.

In [13], the UML profiling mechanism is adapted for EMF-based DSMLs. This is another example of DSMM as users need a language to define new profiles and apply them at the meta-level below. Again, a two meta-level setting forces the use of workarounds. In this case, they emulate the existence of attribute instances at the lowest meta-level by the run-time adaptation of the meta-model, injecting new attribute types and classes.

Instead of emulating several meta-levels within two [8] or using artificial workarounds [13,16], we claim that a more natural way to define DSMM languages is the native use of multi-level meta-modelling, also known as deep meta-modelling [6]. Previously, Jablonski et al. [9] used multiple levels to build domain-specific process modelling notations. However, their approach is restricted to meta-modelling, and does not consider the language concrete syntax or its manipulation through model management languages, hindering its use in MDE.

Here, we propose some mechanisms to handle these deficiencies based on some multi-level meta-modelling techniques developed originally by Atkinson and Kühne [3]. There are several multi-level meta-modelling frameworks [1,2,12]. For example, DeepJava [12] extends Java to allow multiple instantiations, whereas the main concern in [1] is the efficient navigation between meta-levels. In [2], the authors discuss the visualization of multi-level languages but do not consider linguistic extensions or the integration with model management languages. All these frameworks either do not consider concrete syntaxes [1,12] or do not integrate model manipulation languages enabling their use for MDE [2].

Although there are many approaches to define textual concrete syntaxes for DSMLs [7,10], their definition for DSMM languages poses new challenges. For instance, there is the need to define the concrete syntax for models several meta-levels below, for which the concrete types that will be available in the models are unknown in advance. Sometimes, it is also necessary to extend the predefined concrete syntax for a particular DSML built using a DSMM language. This enables a progressive refinement of concrete syntaxes at different meta-levels.

Altogether, our contribution is a comprehensive framework to define DSMM language environments based on multi-level meta-modelling. Our approach covers the definition of textual concrete syntaxes, a fine grained customization of the meta-modelling facilities offered to the DSMM language users, and model management languages tailored to a multi-level setting.

3 Deep Meta-Modelling for Domain-Specific Meta-Modelling

In DSMM, users are not given the full power of a general-purpose meta-modelling language, but a more suitable meta-modelling language that contains primitives of the domain, and that is restricted for a particular meta-modelling task.

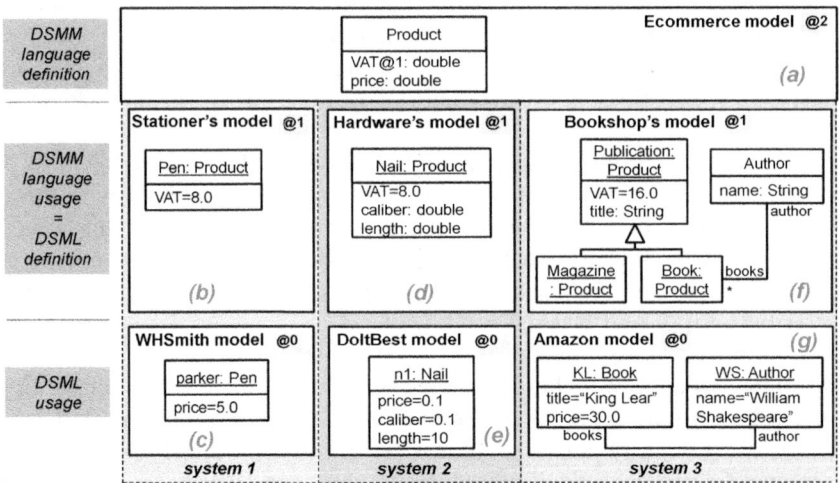

Fig. 1. Definition of a DSMM language for e-commerce (a). Using the language with increasing degrees of extension: no extension (b,c), property extensions (d,e), concept extensions (f,g).

For instance, assume we need to model information systems for e-commerce in various domains. For this purpose, we can build a specialized meta-modelling language that facilitates the construction of DSMLs for each one of these domains. An over-simplified definition of such a meta-modelling language and some of its uses for different scenarios are shown in Fig. 1. Model (a) defines the DSMM language, which is made of a single class Product. This language can be used to define a DSML for a stationer system (model (b)), for which we just use the primitives of the domain (e.g., we create an instance of Product called Pen). Finally, this DSML can be used to define the items in a particular stationery store (i.e., we can create instances of Pen, as done in model (c)).

In this way, the definition of a DSML spans three meta-levels: the Stationer model is an instance of Ecommerce, and WHSmith is an instance of Stationer. Therefore, it is natural to use a multi-level framework to support the definition and usage of our DSMM language, as these frameworks natively support instantiation across several meta-levels without recurring to artificial workarounds. In a multi-level framework, elements retain both a *type facet* which allows their instantiation in the next meta-level, and an *instance facet* as they are instances of an element at the meta-level above. Thus, model elements become *clabjects* (from the union of "class" and "object") enabling a more uniform way of modelling [3].

DSMM languages normally comprise three meta-levels. To enforce this depth in a multi-level framework, we can use *deep characterization* through the concept of *potency* [3]. The potency is an integer number that can be attached to models, clabjects, attributes and references. If an element is not explicitly given a potency, it receives the one of its immediate container. The potency of an element gets decremented at each meta-level, and when it reaches zero, the element cannot be instantiated further. Thus, the definition of our DSMM language has potency 2 (see model (a) in Fig. 1, its potency is indicated by '@2'), it gets instantiated into models with potency 1 (middle models), and the instances of these have potency 0 and therefore cannot be instantiated in subsequent meta-levels. In this way, the DSMM language user is effectively performing DSMM because he builds models with potency 1, which are instantiated as models of potency 0.

The potency is also a way for the deep characterization of properties, in order to control the meta-level in which they can be assigned a value. For example, in our DSMM language, all products will receive a price. Hence, Product declares an attribute price with potency 2, so that it will receive a value two meta-levels below (i.e., each pen has its own price). The potency of the attribute is not explicit, but it is received from the enclosing model. In contrast, the VAT is the same for all products of the same type, hence it has potency 1.

DSMM languages are used to build meta-models for related but different domains. Hence, a particular domain may need to extend the meta-modelling concepts offered by the DSMM language with new domain-specific properties. For example, model (d) in Fig. 1 shows that, in the hardware domain, we need to increase the attributes offered by Product. In particular, Nails need to define their caliber and length. These two attributes are specific for nails and therefore cannot be included in the definition of Product as they are not general for every domain. Similarly, we may also need to declare domain-specific constraints, e.g., stating that the caliber should be larger than 0.1. Finally, some domains may need to make available new primitives to the users of the DSMLs. For instance, in the bookshop domain, the manipulated products are Books, which have exactly one Author (see model (f) in Fig. 1). The concept of Author is not included in the DSMM language, and hence we need to include it in the meta-model for bookshops. This is only possible if the DSMM language provides facilities to define new clabjects, references and multiplicities. Moreover, one may wish to group several products in an inheritance hierarchy. For example, both Magazines and Books have a title and share the same VAT value.

The previous *linguistic extensions* can be supported by a multi-level framework if we use a dual ontological/linguistic typing for the model elements. The ontological typing is a relation within the domain, and refers to the type of which an element is instance. For example, the ontological type of Pen is Product, and the ontological type of parker is Pen. Hence, *ontological meta-modelling* is concerned with describing the concepts in a certain domain and their properties [4]. All elements in the top-most model (model (a) in Fig. 1) and some elements in the domain-specific meta-models (e.g., Author) may not have ontological type. In contrast, all elements have a linguistic type, which refers to the meta-modelling primitive used to create the element. For example, the linguistic type of Product, Pen and parker is clabject, while the linguistic type of books is reference.

One can interpret the union of the three models in each column of Fig. 1 as being conformant to a linguistic meta-model, as shown in Fig. 2(a) (the linguistic meta-model is only partially shown). In our approach, a *linguistic extension* is

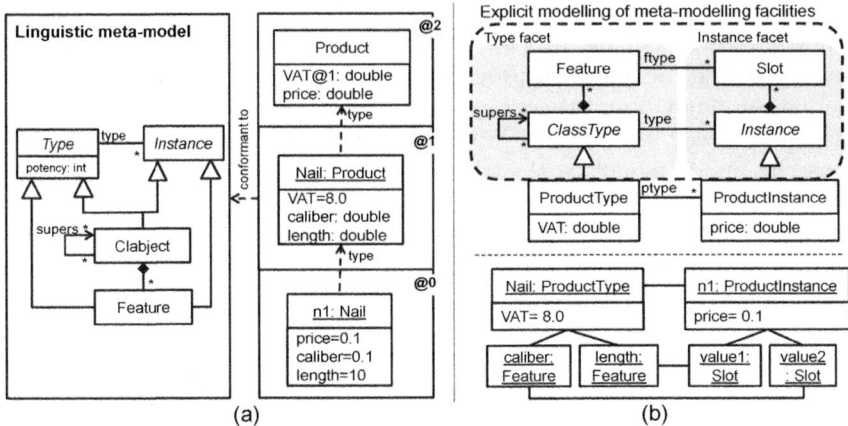

Fig. 2. Defining a DSMM language using: (a) 3 levels and dual typing, (b) 2 levels

an element without ontological typing, like Author or the caliber attribute in Nail. The dual ontological/linguistic typing is very convenient for DSMM as it makes available standard meta-modelling facilities at each meta-level.

Alternatively, Fig. 2(b) shows the definition of our DSMM language using only two meta-levels. This solution makes necessary to explicitly model the desired meta-modelling facilities, and to manually encode the machinery to emulate built-in support for instantiation and constraint checking. Thus, one should build mechanisms taking care of type conformance, data types, definition and evaluation of constraints, and so on.

Altogether, deep meta-modelling facilitates the construction of DSMM languages. However, the following challenges remain:

- We need mechanisms to control the linguistic extensions offered by the DSMM languages, as not any extension may be valid in any domain.
- To be usable in practice, we need to provide a suitable concrete syntax for the DSMM languages and for the DSMLs defined with them. Ideally, both syntaxes should be defined once together with the DSMM language definition, and it should be possible to refine or extend them to take into account the particularities of specific domains.
- To enable the integration of DSMM in MDE projects, we need appropriate model management languages able to work in this multi-level setting.

These three challenges are tackled in the next three sections.

4 Customising the Meta-Modelling Facilities

Designers need to control the way in which the designed DSMM languages will be used and extended. For this purpose, we propose the use of tags to identify the non-extendable language elements, and the use of constraints to ensure a certain extensibility degree. We will illustrate both control mechanisms using the textual syntax of the METADEPTH [6] tool. For example, the listing shown in Fig. 3 defines our DSMM language for e-commerce systems (lines 1–7), its usage to define a stationer's model (lines 8–10), and an instance of this (lines 12–14), corresponding to models (a, b, c) in Fig. 1.

```
1  strict Model Ecommerce@2 {              8  Ecommerce Stationer {
2    strict Node Product {                 9    Product Pen { VAT = 8; }
3      VAT@1 : double;                     10 }
4      price : double;                     11
5      minPrice: $self.price > 0$          12 Stationer WHSmith {
6    }                                     13   Pen parker { price = 5.0; }
7  }                                       14 }
```

Fig. 3. Definition and use of the DSMM language for e-commerce in METADEPTH

The top-model `Ecommerce` lacks ontological type and hence is declared using the keyword `Model` (line 1). This model defines clabject `Product` using the keyword `Node` (line 2). Potencies are specified using the "@" symbol. Constraints can be defined using Java or the Epsilon Object Language (EOL), a variant of OCL that permits side effects [11]. For example, the constraint `minPrice` in line 5 demands a positive price for the products. It receives potency 2 from the model, therefore it will be evaluated two meta-levels below. The model instantiated in lines 8–10 has `Ecommerce` as ontological type, which is used instead of the keyword `Model`.

By default, the meta-models built with a DSMM language can be extended with new primitives (i.e., new clabjects), and any element in the meta-models can be extended with new features. To fine tune the extensibility of a DSMM language, our first proposal is a tagging control mechanism to identify the non-extensible elements. In this way, if the model with the DSMM language definition is tagged as `strict`, it will not be possible to add clabjects without an ontological typing in the next meta-level. If a clabject is tagged `strict`, their instances are forbidden to define new attributes, references or constraints. In the previous listing, both the `Ecommerce` model and the `Product` node are `strict`. Thus, we can use the DSMM language to build the stationer's model in Fig. 1, but not the hardware model (as `Product` instances cannot be extended) or the bookshop model (as `Author` has no ontological type).

If an element is not tagged `strict`, then we may need to control its allowed linguistic extensions. For example, we may like each `Product` instance at potency 1 to declare an attribute acting as identifier, which will receive a value at potency 0. Even though we could declare such a field at meta-level 2 with potency 2, here we may wish to let the decision of the attribute name and type (e.g., `String` or `int`) to the meta-level 1. For this purpose, we propose defining constraints that can make use of facilities of the linguistic meta-model. Fig. 4 shows a constraint, with potency 1, demanding the linguistic extension of all `Product` instances with some attribute tagged as identifier. The method `newFields` belongs to the API of METADEPTH's linguistic meta-model, and returns a collection with the new attributes declared in a meta-level. The method `isId` checks if a field is an identifier. As this constraint has potency 1, it will be evaluated at the next meta-level, where the DSMM language is used.

```
1  Node Product {
2      ...
3      extid@1: $self.newFields(). exists(f | f.isId())$
4  }
```

Fig. 4. Constraint demanding a linguistic extension

Finally, as the next section shows, we can also control the allowed linguistic extensions syntactically through the design of an appropriate concrete syntax.

5 Designing the Concrete Textual Syntax

Even though deep meta-modelling enables DSMM, our goal is building DSMM languages, and therefore we need to design a concrete syntax for them (in addition to their abstract syntax). In the previous section, we used the default textual concrete syntax that METADEPTH makes available to model uniformly at every meta-level. However, this syntax usually leads to verbose model specifications, while we may prefer a more compact, domain-specific representation. For example, instead of creating instances of Product using Product Pen{VAT=8;}, we may like a more concise syntax for product instantiation like Pen(8%).

Should the designer only had to define the syntax of the DSMM language, he may use existing tools for describing textual syntaxes like xText [15], TCS [10] or ANTLR [14]. However, as Fig. 5 illustrates, a multi-level architecture poses some challenges that these tools are not able to deal with, since the designer has to provide a syntax for the languages built with the DSMM language as well. In this way, when defining a DSMM language, the designer has to provide both the syntax of the models at meta-level 1 (i.e., of the domain-specific meta-models) and the syntax of the models at level 0 (i.e., of the meta-model instances). For this purpose, we assign to each concrete syntax definition a potency governing the meta-level at which it is to be used. Thus, the syntax with potency 1 will be used in the next meta-level, and the one with potency 2 will be used two meta-levels below. Moreover, it should be possible to refine the syntax initially defined for the models at meta-level 0, in order to introduce domain-specific constructs and describe the syntax of any linguistic extension.

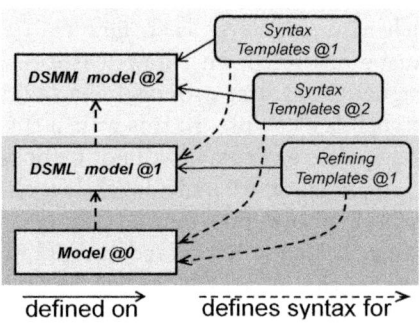

Fig. 5. Defining the concrete syntax

Following this idea, we have created a template-based language to define textual concrete syntaxes in METADEPTH. Using this language, the syntax of each clabject is defined through a template, which has a potency attached, controlling the meta-level at which the template will be applied. Another template declares the syntax of the model itself. As an example, Fig. 6 shows to the left the definition of the concrete syntax for our example DSMM language, whereas the right corresponds to the syntax for models at meta-level 0.

```
1  Syntax for Ecommerce [".ecommerce_mm"] {         7  Syntax for Ecommerce [".ecommerce"] {
2    template@1 TEcommerce for Model Ecommerce:     8    template@2 DeepProds for Model Ecommerce:
3      "id '{' &TProduct* '}'"                      9      "typename id '{' &DeepProd* '}'"
4    template@1 TProduct for Node Product:         10    template@2 DeepProd for Node Product:
5      "id '(' #VAT '%' ')'"                       11      "typename id '(' #price '€' ')'"
6  }                                               12  }
```

Fig. 6. Defining the concrete syntax for models at levels 1 (left) and 0 (right)

The first line in the definition to the left declares the language to which the syntax applies (the Ecommerce model) as well as the associated file extension (*ecommerce_mm*). Its two templates have potency 1, therefore they correspond to the syntax of the DSMM language (i.e., the templates will be used in the next meta-level). In particular, lines 2–3 define the syntax of the instances of the Ecommerce model, whereas lines 4–5 define the syntax of the clabject Product. The keyword "id" stands for the identifier of an element (see lines 3 and 5), whereas the attributes of a clabject can be referenced by using the prefix "#" (like VAT in line 5). Templates can refer to other templates, as in line 3, where it is indicated that the instances of Ecommerce can contain zero or more Product instances ("&TProduct*"). Using this textual syntax, we can specify the Stationer model as Stationer{ Pen(8%) }.

The right of the same listing declares the syntax for the models at meta-level 0, which will be stored in a separate file with extension *ecommerce*. In this case, all templates have potency 2. At this point, we do not know the model type for which the syntax is defined, but we only know that it will be an indirect instance of Ecommerce (line 8). To access the name of the concrete type we use the keyword "typename", which is interpreted by the parser to check that it is an indirect instance of Ecommerce (line 9). The same applies to the definition of templates for clabjects (lines 10–11). With this syntax we can write Stationer WHSmith { Pen parker(5.0€) } to instantiate model Stationer.

Templates can include "semantic" actions (e.g., to initialize fields of the created clabjects) and may have several syntactic expressions. For instance, we can insert in line 12 of the previous listing ''typename id'' with ''#price = 0'' to permit defining products without a price, which gets initialized to 0.

Finally, similar to [7], we can use a single template to define the syntax of several clabjects in the same inheritance hierarchy. Thus, if a clabject does not have an associated template, it uses the template of its closest ancestor in the inheritance hierarchy. A useful keyword in this case is "type", which gets substituted by the name of the clabject. For example, given a clabject "B" inheriting from "A", and a template attached to "A" with body ''type id'', then writing "A a" creates an A instance, while typing "B b" creates a B instance. As a difference with "typename", "type" is used for direct types (i.e., at adjacent meta-levels) expecting exactly A or B. In contrast, "typename" is used for indirect types (i.e., at non adjacent meta-levels) and induces a checking that the name typed in place of "typename" is an indirect instance of the clabject the template is attached to.

5.1 Customising the Meta-Modelling Facilities at the Syntax Level

In Section 4, we showed how to customise the extensibility of a DSMM language at the abstract syntax by identifying strict (i.e., non-extensible) elements and constraining the kind of allowed extensions. These design decisions should be reflected in the concrete syntax of the DSMM language as well, to discard forbidden extensions syntactically even before than semantically.

Our template language provides the following keywords to customise the allowed extensions for a DSMM language at the concrete syntax: flingext to allow declaring new fields with no ontological type, lingext to allow the addition of new clabjects with no ontological type, constraint for declaring constraints, and super to define new inheritance relations for clabjects. Moreover, two additional keywords allow defining how these extensions should be instantiated at level 0: flinginst for field instances and linginst for clabject instances.

For example, the listing shown to the left of Fig. 7 provides a concrete syntax enabling the definition of new fields and constraints in the instances of Product, due to the expression in line 6. Moreover, line 10 enables the instantiation of those extra fields in indirect instances of Product. Note that, this time, the concrete syntaxes of models at levels 0 and 1 are defined together, and have associated the same file extension. The listing to the right of the figure shows the definition of two models using this concrete syntax. The model Hardware in lines 1–7 (in the column to the right of Fig. 7) is an instance of Ecommerce, while the model in lines 9–11 is an instance of Hardware.

```
1  Syntax for Ecommerce [".ecommerce"] {
2    template@1 TEcommerce for Model Ecommerce:
3      "id '{' &TProduct* '}'"
4    template@1 TProduct for Node Product:
5      "id '(' #VAT '%' ')' '{'
6         (flingext ';' | constraint)* '}' "
7    template@2 DeepProds for Model Ecommerce:
8      "typename id { &DeepProd* }"
9    template@2 DeepProd for Node Product:
10     "typename id '(' #price '€' flinginst* ')' "
11 }
```

```
1  Hardware {
2    Nail (8.0%){
3      caliber : double;
4      length : double;
5      bigger : $self.caliber>=0.1$
6    }
7  }
8
9  Hardware DoItBest {
10   Nail n1(0.1€ caliber=0.1 length=10)
11 }
```

Fig. 7. Extensible textual syntax (left), and its use (right)

The listing to the left of Fig. 8 illustrates the use of lingext to allow the definition of new clabjects at meta-level 1 (line 4), and the use of supers to allow inheritance between instances of Product (line 7). The right of the same figure uses this syntax to define model (f) in Fig. 1. In the listing, Magazine (line 18) and Book (line 19) inherit from Publication, Book defines a new field author (line 20), and there is a new clabject Author with no ontological type (lines 22–24).

```
1  Syntax for Ecommerce [".ecommerce"] {
2
3    template@1 TEcommerce for Model Ecommerce
       :
4    "id '{' (&TProduct | lingext )* '}' "
5
6    template@1 TProduct for Node Product:
7    "id ('(' #VAT '%' ')')? ('extends' supers)?
8    (';' | '{' (flingext ';' | constraint)* '}') "
9
10   ...
11 }
12
13
14 Bookshop {
15   Publication (16%){
16     title : String;
17   }
18   Magazine extends Publication;
19   Book extends Publication {
20     author : Author;
21   }
22   Node Author {
23     name : String;
24   }
25 }
```

Fig. 8. Syntax template allowing inheritance and new clabjects (left), and its use (right)

5.2 Refining the Syntax of Domain-Specific Modelling Languages

Even if the DSMM language defines a syntax for the instances of the created domain-specific meta-models, the builder of a particular domain-specific meta-model may wish to design a special concrete textual syntax for some of the instantiated clabjects or for the linguistic extensions (see Fig. 5).

For example, we can design a template especially for Nails, as Fig. 9 shows. This template would be defined by the builder of the stationer's domain-specific meta-model at meta-level 1, and attached to it. The template refines the default one defined for products, so that the instances of Nail can be defined using this more specialised syntax (in addition to the default one). Hence, we can write n1(0.1€, 0.1, 0.1), in addition to Nail n1(0.1€ caliber=0.1 length=0.1). In order to disable the instantiation of nails using the latter, more general syntax, we should add the modifier overwrite to template TNail.

```
1  template@1 TNail for Node Nail:
2    "id '(' #price '€', #caliber, #length ')' "
```

Fig. 9. Refining the syntax template for nails at level 1

To conclude, as an implementation note, our template language for specifying concrete syntaxes has been implemented using a meta-model, whereas its concrete syntax has been specified with itself through bootstrapping. The parser generation relies on ANTLR [14]. Moreover, METADEPTH includes a registry of parsers and automatically selects the appropriate parser according to the file extension of the model to be loaded.

6 Model Management for DSMM Languages

To integrate DSMM languages in MDE, we need to provide suitable model management languages able to deal with multiple meta-levels. In METADEPTH we have adapted the Epsilon family of model management languages[1] to work in a multi-level setting. Hence, we can define model manipulation operations and constraints for DSMM languages using the Epsilon Object Language (EOL), code generators working at several meta-levels using the Epsilon Generation Language (EGL), and model-to-model transformations spanning several meta-levels using the Epsilon Transformation Language (ETL). As the working scheme and challenges are similar in all cases, we will illustrate our solution only in the context of model-to-model transformations.

As an example, assume we want to generate a graphical user interface that allows the customers of an e-commerce system to select the products (at level 0) they want to buy. For this purpose, we need to transform the products to a model representation of the graphical user interface, from which we can generate code for different platforms like Java Swing or HTML. Based on this example, in the following we illustrate the four typical transformation scenarios in a multi-level setting: *deep transformations, co-transformations, refining transformations* and *reflective and linguistic transformations*.

Deep Transformations. Oftentimes, a transformation needs to be defined using the meta-model of the DSMM language, and applied to the instances of the DSMLs built with it (i.e., at the bottom level). This scenario is depicted to the right of Fig. 10. In this case, the transformation definition needs to use indirect types because the direct types at level 1 are unknown when the transformation is defined. For example, if we want to generate a graphical user interface for any model of products at level 0, we would like to define the transformation only once at meta-level 2 together with the DSMM language definition. The left of Fig. 10 shows the ETL deep transformation to achieve this goal, which will be executed on indirect instances of the Ecommerce model. Rule Product2CheckButton creates a CheckButton for each indirect instance of Product (lines 3–8). The rule is annotated with the top-level meta-model needed by the transformation (line 1), and the level at which the transformation is to be executed (line 2). The *post* block (lines 10–15), which is executed when the transformation finishes, creates the *GroupBox* for the checkbuttons and the container *Window*.

Co-transformations. In this kind of transformations, a model and its meta-model need to be transformed at the same time, as the right of Fig. 11 illustrates. Here, the same transformation has to deal with direct and indirect instances of the clabjects in the meta-model of the DSMM language; therefore, a mechanism is needed to select the level at which the rules will be applied.

As an example, we may wish to generate a menu for each product type defined at level 1, and checkbuttons for each product instance at level 0. For this purpose, we can use the transformation in Fig. 11. Line 1 imports the previous

---

[1] See http://www.eclipse.org/epsilon/

```
1  @metamodel(name=Ecommerce,file=Ecommerce)
2  @model(potency=0)
3  rule Product2CheckButton
4     transform pr : Source!Product
5     to cb : Target!CheckButton {
6        cb.name := pr.name()+'_cbutton';
7        cb.text := pr.name()+'('+pr.price+')';
8     }
9
10 post {
11    var wd: Target!Window := new Target!Window();
12    var gb: Target!GroupBox := new Target!GroupBox();
13    wd.children := gb;
14    gb.children.addAll(Target!CheckButton.all());
15 }
```

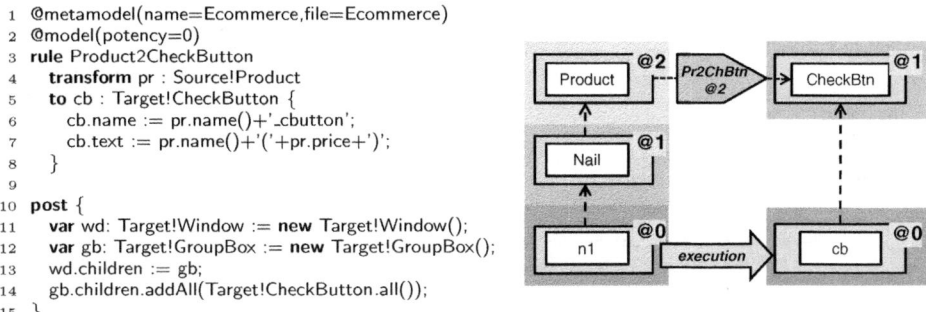

Fig. 10. Deep transformation example (left) and scheme (right)

transformation which transforms the products at level 0. Then, rule ProductType2Menu is executed for each Product at level 1. The level at which the rule is executed is specified by the model alias, before the '!' symbol (see line 4). Hence, we use Level0 for a model with potency 0 and Level1 for a model with potency 1. We can also use the alias Source to refer to the source model regardless its potency. This is the alias used in the listing of Fig. 10, where the annotation in line 2 forces the execution of the transformation on models with potency 0. Hence, our framework implicitly makes available all (meta-)*-models of the context model for the transformation.

Refining Transformations. Sometimes, a deep transformation needs to be refined for particular instances defined at level 1. This situation is depicted to the right of Fig. 12. For example, if we decide to transform the instances of Nail in a different way to consider the specific attributes that we added to it (caliber and length), we need to refine the transformation rule defined for Products in Fig. 10. The refined rule is shown in Fig. 12. The rule extends Product2CheckButton, but it is refined for type Nail. To support this kind of transformations, we adapted ETL to allow extending a rule if the child rule transforms a direct or indirect instance of the clabject type transformed by the parent rule. The child rule will be applied whenever is possible, executing the body of the rules of both parent and child. In our example, rule Nail2CheckButton will

```
1  import 'file:///Prod2GUI.etl';
2
3  rule ProductType2Menu
4     transform pr : Level1!Product
5     to mn : Target!Menu {
6        mn.name := pr.name()+'_menu';
7        mn.text := pr.name()+'('+pr.VAT+')';
8     }
```

Fig. 11. Co-transformation example (left) and scheme (right)

```
1  import 'file:///Prod2GUIDeep.etl';
2
3  @metamodel(name=Ecommerce,file=Ecommerce.mdepth
   )
4  @model(potency=0)
5  rule Nail2CheckButton
6    transform pr : Source!Nail
7    to mn : Target!CheckButton
8    extends Product2CheckButton {
9      mn.name := pr.name()+'_check_nail';
10     mn.text := pr.name()+'('+pr.price+',
11       caliber='+pr.caliber+', length='+pr.length+')';
12   }
```

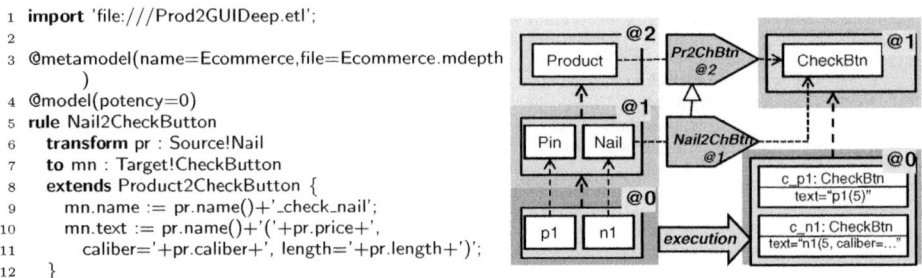

Fig. 12. Refining transformation example (left) and scheme (right)

be executed for instances of Nail, whereas rule Product2CheckButton will be executed for indirect instances of Product that are not instances of Nail.

Reflective and Linguistic Transformations. When defining a deep transformation, we may want to account for the linguistic extensions that can be performed at level 1. For this purpose, the transformation language needs reflective capabilities to access any new declared field, and it has to be possible to perform queries using linguistic types (i.e., Node, Edge and Model). The combination of these two capabilities enables the construction of generic transformations, applicable at any meta-level, and to elements of any ontological type. The working scheme of this kind of transformations is shown to the right of Fig. 13.

```
1   rule Product2CheckButton
2     transform pr : Level0!Product
3     to cb : Target!CheckButton {
4       cb.name := pr.name()+'_cbutton';
5       cb.text := pr.name()+'( price='+pr.price+' ';
6       for (f in pr.newFields())
7         cb.text := cb.text+f.name()+'= '+
8                    f.getValue()+' ';
9       cb.text := cb.text+')';
10    }
11
12  rule Node2Label
13    transform pr : Level0!Node
14    to cb : Target!Label {
15      guard: not pr.isKindOf(Level0!Product)
16      cb.name := pr.name()+'_label';
17      cb.text := pr.name()+'(';
18      for (f in pr.fields())
19        cb.text := cb.text+f.name()+'= '+
20                   f.getValue()+' ';
21      cb.text := cb.text+')';
22    }
```

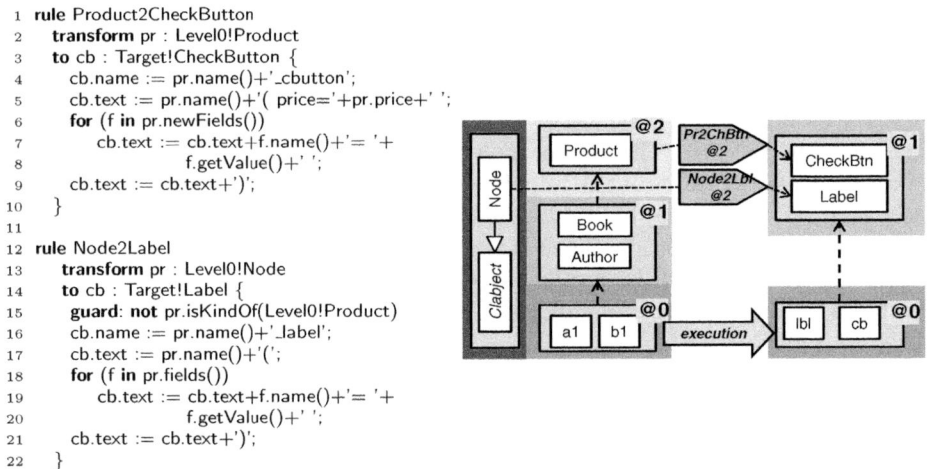

Fig. 13. Linguistic transformation example (left) and scheme (right)

The listing in Fig. 13 shows a transformation with one reflective rule and another one defined on a linguistic type. Rule Product2CheckButton is reflective. It gets executed for each indirect instance of Product at level 0, creating a CheckButton. The rule takes into account that Product instances at level 1 may have been extended with new attributes. Thus, the rule iterates on the new attributes in line 6 (returned by newFields), concatenating their name and value. Technically, this reflection is possible because ETL is also reflective, being able to call transparently methods of the METADEPTH API.

In its turn, rule Node2Label uses linguistic typing, being applicable to all Node instances (all elements) of potency 0 which are not indirect instances of Product (forbidden by the guard in line 15). In this way, if we apply this transformation to the Amazon model in Fig. 1, we obtain one CheckButton (the transformation of the KL book by rule Product2CheckButton) and one Label (the transformation of the WS author by Node2Label).

In the presented transformation examples, the target language has two meta-levels. We also allow DSMM languages as target, and currently we only support rules specifying the creation of direct instances of clabjects. One may consider *abstract* rules specifying the creation of indirect instances, which would need to be refined at level 1 stating which clabject to instantiate. This is left for future work.

7 Discussion and Future Work

In this paper, we have presented our approach to define DSMM languages supporting the flexible definition of a textual concrete syntax, a fine control of the exposed meta-modelling facilities, and integration in MDE projects by making available multi-level model management languages.

We also discussed the typical transformation scenarios in a multi-level setting (deep transformations, co-transformations, refining transformations and linguistic/reflective transformations) and illustrated their support using ETL. These scenarios apply to other model management languages and tasks as well. In particular, they apply to the definition of textual syntaxes: at the top-level, we can define syntactic templates for level 0 models (similar to deep transformations), or for both level 0 and level 1 models (similar to co-transformations); we can add refining templates at level 1 (like in refining transformations); and we can define templates dealing with linguistic extensions (as in linguistic transformations). Each model management language needs to provide appropriate constructs to deal with each scenario, namely: the ability to select the meta-level at which a certain operation is to be applied (e.g., potencies for rules and templates), the ability to select clabjects of specific meta-levels (e.g., aliases Level0 and Level1 in rules), the possibility to obtain indirect instances of clabjects (transparently in our case), to access clabjects by their linguistic type (e.g., Node) and to reflectively access linguistic extensions (e.g., method newFields).

We are currently using METADEPTH to define DSMM languages in different domains: component-based systems, web engineering and mobile devices. We are also exploring the definition of visual syntaxes for DSMM languages, and extending the integration of the tool with multi-level meta-modelling languages.

Acknowledgements. This work was funded by the Spanish Ministry of Economy and Competitivity (project "Go Lite" TIN2011-24139) and the R&D programme of the Madrid Region (project "e-Madrid" S2009/TIC-1650).

References

1. Aschauer, T., Dauenhauer, G., Pree, W.: Representation and Traversal of Large Clabject Models. In: Schürr, A., Selic, B. (eds.) MODELS 2009. LNCS, vol. 5795, pp. 17–31. Springer, Heidelberg (2009)
2. Atkinson, C., Gutheil, M., Kennel, B.: A flexible infrastructure for multilevel language engineering. IEEE Trans. Soft. Eng. 35(6), 742–755 (2009)
3. Atkinson, C., Kühne, T.: Rearchitecting the UML infrastructure. ACM Trans. Model. Comput. Simul. 12(4), 290–321 (2002)
4. Atkinson, C., Kühne, T.: Model-driven development: A metamodeling foundation. IEEE Software 20(5), 36–41 (2003)
5. Atkinson, C., Kühne, T.: Reducing accidental complexity in domain models. Software and System Modeling 7(3), 345–359 (2008)
6. de Lara, J., Guerra, E.: Deep Meta-modelling with METADEPTH. In: Vitek, J. (ed.) TOOLS 2010. LNCS, vol. 6141, pp. 1–20. Springer, Heidelberg (2010)
7. Espinazo Pagán, J., Menárguez, M., García-Molina, J.: Metamodel Syntactic Sheets: An Approach for Defining Textual Concrete Syntaxes. In: Schieferdecker, I., Hartman, A. (eds.) ECMDA-FA 2008. LNCS, vol. 5095, pp. 185–199. Springer, Heidelberg (2008)
8. Herrmannsdörfer, M., Hummel, B.: Library concepts for model reuse. Electron. Notes Theor. Comput. Sci. 253, 121–134 (2010)
9. Jablonski, S., Volz, B., Dornstauder, S.: A meta modeling framework for domain specific process management. In: COMPSAC 2008, pp. 1011–1016 (2008)
10. Jouault, F., Bézivin, J., Kurtev, I.: TCS: a DSL for the specification of textual concrete syntaxes in model engineering. In: GPCE. ACM (2006)
11. Kolovos, D.S., Paige, R.F., Polack, F.A.C.: The Epsilon Object Language (EOL). In: Rensink, A., Warmer, J. (eds.) ECMDA-FA 2006. LNCS, vol. 4066, pp. 128–142. Springer, Heidelberg (2006)
12. Kühne, T., Schreiber, D.: Can programming be liberated from the two-level style? – Multi-level programming with DeepJava. In: OOPSLA 2007, pp. 229–244 (2007)
13. Langer, P., Wieland, K., Wimmer, M., Cabot, J.: From UML Profiles to EMF Profiles and Beyond. In: Bishop, J., Vallecillo, A. (eds.) TOOLS 2011. LNCS, vol. 6705, pp. 52–67. Springer, Heidelberg (2011)
14. Parr, T.: The Definitive ANTLR Reference: Building Domain-Specific Languages. Pragmatic Bookshelf (2007), http://www.antlr.org/
15. xText, http://xtext.org
16. Zschaler, S., Kolovos, D.S., Drivalos, N., Paige, R.F., Rashid, A.: Domain-Specific Metamodelling Languages for Software Language Engineering. In: van den Brand, M., Gašević, D., Gray, J. (eds.) SLE 2009. LNCS, vol. 5969, pp. 334–353. Springer, Heidelberg (2010)

Metamodel Based Methodology for Dynamic Component Systems

Gabor Batori[1], Zoltan Theisz[2], and Domonkos Asztalos[1]

[1] Software Engineering Group, Ericsson Hungary Ltd.
{gabor.batori,domonkos.asztalos}@ericsson.com
[2] evopro Informatics and Automation Ltd.
zoltan.theisz@evopro.hu

Abstract. MBE solutions, including their corresponding MDA frameworks, cover many parts of industrial application development processes. Although model based development methodologies are in abundance, fully integrated, domain specific methodologies still find their niche in specialized application scenarios. In this paper, such an alternative methodology will be presented that targets reconfigurable networked systems executing on top of interconnected heterogeneous hardware nodes. The methodology covers the whole development cycle; it even utilizes a configuration model for component reconfigurability, and also involves a first-order logic based structural modeling language, Alloy, in the analysis of component deployment and reconfiguration. The methodology is supported by both a metamodel based tooling environment within GME and a robust distributed middleware platform over Erlang/OTP. Due to its special applicability, the methodology is limited in scope and scaling, though core parts have been successfully showcased in a sensor network demonstrator of the IST project RUNES.

1 Introduction

Dynamic component systems provide a versatile platform for creating autonomic distributed peer-to-peer applications in various industrial domains. A particularly challenging case of these domains is the area of intelligent sensor networks, that combine sensory and effectory facilities within their control loops. Due to the frequent reconfiguration of software components, this field of applicability is characterized by the inherent complexity of such environments; therefore creating an effective, high-quality software development methodology that seriously unburdens the day-to-day tasks of application developers is a rather ambitious endeavor. However, the Reconfigurable Ubiquitous Network Embedded Systems (RUNES) IST project [1] successfully addressed this challenge by providing a common distributed component-based platform architecture on top of heterogeneous networks of computational nodes. The RUNES middleware platform [2] is accompanied by a corresponding model-based software development methodology and tooling support. In effect, the approach and the implemented framework are based on well–known concepts of Model-Integrated Computing [3] and support a rapid application development environment in GME [4]. Nevertheless, the validation and eventual verification of the produced dynamic networked components turn out to be a rather ambitious endeavor, which requires detailed software engineering know-how. Hence, the original RUNES MBE methodology [5] had to be extended by some practical, formal logic based techniques in Alloy [6] in order to establish an overarching metamodel based methodology. This covers the whole development cycle, including formal scenario validation and better quality insurance for some MBE modeling tasks by eliminating non-trivial dynamic errors or failure situations that may frequently reoccur in the application design of reconfigurable component systems.

The paper is structured as follows: Section 2 provides a background on the technical domain of networked reconfigurable component systems, establishing this way the conceptual frame for the rest of the paper. In Section 3, the metamodel based development process is presented covering the whole life-cycle of component applications. Next, Section 4 describes, in relative details, the modeling assets used in the various stages of the development process, from scenario analysis up to its validation. Then, Section 5 mentions some of the case studies and Section 6 gives some insight onto the practical side of the methodology. Finally, in Section 7, the conclusions are provided.

2 Networked Reconfigurable Dynamic Component System

The architecture of the targeted networked reconfigurable dynamic component system consists of a reflective, reconfigurable middleware model of the component system and a corresponding Component Run-Time Kernel (CRTK) that provides the management APIs. The reflective components are linked together by their interfaces, they communicate via message sending and store their meta-data in a distributed database within the middleware. Each computational node incorporates an instance of the CRTK, which provides the basic middleware APIs of component management. These architectural concepts are mirrored by an effective reference implementation, called ErlCOM [7], which runs on Ericsson's Erlang/OTP distributed infrastructure [8] utilizing Mnesia [9] for the distributed database.

The component is the basic unit of the system that corresponds to an active actor-like process, it owns snippets of executable code and has a uniquely registered name in the middleware's global registry. The components are organized into caplet hierarchies the root of which is occupied by a capsule, which is the main process entity of the node. The caplets' main purpose is to provide supervisory facilities for the maintenance of robustness and longevity of the whole component system. The supervisory decisions are taken according to a set of predefined constraints stored within a particular component framework. The interaction between components is carried out via pure message passing that is managed by the bindings representing the behavioral policy of the communication channels. The bindings are also components with special communication properties. Message passing is synchronous; messages can be intercepted both before they enter the interfaces of the recipients and after the replies have left those same interfaces. The pre- and post-actions of the bindings constitute a list of additional transformations on individual messages. Bindings are created when a receptacle, that is, a required interface, of a particular component is to be bound to a provided interface of another component, provided that their compatibility has been checked and validated. Finally, both components and bindings possess explicit state information which is stored as metadata in the global repository within the distributed middleware deployed over the networked nodes.

3 Development Process

Professional software developments are always accompanied by corresponding development processes that safeguard industrial scale applicability of the chosen technology. Although there is a plethora of such MBE approaches, e.g. Rational Unified Process, the ambition level of our process design was influenced by the aim of being able to cover all stages of component based application development, including generative metamodeling technologies and scenario validation and verification. The overview of the process stages are depicted in Figure 1. The process is layered into five stages; namely, Scenario, Application Model, Platform Model, Code Repository and Running System. The arrows of the non-iterative part of the process, connecting together the artifacts of the various stages, are labeled by sequence numbers in accordance to their timing. Here, the stages are only briefly introduced, the assets these stages are operating on will be described in Section 4.

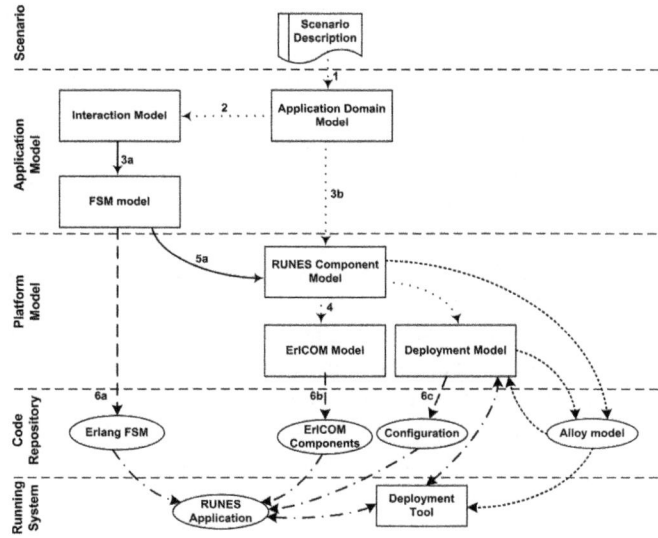

Fig. 1. MBE development process

The Scenario evaluates and finalizes a set of scenario descriptions by establishing the scope of the application domain. Based on our experience, real-life distributed applications usually involve intense interactions among application components, thus both structural and interaction modeling are of equally importance. Therefore, the Application Domain Model is created to cover the scenario in such a way that all use case details are taken adequately into account and all stakeholders' roles have been discovered.

The roles make up the basic elements of the interaction model, hence the dynamicity of the use cases must be translated into corresponding Message Sequence Charts (MSC). The Application Domain Model and the Interaction Model must be detailed enough so that quality investigations could be carried out in order to check the feasibility of the design. Moreover, this stage involves many creative decisions, so both arrow 1 and 2 in Figure 1 are dotted, this way showing that the activity is mainly manual in nature.

The Interaction Model is transformed into a FSM Model and then a further translation maps it onto the RUNES Component Model. The solid arrow indicates that the translation is executed via non-trivial graph transformations as reported in [5]. The Application Domain Model usually requires creative refinements and only semi-automatically (dotted line) can be translated into a RUNES Component Model.

The Platform Model stage has been conceived to support total semantics elaboration, that is, the RUNES Component Model is extended by the semantics of the platform, the components and the FSMs. This step involves some manual coding in Erlang so that the total executable specification of the application can be fully established.

The final application model takes into consideration the distributed nature of the application; hence, a Deployment Model is also getting populated. It entirely specifies the total component allocation of the application over the available hardware nodes of the underlying network.

The Code Repository is the stage which copes with source code management. The code production is fully automated, which is indicated by dashed lines, and the resulted code snippets of the components are stored within the global repository of the middleware as modules ready to be loaded. The Deployment Model is translated into an initial run-time configuration which is deployed over the participating ErlCOM nodes. Any changes of the component configuration at run-time are managed by the Deployment Tool, which continuously updates the Deployment Model.

The Deployment Tool implements a kind of metamodel-driven component management, which generalizes policy-based network management in such a way that the information model used by the network management infrastructure mirrors the software assets of the component based system produced during the generative model translators. In effect, it establishes a soft real-time synchronization loop between the GME model repository and the running component application. In other words, the Deployment Tool, which is a protocol independent abstraction of GANA's Decision Making Element [10], first deploys the initial component configuration of the application then it constantly readapts the component configuration by listening to both application and middleware notifications and by observing all changes within the Deployment Model stored inside the model repository. Therefore, with the control logic properly established, the Deployment Tool is able to manage both re-active and pro-active component reconfigurations as reported in [5,11].

The Alloy based model verification step extends this standard operation of the Deployment Tool. It contains two additional model transformations; one that originates from the RUNES Component Model and another that takes a compatible RUNES Deployment Model and it turns them into a configuration scenario that can be verified within Alloy Analyzer [12]. The model transformations produce configuration scenarios, which include both the structural and the behavioral specifications of the application. However, only those parts of the FSM action semantics are kept from the total dynamic behavior that either directly relate to important control logic elements of the scenario or which belong to the operations provided by the underlying ErlCOM middleware. These steps simplify, though, more precisely specify when and with which parameters the application invokes the operations of the CRTK. Hence, the validation of a particular scenario investigates mainly the evolution of the application from the point of view of its component reconfigurations that are allowed by the semantics of the ErlCOM middleware. The results of this verification step provide useful hints to the run-time autonomic control mechanisms which will either be embedded into the application or be defined as explicit rules of the policy engine. The validation and verification step is rather iterative in nature, which is luckily well supported by Alloy Analyzer.

4 Modeling Assets

4.1 Interaction Model

Large-scale networked systems can be efficiently represented by a large number of interacting services. By combining all those services an entity is getting involved in the complete behavior specification for that particular entity can be established. Hence, our service concept is effectively based on the interaction patterns between cooperating entities. The notion of a role describes the contribution of an entity within a given interaction pattern. In our methodology we follow a particular service oriented approach [13], which maps service specifications onto a set of interconnected components, each of them having an internal Finite State Machine (FSM), and a corresponding pool of abstract communication channels. This techniques also incorporates an effective state machine synthesis algorithms so that scenarios can be easily turned into a corresponding set of FSMs, that fully specify the intended dynamic behavior of the specified system (see Figure 2). The state machine generation is carried out automatically and relies on two types of MSCs, the basic MSCs and the high level MSCs (HMSC). The output of the transformation is one FSM per role within the domain model; that is, the FSM implementing the respective role's contribution to the services it is associated with. The FSMs are incorporated in stage Application Model.

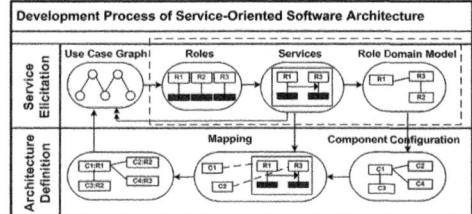

Fig. 2. Service-based interaction model

4.2 Structural Model

The core part the component metamodel is illustrated in Figure 3. The metamodel mirrors the constituents of the networked reconfigurable dynamic component systems (see

Section 2). Hence, Components, short for ErlCOMComponent, are encapsulated units of functionality and deployment, which interact with each other only via interfaces and receptacles. Interfaces are defined by a list of related operation signatures and associated data types. Components can also provide multiple interfaces, this way embodying a clear separation of concerns (e.g. between base functionality and component management). Capsules and Caplets are platform containers providing access to the run-time APIs. Bindings ensure consistent connection setup between a compatible Interface and a Receptacle. The compatibility checks take into account the list of Operations describing the service specification of a particular Interface or Receptacle. The Operations are further specified by their signatures containing the list of incoming parameters and the outgoing ReturnValue if it exists. The component model itself is complemented by two other architecture elements: component frameworks and reflective extensions. ComponentFrameworks (CF) are groupings of Components with embedded constraints that guarantee that only "meaningful" component configurations can be built. All entities of the metamodel (Component, Capsule, Interface, Receptacle, Binding, ComponentFramework) can store arbitrary <key,value> attributes, which describe the reflective behavior of the ErlCOM middleware. Component interactions can be intercepted at the Bindings by pre- and post-actions to enable additional processing on the level of individual messages. These last two features of the middleware are specified in a different part of the component metamodel. The structural model of a component application is designed in stage Platform Model.

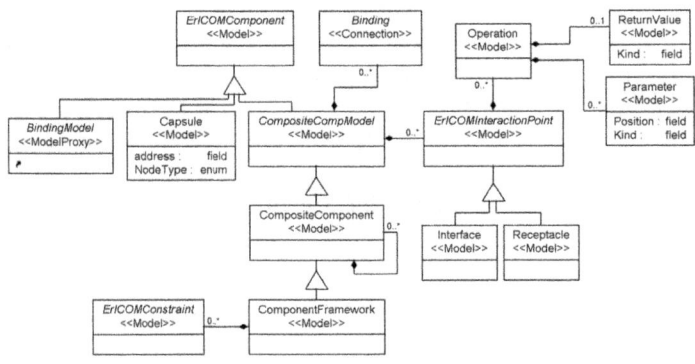

Fig. 3. Structural metamodel

4.3 Behavior Model

The component behavior description is formalized in an abstract model of action semantics (see Figure 4). This Behavior Model is rather generic, though it provides a selection attribute for specifying the modeled behavior within the selected implementation language(s). The entities that can contain behavior descriptions are the Interface and the Component. A fully specified component model is later translated into the chosen target implementation language(s) by language optimized model interpreter(s). By

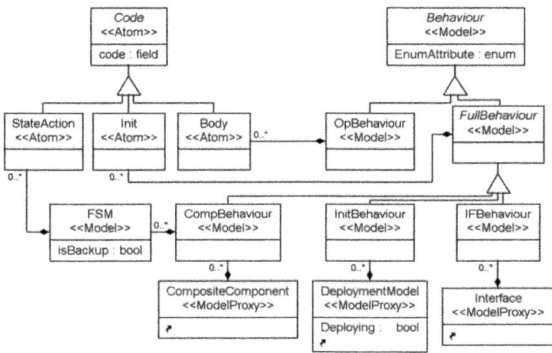

Fig. 4. Behavior metamodel

this means, Components can be operationally described in various programming languages; however, they must rely on the same modeling framework. A language specific model interpreter processes only those parts of a component model which contain relevant information for the desired target language environment. Therefore, the metamodel embodies various code snippets; the snippets are later woven together into executable component implementations by the corresponding model interpreters. Although this facility is rather versatile, over the ErlCOM CRTK only Erlang has been used as the language of executable specification of dynamic behavior. The core building blocks of such a specification are as follows:

- Init - Initialization code for a component, an interface or the system.
- Body - Executable specification of the operation of an interface. The signature of the operation is defined in the model and automatically generated by the interpreter.
- StateAction - Specifies the action semantics inside an FSM state which is automatically injected into the corresponding connection point within the generated FSM.

4.4 Deployment Model

The complete synthesized platform specific application model contains both the structural configuration and the behavioral semantics of all the constituent components, including their interconnecting bindings and component framework constraints. That model represents the functional view of the application; however, it neither specifies how the application is deployed on the available networked nodes nor how it has to start. Therefore, the deployment configuration (see Figure 5) must be modeled, too. The deployed component configuration, which contains the complete synthesized platform specific application model and the initial configuration of the components, is called in our methodology as the total synthesized platform specific distributed application model.

From the point of view of out model based framework, one of the most important elements of the deployment infrastructure is the Deployment Tool. The schematics of the Deployment Tool based reconfiguration is shown in Figure 6. The Deployment Tool

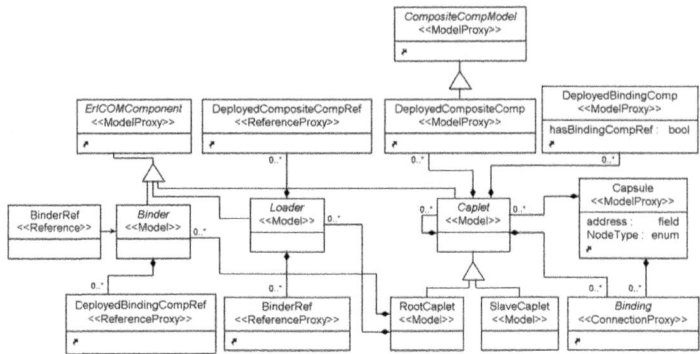

Fig. 5. Deployment metamodel

analyzes the initial component configuration of the total synthesized platform specific application model and creates the needed ErlCOM run-time elements by invoking the corresponding operations of the ErlCOM API. (The complete ErlCOM API semantics, including dynamic behavior of the middleware, has been published in [7]) After the initial deployment has been completed the application starts running and the ErlCOM CRTK continuously monitors all component reconfiguration and in case of observable component changes events are sent containing descriptive notifications to the Deployment Tool. The Deployment Tool keeps track of the actual component configuration of the running system by updating the total synthesized platform specific RUNES application model. Deployment Tool plug-ins can also execute policy based rules either re-actively or pro-actively. Any corrective changes on the modeled component configuration of the component application will be reflected by the run-time deployment.

4.5 Validation and Verification Model

Distributed reconfigurable component systems are complex by nature, hence, the importance of formal description techniques in system design is well known. In our methodology, we have based the formal model analysis on the usage of Alloy [6], a first order logic based description language, that is powered by SAT solvers. This formal description technique has been successfully used for modelling various complex systems in a wide range of application domains. It has been applied in [14] for the analysis of some critical correctness properties that should be satisfied by any secure multicast protocols. The idea of applying Alloy for component based system analysis was also suggested by Warren et al. [15], where OpenRec's Alloy model is investigated. This Alloy model served as a conceptual basis for our own Alloy component model, which specifies all the core items of the ErlCOM metamodel and middleware semantics, including structural elements, the precise dynamics of finite state machines and the major concepts of the deployment metamodel, in their first order logic based semantics. The precise definition of this Alloy model,that enables the detailed analysis of dynamic component behavior has been published in [16]. There are similar techniques that aim to identify various types of dynamic system reconfigurations [17]; however, our approach is a better fit

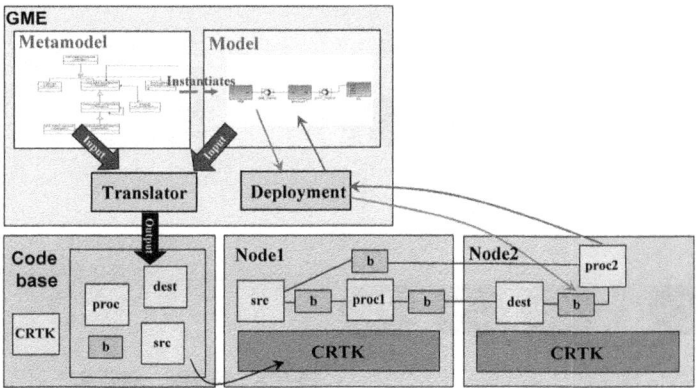

Fig. 6. Deployment Tool based component reconfiguration

for the networked reconfigurable dynamic component systems. Nevertheless, all these attempts provide a rather good categorization of various problems and corresponding solutions related to dynamic software evolution. Considering the tooling support, Aydal et al. [18] found Alloy Analyzer one of the best analysis tools for state-based modeling languages, which has been a serious concern in our selection of Alloy for scenario validation and verification purposes.

The graphical visualization of the structural model of a scenario example in Alloy Analyzer is depicted in Figure 7. It shows a model that represents a snapshot of a dynamically evolving component configuration of a sensor network scenario example taken from the RUNES project [1]. The components (black hexagons) have been deployed over a cross shaped capsule (gray pentagons) topology. The connections among the capsules of this topology are indicated by green arrows. The internal resources, here the maximum number of deployed components/bindings, of the capsules are limited in capacity. The concrete mapping of the components and bindings (white rhombuses) onto the capsules, at a particular instance of time, is visualized by the brown and red arrows, respectively.

Regarding the dynamic behavior of the FSMs, Figure 8 shows the state machine of the NetworkDriver component as an example from the same scenario. The initial status of the FSM is given by the start state (black ellipse) and the initial transition (white rectangle). The other states are represented by gray colored ellipses, while the transitions are shown via red rectangles.

Due to page limitation, this paper cannot detail on a full analysis example (simplified example is reported in [16]), so the validation/verification session is only summarized. Basically, such a session is carried out within Alloy Analyzer and it is driven by the Alloy model of the scenario under investigation. Validation only generates a set of potential runs of the scenario, while verification also injects logical properties into the Alloy specification of the component application before it looks for counter-examples, and locates them if found. In general, the approach helps to analyze configuration sequences so that they both comply with some application constraints and avoid non-trivial pitfalls. The result of these analyses is fed back to the control logic of the Deployment Tool (see Section 4.4).

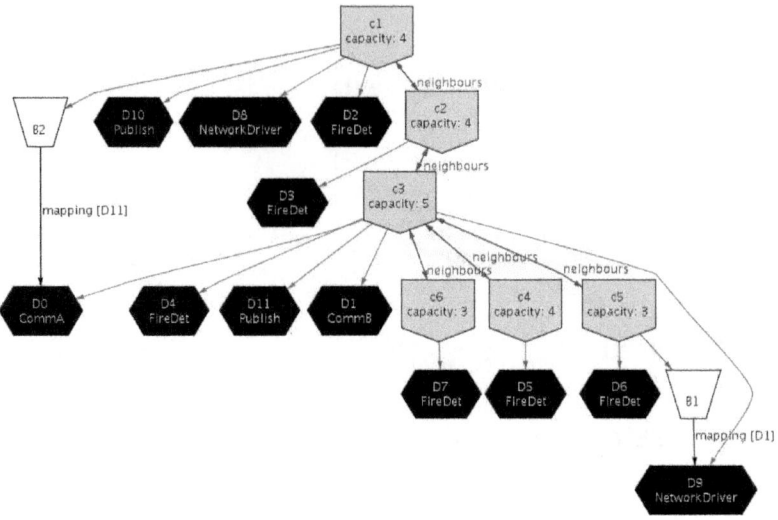

Fig. 7. Structural analysis model

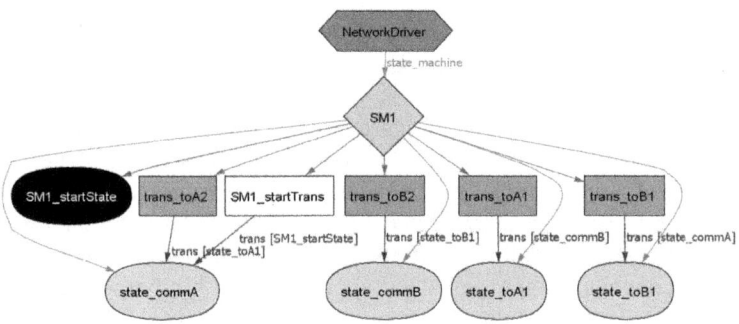

Fig. 8. Dynamic analysis model

5 Case Studies

There had been many prototypical case studies during the frame of the RUNES IST [1] project. The aim of the studies had been to successively evaluate the methodology and its applied modeling and platform technology. The efforts of this continuous evaluation resulted in the process described in Section 3. The final RUNES demonstrator [19] based around a scaled down model of the road tunnel scenario consisting of ten TMote Sky motes and an embedded Gateway hardware, which connected the motes to a local visualization infrastructure, had been mostly developed following this process and relying on the available modeling assets. The Alloy based verification has been an internal research activity aimed to exploit the results of the RUNES project and directly targeted scenario verification and validation in Alloy. One of such a scenario validation use case has been reported publicly in [16]. Finally, this validation step has been integrated into our methodology.

6 Evaluation

Every methodology has its limits, our approach not being an exception. The research challenges of the RUNES project focused on the effective component based software generation in the domains of embedded systems and sensor networks. Therefore, the resulting methodology and tooling had to satisfy these challenges. The final demonstrator had been developed following the described process, however, not all the code assets could be automatically generated for each hardware nodes. The limitation was due to the non-existence of ErlCOM CRTK on the TMote Sky motes. Although semantically correct FSMs had been generated for the ErlCOM simulation of the mote CRTK, these code snippets had to be manually ported to the target platform. Though, we regard it as a platform limitation that may change in the future. Concerning our verification and validation efforts, we have hit the same practical barriers that are all too known in the model checking community. Without applying adequate abstraction scenario use cases are impossible to be analyzed verbatim from the development model. Our practical approach relied on case-by-case scenario selection and expert validation via Alloy Analyzer, however much of the Alloy description can be produced from the scenario models.

7 Conclusion

This paper disseminated a multi-stage, metamodel based software development methodology for the domain of networked reconfigurable dynamic component systems. After the brief introduction of the underlying technology, the steps of the development process have been explained, then, the various model assets have been described one-by-one. Although the production part of the development methodology had been thoroughly tested within the RUNES IST project, the validation/verification part is still under further investigation. The results are promising, but we are fully aware of the limitations of first order logical based verification tools and the related scalability issues. Nevertheless, we firmly believe that this proposed MBE methodology well served the original challenges of our motivation.

References

1. Arzén, K.-E., Bicchi, A., Dini, G., Hailes, S., Johansson, K.H., Lygeros, J., Tzes, A.: A component-based approach to the design of networked control systems. European Journal of Control (2007)
2. Costa, P., Coulson, G., Mascolo, C., Picco, G.P., Zachariadis, S.: The RUNES Middleware: A reconfigurable component-based approach to networked embedded systems. In: Proc. of the 16th Annual IEEE International Symposium on Personal Indoor and Mobile Radio Communications (PIMRC 2005), Berlin, Germany (September 2005)

3. Karsai, G., Sztipanovits, J., Ledeczi, A., Bapty, T.: Model-integrated development of embedded software. Proceedings of the IEEE 91, 145–164 (2003)
4. Ledeczi, A., Maroti, M., Bakay, A., Karsai, G., Garrett, J., Thomason, C., Nordstrom, G., Sprinkle, J., Volgyesi, P.: The generic modeling environment. In: Proceedings of WISP 2001, Budapest, Hungary, pp. 255–277 (May 2001)
5. Batori, G., Theisz, Z., Asztalos, D.: Domain Specific Modeling Methodology for Reconfigurable Networked Systems. In: Engels, G., Opdyke, B., Schmidt, D.C., Weil, F. (eds.) MODELS 2007. LNCS, vol. 4735, pp. 316–330. Springer, Heidelberg (2007)
6. Jackson, D.: Software Abstractions: Logic, Language, and Analysis. The MIT Press, London (2006)
7. Batori, G., Theisz, Z., Asztalos, D.: Robust reconfigurable erlang component system. In: Erlang User Conference, Stockholm, Sweden (2005)
8. Armstrong, J.: Making reliable distributed systems in the presence of software errors. SICS Dissertation Series 34 (2003)
9. Mattsson, H., Nilsson, H., Wikström, C.: Mnesia – A Distributed Robust DBMS for Telecommunications Applications. In: Gupta, G. (ed.) PADL 1999. LNCS, vol. 1551, pp. 152–163. Springer, Heidelberg (1999)
10. Prakash, A., Theisz, Z., Chaparadza, R.: Formal Methods for Modeling, Refining and Verifying Autonomic Components of Computer Networks. In: Gavrilova, M.L., Tan, C.J.K., Phan, C.-V. (eds.) Transactions on Computational Science XV. LNCS, vol. 7050, pp. 1–48. Springer, Heidelberg (2012)
11. Batori, G., Theisz, Z., Asztalos, D.: Configuration aware distributed system design in erlang. In: Erlang User Conference, Stockholm, Sweden (2006)
12. Jackson, D.: Alloy analyzer (2008), http://alloy.mit.edu/
13. Krüger, I.H., Mathew, R.: Component Synthesis from Service Specifications. In: Leue, S., Systä, T.J. (eds.) Scenarios. LNCS, vol. 3466, pp. 255–277. Springer, Heidelberg (2005)
14. Taghdiri, M., Jackson, D.: A Lightweight Formal Analysis of a Multicast Key Management Scheme. In: König, H., Heiner, M., Wolisz, A. (eds.) FORTE 2003. LNCS, vol. 2767, pp. 240–256. Springer, Heidelberg (2003)
15. Warren, I., Sun, J., Krishnamohan, S., Weerasinghe, T.: An automated formal approach to managing dynamic reconfiguration. In: 21st IEEE International Conference on Automated Software Engineering (ASE 2006), Tokyo, Japan, pp. 37–46 (September 2006)
16. Theisz, Z., Batori, G., Asztalos, D.: Formal logic based configuration modeling and verification for dynamic component systems. In: MOPAS 2011 (2011)
17. Walsh, D., Bordeleau, F., Selic, B.: A Domain Model for Dynamic System Reconfiguration. In: Briand, L.C., Williams, C. (eds.) MoDELS 2005. LNCS, vol. 3713, pp. 553–567. Springer, Heidelberg (2005)
18. Aydal, E.G., Utting, M., Woodcock, J.: A comparison of state-based modelling tools for model validation. In: Tools 2008 (June 2008)
19. 5th RUNES Newsletter, p. 6 (2007), http://www.socrades.eu/Documents/objects/file1201161327.23

Bidirectional Model Transformation with Precedence Triple Graph Grammars

Marius Lauder*, Anthony Anjorin*, Gergely Varró**, and Andy Schürr

Technische Universität Darmstadt, Real-Time Systems Lab,
Merckstr. 25, 64283 Darmstadt, Germany
name.surname@es.tu-darmstadt.de

Abstract. Triple Graph Grammars (TGGs) are a rule-based technique with a formal background for specifying bidirectional model transformation. In practical scenarios, the unidirectional rules needed for the forward and backward transformations are automatically derived from the TGG rules in the specification, and the overall transformation process is governed by a control algorithm. Current implementations either have a worst case exponential runtime complexity, based on the number of elements to be processed, or pose such strong restrictions on the class of supported TGGs that practical real-world applications become infeasible. This paper, therefore, introduces a new class of TGGs together with a control algorithm that drops a number of practice-relevant restrictions on TGG rules and still has a polynomial runtime complexity.

Keywords: triple graph grammars, control algorithm of unidirectional transformations, node precedence analysis, rule dependency analysis.

1 Introduction

The paradigm of Model-Driven Engineering (MDE) has established itself as a promising means of coping with the increasing complexity of modern software systems and, in this context, *model transformation* plays a central role [3]. As industrial applications require reliability and efficiency, the need for formal frameworks that guarantee useful properties of model transformation arises. This is especially the case for *bidirectional* model transformation, where defining a precise semantics for the automatic manipulation and synchronization of models with a corresponding efficient tool support is quite challenging [4]. Amongst the numerous bidirectional model transformation approaches surveyed in [18], the concept of *Triple Graph Grammars (TGGs)* features not only solid formal foundations [5,12] but also various tool implementations [7,11,12].

TGGs [16] provide a declarative, rule-based means of specifying the consistency of source and target models in their respective domains, and tracking

---

* Supported by the 'Excellence Initiative' of the German Federal and State Governments and the Graduate School of Computational Engineering at TU Darmstadt.
** Supported by the Postdoctoral Fellowship of the Alexander von Humboldt Foundation and associated with the Center for Advanced Security Research Darmstadt.

inter-domain relationships between model elements explicitly by automatically maintaining a correspondence model. Although TGGs describe how *triples* consisting of source, correspondence, and target models are simultaneously derived, most practical software engineering scenarios require that source or target models already exist and that the models in the correspondence and the opposite domain be consistently constructed by a unidirectional forward or backward transformation. As a consequence, TGG tools that support bidirectional model transformation (i) rely on unidirectional forward and backward operational rules, automatically derived from a single TGG specification, as basic transformation steps, and (ii) use an algorithm that controls which rule is to be applied on which part of the input graph. As a TGG rule in the specification might require *context elements* created by another TGG rule, the control algorithm must consider these *precedences/dependencies* at runtime when (a) determining the order in which graph nodes can be processed, and (b) selecting the rule to be applied.

In this paper, we introduce a *node precedence analysis* to provide a global view on the dependencies in the source graph and to guide the transformation process. Additionally, we combine the node precedence analysis with *a rule dependency analysis* to support the control algorithm in determining the node processing order and selecting the next applicable rule. This approach can now exploit global dependency information, and perform an iterative, top-down resolution which is more expressive (can handle a larger class of TGGs) and fits better into future incremental scenarios. Finally, we prove that the improved control algorithm is still correct, complete, and polynomial.

Section 2 introduces fundamental definitions using our running example while Sect. 3 discusses existing TGG batch algorithms. Sect. 4 presents our rule dependency and node precedence analysis, used by the TGG batch algorithm presented in Sect. 5. Finally, Sect. 6 gives a broader overview of related *bidirectional* approaches and Sect. 7 concludes with a summary and future work.

2 Fundamentals and Running Example

In this section, all concepts required to formalize and present our contribution are introduced and explained using our running example.

2.1 Type Graphs, Typed Graphs and Triples

We introduce the concept of a *graphs*, and formalize *models* as *typed graphs*.

Definition 1 (Graph and Graph Morphism). *A graph $G = (V, E, s, t)$ consists of finite sets V of nodes, and E of edges, and two functions $s, t : E \to V$ that assign each edge source and target nodes. A graph morphism $h : G \to G'$, with $G' = (V', E', s', t')$, is a pair of functions $h := (h_V, h_E)$ where $h_V : V \to V'$, $h_E : E \to E'$ and $\forall e \in E : h_V(s(e)) = s'(h_E(e)) \land h_V(t(e)) = t'(h_E(e))$.*

Definition 2 (Typed Graph and Typed Graph Morphisms).

A type graph *is a graph* $TG = (V_{TG}, E_{TG}, s_{TG}, t_{TG})$.
A typed graph $(G, type)$ *consists of a graph* G *together with
a graph morphism* type: $G \to TG$.
Given typed graphs $(G, type)$ *and* $(G', type')$, $g : G \to G'$ *is
a typed graph morphism iff the diagram commutes.*

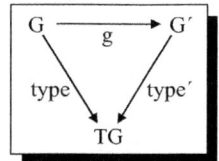

These concepts can be lifted in a straightforward manner to *triples* of connected graphs denoted as $G = G_S \xleftarrow{h_S} G_C \xrightarrow{h_T} G_T$ as shown by [6,12]. In the following, we work with *typed graph triples* and corresponding morphisms.

Example. Our running example specifies the integration of *company structures* and corresponding *IT structures*. The *TGG schema* (Fig. 1) is the type graph triple for our running example. The *source domain* is described by a type graph for company structures: A Company consists of a CEO, Employees and Admins. In the *target domain*, an IT structure (IT) provides PCs and Laptops in Networks controlled by a Router. The *correspondence domain* specifies valid links between elements in the different domains.

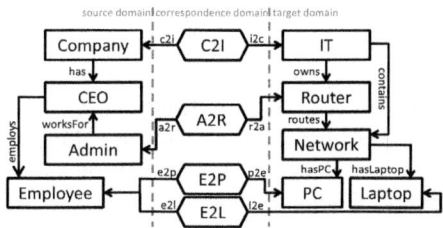

Fig. 1. TGG Schema for the integration of a company with its IT structure

A schema conform (typed graph) triple is depicted in Fig. 2. The company ES has a CEO named Andy for whom administrator Ingo works. Additionally, Andy employs Tony and Marius. The corresponding IT structure ES-IT consists of a router WP53 for the network ES-LAN with a PC PC65 and a laptop X200.

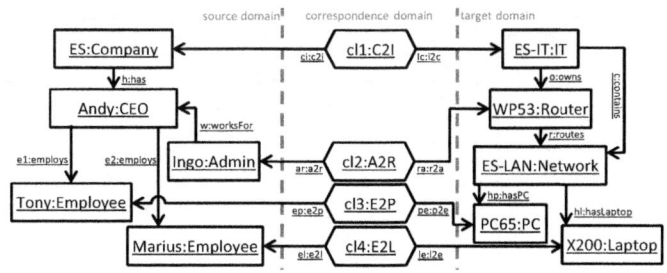

Fig. 2. A TGG schema conform triple

2.2 Triple Graph Grammars and Rules

The simultaneous evolution of typed graph triples such as our example triple (Fig. 2) can be described by a *triple graph grammar* consisting of *transformation rules*. This is formalized in the following definitions.

Definition 3 (Graph Triple Rewriting for Monotonic Creating Rules). A monotonic creating rule $r := (L, R)$, is a pair of typed graph triples such that $L \subseteq R$. A rule r rewrites (via adding elements) a graph triple G into a graph triple G' via a match $m: L \to G$, denoted as $G \stackrel{r@m}{\rightsquigarrow} G'$, iff $m': R \to G'$ is defined by building the pushout G' as denoted in the diagram.

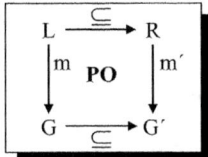

Elements in L denote the precondition of a rule and are referred to as *context elements*, while elements in $R \setminus L$ are referred to as *created elements*.

Definition 4 (Triple Graph Grammar). A triple graph grammar $TGG := (TG, \mathcal{R})$ consists of a type graph triple TG and a finite set $\mathcal{R}$ of monotonic creating rules. The generated language ($G_\emptyset$ denotes the empty graph triple) is
$$\mathcal{L}(TGG) := \{G \mid \exists\, r_1, r_2, \ldots, r_n \subset \mathcal{R}: G_\emptyset \stackrel{r_1@m_1}{\rightsquigarrow} G_1 \stackrel{r_2@m_2}{\rightsquigarrow} \ldots \stackrel{r_n@m_n}{\rightsquigarrow} G_n = G\}.$$

Example. The rules depicted in Fig. 3 build up an integrated company and IT structure simultaneously. Rule (a) creates the root elements of the models (a Company with a CEO and a corresponding IT), while Rule (b) appends additional elements (an Admin and a corresponding Router with the controlled Network). Rules (c) and (d) extend the models with an Employee, who can choose a PC or a Laptop. We use a concise notation by merging L and R of a rule, depicting context elements in black without any markup, and created elements in green with a "++" markup.

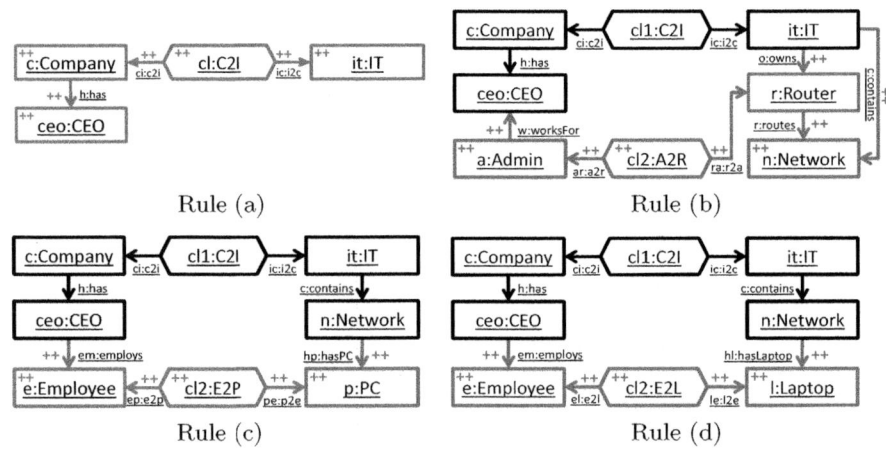

Fig. 3. Rules (a)–(d) for the integration

2.3 Derived Operational Rules

The real potential of TGGs as a bidirectional transformation language lies in the automatic derivation of *operational rules*. Such operational rules can be used to transform a given source domain model to produce a corresponding target domain model and vice versa. Although we focus in the following sections only on a forward transformation, all concepts and arguments are symmetric and can be applied analogously for the case of a backward transformation.

It has been proven by [5,16] that a sequence of TGG rules, which describes a simultaneous evolution, can be uniquely decomposed into (and conversely composed from) a sequence of *source rules* that only evolve the source model and *forward rules* that retain the source model and evolve the correspondence and target models. These operational rules serve as the building blocks used by a control algorithm for unidirectional forward and backward transformation.

Definition 5 (Derived Operational Rules). *Given a $TGG = (TG, \mathcal{R})$ and a rule $r = (L, R) \in \mathcal{R}$, a source rule $r_S = (SL, SR)$ and a forward rule $r_F = (FL, FR)$ can be derived according to the following diagram:*

$$\begin{array}{ccccccccccc}
SL = L_S & \xleftarrow{\varepsilon} & \emptyset & \xrightarrow{\varepsilon} & \emptyset & | & L = & L_S & \xleftarrow{\sigma_L} & L_C & \xrightarrow{\tau_L} & L_T & | & FL = R_S & \xleftarrow{\sigma \circ \sigma_L} & L_C & \xrightarrow{\tau_L} & L_T \\
\downarrow n & & \downarrow \sigma & & \downarrow \varepsilon & & \downarrow \varepsilon \Leftarrow n & & \downarrow \sigma & & \downarrow \gamma & & \downarrow \tau \Rightarrow n & & \downarrow id & & \downarrow \gamma & & \downarrow \tau \\
SR = R_S & \xleftarrow{\varepsilon} & \emptyset & \xrightarrow{\varepsilon} & \emptyset & | & R = & R_S & \xleftarrow{\sigma_R} & R_C & \xrightarrow{\tau_R} & R_T & | & FR = R_S & \xleftarrow{\sigma_R} & R_C & \xrightarrow{\tau_R} & R_T \\
& \text{source rule } r_S & & & & & & \text{TGG rule } r & & & & & & \text{forward rule } r_F
\end{array}$$

Example. From Rule (c) of our running example (Fig. 3), the operational rules r_S and r_F depicted in Fig. 4 can be derived. The source rule extends the source graph by adding an Employee to an existing CEO in a Company, while the forward rule r_F *transforms* an existing Employee of a CEO by *creating* a new E2P link and a PC in the corresponding Network.

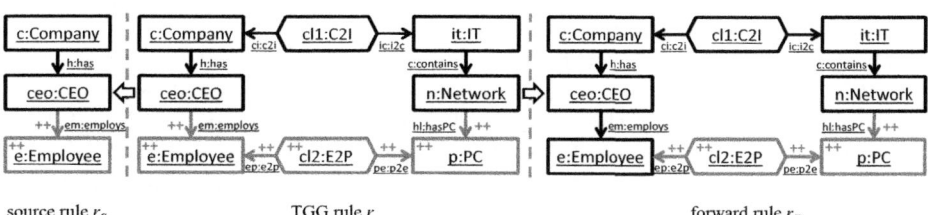

Fig. 4. Source and forward rules derived from Rule (c)

3 Related Work on TGG Control Algorithms

Constructing forward (and conversely backward) transformations from operational rules requires a *control algorithm* that is able to determine a sequence of forward rules to be applied to a given source graph. The challenge is to specify a control algorithm that is correct (only consistent graph triples are produced), complete (all consistent triples, which can be derived from a source or a target graph, can actually be produced), efficient (runtime complexity scales polynomially with the number of nodes to be processed), and still expressive enough for real-world applications. To better understand this challenge, we discuss how existing algorithms handle the source graph of our example triple (Fig. 2).

(I) Bottom-Up, Context-Driven and Recursive: An established strategy is to transform elements in a bottom-up context-driven manner, i.e., to start with a random node and check if all context nodes (dependencies) are already transformed *before* the selected initial node can be transformed. If a context node is not yet transformed, the algorithm transforms it, by recursively checking and transforming its context. Context-driven algorithms always start their transformation process with an arbitrarily selected node, without "knowing" if this was a good choice, i.e., if the node can be transformed immediately or if the input model as a whole is even valid. Such algorithms are correct, but, in general, have problems with completeness due to wrong *local* decisions.

(I.a) Backtracking: A simple backtracking strategy could be employed to cope with wrong local decisions. For our example, a first iteration over all nodes would determine that only ES together with Andy can be transformed by applying Rule (a). In a second iteration the algorithm would determine again in a trial and error manner that only Ingo can be transformed next with Rule (b), as neither Tony nor Marius can be transformed using Rule (c) or (d) (a Network is missing in the opposite domain). Finally, Tony and Marius can be transformed. This algorithm is correct and complete as shown in [5,16] but has exponential runtime and is, therefore, impractical for real-world applications.

It is, however, possible to guarantee polynomial runtime of the context-driven recursion strategy by restricting the class of supported TGGs appropriately as in case of the following approaches.

(I.b) Functional Behavior: Demanding *functional behavior* [7,9] guarantees that the algorithm can choose freely between applicable rules at every decision point and will always get the *same result* without backtracking. Although functional behavior might be suitable for fully automatic integrations, our experience with industrial partners [14,15] shows that user interaction or similar guidance (e.g., configuration files) of the integration process is required and leads naturally to non-functional sets of rules with certain degrees of freedom [13,14,15]. Please note that our running example is clearly non-functional due to Rules (c) and (d), which can be applied to the same elements on the source side, but create different elements on the target side. Therefore, depending on the choice of rule applications, *different* target graphs are possible with our running example. Demanding functional behavior is a strong restriction that reduces the expressiveness and suitability of TGGs for real-world applications [12,17].

Nevertheless, such a strategy has polynomial runtime and its applicability can be enforced statically via critical pair analysis [6].

(I.c) Local Completeness: Algorithms that allow a non-functional set of rules to handle a larger set of scenarios exploit the explicit traceability to cope with non-determinism and non-bijectivity [19], while still guaranteeing completeness for a certain class of TGGs. Hence, [12] demands *local completeness*, i.e., that a local decision between rules that can transform the current node *cannot* lead to a dead-end. This means that a local choice (which can be influenced by the user or some other means) might actually result in *different* output graphs, which are, however, always consistent, i.e., in the defined language of the TGG ($\mathcal{L}(TGG)$). For our running example, we could start with an arbitrary node, e.g., Ingo. According to Rule (b), a CEO and a Company are required as context and Rule (a) will thus be applied to ES and Andy. After processing Ingo, Tony and Marius can be transformed in an arbitrary order, each time making a local choice if a PC (Rule (c)) or Laptop (Rule (d)) is to be created. Furthermore, a *dangling edge check* is introduced in [12] to further enlarge the class of supported TGGs via a look-ahead to prevent wrong local decisions that would lead to "dangling" edges that can no longer be transformed. Note that our running example is *not* local complete, as it cannot be decided whether an Admin or an Employee should be transformed first (Rules (c) and (d) demand an element on the *target* side that can only be created by Rule (b)). For this reason, the algorithm might fail if it decides to start with one of the Employees. In this case, Rules (c) and (d) would state that ES and Andy are required as context and have to be transformed first. This is, however, insufficient as a Network must be present in the target domain as well. This context-driven approach fails here as transforming ES and Andy with Rule (a) *does not* guarantee that the employees Marius and Tony can be transformed. The problem here is that context-driven algorithms only regard the given input graph for controlling the rule application and do not consider *cross-domain context dependencies* such as Network in this case.

(II) Top-Down and Iterative: In contrast to context-driven recursive strategies, which lack a *global view* on the overall dependencies and seem to be unsuitable for an *incremental* synchronization scenario, algorithms can operate in a top-down iterative manner exploiting a certain global view on the whole input graph instead of arbitrarily choosing a node to be transformed.

(II.a) Correspondence-Driven: The algorithm presented by [11] requires that all TGG rules demand and create at least one correspondence link, i.e., a hierarchy of correspondence links must be built up during the transformation. The correspondence model can be used to store dependencies between links in this case and is interpreted as a directed acyclic graph, which is used to drive and control the transformation. This algorithm is both batch *and* incremental but it is unclear from [11] for which class of TGGs completeness can be ensured.

(II.b) Precedence-Driven: A precedence-driven strategy defines and uses a partial order of nodes in the source graph according to their *precedence*, i.e., the sorting guarantees that the nodes can only be transformed in a sequence that is compatible with the partial order.

4 Rule Dependency and Precedence Analysis for TGGs

In this section, we present a node precedence analysis that provides a partial order required for a precedence-driven strategy, together with a rule dependency analysis that partially solves the problem of cross-domain context dependencies caused by context elements in the domain under construction.

4.1 Rule Dependency Analysis

To handle cross-domain context dependencies, we utilize the concept of *sequential independence* as introduced by [6], to statically determine which rules depend on other rules. The intuition is that a rule r_2 depends on another rule r_1, if r_1 creates elements that r_2 requires as context.

Definition 6 (Rule Dependency Relation $<_R$). *Given rules $r_1 = (L_1, R_1)$ and $r_2 = (L_2, R_2)$, r_2 is sequentially dependent on r_1 iff a graph D and morphisms f, h exist, such that there exists no morphism g as depicted to the right, i.e., at least one element required by r_2 (an element in L_2), is created by r_1 (this element is in R_1 but not in L_1).*
The precedence relation $<_R \subseteq \mathcal{R} \times \mathcal{R}$ is defined for a given TGG as follows:
$r_1 <_R r_2 \Leftrightarrow r_2$ is sequentially dependent on r_1.

In practice, $<_R$ can be calculated statically by determining all possible intersections of R_1 and L_2. If at least one element in an intersection is not in L_1 then r_2 is sequentially dependent on r_1 (i.e., $r_1 <_R r_2$).

Example. For the TGG rules of our running example (Fig. 3), the following pairs of rules constitute $<_R$: Rule (a) $<_R$ Rule (b), Rule (a) $<_R$ Rule (c), Rule (a) $<_R$ Rule (d), Rule (b) $<_R$ Rule (c), and Rule (b) $<_R$ Rule (d).

4.2 Precedence Analysis

The following definitions present our path-based node precedence analysis which is used to topologically sort the nodes in a source graph and thus control the iterative transformation process:

Definition 7 (Paths and Type Paths). *Let G be a typed graph with type graph TG. A path p between two nodes $n_1, n_k \in V_G$ is an alternating sequence of nodes and edges in V_G and E_G, respectively, denoted as $p := n_1 \cdot e_1^{\alpha_1} \cdot n_2 \cdot \ldots \cdot n_{k-1} \cdot e_{k-1}^{\alpha_{k-1}} \cdot n_k$, where $\alpha_i \in \{+, -\}$ specifies if an edge e_i is traversed from source $s(e_i) = n_i$ to target $t(e_i) = n_{i+1}$ (+), or in a reverse direction (−). A type path is a path between node types and edge types in V_{TG} and E_{TG}, respectively. Given a path p, its type (path) is defined as $type_p(p) := type_V(n_1) \cdot type_E(e_1)^{\alpha_1} \cdot type_V(n_2) \cdot type_E(e_2)^{\alpha_2} \cdot \ldots \cdot type_V(n_{k-1}) \cdot type_E(e_{k-1})^{\alpha_{k-1}} \cdot type_V(n_k)$.*

For our analysis we are only interested in paths that are induced by certain *certain patterns* present in the *TGG rules*.

Definition 8 (Relevant Node Creation Patterns). *For a $TGG = (TG, \mathcal{R})$ and all rules $r \in \mathcal{R}$, where $r = (L, R) = (L_S \leftarrow L_C \rightarrow L_T, R_S \leftarrow R_C \rightarrow R_T)$. The set Paths_S denotes all paths in R_S (note that $L_S \subseteq R_S$). The predicates $\text{context}_S : \text{Paths}_S \rightarrow \{true, false\}$ and $\text{create}_S : \text{Paths}_S \rightarrow \{true, false\}$ in the source domain are defined as follows:*
$\text{context}_S(p_r) := \exists \, r \in \mathcal{R}$ *s.t. p_r is a path between two nodes $n_r, n'_r \in R_S$:
$(n_r \in L_S) \wedge (n'_r \in R_S \setminus L_S)$, i.e., a rule r in $\mathcal{R}$ contains a path p_r which is isomorphic to the node creation pattern depicted in the diagram to the right.*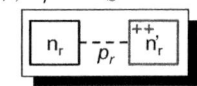
$\text{create}_S(p_r) := \exists \, r \in \mathcal{R}$ *s.t. p_r is a path between two nodes $n_r, n'_r \in R_S$:
$(n_r \in R_S \setminus L_S) \wedge (n'_r \in R_S \setminus L_S)$, i.e., a rule r in $\mathcal{R}$ contains a path p_r which is isomorphic to the node creation pattern depicted in the diagram to the right.*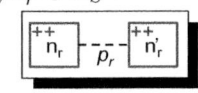

We can now define the set of interesting type paths, relevant for our analysis.

Definition 9 (Type Path Sets). *The set TPaths_S denotes all type paths of paths in Paths_S (cf. Def. 8), i.e., $\text{TPaths}_S := \{tp \mid \exists \, p \in \text{Paths}_S \text{ s.t. } type_p(p) = tp\}$. Thus, we define the restricted* create *type path set for the source domain as $TP_S^{create} := \{tp \in \text{TPaths}_S \mid \exists \, p \in \text{Paths}_S \wedge type_p(p) = tp \wedge create_S(p)\}$, and the restricted* context *type path set for the source domain as $TP_S^{context} := \{tp \in \text{TPaths}_S \mid \exists \, p \in \text{Paths}_S \wedge type_p(p) = tp \wedge context_S(p)\}$.*

In the following, we formalize the concept of *precedence between nodes*, indicating that one node could be used as context when transforming another node.

Definition 10 (Precedence Function $\mathcal{PF}_S$). *Let $\mathcal{P} := \{<, \doteq, \cdot \not\leftrightarrow \cdot\}$ be the set of precedence relation symbols. Given a $TGG = (TG, \mathcal{R})$ and the restricted type path sets for the source domain TP_S^{create}, $TP_S^{context}$. The precedence function for the source domain $\mathcal{PF}_S : \{TP_S^{create} \cup TP_S^{context}\} \rightarrow \mathcal{P}$ is computed as follows:*

$$\mathcal{PF}_S(tp) := \begin{array}{l} < \text{ iff } tp \in \{TP_S^{context} \setminus TP_S^{create}\} \\ \doteq \text{ iff } tp \in \{TP_S^{create} \setminus TP_S^{context}\} \\ \cdot \not\leftrightarrow \cdot \text{ otherwise} \end{array}$$

Example. $\mathcal{PF}_S$ for our running example consists of the following entries:
Rule (a): $\mathcal{PF}_S(\texttt{Company} \cdot \texttt{has}^+ \cdot \texttt{CEO}) = \doteq$ and $\mathcal{PF}_S(\texttt{CEO} \cdot \texttt{has}^- \cdot \texttt{Company}) = \doteq$
Rule (b): $\mathcal{PF}_S(\texttt{Company} \cdot \texttt{has}^+ \cdot \texttt{CEO} \cdot \texttt{worksFor}^- \cdot \texttt{Admin}) = <$ and
$\quad\quad\mathcal{PF}_S(\texttt{CEO} \cdot \texttt{worksFor}^- \cdot \texttt{Admin}) = <$
Rules (c) and (d): $\mathcal{PF}_S(\texttt{Company} \cdot \texttt{has}^+ \cdot \texttt{CEO} \cdot \texttt{employs}^- \cdot \texttt{Employee}) = <$ and
$\quad\quad\mathcal{PF}_S(\texttt{CEO} \cdot \texttt{employs}^- \cdot \texttt{Employee}) = <$

Restriction. As our precedence analysis depends on paths in rules of a given TGG, the presented approach requires TGG rules that are (weakly) connected in each domain. Hence, considering the source domain, the following must hold:
$\forall \, r \in \mathcal{R}, \forall \, n, n' \in R_S : \exists \, p \in \text{Paths}_S$ between n and n'.

Based on the precedence function $\mathcal{PF}_S$, relations $<_S$ and $\doteq^*_S$ can now be defined and used to topologically sort a given input graph and determine the sets of elements that can be transformed at each step in the algorithm.

Definition 11 (Source Path Set). *For a given typed source graph G_S, the source path set for the source domain is defined as follows:*
$P_S := \{p \mid p \text{ is a path between } n, n' \in V_{G_S} \wedge type_p(p) \in \{TP_S^{create} \cup TP_S^{context}\}\}$.

Definition 12 (Precedence Relation $<_S$). *Given $\mathcal{PF}_S$, the precedence function for a given TGG, and a typed source graph G_S. The precedence relation $<_S \subseteq V_{G_S} \times V_{G_S}$ for the source domain is defined as follows: $n <_S n'$ if there exists a path $p \in P_S$ between nodes n and n' such that $\mathcal{PF}_S(type_p(p)) = <$.*

Example. For our example triple (Fig. 2), the following pairs constitute $<_S$: (ES $<_S$ Ingo), (ES $<_S$ Tony), (ES $<_S$ Marius), (Andy $<_S$ Ingo), (Andy $<_S$ Tony), and (Andy $<_S$ Marius).

Definition 13 (Relation $\doteq_S$). *Given $\mathcal{PF}_S$, the precedence function for a given TGG, and a typed source graph G_S. The symmetric relation $\doteq_S \subseteq V_{G_S} \times V_{G_S}$ for the source domain is defined as follows: $n \doteq_S n'$ if there exists a path $p \subset P_S$ between nodes n and n' such that $\mathcal{PF}_S(type_p(p)) = \doteq$.*

Definition 14 (Equivalence Relation $\doteq^*_S$). *The equivalence relation $\doteq^*_S$ is the transitive and reflexive closure of the symmetric relation $\doteq_S$.*

Example. For our example triple (Fig. 2), the following equivalence classes constitute $\doteq^*_S$: {Andy, ES}, {Ingo}, {Tony}, and {Marius}.

Definition 15 (Precedence Graph $\mathcal{PG}_S$). *The precedence graph for a given source graph G_S is a graph $\mathcal{PG}_S$ constructed as follows:*
(i) The equivalence relation $\doteq^*_S$ is used to partition V_{G_S} into equivalence classes $EQ_1, \ldots EQ_n$ which serve as the nodes of $\mathcal{PG}_S$, i.e., $V_{\mathcal{PG}_S} := \{EQ_1, \ldots, EQ_n\}$.
(ii) The edges in $\mathcal{PG}_S$ are defined as follows:
$E_{\mathcal{PG}_S} := \{e \mid s(e) = EQ_i, \; t(e) = EQ_j : \exists \, n_i \in EQ_i, n_j \in EQ_j \text{ with } n_i <_S n_j\}$.

Example. The corresponding $\mathcal{PG}_S$ constructed from our example triple is depicted in Fig. 5(a) in Sect. 5.

5 Precedence TGG Batch Algorithm

In this section, we present our batch algorithm (cf. Algorithm 1) and explain how the introduced rule dependency and node precedence analyses are used to efficiently transform a given source graph. For a forward transformation (a backward transformation works analogously), the input for the algorithm is a graph G_S, the statically derived rule dependency relation $<_R$, and the precedence function for the source domain $\mathcal{PF}_S$.

Procedure TRANSFORM determines a graph triple $G_S \leftarrow G_C \rightarrow G_T$ as output. The first step (line (2)) of the algorithm is to build the precedence graph

Algorithm 1. Precedence TGG Batch Algorithm

1: **procedure** TRANSFORM($G_S, <_R, \mathcal{PF}_S$)
2:     $\mathcal{PG}_S \leftarrow$ BUILDPRECEDENCEGRAPH($G_S, \mathcal{PF}_S$)
3:     **while** ($\mathcal{PG}_S$ contains equivalence classes) **do**
4:        $readyNodes \leftarrow$ all nodes in equiv. classes in $\mathcal{PG}_S$ without incoming edges
5:        $readyNodes \leftarrow$ sort $readyNodes$ utilizing $<_R$
6:        **for** (node n in $readyNodes$) **do**
7:           $transformedNodes \leftarrow$ CHOOSEANDAPPLYRULE(n)
8:           **if** $transformedNodes \neq \emptyset$ **then**
9:              $\mathcal{PG}_S \leftarrow$ remove all nodes in $transformedNodes$ from $\mathcal{PG}_S$
10:            **break**
11:           **end if**
12:        **end for**
13:        **if** $transformedNodes = \emptyset$ **then**
14:           **terminate with error**   ▷ *Local Completeness Criterion* violated
15:        **end if**
16:     **end while**
17:     **return** $G_S \leftarrow G_C \rightarrow G_T$
18: **end procedure**

$\mathcal{PG}_S$ according to Def. 15. Note that the procedure BUILDPRECEDENCEGRAPH will terminate with an error if there is a cycle in the precedence graph and it is thus impossible to sort the elements of the source graph according to their dependencies. Starting on line (3), a while-loop iterates over equivalence classes in $\mathcal{PG}_S$ until there are none left. In the while-loop, the set *readyNodes* contains all nodes that can be transformed next, i.e., whose context elements have already been transformed (line (4)). This set is determined by taking all nodes in the equivalence classes of $\mathcal{PG}_S$, which do not have incoming edges (dependencies). On line (5), *readyNodes* is sorted according to the partially ordered relation $<_R$, i.e., the rules that can be used to transform nodes in *readyNodes* are determined, sorted with $<_R$ and reflected in *readyNodes*. This could be achieved by assigning an integer to each rule according to the partial order of $<_R$ and then selecting the largest number of all rules that translate $n \in readyNodes$ for n.[1] Next, a for-loop iterates over the sorted *readyNodes* (line (6)). On line (7) the procedure CHOOSEANDAPPLYRULE is used to determine and filter the rules as presented in [12], allowing for user input or choosing arbitrarily from the final applicable rules. If a rule could be successfully chosen and applied to transform n on line (7), a non-empty set of *transformedNodes* is returned that is used to update $\mathcal{PG}_S$ on line (9). In this case, the for-loop is terminated and the while-loop is repeated with the updated and thus "smaller" $\mathcal{PG}_S$. If *transformedNodes* is empty, the for-loop is repeated for the next node in *readyNodes*. If *transformedNodes*, however, *remains* empty on line (13), we know that no node in *readyNodes* has been transformed and that the algorithm has hit a dead-end. This can only

---

[1] If it is not possible to sort *readyNodes* due to cycles in $<_R$, this additional analysis supplies no further information and *readyNodes* remains unchanged.

happen for TGGs that violate the *Local Completeness Criterion* (cf. algorithm strategy I.c in Sect. 3) and are *not* in the class of supported TGGs.

Example. To demonstrate the presented algorithm, we apply a forward transformation for the source graph of our example triple depicted in Fig. 2. Given as input is G_S, the rule dependency relation $<_R$ (depicted as a graph in Fig. 5(b)), and the precedence function $\mathcal{PF}_S$ (cf. example for Def. 10). On line (2), the precedence graph $\mathcal{PG}_S$ for G_S, depicted in Fig. 5(a), is built. $\mathcal{PG}_S$ is acyclic, hence the transformation can continue.

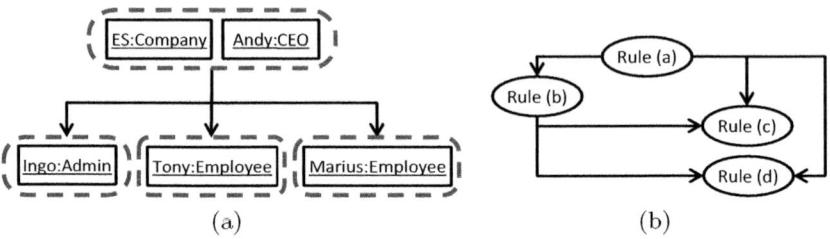

Fig. 5. $\mathcal{PG}_S$ for the input graph (left) and relation $<_R$ for all rules (a)–(d) (right)

On line (4), the set *readyNodes* is determined, consisting in this case of the nodes ES and Andy from a single equivalence class of $\mathcal{PG}_S$. On line (5), only one rule can be used to transform both nodes and, therefore, the sorting is trivial. On line (6) ES or Andy is chosen randomly, and in either case, the only candidate rule is Rule (a) (Fig. 3), which can be directly applied on line (7). Again in either case, *transformedNodes* contains both nodes as Rule (a) transforms ES and Andy simultaneously. $\mathcal{PG}_S$ is updated on line (9) to consist of three unconnected equivalence classes Ingo, Tony, and Marius, and the for-loop terminates. In the second iteration through the while-loop, *readyNodes* now contains all these three elements and will be sorted according to $<_R$ on line (5). This time, the sorting reveals that Ingo must be transformed before Tony and Marius as Rules (c) and (d) both require a Network as context in the target domain, which can only be created by applying Rule (b) first, i.e., *Rule (b)*$<_R$*Rule (c)*, *Rule (b)*$<_R$*Rule (d)* (Fig. 5(b)). The for-loop in line (6), therefore, starts with Ingo. Applying Rule (b) (line (7)) puts Ingo in *transformedNodes*, $\mathcal{PG}_S$ is updated on line (9) to now contain only Tony and Marius and the for-loop is terminated with the break on line (10). In the third iteration, *readyNodes* contains Tony and Marius, and no sorting is needed as Rules (c) and (d) do not depend on each other. On line (6) Tony could be randomly selected first and (arbitrarily or via user input) Rule (c) could be chosen to be applied on line (7). After updating $\mathcal{PG}_S$ again and breaking out of the for-loop, only Marius remains untransformed. Similar to the penultimate iteration, Rule (d) could be selected and applied this time. Updating $\mathcal{PG}_S$ on line (9) empties the precedence graph, which terminates the while-loop on line (3). The created graph triple depicted in Fig. 2 is returned on line (17).

Formal Properties of the Precedence TGG Batch Algorithm

In the following we argue that the presented algorithm retains all formal properties stipulated in [17] and proved for the context-driven algorithm of [12].

Definition 16 (Correctness, Completeness and Efficiency).
Correctness: Given a source graph G_S, the transformation algorithm either terminates with an error or produces a graph triple $G_S \leftarrow G_C \rightarrow G_T \in \mathcal{L}(TGG)$.
Completeness: For all triples $G_S \leftarrow G_C \rightarrow G_T \in \mathcal{L}(TGG)$, the transformation algorithm produces a consistent triple $G_S \leftarrow G'_C \rightarrow G'_T \in \mathcal{L}(TGG)$ for the input source graph G_S.
Efficiency: According to [17], a TGG batch transformation algorithm is efficient if its runtime complexity class is $O(n^k)$, where n is the number of nodes in the source graph to be transformed and k is the largest number of elements to be matched by any rule r of the given TGG.

All properties are defined analogously for backward transformations.

Theorem. *Algorithm 1 is correct, complete and efficient for any source-local complete TGG [12].*

Proof.
Correctness: If the algorithm returns a graph triple, i.e., does not terminate with an error, it was able to determine a sequence of source rules $r_{1_S}, r_{2_S}, \ldots, r_{n_S}$ that would build the given source graph G_S and, thus, the corresponding sequence of forward rules $r_{1_F}, r_{2_F}, \ldots, r_{n_F}$ that transform the given source graph (Def. 5). The *Decomposition and Composition Theorem* of [5] guarantees that it is possible to compose the sequence $r_{1_S}, r_{2_S}, \ldots, r_{n_S}, r_{1_F}, r_{2_F}, \ldots, r_{n_F}$ to the sequence of TGG rules $r_1, r_2, \ldots, r_n$ which proves that the resulting graph triple is consistent, i.e., $G_S \leftarrow G_C \rightarrow G_T \in \mathcal{L}(TGG)$. □
Completeness: Showing completeness is done in two steps: First of all, we consider the algorithm without the additional concept of rule dependencies via the relation $<_R$.

The remaining algorithm transforms nodes with the same concepts (e.g., dangling edge check) as the previous algorithm in [12], but iteratively *in a fixed sequence*, for which we guarantee, by definition of the precedence graph (cf. 15), that the context of every node is always transformed first. As the context-driven strategy taken by the algorithm in [12] is able to transform a model by arbitrarily choosing an element and transforming its context elements in a bottom-up manner (cf. Sect. 3), the fixed sequence taken by our algorithm must be a possible sequence that could be chosen by the algorithm in [12]. Algorithm 1 can, therefore, be seen as forcing the context-driven algorithm to transform elements in one of the possible sequences, from which it can arbitrarily choose. This shows that all completeness arguments from [12] can be transferred to the new algorithm, i.e., Algorithm 1 is complete for the class of local complete TGGs.

In a second step, we now consider the algorithm with the additional relation $<_R$ and, therefore, the capability of handling specifications with cross-domain context dependencies as in our running example. We have shown in Sect. 3 that the algorithm presented in [12] cannot cope with such specifications as they violate the local-completeness criterion. We can, hence, conclude that Algorithm 1 is more expressive than the previous context-driven algorithm as it can handle certain TGGs that are not local complete. We leave the precise categorization of this new class of TGGs to future work. □

Efficiency: Building the precedence graph $\mathcal{PG}_S$ on line (2), essentially a topological sorting, is realizable in $O(n^l)$, where l is the maximum length of relevant paths according to $\mathcal{PF}_S$. Note that l can be at most of size k (the largest number of elements to be matched by any rule r of the given TGG), thus we can estimate this with $O(n^k)$. The while-loop starting on line (3) iterates through $\mathcal{PG}_S$, which will be decreased every time by at least one node from an equivalence class. The while-loop is, thus, run in the worst-case (equivalence classes in $\mathcal{PG}_S$ all consisting of exactly one node) n times. In the while-loop, we select equivalence classes without incoming edges in line (4). This can be achieved in $O(n)$ by iterating through $\mathcal{PG}_S$. Building the topological order on line (5) requires inspecting all nodes in *readyNodes* and their appropriate rules in $O(n)$. The for-loop starting on line (6) iterates in the worst-case over all nodes in *readyNodes* where updating $\mathcal{PG}_S$ on line (9), requires traversing all successor nodes which is at most $n - 1$ (i.e., $O(n)$). As argued in [12], transforming a node, i.e., checking all conditions and performing pattern matching (line (7)), is assumed to run in $O(n^k)$ (cf. Def. 16). Summarizing, we obtain: $n^k + n \cdot (n + n + n \cdot (n^k + n)) \in O(n^k)$. □

As TGGs are symmetric [8], all arguments can be transferred analogously to backward transformations.

6 Related Work on Alternative Bidirectional Languages

Complementing our related work on TGG batch algorithms (cf. Sect. 3), we now focus on *alternative bidirectional languages* that share and address similar challenges as TGGs but take fundamentally different strategies. As bidirectionality is a challenge in various application domains and communities, there exists a substantial number of different approaches, formalizations and tools [18]. The lenses framework is of particular interest when compared to TGGs, as [8] has shown that incremental TGGs can be viewed as an implementation of a *delta-based* framework for *symmetric lenses*. Although we have presented a batch algorithm for TGGs, our ultimate goal is to provide a solid basis for an efficient incremental TGG implementation. As compared to existing lenses implementations for string data or trees such as *Boomerang* [2], TGGs are better suited for MDE where model transformations operate on complex *graph-like* structures. Similar to TGGs, *GRoundTram*, a bidirectional framework based on graph transformations [10], aims to support model transformations in the context of MDE. There are, however, a number of interesting differences: (i) While GRoundTram demands a forward transformation from the user and automatically generates a consistent backward transformation, TGGs (in this respect similar to lenses) provide a language from which both forward and backward transformations are automatically derived. Both approaches face a different set of non-trivial challenges. (ii) GRoundTram uses UnQL+, which is based on the graph query algebra UnCAL, with a strong emphasis on compositionality, while TGGs are rule-based algebraic graph transformations. (iii) GRoundTram maintains traceability in an implicit manner while TGGs create explicit typed traceability links between integrated models, which can be used to store extra information for incremental model synchronization or manual reviews. In contrast to both Boomerang and GRoundTram, TGGs adhere to the fundamental *unification* principle in MDE (everything is a model) and as such, a bidirectional model transformation specified as a TGG is a model which is conform to a well defined TGG metamodel. Unification has wide-reaching consequences including enabling a natural *bootstrap* and *higher order transformations*. Finally, TGGs served as an inspiration and basis for the standard OMG bidirectional transformation language QVT and can be regarded as a valid implementation thereof [18].

7 Conclusion and Future Work

In this paper, an improvement of our previous TGG batch algorithm was presented. We introduced a novel *node precedence analysis* of TGG specifications combined with a *rule dependency analysis* to further support the batch transformation control algorithm in determining the node processing order. The result is an iterative batch transformation strategy in a top-down manner with increased expressiveness. We have shown that this algorithm runs in polynomial runtime and complies to the formal properties for TGG implementations according to [17], and, therefore, is well-suited for real-world applications where efficiency is almost as important as the reliability of the expected result.

As a next step, we shall implement the presented algorithm as an extension of our current batch implementation in our metamodeling tool eMoflon[2][1], and start working on an efficient incremental TGG algorithm based on our rule dependency and node precedence analyses. Finally, providing a *rule checker* that decides at compile time if a given TGG can be transformed by our algorithm is a crucial task to improve the usability of our tool.

References

1. Anjorin, A., Lauder, M., Patzina, S., Schürr, A.: eMoflon: Leveraging EMF and Professional CASE Tools. In: Heiß, H.U., Pepper, P., Schlingloff, H., Schneider, J. (eds.) Proc. of MEMWe 2011. LNI, vol. 192. GI (2011)
2. Bohannon, A., Foster, J., Pierce, B., Pilkiewicz, A., Schmitt, A.: Boomerang: Resourceful Lenses for String Data. ACM SIGPLAN Notices 43(1), 407–419 (2008)
3. Czarnecki, K., Helsen, S.: Feature-based Survey of Model Transformation Approaches. IBM Systems Journal 45(3), 621–645 (2006)
4. Czarnecki, K., Foster, J.N., Hu, Z., Lämmel, R., Schürr, A., Terwilliger, J.F.: Bidirectional Transformations: A Cross-Discipline Perspective. In: Paige, R.F. (ed.) ICMT 2009. LNCS, vol. 5563, pp. 260–283. Springer, Heidelberg (2009)

---

[2] http://www.moflon.org

5. Ehrig, H., Ehrig, K., Ermel, C., Hermann, F., Taentzer, G.: Information Preserving Bidirectional Model Transformations. In: Dwyer, M.B., Lopes, A. (eds.) FASE 2007. LNCS, vol. 4422, pp. 72–86. Springer, Heidelberg (2007)
6. Ehrig, H., Ehrig, K., Prange, U., Taentzer, G.: Fundamentals of Algebraic Graph Transformation. Monographs in Theoretical Computer Science. An EATCS Series. Springer, New York (2006)
7. Giese, H., Hildebrandt, S., Lambers, L.: Toward Bridging the Gap between Formal Semantics and Implementation of Triple Graph Grammars. In: Lúcio, L., Vieira, E., Weißleder, S. (eds.) Proc. of MoDeVVA 2010, pp. 19–24. IEEE (2010)
8. Hermann, F., Ehrig, H., Orejas, F., Czarnecki, K., Diskin, Z., Xiong, Y.: Correctness of Model Synchronization Based on Triple Graph Grammars. In: Whittle, J., Clark, T., Kühne, T. (eds.) MODELS 2011. LNCS, vol. 6981, pp. 668–682. Springer, Heidelberg (2011)
9. Hermann, F., Golas, U., Orejas, F.: Efficient Analysis and Execution of Correct and Complete Model Transformations Based on Triple Graph Grammars. In: Bézivin, J., Soley, M.R., Vallecillo, A. (eds.) Proc. of MDI 2010. ICPS, vol. 482, pp. 22–31. ACM (2010)
10. Hidaka, S., Hu, Z., Inaba, K., Kato, H., Nakano, K.: GRoundTram: An Integrated Framework for Developing Well-Behaved Bidirectional Model Transformations. In: Alexander, P., Pasareanu, C., Hosking, J. (eds.) Proc. of ASE 2011, pp. 480–483. IEEE (2011)
11. Kindler, E., Rubin, V., Wagner, R.: An Adaptable TGG Interpreter for In-Memory Model Transformations. In: Schürr, A., Zündorf, A. (eds.) Proc. of Fujaba Days 2004, pp. 35–38 (2004)
12. Klar, F., Lauder, M., Königs, A., Schürr, A.: Extended Triple Graph Grammars with Efficient and Compatible Graph Translators. In: Engels, G., Lewerentz, C., Schäfer, W., Schürr, A., Westfechtel, B. (eds.) Nagl Festschrift. LNCS, vol. 5765, pp. 141–174. Springer, Heidelberg (2010)
13. Königs, A.: Model Transformation with Triple Graph Grammars. In: Proc. of MTIP 2005 (2005)
14. Lauder, M., Schlereth, M., Rose, S., Schürr, A.: Model-Driven Systems Engineering: State-of-the-Art and Research Challenges. Bulletin of the Polish Academy of Sciences, Technical Sciences 58(3), 409–422 (2010)
15. Rose, S., Lauder, M., Schlereth, M., Schürr, A.: A Multidimensional Approach for Concurrent Model Driven Automation Engineering. In: Osis, J., Asnina, E. (eds.) Model-Driven Domain Analysis and Software Development, pp. 90–113. IGI (2011)
16. Schürr, A.: Specification of Graph Translators with Triple Graph Grammars. In: Mayr, E.W., Schmidt, G., Tinhofer, G. (eds.) WG 1994. LNCS, vol. 903, pp. 151–163. Springer, Heidelberg (1995)
17. Schürr, A., Klar, F.: 15 Years of Triple Graph Grammars. In: Ehrig, H., Heckel, R., Rozenberg, G., Taentzer, G. (eds.) ICGT 2008. LNCS, vol. 5214, pp. 411–425. Springer, Heidelberg (2008)
18. Stevens, P.: A Landscape of Bidirectional Model Transformations. In: Lämmel, R., Visser, J., Saraiva, J. (eds.) GTTSE 2007. LNCS, vol. 5235, pp. 408–424. Springer, Heidelberg (2008)
19. Stevens, P.: Bidirectional Model Transformations in QVT: Semantic Issues and Open Questions. SoSym 9(1), 7–20 (2008)

A Timed Automata-Based Method to Analyze EAST-ADL Timing Constraint Specifications

Tahir Naseer Qureshi, De-Jiu Chen, and Martin Törngren

KTH – The Royal Institute of Technology, Stockholm, Sweden
{tnqu,chen,martin}@md.kth.se

Abstract. The increasing development complexity of automotive embedded systems has led to industrial needs of improved information management, early verification and validation of a system etc. EAST-ADL; an automotive-specific architectural description language provides a structured model-based approach for information management throughout the development process. A method to formally analyze consistency of EAST-ADL based timing constraint specifications using timed-automata is presented. A mapping scheme providing a basis for automated model-transformations between EAST-ADL and timed-automata is the main contribution. The method is demonstrated with a case study of a brake-by-wire system. Guidelines for extending the mapping framework are also provided.

Keywords: Model-based development, EAST-ADL, Timed-Automata, UPPAAL, Timing Constraints.

1 Introduction

Model-based development (MBD), i.e. the use of computerized models for different activities [1], is being applied in various engineering domains to manage complexities and increase development efficiency. In case of automotive embedded control systems, MBD is being used extensively in many different forms such as automatic code generation from design models using tools like Simulink. Traditionally, the development starts with algorithm (e.g. control algorithm for fuel control) formalization followed by steps like rapid prototyping, generation of production code, hardware-in-the-loop (HIL) testing and final calibrations [2]. The process is efficient for single ECUs (Electric Control Units) but several issues related to timing, interface and communication occur during ECU integration [2]. There is a need for efficient information management and integration of models, tools and languages related to different views and abstraction levels. The views can be product-related, such as hardware, software and infrastructure, or concern related, such as safety, dependability etc. Information traceability, reusability of solutions, early verification and validation, reduced time and cost are examples of the intended benefits from an efficient information management and integration.

One approach to deal with multiple views and structured information management is to base the development on a comprehensive system model to which the views can be related. There exist several generic as well as domain-specific solutions. SysML[1], EAST-ADL (Electronics Architecture and Software Technology- Architecture Description Language) [3] and AUTOSAR (AUTomotive Open System ARchitecture) [4] are examples of such solutions. EAST-ADL is automotive specific having a broad coverage of system lifecycle and specification support with different views and concerns in a well-structured manner. It is also aligned with AUTOSAR and other automotive standards such as ISO26262 [5]. It relies on external tools for activities like analysis of specifications related to functionality, requirements or safety, verification and validation etc. Wide industrial acceptance of EAST-ADL is hindered by its limited tool support.

The presented work is motivated by the fact that ensuring consistency between the constraints specified for different parts of a system can lead to decreased integration issues. A method which paves a way for automated model-transformation between EAST-ADL and timed automata is presented in this paper. It is shown that EAST-ADL timing constraint specifications and the execution behavior of a component can be abstracted as a network of timed-automata. The main contribution is a mapping framework based on pre-defined timed-automata templates, its usage as well as extension guidelines for checking specification consistency. A case-study of a brake by-wire system is used to demonstrate the usage of the framework with PapyrusUML[6] and UPPAAL[7] as the tools for modeling and analysis respectively.

2   EAST-ADL and Timing Extension – Concept and Notations

EAST-ADL evolved through several European projects during the last decade complementing the best industrial practices such as Hardware-In-Loop (HIL) and Software-In-Loop (SIL) simulations with the goal to provide an architectural description language to facilitate the development of automotive embedded systems. The core of the EAST-ADL language definition [3] consists of structural specifications at four different abstraction levels (namely vehicle, analysis, design and implementation). For example product line features (end-to-end functionality) and their variations are specified at the vehicle level whereas the detailed design of functional components, connections and allocations to various hardware components is carried out at the design level. The core supports hierarchical specifications of a system with the concepts of function types and prototypes together with various types of ports and connectors with automotive specific attributes. Specifications of requirements, dependability, variability, and behavioral and timing constraints are supported by corresponding language extensions which refer to the core functional artifacts of EAST-ADL. This modular approach not only separates the definition of functional and non-functional aspects but also enables the use of existing tools for various development activities.

The presented work focuses on a subset of EAST-ADL artifacts applicable to the design level of abstraction and described as follows:

---

[1] http://www.omgsysml.org/#Specification

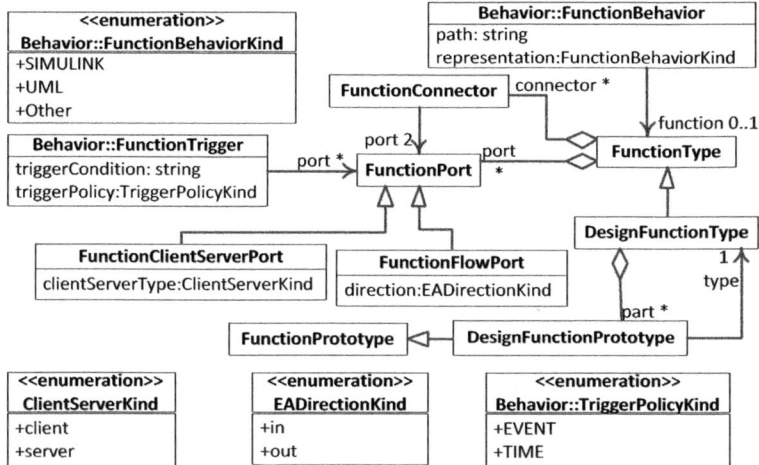

Fig. 1. EAST-ADL core structure and behavior extension

The core and behavior artifacts focused in this paper are shown in Fig. 1 where the artifacts prefixed with *Behavior::* are part of the behavior annex and the rest belongs to the core language definition.. The behavior of a function (FunctionType or DesignFunctionType in Fig. 1) can be classified as the execution behavior and the internal behavior. EAST-ADL relies on external representations like Simulink for internal behavior representation and specifies its execution behavior in the form of triggering information (determined by the triggerPolicy of the associated FuncitonTrigger) i.e. if a function is event triggered (e.g. arrival of data at its port) or time-triggered. The behavior of an EAST-ADL function has three main steps consisting of reading data at input ports, performing computations and writing data on the output port. All functions have run-to-completion semantics i.e. a function runs all the steps before it starts to execute again. All the functions run concurrently unless specified by the designer. Moreover, the ports of an EAST-ADL function have single-sized overwritable and non-consumable buffer semantics.

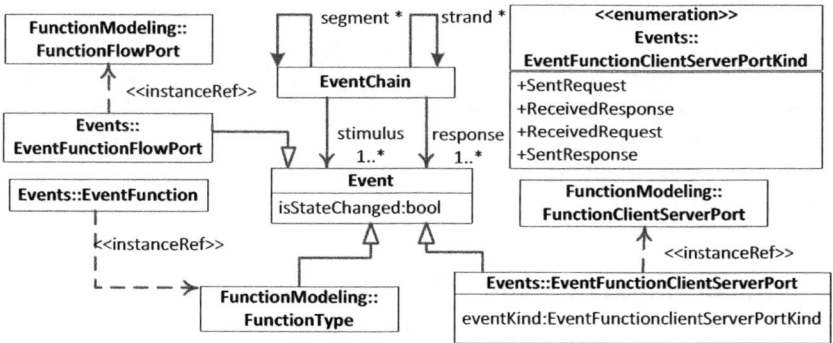

Fig. 2. Events and event chains in EAST-ADL

The timing extension of EAST-ADL is derived from TADL (Time Augmented Description Language) [12]. It can be used to specify the timing constraints on the execution behavior of a function and precedence between different functions. As shown in Fig. 2 the timing extension is based on the concepts of events and event chains. *EventFunction*, *EventFunctionFlowPort* and *EventFunctionClientServerPort* are the three event kinds referring to the triggering of a function by some sort of dispatcher, arrival of a data at a port and service requested (or received) by a client-server port respectively.

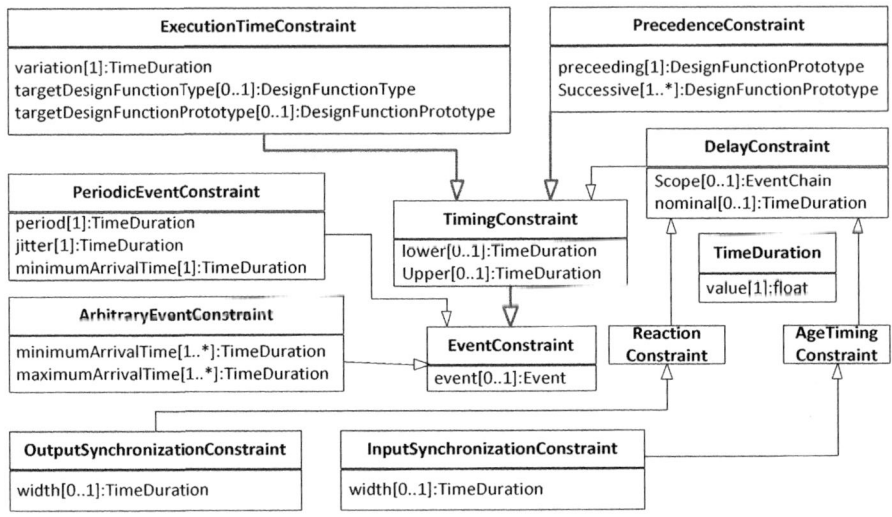

Fig. 3. EAST-ADL timing constraints

A function or a group of functions perform some kind of transformation of data present at their input ports and send the output through their output ports. *Event chains* and the constraints applied on them as well as individual events enable a designer to specify end-to-end timing constraints such as the minimum and maximum time allowed from the occurrence of one event called *stimulus* to the occurrence of another event called *response*. An event chain can further be refined into smaller event chains called *strands* (parallel chains) or *segments* (sequenced). The constraints addressed in this paper are shown in Fig. 3. The periodicity of an event occurrence is an example of possible constraints on the events shown as *PeriodicEventConstraint* in Fig. 3. In addition to above it is also possible to specify constraints on internal behavior (shown as FunctionBehavior in Fig. 1). For additional information, the readers are referred to [3, 9, 12].

3 Timed Automata and UPPAAL

Timed automata (TA) [8] is essentially an automata augmented with clock and time semantics to enable formal model-checking of real-time systems. It has been used for modeling and verification of several systems and scenarios. Let C be a set of clocks, $F(C)$ a set of clock constraints in the form $x \circ y$ or $x + y \circ c$ where $x, y \in C, c \in N$ and $\circ \in \{<, \leq, =, \geq, >\}$. A timed-automata TA is a tuple (L, Lo, C, Σ, I, E) where,

- L is a finite set of locations, nodes or states.
- Lo is the initial location.
- Σ is a set of actions
- $E \subseteq L \times F(C) \times \Sigma \times 2^C \times L$ is a set of edges or transition.
- $I: L \to F(C)$ assigns invariants to locations

The semantics of timed-automata is a transition system where state and pairs (l, u), and transition are defined by rules

$(l, u) \xrightarrow{d} (l, u + d) if\ u \in I(l) and\ (u + d) \in I(l)$ for a non-negative real $d \in \mathbb{R}_+$
$(l, u) \xrightarrow{a} (l', u') if\ l \xrightarrow{g,a,r} l', u \in g, u' = [r \mapsto 0]u\ and\ u' \in I(l')$
where

- u, v denote functions known as clock assignments C mapping to $\mathbb{R}_+$. In addition $u \in g$ is used to denote that u satisfy the guard g.
- For $d \in \mathbb{R}_+$, $u+d$ is the clock assignment which maps all $x \in C$ to $u(x) + d$
- For $r \subseteq C$, $[r \mapsto 0]u$ denote the clock reset mapping all clocks in r to 0 with u for the other clocks in C.

Often a set of timed-automata are used in a networked form with a common set of clocks and actions. A special synchronization action denoted by an exclamation sign (!) or a question mark (?) is used for synchronization between different timed automata. A timed automata in a network is concurrent unless and until mechanisms like synchronization actions are applied. The readers are referred to [8] for a formal definition and semantics of a network of timed-automata. .

3.1 UPPAAL

UPPAAL is a timed-automata based model checking tool for modeling, validation and verification of real-time systems. The tool has three main parts: an editor, a simulator and a verifier, for modeling, early fault detection (by examination i.e. without exhaustive checking) and verification (covering exhaustive dynamic behavior) respectively. A system in UPPAAL is modeled as a network of timed automata. A subset of CTL (computation tree logic) is used as the query language in UPPAAL for verification. In addition to the generic timed-automata UPPAAL uses the concept of *broadcast* channels for synchronizing more than two automata. The concept of urgent and committed state is also introduced to force a transition as soon as it is enabled. The three kinds of properties which can be checked with UPPAAL are (i) *Reachability* i.e. some condition can possibly be satisfied, (ii) *Safety* i.e. some condition will never occur and (iii) *Liveness* i.e. some condition will eventually become true.

UPPAAL uses the concept of templates for reusability and prototyping of system components. Each template can be instantiated multiple times with varying parameters. The instantiation is called a process. The tool has been used in many industrial cases such as a gear box controller from Mecel AB and Philips Audio protocol and several more[2].

4 EAST-ADL and Timed-Automata Relationship

Both timed-automata and EAST-ADL are developed for real-time embedded systems. While the purpose of TA is model-checking of generic real-time system, EAST-ADL on the other focuses on describing structural and some behavioral aspects of embedded systems. There exist at least four different possibilities for mapping and relating EAST-ADL with timed-automata. (i) One possibility is to use timed-automata for defining the behavior of a system by exploiting EAST-ADL external behavior representation support (FunctionBehavior in Fig. 1) as done in [15]. (ii) Another possibility is to transform EAST-ADL behavior extension artifacts [9] to timed-automata for behavioral analysis. (iii) A third possibility is to model timing constraints with timed-automata with a suitable behavior abstraction. (iv) Finally, a combination of both timing constraints and EAST-ADL behavior constraints [9] can also be considered for formal analysis using timed-automata. As the internal functional behavior and hence the associated constraints are out of scope of the work, only the timing constraints and design level of abstraction is considered, corresponding to possibilities (iii), with the following assumptions and limitations:

- Only the *Functional Design Architecture* (FDA) is considered. The design level has two parts namely Functional design architecture (FDA) and *Hardware Design Architecture* (HDA). While HDA covers hardware topology, FDA is used to model software components, middleware functions, device drivers and hardware transfer-functions. Hence, FDA together with and constraints such as time budgets applied on its contained functions can provide a suitable abstraction for the target analysis.
- Only one function type i.e. the FDA is allowed to have prototypes of other functions in its composition for the sake of simplicity. An FDA is a DesignFunctionType (Fig. 1) which can contain several parts (DesignFunctionPrototype). Each prototype refers to a type (DesignFunctionType). This kind of modeling allows a hierarchical composition with infinite depth. Such concept of hierarchical decomposition is not possible with timed-automata; therefore, an additional mechanism for flattening the functional hierarchy (if allowed) of EAST-ADL models will be required if hierarchy is allowed.

4.1 Mapping Scheme

This subsection presents a mapping scheme between EAST-ADL and timed-automata. The proposed scheme is based on the experiences from a previous work [10] where a timed-automata model of an existing emergency braking system (EBS)

---

[2] http://www.uppaal.com/

was utilized to identify relevant EAST-ADL artifacts followed by the verification of the mapping by transformation of a representative industrial case-study of a brake-by-wire system in EAST-ADL to timed-automata. The same approach is used for the proposed mapping scheme and its validation. This mapping consists of templates for each function and timing constraint type. The templates for the timing constraints act as monitors indicating if a constraint is met or not. In addition to the description of the semantics of the mapped EAST-ADL artifacts, template implementations in UPPAAL are also presented for illustration.

Event. In terms of timed automata, an event can be modeled as a synchronization action. For example, the synchronization action *output!* for the transition to the final from the execute state shown in b can be considered as an event corresponding to an *EventFunctionFlowPort* referring to a port with direction *out* or *EventFunctionClientServerPort* with kind of either *sentRequest* or *sentResponse*.

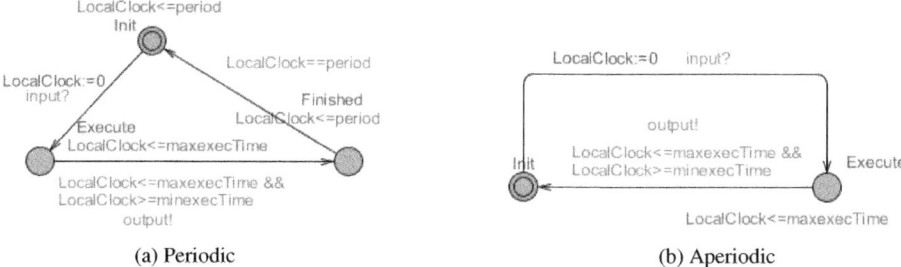

(a) Periodic (b) Aperiodic

Fig. 4. Function templates

Function Execution Behavior. As shown in Fig. 4, a function can be modeled with three or two locations for time-triggered and event triggered systems respectively. The type is determined by the triggering policy of its function trigger shown in Fig. 1. In Fig. 4 , the *Init, Execute* and *Finished* states represent the initial, execution (related to internal behavior) and waiting for the execution period to finish. The parameters *maxexecTime* and *minexecTime* are obtained from *ExecutionTimeConstraint* (Fig. 3) where *max-* and *minexecTime* correspond to the upper and lower limits of timing constraint. On the other hand the period is obtained from *PeriodicEventConstraint* applied on the *EventFunction* referring to the *DesignFunctionType* under consideration. The *input?* and *output!* synchronization actions correspond to reading and writing on all the input and output ports respectively of an EAST-ADL function.

Timing and Event Constraints. A constraint is either satisfied or not satisfied; therefore, four locations corresponding to initial, intermediate, success, fail states are necessary to model a constraint. On occurrence of an event, the automaton proceeds to the intermediate state(s). Based on the applicable guard conditions the *(fail) success* state is reached if a particular constrained is (not) satisfied. Both the timing (related to event chain) and event constraints refer to one or more events. The transition(s) to reach a *fail (safe)* state is enabled by clock guards and synchronization actions representing the timing bounds and event occurrences respectively. Each automaton has a local clock denoted by *LocalClock* in the following text. The event and timing constraint templates are as follows:

Periodic event constraint: A periodic event constraint is used to specify constraints on the periodicity of an event. An UPPAAL template for a periodic event constraint is shown in Fig. 5. The three applied parameters (also shown in Fig. 3) in this template *are period (P), jitter (J) and the minimum arrival time* of the event. The synchronization action "event?" can refer to any event whose periodicity is required to be constrained.

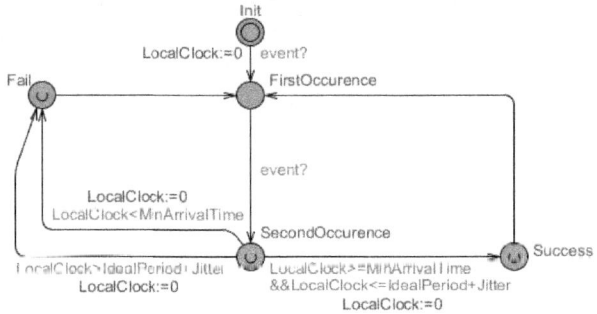

Fig. 5. Periodic event constraint template

Reaction constraint: A reaction constraint specifies a bound between the occurrences of stimuli? and responses of an event chain. According to [3] there exist five possible specification combinations ({upper, lower}, {upper, lower, jitter}, {upper}, {lower}, {nominal, jitter}) for a delay constraint. The presented work considers only one combination i.e. {upper} which corresponds to the maximum time allowed.

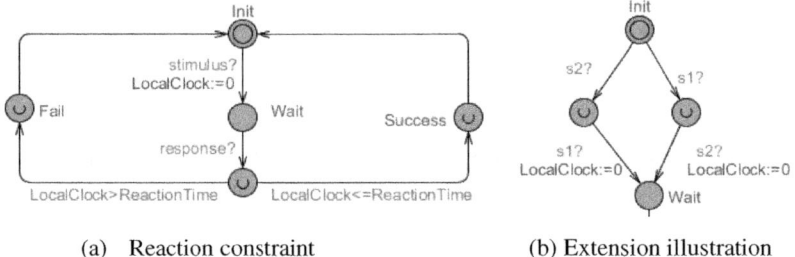

(a) Reaction constraint   (b) Extension illustration

Fig. 6. Reaction constraint template

In the reaction constraint template (Fig. 6a) the clock is reset when a *stimulus* event occurs. As soon as the response event occurs the automata transits to *Fail* or *Success* state depending on the elapsed time i.e. the *LocalClock* value. The template considers only one stimulus and one response. It can be extended for multiple stimuli and responses by adding additional states and parallel transitions. For example, in case of two stimuli, two states between the *Init* and *Wait* states e.g. *s1* and *s2* can be added where the transition from *Init* to *s1* can correspond to the first stimulus occurrence, *s1* to *Wait* corresponding to the second stimulus and vice versa. This is illustrated in Fig. 6b.

Precedence constraint: A precedence constraint specifies the constraint on the order of execution of events. A template for two events is shown in Fig. 7 where *input2* is constrained to occur after *input1*. In order to extend this template for more events additional states can be added similar to reaction constraint leading to the *Fail* and *Success* states.

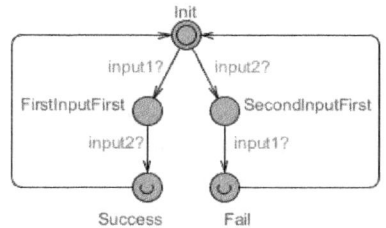

Fig. 7. Precedence event constraint template

Arbitrary event constraint: An arbitrary event constraint specifies bounds on an aperiodic event. The event can occur singly, occasionally or irregularly. The bounds can be specified between two or more occurrences of an event by minimum and maximum arrival time attributes in the form of an array. The element of the array corresponds to the time between the first and later occurrences of an event. For example, the third element corresponds to the time constraint between the first and the fourth event occurrences.

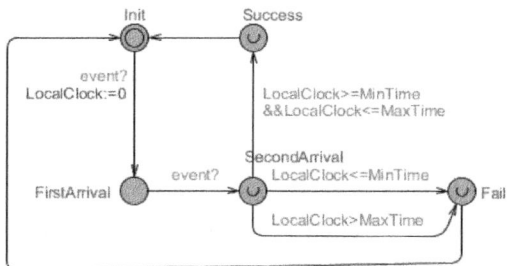

Fig. 8. Arbitrary event constraint template

The template shown in Fig. 8 models bounds on two consecutive occurrence of an event. If it is desired to constraint occurrence of the first and third event then a new state and transition can be added before the clock value is checked. The template can be extended for more than three occurrences in a similar fashion.

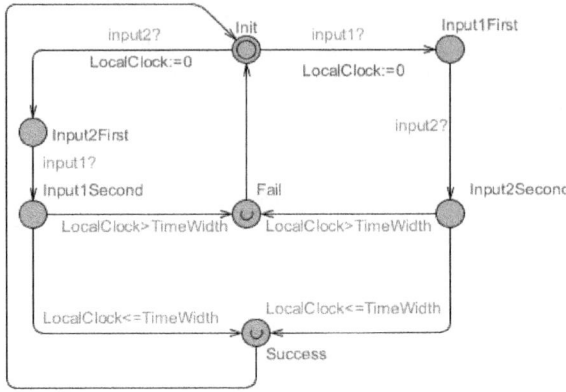

Fig. 9. Input synchronization constraint template

Input and output synchronization constraints: An input synchronization constraint specifies the time width within which a set of stimuli of an event chain should occur. In order to model the input synchronization constraint the automata shown in Fig. 9 is used. The actions *input1?* and *input2?* represent two stimuli and the parameter *Time Width* (represented as *width* in Fig. 3) determines the maximum time allowed between two stimuli.

The output synchronization event is similar to the input synchronization except that instead of response the stimuli are constrained to occur in a specified time width. Therefore, the same template can be used with the responses as inputs. In order to incorporate more events, additional states and transitions corresponding to different combinations of occurrences can be added between *Init* and *Fail* states similar to the reaction time constraint.

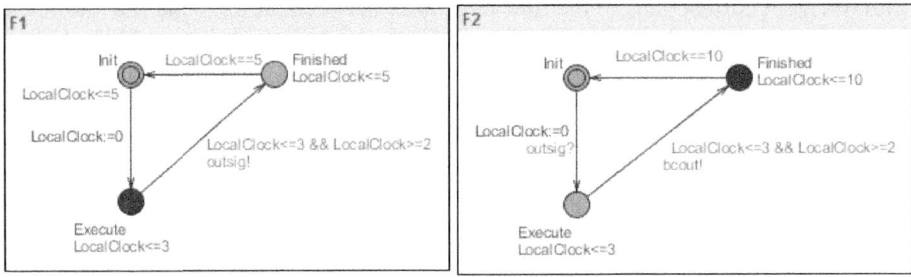

Fig. 10. Execution rate difference illustration

Port Buffer and Execution Rate Difference. An EAST-ADL system is inherently deadlock free due to the semantics of ports discussed in section 2. However, two UPPAAL processes with different periodicities synchronized using channels can theoretically lead to a deadlock situation due to timing mismatch. For example, the two functions *F1* and *F2* are in a deadlock condition shown in Fig. 10. Both *F1* and *F2* have the same minimum and maximum execution time but *F1* has a faster rate of execution (twice in Fig. 10). The deadlock is due to the fact that sender *F1* is ready to output a signal but *F2* is not in the state where it can receive it.

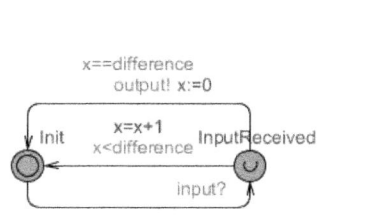 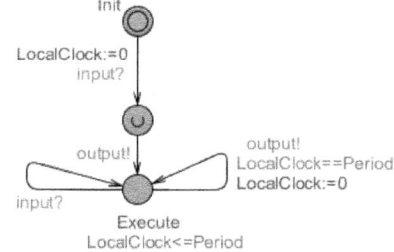

(a) Fast to slow rate transition (b) Slow to fast rate transition

Fig. 11. Rate transition templates

Due to the above mentioned issue, we introduce the concept of rate-transition templates shown in Fig. 11 inspired by the Matlab rate-transition block[3]. The template in Fig. 11a is used when the sender is running at a faster rate (less period) than the receiver. The actions *input?* and *output!* correspond to the input from the sender and output to the receiver respectively. The *difference* parameter is the *difference of frequency* obtained by dividing the period of the receiver with that of sender. For the case where the sender has low frequency, the template in Fig. 11b is used. This template mimics the the EAST-ADL assumed communication mechanism (over-writing semantics). The parameter *Period* corresponds to the period of the receiving function. This solution acts similar to a zero-order hold function in Simulink.

4.2 Verification

With the above defined relationship between EAST-ADL and timed-automata, the verification essentially becomes a reachability analysis in the following form:

1. A given constraint is satisfied iff for all initial conditions, the state "Fail" is never reached for all cases.
2. A system is free of any inconsistencies iff there is not deadlock and all the constraints are satisfied.

4.3 Usage Considerations and Limitations

Template Usage. The templates discussed above exist in several variants depending on the composition of EAST-ADL function and the applied timing constraints. The first variation is the existence of input and output channels. If an EAST-ADL function does not have any input port then a template without an input channel will be chosen and vice versa. Such type of function is shown as *F1* in Fig. 10. The second variation is the type of channel used for synchronization where the rule applied is that *"if an output of a function is an input for two or more functions then the channel is of type broadcast otherwise"*. A function in this case also includes the modeled timing constraints. For example, the output of *F1* in Fig. 10 will be of type broadcast if there

---

[3] http://www.mathworks.se/help/toolbox/simulink/slref/ratetransition.html

another function *F3* exists whose input is the output of *F1*. The function *F3* can be another function or a timing constraint.

In addition to above, consistency between time measurements units have to be ensured by the user. For example, it is now allowed to use *ms* for timing constraint and *ns* for another. In addition, the UPPAAL processes have to be updated with new channel names when rate-transition is used. This is shown in Fig. 13 where BTC and GBC were supposed to communicate with *CalculatedTorque* channel but due to the use of rate-transition *CalcualatedTorque2* channel is introduced in the system description.

To verify a given set of timing constraints of a system specification, the following two query language syntaxes have to be used.

- *A [] (not deadlock)* to verify if there exist any deadlock.
  - Two possible reasons for a deadlock can be (i) the absence of one or more rate-transition templates in case of different frequency between two communicating functions and (ii) an incorrect synchronization channel type. This typically occurs if an ordinary channel type where a broadcast type is required.
- *A [] (not XX.Fail)* to verify that a timing constraint modeled with an UPPAAL process named XX never reaches the failed state.
  - In case a fail state is reached, the timing constraints have one or more inconsistencies.

4.4 Mapping Summary

EAST-ADL	UPPAAL	Remarks
Function Prototype	Fig 4	Type determined by the associated function trigger policy. *Min-* and *max* execution time from the associated execution time constraint and period from the periodic event constraint referring to the *EventFunction* associated with the function.
Periodic event constraint	Fig 5	Direct mapping of event name. *MinArrivalTime* is the *lower* time limit specified by the constraint. Other parameters are directly mapable.
Reaction constraint	Fig 6	Stimulus and response names from the *event chain* in scope, *reaction time* from the *upper* value the timing constraint.
Precedence constraint	Fig 7	Direct mapping of event names.
Arbitrary event constraint	Fig 8	Direct mapping of event name and parameters.
Input synchronization constraint	Fig 9	Event names from list of *stimuli* of the event chain in scope, time width from the upper time limit of the reaction time constraint associated with the event chain.
Output synchronization constraint	Fig 10	Event names from list of *responses* of the event chain in scope, time width from the upper time limit of the reaction time constraint associated with the event chain.
Functional Design Architecture	System	Each of the prototypes in FDA take the form of a process in UPPAAL. The connectors will take the form of synchronization channel.

5 Brake-by-Wire Case Study

The brake-by-wire (BBW) system is a representative industrial case study. This case has been used in several EAST-ADL related projects like ATESST2 and TIMMO. It provides coverage of EAST-ADL artifacts and methodology at multiple abstraction levels. A simplified version of the case is shown in Fig. 12. The figure is a snapshot from its EAST-ADL (UML profile[4]) implementation. For simplicity, three actuators, ABS functions and their connections are not shown in the figure. The triggers, events and constraints of the case study are listed in the following tables:

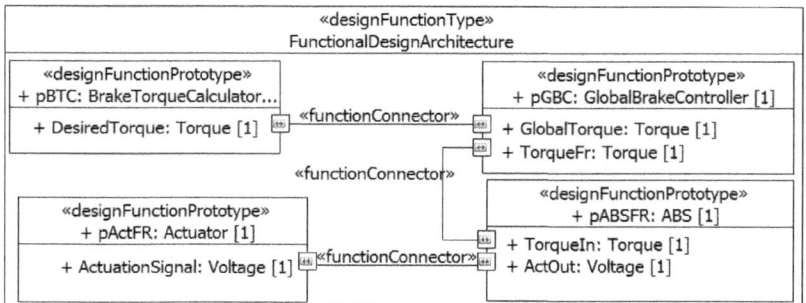

Fig. 12. UML implementation of the Brake-by-wire system

Table 1. Function Triggers

Trigger Name	Attributes
BTCTriggerEvent	TargetFunctionPrototype=pBTC, TriggerPolicy = Time
GBCTriggerEvent	TargetFunctionPrototype=pGBC, TriggerPolicy = Time
ABSFRTrigger	TargetFunctionFlowPort=pABSFR, TriggerPolicy=Event
ABSFLTrigger	TargetFunctionFlowPort=pABSFL, TriggerPolicy =Event
ABSRRTrigger	TargetFunctionFlowPort=pABSRR, TriggerPolicy =Event
ABSRLTrigger	TargetFunctionFlowPort=pABSRL, TriggerPolicy =Event

Table 2. Events

Event Name	Type	Attributes
BTCTriggerEvent	EventFunction	TargetFunctionPrototype=pBTC
GBCTriggerEvent	EventFunction	TargetFunctionPrototype=pGBC
CalculatedTorque	EventFunctionFlowPort	TargetFunctionFlowPort=DesiredTorque TargetFunctionPrototype=pBTC
actuation1	EventFunctionFlowPort	TargetFunctionFlowPort=ActOut TargetFunctionPrototype=pABSFR

---

[4] http://www.maenad.eu/public/
EAST-ADL-ProfileSpecification_M2.1.9.pdf

Table 3. Event Chain

Event Chain Name	Attributes
EC1	Stimulus = CaclulatedTorque, Response = actuation1

Table 4. Constraints

Constraint Name	Type	Attributes
BTCExecution	Execution time	TargetFunctionPrototype=pBTC , Lower = 3 , Upper =5
GBCExecution	Execution time	TargetFunctionPrototype=pGBC, Lower = 2, Upper =6
ABSFRExecution	Execution time	TargetFunctionPrototype=pABSFR, Lower = 2, Upper =3
ABSFLExecution	Execution time	TargetFunctionPrototype=pABSFL, Lower = 2, Upper =3
ABSRRExecution	Execution time	TargetFunctionPrototype=pABSRR, Lower = 2, Upper =3
ABSRLExecution	Execution time	TargetFunctionPrototype=pABSRL, Lower = 2, Upper =3
RC1	Reaction	Scope = EC1, ReactionTime = 50 ms
PEC1	Periodic event	TargetEvent= CaculatedTorque, MinArrivalTime= 3ms, IdealPeriod = 10 ms, Jitter = 9 ms
PCC1	Precedence	Preceding – CalculatedTorque, Successive = actuation1

An UPPAAL model of a subset of the constraints and functions described above is shown in Fig. 13.

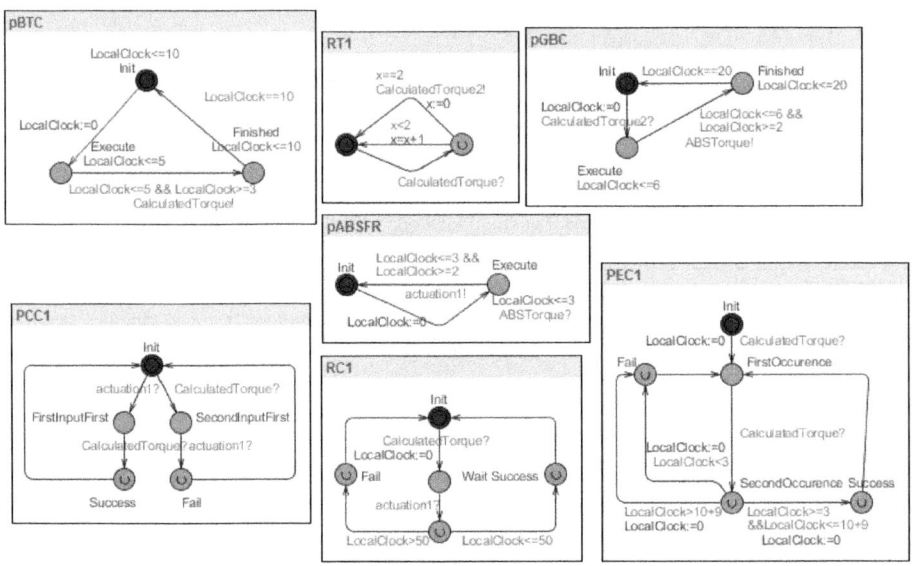

Fig. 13. Brake-by-wire model in UPPAAL

In the above figure, pBTC, pGBC and pABSFR are function prototypes shown in Fig. 12b. RT1 is a rate transition process added between pBTC and pGBC. PCC1, RC1 and PEC1 are listed in Table 4 where clock guards (in green) correspond to the listed timing values. As listed in Table 1 pABSFR is event triggered whereas pBTC and pGBC are time triggered. The stimulus and response of the event chain in scope of RC1 is listed in Table 3 with the corresponding events in Table 2.

All the constraints were found to be satisfying the specifications for the BBW system. Experiments were made to validate the templates. It included changing the periodicity of BTC and the order of inputs for the precedence constraint i.e. by using BTC output as the successive event instead of the preceding one. The latter case is shown in Fig. 13. Intuitively an increase in the period of BTC to a particular level should violate the periodicity constraint. The same observation was made with the UPPAAL model. Similarly, the change in the order of sequence leads to the *Fail* state of the precedence constraint.

6 Related Work

A number of efforts have been carried out to enable the analysis, verification and validation of system architecture design captured in EAST-ADL. This paper is an extension of [10] where the work was limited to the reaction time constraint and evaluation of the possibility of model transformation between EAST-ADL and UPPAAL. [11] presents an effort to integrate the SPIN model checker for formal verification of EAST-ADL models. The automata addressed by SPIN are untimed and the SPIN transformation needs to be updated for the latest EAST-ADL release. Furthermore, the timing constraint package used in this work is a subset of TADL (Timing Augmented Description Language) [12] developed by the TIMMO project consortium[5]. The authors of [13] proposed the use of MARTE[6] for complementing EAST-ADL to enable timing analysis. A method for timed-automata based analysis of EAST-ADL models is presented in [15] where timed-automata are used for behavior analysis and modeling. The work in this paper complements the above cited references by providing a method to check the consistency of the timing constraints before they are actually used for detailed timing analysis of any kind.

7 Discussion

A method to analyze consistency in timing constraints specified using EAST-ADL is presented. The proposed mapping scheme is a basis for transformations between EAST-ADL and timed-automata based tools. Our earlier work [10] shows that it is possible to automate model transformations between EAST-ADL and UPPAAL based on their meta-models. The transformation using the concept of templates is a part of the planned future work where the main challenge is the absence of one-to-one mappings, unidirectional links from EAST-ADL extensions to core language constructs and, the variations due to the usage criteria mentioned in section 4.

---

[5] `http://timmo-2-use.org/`
[6] `http://www.omg.org/spec/MARTE/1.0/`

There also exists possibility to generate test cases from the timing constraints which can later be used to test the final product or its prototype. A further investigation of EAST-ADL is required for such support. Another issue which requires investigation is the combined analysis of internal behavior and timing constraints and the method to transfer the results of analysis back for storing them as part of the EAST-ADL model using its verification and validation extension.

References

1. Törngren, M., Chen, D., Malvious, D., Axelsson, J.: Model-Based Development of Automotive Embedded Systems. In: Automotive Embedded Sytems Handbook (2009)
2. Lönn, H., Freund, U.: Automotive Architecture Description Languages. In: Automotive Embedded Systems Handbook (2009)
3. The ATESST2 Consortium, EAST-ADL Domain Model Specification, Project Deliverable 4.1.1 (June 2010), http://www.atesst.org/home/liblocal/docs/ATESST2_D4.1.1_EAST-ADL2-Specification_2010-06-02.pdf
4. AUTOSAR Website, http://www.autosar.org/ (accessed January 2011)
5. Road vehicles – Functional Safety, International Organization for Standardization, ISO 26262 (Draft International Standard) (2009)
6. PapyrusUML Website, http://www.papyrusuml.org (accessed January 2011)
7. Behrmann, G., David, A., Larsen, K.G.: A Tutorial on UPPAAL. In: Bernardo, M., Corradini, F. (eds.) SFM-RT 2004. LNCS, vol. 3185, pp. 200–236. Springer, Heidelberg (2004)
8. Bengtsson, J.E., Yi, W.: Timed Automata: Semantics, Algorithms and Tools. In: Desel, J., Reisig, W., Rozenberg, G. (eds.) ACPN 2003. LNCS, vol. 3098, pp. 87–124. Springer, Heidelberg (2004)
9. The ATESST2 Consortium, Update Suggestions for Behavior Support, Project Deliverable 3.1, Appendix A3.4 (June 2010), http://www.atesst.org/home/liblocal/docs/ATESST2_Deliverable_D3.1_A3.4_V1.1.pdf
10. Qureshi, T.N., Chen, D.J., Persson, M., Törngren, M.: Towards the Integration of EAST-ADL and UPPAAL for Formal Verification of EAST-ADL Timing Constraint Specification. Presented at TiMoBD (Time Analysis and Model-Based Design, from Functional Models to Distributed Deployments) Workshop, October 9 (2011)
11. Feng, L., Chen, D.J., Lönn, H., Törngren, M.: Verifying System Behaviors in EAST-ADL2 with the SPIN Model Checker. In: IEEE International Conference on Mechatronics and Automation, Xi'an, China, August 4-7 (2010)
12. The TIMMO Consortium, TADL: Timing Augmented Description Language Version 2, Project Deliverable 6 (2009),
http://www.timmo.org/pdf/D6_TIMMO_TADL_Version_2_v12.pdf
13. Mallet, F., Peraldi-Frati, M.A., André, C.: Marte CCSL to Execute East-ADL Timing Requirements. In: Proceedings of ISORC 2009, pp. 249–253 (2009)
14. Object Management Group. UML Profile for MARTE: Modeling and Analysis of Real-Time Embedded Systems, formal/2009-11-02 (2009),
http://www.omg.org/spec/MARTE/1.0/PDF
15. Kang, E.-Y., Schobbens, P.-Y., Pettersson, P.: Verifying Functional Behaviors of Automotive Products in EAST-ADL2 Using UPPAAL-PORT. In: Flammini, F., Bologna, S., Vittorini, V. (eds.) SAFECOMP 2011. LNCS, vol. 6894, pp. 243–256. Springer, Heidelberg (2011)

Code Generation Nirvana

Petr Smolik and Pavel Vitkovsky

Metada
{petr.smolik,pavel.vitkovsky}@metada.com

Abstract. Life is fun and prospect of reincarnations is thus very attractive. People enjoy various ways how models may be transformed to executable code, how information may be derived, enriched, superimposed. It could take a number of complex transformations to reach the state of nirvana of a finally running application. Each such model transformation is like a reincarnation, new existence in a different body, the spirit mostly staying the same. We have been for years fascinated with this and tried different ways and approaches and we are experiencing a progress. We have extensively applied code generation in areas of enterprise systems integration and enterprise frontends. During time we have done code generation different ways into different target languages and we have also done a lot of direct model interpretation. More and more we value nirvana over many reincarnations, nevertheless there is still place left for code generation. In this paper we share our model-driven experience.

Keywords: Code Generation, Domain-Specific Modeling (DSM), Domain-Specific Modeling Languages (DSML), Model-Driven Engineering (MDE), Model Interpretation, Executable Models, XML, XSLT, XQuery.

1 Introduction

Model-driven approaches deal with system complexity by introducing higher levels of abstraction. Models abstract from technology specifics and attempt to focus on the important aspects of a given problem domain. The best models talk in terms of the domain expert's concepts and enable definition of systems by means of defining and relating instances of these concepts. The ability to directly express the domain-specific knowledge in models leads to higher efficiency in systems design and implementation. [1][2][3][4][5]

Nevertheless there are obstacles. It is hard to identify the right concepts on the right levels of abstraction. It is always easier to settle down on abstractions that are closer to the solution space where the resulting systems or applications are actually implemented, but it is much harder to find the right abstractions that are closer to the actual problem domain and its concepts.

Our experience comes mostly from the financial services domain, where one would expect to manipulate concepts like account, payment, transaction, or loan. But we did not manage to reach this level of abstraction in our models yet. We still do not configure current accounts and loan accounts, and enact their models in running applications. One of the reasons may be that financial institutions have many core systems already in place and their new needs are being satisfied by introducing dozens of new systems around the old ones and then heavily integrating their functionalities via integration layers, while trying to build unified frontends, since it is unbearable for the branch employees to tackle thirty different unintegrated ways to manage several customer's financial products.

For this reason the domain-specific modeling languages that we have so far designed were centered more around integration and frontends. The abstractions that are defined, manipulated, related, documented, and managed are not accounts, but components, operations, action flows, mappings, mapping tables, forms and their widgets, all this being composed into specific channel applications within multi-channel solutions. We still consider these modeling languages domain-specific, but their focus is in the integration or channel application domains, not in the financial services domain. Nevertheless, our ongoing goal is to reach higher and tackle the real business.

In the following chapters of this paper we do not present specifics of our metamodels for integration and multi-channel applications. These are not that interesting and could be shown on tools presentations. What we found interesting during the process of designing model-driven systems is the process of reaching model execution, either via code generation, or direct model interpretation, or something between.

2 Model Executability

Executability of models means that it is possible to transform models into executable form without any further coding in some general-purpose programming language. Models defined in domain-specific modeling languages (DSMLs) may be executable if these languages are designed to be executable.

Model is executable when it is possible to create a running application just by creating the model. The goal is to model as little as possible, but still all that is needed. The core thing that makes models to be relatively simple and abstract is constraint. Only as little as possible set of concepts should be manipulated in the model and limits should be imposed on the variabilities provided by these concepts. Everything else is „an execution framework" (or "domain framework"). An execution framework enables the models to „live". It interprets the attributes of entities defined in the model. It enacts them. Framework may be written as components constructed using a general-purpose programming language. Framework may be composed also from various interpreters interpreting different transformed representations of models. It is possible to explore these various ways to make models executable.

We think of code generation as means to make models executable. Not to generate skeletons that need to be completed with hand-written final code. Code generation transforms, maybe in several steps (reincarnations), models into machine-executable code. It is also possible to directly execute models with interpreters specifically written to execute them based on their metamodels. Code generation and model interpretation are then two different alternative strategies to "implement" execution tools [6]. Interestingly, the process of code generation is a process of model interpretation. The execution of the resulting code is not.

3 Chicken or an Egg

The evolution of programming languages in themselves (bootstrapping) is well known [7]. It is interesting to see this in the domain-specific languages. Take for example a language to define how specific XML data should be retrieved from tables of a relational database. Such language is for example the XML Data Access (XDA) language [8]. This language has been used in our modeling tool and it represents a modeling language in the domain of retrieval of XML data from relational databases. Models in the XDA language are mostly concerned with "concepts" that correspond to tables in a relational database and "concept views" that define tree structures over the graph of related concepts.

XDA interpreter executes models defined in the XDA language. This interpreter will always take an XML definition of what data should be retrieved and will perform the actual retrieval by calling a relational database and join data from various tables into a complex XML document.

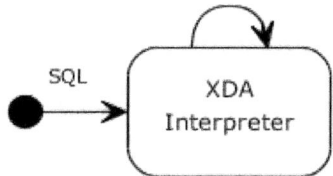

```
(start)-SQL>(XDA\nInterpreter)-resulting XML data used as
its own model>(XDA\nInterpreter)¹
```

It starts to be interesting when we store the specific XDA models in the database. In such a case, in order to retrieve the XDA model from the database we need the model itself. Without itself the model could not be retrieved. The model is like a chicken and the result of interpretation is like an egg. But there is no egg without a chicken. In the beginning there had to be some, if the simplest, chicken or an egg. Thus for the XDA interpreter to start working, it is necessary to hand-create the chicken-like XDA model.

This seems to be also applicable in the area of GUI interpreters. Take for example an "Editor Interpreter". The purpose of an editor interpreter is to enable editing of a structure of data. This structure may be expressed as an XML. For a specific editor, the editor interpreter is configured with an editor model. We could imagine that this is also expressed as an XML, though it generally does not have to.

The editor interpreter takes the editor model and provides user a GUI for editing a chunk of data. Initially an editor model (a chicken) has to be hand-created, nevertheless it is thereafter possible to use the proto-editor to edit its own definition (an egg) and expand it to increase its ability. Of course this means that the editor interpreter may also need some expanding.

---

[1] Images were generated via simple UML activity diagram DSL and image generator available at http://yuml.me/.

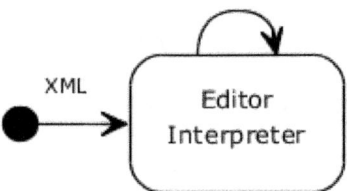

XML editor model edited with its own editor

```
(start)-XML>(Editor\nInterpreter)-XML editor definition
edited with its own editor>(Editor\nInterpreter)
```

When creating executable models this self-defining property is often encountered. It does not matter if interpreters are simple or complex, or whether there are many or few model transformation stages. Initially we started with interpretation via many complex transformations and intermediary interpretations and later we progressed to more directly interpreted solutions as shown in the following sections.

4 Integration Reincarnations

Enterprise application integration (EAI) enables several independent systems to communicate chunks of data among each other to fulfill particular purpose. Technically this may be implemented in various ways based on different technologies. From the modeling perspective the format is not really important. What is important is the way how data are structured, how the system interfaces differ, and how they are mapped to each other.

4.1 Many Reincarnations

We faced situation that large amount of integration was to be done and C++ was the required target language because of speed concerns. XSLT [9] and XQuery [10] were then too new and too slow. In order to get the large amount of production grade C++ integration code we created an integration modeling language.

In our case integration models define specific integration services and their operations. Each operation has an input and output interface defined as a tree structure of data that may be composed directly or with the help of reusable complex types. An operation may directly represent some external functionality to be called, or may define a composite flow that calls several other operations. Each composite flow is composed of actions, mainly call actions that call other operations and decision actions that decide on what routes should be taken in the flow. Data mappings are defined on each action call to provide proper inputs to operations being called. These mappings use a simple expression language modeled as a computation tree that enables mapping of diverse structures to each other.

Models in the integration modeling language were persisted in a database and edited with our generated editors.

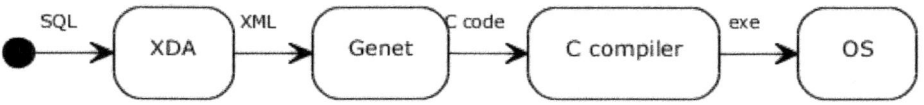

```
(start)-SQL>(XDA)-XML>(Genet)-C code>(C compiler)-
exe>(OS)
```

XML Data Access (XDA) [8] interpreter was used to obtain the model from a relational database. We hand-created several transformation XSLTs and used Genet interpreter to orchestrate complex transformations to create high-quality and optimized C++ code.

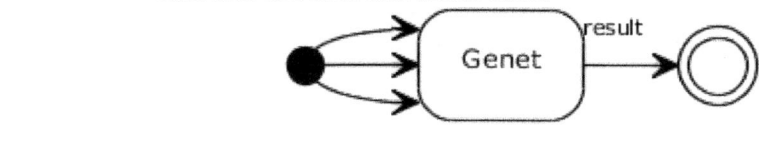

```
(start)->(Genet)-result>(end),
(start)->(Genet),
(start)-XML data and XSLs and Genet model>(Genet)
```

The Genet interpreter itself executes several steps of model transformations based on a Genet model. Genet is an interpreter of a configuration of a transformation pipeline. It interprets a network of gen nodes where each gen node represents one particular XSLT or XQuery transformation that may have outputs of several other gen nodes as its sources. So before resulting C++ comes out, there may be several intermediary transformations. Intermediary transformations are partial derivations of the source model, so that it is in the end easier to come-up with cleanest and nicest code possible. Intermediary transformations are themselves further model reincarnations into intermediary languages.

Finally, the resulting generated C++ code was compiled and executed. The mapping model contained service interface definitions on a service bus, service interfaces of backend services, and large amount of mapping and routing rules. The resulting executable implements transformation from one structure of message to another, for many message types, data formats (not only XML), and many integrated systems.

In order for the model to be morphed into an executable code this way it takes many transformations (SQL->XML....->XML...->XML->C code->exe).

4.2 Fewer and Fewer Reincarnations

The previous many-reincarnations integration solution lived for several years before new integration solutions came to the market and enabled XQuery to be used for data mapping and routing effectively. We switched from C++ generation to XQuery generation. The models did not have to change, only model transformations did. It became easier to develop and test the integration solution because the step of lengthy C++ compilation was skipped.

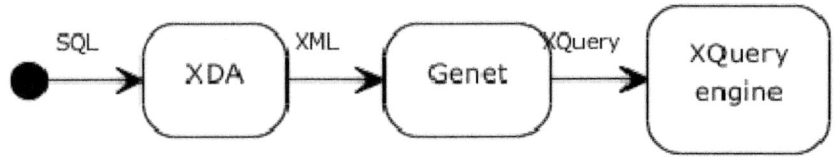

(start)-SQL>(XDA)-XML>(Genet)-XQuery>(XQuery\nengine)

Model transformations were now less complex, because XQuery is a transformation language (a transformation DSL) whereas C++ is a general-purpose language. The step of lengthy compilation was also removed since XQuery is directly executed by the XQuery engine.

Further on, it slowly became clear that the relational database is not the greatest place to store models. So we decided that direct representation of models in XML would improve the situation.

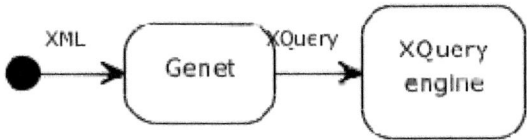

(start)-XML>(Genet)-XQuery>(XQuery\nengine)

The situation was better, but it still took quite a while for the whole solution of hundreds to thousands of XQueries to be generated from models. So in the end one of our colleagues wrote a mapping interpreter. The interpreter takes an XML representation of the model and directly interprets it to provide the data mapping services.

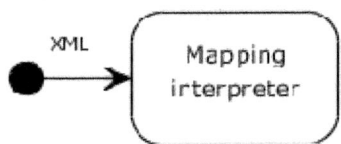

(start)-XML>(Mapping\ninterpreter)

Now there is no transformation at all. No code generation whatsoever. No reincarnations. Direct nirvana. Nevertheless, at the moment we do not have enough long-term experience with the mapping interpreter. The complexity of code generation may or may not have just moved into the complexity of the interpreter. Metamodel concepts are now represented as entities in the general-purpose programming language that the interpreter is written in (Java). Interpretation is provided real-time by manipulating the input data based on the metamodel entities. It is completely different than code generation. Interpretation directly produces behavior, not code to be executed.

5 User Interface Reincarnations

To enable creation and use of domain-specific modeling languages on our projects we developed a web-based modeling and metamodeling solution. Interestingly, with this solution we have also experienced similar history of lowering number of transformations. In this case it was about transformations of metamodels into functioning model editors.

In these user interface models we are mainly concerned with defining tree-structured editors for individual model object types. Model objects need to be listed, edited, and each object, based on its type, may have any number of levels with composite sub-objects that again need to be listed and edited.

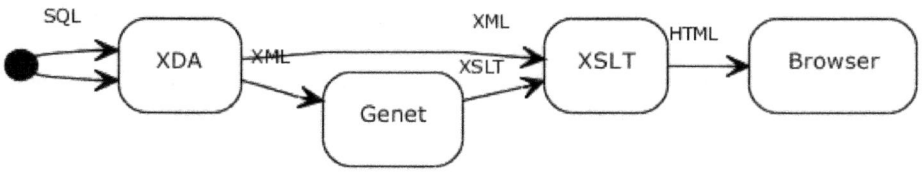

```
(start)->(XDA)-XML>(XSLT)-HTML>(Browser),
(start)-SQL>(XDA)-XML>(Genet)-XSLT>(XSLT)
```

We started with a system that utilized XSLs to build an application GUIs and required a set of XML definition files to configure the XML Data Access interpreter used to obtain XML data from a relational database. In order to be able to create GUIs effectively, we developed an editor modeling language that was used to define editors and all the XML configurations for the data access. All the XSLT transformations were suddenly generated for the GUIs. There were XSLTs that were used to generate XSLTs. This enabled fast creation of modeling GUIs without having to write SQL queries or transformations to HTML.

Although this solution is quite interesting, it is also very complex and hard to maintain and extend. There are probably too many reincarnations of the model before it is really executed. Recently we work on removing this complex set of transformations and would like to reach the nirvana of a running application as fast as possible.

The newly designed editor interpreter will directly interpret the editor definition (a model) and enable to edit the corresponding data. Apart from producing HTML that is still interpreted at the browser, nirvana will be reached quickly without many complex reincarnations.

```
(start)->(Editor\ninterpreter)-HTML>(Browser),(start)-XML
editor definition and data>(Editor\ninterpreter)
```

We hypothesize that an ecosystem of various model interpreters will enable faster construction of applications. It is possible that there will be model interpreters that will encapsulate within themselves the actual stages of code generation, compilation, and final execution. The question may not be whether code generation or direct interpretation. Both may suit some situations better. They may also be combined. Interpretation and code generation should thus be seen as continuum and not as two alternatives [11].

6 Conclusion

Reaching code generation nirvana means getting out a running application out of a set of executable models. Models may be expressed in domain-specific modeling languages (DSMLs) that are interpreted by code generators that generate executable code or directly interpreted by purpose-built model interpreters. Such interpreters use their internal representation of a model to provide expected useful behavior. Direct model interpretation is different than code generation, because code generation focuses on creating an executable code. The code generation process itself is the process of model interpretation, but the final result of code generation is an executable that does the real work, not interpretation.

There are pros and cons of both approaches [12]. The complexity of code generation could just move into complexity of interpreters, though we hope not. Code generation may result in highly optimized code and faster execution, whereas interpretation removes the steps of generation and code compilation so that the models can be executed directly as they change, which may result in faster development. It is possible to generate code into several target languages and environments at the same time. Similarly it is possible to write the same interpreters in different languages or run the same on different platforms. Model interpreters just may have been undervalued and should be used more in practice [13]. There are arguments that model interpretation is a superior approach for developing the models themselves [14] and importance of in-IDE interpretation and testing is also being stressed [11].

An interesting area of research is what general-purpose languages are best for what types of model interpreters. Dynamic languages that enable to program themselves during runtime provide facilities for executing some steps of code generation during interpretation itself.

Life has its twists and turns and reincarnations will remain attractive. Not all code generation will be replaced by direct interpretation, but we expect there will be a growing number of various interpreters of different domain-specific modeling languages. If these interpreters will internally use code generation or not may remain their private implementation detail.

References

1. Stahl, T., Völter, M.: Model-Driven Software Development Technology, Engineering, Management. Wiley (2006)
2. Schmidt, D.: Model-Driven Engineering. IEEE Computer 39(2), 25–32 (2006)

3. Kelly, S., Tolvanen, J.P.: Domain-Specific Modeling. Enabling Full Code Generation. John Wiley & Sons, Inc. (2008)
4. Favre, J.M.: Towards a basic theory to model model driven engineering. In: Proceedings of the Workshop on Software Model Engineering, WiSME (2004)
5. Smolik, P.: Mambo Metamodeling Environment, Doctoral Thesis, Brno University of Technology (2006), http://www.mambomde.com/MamboMDE.pdf
6. Cabot, J.: Executable models vs code-generation vs model interpretation (2010), http://modeling-languages.com/executable-models-vs-code-generation-vs-model-interpretation-2/
7. Terry, P.T.: Compilers and Compiler Generators: An Introduction With C++. International Thomson Computer Press (1997)
8. Smolik, P., Tesacek, J.: Data Source Independent XML Data Access. In: Proceedings of Information System Modeling Conference 2000, Rožnov pod Radhoštěm, CZ, MARQ, pp. 17–22 (2000)
9. Kay, M. (ed.): XSL Transformations (XSLT) Version 2.0. W3C Recommendation (January 23, 2007)
10. Boag, S., Chamberlin, D., et al. (eds.): XQuery 1.0: An XML Query Language, 2nd edn. W3C Recommendation (December 14, 2010)
11. Völter, M.: MD*/DSL Best Practices (2011), http://www.voelter.de/data/pub/DSLBestPractices-2011Update.pdf
12. Den Haan, J.: Model Driven Development: Code Generation or Model Interpretation? (2010), http://www.theenterprisearchitect.eu/archive/2010/06/28/model-driven-development-code-generation-or-model-interpretation
13. Völter, M.: Model-Driven Development of DSL Interpreters Using Scala and oAW (2008), http://www.voelter.de/data/presentations/MDInterpreterDevelopment.pdf
14. Chaves, R.: Model interpretation vs. code generation? Both (2010), http://abstratt.com/blog/2010/08/07/model-interpretation-vs-code-generation-both/

A Plug-in Based Approach for UML Model Simulation

Alek Radjenovic, Richard F. Paige, Louis M. Rose, Jim Woodcock,
and Steve King

Department of Computer Science, The University of York, United Kingdom
{alek,paige,louis,jim,king}@cs.york.ac.uk

Abstract. Model simulation is a credible approach for model validation, complementary to others such as formal verification and testing. For UML 2.x, model simulations are available for state machines and communication diagrams; alternative finer-grained simulations, e.g., as are supported for Executable UML, are not available without significant effort (e.g., via profiles or model transformations). We present a flexible, plug-in based approach to enhance UML model simulation. We show how an existing simulation tool applicable to UML behavioural models can be extended to support external action language processors. The presented approach paves the way to enrich existing UML-based simulation tools with the ability to simulate external action languages.

1 Introduction

The UML 2.x standard supports modelling of behaviour through a number of mechanisms, including state machines and activity diagrams, and pre- and postconditions expressed in OCL. In parallel, executable dialects of UML have been developed to support more fine-grained specification of behaviour using *action languages*. As a result, these languages support rich simulation and code generation from models, but they are not directly supported by UML 2.x compliant tools, nor are they based on the same metamodels as UML 2.x. If modellers want to use action languages (and supporting simulators) with UML 2.x models and tools, they either have to acquire a tool that already provides such capabilities (which may not support their exact simulation requirements), or make use of, e.g., model transformations to a different set of languages and supporting tools.

We present a flexible, plug-in based approach for UML model simulation. We show how existing modelling and simulation tools capable of processing UML behavioural models can be extended to support external action language processors, including for their simulation. This is achieved through precisely modelling the interfaces between the modelling tool and an external action language processor, and implemented using a plug-in mechanism. The approach supports enrichment of UML modelling and simulation tools with simulation capability for action languages. The approach even enables addition of *further* action languages to UML tools that already possess one, thus allowing engineers to increase and tailor the simulation support available in the existing tools.

This approach has been developed to meet industry requirements, in the context of the European FP7 project INESS, to (i) provide enhanced simulation support for existing railway interlocking models, particularly for safety analysis and validation; and (ii) without requiring new modelling tools to be purchased or developed.

As a result of our work, we have modified an existing UML 2.x modelling and simulation tool in several ways. We have: (i) extended its internal behavioural metamodel to support embedded expressions specified in external languages, (ii) enabled the tool to support a plug-in mechanism, and (iii) extended the tool's functionality with a new set of services compliant with the interfaces mentioned above. Importantly, the operation of the tool in the absence of external plug-ins is identical to the normal operation of the tool prior to the modifications. We have also implemented a plug-in based on an existing action language, and validated our approach using a number of real-world case studies from the railway signalling domain, as we describe later in the paper.

As opposed to existing approaches, we tried to generalise the interactions between a UML simulation tool and an *external* language processor, allowing the capability of existing tools to be augmented without further tool development.

The remainder of the paper is structured as follows. Section 2 presents the background and context. Section 3 presents the overall requirements for tool support (both modelling and simulation), and the mechanisms used to flexibly extend existing tools to support external action languages. Section 4 presents examples of industrial application and describes how the approach exploiting the plug-in based approach was assessed. Section 5 summarises related work, and we analyse the effectiveness of the approach in the conclusions in Section 6.

2 Context and Background

This work was undertaken within the INESS (Integrated European Signalling System), funded by the FP7 programme of the European Union. This industrial project focused on producing a common, integrated, railway signalling system within Europe. Signalling systems are perhaps the most significant part of the railway infrastructure. They are essential for the performance and safety of train operations. A significant number of large UML models produced by the signalling experts using a tool called CASSANDRA [7] (a plug-in for the UML tool Artisan [1]) had been developed. The input models comprise UML class and state machine diagrams and are used to model railway signalling systems and simulate their execution. In addition, the models were enriched with expressions described in CASSANDRA's bespoke action language, SIML. A strict requirement in the project was that modelling tools (Artisan) remain unchanged, for the purposes of validation (engineers were unwilling to change the tools or the way in which they used them, partly because model modification was too expensive).

Engineers also used CASSANDRA to perform simulations, in order to check functional properties and explore safety requirement violations. The simulations were executed via a Prolog-based engine [8], and as such the simulator was considered to be slow and inefficient by engineers. Additionally, customisation of the simulator was not possible. Requirements for more fine-grained control of simulations were expressed by the industry engineers.

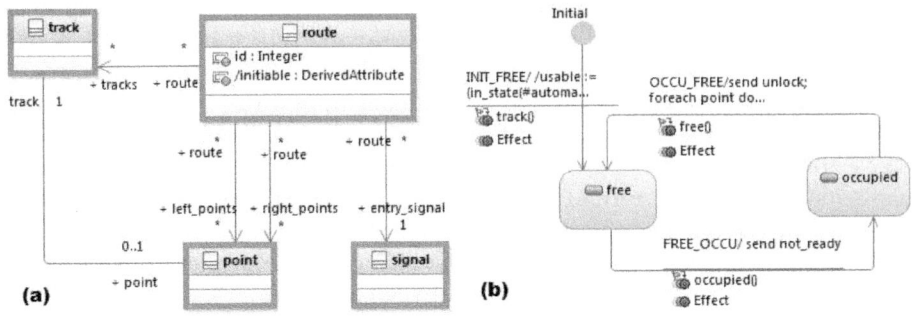

Fig. 1. (a) Class diagram; and (b) State machine for Track class

A simplified excerpt of a class diagram is shown in Fig 1 (a). The UML state machine in Fig. 1 (b) models the behaviour of Track objects. The expressions that follow the transition names, such as '*send not_ready*' are written using SIML [7]. SIML is composed of *four parts* that roughly deal with the following concerns of model simulation:

- *declaration* – allows users to define basic elements, typically corresponding to the UML model elements (classes, events, etc.) that can be read directly from the input model *only if CASSANDRA is used*; also, define elements not present in the original model (e.g. inputs from the environment)
- *expression* – assists users in building and evaluating complex expressions (classified according to the data type) formed from multiple elements
- *action* – provides mechanisms to define elementary pieces of behaviour (e.g. creation/deletion of instances and association links); invocation of behaviours defined in the source model (e.g. class operations or transition triggers)
- *control* – allows users to combine elementary actions into ordered sequences and iterations

Engineers working on INESS had created a substantial number of railway signalling models using the CASSANDRA extensions to Artisan. The simulation capabilities of CASSANDRA did not provide adequate performance or scalability to sufficiently validate the models, explore them, and provide assurance that safety properties were met. As a result, new requirements for simulation were specified. In particular, it was mandated that engineers would still be able to use CASSANDRA (and Artisan), that the existing action language would still be supported, but external simulators (that were more efficient, more scalable, or performed better) that would also simulate the action language could be exploited.

To satisfy the industrial requirements to provide richer and higher performance simulation capabilities while still retaining use of CASSANDRA/Artisan, we have developed a plug-in based approach, detailed in the next section. Our development so far has connected a specific external language processor and a simulation tool as proof-of-concept to the railway signalling engineers. The external processor is capable of parsing an action language and making requests into the simulation tool's API (e.g. to create objects, or fire events), but has awareness of the global clock, tasks, message queues, and other standard simulation tool's resources. The simulation tool is based on the SMILE platform [15,14]. The tool's architecture is shown in Fig. 2, and its operation is best described using the following scenario.

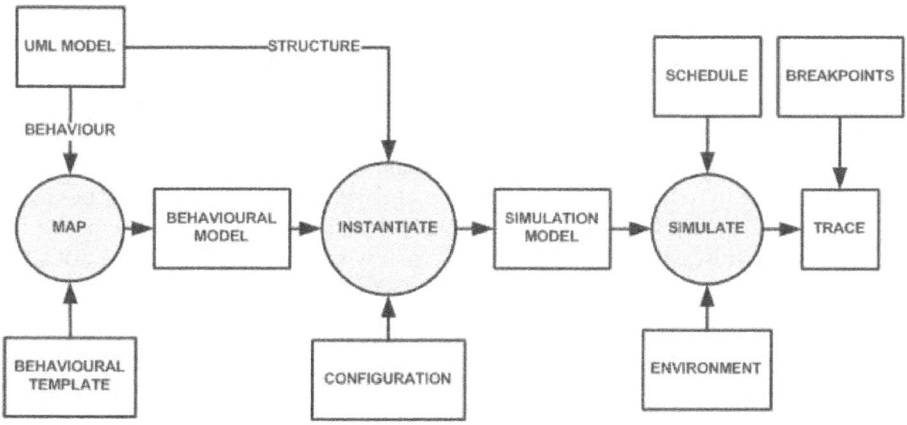

Fig. 2. Simulation tool architecture

The input UML model (created by any UML compatible tool) is first queried (as explained in [15]) in order to extract the behavioural information from state diagrams (states, transitions, triggers, etc.). This is then mapped to a state machine *behavioural template* defined in one of the SMILE family of languages to produce a set of types which describe only the behaviour of UML model components. The set of types is stored in a *behavioural model*. In parallel, the input model is also queried to generate structural information (e.g. from class diagrams). The next step involves using manual *configuration* (supported graphically by the tool) to create a *simulation model*. The simulation model is a set of instances of types from the behavioural model that also take into consideration the structural hierarchy obtained in the previous step.

The simulation tool supports concurrency in the form of tasks which provide execution separation. Consequently, in the *configuration* step, users may define multiple tasks and map each simulation object to one of them. After selecting a *scheduling mode*, the simulation can be run. Optionally, users can define the system's environment in the form of one or more stimuli. The tool produces a simulation trace, providing a detailed report on events that occurred during the simulation (e.g. triggers, transitions, message queues, or unsatisfied conditions).

3 The Plug-in Based Approach

The existing tool could simulate basic UML behaviours (described by standard UML behaviour diagrams). More fine-grained behaviour descriptions could only be provided using external action language expressions. Thus, the key objective was to provide a flexible plug-in mechanism to allow connection and interoperation between the tool and the external language processor, and to allow us to detach, disable or replace the new simulation capability when not needed. The work was divided into the following packages:

1. Inclusion of *external* (SIML) behavioural data from the input model into the *simulation models* (Fig. 2.), ensuring additional data in the simulation model is ignored by default, avoiding disruption of the existing tool operation.
2. Enhancement of the simulation tool so that it provides a mechanism for plug-ins capable of processing expressions in an action language
3. The implementation of the plug-in for the SIML action language
4. Evaluation by performing simulations and verifying model correctness
5. Generalising and formalising the interface(s) between the tool and the language plug-ins, enabling usage with a variety of (Executable UML) notations

3.1 Extensions to the Behavioural Metamodel

Behavioural templates are used to create *behavioural types* based on information extracted from a source UML model. Fig. 3. shows an extended metamodel for the types created based on the behavioural template for state machines. We observe that the behavioural types are composed of one or more *properties* (e.g. states) and *transitions*, which in turn comprise a *trigger* and one or more *conditions* (guards) and *actions*. The existing behavioural type metamodel was extended with the External class to enable the inclusion of the embedded action language expressions from the source model into the simulation. This class defines three attributes: *language* – to signify which action language is used, *classifier* – to describe which particular part of the behaviour the expression applies to (e.g. *effect*, for transitions; *exit* or *entry*, for a state change), and a *body* – which contains (external notation) expressions unknown to the simulation tool.

3.2 The Simulation Tool Plug-in Mechanism

To allow for an arbitrary action language to be used on the core UML models, a plug-in mechanism has been chosen. This choice ensures that there will be no need to modify the simulation tool to accommodate different kinds of executable UML. The loading of plug-ins (one per project) is dynamic. (A project includes input models, queries, a behavioural template, configuration files, schedule, breakpoints, etc.). The mechanism's implementation details are specific to the implementation platform and are not relevant here.

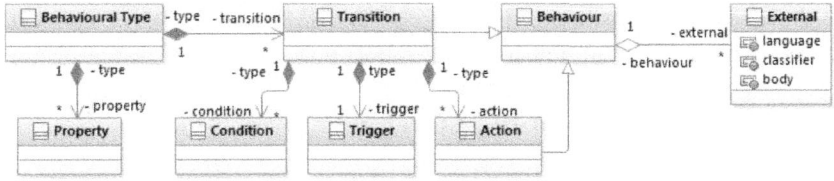

Fig. 3. Extended behavioural type metamodel

3.3 The SIML Plug-in

The SIML plug-in is the SIML-specific implementation of the external language processor interface, IPlugin (Fig. 4. (a)), and was developed incrementally, adding the functionality found in SIML expressions in a gradual manner.

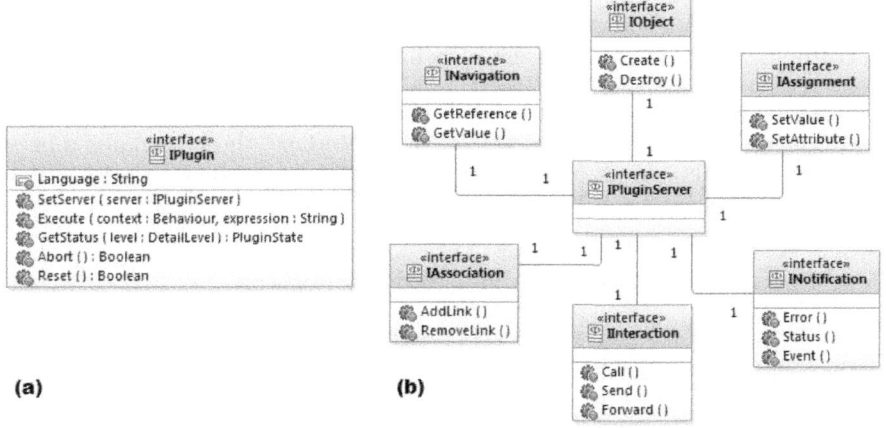

Fig. 4. (a)IPlugin and (b) IPluginServer interfaces

The SetServer method is called when the plug-in is loaded. The simulation tool then uses the Language attribute in order to determine which action language it is capable of processing. The SetServer method passes a reference to the simulation tool's component that is the implementation of the IPluginServer interface (described in the next section). When the SetServer call is made, the plug-in resets its internal state to the default initial state. The tool can also force this operation by using the Reset method. The Execute method is called when the plug-in is required to process an action language expression. This method takes two parameters: context – informing the plug-in which (behavioural) object is requesting the processing, and expression – the action language expression that needs to be processed. For debugging, management or reporting purposes, the tool can also request a snapshot of the plug-in's internal state through the `GetStatus` method, as well as issue an `Abort` request as a safety mechanism to abandon further proecssing.

3.4 The Simulation Tool Plug-in API

`IPluginServer` essentially describes an API (a set of simulation tool's services that `IPlugin`–compatible plug-ins can use). The API is described by the `IPluginServer` interface (Fig. 4. (b)), and consists of the following (sub-) interfaces grouped by the functionality:

- **navigation** – providing access to model elements
- **object** – required to create and destroy objects
- **assignment** – required to set values to object references and to allocate values to objects' attributes
- **association** – required to create and remove relationships between objects
- **interaction** – providing mechanisms to pass data between objects in synchronous and asynchronous manner
- **notification** – asynchronous mechanism for providing management and operational notifications from the plug-in to the tool

Basic methods associated with each section are also shown in Fig. 4(b). With the exception of those in the `INotification` interface, these methods represent a minimum set of services required to 'drive' a state-machine based simulation scenario from an executable UML plug-in.

3.5 Normal Operation, Control, and Exceptions

The simulation tool was also required to implement a mechanism to control the overall simulation execution in the presence of an external plug-in (e.g. in order to avoid deadlock scenarios, either because of a faulty or partial plug-in implementation, or an incomplete/erroneous behavioural specification in the input model). The tool and the plug-in operate collaboratively during the simulation runs, using a master-slave mode of operation. The simulation tool is a passive master of the workflow, at times relinquishing control to the plug-in in full, but continually monitoring the execution and intervening in case of a problem by: disabling the plug-in, aborting the simulation, and reporting back to the user. In a nutshell, a simulation run goes through the following stages and sub-stages:

- **Power-up** – initialisation of tool and plug-in internal states and variables
- **System execution** – composed of *simulation steps*; in each step, the tool sequentially executes all system tasks; this stage is repeated until either (a) the simulation runs its natural course where all simulation objects have become idle, (b) the users halts the execution, either manually or through a breakpoint, (c) an error is reported by a plug-in, or (d) the plug-in has become unresponsive
    - **Task execution** – task's simulation objects are executed sequentially; if an object's message queue is empty or blocked, the object is skipped

* **Object execution** – executing object's current behaviour (e.g. a transition in a state machine scenario, comprising multiple actions)
- **Power-down** – in this stage, the simulation trace may be logged, or perhaps a report generated if particular analysis is required

The above execution flow is controlled by the tool. The control is partially relinquished to the plug-in at the *object execution* level, if and when an external action language expression is read from the object's message queue. Before doing so, the tool sets a timer to guard against situations when the plug-in blocks further operation of the tool. If the control is returned to the tool before the time-out, the timer is cancelled; if not, the plug-in is forcefully disabled, the simulation is aborted, and feedback is given to the user.

4 Industrial Application and Assessment

The work presented is in response to strong industrial demands to provide enhanced simulation support for railway interlocking models, particularly for safety analysis and validation, without requiring new modelling tools to be purchased or developed. The enhanced control of simulations is achieved through external action languages that allow a more fine-grained specification of behaviours in UML models. We have demonstrated how to extend a simulation tool's capabilities to exploit external action languages, achieved through a dynamic integration of the tool and the external module using the plug-in mechanism. We have also formalised the interaction between these two by precisely modelling their interfaces.

Following the implementation of the extension to the tool and the SIML plug-in, we have used the following criteria in order to validate our approach, by verifying the tool operation:

- *without a plug-in* – in the absence of a plug-in, the tool's operation must be equivalent to that prior to the modifications made
- *with a plug-in* – in the presence of a relevant language plug-in, simulation is either fully automatic or hybrid (largely driven by the executable UML expressions embedded in the model, but manual user input is also supported)
- *with a malfunctioning plug-in* – the tool must prevent the plug-in from blocking the simulation indefinitely by disabling the plug-in under such circumstances, aborting the execution, and providing the feedback to the user

All scenarios above were tested and the criteria satisfied. In particular, the 'malfunctioning plug-in' was repeatedly tested during the incremental development; during this period, when the plug-in's functionality was only partially implemented, blocking situations were in abundance. The verification of the normal operation of the tool (without a plug-in) was compared against the unmodified version of the tool on the same set of case studies. Finally, the hybrid operation was tested by disabling selected functionality in the plug-in (e.g. sending a message) and replacing it by issuing a prompt to provide a manual user input.

The fully-automatic operation was tested on a number of case studies from the railway signalling domain, the smallest containing 7 classes and 25 SIML statements, and the largest 89 classes and several hundred SIML statements. Every class had its own state machine defined. Simulation runs were performed on all case studies, validating the approach and the tool/plug-in operation. Due to project's time constraints, it was not possible to fully verify the correctness ([2]) of the larger models. The modified tool outperformed Artisan-CASSANDRA combination, if only just – possibly attributed to the 'lightweightedness' of the tool, but because of its prototype status, further improvements are expected. The real power of the approach, however, lies in its extensibility and generalisation. The SIML plug-in was implemented in 3 weeks, but after the initial learning curve, we anticipate the future plug-in development to shrink to several days.

The following are typical scenarios in which the integrated solution (the simulation tool and the plug-in) was (can be) used:

- *normal execution* – performing a simulation run according to the specification derived from the source models. Two most typical outcomes are: (a) execution runs its natural course (i.e. no further activity detected), a snapshot of the current state of the system is taken, then analysed together with the simulation trace; (b) simulation runs indefinitely; user forcefully halts the execution and analyses trace.
- *property checking* – checking if specified property is satisfied. We use conditions (Boolean expressions composed of model elements, attributes, and Boolean operators) specified in breakpoints to signify properties. A breakpoint causes the simulation to pause (or come to a halt) when its condition evaluates to true.
- *error injection* – analysing the robustness of the modelled system, i.e. its behaviour in the presence of errors. Errors are purposely introduced into the system through user input.

Property checking and error injection are illustrated using the example in Fig. 5. Two routes R1 and R2 (comprising tracks T, signals S, and points P) are defined as:

```
R1 = {S1; T1,P1(left),T3} and R2 = {S1; T1,P1(right),T2}
```

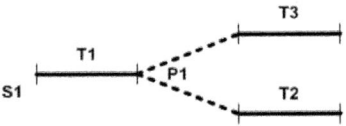

Fig. 5. An example railway interlocking model used for assessing the approach

We observe that that the routes share elements such as the entry signal S1 or track T1. When specifying properties, we use *negative application conditions* (NACs) (e.g. to verify that a system is safe, we define conditions that make the system unsafe). For instance, we may want to verify that signal S1 is not in the `proceed` state if, at the same time, track T1 is in the `occupied` state. Thus the property that we want to check is defined using the Boolean expression:

(S1.state == 'proceed') AND (T1.state == 'occupied')

specified as a breakpoint condition. If, during a simulation run, the expression evaluates to *true*, the execution of the model is stopped. The user is then able to see which breakpoint triggered this, and can analyse the trace to find the design fault.

We can also deliberately inject errors into the system's behaviour. Using the same scenario, we can define a different breakpoint, as follows:

(R1.state == 'active') AND (R2.state == 'active') AND
(T1.state == 'occupied')

Routes essentially have two main states: *idle* and *active*. Since R1 and R2 share a common track, they cannot be both *active* at the same time when T1 is *occupied*. During the simulation, for instance, when R1 is active and T1 occupied, we can (through user input) change R2's state to 'active' and observe how the system behaves afterwards. This method works well; however, the simulation clock has to be slowed down substantially in order to inject errors at the right time. Work is in progress to provide a mechanism to use rule-based scripts for error injection.

5 Related Work

Shlaer and Mellor [18,19,17] developed a method in which objects are given precise behaviour specifications using state machine models annotated with a high-level action language. In the late 1990s, OMG started working on Action Semantics for the UML with an objective to extend the UML with a compatible mechanism for specifying action semantics in a platform-independent manner.

There are a number of research and academic platforms and tools that attempt to define behaviours in UML models more precisely, and to execute such enriched models [10,6,16]. There are also several commercial tools that define their own semantics for model execution [7,5,4,9,3]. They often include a proprietary (action) language. Consequently, models developed with different tools cannot be easily interchanged and cannot interoperate.

The Foundational UML (fUML) [12] specification (adopted in 2008) provided the first precise operational and base semantics for a subset of UML encompassing most object-oriented and activity modelling. fUML, however, does not provide a new concrete *surface* syntax; rather, it ties the precise semantics solely to the existing abstract syntax model of UML. Subsequently, OMG issued an RFP for Concrete Syntax for a UML Action Language. Currently, what is known as the Action Language for fUML (or Alf) [11] is in beta 2 phase (since 2010).

Alf is a textual surface representation for UML behaviours. Expressions in Alf can be attached to a UML model in any place where a UML behaviour can be. Any Alf text that can be mapped to fUML can be reduced to a set of statements in first-order logic. Unfortunately, it does not allow us to use model-checking features or a theorem prover for validation or verification. In that respect, significant additional work remains in order to provide a complete formal verification for a system [13]. This is exactly why simulation in combination with Alf (or indeed any other executable UML language) is beneficial. Simulations do not provide formal proofs; nevertheless, they can significantly increase confidence in the tested models.

There is one other significant gap. Although we now have the action semantics (in fUML) and are close to seeing a fully adopted concrete syntax (in Alf), the question of *how* the models will be executed still remains. In other words, there are currently no attempts to standardise or even specify a simulation environment for UML that would define how such platform should connect to Alf or another (proprietary) action language. In the meantime, we should do as best as we can with what is available and try to adapt the existing UML compatible simulation tools for use with diverse executable UML notations. This paper contributes to this objective.

6 Conclusion

Model simulation is increasingly seen as a reliable complementary approach to formal verification or testing that attempts to establish the validity of model behaviours. Standard UML's limitation to describe these behaviours in greater detail is addressed by a number of action languages. Although the majority of these languages were designed following the same or similar philosophy, there is no common metamodel from which they can be derived. This presents a significant challenge for UML tool makers if they were to support a number of such languages in their tools.

We have tried to address this problem and have proposed a modular approach to UML model execution through simulation. We have demonstrated a scenario in which a UML-based simulation tool is extended in a non-disruptive, modular, manner to accommodate multiple action language 'engines' to collaborate with the tool during simulation runs. This was achieved by augmenting the tool's capability using a simple plug-in paradigm. We have formalised the solution by defining the interfaces required by the plug-in and the tool so that the two can be integrated. We have also illustrated the normal operation, the workflow control, as well as the exception handling mechanisms. We have evaluated our approach on examples from the railway signalling domain. The tool we used in our study was an in-house tool (based on the SMILE platform), while the language was CASSANDRA's action language SIML.

Our next steps will include investigation into more action languages, other simulation platforms, as well as further generalisation and formalisation of the approach. We anticipate an increased activity in the model simulation arena and are also mindful of the fact that new domain-specific action languages may emerge. As part of our desire for a broader research impact, our intention is to standardise the interaction between the simulation tools and action languages.

References

1. Atego. Artisan Studio (2011), http://www.atego.com/products/artisan-studio/
2. dos Santos, O.M., Woodcock, J., Paige, R.F., King, S.: The Use of Model Transformation in the INESS Project. In: de Boer, F.S., Bonsangue, M.M., Hallerstede, S., Leuschel, M. (eds.) FMCO 2009. LNCS, vol. 6286, pp. 147–165. Springer, Heidelberg (2010)
3. Dotan, D., Kirshin, A.: Debugging and Testing Behavioral UML Models. In: Companion to the 22nd ACM SIGPLAN Conference on Object-Oriented Programming Systems and Applications Companion (OOPSLA 2007), pp. 838–839 (2007)
4. IBM, Rational Rhapsody (2012), www.ibm.com/software/awdtools/rhapsody/
5. IBM, Rational Software Architect RealTime Edition (RSA–RTE) (2012), http://www.ibm.com/software/rational/products/swarchitect/
6. Jiang, K., Zhang, L., Miyake, S.: An Executable UML with OCL-based Action Semantics Language. In: 14th Asia-Pacific Software Engineering Conference (APSEC 2007), pp. 302–309 (December 2007)
7. Know Gravity. CASSANDRA (2011), http://www.knowgravity.com/eng/value/cassandra.htm
8. Mellish, C.S., Clocksin, W.F.: Programming in Prolog: Using the ISO Standard. Springer (2003)
9. Mentor Graphics. BridgePoint (2012)
10. Mooney, J., Sarjoughia, H.: A Framework for Executable UML Models. In: 2009 Spring Simulation Multiconference. Society for Computer Simulation International (2009)
11. OMG. Action Language for Foundational UML (Alf). Technical Report October 2010, OMG (2011)
12. OMG. Semantics of a Foundational Subset for Executable UML Models (fUML), v1.0. Technical Report, OMG (February 2011)
13. Perseil, I.: ALF formal. Innovations in Systems and Software Engineering 7(4), 325–326 (2011)
14. Radjenovic, A., Paige, R.F.: Behavioural Interoperability to Support Model-Driven Systems Integration. In: 1st Workshop on Model Driven Interoperability (MDI 2010), at MODELS 2010, Oslo, Norway. ACM Press (2010)
15. Radjenovic, A., Paige, R.F.: An Approach for Model Querying-by-Example Applied to Multi-Paradigm Models. In: 5th International Workshop on Multi-Paradigm Modelling (MPM 2011), at MODELS 2011. ECEASST, vol. 42, pp. 1–12 (2011)
16. Risco-Martín, J.L., de La Cruz, J.M., Mittal, S., Zeigler, B.P.: eUDEVS: Executable UML with DEVS Theory of Modeling and Simulation. Simulation 85(11-12), 750–777 (2009)
17. Shlaer, S., Mellor, S.J.: Object-Oriented Systems Analysis: Modeling the World in Data. Prentice Hall (1988)
18. Shlaer, S., Mellor, S.J.: Recursive Design. Computer Language 7(3) (1990)
19. Shlaer, S., Mellor, S.J.: Object Lifecycles: Modeling the World in States. Prentice Hall (1992)

MADES: A Tool Chain for Automated Verification of UML Models of Embedded Systems

Alek Radjenovic[1], Nicholas Matragkas[1], Richard F. Paige[1], Matteo Rossi[2], Alfredo Motta[2], Luciano Baresi[2], and Dimitrios S. Kolovos[1]

[1] Department of Computer Science, The University of York, United Kingdom
{alek,nikos,paige,dkolovos}@cs.york.ac.uk
[2] Politecnico di Milano, Italy
{rossi,motta,baresi}@elet.polimi.it

Abstract. The benefits of Model Driven Development may be achieved through exploitation of its potential for automation. Automated model verification is one of the most important examples of this. The usage of automated model verification in everyday software engineering practice is far from widespread. One of the reasons for this is that model designers do not have the necessary background in mathematical methods. An approach where model designers can remain working in their domain while the verification is performed on demand, automatically and transparently, is desirable. We present one such approach using a tool chain built atop mature, popular and widespread technologies. Our approach was verified on industrial experiments from the embedded systems domain in the fields of avionics and surveillance.

1 Introduction

Our research project – MADES (*Model–based methods and tools for Avionics and surveillance embeddeD SystEmS*) [16] – was born out of demand from the embedded systems industry to develop a model–driven approach to improve current practice in the development of embedded systems. This approach was to cover all phases, from design to code generation and deployment. Many embedded software systems, and particularly those from the avionics and surveillance domains, require high integrity, where verification is essential before deployment. Verifying properties of the system at the start of the development is highly desirable as the first line of defence against design faults which if detected at a later stage are very costly. At the same time, system verification at the model level is hard because model designers typically do not possess the necessary mathematical background. In this paper we present a tool chain that allows system designers to perform model verification on demand, automatically and transparently (without the need to understand the complexities of the mathematical formalisms that underpin the approach).

A model designer and a formal methods expert focus on significantly different things. Even the tools and techniques they use are at the opposite end of the software engineering spectrum. The former typically uses graphical modelling tools, whilst the latter uses textual notations that rely heavily on mathematics. Inadequate knowledge of model checking techniques can limit the scope of the types of verifications that can be performed. On the other hand, inadequate knowledge of the system under development can weaken the validity of the verification itself. The majority of research efforts have been on low–level detail, such as: how can we translate an OCL constraint into a mathematically sound form that we can use with a SAT solver? Or, how can we define correctness properties for UML class diagrams?

This paper addresses the big picture: how can we make the verification process more practical? How can we provide the model designers with a tool that enables them to automatically check the correctness of their models without the need to understand model checking? The solution we provide is a tool chain – a set of domain–specific tools communicating with each other. Two of the key traits of a successful tool chain are: (i) *transformational capabilities* – e.g., to transform models into transformation scripts and (ii) *usability* – a tool's ability to allow the user to specify another domain's documents using concepts from its own domain. Consequently, the work described in this paper focuses on providing one such tool chain that enables model designers to utilise mathematical methods 'under the hood'.

We were able to use and combine several existing and mature technologies. On the verification side, we build on current model–checking technology to provide decision procedures more specifically tailored to the project domain. By exploiting domain abstractions and model fragments, the designers are allowed to define properties in a way close to their domains that hides the formalism. An enabling technology that underpins our framework is model transformation. We provide support via Epsilon [15] for various kinds of model transformations. The transformations support the verification tasks by allowing platform models (e.g., in subsets of UML/MARTE [19]) to be mapped to verification technology, such as Zot [24] or Alloy [17].

Our solution provides model designers with the ability to verify their design without the need to understand underlying formalisms. It allows on–demand and automatic verification at *any* stage of the development process. Our approach works with the entire system model, a segment of it, or even a partial model implementation. In case of verification failures, counter examples are provided with the ability to trace back to the source of errors. Our solution is practical, usable, reusable, generic, and underpinned by proven mature technologies. Importantly, it is in direct response to specific industrial requirements.

The remainder of the paper is structured as follows. Section 2 presents the background and context. Section 3 summarises the related work. Sections 4 and 5 present the overview of the approach, and the details of the implementation. Section 6 presents an example of industrial application and describes how the approach was assessed. We conclude by analysing the effectiveness of the approach in Section 7.

2 Background

The key ambition of the MADES project [2] is to develop a model–driven approach to improve the current practice in the development of embedded systems. The proposed approach is holistic in that it covers all phases of the development life–cycle, from design to code generation and deployment.

MADES makes several key contributions. Firstly, a dedicated (MADES) language was developed as an extension to OMG's MARTE Profile [19]. Secondly, approaches have been developed for verification of key properties on designed artefacts, closed-loop simulation based on detailed models of the environment, and the verification of designed transformations. And thirdly, code generation techniques have been devised which addresses both hardware description languages as well as conventional programming languages, with features for compile–time virtualisation of common hardware architecture features, including accelerators, memory, multiprocessor and inter–processor communication channels, to cope with the fact that hardware platforms are getting more and more complex.

Our work is part of the validation effort in which we use model transformations to generate various software artefacts from the MADES models. The documents include verification scripts, simulation scripts, hardware architecture descriptions, architecture agnostic source code, software and hardware mappings for compile–time virtualisation, and hardware architecture descriptions for compile–time virtualisation. The model transformation work is in direct response to the high level requirements to achieve tool interoperability, code generation, and traceability of the model–based activities of the development life–cycle of embedded systems.

3 Related Work

3.1 Model Checking

Over three decades ago, two seminal papers [25], [9] founded what has become the highly successful field of *model checking*, for automatically assessing whether a system model satisfies specified properties. In recent times, as model driven development (MDD) became more widespread, model verification has come at the forefront of research in this arena. Model verification can take many different forms, including formal (mathematical) analyses such as performance analysis based on queuing theory or safety–and–liveness property checking. Very often, it means executing models on a computer as an empirical approach to verification [27].

Holzmann [13] states that in the classic approach to logic model checking, verification requires a manually constructed model to be written in the language that is accepted by the model checker. The construction of such a model typically requires good knowledge of both the application being verified and of the capabilities of the model checker that is used for the verification.

Schmidt [26] points out that traditionally model checking has been performed very late in the development (in the testing phase), though he argues for the necessity to be able to do this at any stage of the development lifecycle. Moreover, now that many of the verification technologies have matured, there is an emergent need for verification to be usable in practice [6].

Unsurprisingly, because of its widespread usage, the focus of attention in recent years has been the Unified Modeling Language (UML) [20,21]. A lot of research activity has been around OCL (Object Constraint Language) [23] used in UML specifications. Some examples include [6,7,5,8,12,28,29]. Despite some insightful approaches, the majority of these valuable contributions focus solely on the structural aspects (namely, UML Class Diagrams).

In "Verified Software: A Grand Challenge" [14], Jones et al. point out that formal methods used in verification are intended to predict software behaviour. A verification method for UML cannot therefore be complete if it does not include behaviours described, for instance, through UML state machine or sequence diagrams. Approaches such as [31] which uses formal analysis on concurrent systems specified by collections of UML state machines, or [4] that deals with automatic translation of statecharts and sequence diagrams into generalized stochastic Petri nets, are a steps in the right direction.

3.2 Model Transformation

Model transformation plays a key role in model driven development. Although there is still no mature foundation for specifying transformations among models [10], there are many worthwhile theoretical approaches as well as several that are practical, too.

One of the platforms that is at the forefront of model transformations, not only due to its maturity, but more importantly in terms of its usability, is Epsilon [15] a family of interoperable task specific languages for interaction with EMF (Eclipse Modeling Framework) [11] models. In particular, the Epsilon Transformation Language (ETL), a hybrid, rule–based language, provides not only the usual transformation features but can be used to query, navigate, or modify both source and target models. ETL can transform many input to many output models. In addition, the Epsilon Generation Language (EGL) is typically used hand–in–hand with ETL for model–to–text transformations (e.g. translating UML models into Java code).

The enabling technology that helps us achieve full automation in model driven system verification is model transformation.

4 Approach/Framework

As stated earlier, the overall objective of the MADES project is to improve the model–driven design for embedded platforms. The overview of the various artefacts in the MADES approach can be found in [1]. Verification of system properties at different phases of the development process plays a key role.

Fundamental to this is reducing the overall effort associated with the verification process. One way to achieve this is to hide the complexity of the formal models from the domain experts and allow them to specify the system of interest in a notation they are familiar with. To this end, the MADES approach uses model transformations to provide a seamless integration between design tools and the verification tools. We have accomplished this by means of a tool chain whose workflow has three main stages. In *Modelling*, a modelling tool (Modelio [30]) is used to generate design models using the MADES modelling language (a combined subset of OMG MARTE [19] a UML profile for modelling real–time embedded systems and SysML [18] – a general–purpose modelling language for systems engineering applications). These models serve as the input to the next stage – the *Transformation*. In this stage, Java code is generated, instantiating objects needed for the verification platform. The final stage – *Verification* – uses the objects from the previous stage to produce verification scripts (containing lists of temporal logic formulae) as an input to the Zot tool [22] that performs formal proofs.

Most importantly, users interact only with the modelling tool. The transformation and the verification take place 'under the hood', transparently to the users, who do not have to deal with anything beyond their domain, making this a true MDE approach.

5 Implementation

5.1 Modelling

The proposed approach is model–driven. Hence, the verification process is entirely guided by the MADES design model, comprising a set of mandatory and optional UML/MARTE diagrams, including:

- *Class diagrams* – besides standard UML features, these may define MARTE clock types (CT) that constrain the temporal behaviour of components (e.g. associating a CT with a class is equivalent to declaring clock instance associated with all the objects of that class)
- *Object diagrams* – contain class and clock instances declared in class diagrams
- *State diagrams* – describe the state–based behaviour of system objects. These include standard features like states, transitions, triggers, guards and actions
- *Sequence diagrams* – describe partial behaviours in the system, capturing message (class operation instance) exchanges between objects (as defined in the Object Diagram). Time constraints (capturing metric timing relationships between events in the diagram) can be also added using MARTE stereotypes
- *Interaction Overview Diagrams* – provide a high–level structuring mechanism to compose sequence diagrams through common operators such as *sequence, iteration, concurrency,* or *choice* (this compositional solution differs from the one used in scenario–based approaches, because sequence diagrams are not used to render valid, invalid, or contingent traces, but rather to describe portions of the behaviour of the system)

Finally, diagrams share a common set of events such as interrupts, beginnings and ends of messages, or clock ticks, enabling different diagrams (system views) to communicate with each other.

5.2 Tool Chain

In real-time embedded systems, the most intuitive way to describe operational behaviours has the following main characteristics: (i) time is explicitly represented in the diagram, (ii) the timing constraints can be represented directly in the diagram, and (iii) the level of abstraction can be easily refined through the development process. For example, in this context, the sequence diagrams represent what is performed by different functional blocks in a time-based visualisation, and they can be used as a starting point to determine if various timing properties of interest remain valid during the development process. Some examples of timing properties are:

- Is the system able to complete *Task X* within *t* time units?
- Does *Event E* always precede *Event F*?
- If *Event E* occurs, will *Event F* occur within *t* time units?

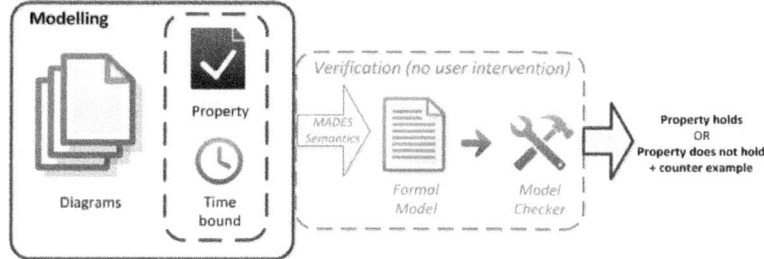

Fig. 1. Verification workflow

The MADES verification workflow (Figure 1) comprises a modelling stage and a verification stage (that requires no user intervention). As stated earlier, the entire verification process is fully automatic. However, minor user input is required as explained next. During the modelling stage, in addition to the UML diagrams, the user defines a *property* to be verified, as well as and the *time bound*. In MADES approach, this is achieved through a user-friendly interface (Figure 2), where users can also choose a SAT solver and a model checker they wish to use. The current implementation model checker is Zot, but any model checker that supports TRIO temporal logic can be used instead.

Once the models, the property to be checked, and the time bound are defined, the user can automatically run the verification and check whether the property is satisfied or not. If the property is not satisfied, the model checker generates

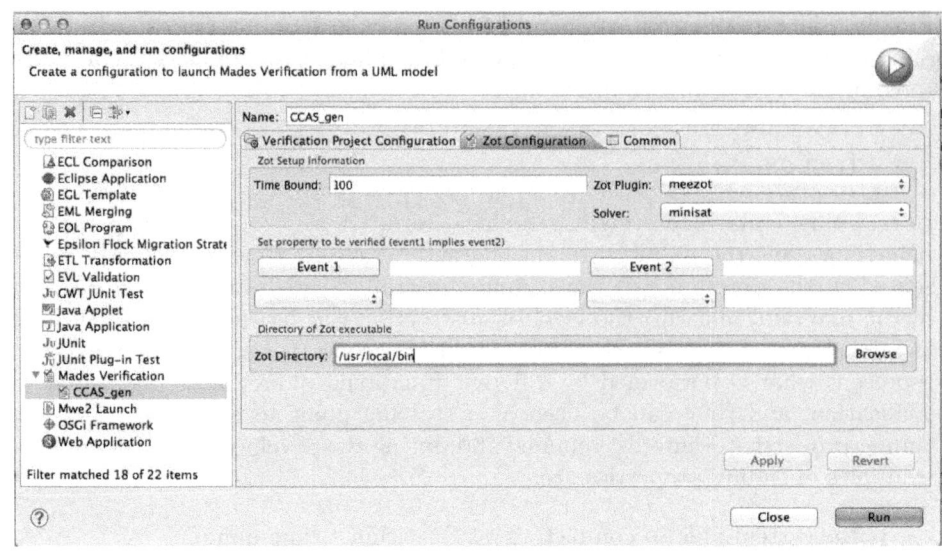

Fig. 2. Property and time bound configuration

a counter–example showing a system execution that violates the property. An integrated traceability mechanism allows us to trace back from the elements in the counter–example to the original UML model using trace links that are visualised in a dedicated editor. As it is apparent from this workflow, the user does not need to be familiar with temporal logic formulas to be able to formally verify the design models.

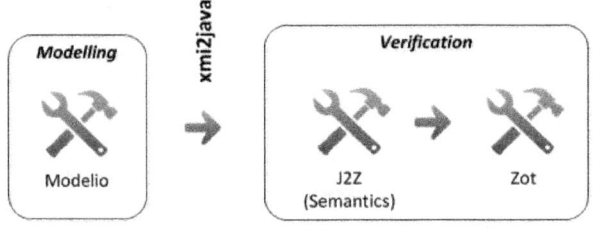

Fig. 3. MADES verification tool chain

MADES verification tool chain is shown in Figure 3. The generated models (using an XMI–compliant CASE tool, such as *Modelio* or *Papyrus*) are transformed (xmi2java) to Java code that acts as an input to the Java–to–Zot tool (*J2Z*). J2Z then produces a corresponding set of TRIO formulae that are fed into the verification engine (*Zot*). Zot encodes satisfiability (SAT) and validity problems for discrete time TRIO temporal logic formulae as propositional SAT problems, which are in turn checked with off–the–shelf SAT solvers. The TRIO formulae define the semantic representation and provide a formal semantics to MADES diagrams [3].

The code snippet below illustrates the Java primitives associated with an Interaction Overview Diagram, using the API provided by J2Z. The bottom part shows the commands to start generating the semantic representation written in Lisp for Zot.

```
...
//IOD declaration
core.diagrams.IOD CCAS_IOD=new IOD();
iod.Node i_n1= new InitialNode();
iod.Node i_n2= new Merge();
iod.Node i_n3= new InterruptNode(BrakeInterrupt);
iod.Node i_n4= new FlowFinalNode();
CCAS_IOD.addControlFlow(i_n1,i_n2);
CCAS_IOD.addControlFlow(i_n2,SDSendSensorDistance);
CCAS_IOD.addControlFlow(SDSendSensorDistance,i_n2);
CCAS_IOD.addControlFlow(SDSendBrakeCommand,i_n4);
CCAS_IOD.addControlFlow(i_n3,SDSendBrakeCommand);
//J2Z Wrap--up
MadesModel madesModel=new MadesModel();
//[...] Add diagrams to the MADES UML model
madesModel.addIod(CCAS_IOD);
//ZOT Configuration
ZOTConf zot=new ZOTConf(100, ``meezot'', ``minisat'', madesModel);
zot.writeZOTFile(``CCAS_Verification.zot'');
```

5.3 Transformation

The transformation of XMI files (the output of the modelling stage) into Java code (the input to the verification stage) is performed using the xmi2Java script (Figure 3) that uses the model transformation technology in order to convert various relevant portions of the input model into Java code. The transformations are specified using ETL (Epsilon Transformation Language) and the output code is generated in EGL (Epsilon Generation Language).

6 Industrial Application and Assessment

The operation of the MADES verification tool chain is illustrated using a real-world case study from the real-time embedded systems domain (the automotive industry) - a *Car Collision Avoidance System* (CCAS). One of the key functions of CCAS is to detect the position of the car on which it is installed relative to other objects in its environment (such as other vehicles or pedestrians). The distance between the car and the external objects is read through the on-board *Radar* that sends data to the *Controller* every 100ms via the system bus (CAN).

The full CCAS specification includes a large number of properties for timing (e.g. data transfer), safety (e.g. when to brake if in a critical state) or liveness. Using the MADES modelling language, CCAS is described with one class diagram, one object diagram, one interaction overview diagram, two sequence diagrams, and three state diagrams. Examples of these are provided in Figure 4 and Figure 5.

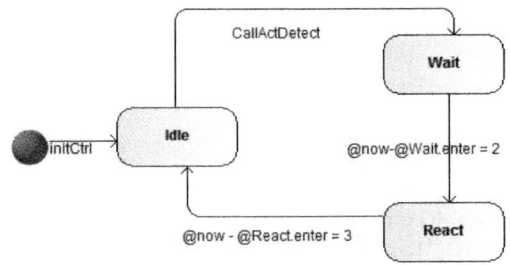

Fig. 4. One of CCAS state diagrams

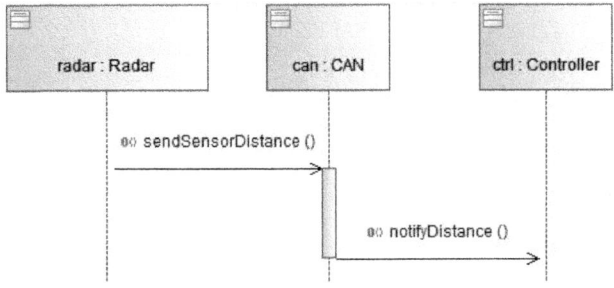

Fig. 5. An example sequence diagrams in CCAS

Consider the following safety requirement as an example of property checking:
*"If the sensor measuring the distance between the car and
the external objects continuously reads a value that is less than
2 meters for a period of 50 time units, then the system should
brake within those same 50 time units."*
This requirement can be expressed as a property formalised by the following TRIO formula:

$$\text{Alw(Lasted([distance<2],50)} \rightarrow \text{WithinP(brakeS braking,50))} \quad (1)$$

where [distance<2] represents a Boolean predicate. The formula did not initially hold, and the Zot tool produced a counter-example within around 30 seconds (we used the meezot plugin and the minisat SAT solver, and the time bound was set to 100). The counter-example showed that the violation of the property was the consequence of a cumulative delay composed of the delay related to the *radar* component (governed by a logical clock with a period of 10 time units), and the transmission and reaction delays that are present throughout the model. By modifying the time bounds in above formula we can show that, by giving the system a little more leeway in the required reaction time, we can make the property hold. Specifically, the time bounds in formula were changed from 50 to 56 time units. By repeating the verification with the new values, the Zot tool reported (within 20 seconds) the UNSAT result. This is interpreted as: *"it is not possible to find a system trace that violates the property, hence the property holds for the system"*.

For reference, the output is produced in two steps: (i) initially, Zot shows the Boolean predicates used to represent the UML model in temporal logic, and (ii) *z3* (a well-known and efficient SMT solver by Microsoft Research) solves the satisfiability problem and reports the UNSAT result.

This simple example illustrates how the MADES tool chain enables modellers to conduct their own experiments, detect and better understand design faults, and improve the system models.

7 Conclusion

This work was done within the MADES project in response to a strong and specific demand from the real–time embedded (avionics and surveillance) industry to develop a holistic, model–driven approach to improve the current practice in the development of hardware and software systems. By holistic we mean encompassing all stages of the development life–cycle, from design to code generation, testing and deployment. In this document we have discussed a particular solution that addresses the verification aspect of system development. In particular, this solution was in response to specific industrial requirements to enable modellers to verify their designs on demand, automatically and transparently (i.e. protecting them from the need to understand the underlying complexities of the formal methods).

Here, we have presented an approach in the form of an interoperable tool chain that builds exclusively on technologies that are mature, widespread and open source. In addition, all the new tools built for this project are (or will be) open source and widely available to the public. Importantly, our approach is complete in that it provides support for both structural models (e.g. UML class and object diagrams) as well as behaviour models (e.g. UML sequence and state machine diagrams).

The approach has been evaluated on a number of real world case studies from the embedded domain in collaboration with our industrial partners Cassidian and TXT.

Future work includes a more elaborate, bidirectional, traceability mechanism as well as a tool extension to support system simulation for validating dynamic behaviours.

Acknowledgements. This research was supported by the European Community's Seventh Framework Program (FP7/2007-2013) under grant agreement n. 248864 (MADES), and by the Programme IDEAS-ERC, Project 227977-SMScom.

MADES is a Specific Targeted Research Project (STREP) of the Seventh Framework Programme for research and technological development (FP7) – the European Union's chief instrument for funding research over the period 2007 to 2013.

References

1. Audsley, N.C., Gray, I., Indrusiak, L.S., Kolovos, D., Matragkas, N., Paige, R.: Model-based development of embedded systems - the MADES approach. In: 2nd Workshop on Model Based Engineering for Embedded Systems Design (MBED 2011), pp. 1–4 (2011)
2. Bagnato, A., Sadovykh, A., Paige, R.F., Kolovos, D.S., Baresi, L., Morzenti, A., Rossi, M.: MADES: Embedded Systems Engineering Approach in the Avionics Domain. In: 1st Workshop on Hands-on Platforms and Tools for Model-Based Engineering of Embedded Systems (HoPES 2010), p. 5 (2010)
3. Baresi, L., Morzenti, A., Motta, A., Rossi, M.: Towards the UML-Based Formal Verification of Timed Systems. In: Aichernig, B.K., de Boer, F.S., Bonsangue, M.M. (eds.) FMCO 2010. LNCS, vol. 6957, pp. 267–286. Springer, Heidelberg (2011)
4. Bernardi, S., Donatelli, S., Merseguer, J.: From UML Sequence Diagrams and Statecharts to analysable Petri Net models. In: 3rd International Workshop on Software and Performance, pp. 35–45 (2002)
5. Brucker, A.D., Wolff, B.: HOL-OCL: A Formal Proof Environment for UML/OCL. In: Fiadeiro, J.L., Inverardi, P. (eds.) FASE 2008. LNCS, vol. 4961, pp. 97–100. Springer, Heidelberg (2008)
6. Cabot, J., Clariso, R.: UML/OCL Verification In Practice. In: ChaMDE Workshop (MODELS 2008), pp. 31–35 (2008)
7. Cabot, J., Clariso, R., Riera, D.: UMLtoCSP: A Tool for the Formal Verification of UML/OCL Models Using Constraint Programming. In: 22nd IEEE/ACM International Conference on Automated Software Engineering (ASE 2007), pp. 547–548. ACM, New York (2007)
8. Cabot, J., Clariso, R., Riera, D.: Verification of UML/OCL Class Diagrams using Constraint Programming. In: IEEE International Conference on Software Testing Verification and Validation Workshop (ICSTW 2008). IEEE (2008)
9. Clarke, E.M., Emerson, A.: Design and synthesis of synchronization skeletons using branching time temporal logic. In: Workshop on Logics of Programs. Springer, Heidelberg (1981)
10. Czarnecki, K., Helsen, S.: Feature-based survey of model transformation approaches. IBM Systems Journal 45(3), 621–645 (2006)
11. The Eclipse Foundation. Eclipse Modeling Framework (EMF) (2012), http://www.eclipse.org/modeling/emf/
12. Gogolla, M., Kuhlmann, M., Hamann, L.: Consistency, Independence and Consequences in UML and OCL Models. In: Dubois, C. (ed.) TAP 2009. LNCS, vol. 5668, pp. 90–104. Springer, Heidelberg (2009)

13. Holzmann, G.J., Joshi, R.: Model-Driven Software Verification. In: Graf, S., Mounier, L. (eds.) SPIN 2004. LNCS, vol. 2989, pp. 76–91. Springer, Heidelberg (2004)
14. Jones, C., O'Hearn, P., Woodcock, J.: Verified software: a grand challenge. Computer 39(4), 93–95 (2006)
15. Kolovos, D.S., Paige, R., Rose, L., Polack, F.: The Epsilon Book. Technical report, The University of York, York, UK (2010)
16. MADES. Model-based methods and tools for Avionics and surveillance embeddeD SystEmS (2012), http://www.mades-project.org/
17. MIT. alloy (2012), http://alloy.mit.edu/alloy/
18. OMG. OMG Systems Modeling Language (OMG SysML), v1.2. Technical report, OMG (2007)
19. OMG. UML Profile for MARTE : Modeling and Analysis of Real-Time Embedded Systems. Technical Report, OMG (November 2009)
20. OMG. Unified Modeling Language - Infrastructure. Technical Report, OMG (May 2010)
21. OMG. Unified Modeling Language - Superstructure. Technical Report, OMG (May 2010)
22. OMG. MOF 2 XMI Mapping Specification. Technical report, OMG (2011)
23. OMG. OMG Object Constraint Language (OCL) v2.3.1. Technical Report, OMG (January 2012)
24. Pradella, M., Morzenti, A., Pietro, P.S.: The symmetry of the past and of the future: bi-infinite time in the verification of temporal properties. In: Proceedings of the the 6th Joint Meeting of the European Software Engineering Conference and the ACM SIGSOFT Symposium on The Foundations of Software Engineering, ESEC-FSE 2007, pp. 312–320. ACM, New York (2007)
25. Queille, J.P., Sifakis, J.: Specification and verification of concurrent systems in CESAR. In: 5th International Symposium on Programming, Springer, Heidelberg (1982)
26. Schmidt, D.C.: Model Driven Engineering. Computer 39(2), 25–31 (2006)
27. Selic, B.: The pragmatics of model-driven development. IEEE Software 20(5), 19–25 (2003)
28. Shaikh, A., Wiil, U.K., Memon, N.: UOST: UML/OCL Aggressive Slicing Technique for Efficient Verification of Models. In: Kraemer, F.A., Herrmann, P. (eds.) SAM 2010. LNCS, vol. 6598, pp. 173–192. Springer, Heidelberg (2011)
29. Soeken, M., Wille, R., Kuhlmann, M., Gogolla, M., Drechsler, R.: Verifying UML/OCL Models Using Boolean Satisfiability. In: Conference on Design, Automation and Test in Europe (DATE 2010). European Design and Automation Association, pp. 1341–1344 (2010)
30. SOFTEAM. Modelio (2012), http://modelio.org/
31. ter Beek, M.H., Fantechi, A., Gnesi, S., Mazzanti, F.: A state/event-based model-checking approach for the analysis of abstract system properties. Science of Computer Programming 76(2), 119–135 (2011)

Time Properties Verification Framework for UML-MARTE Safety Critical Real-Time Systems

Ning Ge and Marc Pantel

University of Toulouse, IRIT/INPT
2 rue Charles Camichel, BP 7122, 31071 Toulouse cedex 7, France
{Ning.Ge,Marc.Pantel}@enseeiht.fr

Abstract. Time properties are key requirements for the reliability of Safety Critical Real-Time Systems (RTS). UML and MARTE are standardized modelling languages widely accepted by industrial designers for the design of RTS using Model-Driven Engineering (MDE). However, formal verification at early phases of the system lifecycle for UML-MARTE models remains mainly an open issue.

In this paper[1], we present a time properties verification framework for UML-MARTE safety critical RTS. This framework relies on a property-driven transformation from UML architecture and behaviour models to executable and verifiable models expressed with Time Petri Nets (TPN). Meanwhile, it translates the time properties into a set of property patterns, corresponding to TPN observers. The observer-based model checking approach is then performed on the produced TPN. This verification framework can assess time properties like upper bound for loops and buffers, Best/Worst-Case Response Time, Best/Worst-Case Execution Time, Best/Worst-Case Traversal Time, schedulability, and synchronization-related properties (synchronization, coincidence, exclusion, precedence, sub-occurrence, causality). In addition, it can verify some behavioural properties like absence of deadlock or dead branches. This framework is illustrated with a representative case study. This paper also provides experimental results and evaluates the method's performance.

Keywords: Real-Time System, Time Property Verification, Model Transformation, UML, MARTE, Time Petri Net, Model Checking.

1 Introduction

Safety Critical Real-Time Systems (RTS) have strong timing requirements concerning system's reliability. Model-Driven Engineering (MDE) allows verifying system's properties since the early phases of system lifecycle and iteratively improving the models according to the verification results. One important issue

---

[1] This work was funded by the French ministries of Industry and Research and the Midi-Pyrénées regional authorities through the ITEA2 OPEES and FUI Projet P projects.

is how to assess the properties for semi-formal models. UML [14] and its profile for modelling non-functional concerns, MARTE [15] are standardized modelling languages widely accepted by industrial designers for RTS. However, to our knowledge, no formal specification for the whole language is currently available. Thus, before verification, UML models must be transformed to executable and verifiable models, supported by state-of-the-art model checkers. Meanwhile, time properties must also be transformed to verifiable time assertions. A key issue in the use of model checkers is to avoid the combinatorial explosion of state space and to guarantee the verification method's performance. Combemale et al. have proposed in [5] to design *Property-driven* formal verification tools to handle many different kinds of properties for complex system models. The translation is thus dedicated to each kind of properties to improve verification performance. This work follows the same approach to design a time property verification toolset for UML-MARTE models of safety critical RTS.

This paper presents the resulting verification framework that can assess time properties like upper bounds for loops and buffers, Best/Worst-Case Response Time (B/WCRT), Best/Worst-Case Execution Time (B/WCET), Best/Worst-Case Traversal Time (B/WCTT), schedulability, and synchronization-related properties (synchronization, coincidence, exclusion, precedence, sub-occurrence, causality). In addition, it can verify some behavioural properties like absence of deadlock or dead branches. The framework relies on three steps.

Firstly, the property-driven transformation from UML-MARTE to Time Petri Nets (TPN). This method translates semi-formal UML models into executable TPN models for verification purpose. TPN [13] is selected as the verification model, as it allows expressing and verifying time properties under both logical and chronometric time models. This framework uses the TINA toolset [3] as model checker. Fig. 1 is a TPN example. Compared to Petri Nets, the transitions in TPN are extended with a time constraint that controls the firing time. For example, transition T_1 is attached with time constraint [19,27]. When the token arrives at place P_1, the local timer of T_1 starts. Between 19 and 27 time units, T_1 can be fired. This transformation covers UML architecture models (using the full Composite Structure Diagram) and behaviour models (using the full State Machine Diagram and a major subset of Activity Diagram). It is property-driven in order to limit the state space during model checking. Property-driven means that the transformation of some UML elements can be different depending on the assessed property; meanwhile the transformation does not conserve all the information in UML, but only those concerning the property verification. Another issue is raised from TPN theoretical limits. As model checking and reachability are undecidable in TPN when using stopwatch [4], the transformation method should avoid using stopwatches.

Secondly, the translation from time properties into time property patterns. Time properties are expressed using MARTE. These expressions cannot be directly verified by TPN model checker. The proposed method translates them into a set of verifiable property patterns, which are quantitative. Their values can be computed in our proposal by iterative use of the model checker relying on

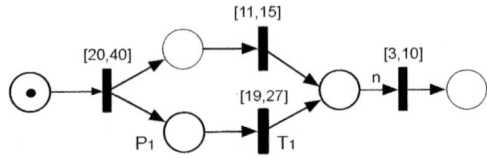

Fig. 1. Time Petri Net Example

dichotomy search. The time property patterns are independent of both the user modelling language and the verification language, making the method reusable in other verification frameworks. To make our method practical for end users, we focus on the time properties at both the event and the task levels. For the synchronization-related properties, we introduce the concept of *time tolerance*, because two simultaneous events cannot be measured without errors in the real world. The related work CCSL [2] focuses only on more symbolic time constraints at the event level without time tolerance.

Finally, the verification of time property patterns. The usual methods for verifying time properties in TPN rely mostly on LTL (Linear Time Logic), CTL (Computation Tree Logic) and μ calculus. First, end users are not accustomed to their use. Second, these languages are not always powerful enough for some quantitative properties, in terms of both their semantic expressiveness and computation resource consummation. This issue is reduced by using the observer-based model checking. For one property pattern, an additional TPN structure extends the original TPN, then the reachability graph is generated using the highest abstraction. Complex LTL assertions become marking existence assertions, which can be cheaply computed. The observers do not change the original TPN's behaviour. This observer-based verification method relying on TPN is independent of the user modelling language, making it reusable.

This paper is structured as follows: Section 2 compares this proposal with the related works; Section 3 briefly presents the verification framework for UML-MARTE; Section 4 introduces a representative case study; Section 5 presents the property-driven transformation method from UML-MARTE models to the target TPN models; Section 6 proposes the time property translation method and the time property patterns verification method based on observers in TPN; Section 7 evaluates the proposed framework by verifying the time property in the case study and analyses the method's performance; Finally, comments on conclusion and further works are discussed in Section 8.

2 Related Works

Some works are also aimed to verify the properties in UML. The difference lies in the type of verification model and the capacity of the verification methods. Lilius and Paltor use the PROMELA language in [11] to specify UML models and exploit the SPIN model checker. This method did not involve LTL verification and the author thought SPIN is not the most efficient solution. André and Mallet use

Esterel in [2] as verification language. Although its time constraint specification language CCSL covers logical and chronometric constraint in UML, its verification approach only supports logical constraints so far to our understanding. Gagnon et al. translate UML diagrams into Maude language and verify deadlock property using LTL in [6]. This work does not handle other time properties. In terms of performance, this work denotes that they still need to test this approach on larger examples. Knapp1 and Wuttke transform UML to a special class of timed automaton in [10], then translate them to concrete programs for model checkers SPIN. It verifies the consistency between different system descriptions. This work does not concern the time aspect. Medina and Cuesta present in [12] MARTE2MAST, a tool that enables the extraction of schedulability analysis models and their direct analysis using MAST [9]. It supports analysis by using simulation tool and static analysis techniques. It defines a complete package for system analysis including the scheduling algorithms. However, as the simulation is not exhaustive, it cannot prove the correctness in all possible cases. Shousha et al. describe in [16] a search-based UML-MARTE model analysis method for starvation and deadlock detection. It uses genetic algorithms to search through the state space. As the genetic search method cannot ensure the building of the full state space including all the final states, this method cannot guarantee that the whole space will be exhaustively searched. It can detect errors but cannot prove their absence, which is a significant drawback for safety critical systems.

Petri Nets are powerful models for describing system behaviour and for verifying the properties. In [1] Andrade et al. map SysML Activity to ETPN (extended TPN with energy constraints) to estimate the energy consumption and the execution time of system. Compared with this work, the advantages of our work lie in 3 aspects: for the time property scope, we verify a large scope of time properties, while [1] covers only the execution time; for the transformation method, we propose the property-driven transformation method and consider both the architecture and the behaviour models, while [1] only considers the behaviour model; for the verification method, we propose a novel observer-based TPN verification method.

3 Overview of UML-MARTE Verification Framework

The objective of the UML-MARTE verification framework (Fig. 2) is to verify whether the design of *UML-MARTE RTS Model* satisfies the expected *Time Property*. The *System Model* consists of both *Behaviour Model* and *Architectural Model*. The former defines how the system will act and response to the outside world, while the latter describes the interconnection relation between sub-components of the system. In practice, the behaviour model is described by Activity and State Machine diagrams, and the architecture is defined by Composite Structure diagrams. All time related specifications and *Time Properties* are modelled using MARTE profile. *System Models* are translated into *TPN* models through *Behaviour/Structure Transformation*. *Time Properties* are translated into *Time Property Patterns* by *Time Property Transformation*. All the transformations are performed automatically and the formal activities are transparent to the end user. The model checking is performed on the generated *Tag Pattern TPN* models and the corresponding *LTL/CTL/Marking Assertion* by using TINA model checker. The verification is based on the observers added in the TPN. An observer is used to observe the value of one *Property Pattern*. Finally, *Verification Result Computation* is performed to combine the *Property Pattern Results*, then the target *Time Property Verification Result* is available.

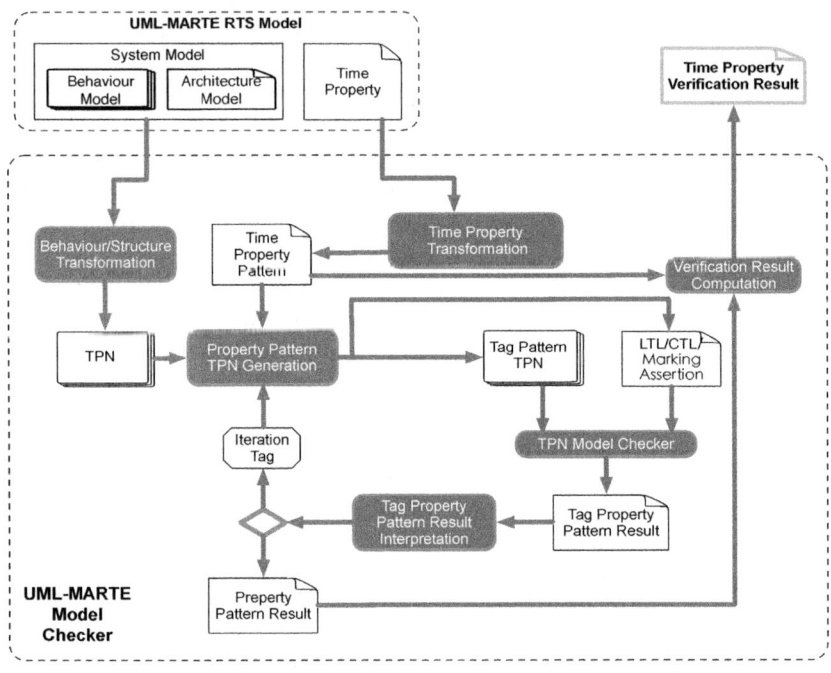

Fig. 2. UML-MARTE Model Checker

4 Case Study

We use a classical asynchronous RTS model, IMA-based airborne system, to present the application of the proposed methods. According to the general asynchronous message-driven pattern, the *sender* will regularly distribute data to the two *receivers* through the communication networks that have transfer delays and jitters. The receivers will do some computation. Fig. 3 presents the architecture model. The *sender* represents a data-collecting sensor. The *router* represents a virtual link of Avionics Full DupleX (AFDX). The two *receivers* represent two identical calculators that provide redundant control. The input data of computation is sent by the *sender* through the *router*.

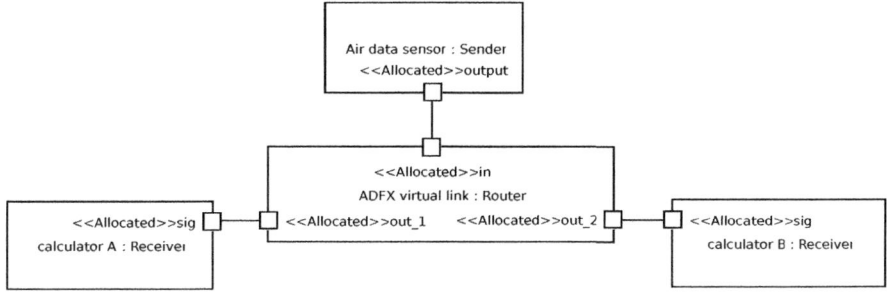

Fig. 3. IMA-based Airborne Architecture Model

The elements from MARTE in Table 1 are used to describe time specification. The redundant controller design requires that the output of the two calculators must be available at the same time in each working cycle; otherwise, the servo of the corresponding actuator cannot correctly unify the redundant command. In this case, we need to verify *the coincidence of computation tasks between calculators A and B*. As it is impossible to respect a strict simultaneous timing with an explicit local synchronisation, a time tolerance is defined. Once the two time instants fall into the same time window (size of window equals to tolerance), they are considered as coincident.

Table 1. MARTE Profile Usage

MARTE Profile	Time Specification
GRM::ResourceUsage	task's execution time
GRM::CommunicationMedia	communication delay
Alloc::Allocated	mapping the soft data pin to the hard data port

The AFDX only guarantees the communication delay upper bound, which means that the delay varies in $[t_{min}, t_{max}]$. Thus, it is obvious that the computation of calculators A and B are coincident only if the time tolerance is superior to $(t_{max} - t_{min})$, which is twice of the network jitter. In some cases, however, we need to design some supplementary protocol between the receivers to decrease the coincidence time window in order to get better system robustness.

The designer implements a *naive* protocol relying on the *hand shake* paradigm of Fig. 4, in which the two receivers are distinguished by respectively setting as active and passive modes (Fig. 5). The active one, after getting the data from the sender, sends an asynchronous notification to the passive one and automatically waits for a fixed time duration to launch its computation. The passive one will start its redundant computation once it gets the notification from its active master. As the notification message is also passed by the same AFDX network, the designer could wonder if this protocol really solves the tolerance-reduction requirement. By modifying the wait time of the active receiver and the network jitter, the designer can use the proposed methods to verify whether the computations are still coincident under the new protocol, and then refine his design according to the verification results. In this case study, we illustrate how our approach helps verifying time properties and assists the protocol designer with guaranteed correctness and performance.

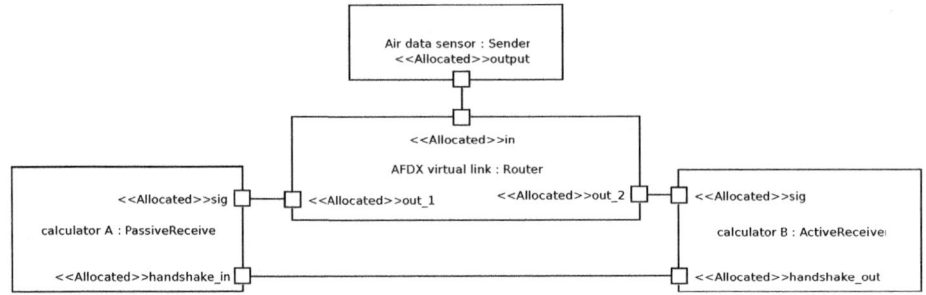

Fig. 4. IMA-based Airborne System Architecture Model with Handshake Protocol

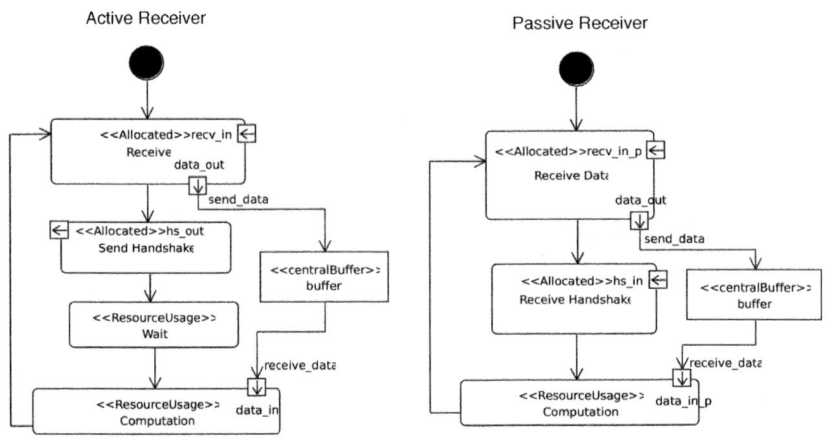

Fig. 5. IMA-based Airborne System Behaviour Model with Handshake Protocol

5 Transformation from UML-MARTE to TPN

We present the principles of the UML transformation method and illustrate the transformation for a significant subset of UML elements of both the architecture and behaviour models. Due to page limits, the complete transformation rules for UML Activity Diagram can be consulted in [8]. The description of the UML State Machine Diagram transformation will be submitted later on.

5.1 Principles

The transformation approach is property-driven, aiming to limit the state space of model checking. The approach respects the following 6 principles:

1. The framework verifies each time property in one state space generation. This means one transformation keeps only the information for one property to be verified.
2. The transformation of one UML element may be different according to the time property.
3. For some UML elements not influencing time properties, the target TPN semantics can be standardized and homogeneous for all the properties.
4. The transformation should guarantee the consistency between high-level and lower-level models. However, a correct transformation here does not imply a 100% semantic preservation, but rather to ensure the semantics necessary for the property verification are preserved through the transformation.
5. The target TPN models should ensure high performance verification, especially for large-scale asynchronous applications.
6. The patterns resulted from each element transformation should be easy to assemble. This may degrease the verification performance. But it can be compensated later by a model optimization phase that eliminates the elements irrelevant to the verification.

5.2 Architecture Model Transformation

The architecture parts in the model aim to connect the different parts to build a whole system, using communication media or shared resource. The transformation method aims to replace each component of the architecture part by its relevant behaviour part, respecting a correct instance-mapping, context-based naming and their connection relationship. In the Composite Structure Diagram (CSD) from the case study, the significant elements are *Part*, *Port* and *Connector*. The others remain important, but due to page limits, we only describe the mapping rules for *Part* and *Port* in this paper.

Part. There are two patterns for *Part*: hierarchical and primitive (Fig. 6). The behaviour is described, for the former, by the Part's inner structure, and, for the later, by the Part's associated behaviour model. For the hierarchic pattern, the architecture model is considered as a tree-like structure, and the mapping approach is applied recursively.

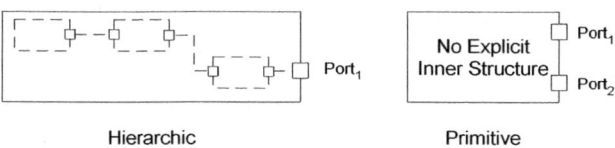

Fig. 6. CSD-Part

Port. *Port* is used to connect outside structure and inner behaviour. MARTE *Alloc::Allocated* profile is used to map the logical *PIN* in behaviour model and the physical *Port* in architectural model. *Port* is transformed to an empty TPN place to represent a data buffer concept. In a bad designed system, data quantity may overfill the buffer size, it is thus important to detect this undesired property before doing the verification, as this may cause an undecidable boundedness problem in TPN verification. In order to avoid a non-terminating verification problem, a supplementary structure is added (Fig. 7). It ensures that if the buffer is overfilled, it will raise an overflow. The overflow is represented by an ever-large marking that cannot exist in normal system. As TINA can detect on-the-fly any marking exceeding the pre-set threshold and stop state graph generation at once, this transformation method guarantees that all verification will finally terminate.

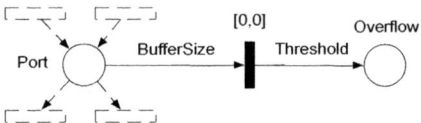

Fig. 7. CSD-Port

5.3 Behaviour Model Transformation

A general transformation pattern is defined (see Fig. 8) to automate the assembly of the TPNs generated from the behaviour model. For all non-link elements in UML, the generated TPN must contain some *C_IN* transitions to connect with other predecessors in static model structure. In the same manner, some *C_OUT* places must exist to connect with its structural successors.

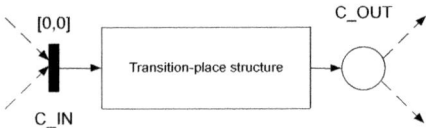

Fig. 8. General Transformation Pattern

The main elements in the UML Activity Diagram (AD) are related to control, action, resource, object, and connection. We present the transformation for *OpaqueAction* for system with single and multiple clocks (see later). An action is the fundamental unit of executable behaviour. It takes a set of inputs and converts them into a set of outputs. Depending on the abstraction level, an action could represent either a complex processing flow or a primitive one carrying out a computation. In UML-AD, there are 55 kinds of actions. Each kind covers a certain range of semantics for different usage. In order to focus on the core semantics related to time properties, we generalize the concept using the *OpaqueAction*.

Action Transformation Pattern. The transformation method is illustrated by Fig. 9. All input data-related flows should link to B. All output data-related flows should link to C. All input resource-related flows should link to A. All output resource-related flows should link to D. The execution time of one action is specified by the time constraint on transition C.

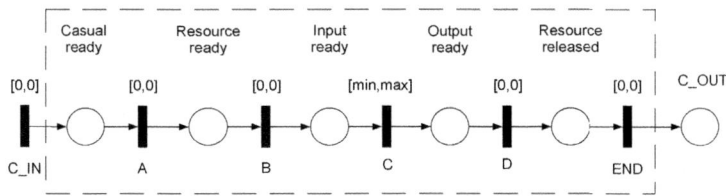

Fig. 9. UML Action Transformation to TPN

Mono-clock & Multi-clock. In the real world, each clock has an independent drift. For systems with a single clock (mono-clock) this drift can be ignored, because the difference between tick duration and real physical time is of the same proportion at any given time for any part of the system. However, in systems with several clocks (multi-clock), the model transformation should be able to represent the correct time semantic of the system by considering the different clocks' drifts. The solution is to assume a global physical clock and to project each time consumption and drift on this unique precise time reference. In our study, we use strictly the physical time notion as the exact reference for both mono and multi-clock base system.

Mono-clock Action. For mono-clock actions, the execution time is directly used after a global normalization of the time units. For example, if action A takes [3.4 ms, 4.7 ms] and actions B [78.9 us, 463.5 us], the correspondent min time and max time on the TPN transition is [34000, 47000] and [789, 4635] respectively, with the common unit of 0.1 us.

Multi-clock Action. For multi-clock actions, the execution time is specified by the expected physical time. Before integrating this time into a multi-clock based system, first we need to translate the expected physical time into tick numbers. Then its real physical time can be deduced by associating the clock's drift. We use the same example as the previous one. Let clock A and B tick theoretically every 1 us, and their backward and forward drift are both 1%, therefore action A's tick number is [3400, 4700] and B's is [78.9, 463.5]. As tick number must be integer, a rounding strategy must be taken, without introducing unreasonable conversion error. In our study, we use the floor function for t_{min} and ceiling function for t_{max}. Therefore, we have A for [3400, 4700] and B for [78, 464] as tick numbers after the rounding.

As the method assumes each component has independent clock, the drawback is that it can be too strict for those devices that share a clock. We still decide to choose this abstraction paradigm, because in the verification viewpoint, this will only lead to a false-violation. It means that if a time property is satisfied under independent-clock hypothesis, it must be also satisfied in a shared-clock system. This sufficient but not necessary condition may only cause a performance trade-off in practice, but never gives out a wrong verification result when property's proof is positive.

6 Translation and Verification of Time Property

The time properties should be translated into TPN-compatible analyzable formalism. In our case study, the property is the coincidence between two tasks. We illustrate the property translation and verification methods for this property. The translation for all the synchronization-related properties can be consulted in [7]. The verification of other properties will be presented in other papers.

6.1 Translation of Coincidence Property

Definition (Task Level Coincidence). *Task X and Y are coincident iff. the nth occurrence of X occurs simultaneously with the nth occurrence of Y, $n \in \mathbb{N}$.*

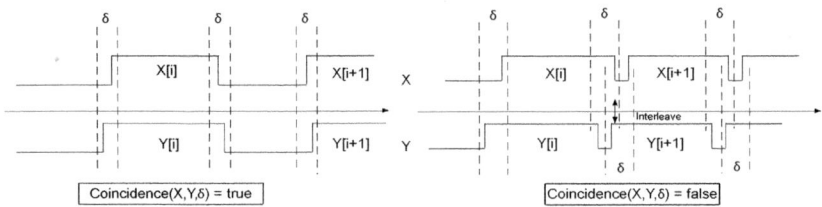

Fig. 10. Coincidence Property

As shown in Fig. 10, the coincidence between two tasks is determinated by the coincidence between the $Event_{start}$ and the $Event_{end}$ of tasks. For the nth occurrence of task X and Y, if the two $Event_{start}$ are coincident and the two $Event_{end}$ are coincident within time tolerant δ, task X and Y are coincident. Formally, task coincidence is translated into the following 3 equivalent assertions.
$Coincidence(X, Y, \delta) \equiv$

$$\forall t \in \mathbb{R}_+ : (|O(X_s^t) - O(Y_s^t)| < 2) \wedge (|O(X_e^t) - O(Y_e^t)| < 2) \qquad (1)$$

$$\forall t \in \mathbb{R}_+ : (|T(X_s^t) - T(Y_s^t)| < \delta) \wedge (|T(X_e^t) - T(Y_e^t)| < \delta) \qquad (2)$$

$$\forall i \in \mathbb{N}^* : (T(X_e^i) + \delta < T(Y_s^{i+1})) \wedge (T(Y_e^i) + \delta < T(X_s^{i+1})) \qquad (3)$$

In the above assertions, X represents task; X_a the inner event a of task X, particularly X_s for start event, X_e for end event; X_a^i the ith occurrence of inner event of task X; X_a^t the occurrence of X_a which is the nearest (forward or backward) to the time instant t; $T(X_a^i)$ the occurring time instant of X_a^i; $T(X_a^t)$ the occurring time instant of X_a^t; $O(X_a^t)$ the occurrence count for X_a at time t; and δ is the time tolerance for coincidence. There are 4 time property patterns in the assertions (Table 2). The task-level property is then represented by a set of event-level property patterns.

Table 2. Time Property Patterns

Time Property Pattern	Definition
X_s^{i+k}	Representation of event X_s^{i+k}
$\|O(X_a^t) - O(Y_a^t)\| < \delta$	Occurrence difference between events X_a^t and Y_a^t
$\|T(X_a^t) - T(Y_a^t)\| < \delta$	Relative T_{max} between events X_a^t and Y_a^t
$T(X_e^i) + \delta < T(Y_s^{i+1})$	Relative T_{min} between events X_a^t and Y_b^t

6.2 Verification of Time Property Pattern $|T(a^t) - T(b^t)| < \delta$

To assess the time property, the observer pattern is added into the original TPN, and then the TINA model checker is used to verify the observer-dedicated LTL/CTL/Marking assertions for the TPN. As model checking significantly consumes time and memory resource, we use the following 2 approaches to ensure the verification performance.

- When doing the model checking, the TPN shall perform the highest possible abstraction to unfold the reachability graph. This high abstraction model should preserve the desired time property. The model-checking is on-the-fly.
- Each assertion's verification is independent in terms of reachability graph generation, so a parallel computation is possible.

We choose one of the property patterns, $|T(a^t) - T(b^t)| < \delta$, to illustrate the verification method. The principle of deciding whether two events are always occurring in a given bound is to find out whether one could advance another by time δ.

An observer pattern (Fig. 11) is added in the original TPN. The middle transition will always instantly neutralize the tokens from the places $Occ\ A$ and $Occ\ B$ except when one token waits for a time longer than δ that leads to the firing of $Pass$ transition. To guarantee the termination of model checking, the pattern is extended by adding a large overflow number on the tester's incoming arc. We use places $tester\ A$ and $tester\ B$ to detect this exception. In the generated reachability graph, it only requires to verify if $tester\ A$ or $tester\ B$ has marking. The assertion is: $\Diamond(testerA = 1) \vee \Diamond(testerB = 1)$.

Once it is known how to verify $|T(a^t) - T(b^t)| < \delta$, it is possible to change δ to compute a near optimal tolerance. If $|T(a^t) - T(b^t)| < \delta + 1$ is verified as true, but false for $|T(a^t) - T(b^t)| < \delta$, then the near optimal tolerance is $\delta + 1$.

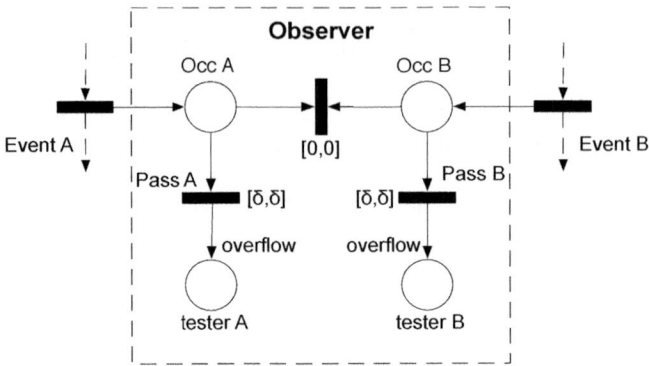

Fig. 11. $|T(a^t) - T(b^t)| < \delta$ Pattern TPN Observer

In order to improve the computation efficiency, a dichotomy search is used to reduce the complexity from $O(N)$ to $O(\log N)$.

7 Verification Result and Performance Analysis

7.1 Verification Result

In the case study, the designer aims to design a protocol relying on our verification framework, and then evaluate the system performance. The designer alters the *wait time of the active receiver* and the *jitter*, selects the *network average delay* and computes the *coincidence tolerance*. The result is shown in Fig. 12. Different coloured lines represent the result with different jitters. The variation is regular and linear because the modelled system is conceptually simple without resource sharing. It is obvious that the best wait time of the protocol is 1600ms.

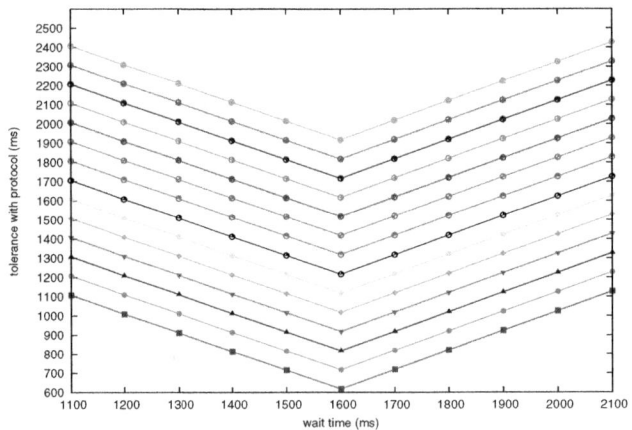

Fig. 12. Verification Result: Best Wait Time of Active Receiver

Then the user aims to evaluate this protocol by verifying the coincidence property. In the verification result (see Table 3), comparing the minimum coincidence tolerance in original system and that in the protocol system, it is obvious that the protocol succeeds in decreasing the tolerance value. We can say the system is more robust than the original.

Table 3. Verification Result: Independence with Designed Hand shake Protocol (ms)

Network Average Delay	Network Jitter	Time Window	Min Coincidence tolerance	
			Original System	Protocol System
1600	100	200	685	617
1600	300	600	1085	817
1600	500	1000	1485	1017
1600	700	1400	1885	1217
1600	900	1800	2285	1417
1600	1100	2200	2685	1617
1600	1300	2600	3085	1817
1600	1500	3000	3485	2017

7.2 Verification Performance Analysis

The performance of model checking is a very important issue for the end user. In this verification framework, we have used property-driven transformation, observer-based verification in highest abstraction mode and parallel computation methods to avoid the explosion of state space problem and to ensure a high performance. To validate the performance, we focus on two aspects: efficiency and scalability. The objective is to find out that within an acceptable time range

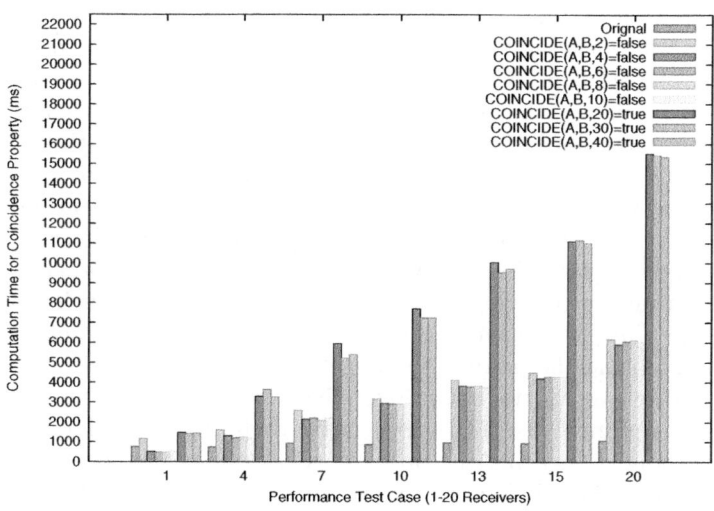

Fig. 13. Performance Evaluation

for rapid system prototyping (less than 1 minute), the framework is able to verify the coincidence property of system with a scale of *2 senders, 2 routers, and 1-20 pairs of active-passive receivers* which is representative of current avionics systems.

The performance evaluation result (Fig. 13) shows both the efficiency and the scalability of the performance. The efficiency is shown by the verification's computation time. For a system with 20 pairs of receivers, the original reachability graph generation time is less than 1000ms on a common computer; the computation time proving that the property is true is less than 16000ms, and the computation time proving that the property is false is about 6000ms. It is straightforward that proving a property false needs less time than the truth proof, because once a violation is detected the checking terminates. The scalability is shown by the linear relation between the time-over-cost of verification and the system's scale. When the increasing ratio is constant, it guarantees that if the original system reachability graph could be generated, then all the verifications of its time properties using our framework will take an appropriate time.

8 Conclusion and Further Works

In this paper, we propose a time property verification framework for UML-MARTE safety critical RTS. This verification framework can assess time properties like upper bound for loops and buffers, B/WCRT, B/WCET, B/WCTT, schedulability and synchronization-related properties (synchronization, coincidence, exclusion, precedence, sub-occurrence, causality). In addition, it can verify some behavioural properties like the absence of deadlock or dead branches. We evaluate the framework with a representative case study focusing on the property of coincidence between two tasks. The verification result demonstrates this framework can not only verify the time properties, but also assist the system's design at early phases of the lifecycle. The performance test and analysis illustrate the efficiency and scalability of the framework. Due to page limits, we will present the other properties' verification in other contributions.

One contribution is the proposition of the property-driven transformation, time property translation and observer-based verification methods. The time property translation method is independent of both the design modelling language and the verification language; the observer-based verification method is independent of the design modelling language. This independence allows these methods to be integrated in other verification frameworks. Another contribution is the approaches for reducing the state space combinatorial explosion problem, including the property-driven transformation, the highest abstraction on-the-fly model checking, and the parallel computation.

In the future, we will focus on extending this framework. On the technical side, we will optimize the TPN models by finding some reducible structural patterns without influencing the property. On the methodological side, we will experiment with other kind of properties, like the functional property, to improve the *Property-driven* approach to DSML (Domain Specific Modelling Language) model verification that started in the TOPCASED project.

References

1. Andrade, E., Maciel, P., Callou, G., Nogueira, B.: A methodology for mapping sysml activity diagram to time petri net for requirement validation of embedded real-time systems with energy constraints. In: Digital Society, ICDS 2009 (2009)
2. André, C., Mallet, F.: Specification and verification of time requirements with ccsl and esterel. In: Proceedings of the 2009 ACM SIGPLAN/SIGBED Conference on Languages, Compilers, and Tools for Embedded Systems, LCTES 2009, pp. 167–176. ACM, New York (2009)
3. Berthomieu, B., Ribet, P.-O., Vernadat, F.: The tool tina - construction of abstract state spaces for petri nets and time petri nets. International Journal of Production Research 42(14), 2741–2756 (2004)
4. Berthomieu, B., Lime, D., Roux, O.: Reachability problems and abstract state spaces for time petri nets with stopwatches. Discrete Event Dynamic Systems 17, 133–158 (2007)
5. Combemale, B., Crégut, X., Garoche, P.L., Thirioux, X., Vernadat, F.: A Property-Driven Approach to Formal Verification of Process Models. In: Filipe, J., Cordeiro, J., Cardoso, J. (eds.) ICEIS 2007. LNBIP, vol. 12, pp. 286–300. Springer, Heidelberg (2008)
6. Gagnon, P., Mokhati, F., Badri, M.: Applying model checking to concurrent uml models. Journal of Object Technology 7(1), 59–84 (2008)
7. Ge, N., Pantel, M.: Verification of synchronization-related properties for uml-marte rtes models with a set of time constraints dedicated formal semantic, http://hal.archives-ouvertes.fr/hal-00677925
8. Ge, N., Pantel, M., Crégut, X.: Time properties dedicated transformation from uml-marte activity to time petri net. Submitted to 5th International Workshop UML and Formal Methods (UML&FM 2012) (August 2012), http://hal.archives-ouvertes.fr/hal-00686986
9. Gonzalez Harbour, M., Gutierrez Garcia, J., Palencia Gutierrez, J., Drake Moyano, J.: Mast: Modeling and analysis suite for real time applications. In: 13th Euromicro Conference on Real-Time Systems (2001)
10. Knapp, A., Wuttke, J.: Model Checking of UML 2.0 Interactions. In: Kühne, T. (ed.) MoDELS 2006. LNCS, vol. 4364, pp. 42–51. Springer, Heidelberg (2007)
11. Lilius, J., Paltor, I.: vuml: a tool for verifying uml models. In: 14th IEEE International Conference on Automated Software Engineering, pp. 255–258 (October 1999)
12. Medina, J.L., Cuesta, Á.G.: From composable design models to schedulability analysis with uml and the uml profile for marte. SIGBED Rev. 8(1), 64–68 (2011)
13. Merlin, P., Farber, D.: Recoverability of communication protocols–implications of a theoretical study. IEEE Transactions on Communications 24(9), 1036–1043 (1976)
14. Object Management Group, Inc.: OMG Unified Modeling Language^{TM}, Superstructure (February 2009)
15. Object Management Group, Inc.: UML profile for MARTE: modeling and analysis of real-time embedded systems version 1.0 (November 2009)
16. Shousha, M., Briand, L., Labiche, Y.: A uml/marte model analysis method for uncovering scenarios leading to starvation and deadlocks in concurrent systems. IEEE Transactions on Software Engineering 1, 99 (2010)

Unification of Compiled and Interpreter-Based Pattern Matching Techniques

Gergely Varró[*], Anthony Anjorin[**], and Andy Schürr

Technische Universität Darmstadt,
Real-Time Systems Lab,
D-64283 Merckstraße 25, Darmstadt, Germany
{gergely.varro,anthony.anjorin,andy.schuerr}@es.tu-darmstadt.de

Abstract. In this paper, we propose a graph pattern matching framework that produces both a standalone compiled and an interpreter-based engine as a result of a uniform development process. This process uses the same pattern specification and shares all internal data structures, and nearly all internal modules. Additionally, runtime performance measurements have been carried out on both engines with exactly the same parameter settings to assess and reveal the overhead of our interpreter-based solution.

Keywords: model transformation, pattern matching interpreter, compiled pattern matcher.

1 Introduction

As model transformation undoubtedly plays an immense role in the process of model-driven development, efficiency and scalability are, therefore, important issues. In many state-of-the-art tools [1,2], model transformations are governed by imperative control flow statements, which apply declarative rules as basic transformation units. Such tools offer the usual advantages of declarativity like an easily understandable specification language, and readily available solutions provided by the underlying execution engine for many performance-critical tasks, whose optimal implementation requires years of specialized expertise. One such task is the efficient checking of the application conditions of rules, which requires identifying those parts in the system model on which the rule is executable.

This application condition checking process (as well as several other subtasks in bidirectional model synchronization and on-the-fly consistency checking scenarios) can be described as a general pattern matching problem. In this context, a pattern consists of constraints, and the matching process determines those parts of the underlying model that fulfill all these constraints. Structural constraints

---

[*] Supported by the Postdoctoral Fellowship of the Alexander von Humboldt Foundation and associated with the Center for Advanced Security Research Darmstadt.
[**] Supported by the 'Excellence Initiative' of the German Federal and State Governments and the Graduate School of Computational Engineering at TU Darmstadt.

express restrictions that can be checked by using the services of the modelling layer (e.g., type checks, navigation along links), while non-structural constraints are handled by some other means (like integer or textual comparison). The rest of the paper will focus on handling structural constraints, which corresponds to the graph pattern matching problem [3]. Nonetheless, our approach is left open w.r.t. the integration of non-structural constraints as well.

When implementing a pattern matching engine, developers must decide on several important issues (see Sec. 2) already in the early phase of design, which are hardly modifiable in later development phases as they have radical consequences on the overall architecture. One of these critical topics is the decision whether a compiled or an interpreter-based engine is to be built.

A *compiled engine* only consists of program code that is directly executable on a certain platform without an extra module for performing pattern matching. A compiled engine typically features better runtime performance, as the algorithms are represented as machine or byte code of the underlying execution system and no operation handling layer is needed. In contrast, an *interpreter-based engine* requires a specific module (the interpreter), which is responsible for executing the operations needed to perform pattern matching. Such a technique could offer more flexibility (e.g., model-sensitive performance optimization [4]) and provide additional services such as high-level debug support, as the interpreter can access and exploit runtime information more easily.

There exists a large variety of advanced compiled pattern matcher implementations [1,5], and several sophisticated interpreter-based approaches [2,6] in different rule-based model transformation tools. Although some of them provide solutions for both cases, the resulting engines can be considered to be separate programs. The following statement [7] is, therefore, still valid: "Interpretation and code generation are often seen as two alternatives, not as a continuum". In order to allow different combinations of these alternatives, techniques are needed that handle compiled and interpreter-based pattern matchers in a uniform and tightly integrated way.

In this paper, we propose a pattern matching framework that can produce both a standalone compiled and an interpreter-based engine as a result of a uniform development process, which shares (i) the pattern specification, (ii) all internal data structures, and (iii) all internal activities except for one engine-specific module. Furthermore, applying exactly the same settings in this uniform process wherever possible, runtime performance measurements are carried out on both engines to assess and reveal the overhead of our interpreter-based solution. To our best knowledge, our proposed approach can be considered the first pattern matcher to support both a compiled and an interpreter-based setup in a unified, configurable and integrated manner and can, therefore, be easily embedded and used by different rule-based model transformation tools.

The remainder of the paper is structured as follows. Related work is discussed in Section 2. Section 3 introduces basic metamodelling terminology, pattern specification constructs, and the process of pattern matching. Sections 4 and 5 present our data structures and algorithms used in the unified pattern matching engine.

Section 6 gives a quantitative assessment and performance comparison of our compiled and interpreter-based engines. Section 7 concludes our paper.

2 Design Space of Pattern Matchers and Related Work

A widely deployable pattern matching engine should support many different application scenarios like the execution of rule-based model transformations on a desktop computer, as well as performing security monitoring tasks on an embedded system. As the computational power and the amount of available resources of these architectures significantly differ, the development of a pattern matcher requires considering several design issues that influence the applicability and performance of the approach.

The design space of pattern matching engines can be characterized by the following properties:

(1) Dependency on separate pattern matching modules. The first property, which has the closest relation to the topic of this paper, expresses whether pattern matching requires a specific interpreter (I), or can be performed without any separate modules in a standalone manner as a compiled program (C).

(2) Existence and granularity of intermediate data structures. Pattern matching interpreters and code generators that produce compiled engines usually operate on data structures with different granularity. One group of solutions directly processes the declarative, pattern specification either in a low-level form as an abstract syntax tree representation (AST), or in a high-level form as a pattern definition (P). The other group operates on a preprocessed (and typically optimized) intermediate data structure, which can either be a low-level byte code representation (BC), or a high-level search plan (SP).

(3) Generation schedule of intermediate data structures. When intermediate data structures are used by the pattern matcher, their generation schedule can also be an important design decision due to its time consuming nature. Intermediate data structures can be calculated clearly at compile time (CT), at runtime in an on-demand fashion (OD) by using a caching mechanism, or at runtime (RT) before each pattern matching process.

(4) Availability of model sensitive pattern matching strategies. The size and the structure of the underlying model often influence the runtime performance of a pattern matcher. As both characteristics can significantly change as a transformation proceeds, the runtime selection of a pattern matching strategy in a model sensitive (MS) way (i.e., by using statistics from the model) is a feasible optimization compared to approaches that rely only on metamodel-level, domain-specific (DS) information.

(5) Incrementality. As matches for a given pattern are often requested several times during the life cycle of several application scenarios, exploiting the reuse of already calculated matches is a feasible optimization possibility. In this sense, batch engines (B) restart the pattern matching process from scratch at each invocation, while incremental approaches (I) store a set of (partial) matches, and update this set according to a defined schedule that depends on changes in the underlying model.

(6) Implementation/target language. As the applicability of a pattern matcher in a specific environment is largely determined by the implementation language of the interpreter, or the target language of the code generator, this property has also been included in our survey. The categorization here indicates support for a single (1) or multiple (*) languages.

(7) Reusability in different modelling spaces. Another important factor, in the evaluation of pattern matchers, is their reusability in different modelling environments. In this sense, an engine can operate on non-standard (NS) or standard (S) (e.g., EMF, MDR) model repositories. In the latter case, a star (*) suffix is added, if a tool provides clear interfaces to several standard modelling environments.

(8) Model access. When a tool operates in a standard compliant modelling environment, the underlying model can be accessed via tailored (T) or reflective (R) interfaces, which obviously affects both the runtime performance, and the resource (disk and memory) demand of an approach.

As a categorization of general model transformation tools is already available [8], this survey, which cannot be complete due to space restrictions, focuses on the pattern matching modules of state-of-the-art, rule-based transformation engines, and systematically compares them based on the previously listed criteria, which has been preceded by a manual inspection of the available source code (or a related publication). Table 1 presents the evaluation of these pattern matchers, which are enumerated in alphabetical order.

Table 1. Tool comparison

Tool name	(1)	(2)	(3)	(4)	(5)	(6)	(7)	(8)
ATL [2]	I	BC	CT	DS	B	1	S*	R
Epsilon [9]	I	AST	N/A	DS	B	1	S*	R
Fujaba @ KS [1]	C	SP	CT	DS	B	1	S*	T
Fujaba @ PO [10]	I	SP		RT	MS B	1	S	T – R
GReAT [11]	I C	P	N/A	DS	B	1	NS	T
GrGen [5]	C	SP	OD		MS B	1	NS	N/A
Groove [12]	I	SP	OD		MS B I	1	NS	N/A
Henshin [13]	I	P	N/A	DS	B	1	S	R
PROGRES [14]	I C	BC	OD	DS	B I	*	NS	N/A
VIATRA [15,6]	I	SP	OD	DS	MS B I	1	NS S	T
Our approach	I – C	SP	CT OD – RT	DS	B	1	S	T
Perfect tool	I – C	BC,SP	CT – OD – RT	DS – MS	B – I	*	NS – S*	T – R

The N/A mark shows if a categorization is non-applicable, while the '–' notation is used to express that a tool is able to cover the whole range of values in an integrated and configurable manner. The last two lines represent the evaluation of our current approach, and a hypothetic ideal pattern matching engine that could be deployed in many different application scenarios.

Table 1 clearly shows that many aspects of the ideal solution have already been solved separately by the different existing tools; however, the coverage of *design space ranges* along several properties is still not satisfactory. The main challenge here is that each of the above-mentioned design space properties represents a decision that is hard-wired into the tool architecture making reengineering tasks difficult in this context.

3 Modelling Concepts and Data Structures

In this section, we introduce basic metamodelling terminology required to present our approach, define concepts related to pattern specification, and illustrate the process of pattern matching and its runtime data structures.

3.1 Metamodels and Models

A *metamodel* is the specification of the concepts and relationships in a certain domain. Figure 1(a) depicts an excerpt of the metamodel from a case study [16] for the GraBaTs'09 transformation tool contest [17], which poses a program comprehension challenge based on the Eclipse Java Development Tools (JDT) API [18]. Using the common UML class diagram notation, parts that are relevant for our running example are depicted. The metamodel has been taken unchanged from the case study, and defines concepts as *classes* (e.g., a CompilationUnit). Classes can *inherit* from other classes (e.g., every MethodDeclaration is a BodyDeclaration), can contain *attributes* (every Name has an fqn as an attribute of type String), and can *reference* other classes (CompilationUnits contain arbitrary many AbstractTypeDeclarations, which each have exactly one SimpleName). Attributes and references are referred to as *structural features* in the rest of the paper.

A *model* is an abstraction of a system, created with an intended goal in mind. In alignment with the UML notation, nodes and edges are referred to as *objects* and *links*, respectively. A model that is expressed using concepts specified in a metamodel is said to *conform to* the metamodel. Figure 1(b) depicts a model, which corresponds to the Eclipse JDT representation of a Java class Client with a single public method, which returns a Client.

3.2 Pattern Specification

This subsection introduces the concepts needed for specifying patterns. The following definitions are based on [19].

A *pattern* is a set of constraints over a set of variables. A *variable* is a placeholder for an object in a model. *Interface variables* constitute a subset of all variables used in a pattern, and represent the variables that can be accessed outside of the pattern. All other *local* (i.e., non-interface) variables can only be

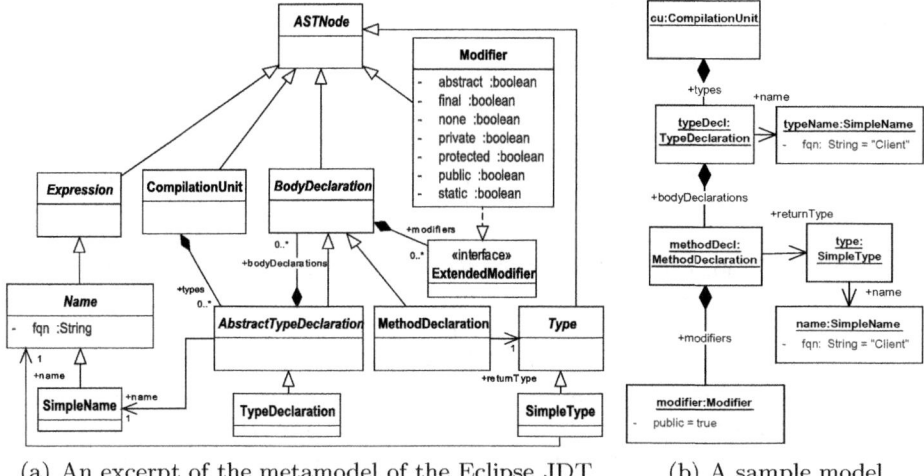

(a) An excerpt of the metamodel of the Eclipse JDT   (b) A sample model

Fig. 1. An excerpt of the metamodel of the Eclipse JDT API and a sample model

accessed and used internally in the pattern. A *constraint* specifies a condition on a set of variables that must be fulfilled by the objects, which are assigned to the variables during pattern matching. A constraint consists of a *constraint type* and a set of variables (also referred to as *parameters* in this context), for which the constraint must hold. In the following, an explicit reference to the type of a constraint shall be denoted by adding a 'type' suffix.

The pattern matcher has a pluggable infrastructure for the constraints that can be used for specifying patterns.[1] In this paper, only a subset of constraints is presented. The support for extending the framework with constraints for attribute handling, positive and negative pattern invocations is already available, however, the implementation for pattern calls is still a task for the future.

A *class constraint* (cls) restricts the type of the objects that can be assigned to its single parameter. A *structural feature constraint* (sf) prescribes the existence of a link, which connects the assigned objects and conforms to a given structural feature. Both constraints cls and sf have references to types in the corresponding metamodel. A *Boolean constraint* must evaluate to true for the assigned values to its single parameter.

The textual specification of patterns, used in this paper, is defined by the following simplified EBNF grammar:

```
patternSpecification ::= "pattern" signature "=" body
signature ::=  NAME "(" interfaceVariables ")"
body ::= "{" constraint* "}"
constraint ::= NAME typeReference? "(" variables ");"
typeReference ::= "<" NAME ">"
```

---

[1] Quantifiers can be defined at runtime in our framework, when the pattern matching is invoked, and consequently, they are not part of the pattern specifications.

```
interfaceVariables ::= variables
variables ::= ( NAME ",")* NAME
NAME ::= [a-zA-Z]+
```

Example. The graphical representation and the textual specification of pattern publicMethods[2] are presented in Fig. 2. This pattern requires the existence of a compilation unit CU, which has a type declaration TD with a public method declaration MD. Pattern publicMethods has three interface variables CU, TD, and MD (line 1). The class constraint on line 3 prescribes that variable CU must be mapped to a CompilationUnit. The structural feature constraint on line 10 requires a types reference that connects the objects that are assigned to variables CU and TD. The Boolean constraint on line 16 prescribes that the object assigned to variable PublicTag must be true. Please note that (i) the order of constraints (rows) in the textual representation of a pattern is arbitrary, (ii) constraints on references and attributes are handled in a uniform way (line 13), and (iii) the pattern matcher has access to all the properties of a metamodel element (information whether a class is abstract, a reference is a composition, etc.) via the references maintained in the class and structural feature constraints.

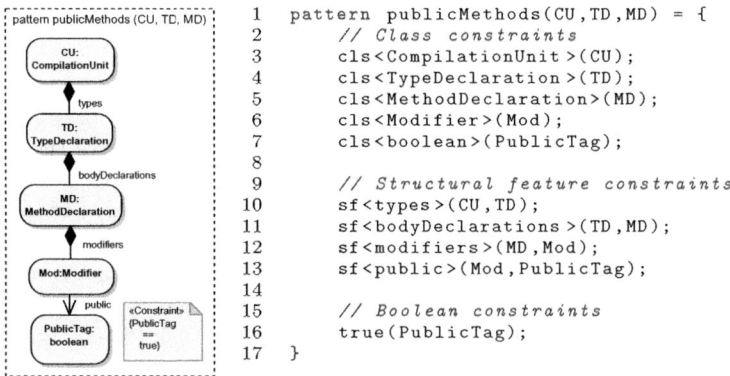

Fig. 2. Pattern publicMethods in a graphical and textual representation

3.3 Pattern Matching and Runtime Data Structures

Pattern matching is the process of determining mappings for all variables in a given pattern, such that all constraints in the pattern are fulfilled. The mappings of variables to objects are collectively called a *match*, which can be a *complete match* when all the variables are mapped, or a *partial match* in all other cases.

An *adornment* represents binding information for a sequence of variables and is indicated in the textual syntax by a sequence of letters B and F of the same length, which appears as a superscript on the name of the concept to which

---
[2] A more complex example scenario can be found in [4].

the adornment is attached. The letter B or F in an adornment, means that the variable in that position is bound or free, respectively.

When pattern matching is invoked, interface variables can be already bound to objects to restrict the search. The corresponding binding information of all interface variables is called a *pattern adornment*.

An *operation* represents a single atomic step in the matching process and it consists of a constraint and a constraint adornment. A *constraint adornment* prescribes which parameters must be bound when the operation is executed. A *check operation* has only bound parameters. An *extension operation* has free parameters, which get bound when the operation is executed.

Example. Suppose a matching process for the pattern `publicMethods` (Fig. 2) is to be run on the model of Fig. 1(b), with the interface variable CU bound to the compilation unit cu at pattern invocation. This single mapping itself constitutes a partial match, and the corresponding pattern adornment is BFF,[3] since only the first interface variable has been bound. When the pattern matching process terminates, a complete match is returned, which maps variables CU, TD, MD, Mod, and PublicTag to objects cu, typeDecl, methodDecl, modifier, and a Boolean true value, respectively.

4 Workflow of Compiled Pattern Matching

This section presents the workflow for generating a compiled pattern matching engine. In this process, a pattern matcher class is generated for every pattern. Although an adornment is part of runtime binding information, the generated engine must be prepared to handle a fixed set of pattern adornments, which are selected in advance at compile time. For each selected pattern adornment, a method that performs the actual pattern matching is generated into the corresponding pattern matcher class according to the approach depicted in Fig. 3, which operates as follows:

Section 4.1 For each constraint type used in the pattern specification, the set of allowed constraint adornments is calculated.
Section 4.2 For each pair of constraint and allowed constraint adornment, an operation is loaded.
Section 4.3 Operations are filtered and ordered by a search plan algorithm to produce an efficient search plan.
Section 4.4 Based on the search plan, generators are created, which control the code generation process.

When the pattern matcher is invoked at runtime, the pattern adornment is determined and used to select and execute the corresponding generated method.[4] The selected method performs the complete pattern matching process, collecting

---

[3] The pattern adornment only contains binding information for interface variables (CU, TD and MD in this example).
[4] If no such method exists, an exception is thrown, which might initiate a pattern matcher regeneration process.

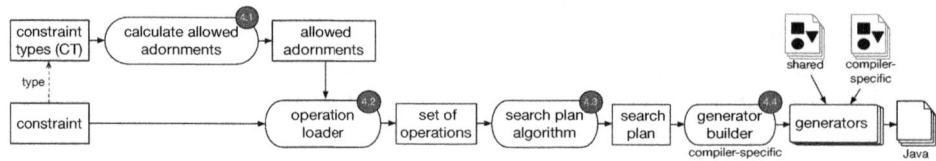

Fig. 3. Process for producing a compiled pattern matching engine

complete matches in a result set. The following subsections discuss the steps of the process in detail.

4.1 Allowed Adornment Calculation

In general, not every possible adornment is valid for every constraint type. Our framework allows the underlying modelling layer to define the set of allowed adornments for every available constraint type in a configurable way. For presentation purposes, standard Ecore/EMF is assumed as the modelling layer in the following: A structural feature constraint type, referring to a bidirectional reference, would allow adornments BB, BF, and FB, where BB means checking the existence of a link, while BF and FB denote forward and backward navigations, respectively. In the case of unidirectional references, only BB and BF adornments make sense. Analogously, only BB and BF adornments are allowed for structural feature constraint types referring to an attribute. Only the adornment B is allowed for class and Boolean constraint types.[5]

Example. The framed part of Figure 4(a) shows the complete list of constraint types and allowed adornments for pattern publicMethods. Lines 1–5 show that class constraint types have the adornment B as type checks can be performed only on a bound parameter. Line 6 represents a check for the existence of a types link, while line 7 means a forward navigation along a link of type types.

4.2 Operation Loading

The operation loader prepares all the operations that might be needed to execute pattern matching by iterating through all constraints of a pattern. It looks up the allowed adornments for the type of the constraint, and creates a new operation for each combination of constraint and allowed adornment.

Example. Figure 4(a) lists the set of operations that might be needed to calculate matches for pattern publicMethods. For example, line 1 shows that variable CU must already be mapped to an object before a corresponding type check can be performed. Line 7 expresses that a forward navigation along types links is executable only when an object has already been bound to variable CU.

---

[5] The set of allowed adornments for standard MOF/JMI, in contrast to Ecore/EMF, would also allow FF for associations, and F for class constraint types. Similarly, a modelling layer with additional EMF services could also support an extended set of allowed adornments for EMF supporting e.g., FB for indexed attributes.

```
 1  cls<CompilationUnit>^B(CU)
 2  cls<TypeDeclaration>^B(TD)
 3  cls<MethodDeclaration>^B(MD)
 4  cls<Modifier>^B(Mod)
 5  cls<boolean>^B(PublicTag)
 6  sf<types>^{BB}(CU,TD)
 7  sf<types>^{BF}(CU,TD)
 8  sf<bodyDeclarations>^{BB}(TD,MD)
 9  sf<bodyDeclarations>^{BF}(TD,MD)
10  sf<modifiers>^{BB}(MD,Mod)
11  sf<modifiers>^{BF}(MD,Mod)
12  sf<public>^{BB}(Mod,PublicTag)
13  sf<public>^{BF}(Mod,PublicTag)
14  true^B(PublicTag)
```

(a) Operations

```
 1  publicMethods^{BFF}(CU,TD,MD) = [
 2    cls<CompilationUnit>^B(CU);
 3    sf<types>^{BF}(CU,TD);
 4    cls<TypeDeclaration>^B(TD);
 5    sf<bodyDeclarations>^{BF}(TD,MD);
 6    cls<MethodDeclaration>^B(MD);
 7    sf<modifiers>^{BF}(MD,Mod);
 8    cls<Modifier>^B(Mod);
 9    sf<public>^{BF}(Mod,PublicTag);
10    cls<boolean>^B(PublicTag);
11    true^B(PublicTag);
12  ]
```

(b) Search plan for the sample pattern publicMethods

Fig. 4. Data structures used by both engines

4.3 Search Plan Generation

Operations are filtered and ordered by a search plan algorithm to produce efficient search plans. Due to space restrictions, search plans generation techniques like [1,4,6] and their details (e.g., cost functions, optimization algorithms) are not discussed in this paper.

A *search plan* is defined as a sequence of operations satisfying the following conditions:

1. Each constraint in the pattern has exactly one corresponding operation in the search plan.
2. Each variable that must be *bound* according to the constraint adornment of an operation is either already bound in the pattern adornment, or appears as a free variable in one of the preceding operations.
3. Each variable that must be *free* according to the constraint adornment of an operation is not bound in the pattern adornment and does not appear in any of the preceding operations as free variables.
4. Each extension operation must be immediately followed by class check operations that perform the type checking of the free variables of the extension operation.

Example. Figure 4(b) shows a search plan for pattern publicMethods, when the first interface variable (CU) is bound when pattern matching is invoked. The search plan has been derived from the set of operations (Fig. 4(a)) by filtering and reordering, and it fulfills all conditions 1–4. The constraint adornment on line 3, for example, is valid, as CU, which must be bound, is indeed bound in the pattern adornment. Similarly, TD, which must be free, is free in the pattern adornment, and does not appear in any preceding operation as a free variable.

4.4 Code Generation for a Compiled Pattern Matcher

The final step is code generation, which is controlled by a set of different *generators* that each maintain a link to a template.[6] As depicted in detail in Fig. 5 for the pattern adornment BFF, a *method generator* references a series of *operation generators*, responsible for navigation in the model (e.g., lines 2 and 5), which in turn reference *variable generators*, that store the determined values for variables on the JVM stack (e.g., lines 3–4 and 6–7). A *match generator* is responsible for the code that should be executed when a (complete) match is found (line 15). Code generation is initiated by starting the template of the method generator.

```
 1  private void matchBFF(CompilationUnit cu) {
 2    for (AbstractTypeDeclaration tempTD : cu.getTypes()) {
 3      if (tempTD instanceof TypeDeclaration) {
 4        TypeDeclaration td = (TypeDeclaration) tempTD;
 5        for (BodyDeclaration tempMD : td.getBodyDeclarations()) {
 6          if (tempMD instanceof MethodDeclaration) {
 7            MethodDeclaration md = (MethodDeclaration) tempMD;
 8            for (ExtendedModifier tempMod : md.getModifiers()) {
 9              if (tempMod instanceof Modifier) {
10                Modifier mod = (Modifier) tempMod;
11                Boolean tempPublicTag = mod.getPublic();
12                if (tempPublicTag != null) {
13                  Boolean publicTag = tempPublicTag;
14                  if (publicTag.booleanValue()) {
15                    // Complete match
16  } } } } } } } }
```

Fig. 5. Generated code to handle pattern matching

5 Workflow of Interpreter-Based Pattern Matching

Interpreter-based engines typically carry out all their pattern matching related tasks at runtime. As such, the pattern specification should be considered as a starting point when the matching process is invoked. Furthermore, in order to avoid any dependencies on generated data structures, interpreter-based pattern matchers typically use a reflective API of the modelling layer to access objects and to navigate along links.

In contrast to this general tendency, our interpreter-based solution (whose workflow is presented in Fig. 6) uses tailored interfaces (just like the compiled pattern matcher) to completely eliminate the performance effects that would be caused by the different model access strategies, and thus, to enable a fair quantitative comparison of our compiled and interpreter-based engine variants. This requires generated operation classes (and a loader class), which are subclasses of their generic counterparts and are produced at compile time (as shown by the solid arrows). A generated operation, thus, represents an atomic step in the pattern matching process and uses a tailored interface for model access purposes.

---

[6] Velocity is used as a template language and engine.

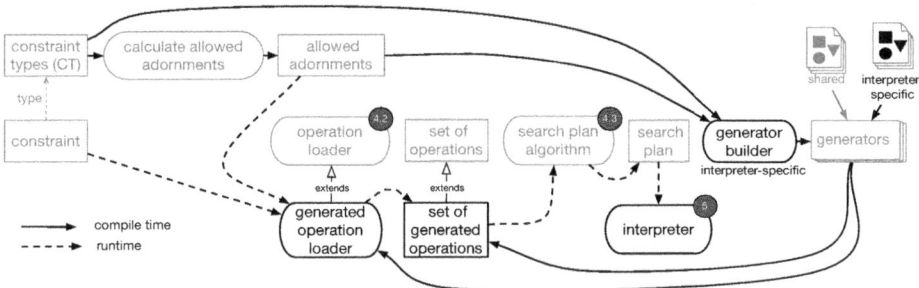

Fig. 6. Process for producing an interpreter-based engine

Although generated operations are produced at compile time, *all the remaining activities* are executed at *runtime* as highlighted by dashed arrows in Fig. 6. The runtime part of the interpreter-based pattern matching approach, which reuses all parts from Sec. 4 that are shaded in grey, works as follows:

Section 4.2. When the pattern matcher is invoked, a (generated) operation is loaded for each pair of constraint and allowed constraint adornment. As constraints are part of the pattern, this behaviour completely aligns with the expectation that an interpreter-based engine should start processing the pattern specification at runtime.

Section 4.3. Operations are filtered and ordered by a search plan algorithm to produce a search plan. The algorithm is obviously influenced by the pattern adornment, that has been determined by examining which interface variables have been mapped to objects in the model at pattern invocation.[7]

Section 5. Finally, the interpreter performs pattern matching by executing the search plan. The details of this interpreter module are presented in the remaining part of this section.

The interpreter uses a *match array* for storing the current match and the operations in the search plan. Every operation has a link to the next operation and a mapping, that identifies the slots in the match array, which correspond to the parameters of the operation.

When the interpreter is invoked, it prepares the initial match array, whose size is determined by the number of variables in the pattern. The initial match array is filled according to the input mapping of interface variables to objects in the model, and is passed to the first operation in the search plan. When an extension operation is performed, the structural feature is traversed forwards (BF) or backwards (FB) to bind the corresponding free variable, the type of the accessed object is validated, and the execution is passed on to the following operation for subsequent processing together with the extended match array. For a check operation, the operation is performed and, in case of success, the current match array is simply left unchanged and passed on. When the match

---

[7] Search plans can be cached and reused depending on the configuration settings.

array passes beyond the last operation, it represents a complete match and is stored in a result set. A single match array is used for storing all (partial) matches, and only complete matches are copied and stored in a result set.

This behaviour is a depth-first traversal[8] of a state space (just like the compiled approach), where a *state* represents the processing of a partial match by an operation. The state space can alternatively be described as a tree, whose root is the initial match, while internal nodes and leaves correspond to partial and complete matches, respectively.

6 Measurement Results

In this section, we present measurement results from comparing our compiled engine with our interpreter-based pattern matching engine, both produced via a uniform process, using our framework as discussed in Sec. 4 and Sec. 5. The pattern used for the measurements is from [16] and describes all classes, excluding inner classes, that contain at least one public static method, whose return type is the same as the class itself. Five models (Set0 – 4) of different size were taken unchanged from the same case study.

A 1.57 GHz Intel Core2 Duo CPU with 2.96 GB RAM was used for all measurements. Windows XP Professional SP 3 and Java 1.6 served as the underlying operating system and virtual machine, respectively. The maximum heap size was set to 1536 MB. *User time*, which is the amount of time the CPU spends performing actions for a program, was measured. On the used machine, this could only be measured with a precision of ± 12.625 ms. As a single pattern matching task takes less time than this value, each measurement was performed as a series of blocks. In a measurement block, the pattern matching task of the compiled engine was performed 100 times, while in the case of the interpreter-based engine, search plan generation and pattern matching were executed 500 times, and 20 times, respectively.[9] This block-based measurement was repeated 50 times in all cases to provide stable average values.

The generated search plans and resulting matches in both cases were validated manually to be equivalent. To obtain a fair comparison, search plan generation and pattern matching were measured separately for the interpreter.

Table 2 presents the measured execution times. The first column indicates the model used (Set0 – 4), the second and third columns the size of the model in number of Java classes and objects, respectively. The fourth column denotes the corresponding state space size in number of states, the fifth column the time (ms) for the compiled engine, while the last two columns show the time (ms) for search plan generation and pattern matching for the interpreter-based engine.

---

[8] Alternative strategies (e.g., breadth-first traversal) would typically duplicate match arrays during the execution of extension operations, which would cause an increased memory consumption.

[9] The only reason for selecting different block length values was to have raw data approximately on the same scale, which already belongs to the measureable range.

Table 2. Measurement results

	Java classes #	Model size #	State space #	Compiled PM ms	Interpreter-based SP ms	Interpreter-based PM ms
Set0	14	70447	232	0.03	0.12	0.19
Set1	40	198466	549	0.08	0.12	0.53
Set2	1605	2082841	37348	12.99	0.12	41.91
Set3	5769	4852855	94300	31.17	0.41	142.34
Set4	5984	4961779	103122	36.01	0.84	230.38

Table 2 shows that the compiled engine, which represents algorithms in a byte code form, and thus, requires no operation handling tasks to be executed, outperformed the interpreter-based engine in all cases, and was about 4–6 times faster. For the interpreter-based engine, the time spent for search plan generation increased for the larger models (Set3 and Set4), which are loaded into memory prior to search plan generation. We believe this is caused by garbage collection, which becomes necessary due to the substantial difference in size of the models as compared to Set0 or Set1.

In order to clarify the exact reason for the large execution times of the interpreter-based engine in case of large models, and to justify our assumption on the role of garbage collection, further measurements should be performed in the future with larger heap size settings, on more patterns and on different application domains e.g., like the ones mentioned in [20]. An additional comparison using reflective interfaces for our engines would also be interesting. Furthermore, other dimensions could be measured including memory footprint, number of loaded classes and RAM consumption.

Note that the main goal of our measurements was neither to quantitatively analyze pattern matchers with search plans [4,20], nor to draw any conclusion regarding the performance of compiled and interpreter-based engines in general, nor to repeatedly justify the obvious comparative statements about the runtime superiority of compiled techniques, but to assess the *exact extent* of performance differences between our pattern matcher variants. In our measurements, both variants accessed the EMF-based modeling layer via the same tailored interfaces. Additionally, they applied the same algorithm to produce the same search plan, which resulted in the same state space traversed in the same depth-first order. We think that this unified measurement setup could only be achieved by using a framework-based solution, and any modification in this setup would introduce performance influencing factors that are independent from the main issue under investigation (i.e., the exact effects caused by the selection of our compiled or interpreter-based engine).

7 Conclusion

In this paper, we proposed a pattern matching framework that can produce both a standalone compiled and an interpreter-based engine in a uniform process that shares all internal data structures and the majority of modules. As main advantages, our framework-based solution (1) eases the task of reengineering a tool with respect to its pattern matcher module, and (2) enables a switching possibility between the compiled and interpreter-based engines at runtime. Additionally, we carried out performance measurements on both engines with the same parameter settings to assess the overhead of our interpreter-based solution.

The proposed approach has been implemented in the context of the Democles project, whose goal is to provide a model-based pattern matcher implementation, which integrates several advanced pattern matching algorithms in one framework, and can be embedded into different tools. Contributions of this paper cover one aspect of this project, which was to present the unified process for handling compiled and interpreter-based pattern matchers. The model-sensitive search plan algorithm of the pattern matcher has been published in [4]. The interpreter additionally supports (a yet unpublished) step by step execution possibility, which can be the basis of a high-level debugger in the future.

References

1. Geiger, L., Schneider, C., Reckord, C.: Template- and modelbased code generation for MDA-tools. In: Giese, H., Zündorf, A. (eds.) Proc. of the 3rd International Fujaba Days, Paderborn, Germany, pp. 57–62 (2005),
ftp://ftp.upb.de/doc/techreports/Informatik/tr-ri-05-259.pdf
2. Jouault, F., Kurtev, I.: Transforming Models with ATL. In: Bruel, J.-M. (ed.) MoDELS 2005. LNCS, vol. 3844, pp. 128–138. Springer, Heidelberg (2006)
3. Rozenberg, G. (ed.): Handbook of Graph Grammars and Computing by Graph Transformation, vol. 1: Foundations. World Scientific (1997)
4. Varró, G., Deckwerth, F., Wieber, M., Schürr, A.: An Algorithm for Generating Model-Sensitive Search Plans for EMF Models. In: Hu, Z., de Lara, J. (eds.) ICMT 2012. LNCS, vol. 7307, pp. 224–239. Springer, Heidelberg (2012)
5. Geiß, R., Batz, G.V., Grund, D., Hack, S., Szalkowski, A.: GrGen: A Fast SPO-Based Graph Rewriting Tool. In: Corradini, A., Ehrig, H., Montanari, U., Ribeiro, L., Rozenberg, G. (eds.) ICGT 2006. LNCS, vol. 4178, pp. 383–397. Springer, Heidelberg (2006)
6. Varró, G., Varró, D., Friedl, K.: Adaptive graph pattern matching for model transformations using model-sensitive search plans. In: Karsai, G., Taentzer, G. (eds.) Proc. of International Workshop on Graph and Model Transformation. ENTCS, vol. 152, pp. 191–205. Elsevier (2005)
7. Voelter, M.: Best practices for DSLs and model-driven development. Journal of Object Technology 8(6), 79–102 (2009)
8. Czarnecki, K., Helsen, S.: Feature-based survey of model transformation approaches. IBM Systems Journal 45(3), 621–645 (2006)
9. Kolovos, D., Rose, L., Paige, R.: The Epsilon book,
http://www.eclipse.org/gmt/epsilon/doc/book/
10. Giese, H., Hildebrandt, S., Seibel, A.: Improved flexibility and scalability by interpreting story diagrams. In: Margaria, T., Padberg, J., Taentzer, G. (eds.) Proc. of the 8th International Workshop on Graph Transformation and Visual Modeling Techniques, ECEASST, vol. 18 (2009)

11. Agrawal, A., Karsai, G., Neema, S., Shi, F., Vizhanyo, A.: The design of a language for model transformations. Software and Systems Modeling 5(3), 261–288 (2006)
12. Rensink, A.: The GROOVE Simulator: A Tool for State Space Generation. In: Pfaltz, J.L., Nagl, M., Böhlen, B. (eds.) AGTIVE 2003. LNCS, vol. 3062, pp. 479–485. Springer, Heidelberg (2004)
13. Arendt, T., Biermann, E., Jurack, S., Krause, C., Taentzer, G.: Henshin: Advanced Concepts and Tools for In-Place EMF Model Transformations. In: Petriu, D.C., Rouquette, N., Haugen, Ø. (eds.) MODELS 2010, Part I. LNCS, vol. 6394, pp. 121–135. Springer, Heidelberg (2010)
14. Schürr, A., Winter, A.J., Zündorf, A.: The PROGRES Approach: Language and Environment. In: Handbook on Graph Grammars and Computing by Graph Transformation, vol. 2: Applications, Languages and Tools, pp. 487–550. World Scientific (1999)
15. Bergmann, G., Ökrös, A., Ráth, I., Varró, D., Varró, G.: Incremental pattern matching in the VIATRA model transformation system. In: Karsai, G., Taentzer, G. (eds.) Proc. of the 3rd International Workshop on Graph and Model Transformation, pp. 25–32. ACM (2008)
16. Sottet, J.S., Jouault, F.: Program comprehension, http://is.tm.tue.nl/staff/pvgorp/events/grabats2009/cases/grabats2009reverseengineering.pdf
17. Levendovszky, T., Rensink, A., van Gorp, P.: 5th International Workshop on Graph-Based Tools: The Contest, http://is.tm.tue.nl/staff/pvgorp/events/grabats2009/
18. Beaton, W., des Rivieres, J.: Eclipse platform technical overview. Technical report, The Eclipse Foundation (2006)
19. Horváth, Á., Varró, G., Varró, D.: Generic search plans for matching advanced graph patterns. In: Ehrig, K., Giese, H. (eds.) Proc. of the 6th Int. Workshop on Graph Transformation and Visual Modeling Techniques, vol. 6 of ECEASST (2007)
20. Varró, G., Schürr, A., Varró, D.: Benchmarking for graph transformation. In: Proc. of the 2005 IEEE Symposium on Visual Languages and Human-Centric Computing, Dallas, Texas, USA, pp. 79–88. IEEE Computer Society Press (2005)

OCL-Based Runtime Monitoring of Applications with Protocol State Machines

Lars Hamann, Oliver Hofrichter, and Martin Gogolla

University of Bremen, Computer Science Department
Database Systems Group, D-28334 Bremen, Germany
{lhamann,hofrichter,gogolla}@informatik.uni-bremen.de

Abstract. This paper presents an approach that enables users to monitor and verify the behavior of an application running on a virtual machine (like the Java virtual machine) at an abstract model level. Models for object-oriented implementations are often used as a foundation for formal verification approaches. Our work allows the developer to verify whether a model corresponds to a concrete implementation by validating assumptions about model structure and behavior. In previous work, we focused on (a) the validation of static model properties by monitoring invariants and (b) basic dynamic properties by specifying pre- and postconditions of an operation. In this paper, we extend our work in order to verify and validate advanced dynamic properties, i.e., properties of sequences of operation calls. This is achieved by integrating support for monitoring UML protocol state machines into our basic validation engine.

1 Introduction

When one faithfully follows the Model-Driven Development (MDD) paradigm, abstract representations of all artifacts, in particular of code, are needed in form of models. Model-like descriptions can be used as central parts in the software development process and are considered to be a promising paradigm for effective software production. Models can be employed in all development phases and for different purposes. Consequently and despite all justified criticism, the Unified Modeling Language (UML) is playing a pivotal role as a modeling language. Nearly every software engineer understands at least the UML core concepts, while other more specialized modeling languages first need to be explained from the scratch. This central role of the UML can also be observed by looking for transformation approaches from UML to more formal and specialized languages or tools such as the Alloy [24] language, SAT [25] or model checkers [19].

When using UML models for abstractions of concrete software systems, model quality is important. It has to be ensured that the developed models correspond to the implementation to be abstracted from. Otherwise formal quality assurance techniques would verify some disconnected abstract model and not the concrete implementation. This is especially true, if the implementation is not fully generated from the model and finalized by a developer. This is currently the most common case.

In [17] simulation of the model is proposed in the overall process of model checking. The process is shown in Fig. 1 which is adapted from [17, p. 8]. Our contribution and extension to the process is shown in the parts having a grey background.

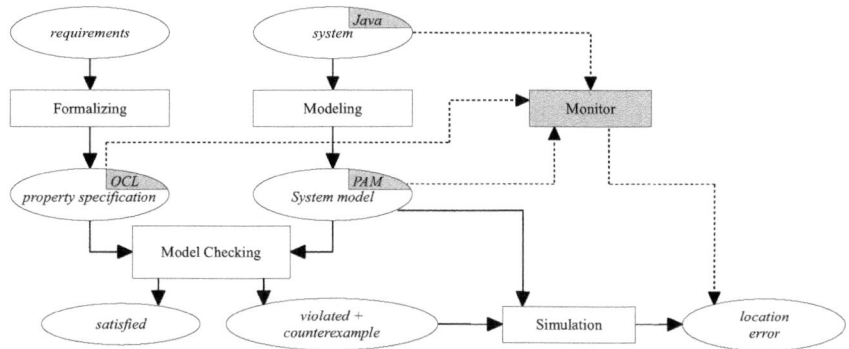

Fig. 1. Monitoring in the context of Model Checking (c.f. [17])

In our approach, we do not only simulate the model. We combine the system model with the implementation (the system) in order to be able to detect mismatches between the implementation, the system model and the property specification. We do so while executing the actual implementation. As systems we consider applications running inside a virtual machine, such as Java application running inside the Java Virtual Machine (JVM). Our system model will be defined as a UML class model extended by UML protocol state machines [20] and augmented with property specifications resp. assumptions formulated as OCL (Object Constraint Language) [21] state invariants and OCL operation pre- and postconditions. Since the elements of this system model need to be identified by our monitor, the system model needs to be aligned to the implementation. We call such a model a platform aligned model (PAM). We connect these components with a monitor in order to verify assumptions about the components at runtime. Our monitor can be started at any time that the concrete system, i.e., the Java application, is running. As an extension to our work presented in [15] and [16], we show how a state machine extension of the employed validation engine can be used without modifying our monitor component. Here, we show how UML protocol state machines (psms, singular psm) can be used to validate the correct sequence of operation calls, i.e., a protocol definition for a given class. We will further discuss some threads to validity which have to be considered when using a monitor approach like ours.

The rest of this paper is structured as follows. In Section 2 we put forward the basic ideas of our proposal for analyzing applications running in the Java virtual machine. Section 3 gives an overview on the integration of protocol state machines into our validation engine USE [11]. Section 4 explains the employment of protocol state machines in combination with our monitoring approach by means of a middle-sized case study applied in our tool USE. Section 5 discusses related work. The paper ends with a conclusion and ideas for future work.

2 Monitoring

In this section we explain our monitoring approach. A more detailed description can be found in [15]. The main idea of our approach is to monitor a running implementation of a system and to extract a more abstract representation of the current system state into a validation engine. We call this abstract representation a *snapshot* of the system under monitoring (SUM), because in general it is a small subset of the artifacts of the running system. Since we want to focus only on central parts of the implementation we leave out unimportant parts. The basis for this snapshot is a model which is more abstract than the implementation, e. g., by defining associations which are not present in programming languages, but specific enough to be able to find relevant parts inside the SUM, e. g., by specifying concrete package names. Because of this alignment between the most specific platform model, e. g., byte code and platform independent models we call this model level *platform aligned model (PAM)*.

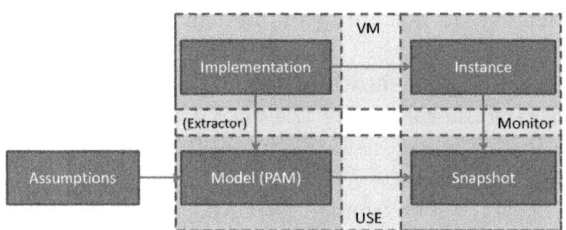

Fig. 2. Overview of the monitoring approach

As shown in Fig. 2 the PAM is enriched with assumptions about the running system. These assumptions are verified during the monitoring process by our validation engine USE. In order to be able to verify assumptions specified in a model USE needs an instance (i. e., objects and links) of it. In the monitoring context we call this instance a snapshot. Figure 2 shows this relation at the bottom. The monitor ensures, that the instance required by USE is a valid snapshot of the monitored instance inside the virtual machine. The virtual machine itself as shown at the top of the figure uses the implementation and an instance, i. e., the (heap) memory, stack, stack pointer, etc. of a running program. The PAM can be defined in several ways. For example, it can be step-wise refined when developing a system or it can be extracted by using reengineering techniques as shown in [16]. Furthermore, it can be generated when using model driven development.

Using modern virtual machine implementations like the JVM or the CLR of Microsoft .NET allows our monitor to use a rich pool of debugging and profiling interfaces. For example, the Java Platform Debugger Architecture[22] enables third party tools to easily access applications running inside a local or remote virtual machine. An important part of this interface is the possibility to retrieve information about instances of a specific type. This is used as an entry point for our monitoring approach described next.

First, the validation engine needs to be configured with the corresponding PAM and the SUM needs to be started. Next, the monitor needs to be connected to the running system. If the startup of a SUM is important, the user can also start the application with specific parameters, so that it suspends directly when started and is resumed only if the monitor signals this to the application. When the monitor is connected after the application is already running, the monitor creates a snapshot of the current system state. The following descriptions of the steps to create this abstract snapshot are explained in more detail in [15].

1. For all classes in the PAM which can be matched to an already loaded class in the VM, all existing instances of them are mapped to newly created instances of the platform aligned model.
2. For each created instance in the previous step the values of the attributes defined in the PAM are read. This step includes a mapping for values of primitive types to built-in OCL types, e. g., String and Real (c. f. [28]). Attribute values with a type of a class defined in the PAM need to be mapped using the mapping created in the first step.
3. For all associations in the PAM, links are created between corresponding instances.
4. By using the current stack-trace of the monitored system the current operation call sequence relevant to the monitored elements can be rebuilt. For this, the deepest operation call to a monitored operation (an operation specified in the PAM) on the call stack acts as an entry point for the following monitored operations on the call stack.

After such a snapshot has been constructed, the monitor needs to register to several events that occur in the VM in order to keep the snapshot synchronized with the running system and to allow a dynamic monitoring of the SUM. Currently our monitor makes use of the following breakpoint and watchpoint locations:

1. At class initialization to allow the registration of all other breakpoints. This ensures, that classes which were not loaded while taking the snapshot are also monitored.
2. At constructors of monitored classes. This allows the monitor to keep track of newly created instances and therefore enables an incremental construction of the system state in contrast to always construct a new snapshot of the running system when needed.
3. At the start of a monitored operation. This enables the monitor to validate preconditions at runtime and to follow the call sequence.
4. Just before the exit of an operation call. This enables the monitor to validate postconditions. The break must occur after the result of the operation is calculated.

5. When a monitored attribute is modified. A monitored attribute might be an attribute or association end inside of the PAM.

Monitoring an application in the presented way in combination with our validation engine USE allows a user to monitor the validity of UML constraints like multiplicities or composition properties, invaraints, pre- and postconditions *without* the need to modify the source code of the application or to use special bytecode injection mechanism. In addition, without changing the monitor component, improvements made to the validation engine can be used. For example after adding support for protocol state machines to USE, as described next, only the PAMs of the monitored systems needed to be extended to allow a more detailed monitoring of call sequences. Without the use of protocol state machines, only a very small part of a call sequence could be validated in one step, because OCL only allows access to the state just before an operation was called. Using protocol state machines it is possible to validate operation call sequences of arbitrary length.

3 Protocol State Machines in USE

The UML specifies two kinds of state machines: behavioral and protocol state machines [20]. As the name suggest, the former kind is used to specify the behavior of UML elements including actions attached to transitions to specify changes inside a system while taking a transition. The latter one specifies the allowed call sequences of a protocol. In USE we added support for protocol state machines in the context of a class. Following the general idea of USE, we start with a small well-defined subset of the many features for UML state machines. In the following we describe this implemented subset and its semantics.

First of all, all state machines in USE are flat, i.e., they have only one region and no composite states. They have only a single initial and a single end state. All other states are proper states and no pseudo states, which means that there are no forks or joins. States can have a state invariant which needs to be valid if a given psm instance is in the corresponding state. The context of a psm instance and also for the state invariant (accessed by using self in an OCL expression) is the instance of the context class of the psm which owns the psm instance. For the initial state only an unnamed transition or a transition with the event create is allowed as an outgoing transition. An initial state has no incoming transitions while an end state has no outgoing transitions. The transitions between states specify the valid call sequences of operations for the context class. As described in the UML the protocol state transitions between states consist of three parts:

1. the referred operation (op),
2. an optional guard (G), i.e., a precondition and
3. a postcondition (PC) which is also optional.

In an state machine diagram the transitions are labeled using the following schema: $\xrightarrow{\text{[G] op()/ [PC]}}$. A state can have multiple outgoing transitions that refer to the same operation. To be still able to choose a single transition the guard, post condition and state invariant of the target state for all transitions referring to the same operations are considered by USE. In some situation the usage of all this information still leads to multiple possible transitions. When USE encounters such a situation it reports an error to the user.

When an operation on an object whose class defines at least one psm is called, the selection of the transition to be taken for each psm is done in the following way. First, it is checked if the operation call needs to be ignored, i.e., no transition must be taken. This is the case if

- none of the transitions inside the protocol state machine covers the called operation (see [20, p. 545]) or
- the psm is not in a stable state, i.e., a transition is currently active.

If the operation cannot be ignored it is checked

- if at least one outgoing transition of the current state is enabled, i.e., the state has one or more outgoing transitions which refer to the called operation while having a valid precondition.

All enabled transitions are saved as possible transitions which could be taken after the operation call is completed. When the called operation finishes its execution, for all possible transitions the postcondition and the state invariant of the target state are validated. If only one transition fulfills the postcondition and the state invariant the transition is taken. Otherwise an error is reported which also explains if either no transition could be taken or multiple transitions would be possible.

3.1 State Determination

One benefit of our monitoring approach is the possibility to connect to a monitored system at any time. While this allows a SUM to run without overhead until the monitoring starts, this ability leads to some issues to be considered. One major problem is the lack of information of previously called operations, so that all protocol state machine instances are in an undefined state. To allow a correct monitoring of psms it is important to determine the correct states of all psm instances. To be able to determine the states after an initial snapshot has been taken we use state invariants. These state invariants need to be well-defined because otherwise the snapshot would be in an unsound state. For example, all psm instances should be in a given state after the state determination check. In this context well-defined means that the state invariants should be independent of each other, i.e., at any state only one state invariant evaluates to true for every instance referring to the psm.

When using complex state invariants the task of verifying the independence of state invariants can be accomplished by using automatic model finding techniques. These are similar to the one presented in [13] which allows a user to show the independence of invariants. In [13] the independence of invariants is slightly different form the independence of state invariants we want to achieve. In [13] an invariant is defined as independent if it cannot be removed without loss of information meaning, there exists at least one system state where this single invariant is violated. For the independence of state invariants required for the state determination, we consider state invariants as independent if for all system states only a single state invariant is fulfilled.

Formally, given the set of all possible system states $\sigma(M)$ of a Model M and the invariants $i_1, \ldots, i_n$ the independence of an invariant i_k is defined in [13] as

$$\exists \sigma \in \sigma(M)(\sigma(i_1) \wedge \cdots \wedge \sigma(i_{k-1}) \wedge \sigma(i_{k+1}) \wedge \cdots \wedge \sigma(i_n) \wedge \neg \sigma(i_k))$$

whereas in this work the independence of state invariants $i_1, \ldots, i_n$ for a single psm is defined as

$$\forall \sigma \in \sigma(M)(\sigma(i_k) \Rightarrow \neg \sigma(i_1) \wedge \cdots \wedge \neg \sigma(i_{k-1}) \wedge \neg \sigma(i_{k+1}) \wedge \cdots \wedge \neg \sigma(i_n))$$

However, the same validation techniques apply, but as the universal quantification indicates, a full verification requires a complete search through all possible system states, which implies the well-known state space explosion problem and is therefore not a trivial task and we restrict ourselves to checking occurring test cases.

4 Case Study

In this section we apply our extensions to the monitoring approach to the public available, mid-sized application we used in [15]. The case study will demonstrate the advantages of our approach.

- Assumptions about a running implementation can be validated without the need to modify the source code.
- The state of an implementation can be examined in an abstract way to discover inconsistencies or design decisions.
- Using protocol state machines the correct usage of the defined protocol of a class can be validated.
- Concrete usage scenarios can be visualized by means of a sequence diagram.

This will be exemplified by the following case study using an open source computer game called *Free Colonization*[1] or in short *FreeCol*. It is a modern Java-based implementation of the 1994 published game *Sid Meier's Colonization*[2]. The game itself is a round-based strategy game with the goal to colonize America and finally to achieve independence. The game takes place on a matrix-like map which consists of tiles with different types, e.g., water, mountain, forest. Different units operate on this map and can explore unknown territory, build

---
[1] Project website: http://www.freecol.org
[2] The corresponding Wikipedia article gives detailed information about the game play. http://en.wikipedia.org/wiki/Sid_Meier%27s_Colonization

colonies, trade goods, etc. Figure 3 shows an example state transition of a running game. One unit (i. e., a pioneer) is placed in the center of the shown map on the left side and is surrounded by several different tile types. The right map shows the game state after the pioneer has build a new colony called Jamestown. The sketched state machines displayed below the two maps exemplify our new contribution. We want to be able to monitor the transition of the pioneer state from one state before she or he built a colony to another state after she or he joined the colony (note, that this is a single step in the game).

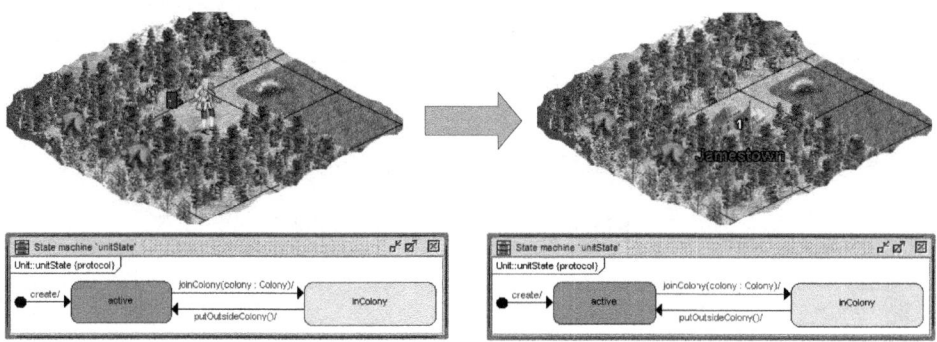

Fig. 3. Sample game situation in FreeCol

To be able to monitor this transition, we extended the PAM presented in [15] in a step-wise manner. First we added the enumeration UnitState to our PAM and defined a new attribute state:UnitState to the class Unit as shown in Fig. 4. The presence of this attribute simplified the definition of the state invariants as we will see later.

For our purpose the class diagram shown in Fig. 4 with an overall of 14 classes is detailed enough. When compared to the 551 classes which are present in version 0.9.2 of FreeCol we used for the monitoring this illustrates that the PAM for an application only needs to represent a small subset of the monitored implementation. Because we focus on state transitions we do not show any constraints defined for the PAM. Examples can also be found in [15].

Except for one case, we modeled attributes of a Java class which use a class present in the PAM as associations. The exception is the attribute Tile::type which reduces the number of links in an object diagram, but still allows to directly see that tiles differ in their type. For a first definition of a psm which monitors the entrance and the exit of a colony for a unit, we only need to consider the class Unit and its operations joinColony(aColony:Colony) and putOutsideColony() in combination with the attribute state:UnitState. These elements are present in the concrete implementation of the class Unit and can directly be monitored. The enumeration UnitState defines nine different enumeration literals which express different states of a unit. Since we are only interested in the state IN_COLONY and do not consider the other states we

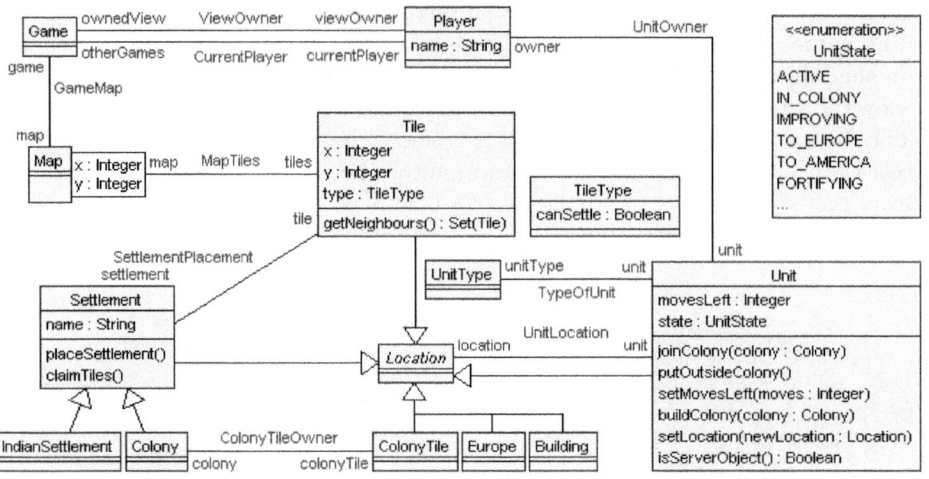

Fig. 4. Platform aligned model

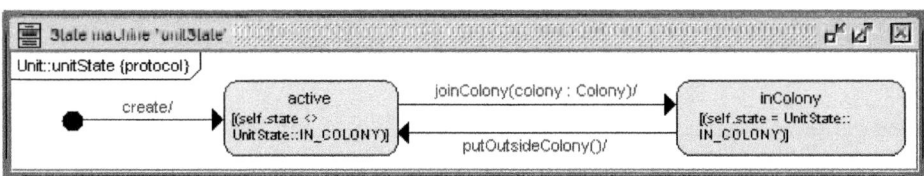

Fig. 5. Protocol state machine for the class Unit

can specify a protocol machine with two states. One for the state IN_COLONY and one for all other game states. Our assumption about the protocol of the class Unit is that an operation call to putOutsideColony() is only valid after the operation joinColony() has been called on the same object sometime before.

To be able to set the correct state of a monitored instance we need to specify state invariants for these two states. As stated earlier, the presence of the attribute state for the class Unit simplifies this task, because we only need to check the value of the attribute to determine the current state after a snapshot has been taken. Therefore, the state invariant for the psm state inColony is self.state = UnitState::IN_COLONY and the other state invariant only changes the comparison from equal to not equal. Given the previously expressed assumptions, this leads to a psm which has two states and two transitions leaving out the transition for the creation. This psm is shown in Fig. 5. A Unit object starts in the state active after it is created and enters the state inColony when the operation joinColony(colony:Colony) was executed. If the operation putOutsideColony() is called the state changes back to active. Any other operation call to a unit instance is ignored as described in the UML specification for operation not mentioned in a psm. This means, the psm only allows a state change when one of the two operations is called.

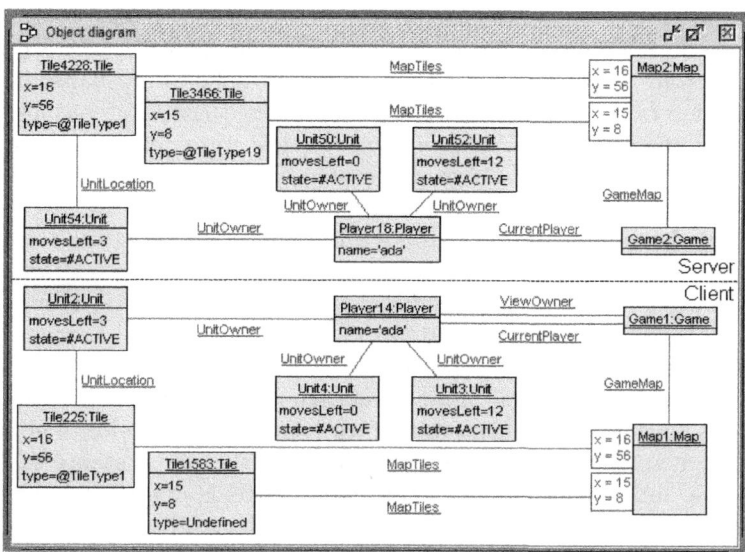

Fig. 6. Parts of the snapshot taken at runtime

Figure 6 shows the relevant part of the snapshot after connecting to the running game when it is in the game state shown on the left of Fig. 3 as an object diagram. The overall snapshot consists of nearly 6000 objects and 4000 links which makes it impossible to manually extract an informative object diagram. USE allows a user to select objects which should be shown or hidden in an object diagram by using several features. Two useful ones are the selection by an OCL expression and the selection of related objects by path length (see [12] for more information). The shown part of the snapshot is divided into two parts, which are important while validating the assumptions about the state transitions. Because we monitored a single user game on a single machine the instance of the game contains both, the data used by the game server and the client. By looking at the instances `Tile3466` on the server side and `Tile1583` on the client side one can see that the server part has more information about the game than the client part. Both instances represent the same tile on a map, because their positions are equal, but the client instance does not know of what type the tile is. To be able to determine if an object belongs to the server or client side we also monitored the class game with the association `ViewOwner`. If a game object is not linked to a player by this association it is the server game. The equivalent OCL expression (`self.owner.ownedView->isEmpty()`) is used as a body for the operation `isServerObject()` of the class `Unit`. This operation is marked as a query operation and is therefore ignored by the monitor. The object diagram further shows the owned units of the player named 'ada' and the object for the tile on which we want to build a colony (`Tile4228` resp. `Tile225`).

After taking this initial snapshot, the states of the protocol state machines for the existing unit objects need to be determined. This can be done by a single command in USE which also informs the user about objects for which the psm instance could not be set to a single state. This happens, if no state invariant or multiple state invariants evaluate to true w. r. t. the given snapshot. Because this state determination is a common task after a snapshot has been taken, the monitor plugin can automatically execute the state determination after the construction of a snapshot. After the states have been determined the states of the relevant units of the snapshot are as expected (active). After resuming the game and building the new colony *Jamestown* we get a valid sequence of operation calls which can be seen in the monitored sequence diagram shown in Fig. 7. We observed, that the execution of the operation joinColony() indeed leads to the attribute value IN_COLONY of the attribute Unit::state, because no violation of a transition is reported.

To get further information about our assumptions we can instruct USE to validate the current state invariants of all psm instances. After the validation of our current snapshot USE reports an error for the psm instance of the client object of the unit which has built the colony. This is due to the fact that the operation buildColony is only called on the server object and only the new values are transfered to the client object. Therefore, USE did not execute a transition from the source state active to the target state inColony for the client unit but monitored the change of the attribute state to IN_COLONY. Now, the new attribute value violates the state invariant of the state active.

Because the separation of the client and server objects seems to be a valid design decision we can ignore these violations and continue the monitoring process to retrieve further information about the validity of our assumptions. To test the defined protocol we use another unit and let it join and exit the colony. While executing this scenario another issue arises because entering an existing colony, i. e., a unit only enters a colony without building it before, does not lead to an operation call to joinColony(). Instead, only setLocation() is called which is not handled by the psm and therefore does not execute a transition keeping the psm instance in the state active, but the attribute value of the runtime instance is set to IN_COLONY which violates the state invariant of the state active.

Using this information a user of the monitor needs to decide where the error is located: in the implementation or in the PAM. For our example, we assume that the PAM needs to be modified although it seems to be an unsound usage of the Unit class. This assumption is backed by the fact, that the developers of FreeCol refactored this part of the game in newer releases. If we want to adapt our psm to the last discovered facts, we need to handle the client server separation and the additional operation calls. The modified psm is shown in Fig. 8. The additional operation setLocation(newLocation:Location) leads to two new transitions in the psm. Both transitions have as their source state the state active but differ in their target and guard. If the new location is of type ColonyTile, which represents special tiles related to a colony, the new state after the execution is inColony otherwise the state does not change. Interestingly, when a Unit object leaves a colony this leads always to a call to putOutsideColony().

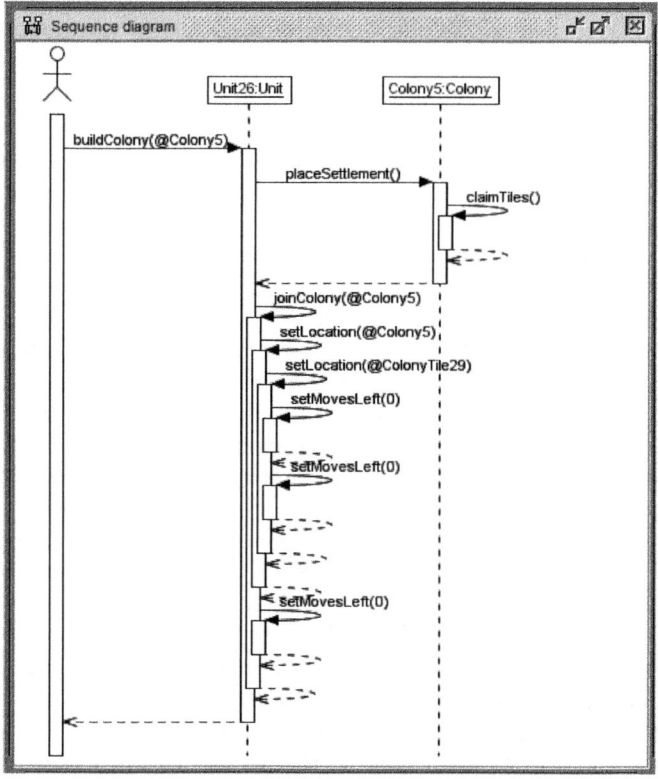

Fig. 7. Sequence diagram of the monitored execution

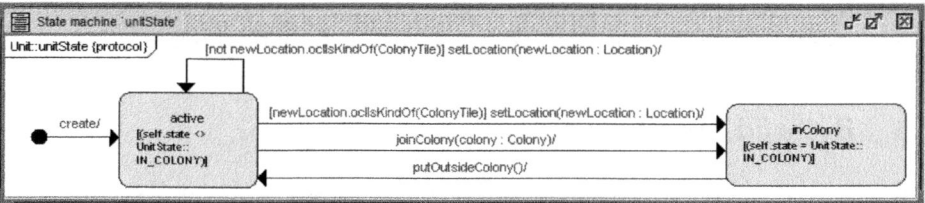

Fig. 8. Extended PSM for the class Unit

However, the problem how to differentiate the server and client objects still exists. When taking a snapshot all state invariants should be independent to allow a valid determination of the current state. If we would introduce a new state for client objects with the state invariant not self.isServerObject() and add a new conjunction self.isServerObject() to the two existing state invariants the state determination would work, because each instance can be mapped to a single state. Either it is a client object or it is a server object and the two server states are independent because of the different comparison operators. The problem with this approach is the dynamic monitoring after existing instances are read. A new instance would be in the state `active` which is now only defined for a server object due to the new conjunction. If a new client instance is created this would violate the state invariant. Further, the new client instance would never change the state because none of the monitored operations is called for client objects as described before. Using an implies condition would violate the independence of the two server states because for client objects both invariants would be fulfilled.

A simple solution would be to add a transition which covers the operation that specifies the new instance to be a client instance. However, FreeCol does this inside of the constructor which is represented as the `create` transition and the UML explicitly forbids multiple outgoing transitions for the initial state and also no post condition on it. If it was allowed the distinction could be done using postconditions on two different create transitions. Another solution for this is to use a change event on a transition. By specifying the change expression `not self.isServerObject()` a psm instance can move to a specify client state. A drawback of this solution is the relative high calculation cost of such change events. Because a change expression can generally access every object or property of the current snapshot all currently valid transitions with change events would need to be checked after every change in the snapshot. The costs can be reduced by using special analysis algorithms which calculate the change expressions that need to be checked after a change as presented in [7]. Currently, such a mechanism is not present in USE, but could be integrated in the future. For now, we need to ignore state violations of the client objects. Note, that the validation of the correct transitions for the server objects still works.

When using this modified psm all scenarios described above lead to the expected changes of the psm states. Beside the manual execution of observed game situations the presence of computer controlled players in the game can be used as a test driver. As with the manual play all analyzed operations are also used by computer controlled players. We used this to strengthen our PAM.

5 Related Work

In our previous work we focused on the runtime verification of static properties (like multiplicity constraints and invariants) of an application running on a virtual machine [15]. Different approaches for checking information extracted from a running system for certain properties exist. [10] and [2] make a comparison between these approaches. According to [10] most constraint validation techniques for Java are based on the design-by-contract-principle introduced by the Eiffel programming language. In contrast to our approach, the approaches compared to each other in [2] require a full access to the source code of the system under monitoring. The Java Modeling Language (JML) is appropriate both for formal verification and runtime assertion checking [18].

In this paper, we extended our validation engine by support for UML protocol state machines in order to be able to verify and validate dynamic sequences of operation calls. Our approach applying protocol state machines differentiates from approaches which are based on the usage of regular expressions. Such an approach is presented in [5]. It enables programmers to define parameterized runtime monitors. For this purpose a temporal ordering over breakpoints, which are used for debugging purposes by programmers, is introduced. The temporal ordering is defined by regular expressions. Another approach uses tracematches for runtime verification [6]. As the previous approaches, this one is also based on regular expressions.

A UML protocol state machine as used in our approach is different from regular expressions through the information of transitions: protocol state machines provide the possibility to specify an initial condition (guard) under which an operation can be called. This possibility makes protocol state machines more powerful than regular expressions. The authors of [23] present an approach which applies UML protocol state machines to produce class contracts. For this purpose they define the structure and the semantics of UML protocol state machines.

With 'ocl2j' a tool exists which allows to enforce OCL constraints in Java through translating OCL expressions into Java code [9]. An analog approach is presented e.g. in [14]. From the authors runtime verification approach the tool 'INVCOP' has arisen. The Dresden OCL toolkit makes available two distinctive approaches for OCL-based runtime verification [8]. While the 'generative' approach is based on the generation of AspectJ code, the 'interpretative' approach integrates the Dresden OCL2 Interpreter into a runtime environment in order to interpret OCL constraints.

In [4] the monitoring of state machines is focused while the usage of OCL is relinquished. With the 'aspect oriented approach', the 'listener approach' and the 'debugging approach', the authors describe three possibilities to extract runtime models.

To synchronize a running system with a runtime model the authors of [26] use 'synchronizers'. Thus the system can be changed immediately when the model has been updated and the model can be immediately adapted if the system progresses.

Java PathFinder (JPF) is a runtime verification and testing environment for Java developed at NASA Ames Research Center [27]. JPF is based upon a special Java Virtual Machine which is called from a model checking engine included in JPF. The authors of [1] present JPF-SE, a symbolic execution extension to JPF. The framework Polyglot has been integrated with the Java PathFinder [3]. Polyglot enables the execution of multiple variants of statecharts including UML statecharts and the verification of their models against properties. It uses an intermediate representation which is translated from a range of modeling tools. The intermediate representation is used to generate Java code representing the structure of a statechart which is analyzed by applying JPF.

6 Conclusion

We have presented an extension to our approach for monitoring assumed properties in form of OCL constraints for a running Java application. Based on this approach, which takes advantage of the powerful features of the Java virtual machine, we have added support for protocol state machines to the underlying validation engine. This allows us to specify assumptions not only formulated as class invariants or operation contracts, but also as state invariants. By using a protocol state machine, more knowledge about the history of an object is available because of the recording of states. We have shown that the definition of state invariants is important for our approach in order to determine the correct states of an object when connecting to a running system without the information about previous operation calls. We explained our work by a non-trivial example of an open-source game.

As future work we want to extend the support for protocol state machines within our validation engine. One major improvement would be the support for change events. To be applicable in practice, an efficient implementation is needed which considers only the transitions with an effective change event. A more detailed study of similar approaches, for example, based on aspect-orientation or approaches considering the Java Modeling Language (JML) as a target language, might introduce alternative features and our monitor could be improved in various directions. For example, one could consider abstract model breakpoints, which are configurable by the user or by extended information about elements that are only present within the running system. Last, but not least, comprehensive case studies must give more feedback about the applicability of our work.

References

1. Anand, S., Păsăreanu, C.S., Visser, W.: JPF–SE: A Symbolic Execution Extension to Java PathFinder. In: Grumberg, O., Huth, M. (eds.) TACAS 2007. LNCS, vol. 4424, pp. 134–138. Springer, Heidelberg (2007)
2. Avila, C., Sarcar, A., Cheon, Y., Yeep, C.: Runtime Constraint Checking Approaches for OCL, A Critical Comparison. In: SEKE (2010)
3. Balasubramanian, D., Pasareanu, C.S., Whalen, M.W., Karsai, G., Lowry, M.R.: Polyglot: modeling and analysis for multiple Statechart formalisms. In: Dwyer, M.B., Tip, F. (eds.) ISSTA, pp. 45–55. ACM (2011)
4. Balz, M., Striewe, M., Goedicke, M.: Monitoring Model Specifications in Program Code Patterns. In: Proc. of the 5th Int. WS Models@run.time, pp. 60–71 (2010)
5. Bodden, E.: Stateful breakpoints: a practical approach to defining parameterized runtime monitors. In: ESEC/FSE 2011. ACM, New York (2011)
6. Bodden, E., Hendren, L.J., Lam, P., Lhoták, O., Naeem, N.A.: Collaborative Runtime Verification with Tracematches. J. Log. Comput. 20(3), 707–723 (2010)
7. Cabot, J., Teniente, E.: Incremental integrity checking of UML/OCL conceptual schemas. Journal of Systems and Software 82(9), 1459–1478 (2009)
8. Demuth, B., Wilke, C.: Model and object verification by using Dresden OCL. In: Proceedings of the Russian-German Workshop Innovation Information Technologies: Theory and Practice, Ufa, Russia, pp. 687–690 (2009)
9. Dzidek, W.J., Briand, L.C., Labiche, Y.: Lessons Learned from Developing a Dynamic OCL Constraint Enforcement Tool for Java. In: Bruel, J.-M. (ed.) MoDELS 2005. LNCS, vol. 3844, pp. 10–19. Springer, Heidelberg (2006)

10. Froihofer, L., Glos, G., Osrael, J., Goeschka, K.M.: Overview and Evaluation of Constraint Validation Approaches in Java. In: Proc. of ICSE 2007, pp. 313–322. IEEE Computer Society, Washington, DC (2007)
11. Gogolla, M., Büttner, F., Richters, M.: USE: A UML-Based Specification Environment for Validating UML and OCL. Science of Computer Programming 69, 27–34 (2007)
12. Gogolla, M., Hamann, L., Xu, J., Zhang, J.: Exploring (Meta-)Model Snapshots by Combining Visual and Textual Techniques. In: Proc. 10th Int. Workshop on Graph Transformation and Visual Modeling Techniques (GT-VMT 2011) (2011)
13. Gogolla, M., Kuhlmann, M., Hamann, L.: Consistency, Independence and Consequences in UML and OCL Models. In: Dubois, C. (ed.) TAP 2009. LNCS, vol. 5668, pp. 90–104. Springer, Heidelberg (2009)
14. Gopinathan, M., Rajamani, S.K.: Runtime Monitoring of Object Invariants with Guarantee. In: Leucker, M. (ed.) RV 2008. LNCS, vol. 5289, pp. 158–172. Springer, Heidelberg (2008)
15. Hamann, L., Gogolla, M., Kuhlmann, M.: OCL-Based Runtime Monitoring of JVM Hosted Applications. In: Proc. WS OCL and Textual Modelling. ECEASST (2011)
16. Hamann, L., Vidács, L., Gogolla, M., Kuhlmann, M.: Abstract Runtime Monitoring with USE. In: Proc. CSMR 2012, pp. 549–552 (2012)
17. Katoen, J.P., Baier, C.: Principles of Model Checking. MIT Press (2008)
18. Leavens, G.T., Cheon, Y., Clifton, C., Ruby, C., Cok, D.R.: How the design of JML accommodates both runtime assertion checking and formal verification. Sci. Comput. Program. 55(1-3), 185–208 (2005)
19. Moffett, Y., Beaulieu, A., Dingel, J.: Verifying UML-RT Protocol Conformance Using Model Checking. In: Whittle, J., Clark, T., Kühne, T. (eds.) MODELS 2011. LNCS, vol. 6981, pp. 410–424. Springer, Heidelberg (2011)
20. UML Superstructure 2.2. Object Management Group (OMG) (February 2009), http://www.omg.org/spec/UML/2.2/Superstructure/PDF/
21. Object Constraint Language 2.2. Object Management Group (OMG) (February 2010), http://www.omg.org/spec/OCL/2.2/
22. Oracle: Java^{TM} Platform Debugger Architecture - Structure Overview (2011), http://download.oracle.com/javase/6/docs/technotes/guides/jpda/architecture.html
23. Porres, I., Rauf, I.: From Nondeterministic UML Protocol Statemachines to Class Contracts. In: Int. Conf. on Software Testing, Verification, and Validation, pp. 107–116. IEEE Computer Society, Los Alamitos (2010)
24. Shah, S.M.A., Anastasakis, K., Bordbar, B.: From UML to Alloy and Back Again. In: Ghosh, S. (ed.) MODELS 2009. LNCS, vol. 6002, pp. 158–171. Springer, Heidelberg (2010)
25. Soeken, M., Wille, R., Drechsler, R.: Encoding OCL Data Types for SAT-Based Verification of UML/OCL Models. In: Gogolla, M., Wolff, B. (eds.) TAP 2011. LNCS, vol. 6706, pp. 152–170. Springer, Heidelberg (2011)
26. Song, H., Huang, G., Chauvel, F., Sun, Y.: Applying MDE Tools at Runtime: Experiments upon Runtime Models. In: Models@run.time, pp. 25–36 (2010)
27. Visser, W., Havelund, K., Brat, G.P., Park, S., Lerda, F.: Model Checking Programs. Autom. Softw. Eng. 10(2), 203–232 (2003)
28. Warmer, J., Kleppe, A.: The Object Constraint Language: Precise Modeling with UML, 2nd edn. Addison-Wesley (2003)

On Model Subtyping

Clément Guy[1], Benoît Combemale[1], Steven Derrien[1],
Jim R.H. Steel[2], and Jean-Marc Jézéquel[1]

[1] University of Rennes1, IRISA/INRIA, France
[2] University of Queensland, Australia

Abstract. Various approaches have recently been proposed to ease the manipulation of models for specific purposes (*e.g.,* automatic model adaptation or reuse of model transformations). Such approaches raise the need for a unified theory that would ease their combination, but would also outline the scope of what can be expected in terms of engineering to put model manipulation into action. In this work, we address this problem from the model substitutability point of view, through model typing. We introduce four mechanisms to achieve model substitutability, each formally defined by a subtyping relation. We then discuss how to declare and check these subtyping relations. This work provides a formal reference specification establishing a family of model-oriented type systems. These type systems enable many facilities that are well known at the programming language level. Such facilities range from abstraction, reuse and safety to impact analyses and auto-completion.

Keywords: SLE, Modeling Languages, Model Typing, Model Substitutability.

1 Introduction

The growing use of Model Driven Engineering (MDE) and the increasing number of modeling languages has led software engineers to define more and more operators to manipulate models. These operators are defined in terms of model transformations expressed at the language level, on the corresponding metamodel. However, new modeling languages are still generally designed and tooled from scratch with few possibilities to reuse structure or model manipulations from existing modeling languages.

To address the need for a more systematic *engineering* of model transformations, various approaches have recently been proposed. These approaches include model transformation reuse [1,2,3,4,5,6] and automatic model adaptation [7,8,9,10]. Although these approaches do meet their goals, they remain somewhat disconnected from each other, and lack a unified theory enabling both their combination and comparison. Such a formalization would also help defining the scope of what can be expected (from a engineering point of view) to put model manipulation into action.

In this paper, we tackle the problem from the model substitutability point of view, through model typing. Model typing provides a well-defined theory that considers models as first-class entities, and typed by their respective model types [3]. In addition to the previous work on model typing focusing on the typing relation (*i.e.,* between a model and its model types), we introduce four model subtyping relations. These relations provide model substitutability, that is they enable a model typed by A to be safely used where a model typed by B is expected, A and B being model types.

This work provides a formal reference specification establishing a family of model type systems. These type systems enable many facilities that are well known at the programming language level, ranging from abstraction, reuse and safety to auto-completion.

This paper is structured as follows. We first illustrate the need for a systematic engineering for model manipulation using examples from the optimizing compilation community (Section 2). We then provide some background on MDE and model typing as introduced by Steel *et al.* [3] in Section 3. In Section 4 we formally define four model subtyping relations, based on two criteria: the structure and the considered subset of the involved model types. Section 5 addresses the ways to declare and check these subtyping relations. Section 6 classifies existing approaches providing reuse facilities for model manipulation with respect to the specification of model-oriented type systems provided in sections 4 and 5. Finally, Section 7 concludes the paper and summarizes our ideas for future work.

2 Illustrative Examples

Optimizing compilers have always used abstractions (*i.e.*, models) of the compiled program to apply numerous analyses, which are often tedious to implement. Thus, optimizing compilation seems a good candidate when looking for a domain in which model manipulation engineering facilities would be valuable.

Most analyses performed by optimizing compilers leverage sophisticated algorithms implemented on different types of compilers' intermediate representations (IRs). Implementation of such algorithms is known to be a tedious and error-prone task. As a consequence, providing modularity and reuse is a crucial issue for improving compiler quality but also compiler designer productivity.

Dead Code Elimination (DCE) is an example of such an algorithm. It is a classical compiler optimization which removes unreachable code from the control flow graph of a program (*e.g.*, the else branch of a if whose condition is always true) [11]. Although the DCE algorithm is relatively straightforward, there exist more complex analyses, such as those leveraging abstract interpretation techniques [12]. Such analyses can infer accurate invariants over the values of the variables of the analyzed program. These invariants can then be used to detect possible program errors (*e.g.*, buffer overflows) or to offer program optimization opportunities.

As with many compiler optimizations, the scope of applicability of these algorithms is wide, including most imperative programming languages. We consider three examples of such languages: two compiler IRs, the GeCoS and the ORCC IRs; and a toy procedural language, Simple. GeCoS[1] is a retargetable C compiler infrastructure targeted at embedded processors. ORCC[2] is a compiler for CAL[3], a dataflow actor language in which actions are described with a standard imperative semantics. Both IRs are

---
[1] Cf. http://gecos.gforge.inria.fr
[2] Cf. http://orcc.sourceforge.net/
[3] Cf. http://ptolemy.eecs.berkeley.edu/papers/03/Cal/index.htm

metamodel-based: models conforming to these metamodels are used as abstractions of the compiled program. Finally, Simple is a language on which is defined P-Interproc[4], an interprocedural analyzer implementing several abstract interpretation analyses.

Rather than being reimplemented for each targeted languages (*e.g.*, GeCoS IR, ORCC IR and Simple), we would expect DCE and our abstract interpretation analyses to be defined once and then reused across these languages. Of course, this reuse should be done safely and should be transparent for the programmer. More precisely, the only thing the programmer should care about when building his compilation flow is whether his model is eligible (or not) for a given model manipulation.

Facilities such as abstraction (hiding unnecessary details from the programmer), reuse (sharing a model manipulation between different metamodels), and safety (forbidding erroneous reuse) could be provided by a type system specifically targeted at models. Such a model-oriented type system would greatly help in increasing both programmers productivity and model-oriented software quality.

3 Background

In this section, we first present the MOF (Meta-Object Facility) metalanguage, the basis for metamodels, and thus model manipulation operators. We then present model types as introduced by Steel *et al.* [3] on which we base our model subtyping relations. Finally, we discuss the limits of the model subtyping relation proposed by Steel *et al.*

3.1 Model Driven Engineering

The Meta-Object Facility. (MOF) [13] is the OMG's standardized meta-language, *i.e.*, a language to define metamodels. As such it is a common basis for a vast majority of model-oriented languages and tools. A metamodel defines a set of models on which it is possible to apply common operators. Therefore, model substitutability must take into account MOF and the way it expresses metamodels.

Figure 1 displays the structure of EMOF (Essential MOF) which contains the core of the MOF meta-language in the form of a class diagram. EMOF supports the definition of the concepts and relationships of a metamodel using Classes and Propertys. Classes can be abstract (*i.e.*, they cannot be instantiated) and have Propertys and Operations, which declare respectively attributes and references, and the signatures of methods available from the modeled concept. Classes can have several superclasses, from which they inherit all Propertys and Operations. A Property can be composite (an object can only be referenced through one composite Property at a given instant), derived (*i.e.*, calculated from other Propertys) and read-only (*i.e.*, cannot be modified). A Property can also have an opposite Property with which it forms a bidirectional association. An Operation declares the Types of the exceptions it can raise and ordered Parameters. Propertys, Operations, and Parameters are TypedElements; their type can be either: a Datatype (*e.g.*, Boolean, String, etc.) or a Class. Parameters, Propertys and Operations are Multiplicity Elements. As such, they have a multiplicity (defined by a lower and an upper bound), as well as orderedness and uniqueness.

---

[4] Cf. http://pop-art.inrialpes.fr/interproc/pinterprocweb.cgi

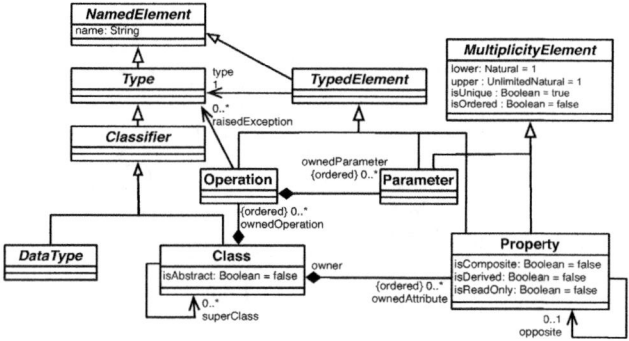

Fig. 1. The EMOF core with class diagram notation

Metamodels can be seen as class diagrams, each of their concepts being instantiable by objects belonging to models. However, metamodel concepts are also instances of MOF elements and thus a metamodel can be drawn as an object diagram where each concept is an instance of one of the MOF elements (*e.g.*, classes Class or Property).

Because model subtyping takes place at the metamodel level, the latter representation facilitates the definition of model subtyping relations by depicting metamodels and their contained concepts as objects with attributes and properties. Thus, we will use the object diagram representation in preference to the more common class diagram one.

3.2 Model Typing

Model Types were introduced by Steel *et al.* [3], as an extension of object typing to provide abstraction from object types and enable model manipulation reuse.

Definition 1. (Model type) *A type of a model is a set of types of objects which may belong to the model, and their relations.*

MOF classes are closer to types (interfaces) than to object classes, thus a model type is closely related to a metamodel. The difference between model types and metamodels lies in their respective relations with models. A model has one and only one metamodel to which it conforms. This metamodel contains all the types needed to instantiate objects of the model. Conversely, a model can have several model types which are subsets of the model's metamodel.

Because model types and metamodels share the same structure, it is possible to extract the type of a model from its metamodel (we call the model type containing all the types from a model's metamodel the *exact type* of the model). Figure 2 represents a model m_1 which conforms to a metamodel MM_1 and is typed by model types MT_A and MT_B, MT_B being the *exact type* of m_1 extracted from MM_1. Both metamodels and model types conforms themselves to MOF.

MOF delegates the definitions of contracts (*e.g.*, pre and post-conditions or invariants) to other languages (*e.g.*, OCL, the Object Constraint Language [14]). Hence neither the original paper on model typing [3] nor this one considers contracts in subtyping relations, but focuses on features of object types contained by model types.

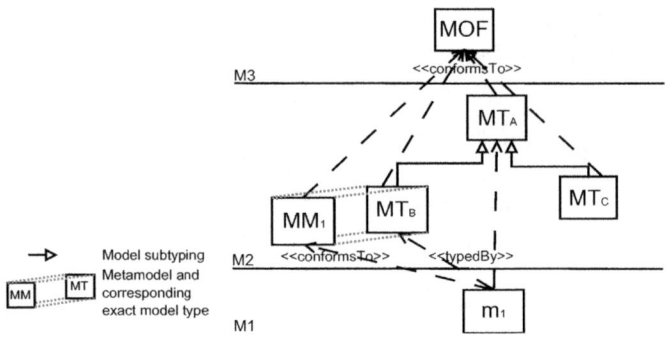

Fig. 2. Conformance, model typing and model subtyping relations

Substitutability is the ability to safely use an object of type A where an object of type B is expected. Substitutability is supported through subtyping in object-oriented languages. However, object subtyping does not handle type group specialization (*i.e.*, the possibility to specialize relations between several objects and thus groups of types).[5] Such type group specialization have been explored by Kühne in the context of MDE [16]. Kühne defines three model specialization relations (specification import, conceptual containment and subtyping) implying different level of compatibility. We are only interested here in the third one, subtyping, which requires an *uncompromised mutator forward-compatibility*, *e.g.*, substitutability, between instances of model types.

Model Type Matching is a model subtyping relation proposed by Steel *et al.* to enable safe model manipulation reuse in spite of limits of object subtyping. To this end, they use the *object type matching* relation defined by Bruce *et al.* [17], which is more flexible than subtyping. For more details, we refer the reader to Steel's PhD thesis [18].

Definition 2. (Model type matching proposed by Steel *et al.* [3]) *Model Type MT_B matches model type MT_A if for each object type C in MT_A there is a corresponding object type with the same name in MT_B such that every property and operation in $MT_A.C$ also occurs in $MT_B.C$ with exactly the same signature as in $MT_A.C$.*

Limits of Model Type Matching. However, *model type matching* as presented by Steel *et al.* is subject to some shortcomings. First, the type rules they present, and their implementation in Kermeta[6], violate their definition of *type matching* by permitting the relaxation of lower multiplicities, i.e. by allowing a non-mandatory attribute to be matched by a mandatory one, which could potentially lead to an invalid model.

In addition, and more significantly, finding a model type common to several model types (*e.g.*, GeCoS IR, ORCC IR and Simple) is not always possible, even if they share numerous concepts (*e.g.*, concepts used in DCE). This impossibility is due to structural heterogeneities between the metamodels [19]. Figure 3 presents such heterogeneities between excerpts from the GeCoS IR and the ORCC IR metamodels representing foreach (from ORCC IR) and for loops (from GeCoS IR, and thus C). The

---
[5] We refer the reader interested in the type group specialization problem to the Ernst's paper [15].
[6] Cf. http://www.kermeta.org

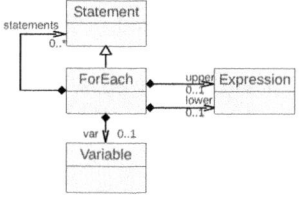 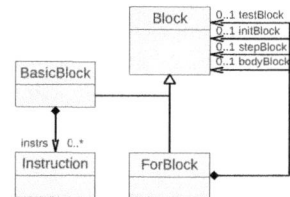

(a) foreach loop in ORCC IR (b) for loop in GeCoS IR

Fig. 3. Extracts of ORCC IR and GeCoS IR metamodels

former (Figure 3(a)) is a simpler loop than the latter (Figure 3(b)), iterating only by steps of one on a given variable between bounds, where a C for can have complete code blocks as initialization, step and test.

Thus to reuse a model manipulation (*e.g.*, DCE), a subtyping mechanism should provide for the definition of an adaptation, needed to *bind* different structures to a single one on which the manipulation is defined. In our example, such an adaptation could be the transformation of foreach loops into more generic for loops, using the variable and the lower bound to produce an initialization block, the variable and the upper bound to produce a test block, and automatically producing a step block with a step of one.

This adaptation should be able to adapt back the result of the manipulation, because this manipulation could modify the model it processes or return a result containing elements of the model. For example, DCE modifies the representation of the program by removing code. Once the optimization has been processed on a common representation, it should be possible to adapt back the structure to impact the result of DCE in the original structure (*i.e.*, an ORCC IR or GeCoS IR model).

Although defining common optimizations on a minimal dedicated structure seems to best fit the need for modularity and reuse, we need to consider the presence of legacy code. For example, DCE is already implemented for the GeCoS IR. Reusing this implementation on ORCC IR would avoid the creation of a generic model type and the reimplementation of the optimization. However, the GeCoS IR does not contain only the concepts required for DCE. More particularly, it contains concepts which do not exist in ORCC IR (*e.g.*, pointers). Therefore, a model subtyping mechanism should be able to accept a subtype which only possesses the concepts of the supertype required for the reuse of a specific model manipulation.

4 Model Subtyping Relations

Object-oriented type systems provide important systematic engineering facilities, including abstraction, reuse and safety. We strongly believe that these facilities can also be provided for model manipulation through a model-oriented type system. However, the existing model subtyping relation has shown some limitations.

For this reason, in this section we review four subtyping relations between model types, based on two criteria: the presence of heterogeneities between the two model types (Subsections 4.1 and 4.2) and the considered subset of the model types (Subsections 4.3 and 4.4). Such a model subtyping relation is pictured in Figure 2 by the generalization arrow between model types MT_A and MT_B. Through this subtyping relation, models typed by MT_A are substitutable to models typed by MT_B, *i.e.*, model manipulations defined on MT_B can be *safely reused* on model typed by MT_A.

4.1 Isomorphic Model Subtyping

An obvious way to safely reuse on a model typed by MT_B a model manipulation from a model type MT_A is to ensure that MT_B contains substitutable concepts (*e.g.*, classes, properties, operations) for those contained by MT_A. As mentioned in Section 3, it is not possible to achieve type group (or model type) substitutability through object subtyping.

MOF Class Matching. Thus, we use an extended definition of *object type matching* introduced by Bruce *et al.* [17] and used by Steel *et al.* to define their *model type matching* relation. Our *object type matching* relation is similar to, but stricter than the latter, because class names must be the same, as must lower and upper bounds of multiplicity elements. Moreover, every mandatory property in the matching type requires a corresponding property in the matched type, in order to prevent model manipulation from instantiating a type without its mandatory properties.

Definition 3. (MOF class matching) *MOF class T' matches T (written $T' <\# T$) iff:*

1. $T.name = T'.name$
2. $T'.isAbstract \Rightarrow T.isAbstract$
3. $\forall op \in T.ownedOperation, \exists S' \in SuperClasses(T')$ such that $\exists op' \in S'.owned Operation$ and:
   3.1 $op.name = op'.name$
   3.2 $op'.type <\# op.type \lor op.type <: op'.type$
   3.3 $\forall p \in op.ownedParameter, \exists p' \in op'.ownedParameter$ such that:
      (a) $\exists U' \in SubClasses(p'.type)$ such that $U' <\# p.type \lor p.type <: p'.type$
      (b) $p.rank = p'.rank$
      (c) $p.lower = p'.lower$
      (d) $p.upper = p'.upper$
      (e) $p.isUnique = p'.isUnique$
   3.4 $\forall e' \in op'.raisedException, \exists e \in op.raisedException$ such that $e' <\# e \lor e' <: e$
4. $\forall a \in T.ownedAttribute, \exists S' \in SuperClasses(T')$ such that $\exists a' \in S'.ownedAttribute$ such that:
   4.1 $a.name = a'.name$
   4.2 $a'.isReadOnly \Rightarrow a.isReadOnly$
   4.3 $a.isComposite = a'.isComposite$
   4.4 $a'.type <\# a.type \lor (a'.type <: a.type \land a.isReadOnly)$
   4.5 $a.lower = a'.lower$
   4.6 $a.upper = a'.upper$
   4.7 $a.opposite \neq void \Rightarrow a'.opposite \neq void \land a.opposite.name = a'.opposite.name$
   4.8 $a.isUnique = a'.isUnique$

5 $\forall a' \in T'.ownedAttribute, a'.lower > 0 \Rightarrow \exists S \in SuperClasses(T)$ such that $\exists a \in S.ownedAttribute \wedge a.name = a'.name$

Where $SuperClasses(T)$, is the set of all superclasses of T, $SubClasses(T)$, the set of all its subclasses, both including T and $<:$ is the object subtyping relation.

Model Type Matching. Given the conditions under which objects may be substitutable in the context of a model type, we can define a *model type matching* relation which ensures the safe type group substitutability. Based on the definition of MOF class matching, we redefine the *model type matching* relation as follows:

Definition 4. (Model type matching) *The* model type matching *relation is a binary relation $\sqsubseteq$ on ModelType, the set of all model types, such that $(MT_B, MT_A) \in \sqsubseteq$ (also written $MT_B \sqsubseteq MT_A$) iff $\forall T_A \in MT_A, \exists T_B \in MT_B$ such that $T_B <\# T_A$.*

The *model type matching* relation can be seen as a kind of subgraph isomorphism which takes into account the MOF specificities (*e.g.*, inherited properties and operations). For this reason we call *isomorphic* model subtyping relation a relation which satisfies the *matching* relation.

4.2 Non-isomorphic Model Subtyping

The fact that MT_B does not match MT_A does not mean that it is not appropriate for substitution. Indeed, the condition for safely substituting a model *m* for another is that *m* contains all the necessary information expected to be handled safely by the called model manipulation or to access the desired features. But this information can be under another form than expected (*e.g.*, with different class names) in which case *m* may be substitutable if the expected form of the information is retrieved.

Model Adaptation is the process of retrieving the information from a model in the form expected. It consists in adapting a model m_B into a model m_A which can be handled by the operation or through which it is possible to access to the desired feature. Thus a *model adaptation* is a way to *create* a *model type matching* relation between two model types. A model adaptation is a function defined at the model type level and applied on models. It takes a model m_B typed by MT_B and returns a model m_A with the same information, but in the form defined by MT_A, *i.e.*, a model whose type matches MT_A.

Definition 5. (Model adaptation) *A model adaptation is a function $adapt_{MT_A}$ from MT_B to MT_C, where MT_A, MT_B and MT_C are model types and such that $MT_C \sqsubseteq MT_A$.*

One way to achieve such an adaptation is to implement a model transformation from MT_B to MT_A, in which case $MT_C = MT_A$. Another way is by adding missing types and derived properties from MT_A to MT_B, creating a new model type MT_C with $MT_C \sqsubseteq MT_B$ and $MT_C \sqsubseteq MT_A$. This is the approach followed by Sen *et al.* [5].

Bidirectional Model Adaptation, that is coupled forward adaptation from MT_B to MT_A and backward adaptation from MT_A to MT_B may be needed, depending whether the adaptation is done to reuse an *endogenous* or an *exogenous* model manipulation [20].

If the adaptation to MT_A is done in order to reuse an *endogenous* manipulation, a backward adaptation is necessary in order to reflect changes made to the adapted model on the original model. Conversely, a backward adaptation is not necessary if the reused feature is an *exogenous* manipulation.

The forward and backward adaptation together form a bidirectional adaptation, which enables the adaptation of a model typed by MT_B into a form which fits the expected model type MT_A but also to reflect the result in the original model. Moreover, a roundtrip adaptation, *i.e.*, applying the forward adaptation then the backward adaptation to the result should lead to an unchanged model. To this end, we use here rules defined by Foster et al. for well-behaved lenses (*i.e.*, bidirectional transformation operators) [21].

Definition 6. (Bidirectional model adaptation) *A bidirectional model adaptation $adapt_{MT_A}$ between model types MT_B and MT_A comprises a function $adapt_{MT_A} \nearrow$ from MT_B to MT_C and a function $adapt_{MT_A} \searrow$ from $MT_B \times MT_C$ to MT_B, where MT_C is a model type such that $MT_C \sqsubseteq MT_A$ and:*

- $adapt_{MT_A} \nearrow (adapt_{MT_A} \searrow (m_B, m_C)) = m_C, \forall (m_B, m_C) \in MT_B \times MT_C$
- $adapt_{MT_A} \searrow (m_B, adapt_{MT_A} \nearrow (m_B)) = m_B, \forall m_B \in MT_B$

Bidirectional adaptation can be provided through bidirectional transformations. Bidirectional transformations are studied in different disciplines of computer science (*e.g.*, MDE, graph transformations and databases) to synchronize two data structures (a *source* and a *view*) [22,23]. In our case, the *source* is the model typed by MT_B found in a context where a model typed by MT_A (our *view*) is expected.

4.3 Total Model Subtyping

When a model of type MT_B can be used in every context in which a model of type MT_A is expected, we talk about *total* substitutability. Therefore, a subtyping relation which guarantees *total* substitutability is a *total* subtyping relation.

Definition 7. (Total subtype) *MT_B is a total subtype of MT_A if any model typed by MT_B can be safely used everywhere a model typed by MT_A is expected.*

4.4 Partial Model Subtyping

Conversely, a *partial* subtyping relation enable a model typed by MT_B to be used in a given context (*e.g.*, a given model transformation) where a model typed by MT_A is expected. This notion of *usage context* have been introduced by Kühne in order to define in which cases a specialization relation holds, while it does not hold in the general case [16]. Typically, a *partial* subtyping relation enables a model typed by MT_B to be substituted for a model a of type MT_A in the context of the call m(a) if MT_B contains the required features for m, even if MT_B is not a *total* subtype of MT_A.

Definition 8. (Partial subtype) *MT_B is a partial subtype to MT_A wrt. f if models typed by MT_B can be safely used where a model typed by MT_A is expected to use the feature f.*

(a) Total subtyping (b) Partial non-isomorphic subtyping

Fig. 4. Two different scenarios of the reuse of DCE between ORCC IR and GeCoS IR

Here, f can be an attribute or an operation from the model or a model manipulation that takes the model as argument. MT_B is a partial subtype to MT_A wrt. f if MT_B is a total subtype of MT_f, where MT_f is a model type which contains only the necessary information to apply or access f safely and such that MT_A is a total subtype of MT_f. We call MT_f the *effective model type* of f.

Definition 9. (Effective model type) *The effective model type MT_f of a feature f extracted from a model type MT_A is the model type which contains all the required features to access or call f and such that $MT_A \sqsubseteq MT_f$.*

This effective model type can be processed using a function which analyzes the model type and extracts its required subset to access a given feature.

Definition 10. (Effective model type extraction) *The effective model type extraction function is a function extractEffectiveMT(MT_A, f), with MT_A a model type and f a required feature belonging to MT_A, and such that $MT_f = extractEffectiveMT(MT_A, f)$ is the effective model type of f extracted from MT_A.*

One possible way to extract this required subset is to use an approach like the one proposed by Sen *et al.* [5]. They compute a metamodel (called the *effective metamodel*) from a larger metamodel using the *footprint* of a model manipulation, *i.e.*, the set of types and features touched by the manipulation. This footprint can be processed statically, by analyzing the code of the model manipulation or dynamically using a trace of the execution of the operation [24]. The dynamic footprint is more accurate because it contains only the types and features of the objects which have been touched by the operation, whereas the static footprint contains all the types and features which may be touched by the operation. However, the dynamic footprint is also costlier and cannot be used for static type checking (cf. Section 5.2).

4.5 Definition of Subtyping Relations for Model Types

From these two criteria (isomorphism of the structures and totality of the subtyping), we define four model subtyping relations to provide model substitutability. In the following MT_A and MT_B are model types and *ModelType* is the set of all model types.

The first model subtyping relation is the *total isomorphic* subtyping relation, to which the three others refer. MT_B is a *total isomorphic* subtype of MT_A if it contains one matching object type for every object type of MT_A, *i.e.*, if $MT_B \sqsubseteq MT_A$. For example, such a subtyping relation could hold between GeCoS IR and a model type extracted from GeCoS IR by selecting only the relevant concepts for Dead Code Elimination (DCE). In Figure 4(a), where the DCE arrow represent the DCE model manipulation defined on a dedicated model type, this case is represented by the generalization arrow between GeCoS IR and the DCE dedicated model type.

Definition 11. (Total isomorphic subtyping relation) *The* total isomorphic *subtyping relation is the matching relation, denoted* $MT_B \sqsubseteq MT_A$.

A *partial isomorphic* subtyping relation wrt. feature f holds between MT_B and MT_A if MT_B contains matching object types for every object type belonging to the *effective model type* of f extracted from MT_A, *i.e.*, MT_B is *partial isomorphic* subtype of MT_A wrt. feature f if MT_B is a *total isomorphic* subtype of the *effective model* type of f extracted from MT_A.

Definition 12. (Partial isomorphic subtyping relation) *The* partial isomorphic *subtyping relation wrt. the feature f is a binary relation* $\sqsubseteq_f$ *on ModelType such that* $(MT_B, MT_A) \in <:_f$ *(also written* $MT_B \sqsubseteq_f MT_A$*) iff* $MT' \sqsubseteq extractEffectiveMT(MT_A, f)$.

MT_B is a *total non-isomorphic* subtype of MT_A if there is a adaptation able to adapt every model typed by MT_B in a model typed by a *total isomorphic* subtype of MT_A. This adaptation must be bidirectional, or it would be impossible to reuse *endogenous* model manipulations from MT_A and the subtyping relation would not be *total*. Figure 4(a) represents such a subtyping relation between ORCC IR and the model type dedicated to DCE mentioned above. Loops from the latter are isomorphic to GeCoS IR ones, thus they cannot be isomorphic to loops from the former. Therefore an adaptation is needed, as the one described earlier (see 3.2).

Definition 13. (Total non-isomorphic subtyping relation) *The* total non-isomorphic *subtyping relation is a binary relation* $\underset{\sim}{\sqsubseteq}$ *on ModelType such that* $(MT_B, MT_A) \in \underset{\sim}{\sqsubseteq}$ *(also written* $MT_B \underset{\sim}{\sqsubseteq} MT_A$*) iff* $\exists adapt_{MT_A}$ *a bidirectional adaptation from* MT_B *to* MT_C *such that* $MT_C \sqsubseteq MT_A$.

Finally, model type MT_B is a *partial non-isomorphic* subtype of MT_A wrt. the feature f if there is an adaptation able to adapt a model typed by MT_B in a model typed by a *total isomorphic* subtype of the effective model type of f extracted from MT_A. This adaptation must be bidirectional if f is an *endogenous* feature. Such a *partial non-isomorphic* subtyping relation is pictured in Figure 4(b), where ORCC IR is subtype of GeCoS IR through an adaptation to the *effective model type* of DCE extracted from GeCoS IR.

Definition 14. (Partial non-isomorphic subtyping relation) *The* partial non-isomorphic *subtyping relation wrt. the feature f is a binary relation* $\underset{\sim}{\sqsubseteq}_f$ *on ModelType such that* $(MT_B, MT_A) \in \underset{\sim}{\sqsubseteq}_f$ *(also written* $MT_B \underset{\sim}{\sqsubseteq}_f MT_A$*) iff* $\exists adapt_{MT_A}$ *an adaptation from* MT_A *to* MT_C *such that* $MT_C \sqsubseteq extractEffectiveMT(MT_A, f)$ *and* $adapt_{MT_A}$ *is a bidirectional adaptation if f is an* endogenous *model manipulation.*

5 Putting Subtyping Relations to Work

Defining model subtyping relations is not sufficient to build a type system. Indeed, a type system implements one or more subtyping relations and provides ways to declare and check them. Thus, we discuss here the ways to declare and check subtyping relations and the respective drawbacks and advantages of these approaches for an implementation of a model-oriented type system.

5.1 Declaration of Subtyping Relations

Subtyping relations can be declared in two ways: *explicitly* and *implicitly*. We call a subtyping relation declaration *explicit* when a syntactic construct is used to state the subtyping relation. Conversely, if the type system infers the subtyping relation from the information it can gather about the types or the use which is done from their instances, the declaration of the subtyping relation is *implicit*. In addition, the declaration of the subtyping relation can take place either *at the definition* of a type or *after the definition* of the subtype and the supertype involved in the subtyping relation.

The way to declare model subtyping relations may affect the possibilities that these relations offer through the type system. For example, a *non-isomorphic* model subtyping relation can be declared *implicitly*. To this end, a tool able to infer adaptations is necessary. Such inference can be done through patterns which are known to be safe or using ontologies to find corresponding class or feature names. However, an *implicit* adaptation mechanism will be more limited in terms of possible adaptations than an *explicit* one, which let the user define its adaptation based on its knowledge of the two model types involved. On the other hand, an *explicit* adaptation mechanism needs appropriate syntactic constructs and analyses to ensure that an adaptation is safe.

Declaration of a subtyping relation *at the definition* of a type is a kind of documentation, letting know what are the subtypes or supertypes of the defined type. Conversely, it is not always possible or desirable to add this information in a type, particularly if the subtyping relation is required for a very specific use (*e.g.*, a *partial* subtyping relation for a single model manipulation) or legacy code where existing model types should be modified. In such cases, declaring the subtyping relation *after the definition* of the involved types may be a solution.

Finally, declaration of a subtyping relation *explicitly at the definition* of a model type could allow inheritance. That is, reuse of the structure of the supertype, with the possibility to redefine or modify it in the subtype without breaking model subtyping. Moreover, if *explicit* declaration *at the definition* is the only way to declare model subtyping relations, it prevents from the type system to use subtyping relations which are unknown from the user, and thus prevents from accidental substitutability.

5.2 Checking of Subtyping Relations

Checking of the subtyping relations is the verification that a subtyping relation holds. Regardless of the way the subtyping relation is declared, this check can be processed either at design time, *i.e.*, during the compilation or interpretation process, or at runtime.

Here again, the way to check model subtyping relations can impact the facilities provided for model manipulations. On the one hand, design time (or static) check enables earlier detection (*i.e.*, than runtime check) of type errors and programming mistakes and thus earlier user feedback. It also enables tools to provide more facilities, such as type-based compiler optimizations, auto-completion or impact analyses. Moreover, compared to runtime checking, design time checking needs significantly fewer tests to achieve the same level of runtime safety.

On the other hand, runtime checking can be processed with more precise type information. When the program is running, the actual type of a variable is known rather than its declared type. Although possibly slower because of the process of the check during the execution of the program, dynamic checking enables valid programs which would be forbidden by a static type checker because of a lack of information. In the context of model types, knowing the actual model would enable the extraction of its model type and would possibly enable subtyping relations forbidden by a static type checker.

6 Discussions

Several approaches have been proposed in the last decade to provide engineering facilities for model manipulation reuse. We show in this section how the fthe different model subtyping mechanisms (*i.e.*, total/partial and isomorphic/non-isomorphic model subtyping, declaration and checking) defined in this paper can be used to classify these approaches through a unified theory. Figure 5 summarizes this classification. The question marks indicate the lack of information about the given mechanism.

6.1 Isomorphic vs. Non-isomorphic Subtyping Relations

To the best of our knowledge, the only approach using an isomorphic subtyping relation is the bidirectional subset of the *adaptation* DSL proposed by Babau *et al.* [9,10]. All

	Total / partial	Iso / non-iso	At / after definition	Explicit / implicit	Checking	Legacy tool reuse
Varró *et al.* [1]	Total	Non-iso (Class renaming)	After	Implicit	?	No
Cuccurru *et al.* [2]	Total	Non-iso (Abstract class renaming)	After	Explicit (Genericity and explicit object subtyping)	?	Yes
Steel *et al.* [3]	Total	Non-iso (Class renaming, multiplicities contraction)	After	Implicit	At compile-time, with possible runtime type errors	Yes
Sanchez Cuadrado *et al.* [4]	Total	Non-iso (Class renaming, multiplicities contraction)	After	Explicit (Binding DSL)	?	Yes
Sen *et al.* [5]	Partial (Effective metamodel)	Non-iso (Potentially any adaptation)	After	Explicit (Static introduction)	At compile-time, with possible runtime type errors	Yes
De Lara *et al.* [6,7,8]	Total	Non-iso (Class renaming, navigation and filtering of properties, $n-1$ bindings)	After (Binding), At definition (Specialization)	Explicit (Binding DSL)	?	No
Babau *et al.* [9,10]	Total (Bidirectional subset)	Iso (Bidirectional subset)	After	Explicit (Adaptation DSL)	?	Yes

Fig. 5. Classification of different model manipulation reuse approaches

other approaches either let class names vary or go further, enabling adaptations such as $n-to-1$ concepts *binding* or navigation and filtering of features. The latter use different mechanisms to *bind* the subtype to its supertype and express the adaptation (*e.g.*, *adaptation* and *binding* DSLs or static introduction). The rarity of *isomorphic* subtyping relations can be explained by the restrictions such relations impose, restrictions which can be safely relaxed in some cases, *e.g.*, class names modification.

6.2 Total vs. Partial Subtyping Relations

Excepting one approach which allows the extraction of the *effective metamodel* from a model manipulation [5], all existing approaches are *total*. To be *total* a *non-isomorphic* subtyping relation must handle bidirectional adaptation. Bidirectionality is tackled in existing approaches by almost *isomorphic* relations [1,2,3,4,9] or by generating an adapted model manipulation rather than adapting the model [6,7,8].

6.3 Declaration of Subtyping Relations

All the existing approaches declare the subtyping relation or *binding after the definition* of the two model types (or their equivalent). However, de Lara *et al.* authorize specialization of model types (called *concepts* in their terminology) using a mechanism close to inheritance (*i.e.*, *at definition*) [6]. Only two approaches declare subtyping relations *implicitly* [1,3] whereas the others use *explicit* mechanisms mainly through DSLs [4,6,7,8,10,9], with the exception of the approaches from Cuccuru *et al.* [2] and Sen *et al.* [5] which use respectively genericity and static introduction.

6.4 Checking of Subtyping Relations

Little is said about the checking of the subtyping relations, apart from the work of Steel *et al.* [3], in which subtyping relations are checked *at compile time*. De Lara *et al.* [6] mention a notion of *valid* binding, but do not formalize it.

6.5 Legacy Tools Reuse

One group of our examples, abstract interpretation analyses, are implemented in an existing tool (P-Interproc). Among the existing approaches, some need to specifically define the model manipulation to be reused [1], or to process it in order to generate an adapted model manipulation [6,7,8]. By doing so, they prevent from reusing existing model manipulations which have not been defined using their own mechanisms or which sources are not available. The other approaches, which enable a subtyping relation with a legacy tool, are the ones with the fewest possible adaptations [2,3,4,10,9], or without any guarantee on the bidirectionality of such adaptations [5].

7 Conclusion and Perspective

This paper provides a review of the overall scope of model substitutability through model typing. To this end we analyze the subtyping relation between two model types wrt. both their structure, and the context of the need for such a substitutability.

First, to be substitutable a model must be structurally equivalent to the expected one. Such a structural equivalence can be achieved if the structures of the two model types are *isomorphic*, or thanks to an adaptation making the two structures *isomorphic*.

Second, such an isomorphism can be *total*, *i.e.*, achieved between the whole structures of the two model types, allowing a substitution of the corresponding models in every possible context where the substitution is necessary. Otherwise, *partial* model substitutability can be achieved according to a given context. In other words, the isomorphism can be achieved between a model type and the *effective model type* of the feature to be reused, *i.e.*, the subset of the model type used in a given context.

From these distinctions, we define four model subtyping relations providing different kinds of model substitutability: *total isomorphic, partial isomorphic, total non-isomorphic* and *partial non-isomorphic*. We review existing approaches to model manipulation reuse wrt. these subtyping relations. It appears that few existing approaches use *partial* subtyping relations or enable adaptations to handle complex structural heterogeneities between model types. Moreover some approaches forbid the reuse of legacy tools. More importantly, most of the approaches lack of a way to forbid erroneous reuse.

In addition to the comparison of existing approaches, the subtyping relations introduced in this paper provide a specification of a family of model type systems that can be implanted in a MDE CASE tool to enable *safe reuse* of model manipulations. In this context, we thus discuss ways to declare a subtyping relation, and how to check it. Depending on the chosen subtyping relation, as well as the way to declare and check it, these type systems enable many facilities that are well known at the programming language level, such as type-based compiler optimizations and auto-completion.

As a direct perspective of this work, we plan to refactor the existing model typing in Kermeta to support the subtyping relations identified in this paper. To this end, we plan to integrate the state-of-the-art of the existing approaches and to study how the work of Vignaga *et al.* [25], focusing on the typing of the relations between models as functions, can be combined with our subtyping relations.

Acknowledgement. This work has been partially supported by VaryMDE, a collaboration between Inria and Thales Research and Technology, and by the French ANR BioWIC (ANR-08-SEGI-005). The authors thank the anonymous reviewers for their constructive feedback which helped us to considerably improve the article.

References

1. Varró, D., Pataricza, A.: Generic and Meta-transformations for Model Transformation Engineering. In: Baar, T., Strohmeier, A., Moreira, A., Mellor, S.J. (eds.) UML 2004. LNCS, vol. 3273, pp. 290–304. Springer, Heidelberg (2004)
2. Cuccuru, A., Mraidha, C., Terrier, F., Gérard, S.: Templatable Metamodels for Semantic Variation Points. In: Akehurst, D.H., Vogel, R., Paige, R.F. (eds.) ECMDA-FA. LNCS, vol. 4530, pp. 68–82. Springer, Heidelberg (2007)
3. Steel, J., Jézéquel, J.M.: On model typing. SoSyM 6(4) (2007)
4. Sánchez Cuadrado, J., García Molina, J.: Approaches for Model Transformation Reuse: Factorization and Composition. In: Vallecillo, A., Gray, J., Pierantonio, A. (eds.) ICMT 2008. LNCS, vol. 5063, pp. 168–182. Springer, Heidelberg (2008)

5. Sen, S., Moha, N., Mahé, V., Barais, O., Baudry, B., Jézéquel, J.-M.: Reusable model transformations. SoSyM 11(1) (2010)
6. de Lara, J., Guerra, E.: From types to type requirements: genericity for model-driven engineering. SoSyM (2011)
7. Sánchez Cuadrado, J., Guerra, E., de Lara, J.: Generic Model Transformations: *Write Once, Reuse Everywhere*. In: Cabot, J., Visser, E. (eds.) ICMT 2011. LNCS, vol. 6707, pp. 62–77. Springer, Heidelberg (2011)
8. Wimmer, M., Kusel, A., Retschitzegger, W., Schönböck, J., Schwinger, W., Cuadrado, J., Guerra, E., de Lara, J.: Reusing model transformations across heterogeneous metamodels. In: International Workshop on Multi-Paradigm Modeling (2011)
9. Kerboeuf, M., Babau, J.-P.: A DSML for reversible transformations. In: OOPSLA Workshop on Domain-Specific Modeling (2011)
10. Babau, J.-P., Kerboeuf, M.: Domain Specific Language Modeling Facilities. In: MoDELS Workshop on Models and Evolution (2011)
11. Aho, A.V., Lam, M.S., Sethi, R., Ullman, J.D.: Compilers: Principles, Techniques, and Tools, 2nd edn. Addison-Wesley (2006)
12. Cousot, P., Cousot, R.: Abstract interpretation: a unified lattice model for static analysis of programs by construction or approximation of fixpoints. In: POPL (1977)
13. OMG: Meta Object Facility (MOF) 2.0 Core Specification (2006)
14. OMG: UML Object Constraint Language (OCL) 2.0 Specification (2003)
15. Ernst, E.: Family Polymorphism. In: Lindskov Knudsen, J. (ed.) ECOOP 2001. LNCS, vol. 2072, pp. 303–326. Springer, Heidelberg (2001)
16. Kühne, T.: On model compatibility with referees and contexts. SoSyM (2012)
17. Bruce, K.B., Schuett, A., van Gent, R., Fiech, A.: Polytoil: A type-safe polymorphic object-oriented language. ACM TOPLAS 25(2) (2003)
18. Steel, J.: Typage de modèles. PhD thesis, Université de Rennes 1 (April 2007)
19. Wimmer, M., Kappel, G., Kusel, A., Retschitzegger, W., Schoenboeck, J., Schwinger, W.: From the Heterogeneity Jungle to Systematic Benchmarking. In: Dingel, J., Solberg, A. (eds.) MODELS 2010. LNCS, vol. 6627, pp. 150–164. Springer, Heidelberg (2011)
20. Mens, T., Gorp, P.V.: A taxonomy of model transformation. Electronic Notes in Theoretical Computer Science 152 (2006)
21. Foster, J.N., Greenwald, M.B., Moore, J.T., Pierce, B.C., Schmitt, A.: Combinators for bidirectional tree transformations: A linguistic approach to the view-update problem. ACM TOPLAS 29(3) (2007)
22. Czarnecki, K., Foster, J.N., Hu, Z., Lämmel, R., Schürr, A., Terwilliger, J.F.: Bidirectional Transformations: A Cross-Discipline Perspective. In: Paige, R.F. (ed.) ICMT 2009. LNCS, vol. 5563, pp. 260–283. Springer, Heidelberg (2009)
23. Hu, Z., Schürr, A., Stevens, P., Terwilliger, J.F.: Bidirectional transformation "bx" (dagstuhl seminar 11031). Dagstuhl Reports 1(1) (2011)
24. Jeanneret, C., Glinz, M., Baudry, B.: Estimating footprints of model operations. In: ICSE (2011)
25. Vignaga, A., Jouault, F., Bastarrica, M., Bruneliére, H.: Typing artifacts in megamodeling. SoSyM (2011)

BOB the Builder: A Fast and Friendly Model-to-PetriNet Transformer

Ulrich Winkler[1], Mathias Fritzsche[2], Wasif Gilani[1], and Alan Marshall[3]

[1] SAP Research, SAP AG,
The Concourse, Belfast, United Kingdom
{ulrich.winkler,wasif.gilani}@sap.com
[2] SAP Modelling and Taxonomy, SAP AG Walldorf, Germany
mathias.fritzsche@sap.com
[3] Queen's Universiy Belfast
Belfast, United Kingdom
a.marshall@ee.qub.ac.uk

Abstract. Petri-Nets are a very expressive modelling concept. However, modelling industrial problems using Petri-Nets is not a trivial task as Petri-Nets do not provide support for constructing large models. Modelling a complete business process, for example, with several activities and associated resources using Petri-Nets becomes a complex task. Model transformations are a promising technology to address this problem. In this paper we present an extended Petri-Net model that supports modelling industrial problems via model transformations. We also introduce a transformation framework that allows to graphically define model transformations by templates.

1 Introduction

Even the simplest form of Petri-Nets (PN), ordinary place/transition nets, are a very expressive modelling concept. Extension, such as inhibitor arcs, time or priorities make Petri-Nets Turing complete.

However, the uptake of Petri-Net based simulations in industry is low as modelling of industrial sized problems using Petri-Nets is not a trivial task. Petri-Nets do not provide support for structuring large models. To model an enterprise scale business process, for example, with several activities and associated resources using Petri-Nets becomes a cumbersome task.

We address this problem by utilising model-driven technologies, such as model-to-model transformations and model tracing. Model transformation allows us to transform an arbitrary model, i.e., a BPMN model, into a Petri-Net model. The Petri-Net model is then used to conduct various analysis, such as simulations and model checking. The results are then transformed back and visualised in the context of the original source model (e.g. the BPMN model). We explain our transformation approach briefly in Section 2.

In our previous work we used ATL [5] to implement model transformations. Although ATL is a very powerful and generic transformation language, we found that developing transformation scripts is time consuming, cumbersome and error prone. Moreover, script based transformation toolkits, such as ATL, tend to be slow.

Our approach uses (a) template based method to define a transformation, (b) graphical editors to model these templates and (c) code generation to transform these templates into the transformation code. Moreover, our framework is deeply integrated into the Eclipse IDE [11] to provide streamlined design, coding, testing, and debugging of transformations.

Our framework comprises:

- BEAM - The Behaviour Analysis Model. BEAM is a modular Petri-Net model with extensions which are useful for model transformations and model tracing. We briefly discuses BEAM in Section 3
- BOB - The BEAM Orchestration and Builder Framework. BOB is a transformation framework for modularised Petri-Nets. Part of BOB are graphical tools to define transformations by providing templates. Using these user provided templates BOB generates the transformer code. We describe BOB in Section 4.

We discuss related work in Section 5 and conclude this paper with an outlook in Section 6.

2 BOB Transformations at a Glance

Before going into details, let us briefly introduce the basic idea of the transformation procedure with modularised Petri-Nets.

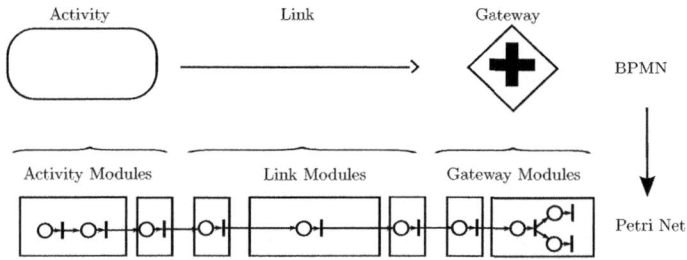

Fig. 1. BOB transformation: the business process model and its transformation into a BEAM instance

In Figure 1 you see a business process modelled in BPMN like notation and its transformation into a Petri-Net. The process comprises three model elements: an *activity*, a *gateway* and an *FlowLink*. The FlowLink connects the activity and the gateway. In bottom half of Figure 1 you see a Petri-Net model which models the behaviour of this business process. Parts of the Petri-Net are grouped by rectangles, which we call modules. For example, the left side module describes the internal behaviour of a process activity, the right side module the functionality of the gateway. The *FlowLink* module describes how the *FlowLink* connects the *activity* and the *gateway*.

The basic idea behind BOB is, that at design time the simulation developer creates templates of the basic Petri-Net structure for all meta-classes of the source meta-model, in this case the BPMN meta-model. We call these template Petri-Net modules *class modules*. If a meta-class contains a reference to other meta-classes (or to itself) the simulation developer also provides templates how class modules should be connected by *reference modules*. These modules are compiled by the BEAM compiler into Java code. The simulation developer may refine this code as required.

At run-time, the BOB transformation process takes a BPMN process model, the provided transformation code and produces a BEAM Net in three steps:

1. A new, empty BEAM Petri-Net is created.
2. The BOB transformer iterates over all elements in the BPMN model. For each source model element the transformation determines the meta-model class of that element and selects the right BEAM module. If a module is available, the transformer creates an instance of that module and inserts that instance in the BEAM model. We call that step the *class module generation*.
3. After all class patterns have been created, the transformer *fuses* the patterns together; that is the transformer creates instances of *reference modules* and connect places and transitions between different class modules and reference modules.

3 BEAM Behaviour Analysis Model

BEAM is a generalised stochastic Petri-Net which supports read, reset and inhibitor FlowLinks. Places and transitions of a BEAM net are grouped in modules. There is nothing special about BEAM; from a pure Petri-Net point of view BEAM is an ordinary Petri-Net as many others, except that we build the support for transformation into the BEAM meta-model. The general idea how we transform arbitrary ECORE based models into a Petri-Net can be applied to other Petri-Net specification as well.

The BEAM meta-model is shown in Figure 2.

BEAM Module: A BEAM module is the basic building block in the BOB transformation framework. A BEAM Module (which is contained in a BEAM file), groups *nodes* (places and transitions) and *arcs* of the BEAM Petri-Net.

Each module (and node) has two identifiers; the *module identifier* (MID) and the *universal unique identifier* (UUID). The UUID, as the name implies, differs for each element in a BEAM-Net. MIDs are only unique for elements within a module and might be the same in two or more modules. Two different modules with the same MID are treated as the same type of module. Module identifiers are used by the BEAM Synchroniser to synchronise modules across files.

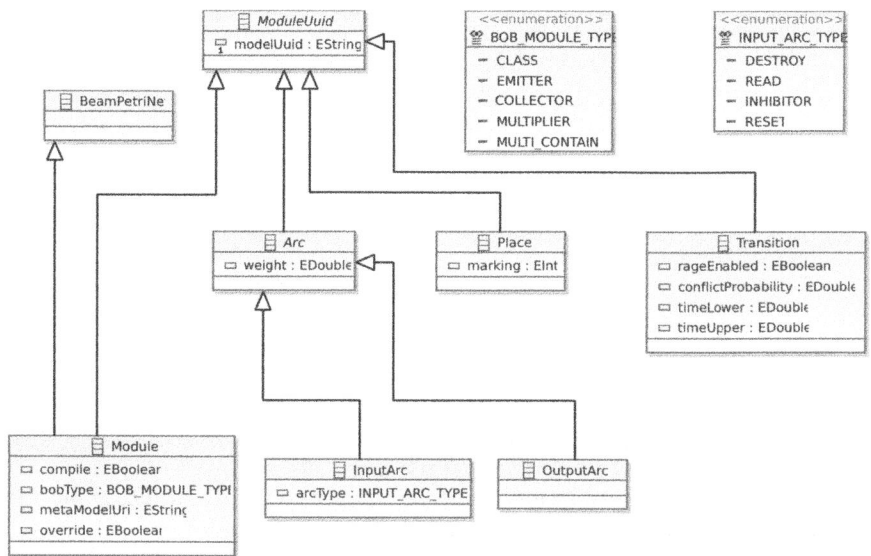

Fig. 2. BEAM meta-model

Each module has a BOB_MODULE_TYPE. The BOB_MODULE_TYPE is used by the transformer to determine how and when to create and fuse modules. We elaborate on these different module types in Section 4.4 and 4.3.

Furthermore we distinguish between *template modules* and *instance modules*. However, this classification is pure linguistics and not expressed in the BEAM meta-model. A template module is provided by the developer and serves as a basic pattern for the BOB transformer to transform a source model object into its Petri-Net representation. We call that process *instantiation*. Once the BOB transformer creates an instance of a *template module* we call it an *instance module*.

Modules may contain other modules and thus may form a hierarchy. This feature is used by the transformation framework to reflect the internal structure of the source model.

4 BOB - The BEAM Orchestration and Builder Framework

Throughout this paper we use a very simple ECORE based meta-model as an accompanying example. The UML diagram of the meta model is given in Figure 3. This example meta-model comprises three classes A, B and X. Class X extends class B. Class A has a zero-to-many reference to B.

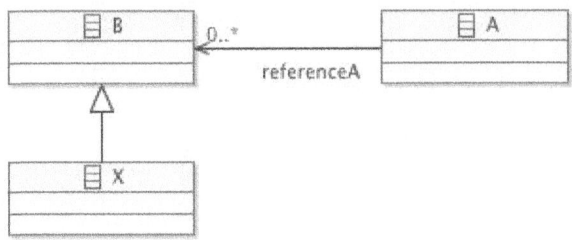

Fig. 3. The meta-model `simple.Example`

4.1 BOB Library Project and BEAM Packages

Let us assume that a simulation developer wants to create an Example-Model-to-BEAM transformation. The simulation developer would start his modelling activities by creating a new BOB library project using the BOB project generator. The BOB project generator loads the source meta-model and initialises the *BOB library project*.

BOB Library Project. A BOB library project is an Eclipse Java project with additional BOB build natures, the BEAM compiler nature and the BEAM synchroniser nature. We elaborate on both natures in Section 4.2. The BOB project generator also initialised the basic project structure and generates *BEAM packages* for all classes of the meta-model.

BEAM package. A BEAM package is a set of *template BEAM modules* and auxiliary Java code that define how a source model object is supposed to be transformed into BEAM modules, orchestrated and composed by the BOB transformer during a transformation. In our example the BOB project generator would produce three BEAM packages for A, B and X. Let us assume that the full qualified name of our meta-model is `simple.Example`. In such a case BOB would create a package `beam.bob.simple.example.a` for class A, `beam.bob.simple.example.b` for B and `beam.bob.simple.example.x` for X.

Once the BOB project generator has initialised the basic project structure and all BEAM packages, the simulation developer starts to fill in the initial empty BEAM module templates and models the basic behaviour using a graphical editors.

4.2 BEAM Module Compiler and Synchroniser

Let us briefly explain what a build-nature does. Every Eclipse project has zero, one or more associated build-natures. Briefly explained, build-natures work like this: the Eclipse runtime-environment observers all files within a project. If a file has been created, changed or deleted all build-natures are notified. Upon a notification the build-nature decides what to do with that received notification. The Java build-nature, for example, would compile a Java source code file into a Java class code file.

BEAM Module Compiler: The BEAM Module Compiler takes a BEAM module and generates the Java code that would produce that module. As the BEAM Module compiler is a part of the build-nature, the BEAM compiler is invoked whenever the simulation developer or the BEAM synchroniser changes a BEAM module definition.

BEAM Synchroniser: BEAM modules of the same type may be used in different BEAM files in a project. We wanted to free the simulation developer of the burden to keeping all BEAM modules in sync. Therefore we provide the BEAM synchroniser which detects changes made to a BEAM module and applies these changes to all BEAM modules in the same project.

4.3 Classes and Interfaces

The Eclipse Modelling Framework and its ECORE meta-model supports object oriented concepts like *classes, interfaces* and *inheritance*.

BEAM does not distinguish between interfaces and classes. The project generator produces a BEAM file with a single BEAM module for all classes and interfaces. In our example the project generator would create a single module in a BEAM file named A.beam in the package bob.simple.example.a

These modules are used to define the internal behaviour of a source model element, for example the internal behaviour of an activity or gateway.

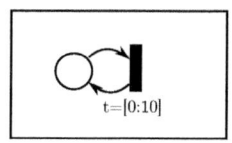

Fig. 4. Class A template

Figure 4 shows the template module of class A which we will use in our example.

4.4 References

In our business process example (Figure 1) the FlowLink object has two references, one reference source to the activity object and one reference targets to the gateway object. In this example the only objective of the FlowLink modules is to transport tokens from the activity module to the gateway module. However, in other use-case that might be different and the simulation developer has to module a more complex behaviour of a reference.

A reference may be regarded as a communication channel between objects. The token would be the message sent over that channel. The transformation of a reference into a BEAM Petri-Net is defined by three modules: the *emitter*, the *multiplier* and the *collector* module.

The emitter module is used to define which object should receive a message and in which order. The multiplier module is the channel itself and might be used to "delay" a message or to lose a message. The multiplier is used to coordinate how messages are "transmitted" or be used to delay a token on it's way to the receiver. The collector might be used to specify in which order a sender receives messages.

For every reference in a meta-model the BOB project generator generates templates for the developer to fill in and to change according to the required need. Let us explain how the developer would model the reference template. In our example class A has a reference to class B. The BOB project generator would create a BEAM file A_referenceA_B.beam in package bob.simple.A. This beam file would contain five modules: the template A, the emitter template, a multiplier template, the collector template and the class template B as shown in Figure 5. Let us assume that the developer filled these templates in as depicted in Figure 5 and 7.

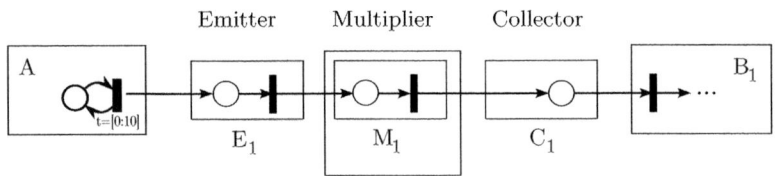

Fig. 5. Template modules for referenceA

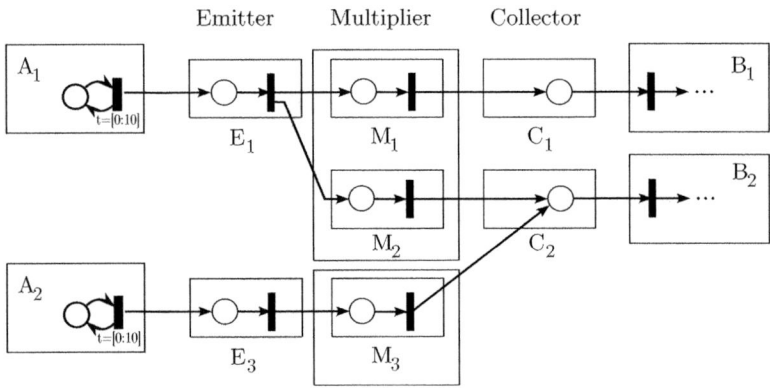

Fig. 6. Transformation result: instance modules (2:2 case)

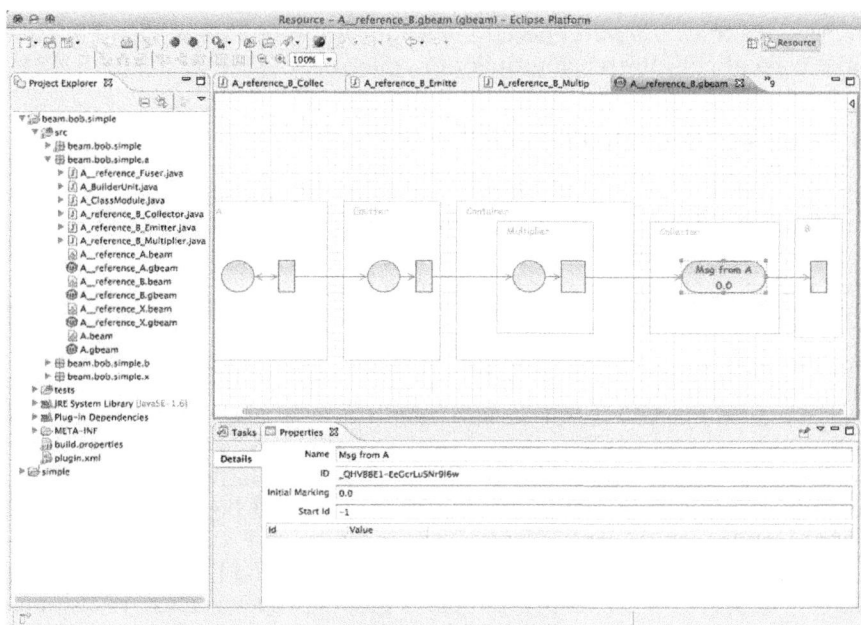

Fig. 7. BOB screen shot. This screen shot shows how the developer uses the graphical BEAM editor (the GBEAM editor) to model the A to B reference templates of the example meta-model. The *Project Explorer View* shows the BOB library project package layout, generated Java code and the BEAM and GBEAM files. BEAM files contain the BEAM model whereas GBEAM contain the graphical details, such as layout, positions and size of elements.

Let us assume that we have a model instance of our example meta-model with four objects; A_1, A_2, B_1 and B_2 as shown in Figure 6. A_1 holds two references to B_1 and B_2 whereas A_3 holds only one reference to B_2. The transformer generates object modules and reference modules as shown in Figure 6 according to the following rules:

1. For each object that holds a reference r the transformer generates an Emitter module. A_1 and A_2 hold a reference to B objects and therefore the transformer produces the Emitter modules E_1 and E_2.
2. For each reference the transformer produces a multiplier module. In our example we have three references and therefore three multiplier modules.
3. For each referenced object the transformer generates a collector pattern. As B_1 and B_2 are referenced objects we have two collectors in our examples.
4. Finally, the BOB transformer creates all arcs between emitter, multiplier and collector.

This schema of modelling references provides a very flexible way to define various scenarios. In most of our use-case we could use this approach to model references.

If it was required to model special behaviour we were able to changed the generated code of the emitter, multiplier or collector.

4.5 Containment References

In some cases we reduce the modelling effort. If, for example a reference is a containment reference then the contained object does not need a collector module, as the containing object is the only object that holds a reference to it. If the reference is a 1:1 reference we can omit the multiplier modules.

4.6 Inheritance

BOB supports inheritance in a very simplistic way. BEAM Modules have the boolean flag `override`. This flag is used to indicate whether the BEAM compiler should compile a template module. The `override` flag is also used by the synchroniser to check whether or not a module should be synchronised with its parent module.

In our simple example, model X inherits from B. The BOB project generator creates the same set of empty template modules as for B. If the simulation developer makes changes in the B module, these changes are applied to the X template module as well unless the `override` flag is set. If the developer change the X module, the `override` flag is set to true. If the `override` flag is set, the synchroniser will no longer synchronise B and X models and the compiler creates the necessary Java code.

If a meta-class has more than one super type this simple mechanism does not work anymore. In this case the BOB project generator disables the inheritance feature by setting the override flag to `true` and the simulation developer has to model this class.

4.7 Module Interfaces and Module Re-use

The BEAM synchroniser uses the BEAM module UMD to synchronise modules across files. This synchronisation mechanism is not limited to modules generated by BOB. The developer may also create modules and assign a unique Universal Module ID to it. This allows the developers to create "libraries" of modules. If they wants to "pull in" a module from a library all they has to do is to create an empty module and give it the same Universal Module ID as the module in the library. The synchroniser then replaces the empty module with the module in the library. With that mechanism we enable the developer to re-use modules and to create interfaces as well.

4.8 Tracing

Model tracing is essential, as tracing relates source model elements to specific places and transitions. Take for example a process activity in Figure 1. The Business Process Expert wants to learn about the queueing length for that particular activity. The queue is symbolised by a place in the BEAM net; the queuing length would be the number of tokens in that place. Tracing establishes the link between process activity and the activity module instance.

Model tracing produces additional *tracing model* [8,3]. We found that using tracing techniques, as for example used by [2], is cumbersome and not needed for BEAM. We were able to build bi-directional tracing into BEAM using a simple, easy to use, and yet sufficient approach: if the source model element has an unique identifier that unique identifier is stored as an attribute by each BEAM module. If the source model element has no unique identifier, the source model URI and the traversal path to the source model element is stored instead.

To identify specific places or transitions, such as the place that symbolises the queue of an process activity, we are using MIDs as well to tag places, transitions and arcs. In our example, the queue place would have the MID `activity-queue`.

Hence, whenever the process expert selects a activity element in the process modelling environment we are able to identify the instance module for that activity and the queueing place of the instance module by utilising MIDs.

4.9 Module Unit Tests and Transformation Verification

In software engineering Unit testing is a method to determine if a small testable part of an application or library meets design requirements and is ready for use. The smallest testable part of a BOB transformation are modules and the BOB project generator creates and initialises for each class and reference a *Unit Test* case. Unit Tests are used by the developer to verify that each template module meets a set of initial design requirements and specifications. For example, a Unit Test for the gateway model may test if the gateway distributes tokens correctly.

BOB provides tools to simplify Unit testing, for example a BEAM simulator that can be executed step by step thus enabling the developer to observe and verify each state during a Unit-Test run.

5 Related Work

The problem of modelling industrial sized Petri-Net has been addressed by a large body of research. Basically four approaches exists: bottom-up/top-down refinements [13,7,1], higher-level Petri-Nets [4], equivalent models [12,6] and Model-to-Petri-Net transformations [10]. The first three approaches have in common that the end-user is required to manually construct Petri-Nets. However, as pointed by Lohmann et al. non-academic people - for example a business process expert - prefer easy-to-use modelling environments tailored to their specific needs [6]. Refinement strategies and Higher-Level Petri-Net are very academic solutions. Equivalent models, such as YAWL [12] for analysing business processes, aim to provide a modelling environment that is less academic, acceptable for a business process experts in terms of usability, and yet is based on strong Petri-Net semantics. However, most commercial products uses BPMN [9] as BPMN is preferred by business process experts as it offers a larger number of modelling elements which YAWL is missing, such as gateway or complex control-flow constructs.

The Petri-Net Kernel (ePNK) is a tool based on Eclipse. It provides graphical editors and a plug-in mechanism to connect various types of Petri-Nets. The ePNK is developed in model driven way, just like BEAM, using the Eclipse Modelling Framework and ECORE, and thus existing model-transformation frameworks as ATL [5] can be used to transform any kind of models to ePNK models. However ATL is a generic transformation language, but we aim to provide a domain specific transformation environment which is tailored to BEAM.

6 Conclusion and Future Work

In this paper we presented BEAM and BOB. BEAM, the Behaviour Analysis Model, is a modular Petri-Net model with extensions which are useful for model transformations and model tracing. BOB, the BEAM Orchestration and Builder Framework an Eclipse based toolkit that comprises a project generator, a compiler, a synchroniser, and a graphical editor to define transformations by providing templates. Using these user templates BOB generates the transformer code.

We found that BEAM/BOB simplify the way that developer model and implement a model-to-PetriNet transformation. In our previous work we used either ATL [5] based scripts or pure Java functions to transform a source model into a BEAM net. Writing code was cumbersome, time consuming and error-prone. Using BOB we are able to develop a transformation much faster and in a user-friendly way using graphical editors to model and test the transformation.

BOB provides a systematic modelling approach to simulation developers. As the BOB project generator generates a complete set of templates the developer has to fill in. The developers can go through these set of templates one by one and model the transformation. If they finished this activity they can be assured that they modelled a transformation completely.

BOB transformation is compiled code rather than an interpreted script. Compared to other script-based transformation, such as ATL [5], a BOB transformation is very fast. Initial tests on 2.4 GHz Intel Core 2 Duo processor with 8 GB RAM demonstrated that a BOB transformation can be 4000 times faster than a ATL based transformation (we compared a BOB transformation with our previous ATL based work [2]). The main reason is that a BOB transformation is compiled code whereas ATL is a script-based transformation. ATL needs to load and parse the transformation scripts, loads the XML models and so on. These steps are not required by BOB and therefore BOB is much faster. Moreover, BOB executes all transformation solely in memory to avoid any disk IO. Comprehensive performance tests of BOB are considered as future work.

References

1. Fehling, R.: A Concept of Hierarchical Petri Nets with Building Blocks. In: Rozenberg, G. (ed.) APN 1993. LNCS, vol. 674, pp. 148–168. Springer, Heidelberg (1993)
2. Fritzsche, M.: Performance related Decision Support for Process Modelling. Phd, Queen's University Belfast (2010)

3. Fritzsche, M., Johannes, J., Zschaler, S., Zherebtsov, A., Terekhov, A.: Application of Tracing Techniques in Model-Driven Performance Engineering. In: Proceedings of the 4th ECMDA Traceability Workshop (ECMDA-TW), pp. 111–120 (2008)
4. Jensen, K.: Coloured petri nets (1987)
5. Jouault, F., Allilaire, F., Bézivin, J., Kurtev, I.: ATL: A model transformation tool. Science of Computer Programming 72, 31–39 (2008)
6. Lohmann, N., Verbeek, E., Dijkman, R.: Petri Net Transformations for Business Processes – A Survey. In: Jensen, K., van der Aalst, W.M.P. (eds.) ToPNoC II. LNCS, vol. 5460, pp. 46–63. Springer, Heidelberg (2009)
7. Mu, D.J., DiCesare, F.: A Review of Synthesis Techniques for Petri Nets. In: Proceedings of Rensselaer's Second International Conference on Computer Integrated Manufacturing, Troy, NY, USA, pp. 348–355. IEEE Comput. Soc. Press, Los Alamitos (1990)
8. Object Management Group: MOF QVT Final Adopted Specification (2005)
9. Object Management Group: Business Process Modeling Notation Specification, Final Adopted Specification, Version 1.0 (2006)
10. Raedts, I.G.J., Petkovi, M., Usenko, Y.S., van der Werf, J., Somers, J.F.G.L.: Transformation of BPMN models for behaviour analysis. In: Proceedings 5th International Workshop on Modelling, Simulation, Verification and Validation of Enterprise Information Systems, MSVVEIS 2007, Funchal, Madeira, Portugal, June 12-13, pp. 126–137. INSTICC Press (2007)
11. und Dan Rubel, E.C.: Eclipse. Building Commercial-Quality Plug-Ins. Addison-Wesley (2006)
12. Vanderaalst, W., Terhofstede, A.: YAWL: yet another workflow language. Information Systems (4), 245–275 (2005)
13. Zuberek, W.M.: Petri nets in hierarchical modeling of manufacturing systems. In: Proc. IFAC Conf. on Control Systems Design (CSD 2000), Bratislava, Slovak Republic, June 18-20, pp. 287–292 (2000)

Solving Acquisition Problems Using Model-Driven Engineering

Frank R. Burton[1,2], Richard F. Paige[2], Louis M. Rose[2], Dimitrios S. Kolovos[2], Simon Poulding[2], and Simon Smith[1]

[1] MooD International, York Science Park, YO10 5ZF, UK
{frank.burton,simon.smith}@moodinternational.com
[2] Department of Computer Science, University of York, YO10 5GH, UK
{paige,louis,dkolovos,smp}@cs.york.ac.uk

Abstract. An acquisition problem involves the identification, procurement and management of resources that allow an organisation to achieve goals. Examples include through-life capability management (in the defense domain), and planning for the *next release* of a software system. The latter is representative of the challenges of acquisition, as solving the problem involves the assessment of the very many ways in which the different requirements of multiple heterogeneous customers may be satisfied. We present a novel approach to modelling acquisition problems, based on the use of Model-Driven Engineering principles and practices. The approach includes domain-specific modelling languages for acquisition problems, and uses model transformation to automatically generate potential solutions to the acquisition problem. We outline a prototype tool, built using the Epsilon model management framework. We illustrate the approach and tool on an example of the next release acquisition problem.

1 Introduction

An *acquisition problem* involves the identification, procurement and management of resources to achieve goals. Consider the following scenario.

> The National Lifeboats Institution is considering its next-generation capability. It has a limited budget, and must satisfy numerous stakeholders such as lifeboat operators, funding bodies, charity workers, and the general public. Its goal is to provide an efficient and effective lifeboat service that protects the public and saves lives. It may acquire improved capability through: better training of current operators, better equipment (e.g., newer lifeboats), better education, etc. It wants to find the most cost-effective capability solution.

This scenario is representative of acquisition problems in numerous domains, including defense, aerospace, logistics, software project management and law. Such problems are complex, and are known to be hard [1,2]. They are challenging for a number of reasons:

- they often involve multiple objectives (e.g., saving lives, minimising cost);
- they are heterogeneous, involving tradeoffs between different types of entities (e.g., better training versus better equipment);

- they are often dynamic: different solutions may be optimal or near-optimal at different times.
- there is rarely a single optimal solution.

Not only is determining optimal or near-optimal solutions to acquisition problems difficult, even understanding the acquisition problem may be challenging, in part because of the uncertainty and imprecision in the problem definition.

We contribute a general approach, based on Model-Driven Engineering (MDE) concepts and technologies, for modelling acquisition problems and calculating solutions that are optimal (Pareto optimality as defined in Section 2.1). The approach consists of a set of domain-specific languages (DSLs) for modelling acquisition goals and scenarios; these scenarios are then manipulated, by a chain of model transformations and model management operations, to produce solutions that are optimal. The advantages of using DSLs and MDE concepts and technologies for modelling and solving acquisition problems are multi-fold:

- Existing techniques used for solving acquisition problems are predominantly domain *dependent*: they rely on domain-specific models and algorithms for expressing how a capability matches a problem. MDE technologies and concepts offer a general, domain *independent* approach to solving such problem while still enabling a domain specific method of expressing the problem itself.
- In particular, the representation of problem concepts, goals and constraints using a DSL-based approach may be more accessible by domain experts.
- Acquisition problems conceptually reduce to manipulating graphs, where nodes typically represent goals and solutions, and edges represent dependencies. MDE technologies allow us to model and attempt to solve acquisition problems in their full generality.
- MDE principles and technologies allow us to abstract away from the complexity of calculating optimal solutions, and to modularise the calculation process. Model transformation, in particular, simplifies mapping (domain) models of problems to optimal solutions.

To illustrate the modelling approach, its novelties and limitations, we apply it to a representative acquisition problem: the software engineering *Next Release Problem (NRP)*. The acquisition objective is to find the 'best' customer requirements to satisfy in a new software release, while staying within budget. This problem, defined in detail in Section 2, is known to be NP-hard [3]. We use it to demonstrate that the MDE-approach can successfully model such complex problems, calculate optimal solutions, and also handle a more general version of the problem that includes dependencies between requirements. We also demonstrate that we can handle continuous variable requirements [2] and provide feedback and explanations of the results, via visualisations.

Beyond offering a solution method for NRP, the presented approach makes multiple generic contributions: the automatic generation of goal models from a partial goal model decomposition with high level descriptions of possible acquirable systems; the automatic evaluation of the generated goal models; calculation of multiple solutions that satisfy multiple stakeholder objectives and that are Pareto optimal, allowing decision-makers to make more informed acquisition; and solution visualisation via MDE tools, particularly EuGENia [4] and GMF [5].

The paper is structured as follows. In Section 2 we present related work and introduce the foundations of NRP, as well as the MDE techniques and technologies we use for our solution. In Section 3 we present our modelling approach, focusing on the DSLs to be used by engineers in representing acquisition goals and scenarios; we also outline the transformations used to produce optimal outputs, and explain how solutions are judged to be optimal. In Section 4 we apply the approach to an instance of NRP. We conclude in Section 5.

2 Background and Related Work

In this section we review the key previous work on acquisition problems, focusing on the Next Release Problem as a representative example. Acquisition problems are, formally, multi-objective optimisation problems. As described in this section we also discuss related work on NRP in more detail, then review the MDE technology that underpins our approach and tools.

2.1 Multi-objective Optimisation Problems

NRP, like other acquisition problems (e.g., Through-Life Capability Management [1]), is an example of a multi-objective optimisation problem. In contrast to single-objective problems, when multiple competing objectives exist, there is normally not a single 'best' solution. Instead, a solution may be the better at one objective but worse than other solutions at a different objective. A solution, X, is said to be *dominated* by another solution, Y, if Y is strictly better than X on at least one objective and as good as X on the remaining objectives. This leads to the notion of a *Pareto front* consisting of those solutions that are not dominated by any other solution. In other words, a solution on the Pareto front may only be bettered on a particular objective if we are willing to accept a worse score on another objective. These solutions on the Pareto front are considered to have *Pareto optimality*. (Deb in [6] presents a detailed explanation of multi-objective optimisation and the concept of a Pareto front.)

When applying search techniques to multi-objective problems it is necessary to quantify how 'good' all solutions are in terms of Pareto optimality, whether or not they are on the Pareto front. An appropriate method is to assign solutions on the Pareto front a *non-domination rank* of 0, then to temporarily ignore the solutions on this front in order to find a new Pareto front which is assigned rank 1, repeating this process until all solutions are ranked [7].

An example of a Pareto front for two objectives, together with solutions having non-domination ranks of 1 and 2, is shown in Fig. 1. For each solution on the Pareto front, it can be seen that no other solution dominates it, but no one solution is optimal for both objectives. Solutions on the Pareto front are the best representatives of different possible trade-offs beyond the competing objectives, and so when making decisions about a multi-objective optimisation problem, typically only the solutions on the Pareto front need be considered.

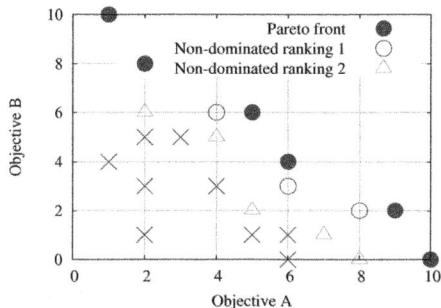

Fig. 1. Example of a Pareto front with the first two non-domination rankings marked. For each objective, a larger value represents a better solution.

2.2 The Next Release Problem

The Next Release Problem involves finding the 'best' set of customer requirements that will be satisfied in the next software release while staying within budget. In the NRP there are multiple customers with numerical weights to indicate their importance to the software company. Each customer requests one or more requirements and each requirement has an associated cost; requirements may also have causal dependencies. The original objective of the NRP was to select which customers should have their requirements satisfied. A consequence of framing the NRP with this objective is that solutions can be unbalanced: a small proportion of customers might have all of their requirements satisfied, and the requirements of some customers might be ignored. The approach to NRP presented by Bagnall et al [3] is limited in this manner, as it is very likely for some customers to have no requirements satisfied at all.

Later work [8–11] overcomes this limitation by having customers place weights of importance on each requirement and hence modifying the NRP so that requirements, instead of customers, are selected for inclusion. The objective in the modified NRP is to select which requirements to satisfy, in order to maximize the total customer satisfaction subject to the provided numerical weights. A further variant on the problem [9] considers the decomposition of a system, where a system is made up of components (typically software features) that work together, and focuses on selecting which new components will be added in the next release.

2.3 The Multi-objective NRP

In the multi-objective Next Release Problem (MONRP) [10], the cost becomes an objective rather than a constraint. The formulation of the problem in terms of customers and requirements is equivalent to variants of NRP described above that consider weights on each requirement indicating the importance of that requirement to the customer. There are now two competing objectives: to maximise the total customer satisfaction, and to minimise the cost to the company (the sum of all the costs of the selected requirements). The solution of the multi-objective NRP problem is therefore a Pareto front of points, each representing a different combination of requirements to include in the release.

Zhang [10] presents an approach to solving MONRP by calculating maximum customer satisfaction for all possible available resources, and hence demonstrates the effects of varying the budget on customer satisfaction. Zhang shows that it is possible to determine situations where increasing the budget only slightly can have a large effect on customer satisfaction, or that the budget can be significantly reduced with only minimal effect on customer satisfaction. However, this approach does not consider dependencies between requirements. In follow-up work, Zhang [2] identifies multiple challenges for MONRP, two of which are: providing sensible feedback and explanation of results; and handling continuous variable requirements (i.e. requirements that can be partially fulfilled, such as increasing the responsiveness of a system). Besides handling requirements dependencies, the modelling approach and tool we present in this paper addresses the latter completely, and the former partially (via visualisations). MDE technologies enable both of these contributions, as we discuss in more detail in the following section.

Various optimisation techniques have been applied to the MONRP, including greedy search, hill climbing, simulated annealing, genetic algorithms, NSGA-II, MoCell and Ant-based search [3, 8, 11, 12]. Since NSGA-II [7] has demonstrated acceptable results in a number of empirical studies on MONRP [10, 11, 13], we choose it as the basis of solution calculation.

2.4 MDE and Model Management

Our modelling approach and supporting tools are based on MDE principles [14] and technologies. The tools we present in later sections exploit Eclipse's EMF/Ecore for defining models and DSLs, and use the Epsilon platform [15] for automatically generating solutions to acquisition problems. Epsilon is a framework of task-specific languages for model management, and comprises a core language (EOL) upon which other task-specific languages are defined. These include a model-to-model transformation language (ETL) [16], a model migration language (Flock) [17], a model-to-text language (EGL), and a tool for generating GMF editors (EuGENia) [4].

The tool that supports our acquisition modelling approach is implemented as a set of DSLs, general model management code and model-to-model (M2M) transformations. Graphical editor support for the tool is provided via EuGENiA and GMF [5].

3 Modelling Approach

As part of a collaboration between MooD International and the University of York, we have developed a general-purpose modelling approach and tool designed to support acquisition problems. The approach is based on a set of DSLs that are used to model an acquisition problem as well as mechanisms and resources that can contribute towards fulfilling the problem's goals. We first describe the modelling approach, and then explain how the tool calculates solutions, using MDE techniques.

3.1 Concept and DSLs

The modelling approach is based on notions of goal modelling [18]. Goal models are normally applied to acquisition problems by first defining the top-level goals of what is required; these top-level goals are then decomposed into sub-goals until it is possible to identify a system or process that enables the goal to be fulfilled. In some cases, it is possible to determine whether a system or process *satisfies* a goal; in others, a looser notion, *satisficing*, is used to indicate that a system or process goes some way to meeting a goal.

Most approaches to calculating solutions to goal models terminate after identifying a complete goal model, i.e., one in which all goals are fulfilled. However, this is insufficient for solving acquisition problems in their full generality. For example, consider Through-Life Capability Management (TLCM) [1]: there are multiple ways for the same goals to be met by completely different supporting systems. Moreover, different acquisition strategies meet the goals to different degrees and have different costs.

Our modelling approach separates the modelling of the goals from the modelling of the systems and processes and how they interact. By underpinning the goal model and the system and process models (component models) with domain specific modelling languages, we can use MDE techniques to freely manipulate them. The use of MDE allows us to manipulate these models to automatically compose completed goals models. Additionally, with the aid of a multi-objective search technique, we can search for a Pareto front of completed goal models representing the various acquisition trade-offs to aid the acquisition decision makers. Goal models are a generic acquisition technique. This means that we can perform trade-off analysis on a very general class of acquisition problem. Being able to manipulate goal models using MDE techniques is the main enabling contribution that enables this. The application of our approach to NRP is purely illustrative.

The modelling of the high level goals and how they decompose is contained in the *Scenario Model*, which is captured in the Scenario DSL, illustrated in Fig. 2.

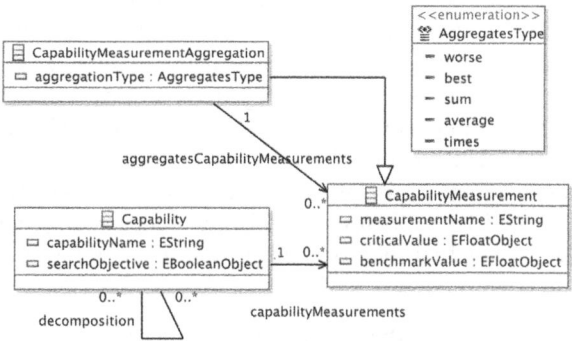

Fig. 2. Scenario Metamodel in Ecore

The main element in the Scenario DSL is the concept of a *Capability*, which is a TLCM term for a Requirement or Goal [1]. Capabilities can be decomposed into sub-capabilities and can have associated quantitative measures. Capability measurements are either fulfilled directly by a *CapabilityProvision* (in a Component Model, see Fig. 3), or indirectly through the *CapabilityMeasurementAggregation* model element. This states how the measure is derived from other capability measurements. Capabilities can either be not fulfilled (typically by the critical value for the measurement not being reached), partially fulfilled (by the critical measurement being met), or completely fulfilled by the benchmark value being met.

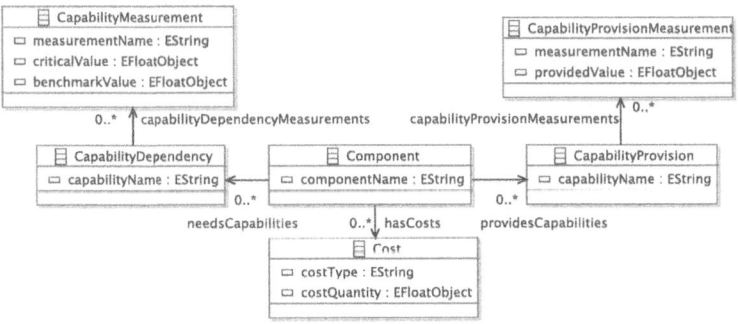

Fig. 3. Simplified Component Metamodel in Ecore

The modelling of the systems/people/processes that can satisfy the goals in the *Scenario Model* are captured in *Component Models*; the abstract syntax is illustrated in Figure 3. The main element in the DSL is *Component*, which represents some system or process that can be acquired. Each component has a name, can provide multiple capabilities, can itself depend on multiple different capabilities, and can have multiple costs (this last element is essential, because some components will cost more in different contexts, e.g., a component used in a safety critical project may require more review by experts, and hence will be more expensive). There is an essential notion of coherency and completeness with components: if a dependency associated with a component is unsatisfied, that component cannot satisfy any other component with a provision.

An end-user models their goals (using the Scenario DSL) and the components (using the Component DSL). We then use MDE techniques to implement search-based algorithms to calculate optimal solutions; this is described in the next section.

3.2 Calculating Solutions to the Acquisition Problem

After specifying a set of goals and available components that can contribute to solutions, we want to calculate solutions to the acquisition problem. This is a search problem. However, it is a non-trivial search problem for reasons discussed earlier: components can contribute to multiple goals; a goal may have multiple possible components that can fulfil it; and, ultimately, the problem may have an arbitrary number of solutions. As such, we need to define a notion of what constitutes an *optimal* solution for such multi-objective problems. Our modelling approach thus calculates a Pareto front. The objectives for the Pareto front are set within the Scenario Model.

The goal model is constructed via a chain of M2M transformations that connect *Capability* model elements from the Scenario DSL with matching *CapabilityProvision* model elements from the Component DSL, thus creating a relationship between them in the Satisfied Scenario DSL. The *CapabilityDependency* in the Component DSL will also be matched with a *CapabilityProvision* in another Component. During this process, when a *Capability* or *CapabilityDependency* model element is connected to a *CapabilityProvision* model element, the provided values from the *CapabilityProvision-Measurement* model elements attached to the *CapabilityProvision* are compared with the critical and benchmark values from the *CapabilityMeasurements* model elements attached to the *Capability* or *CapabilityDependency* model element to determine how well the *Capability* or *CapabilityDependency* is satisfied. There is normally more than one *Component* which can satisfy a *Capability* and in some cases it may be preferable for a *Capability* to remain unfulfilled (e.g. to reduce costs). Consequently, the transformations are *stochastic*.

The overall approach is illustrated in Fig. 4. An end-user provides a single scenario model, multiple component models and a user interface model. The user interface model merely provides the settings for the search algorithm. The scenario model and component models are transformed via a M2M transformation into an intermediate DSL which express a correspondence [19] (Correspondence model). The correspondence model only holds information on *how* the models involved in the search can be *structurally connected* to each other. The next M2M transformation is stochastic and produces a completed correspondence model that captures *exactly one way in which* the models can be connected. This M2M transformation is executed multiple times to generate an initial population for the search method (described below). The completed correspondence model does not capture details such as measurements, costs, etc. A final M2M transformation is used to produce satisfied scenario models, which are the completed goal models that can be evaluated against their objectives. The transformation takes in the structural information from the completed correspondence model and the details from the original scenario and component models. The satisfied scenario metamodel is a composition of the scenario and component meta models with additional relationship for connecting them together.

To derive a Pareto front of solutions, we utilise a search method based on the multi-objective optimisation algorithm NSGA-II [7]. The starting point is the initial population, termed the 'parent' population, of different completed correspondence models produced by the stochastic process described above, and the search proceeds as a sequence of iterations, typically called 'generations', as follows. An 'offspring' population is created by applying a single-point crossover operator that swaps parts of two randomly-chosen models from the parent population to produce a new completed correspondence model. Each new model generated in this way is evaluated against the objectives using a M2M transformation to create a corresponding satisfied scenario model. The parent and offspring populations are then combined and the solutions ordered by non-domination rank. (The concepts of domination and non-domination rank are explained in Section 2.1) The better half of the combined population – the solutions with lowest non-domination rank – are chosen to form a new parent population. The algorithm continues in this way until a specified number of generations is reached. The output is a Pareto front of satisfied scenario models representing the different possible trade-offs between the objectives.

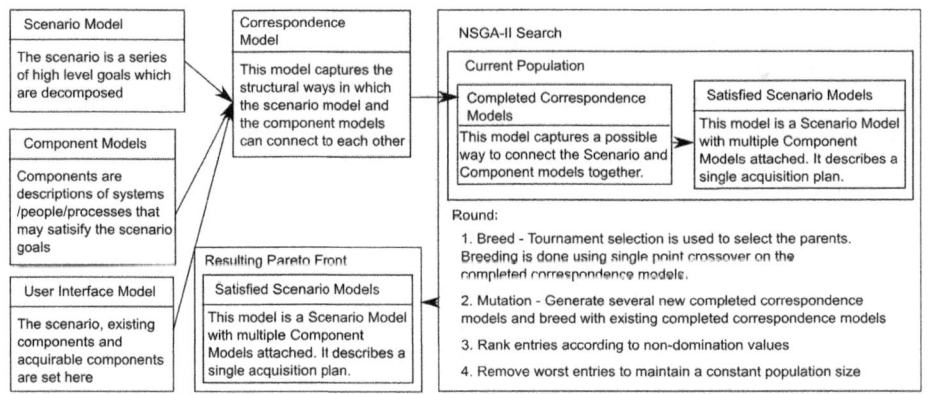

Fig. 4. Solution architecture

The approach offers a number of novelties, including the following.

- *Automatic construction and evaluation of goal models.* The tool uses model management to take a partially decomposed goal model along with components models (representing systems/processes/people) and uses them to automatically generate multiple completed goal models, which represent different viable acquisition plans. The completed goal model is automatically evaluated by using the measures contained in the goal model and the component models used in its construction.
- *Trade-off support between stakeholder goals.* The approach has the ability to find the Pareto front between different stakeholder goals and the different involved costs when generating solutions to the acquisition problem of interest. This enables decision makers to consider trade-offs in the acquisition plans which is useful in cases where there are limited resources and multiple ways to achieve the same goals such as in Through Life Capability Management.
- *Solution visualisation.* The tool generates solutions to acquisition problems using the satisfied scenario DSL. Since a DSL is used, the model, containing the acquisition plan, can be visualised using MDE tools such as EuGENia [4] and GMF [5]. The solution visualisation is illustrated briefly in the next section.

4 Application to the Next Release Problem

We illustrate the modelling approach on instances of the Multi-Objective Next Release Problem (MONRP). First, by using a small representative example, we will demonstrate the modelling approach (and supporting tools, implemented using the Epsilon framework), the calculation of solutions, show how the approach can support problems that are not normally supported by NRP tools. Second, to explore scalability, we apply the approach to a much larger randomly generated dataset for a different instance of the MONRP.

4.1 Stock Control System Example

Our first example is based on the following scenario. A small shop is considering upgrading their existing stock control system. There are two main stakeholders: the shop manager (paying for the upgrade) and shop clerk (who uses the system). The shop manager has three requirements for the upgraded system: monthly reports on the shop's stock flow, email notifications for when stock needs to be reordered, and an automatic ordering system for new stock. The shop clerk also has three requirements: means to track stock (other than manual stock tracking), a better user interface for the system, and a requirement shared with the manager: that of automated stock ordering.

Producing email notifications and automatically ordering stock both depend on common code for determining when stock of an item is likely to run out. There are two different potential improved stock control systems: a cheaper barcode system and a more expensive RFID tag system which is easier to use and better at tracking stock. Such scenarios, where two different component satisfy the same requirement to different degrees, are not supported by existing NRP methods. Additionally, the manager's requirements are deemed more important than the clerk's. Moreover, the manager does not have enough money available to pay for all the upgrades.

4.2 Scenario Model

The first step is to model the acquisition problem in the Scenario DSL (Fig. 5). The Scenario DSL captures both the structure of the MONRP itself, the details of the two customers (manager, clerk) and their requirements. The objective is to calculate the weighted sum of the customer satisfactions. The capability *Next Release Problem* is the search objective and its measure is the sum of the shop manager's and shop clerk's satisfaction, which are weighted. The shop manager and shop clerk are modelled as capabilities which decompose into their requirements, also modelled as capabilities. A requirement whose satisfaction can be measured by a real value (as opposed to a requirement that is either fully met or not met at all) is called a continuous variable requirement. Continuous variable requirements are supported by the approach by giving each requirement a measure with a critical value of 0 and a benchmark value of 1. A

438   F.R. Burton et al.

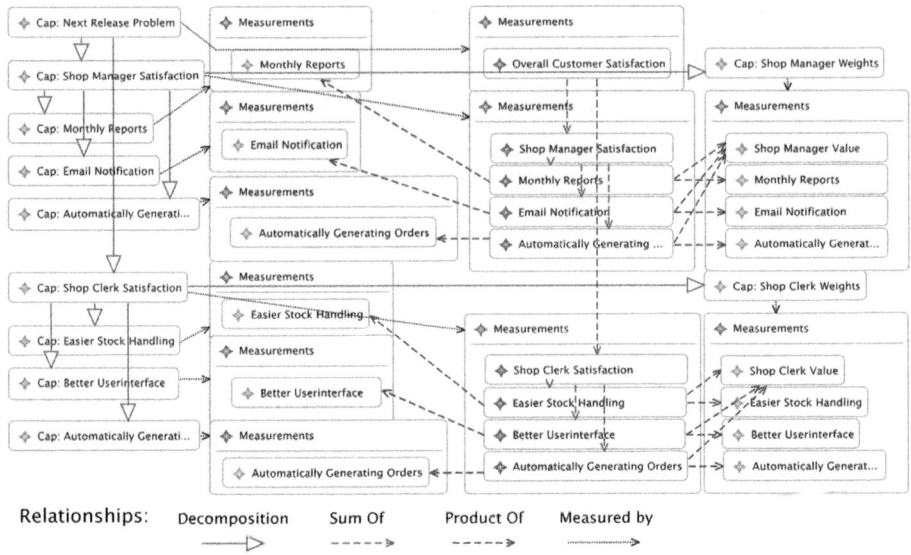

Fig. 5. Shop Case Study Scenario Model

slight modelling quirk is that because the Scenario DSL cannot hold numerical values, the weights have to be modelled in the Component DSL and therefore there are capability decompositions for the shop manager and the shop clerk which take into account the numerical weights for each [1]. The two weight components are set in the User Interface model as pre-existing components and so are always included in the generated goal models. The customer satisfactions have attached measures that are numerical and match the MONRP definition by using the multiplication and sum aggregations relationships.

4.3 Component Models

Examples of the component models for this acquisition problem are shown in Fig. 6. These examples demonstrate, for instance, that the *Barcode Scanning System* is dependent on the *Stock Management System*, will cost £120 to implement, and will provide *Easier Stock Handling*.

Based on these component models, our approach will generate a Pareto front of goal models using the Satisfied Scenario DSL. The search space in this illustrative problem is reasonability small so the tool quickly finds the optimal Pareto front of solutions. The Pareto front has been extracted from the result set using a model-to-text transformation in Epsilon; it is presented in Fig. 8. In this example, suppose that the shop manager has a budget of £250 and initially selects the solution that costs £230. This solution is

---
[1] A dedicated model element for this situation as now been introduced in the tool.

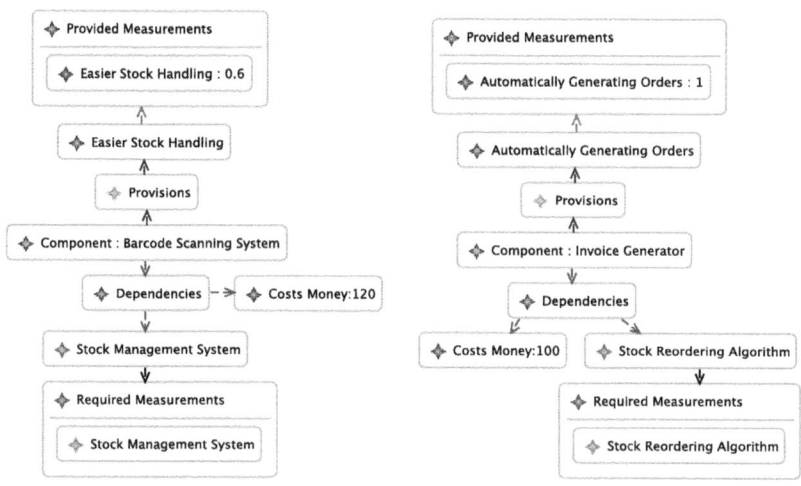

Fig. 6. Shop Case Study Example Component Models

visualised in Fig. 7, which demonstrates how the components are related to the capabilities in order to solve the problem. In the figure, *Capabilities* begin with "Cap:" and *Components* begin with "Comp:".

The shop clerk, seeing that the solution in Fig. 7 only satisfies one of his requirements, is unhappy. To resolve this, the search objectives in the Scenario Model are changed from the Next Release Problem to the two customer satisfactions. This generates a 3-dimensional Pareto front between the shop manager, shop clerk and the cost (Fig. 4.4). After some discussion between the shop manager and the shop clerk, they decide to choose a balanced solution, which gives them both a satisfaction of 0.7 for the cost of £275. The shop clerk agreed to have the extra £25 deducted from his pay.

This illustrates an advantage of an explicitly multi-objective approach to the problem. By deriving a set of potential solutions on the Pareto front, the stakeholders are presented with detailed information on which to base a discussion of trade-offs among the competing objectives.

4.4 Scalability Example

The previous example is small and illustrative; to better assess scalability, we used our approach and tool on a much larger, randomly generated MONRP problem with 5 customers, 50 requirements and 50 components. The customer and requirement weights are all randomly generated and normalised.

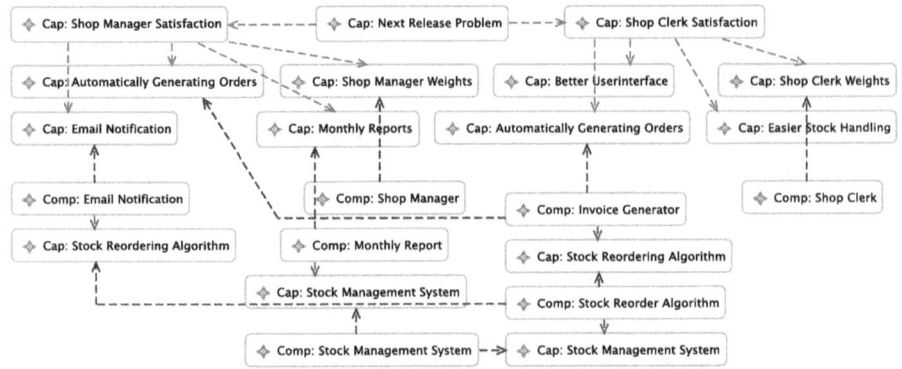

Fig. 7. Shop Case Study Example Solution

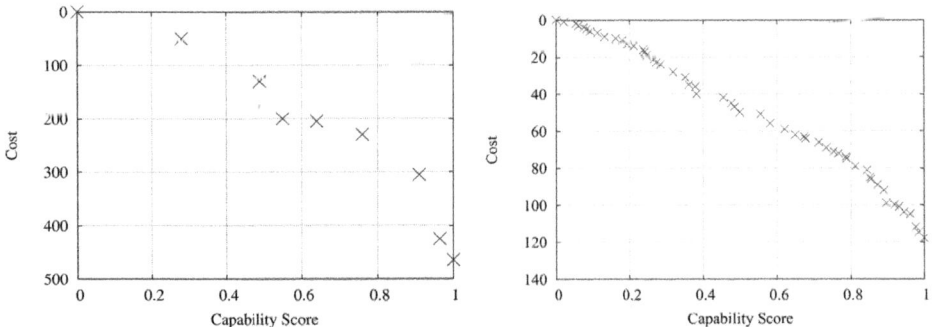

Fig. 8. Shop Case Study Pareto Front

Fig. 9. Scalability Example Pareto Front

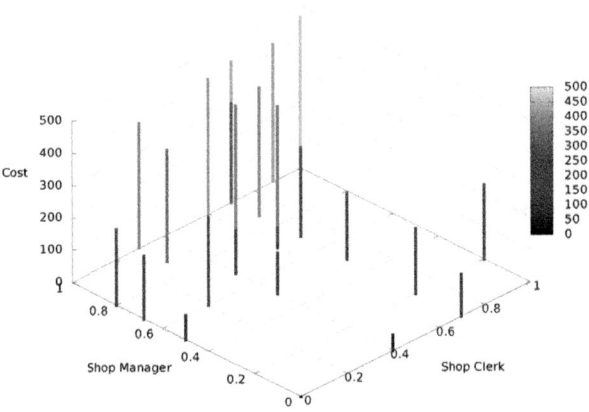

Fig. 10. Shop Case Study 3D Pareto Front

For each requirement a component is generated that provides that requirement. Additionally, there is a 50% chance the component provides another requirement and a 50% chance the component depends on a randomly chosen requirement. The generated Pareto front (shown in Fig. 9) shows that the relationship between customer satisfaction and cost begins near linear, as the software developer can start by selecting software features that are cheap to implement and are highly desirable to their customers. However, as more of the software features are implemented by the software developer, the remaining software features for the software developer to select from contains progressively less desirable and more expensive ones. The result of this is a slight curve in the Pareto front with the last 20% of the customer satisfaction begin twice as expensive to gain as the first 20% of the customer satisfaction.

For the search, a typical population size of 100 and generation count of 100 has being used. The runtime of our prototype on such a problem is approximately 5.5 hours. The randomly generated test data is larger then the largest real world problem in the NRP research field, the Motorola Problem [13]. Our tool is, however, several orders of magnitude slower than dedicated tools for MONRP, which can run in under 1 second [13]. Our focus up until now has not been on performance, but on genericity: our approach supports general acquisition problems and is not specifically tailored for MONRP. Some of the speed reduction we see is however inherent in using general-purpose modelling tools instead of bit strings. A significant reason for lower performance is that the M2M transformation languages are interpreted rather than compiled. In future work, the core M2M transformations may be reimplemented in a compiled language which should significantly reduce the execution time.

4.5 Contributions to the Next Release Problem

Our modelling approach and prototypical tool contribute several specific novelties to the Next Release Problem:

- *Trade-offs in software architecture.* By applying a principled modelling approach, we are able to represent the problem domain concept of customer requirements and the solution domain concept of components separately. In earlier work [9, 10], the customer requirements and components were treated identically. As a result, our approach permits situations in which multiple different components can fulfil the same customer requirement. This corresponds to trade-offs in software architecture and these are not supported by previous work on the NRP.
- *Continuous variable requirements.* A proposed research challenge for the NRP is the handling of continuous variable requirements [2], i.e. requirements whose satisfaction may be partial. For example, a requirement on a web server's response time. It could be a critical that the response time (the continuous variable) is under 300ms and desirable for the response time to be under 100ms. This is easily supported by our tool since it tackles in the problem in a conceptually cleaner way, whereas in previous work [3, 8, 10, 11] on the NRP problem, a requirement can only be satisfied or not satisfied.
- *Visualisation of solutions.* Another research challenge for the NRP is explaining to the stakeholder why solutions are good [2]. By supporting the visualisation of

solutions to show how customer requirements are fulfilled by different components, our tool partially addresses this concern.
- *Tool Flexibility.* Our tool is generic and allows the end-user to change the problem definition. Here, for example, we have used this flexibility to produce a 3-dimensional Pareto Front of two stakeholder's satisfaction against the cost.

5 Conclusions and Further Work

The paper contributes a general approach, based on Model-Driven Engineering (MDE) concepts and technologies, for modelling acquisition problems and calculating optimal solutions. By doing so, the approach supports engineers in carrying out trade-offs between different acquisition strategies, some of which may never have occurred to the engineers, because they were unable to exhaustively identify all the potential solutions.

The paper discussed the typical challenges present in acquisition problems, using the multi-objective Next Release Problem as an example. In particular, we have demonstrated some of the typical problems associated with calculating solutions and presenting them to the end-user. We have presented our modelling approach, which is based on a number of domain-specific languages and is inspired by goal modelling, and explained how the languages are used to specify acquisition scenarios and potential capabilities, and algorithms for matching solutions against acquisition scenarios, in order to present solutions that are Pareto optimal. A prototype tool was presented, which automatically generates solution models. Both the automatic generation of goal models from the problem description, and the descriptions of the available systems, people and processes that can be acquired, as well as the generation of multiple instead of single goal models to show tradeoffs, are novelties of this work.

We then applied the modelling approach to concrete instances of the Next Release Problem, demonstrating that the approach and supporting tool can be used on both significant examples of the NRP, as well as more general NRP problems than those handled by other approaches (e.g., with dependencies between requirements). Overall, the approach that we have taken contributes a more generic capability for handling NRP problems; the price that we pay comes in the form of performance: because our tools are based on general-purpose MDE tools (i.e., Eclipse EMF, Epsilon) instead of dedicated NRP tools, our approach is less efficient; however, the approach does scale, as our example in the previous section demonstrates.

In future work, the tool will be applied to more general acquisition scenarios and on real world case studies. Since the work is primary motivated by the Through Life Capability Management (TLCM), we will enhance the tool to support multiple releases, similar to earlier work by Greer et al [8]. Additionally, we will manage the additional complexities that arise through TLCM, most notably the larger time scales involved (i.e., acquisition processes that take decades). We also intend to investigate mechanisms for performing sensitivity analysis, to check for robustness of acquisition plans.

Acknowledgements. This work is being sponsored by MooD International and the EPRSC (EP/F501374/1) under the Large Scale Complex IT System research programme.

References

1. McKane, T.: Enabling acquisition change - an examination of the Ministry of Defence's ability to undertake Through Life Capability Management. Technical report (June 2006)
2. Zhang, Y.-Y., Finkelstein, A., Harman, M.: Search Based Requirements Optimisation: Existing Work and Challenges. In: Rolland, C. (ed.) REFSQ 2008. LNCS, vol. 5025, pp. 88–94. Springer, Heidelberg (2008)
3. Bagnall, A.J., Rayward-Smith, V.J., Whittley, I.M.: The Next Release Problem. Information and Software Technology 43(14), 883–890 (2001)
4. Kolovos, D.S., Rose, L.M., Abid, S.B., Paige, R.F., Polack, F.A.C., Botterweck, G.: Taming EMF and GMF Using Model Transformation. In: Petriu, D.C., Rouquette, N., Haugen, Ø. (eds.) MODELS 2010. LNCS, vol. 6394, pp. 211–225. Springer, Heidelberg (2010)
5. Eclipse GMF - Graphical Modeling Framework, http://www.eclipse.org/gmf
6. Deb, K.: Multi-objective optimization. In: Burke, E.K., Kendall, G. (eds.) Search Methodologies, pp. 273–316. Springer, US (2005)
7. Deb, K., Pratap, A., Agarwal, S., Meyarivan, T.: A fast and elitist multiobjective genetic algorithm: NSGA-II. IEEE Transactions on Evolutionary Computation 6(2), 182–197 (2002)
8. Greer, D., Ruhe, G.: Software release planning: an evolutionary and iterative approach. Information and Software Technology 46(4), 243–253 (2004)
9. Baker, P., Harman, M., Steinhofel, K., Skaliotis, A.: Search based approaches to component selection and prioritization for the next release problem. In: 22nd IEEE International Conference on Software Maintenance, ICSM 2006, pp. 176–185 (2006)
10. Zhang, Y., Harman, M., Mansouri, S.A.: The multi-objective next release problem. In: Proceedings of the 9th Annual Conference on Genetic and Evolutionary Computation, pp. 1129–1137 (2007)
11. Durillo, J.J., Zhang, Y.Y., Alba, E., Nebro, A.J.: A study of the multi-objective next release problem. In: 1st International Symposium on Search Based Software Engineering, pp. 49–58 (2009)
12. del Sagrado, J., del Águila, I.M., Orellana, F.J.: Ant colony optimization for the next release problem: A comparative study. In: Second International Symposium on Search Based Software Engineering, pp. 67–76 (2010)
13. Durillo, J.J., Zhang, Y., Alba, E., Harman, M., Nebro, A.J.: A study of the bi-objective next release problem. In: Empirical Software Engineering, pp. 1–32 (2011)
14. Schmidt, D.C.: Guest editor's introduction: Model-driven engineering. Computer 39, 25–31 (2006)
15. Kolovos, D.S.: An Extensible Platform for Specification of Integrated Languages for Model Management. PhD thesis, University of York (2008)
16. Kolovos, D.S., Paige, R.F., Polack, F.A.C.: The Epsilon Transformation Language. In: Vallecillo, A., Gray, J., Pierantonio, A. (eds.) ICMT 2008. LNCS, vol. 5063, pp. 46–60. Springer, Heidelberg (2008)
17. Rose, L.M., Kolovos, D.S., Paige, R.F., Polack, F.A.C.: Model Migration with Epsilon Flock. In: Tratt, L., Gogolla, M. (eds.) ICMT 2010. LNCS, vol. 6142, pp. 184–198. Springer, Heidelberg (2010)
18. Lamsweerde, A.V., Dardenne, A., Delcourt, B., Dubisy, F.: The KAOS Project: Knowledge acquisition in automated specifications of software. In: Proceeding AAAI Spring Symposium Series, Track: Design of Composite Systems (1991)
19. Bézivin, J., Bouzitouna, S., Del Fabro, M., Gervais, M.P., Jouault, F., Kolovos, D., Kurtev, I., Paige, R.: A canonical scheme for model composition. In: Model Driven Architecture–Foundations and Applications, pp. 346–360 (2006)

Author Index

Ali, Shaukat 133
Anjorin, Anthony 287, 368
Asztalos, Domonkos 275
Atkinson, Colin 194

Baresi, Luciano 340
Batori, Gabor 275
Behjati, Razieh 226
Blay-Fornarino, Mireille 4
Briand, Lionel 74, 226
Burton, Frank R. 428
Büttner, Fabian 244

Cabot, Jordi 244
Chen, De-Jiu 303
Combemale, Benoît 400
Cordy, James R. 90

de Lara, Juan 259
Derrien, Steven 400
Dingel, Juergen 90
Duchien, Laurence 4

Elaasar, Maged 49

Fritzsche, Mathias 416

Ge, Ning 352
Gerbig, Ralph 194
Gilani, Wasif 416
Gogolla, Martin 32, 384
Goldschmidt, Thomas 62
Gotlieb, Arnaud 226
Guerra, Esther 259
Guy, Clément 400

Hamann, Lars 384
Hegedüs, Ábel 102
Hofrichter, Oliver 384

Jézéquel, Jean-Marc 400

Kennel, Bastian 194
King, Steve 328

Kolovos, Dimitrios S. 118, 340, 428
Kuhlmann, Mirco 32

Labiche, Yvan 49, 74
Lauder, Marius 287
Liu, Yanhua 74
Lönn, Henrik 2

Mahnke, Wolfgang 62
Marshall, Alan 416
Matragkas, Nicholas 118, 340
Mens, Tom 146
Mosser, Sébastien 4
Motta, Alfredo 340

Nejati, Shiva 226

Paige, Richard F. 118, 328, 340, 428
Pantel, Marc 352
Pfeiffer, Rolf-Helge 178
Pinna Puissant, Jorge 146
Poulding, Simon 428

Qureshi, Tahir Naseer 303

Radjenovic, Alek 328, 340
Ráth, István 102
Regnat, Nikolaus 20
Rieke, Jan 210
Rose, Louis M. 118, 328, 428
Rossi, Matteo 340

Schürr, Andy 287, 368
Seidewitz, Ed 1
Selim, Gehan M.K. 90
Smith, Simon 428
Smolik, Petr 319
Steel, Jim R.H. 400
Stelzig, Philipp Emanuel 20
Sudmann, Oliver 210

Theisz, Zoltan 275
Törngren, Martin 303

Van Der Straeten, Ragnhild   146
Varró, Dániel   102
Varró, Gergely   287, 368
Vitkovsky, Pavel   319
Votintseva, Anjelika   20

Wang, Shige   90
Wąsowski, Andrzej   178

Williams, James   118
Winkler, Ulrich   416
Witschel, Petra   20
Woodcock, Jim   328

Yue, Tao   133, 226

Zhang, Gefei   162

GPSR Compliance

The European Union's (EU) General Product Safety Regulation (GPSR) is a set of rules that requires consumer products to be safe and our obligations to ensure this.

If you have any concerns about our products, you can contact us on ProductSafety@springernature.com

In case Publisher is established outside the EU, the EU authorized representative is:

Springer Nature Customer Service Center GmbH
Europaplatz 3
69115 Heidelberg, Germany

Batch number: 09478804

Printed by Printforce, the Netherlands

Crooks and Straights
Copyright © 2014 Masha du Toit

ISBN-13: 978-1499226829
ISBN-10: 1499226829

All rights reserved. No part of this book may be reproduced in any form by any electronic or mechanical means including photocopying, recording, or information storage and retrieval without permission in writing from the author.

This book is a work of fiction. Any resemblance to actual events or real persons, living or dead, is entirely coincidental.

An e-book edition of this title is also available.
This first paperback edition was printed by CreateSpace.

Cover art and design and illustrations by Masha du Toit

masha.co.za

Crooks & Straights

Masha du Toit

Strange Neighbours

The Story Trap
The Broken Path

For Brendon

ROSEMARY AND BURNT RUBBER

"**F**our *roeties!*"

The woman banged on the hatch until it rattled in its frame.

"Hey! Four roeties. Three chicken curry, one veg curry, and two potato wadas."

She shot Gia a look. "Anything to drink?"

"No, thanks."

"That will be thirty-five rand and fifty cents."

Gia handed her a fifty, and tried not to stare as the woman stood on tip-toe to see inside the till drawer.

She's so small! She can't be much taller than Nico.

"Here you go, sweetie." The woman slapped the change on the counter. "Be ready in a minute."

She was clearly curious about Gia, and did not have any inhibitions about staring. Her eyes were sharp and unsettling, and Gia turned away, looking at the shop.

She'd never been in a place like this before, so unlike the clean, modern convenience stores she was used to. It wasn't dirty, but it was old— decades old, she guessed. Vegetables shared shelf space with stationery supplies. Tools and toys crowded the shelves or hung from the ceiling. A refrigerator stood droning against one wall, dripping quietly into an enamel basin.

Gia felt herself relax as she breathed in the scent of Sunlight soap and curry powder.

"You're from that new place down the road?"

The woman was back on her chair behind the counter, and resumed the task that Gia had interrupted — scooping nuts into small paper bags.

"That's right," said Gia.

"It's like a boutique? Ladies clothing and that?"

"Not really," said Gia. "Well, sort of. We design and make the clothing ourselves. Fancy shirts, and wedding gowns. Matric dance dresses. That kind of thing."

The woman's eyebrows went up. "Expensive?"

"Very."

The woman nodded, satisfied. "It looks good. Your daddy did up the shop like that?"

"Yes."

"That was old Mrs Moses's house." Another scoop of nuts was poured into a bag. "She lived there for — oh, many years. Before my time, even. But it's been standing empty too long now. Good to have new people moving in."

She added a few more nuts, then closed the bag with a practised twist, seeming unaware of Gia's fascinated gaze.

She was worth staring at.

Her skin was brown as pastry, and her cheeks and nose were as shiny as if they'd been scorched. A gaudily striped headscarf framed her face and draped her tiny, hunched body. She wore an army of bracelets that clattered and clashed as she moved, and her hands, warped into gnarled roots by arthritis, were loaded with rings.

How could I picture her? thought Gia.

The scent of curry drifting through the hatch suggested the scene.

Gia could see it all perfectly in her mind's eye: *The old woman comfortably ensconced in a cooking pot, stewing herself until she wrinkled like a prune. She might even sprinkle spices over herself, and dip a spoon in to taste the sauce.*

"And that beautiful woman with the long hair? She's your mother?"

Gia came back to reality with a start.

"Oh? Yes. She's my mom."

"She was in here the other day. A real lady. You can *sommer* see it."

As usual, once she'd let her imagination off its leash, Gia found it difficult to rein it in again. It would be too easy to think of this old woman as an odd creature of some kind. She might be a worm-pester, an overgrown hobgoblin, even a witch.

You'd never find someone like this in Claremont or Plumstead, or even Harfield Village.

She glanced surreptitiously at the objects above the counter and was reassured to see the usual horseshoe nailed to the wall, as well as a number of rosemary and wormwood charms dangling among the paper lanterns and garlands of marigolds.

No chance of a magical so close to wards like those.

To her embarrassment she found that the woman was watching her. She shook back the bangles from her hands and picked up another paper packet.

"No need to worry, deary," she said with a far from reassuring cackle. "I'm no witchy. Won't put *muti* in your *roetie*. You can call me Granny. Everybody does. Everybody knows me."

Still smiling, she studied Gia.

"You don't look much like mom. Take after your father?"

"I'm adopted," said Gia, and waited for the usual uncomfortable pause, but Granny took it in her stride.

"And the little one? He your brother?"

The hatch opened and a teenage boy placed several paper parcels on the shelf below. Gia realised he must have been listening to everything they'd said so far.

"Yes," she answered. "My brother Nico. He's seven."

"That funny one," said the boy, leaning through the hatch. He looked very pleased with himself, and even before he said the words, Gia knew what was coming.

"The retard— "

Granny whipped round and slapped him on the side of his head.

"*Skoert jy*," she said. "Hold your mouth about things you don't understand."

The boy ducked back and shut the hatch.

"Don't you mind him," said Granny. "He's an idiot, just like his father. All mouth and no brains. Here's your food. You want a bag?"

Gia nodded, smiling as Granny took a thin plastic bag from under the counter, and packed the food inside it.

"We're open late," said Granny. "You tell your mom, if she ever needs somebody to keep an eye on that little boy of hers, she can leave him here with me. He'll be safe here. Everybody knows Granny."

৪০০৫

Outside, Gia stood taking in her surroundings. It was a sunny, late summer day with the south-easterly wind whipping up a pile of clouds over Table Mountain, and sweeping the sky clear of smog. An alarm wailed in the distance. A line of prayer flags whipped and snapped on a nearby house. A taxi came past, booming out the bass-line, rocking over the speed bumps on its shot suspension, the *gaardjie* hanging out the open door and leering at her.

"Cape Town, girlie?" he shouted, but the taxi sped off before she had a chance to react.

This was so different from Plumstead, where the only pedestrians were street sweepers or security guards. Here, everyone was outside. Children played soccer on the street. Women sat on their doorsteps, chatting and smoking. It was friendly, if a bit intimidating. She felt very visible, the only white person in sight, and a bit too neat in her new school uniform.

Some things were the same, though. Almost every streetlight was strung with newspaper posters bearing slogans of the upcoming referendum.

She set off up the street. As she turned a corner, the alarm she'd been only peripherally aware of became louder. Children were screaming with excitement, but she could not see what attracted their attention. A yellow-and-black Special Branch truck blocked the road. A line of people stood well back, straining to see what was going on. Curious, she walked closer.

"You get back here, Melia, I'm going to *donner* you, you don't listen to Mommy!" A woman dragged a small girl away. "Come inside now, Zaaid, Melia! *Dadelik!*"

Gia found a space next to a middle aged man in overalls with the words "Woodstock Plumbing" embroidered in large yellow letters.

He nodded at her. "They found a nest," he said. "*Haarskeerders.*"

She must have looked baffled.

"Magicals, you know. But small ones. Mr Abrahams was fixing his shed and found a nest. Under the roof."

Beyond the truck a Special Branch officer, muffled in protective clothing, pulled at a sheet of corrugated fencing. He wore a padded jacket and a helmet with nets hanging down from it very much like a beekeeper's outfit, and a large pair of mirrored goggles.

"Isn't it dangerous?" asked Gia.

More uniformed men were moving in to help, tearing back the fence to expose the remains of a shed.

"Ag, no, we should be fine back here," said the plumber. "The cops would get rid of us pretty quick otherwise. Watch— they've got all kinds of tricks."

The fence was partly down, and she could see what must be the nest, a bell-shaped thing in the angle of the roof.

The man whistled.

"That's a big one. Oh— look, there's the lure."

One of the Special Branch men moved toward the nest. He seemed wary, head bent, never looking directly at his target. He placed something on the ground, a nodding bunch of mirrors that dipped and flashed at the end of long wires. He bent over them, did something, and the mirrors started whirling slowly, casting spots of sunlight over the walls.

Another policeman approached with a tube that dribbled dark smoke. The crowd murmured in excited interest, and some people jumped up on garbage bins for a better view.

"They're smoking them out!"

The policeman walked right up to the nest, and cautiously stepped onto the pile of fence sheeting that had been torn down. The pile buckled under his booted feet, and something must have shifted because suddenly he was off balance, and his shoulder struck the corrugated iron of the fence with a resounding bang.

The crowd gasped and drew back.

Gia heard the plumber draw in a hissing breath.

Little shapes separated from the nest, leaping out into the air on glittering wings. The policeman regained his balance and, with one arm crooked protectively over his head, placed the smoking tube next to the lure, and opened it fully.

Black smoke gushed out.

More creatures emerged, but instead of attacking the crowd as Gia expected, they seemed drawn to the sparkling mirrors of the lure, spinning and banking around it, oblivious to the rising smoke.

There was a humming buzz in the air above her. One of the things had flown out of the reach of the smoke and was hovering near. Gia stared at it, a rainbow blur like an enormous dragonfly.

Everything slowed.

The wings moved with infinite grace, drawing lingering shapes like smoke trails in the air. The shrill buzz modulated into a lilting song, oil drifting through water, velvet, rainbow shapes—

"Ow!"

Somebody had jabbed her sharply in the ribs.

"Don't look at it, man!"

The plumber had her by the arm and dragged her back, but the creature was already gone.

"You mustn't look at them," he said angrily. "They'll glamour you, and next thing you wake up and you have no eyes, and your hair's all gone."

"Sorry!"

She blinked and put out a hand to steady herself. The wall felt warm, and for a moment she felt intensely aware of it, as though she could smell it with her fingertips. Then the sensation faded.

"I didn't know it could happen so fast," she said.

"That's why they're so careful, Special Branch," said the plumber. Seeing that she was unhurt, he turned back to the scene by the fence.

The smoke from the policeman's tube drifted close to them, and Gia could smell it now, rosemary and burnt rubber.

A Special Branch policeman poked at the nest, pushing so hard that it rocked and tore open, but no more creatures emerged. The ones who'd been circling the lure must have succumbed to the smoke.

After a few more moments, the Special Branch man picked up the lure and the smoking tube. The smoke was dispersing fast, blown away in the wind. The crowd was moving on too, since nothing more seemed likely to happen.

Gia watched as the truck started up with a roar and bumped down off the pavement, hooting to clear the way. Soon nothing was left except the gaping hole in the fence, and a tinge of burnt rubber in the air.

Gia went closer, expecting to be stopped, but nobody paid her any attention.

There would be no bodies, she knew. Small magicals turned into soil and leaves when they died.

She went right up to the hole in the fence, careful not to lose her balance on the sheets of corrugated metal that still lay scattered about.

The nest itself was interesting, broken though it was. It looked like an enormous wasp's nest, made out of translucent stuff much like waxy paper. Parts of it reminded her of a giant bird's nest woven out of grass and strips of packing tape.

Or was that –

She leaned closer, peering at the nest. The main structure was made out of dried grass, but woven throughout there were finer fibres, strands of what could only be hair.

Human hair?

The plumber's words came back to her.

"...and next thing you wake up and you have no eyes, and your hair's all gone..."

She suppressed a shudder.

The torn-open interior of the nest exposed chambers and spiralling tunnels, lined with down. In places strands of hair and strips of fabric had been knotted and plaited together into intricate whorls like basketwork, threaded with tiny objects.

Plastic beads, the metal tabs from drinking cans, a doll's hand, some empty snail shells.

A slender acacia branch poked out of one side. It made a grim sight.

That must have been their larder, thought Gia.

Little bodies hung impaled on the long, white thorns. Geckos and crickets, a dried-out frog, and even a baby bird.

Gia stepped even closer, and something crunched under her foot. She looked down.

She was standing on a scatter of charred leaves and ash. The leaves lay in curved drifts. If she blurred her eyes, she could almost see them as tiny curled-up figures—

There was a fluttering buzz just behind her.

A shadow on the wall beside her, blurred and hazy.

It swung closer, buzzing almost in her ear for an instant, and was gone.

ഇOര

The rest of the way home, she was too busy thinking to take in much of her surroundings.

She wondered how dangerous the creatures really were. What had the plumber called them?

"Haarskeerders."

That was Afrikaans for "hair shavers." She could see where that name came from. Clearly, the creatures liked to collect human hair, and other things too.

The protective clothing of the Special Branch officers, and their wary tension suggested that the creatures were dangerous. But it was hard to believe that the tiny shapes she'd seen flitting about could inflict much harm. Did they have stings, like wasps, or could they cast spells?

Gia wished she'd had a chance to have a proper look at the one that had hovered over her. It was odd, the way she'd gone all dazed. She must have had time to see it, but all she could remember was a spiralling haze. Thinking about it seemed to bring the strange feeling on again, making her dizzy enough that she had to stand, holding on to a street lamp for balance.

It took a few moments for her vision to clear. Everything seemed fascinating, the silvery wood of the lamppost, the grey and black blobs of the

Probably full of sheets, or shoes, or something boring like that. Although it's not really the right size. Not big enough.

Her curiosity roused, she heaved aside the curtains, and found new places for a box of clothes hangers and another box full of Nico's toys.

I'll just have a peek.

She tried to lift the lid of the trunk, but it would not come open.

Locked. Odd, to lock up an old trunk like this?

A crash from the kitchen distracted her, and she went to see what Nico was up to.

෩O෬

The crash turned out to be less disastrous than it sounded, just Nico dropping an empty mixing bowl.

"Wow," said Gia, impressed by the change in the kitchen.

When she'd last seen it, it had been a gloomy, dusty room. But Mandy had been busy. The linoleum floor, faded though it was, gleamed with polish. The windows were clean, and let in more light than they probably had for decades. The familiar table from their previous kitchen took pride of place in the middle of the room, covered in the same striped cloth she knew so well.

"Tadaa!" Mandy grinned, seeing her surprise. "We've been working, while you were lazing away at school."

"It looks fantastic."

"It's *going* to look fantastic, if I ever find room for all this stuff," said Mandy. "This kitchen must be half the size of the Plumstead one. Lucky thing these old houses have lots of built-in cupboards.

"Gia, put some plates on the table and let's have a sit-down meal for a change. We won't wait for your mom. Once she's in the shower she stays in there all day."

Mandy had been with the family as far back as Gia could remember, cooking, cleaning and babysitting, freeing Saraswati to do her part in the dressmaking business.

Now, Mandy tucked an escaped curl of grey hair out of sight under her headscarf, drew out a chair, and sat in it, as at home in the new kitchen as she had been in the old. She lifted an eyebrow at Nico to stop him rocking on his chair, and picked up her knife and fork with a contented sigh.

"Ah, it's a pleasure to eat something you've not cooked yourself for a change," she said.

Gia ate her roeti straight from its paper wrapping. She was glad to see that Nico ate without any fuss.

That was a good sign. Usually, the slightest deviation from his routine caused him to become anxious, and when he was anxious, Nico did not eat.

Still, he was not completely at ease. Gia could see the signs. He ate mostly with one hand, the other reaching out every now and then to touch Mandy's sleeve. As long as he focused on his food he seemed fine, if a little twitchy. But whenever he caught sight of the unfamiliar kitchen, he flinched, narrowing his eyes as if against a too-bright light.

ഌOര

Nico

Gia and Mandy had started shifting the boxes out of the corridor by the time Saraswati emerged from the shower, rubbing her hair with a towel.

"Those empty boxes are going to recycling, so just pile them up next to the door," she said. "Where's Nico?"

Gia nodded at the corner where her brother was dismantling a toy telephone. Then she pointed at the trunk she'd been wondering about earlier.

"What's in that, Mom? And why's it locked?"

Saraswati turned to look at the trunk and, for a moment, Gia thought that she stared in surprise. Then she seemed to recover herself.

"That goes in our bedroom. Your father can move it when he gets here." She frowned at Gia. "You going to stay in that school uniform all day long?"

Gia was taken aback at the edge in her mother's voice.

Why should Dad move it? It can't be all that heavy.

"Where are my clothes?" she asked, trying to keep her voice neutral.

"They're in your room. Still packed."

Gia went to look.

The room she was to share with Nico was next to her parents', and was far from ready. The furniture had been moved in, but nothing was where it should be. The little tank with Nico's latest watery creature experiment was on the floor in one corner, with only enough water in it to keep the occupants alive. His rat, in its cage for once, was balanced on top of the record player. The posters and drawings that had plastered Nico's walls in their Plumstead home were still in rolls on his bed, and all his toys, books, and other possessions were in boxes.

Her own things were in a stack of boxes and suitcases against one wall.

Gia looked around, calculating.

The room was much smaller than either her or Nico's rooms had been, but it had similar proportions to Nico's old room, with the door and window facing one another.

If I move his bed over there, it will be pretty much in the same place it was at home. Then I can move the bookshelf over there...

After a good deal of shoving and dragging, she'd arranged the furniture to her liking. The second bed went next to the door, as nearly out of sight as possible, and all her boxes were either hidden under it or stacked on top.

She arranged everything else as nearly as possible as it had been in Nico's room in their old house.

The door opened and Mandy looked through. "Can I leave Nico with you?" she asked. "It's hard to clean with him hanging onto me all the time."

"Sure. He can help me in here."

Nico went straight to the tank and peered into it with a worried expression.

"Nico," said Gia. "Do you know where the buckets are? Why don't you fill that tank?"

That kept him busy while she set up the record player. The familiar ritual of preparing the water with purifying chemicals and siphoning it into the tank seemed to calm him.

Gia lowered the needle onto his favourite record, and he looked up with a smile as the first chords played.

"*The solar system,*" said a deep voice. "*This is a journey. A journey into space...*"

Nico settled cross-legged on the floor. He'd taken Poepie out of his cage. The rat sat on Nico's shoulder, whiskers twitching as he surveyed his unfamiliar surroundings. Gia was just putting up the last of Nico's drawings— an enormous dinosaur drawn in cross-section to show its remarkably complicated inner workings— when Saraswati put her head round the door.

"Oh!" she said when she saw the room. "Gia, that's wonderful. But where's *your* stuff going to go?"

Before Gia could reply, keys rattled in the front door.

Nico was on his feet and down the passage in a flash. Saraswati and Gia followed, in time to see the door open and Nico fling himself at his father.

"Whoa, boy, you'll knock me downstairs." Karel grunted. "No, you're too big to pick up now."

He gave Nico a friendly shake, careful not to dislodge the rat, who still perched on Nico's shoulder.

"Sari," he said with a smile at his wife.

"Close the door," said Saraswati, giving her husband a kiss. "The cats will get out—"

"Gia, there's a visitor for you," said Karel.

Gia tried to see who stood behind him.

"Fatima!"

The girls embraced, a little clumsily because Fatima held a motorbike helmet.

"I missed you!" said Fatima. "You should have come with. We had the best time."

"My school started on Monday already," said Gia. "And I had to help here."

"I suppose. Has Ben been round yet?"

"No, I think he's still at that math camp thing."

Karel, one arm still around his wife, said, "Why

don't you two move into the kitchen? It's a bit crowded here."

"Sure," said Fatima, moving down the corridor. "You guys still unpacking boxes? Jeez, I'm hungry. My mother's starving me. This the kitchen? Hi Mandy — did you have a good holiday?"

She plunked her helmet on the kitchen table and stuck her head in the fridge.

Saraswati looked on bemused. "Fatima, if your mother has you on a diet, I don't think—"

"Oh, she'll never know. Anyway, there's nothing here. You guys seriously need to do a shop."

Fatima closed the fridge and sighed dramatically.

"I'm doomed to starvation. Wanna go out Gia? There's a new burger place at the Gardens Centre."

"I'm afraid not," said Saraswati. "Gia has to unpack her bedroom, and I'm sure she has homework. And this evening she has to watch her brother."

She turned a serious look on Gia.

"We have to meet the new client, so I'm relying on you to look after Nico. And it's a week night in any case."

"Oh, Mom!" flashed Gia. "As though I *ever* stay out late. I always get stuck looking after Nico, and I've not seen Fatima for weeks—"

Her mother's lips narrowed. "Gia Rozalia, don't take that tone with me. I'm not repeating myself. You know our rules."

Gia felt her cheeks flush. It was one thing for her mother to nag when they were alone together. But to speak like that in front of her friends—

Karel appeared in the door behind Saraswati.

"Gia, why don't you show Fatima around the house,

and the studio. She's not seen that yet, have you Fatima?"

"Oh cool! I'd love that," said Fatima. "But Mr Grobbelaar, check it out." She struck a model pose, hooking her thumbs under the collar of her leather jacket. "Tibetan Troll-hunter's jacket. Cool, no?"

Karel moved in for a closer look. It was an eye-catching jacket. Blood red leather, figure hugging, with a high ribbed collar and sleeves belling out into exaggerated cuffs.

Karel ran a professional finger down a shoulder seam. "Not bad." He tweaked at the collar. "Quite well made too. Mass produced?"

"Oh, I got it at Edgars! But it's pretty nice."

Fatima unzipped the jacket to reveal the black silk lining. "And look— " She patted her hip. "These loop things are what the troll hunters hook their metal probes on. Red hot. That's why it's all scorched there. But that's just *kamma-kamma*, of course, not the real thing. And these— " She ran a finger and thumb over a series of large metal rivets. "These are supposed to be a record of how many trolls you've killed."

Karel lifted his eyebrows in mock respect. "You are clearly a dangerous young lady."

Saraswati was also studying the jacket with interest. "It's nicely put together, for a mass-market jacket. Lovely colour. This is popular now, Fatima?"

"Oh, it's the hottest thing."

"Well, it's certainly slimming."

Fatima laughed. "There's that, too. Well Gia, you going to show me around?"

"Sure. Let's start downstairs."

ஐOஐ

It was fun showing Fatima around the new studio. She was suitably impressed with the gleaming expanse of floor, and looked with interest as Gia pointed out where the interior walls had been taken down to open the space.

"Your dad did all of this himself?"

"Well, he got people to help him, of course, but he did as much as he could himself. This is the fitting room."

She held aside the curtain so that Fatima could see inside.

"Wow. That's from your old place, isn't it, that mirror? But it looks so much better here." She posed in front of the antique three-way mirror. "Nice light in here. Flattering. People are going to love this."

"You think so?"

"Oh yes. It's all so *exclusive* looking."

They inspected the workroom at the back, a space rarely seen by clients and consequently a lot less glossy. This was where most of the equipment was housed. Overlockers, sewing machines, presses, and shelves full of patterns and rolls of fabric.

Upstairs, they sidled through the main bedroom, which was filled with boxes, and peeked into the en-suite bathroom, still steamy from the shower.

"Good thing your parents have got this," said Fatima. "Just imagine if you all had to share the same bathroom. Why does the shower look like that?"

The shower stall had a waist-high wall, so that the lower half was more like a small, square bathtub.

"Mom likes it like that, so she can soak properly. This is the only bit that's been changed about the upstairs. The rest is all still the same."

Gia showed the other bathroom, a much dingier room with a rusted bath, tiny basin, and a toilet with a cistern high up against the ceiling that had to be flushed by pulling at a dangling chain.

The living room was a jumble of furniture and boxes and they decided not to risk going out onto the balcony.

"That's scary," said Fatima, looking down at the street through the holes in the boards. Then she noticed the work table that had been shoved in between the sofa and the display cabinet.

"That's your mother's spot? Is she working on another dress? Why doesn't she set up downstairs in the studio? Lots more space there."

Gia shrugged. "I think she likes to do that kind of work away from the client stuff. And Dad gets on her nerves when she's working on her own things."

"Is she doing another peacock dress? That was stunning."

"Something like that. But this one is white."

After a quick glance at the door, Gia opened one of the boxes. "Look," she said, lifting a length of white silk. "She's already started embroidering."

"Wow. That's so cool."

The ice-white fabric was criss-crossed with undulating lines of black embroidery that branched and curled like the tendrils of a bramble, studded with tiny, sharp, embroidered thorns. Some of the thorns bore little red glass beads that glinted like drops of blood.

Fatima sighed in admiration.

"Wow," she said again. "It's going to be *gorgeous*."

Gia opened another box, and both girls looked at the rows and rows of little bottles full of beads.

"Look at these!" said Gia, and she lifted out a small box. Inside it nestled four large beads. They were shaped like smooth teardrops, each as large around as one of her fingers. From their weight Gia guessed they must be some kind of semi-precious stone, and they had a depth and lustre that drew the eye. Each was like a tiny clot of blood, living red on the surface, but with a curl of black in its heart.

But now Fatima was getting uneasy. "Better put those back," she said. "Before somebody comes in here and catches us snooping."

Gia replaced the beads reluctantly. She felt the urge to suck her fingertips, as if the beads might have stained them.

"But where's your bedroom?" said Fatima. "You still have to share with the little monster?"

"That's what Mom thinks," said Gia as she closed the boxes and checked to make sure that no one could tell they'd been opened.

"I'll show you."

She led the way through the kitchen, into a narrow room that must once have been a pantry. It was lined all the way to the ceiling with shelves and cupboards.

"These are still full of the previous people's stuff. All kinds of odd things," said Gia. "But we'll look at that later. This is what I want to show you."

She pointed at a set of wooden stairs, almost as steep as a ladder, which ended in a trapdoor in the ceiling.

"You. Are. Not. *Serious*." Fatima looked up. "Up there?"

"Come." Gia climbed the stairs, and pushed open the trapdoor, a heavy wooden thing that slid back stiffly. She climbed through, and was soon followed by Fatima, who looked around at the tiny attic room.

"Wow. Dusty! There must be like a kingdom of spiders up here."

"Come look at the view."

Gia walked over to the dormer window set in one of the slanting walls, and Fatima came to stand beside her.

"Wow. Nice!"

The sun was just about to move behind the mountain. The long, low, golden light of late summer spilled over the houses and streets. In the distance, the harbour lights were on, and below them Eastern Boulevard was a river of red brake lights.

"That is awesome," said Fatima. "And you could put your mattress on here, and sleep right here in the window!" She patted the broad window seat.

"That's what I thought," said Gia.

Fatima gave her a calculating look.

"You want to move your stuff in here, make it nice to convince your mom to let you stay up here?"

"You got it."

Fatima considered the room.

"We'll have to do some more cleaning first then. You go get a bucket and rags. And a vacuum cleaner. Look, there's even a plug point, so we won't need to run an extension cord. But how are we going to fit a mattress through that?"

She pointed at the trapdoor.

"We can scrunch it up," said Gia. "I'm sure we can manage."

"O…kay, if you say so. Ben's going to love this."

Gia was about to climb back down through the trapdoor, when she heard the ladder shake, and Mandy's head appeared.

"What's going on here?" said Mandy. "I thought I

heard something moving around. Ugh. Just look at those cobwebs. What are you up to?"

Gia had hoped to keep things secret until the room was ready to show off, but Mandy might make a valuable ally.

"I want to clean this up, Mandy, to make this my room."

"Your ma will have something to say about that."

Mandy, still only head and shoulders through the trapdoor, looked about the room. Gia said nothing, hoping that the challenge of a thoroughly dirty room would do more than any pleading words from her.

Mandy gave a nod. "But you'll have to purify it first. Once you've got the dust out. No knowing what's magical *goggas* been living up here all these years. I'll give you a salt mixture and show you how to do it. We should probably do a good smudge with some sage too."

"Just show us what to do," said Gia happily. With Mandy on her side, the battle was half-won already.

ೞOಞ

Cleaning the attic room was a lot more difficult than either of the girls had expected.

Mandy gave them old shirts to wear, after making Gia change out of her school uniform.

It was satisfying to see the difference their work made. The floor appeared from under the dust of many years: dark, wooden planks. The walls, that were the sloping sides of the roof, had to be swept clear of cobwebs, but there were not many live spiders among them.

Not that their cleaning was without excitement.

Fatima, sweeping up a thick layer of dust from under the window seat, shrieked with surprise as a clot of dust bunched into a bundle and scrambled up the broom handle at her.

Their screams brought Mandy up the ladder again, just in time to see Fatima slapping wildly with a cloth until the thing exploded in a puff of dust.

"You make that much noise, Madam will be up here," warned Mandy.

"What the hell was that!" said Fatima, eyes wide.

"Dust bunny," said Mandy. "Haven't seen one that big for years. Keep the noise down."

"Looked more like a dust spider to me," said Fatima with a shudder.

They were more careful after that, poking at the dust with the broom handle before sweeping it up, but no more dust bunnies appeared.

Gia found a bundle of newspapers in the angle between the ceiling and a roof beam. It was lined with rags, and smelt strongly of cigarette smoke.

"It looks like a nest," said Fatima. "But what makes a nest like that?"

Now that she looked at it, Gia saw there were other things in the bundle. Scraps of sweet wrappings, all bright colours. Bronze-red, golden-green, emerald, and many other shades, mostly metallic. There were also some lumps of crumbly white stuff that might be sugar, and a tiny plastic-framed mirror.

She looked at these things doubtfully. The nest was already falling apart in her hands, and she could hardly put it back.

"I'll throw the newspapers away," she decided.

"But I'll put these other things in an envelope, and put it back up there."

Fatima stared at her. "You're serious? And you plan to sleep up here, with some *thing* crawling about to get its stuff back?"

She shuddered.

"Well, rather you than me."

When they finished dusting and sweeping, Gia vacuumed while Fatima washed the windows. Then, under Mandy's watchful eye, they purified the room with a mixture of salt and nutmeg, sprinkling the mixture all over the floor and sweeping it up again, careful to always sweep in the direction of the trapdoor.

"Sucks up the bad luck," Mandy explained. "And keeps the *goggas* away."

At the mention of magicals, Gia remembered her experience with the haarskeerder nest, and told Fatima about it as they worked.

"Scary stuff," said Fatima. "I didn't know you still got them in the city. All magicals give me the creeps."

Getting the mattress through the trapdoor proved trickier than Gia had thought. Luckily her parents had taken Nico out to find if there was a park anywhere near for him to play in. Otherwise they would certainly have investigated the amount of noise that was made.

It took Fatima pulling from the top, and Gia balancing on the ladder and pushing from below, and even so the mattress did not go through undamaged.

"Shit," said Fatima, inspecting the tear. "Well, we'll just put the sheets over that and nobody will ever know."

At last, the room was ready.

The mattress fitted on the window seat, and looked inviting, neatly made with blankets and pillows.

Mandy had found a wooden box to act as a bedside table, and a lamp to go on top of it.

Gia looked at it proudly. The room was small, much smaller than the bedroom in their previous house, but that did not matter.

It was hers, and hers alone.

They had even set up the tea corner like the one she'd had in her own bedroom back in Plumstead.

On the floor, for the moment. An electric kettle, some mugs, several tins of tea, and a packet of biscuits.

"So, are you going to show me the doll?" asked Fatima, sitting on the bed and stirring sugar into her tea. "You done more on her?"

"Tons!" said Gia. "Hang on, I'll get her out."

She closed and bolted the trapdoor, then opened one of the suitcases that stood waiting to be unpacked.

"Your parents still don't know about this?"

Gia shook her head and lifted out a cardboard box.

"There's no point in talking to them about it. I'm sick of arguing. I've been working on her when no one else is around. Or at night. Which is partly why I can't share a room with Nico."

She sat next to Fatima and placed the box on the bed between them.

"You still going to take First Exit then?" said Fatima, as Gia opened the box and pulled back the layer of felt.

"Yes," said Gia. "Mom and Dad won't like it, but they can't stop me."

"Oh, Gia, you've given her hair!"

Gia took the doll's head out of its nest of felt.

"Human hair," she said. "It took me ages."

She brushed the fringe back from the doll's forehead

to display the tiny, regular pin holes. "I had to root each lock of hair separately. But it's worth the trouble."

"She's going to look fantastic when you put her all together," said Fatima.

She picked up one of the doll's hands and examined it, holding it in her palm. "You painted this one again. The skin's a different colour."

"No, that's from firing," said Gia. "Makes it change colour like that."

She stroked the doll's hair.

"Do you think she's good enough, Fatima? Will they accept this as an apprentice piece?"

Fatima considered the head.

"Well, I think she's gorgeous," she said at last. "But the thing is, they might not see it as an artwork at all. She's so *pretty*. And she's a doll. Maybe you should — I don't know. Plunge a knife through her neck and make her all gory, or something like that. Say it's a statement about violence against women."

Gia laughed. "Or make her lots and lots of hands," she said. "And sew them all over her body. Except, hands are a mission to make. And anyway, I don't want to do something like that to her."

"I know," said Fatima.

They both looked down at the doll head in Gia's lap.

Is she really good enough? wondered Gia.

Maybe I do have to do something to make her more of an artwork, and not just a doll.

The image of the blood-red beads in her mother's box returned to her. That was the effect she hoped to capture: beautiful and unsettling.

Even just one bead might be enough, if I combined it with embroidery. But I can't ask Mom for them without explaining what I want it for, and she'll notice immediately if I just take one.

The doll was her apprentice piece, her chance to win a scholarship and gain admission to the Ben-Haspeth School of Arts. That was the plan she'd been working towards for more than a year. Instead of finishing high school, she would take First Exit and join the art school as an apprentice. Her parents would never give permission, but that did not matter. She was sixteen, and she could take First Exit without their consent.

As long as the art school accepted her, of course. And that would only happen if her apprentice piece was good enough.

Both girls started as somebody hammered on the trapdoor.

"Open up, Gia," shouted Mandy.

"Coming!" Gia hurriedly tucked the doll back in the box, and put it away.

She opened the trapdoor.

"Madam's home," Mandy said as she climbed through.

"Gia!" came Saraswati's voice from below. "Where are you?"

"I'm here, Mom," called Gia, feeling a flutter of nerves. "Come have a look."

There was a silence. Then her mother's voice, much closer.

"Gia? Where— ?"

"Here, Mom. Up here."

The stairs creaked and her mother appeared, head and shoulders through the trapdoor.

"What's this, Gia?" Saraswati looked around at the room, frowning.

"Move on up!" came Karel's voice from behind her.

"Just wait, Karel—" But Saraswati had to climb all the way through and move aside to make way for Karel and Nico, who were both impatient to see what was at the top of the ladder.

"Just look at this!" said Karel, coming through the trapdoor. "Did you girls clean this up now? Looking pretty good!"

Nico was wide eyed. He looked far too interested for Gia's liking.

"This is *my* room, Nico," she said. "Just like back home. No sneaking in and messing with my stuff, understand?"

She caught her mother's disapproving eye. "I wish you would not talk to your brother like that. And we've decided this already. You are to share the room with Nico—"

"No obvious leaks, and the floor's quite safe," said Karel. He stamped a foot. "Solid. Are the windows warded?"

"Iron wards," said Mandy. "Old-fashioned, but nothing wrong with that. Won't go down in a power failure like these new-fangled electric system, anyhow."

Saraswati turned on her with a frown. "Mandy? Did you help them do this?"

Mandy met her gaze blandly. "You all need more space here, Madam. Nothing wrong with the room. And little Nico will do better on his own, you know that. We've just got him used to sleeping by himself."

Saraswati seemed about to argue back, then she laughed despite her irritation. "True enough. Our one victory." She looked around the room again, rubbing her hands over her upper arms. "You're sure it's safe, Karel?"

"Absolutely," said Karel. "Floor's solid as a rock. No signs of leaks, but we'll know for sure when it starts raining. I can put some bars over the windows, if you like. You'll need some shelving, Gia."

"It seems the decision is made then," said Saraswati. "But I wish you'd asked for permission, Gia. I don't like this sneaking around behind my back."

Gia gave a little jump of joy, and high-fived Fatima.

"Thanks Mom! That's fantastic!" She stepped in for a hug. For a moment her mother was stiff in her arms. Then she relaxed as she relented.

"Just don't fall down that ladder in the dark," she said into Gia's hair.

෨Oര

Fatima left, after a last attempt at getting Gia to go out with her.

"I'm sorry, Fatima," Sariswati had said. "Karel and I have to go out tonight. Meeting a new client. We can't leave Nico on his own."

So that was that.

Gia sat on her parents' bed, watching her mother get ready.

The house was quiet now. Nico was in bed, listening to a record to help him fall asleep. Karel was downstairs in the studio, working on something. Mandy had left for the day.

That was another change.

In Plumstead, Mandy had only gone home on weekends, to see her grown-up daughters and their grandchildren. Now she would be travelling every day, taking train and taxi to get to work here in Walmer Estate.

"Gia, would you brush my hair for me?"

Saraswati sat with her eyes closed, rocking slightly as Gia pulled the brush through her long, black hair.

Gia loved her mother's hair. It was so different from her own, which was short, brown, and tended to curl in unwanted directions. Saraswati's hair was ink-black, dead straight, and hung to her waist. These days it was laced with a few silver strands among the black, but Gia thought those were beautiful too.

"Are you going to put it up?" she asked as she gave back the brush.

Her mother smiled at her in the mirror. "You like that, don't you?"

She reached back and twisted her hair expertly into an ornate loop. Gia handed her the two long wooden pins which Saraswati stuck in at just the right angle to secure the hair.

"There," said Saraswati, tucking an escaped strand behind her ear. "That will do."

Gia watched as Saraswati put kohl around her eyes and deftly applied a touch of lipstick.

She always thought that Saraswati looked like someone from the Tales of the Arabian Nights. Maybe not a princess— her hooked nose and firm chin were too fierce for that. She dressed simply too, and wore no jewelry except for two wide silver bracelets that reached almost from elbow to wrist.

Gia had never seen Saraswati without her silver, and the bracelets seemed as much part of her mother as her hair.

Dressed in white linen, her coiled hair emphasising the graceful length of her neck, Saraswati looked like a queen.

"Gia, could you stay down here with Nico until

we get home?" she said, gathering her things into an evening handbag.

"I know you want to go up into your new room, but if Nico wakes and—"

"It's okay, Mom. I'll stay."

Her mother gave her the lightest of lipstick-saving kisses, surrounding Gia with her jasmine-and-sandalwood scent.

"Thank you, my darling. We'll try not to be out too late."

ഌO☙

The record reached its end, filling Nico's room with its rhythmic bump and scratch until Gia lifted the needle.

She stood over to the bed, and saw that Nico was not yet asleep.

His unhappiness was apparent in the lines of his skinny body lying stiff and tense under the blankets. His eyes were wide open, large and dark, staring up at the ceiling.

She sat on the bed and took one of his hands, which was promptly jerked away again.

Poor old Nico. What was it like for him?

It was going to be a while before he really got used to things. There were going to be some bad dreams tonight.

If only he would talk more.

Gia pictured all the words that Nico did not use building up inside him, looking for ways to escape. No wonder he got so twitchy.

She wondered what went on inside his head. He could speak and understand perfectly well, but he used the words one or two at a time, or strung awkwardly together, as if he were signalling with flags.

Careful to keep her voice to a low monotone, she started reciting: *"If all the seas were one sea..."*

She waited.

Nico stopped twisting his head, and stared up at the ceiling. For a few moments she did not think it was going to work. Then he whispered, *"What-a-great-sea-that-would-be."*

Gia smiled, and continued. *"If all the trees were one tree."*

Once again a pause, and then the response, a little louder this time, *"What-a-great-tree-that-would-be."*

They continued like that, call and response. Gia let her eyes wander over the room. The fish tank was bubbling quietly, the skeekers visible as busy little shadows, swimming about inside. Occasionally one of them would pulse with light. Poepie scratched about in his cage, restlessly moving his bedding around.

Gia looked at the boxes of her clothes and books piled up in a corner. She'd have to cart those up the ladder tomorrow, and figure out a way to store her clothes neatly.

"If all the men were one man."

"What-a-great-man-that-would-be."

She looked down at her brother. His eyes were closing.

He was so sweet like this, all quiet and sleepy, that it was easy to forget how much trouble he could be.

Her saccharine voice put Gia's teeth on edge, but unlike the others, she seemed interested in Nico himself, rather than seeing him as some kind of experiment. Still, Nico would have to go to school soon. Strictly speaking he should have started already, but Saraswati had resisted, saying he was not ready yet.

And these days, could they even afford to send him to school?

"And if the great man took the great axe."

There was no reply.

Nico's eyes were closed, and his breathing slow.

Asleep at last.

Gia sat for a while, leaning back against the headboard, thinking about the events of the day. She was slipping into sleep, and the memories crowded back, in an almost dream. Granny, grinning at her from behind her counter. The charred leaf-bodies of the dead haarskeerders. Fatima, showing off her blood-red jacket. The scent of nutmeg, burnt rubber, and rosemary.

Catching herself nodding, she shook herself awake and stood, careful not to wake Nico. She left softly, leaving the door just open enough so that she could hear if he woke.

ഇOര

BRINK AND MOOLMAN

Gia chose a desk halfway down the classroom. Not too near the front, where she might be noticed, and not too close to the back where the troublemakers hung out. Her fellow students were noisier than usual, excited by the unfamiliar classroom and the prospect of starting on a new, and as yet unknown, subject.

The teacher, a tall, skinny woman, ignored the giggles and scuffles. She stood with her back to the class writing a series of headings on the board.

"*Malifica (evil), comoinis (neutral), utilis (useful), bona (good).*"

She started a second line.

"*Ignis (fire), Aqua (water), Ventus (air), Terra (earth)*".

Although she had her back to the class, she had enough presence to intimidate the worst of the gigglers and whisperers, and the class soon settled down to watch her.

"*Birds, mammals, amphibians, reptiles, fish, insects.*"

By the time she reached the last word, the class had fallen completely silent, so that everyone could hear the grind and squeak of the chalk making the last mark. Dusting her hands, she stood back and regarded the board for a moment, gave a satisfied nod, and faced the class.

She had a long, deeply wrinkled face, and heavy lidded eyes. Her hair was a pile of bright-auburn curls, and she wore hooped earrings, each with a tiny parrot perched inside, heavy enough to stretch her earlobes.

"Good morning," she said, in a voice that suggested a life of brandy and cigarettes. "I'm Miss Huisman."

"Good morning, Miss Huisman," came the dutiful chorus.

"I'm to be your supernatural studies teacher for the rest of the year. Who are the class monitors?"

A boy and girl near the front put up their hands. Miss Huisman peered at their badges.

"Themba, and Rachel, good. Hand these out." She patted a pile of pale blue books on her desk.

"While Themba and Rachel are doing that, there are some things that need to be noted."

The class was dead quiet.

"As you are probably aware, this class has started a little later in the year than is usual. We have to make up the time. If everyone keeps up with their homework, and attends, all should be fine. Understood?"

Everyone nodded, and there were a few shouts of "Yes, Miss!" from the back row.

Soon everyone had a copy of the textbook, and the monitors were back at their desks. Gia looked at the book with interest. It was fairly thick, covered in pale blue paper. The title was *Magical Creatures of Southern Africa* with the authors' names *Brink and Moolman* in smaller type below.

"The book you have before you will be your textbook for this year. If you lose it, or if it is damaged while in your possession, you are liable for the cost of replacement. We will also be referring to other texts, both ancient and modern, as the course progresses. Now."

Miss Huisman picked up a pile of pictures, and held one of them up. "Under which of the headings that I've written there on the board should this go?"

The picture showed a man-like creature, thin to the point of emaciation. It had a big, square jaw thrust forward in a pronounced overbite.

There was a stir and murmur, but no one answered.

"Come now. I know that some of you know this one. Anybody? Yes, you there in the back?"

"That's a crackbottle, Miss!"

"And which heading does it go under?"

But the boy had lost his confidence.

"Anyone else? Is this creature evil, neutral, useful —"

"Evil, Miss," came the answer at last.

Miss Huisman's eyebrows went up.

"Could be. Any other suggestions? How about you, girl. What heading?"

She pointed at a plump girl, who sat pertly upright near the front of the class.

"Earth?" she ventured.

"Why earth?" asked a boy in the row behind her.

"They live underground, don't they?" said the girl. "And they make their babies out of mud."

"No, they don't!"

Miss Huisman's raised hand instantly silenced the argument.

"Crackbottles don't make their babies out of mud. That's an old wives' tale. But you are quite correct, they do live underground. And they're also extremely dangerous. Let's put it under maleus then."

She stuck the picture on the board, and held up another. The answer came quickly now.

"That's a lacefester, Miss!"

"And it's an insect, isn't it?"

"And it flies. That makes it air!"

"But they hunt moldpimps, so it should really go under useful, shouldn't it?"

Miss Huisman looked from one arguing student to the other, eyes bright with amusement.

"Miss?"

A skinny girl with white-blond hair had her hand up. Miss Huisman raised an eyebrow at her.

"Couldn't we rearrange the headings?"

The girl's voice was so soft that the teacher had to lean in to hear her.

"What is your name, girl?"

"Sonella Pretorius, Miss."

"Well, Sonella. How would you suggest we rearrange the headings?"

Sonella pushed up her glasses, and peered at the board. "The most important ones should be at the top," she said. "Then each of the others can be duplicated under them."

"Go on," said Miss Huisman when she paused.

"Like— I think—"

Miss Huisman silently held out the chalk.

Gia thought Sonella would be too shy to go up to the board, but she seemed focused only on the problem she was trying to solve.

First, she copied out the headings *malifica, comoinis, utilis* and *bona,* spacing them widely apart. A girl giggled and there was some whispering, but Sonella did not seem to notice. She wrote *air, earth, fire* and *water* four times, under each of the first headings.

She turned to Miss Huisman. "Like that," she said. "Then, the crackbottle could go under 'malifica - earth' and the lacefester under 'utilis - air'. And you could put in more headings lower down too."

"Good," said Miss Huisman. "And why did you choose malefica and the rest as your first level heading? Why not 'birds, mammals, insects, reptiles'?"

Sonella frowned, and blinked a bit, but Miss Huisman gave her time to answer.

"Not all magicals fit into those categories, do they? Like, um, gloams, and goolies, and things like that? And 'evil, good' and the rest seemed the most general to me. Or maybe the most important?"

"That depends on your purpose in making the categories," said Miss Huisman. "Well done, Sonella. You can return to your desk. The point of this exercise," she said, turning back to the rest of the class, "is to demonstrate that there are many different ways that one can categorise a creature.

"The categories you choose, and how you arrange them, all depend on what you are trying to achieve. Many, many years ago— in fact about two thousand years ago, the famous Greek philosopher and scientist Aristotle created a system by which all beings on earth could be classified. Aristotle's system was called 'the great chain of being' and it listed things from the most to the least important. It started at the top, with God, then followed the angels, then came humans and so on down through the various kinds of animals, insects, and plants. Each thing in its place, unchanging.

"The fascinating thing about Aristotle's scheme is that he did not in any way separate magical beings from the non-magical. Weres, dragons, and the rest were simply placed in the list in among all the other creatures.

"Things changed rather in the Middle Ages. You. What is your name?"

Miss Huisman pointed at one of the boys who always sat at the back of the class. He was lounging so low in his seat that his chin was barely above the desk.

"Charlie, Miss," he said. "But they call me Soutie." He grinned up at Miss Huisman, clearly not intimidated.

"Charlie—?"

"Wexton, Miss."

"Mr Wexton, sit up, and tell me what was the single most important influence in the Middle Ages."

After a pause to make it clear that he might have decided not to obey, Charlie pulled himself up to a more normal sitting position.

"I don't know, Miss? Money?"

There was a rustle of laughter from the rest of the class.

"You could make an argument for that, I suppose, Mr Wexton, but that's not the answer I was looking for. Anyone else?"

When no one else put up a hand, she continued.

"In the Middle Ages it was the Church that dominated every aspect of society. Science, at that time, served the Church and scientists shaped their ideas to fit those espoused by the Church. In medieval times the books that listed all the living creatures were called 'bestiaries'. But these bestiaries were far less rational, less scientific, than Aristotle's lists. The purpose of a bestiary was not to act as a record of knowledge, but to teach moral lessons.

"The bestiaries also made quite a point of indicating which creatures were magical, and which were not.

Some of these distinctions are very different from those we might make today. For example, caterpillars and butterflies were classified as magical, because of the amazing metamorphosis that occurs in their life cycle. And some creatures that we now consider as being magical, were thought perfectly unmagical in those days. For example, whales were not thought magical at all. Maybe it was only when people started sailing into deeper seas, and encountered the songs of the humpback whale— But I'm getting off topic.

"It is in the medieval bestiaries that we find, for the first time, the idea that magical creatures are in some way unnatural. Magical creatures, according to these books, were not part of God's original creation, but were created by the Devil.

"Which led, of course, to the notorious witch burnings, and the purges that swept over Europe in which magical creatures were exterminated, and people were tortured and executed for the crime of having magical talent. The terrible *tormentas*, that continue even in modern times."

"In the thirteenth and fourteenth centuries the Church lost much of its power and science came into its own. As travellers spread out across the world and encountered new cultures and creatures, scientists started finding ways to make sense of all of these discoveries. Instead of relying on existing wisdom, they began to base their theories on what they actually saw— on observation and rational deduction. This became the period we know as the Enlightenment.

"From our point of view, in the subject of supernatural studies, the important individual here is a man called Carl Linnaeuss, who published an exhaustive taxonomy of the natural world. He based his classification, not on ideology, but on the observed attributes. Mammals, reptiles, and all the rest.

"Now. How, would you guess, might Carl Linnaeuss have classified this creature?" She held up another of her pictures. It showed a pale woman with hair that ended in barbed hooks.

Sonella had her hand up. "I think it's a harionago, Miss."

"That is correct. Can anyone tell me its classification?"

Pages rustled as everyone searched their books, but no answers came.

"Nothing? Nobody? Of course, your textbooks only have the most common, local creatures. I have here Linnaeuss's master work, *The Complete Listing of Monsters and Magical Creatures.*" She patted a fat book bound in red leather. "Would you like to come look for it here, Sonella?"

But Sonella shook her head. "It won't be in there, Miss. It's Japanese. Carl Linnaeuss probably did not know about the Harionago."

Miss Huisman bowed and pantomimed ironic applause, clapping her hands soundlessly. "Very good indeed, Miss Pretorius. Linnaeuss's *Complete Listing* is not complete at all. Many creatures are not included, including Chinese, Japanese, Indian, and even some of our own indigenous South African creatures. Can anyone tell me of such a one?"

Charlie Wexton stuck his hand up as far as it could go.

"Mr Wexton?"

"The tokkelossie!" he shouted in triumph, and the class erupted in delighted giggles. Miss Huisman waited for silence as Charlie looked gleefully around, mugging at his friends.

"Indeed, Mr Wexton. The tokkelossie, or tokelosh, as it is also called, is a good example of a South African creature that is not listed here. And what is the defining characteristic of the tokkelosh?"

"Uh?" Charlie lost his smile. Gia was delighted to see a red flush creeping up his neck into his cheeks.

"What, Mr Wexton, would you say is most noticeable about a tokkelosh? Although I hope that you yourself have not had the *misfortune* to actually see one."

Charlie looked desperately at his friends, and seeing no help there, swallowed.

"He has very big— uh— testicles, Miss. That he slings around his—"

But here his voice gave out, and he was reduced to gesture, patting his shoulders.

"That is correct. Well done, Mr Wexton. So, class, you can see that although Linnaeuss's work was essential in establishing a system that could be used for classification, it is not complete. Apart from the fact that not all creatures are included in his lists, many experts, even to this day, disagree with the way that creatures have been classified. And we have not even touched on the problem of humans with magical abilities. Where should they be classified? And then there is the problem of *sentience*."

A hand shot up near the front of the class. It was Rachel, class monitor and daughter of the school inspector.

"Isn't those things political, Miss?"

"Indeed they are, Rachel. And what is the point of your question?"

"I thought—" She faltered, then regained confidence. "We're not supposed to talk politics in school, Miss."

"Oh, indeed? And how would you suggest we study magic and magical creatures, *without* talking about politics?"

When the girl seemed unable to answer, Miss Huisman continued.

"We will be discussing the Grey List, the 'fairy problem' and many other questions of a political nature this year."

As the lesson continued, Gia watched Miss Huisman stalking between the desks, or pacing back and forth in front of the board. She looked just like a bird. Some kind of predatory bird, or maybe a hadeda. She had the same bright eyes and slightly jerky way of moving. Gia could picture her reaching with a long beak and snatching up a student, throwing her head back to gulp them down. She came out of her dream to find Miss Huisman looking down at her, painted eyebrows lifted.

"Well?"

Gia cleared her throat. "I'm sorry, Miss. I did not hear the question."

There was a rustle as the class turned to stare at her. Gia was still new enough to draw attention whenever she spoke.

"My question," said Miss Huisman, enunciating slowly, "was if you could suggest any magical creature that one might encounter here in South Africa?"

"Uh, dust bunnies?" blurted Gia.

The class exploded with laughter and Gia felt her cheeks burn. Still, she refused to be cowed and kept her gaze on Miss Huisman, who inclined her head and waited for silence.

"A pertinent example," she said when order was restored. "*Dust bunnies* is the vernacular, or popular name. You will find it listed in *Brink and Moolman* under 'elementals, household'."

The bell rang. Miss Huisman raised her voice over the hubbub of everyone putting their books away and rising from their desks. "Class! I have some announcements to make before you rush out of here. Homework!" There was a general groan, and a few calls of "Oh, Miss!" which Miss Huisman ignored.

"Each of you must find me at least two examples of a creature or entity that has been re-classified, or that has some controversy over its classification. Secondly, tomorrow a representative of Special Branch will be visiting the school to give a presentation."

This drew a buzz of interest from the class.

"The presentation will take place in the school hall at first period, and the entire school will be in attendance. I expect you all to pay careful attention, and we will be discussing it in tomorrow's lesson. Special Branch, after all, deal with magical creatures, and that is the topic of interest in this classroom. Thank you, that will be all."

As she left the class, Gia found herself walking next to Sonella Pretorius. The girl gave her a shy smile.

"I've seen them," she said. "Dust bunnies." She shuddered. "Horrid!"

Gia laughed. "They are!" she agreed. "What have we got now? Maths?"

Sonella nodded. "Two whole periods of it." She sighed. "And I'm already starving."

༄ O ༅

When Gia got home that afternoon Saraswati was refining a new pattern for a formal jacket, her work spread all across the kitchen table. Mandy grumbled about it, as she wanted to bake a pie for supper, but there was nowhere else for Saraswati to work. One of Karel's designs occupied the large cutting table in the studio.

As Gia crossed the kitchen, Saraswati, both hands occupied with a length of white muslin, was talking with the phone clamped between chin and shoulder. She was also trying to keep Nico away from the paper pattern laid out on the table. Gia kept her head down to avoid catching her mother's eye. She'd had an idea for setting up bookshelves in her new bedroom, and she did not want to be saddled with Nico.

Mandy can help her, she thought as she put her foot on the bottom step. But the phone call must have ended because her mother appeared behind her.

"Gia, could you look after Nico for me? I need Mandy to help me with this job I'm working on. I just don't have enough hands to do it by myself. It'll just be a few minutes."

"More like a few hours," said Gia under her breath, but turned back to the kitchen and, after some persuasion, got her brother to follow her to the living room.

This was a good place for homework. With the balcony door open she could see the street below, as well as a slice of Table Mountain. Nico sat at the table, drawing. Minou, the cat, watched over him, graceful as a vase with her tail curled tightly round her front paws. Pouf lay on the balcony, wistfully watching the scene below. He was a large, black cat who would be impressive if it wasn't for his look of earnest, round-eyed stupidity.

Something beeped in her pocket, and Gia pulled out her texter. It was a message from Fatima, as usual.

Can I come round later?

She quickly typed out her reply.

Just finishing homework. Come in an hour?

She finished her math and English homework as quickly as she could, then spent some time leafing through *Brink and Moolman*.

What had Miss Huisman said? Elementals, Household.

She found the "Elementals", and paged through the sections on air, earth, and fire before finding what she sought under "household".

Vernacular: Dust Crawler, Dust Bunny, Stoffelaar, Lazy Marys, Devil's Dust, Devil's blanket.

A non-sentient accumulation of dust, sand, hair, or other household detritus imbued with the appearance of life. They appear as the result of long-term exposure to magic-working, and as such, Dust Crawlers often occur in the houses or workspaces of practitioners of magic. Dust Crawlers are harmless, and seem to be entirely reactive; they do not move by themselves, but only if disturbed, typically by a broom or duster.

Folk belief: Dust Crawlers are said to be a sign from the Devil to shame a lazy housewife. There are also some references to the use of Dust Crawlers in clay, from which golems can be made. This has not been corroborated through any reproducible experiments.

Classification: Neutral.

Note: There is some controversy over this classification. There are accounts of Dust Crawlers smothering babies or young children. These accounts are, however, as yet unverified.

Gia noticed this last fact with interest.

Great! I've found one controversy already. Just one more, and my Supernatural Studies homework is done for the day.

"Gia—" said Saraswati from the door. Then she stopped, and frowned at the pieces of paper scattered across the table.

"Where's Nico?"

At Gia's blank look, Saraswati's hand went to her heart and she stared at the open balcony door.

"Mom, I think I'd have noticed if he went out there!"

But Saraswati was already striding across the room to look out at the street below. Then she looked in rapid succession behind the couch, the curtains, and the door.

"Nico," she called, her voice deceptively calm.

"Mom, I'm sure—"

But Saraswati was already out of the door. Gia heard her gasp in the corridor. She followed, just in time to see her mother disappear through the open front door, closely followed by the cats.

But that door was closed. I'm sure that door was closed. I locked it, didn't I?

Mandy emerged from the bedroom.

"Nico's gone," said Gia. "Mom thinks he's gone outside."

They both ran downstairs. The burglar gate was also standing open, and outside, in the street, Saraswati stood looking wildly about, completely ignoring Minou and Pouf who disappeared rapidly around the nearest corner.

"Mom, the studio," said Gia, pointing at the open door.

Saraswati darted inside, with Gia and Mandy at her heels.

Nico was nowhere to be seen, and neither was Karel. There was a puzzle of paper pieces on the cutting table to show what he'd been working on, but no sign of the man himself.

Gia, Saraswati and Mandy spread out, looking behind the curtains in the fitting room, in the small toilet at the back, and at last, in the workroom.

There was Nico, sitting cross-legged on the floor, surrounded by the parts of a meticulously dismantled overlocker.

Saraswati gasped with relief. Gia saw that her mother was shaking, could sense her fizzing with shock. As always, her own heart thumped in sympathy to her mother's fear, yet at the same time she felt an overpowering surge of irritation.

Why does she have to react like that? Nothing happened, did it? Nothing ever does. But every time Nico goes out of her sight –

Saraswati took a deep breath and she stared down at her son, taking in the dismantled overlocker.

Gia knew that it was a disaster.

The other overlocker, the newer machine that Mandy used, was in for a service. This older machine was the only one they had going at the moment, and it was needed for several urgent projects.

Well, this old machine's had it now, thought Gia. *Nico's done a thorough job of it. How on earth did he manage to do that so quickly?*

She noticed her keys among the scattered machine parts, and bent to pick them up.

So that's how he got out. Must have snuck them from my bag when I was not looking.

"Nico."

Gia could tell that her mother was trying to sound calm and friendly, but her voice was strained.

"Nico."

Saraswati stepped carefully through the bits of overlocker and crouched in front of her son.

"Nico, look at me."

Gia knew what was coming, and winced as Nico closed his eyes and turned his head away, clamping his chin against one shoulder.

Won't she ever learn? It's best to just leave him alone when he's like that –

Sariswati held out a hand, but withdrew it as Nico leaned away from her. After a moment, she got up and picked her way back to where Gia and Mandy stood watching.

Here it comes, thought Gia.

"Madam, I'm so sorry," said Mandy. "I should have seen—"

"No, Mandy, it is *not* your fault." Saraswati's voice trembled with fury as she turned on Gia.

"How many times, Gia? How many times must this happen?"

She hugged her arms around herself, glaring at her daughter. "I cannot trust you to do even the simplest things. Lock the front door! Lock the gate! Keep the balcony door *closed*. All you had to do was keep an eye on your brother, and once again—"

"But Mom, I *did* lock the door. Nico took—"

But Saraswati was not listening. "Gia, you are always trying to pass the blame on to somebody else. You are no longer a *little girl.* You are *sixteen years old!*"

Gia tried to interrupt, but her mother was unstoppable.

"Do you realise what could have happened, if Nico went wandering off by himself in this neighbourhood? Do you know what kind of people— what kind of *creatures* there are out there?"

Saraswati took a shuddering breath, then glanced over at the workroom door. When she spoke again her voice was softer, but no less vehement. "I don't know what to do anymore, Gia. Really, I don't. You behave as though you are a guest, not a part of the family. I rely on you. Your father relies on you—"

This was too much. Gia felt her face burn as the outraged answers bubbled up inside her.

Why is it always my fault? Why is it always Nico you worry about, and not me? If something happened to me, would you even notice?

But she could say nothing. The whining self-pity of her unspoken thoughts disgusted her. Maybe she really was the self-centred, immature brat that her mother though her. Feeling the tears start, she pushed past Saraswati and made for the door.

"Gia! Come back here. Don't you *dare*—"

The door slammed behind her in a most satisfying way, and Gia was out in the street, running.

៛០ɞ

She ran as hard as she could, deafening herself to the echoes of her mother's words.

Running always calmed her.

Back in Plumstead, she'd gone for a run every evening, but she was unsure where the safe routes were in this new neighbourhood.

A thought made her pull up into a walk, breathing hard. How long had it been since she'd sent that text inviting Fatima?

She swore and patted her pockets, relieved to find that she had both her texter and her wallet.

She tapped out a quick message.

Can we meet somewhere else? Motherfight.

The answer came back almost immediately.
Yuck. Where meet?

Gia thought quickly. The new burger place that Fatima wanted to go to was at the Gardens Centre, wasn't it? That was not so far away. And anyway, she felt like running.

Burger place. Gardens Centre?

Fatima agreed, and Gia set off again, this time at a more measured pace.

It felt good to be moving. Her whole body became a rhythm, legs stretched into an easy stride, the thumping of her feet on the road matched the swing of her arms. Her heart beat strongly and her chest expanded to match the demand for oxygen.

People turned to watch and she felt a touch of pride, knowing that she ran well. Soon she left the narrow roads of Walmer Estate and was into the open spaces where District Six used to be.

The mountain towered over her, and on the other side was Eastern Boulevard, and beyond that, the harbour. The uneven paving forced her to slow down. A slower pace also made it easier to look about, and there was much to see. She'd seen it before, of course, but from a car.

Very different being out on in the middle of it all. It was a little spooky, even in the middle of a sunny afternoon.

Scrubby grass and small thorny bushes covered most of it. There was a church in the distance, the only thing left standing after the government bulldozers, so many years ago. Almost nothing left of the houses and streets that had once been here.

A whole neighbourhood, vanished as if it had never been.

Gia had learnt all about District Six in school, but it was hard to imagine that it had been real. The stories seemed too brightly coloured, too romanticised. A place where black, white and brown, magical and human, had lived together if not quite in harmony, then with energy and gusto. Carnival and sequins, *Ghoema*, choirs and brass bands. The scent of bobotie and yellow rice, sticky koeksisters. Young men in sharp suits, cobblestone streets.

All of it gone.

The people scattered, the homes razed to the ground.

As she walked past the deserted lots, Gia wondered what it had really been like. That made her shiver so she picked up her pace, feeling safer running than she did when she walked. Soon she reached the other side, where the streets were busy with cars and people again.

At the top of Roeland Street she slowed to a walk again, out of breath.

She was not quite as fit as she'd like to be.

She stopped at the intersection across from the Gardens Centre, waiting for the lights to change. Even here there were referendum posters, up to four or five on a single lamppost.

"*Choose the Realistic Choice: Vote Yes for Our Country's Future*" proclaimed one. "*Human Rights Equals Sentient Rights!*" shouted another. "*The Humans Shall Govern,*" stated a third.

"*No to the Gray List, No to Magic Discrimination!*"

"*Trust a Troll With Your Daughter? Then Why Trust It With The Vote?*"

This last one featured a drawing of a troll grasping at a frightened girl, her dress half torn off one shoulder.

The absurdity of it made Gia smile, but the emotion behind the words reached out to her like a bad smell.

Another poster caught her eye; a non-political one, this time, a headline from a newspaper.

"Kavitha: No Virgin?"

This one had a picture of Kavitha Pillay, posing on the arm of her fiancé, Luxulo Langa, the president's son.

Kavitha had been in the news ever since the announcement of her engagement to Luxolo. Multi-racial couples still drew attention, and the alliance of the president's son with the youngest daughter of a prominent Indian businessman had created a feeding frenzy in the media. Hardly a day went by without a front-page picture of Kavitha.

Gia felt a stab of sympathy for the lovely Miss Pillay. No amount of beauty or money could make up for being the centre of this kind of attention. But the lights had changed, and she had a chance to cross the intersection.

At the entrance to the Gardens Centre she stepped through the metal detector and allowed the guard to inspect her pockets. He was not Special Branch, just mall security and she wondered what he would do if he found anything suspicious. What if she were a marrowmaid, with a bag full of blister? Since that horrible spore explosion the Belle Gente had set off at the Golden Acre, everyone was on edge.

෨Oര

Gia had no trouble finding the burger place. An enormous sign dominated the entrance. The sign was shaped like a black wolf, head thrown up in front of a glowing full-moon, with the name of the restaurant spelt out in blood-red neon.

Wolfies.

And in smaller letters below:

We're howl'n good!

Gia heard somebody laugh and there was Fatima, waiting at one of the outside tables, and Ben too, both of them smiling at her reaction.

"Good ain't it!" drawled Ben in an American accent, and then in his normal voice, "wait 'till you see the waitresses."

"Hey Ben, I thought you were still at math camp," said Gia.

"Nope, got back this morning. And then Fatima kidnapped me, as you can see."

"Actually, Mom kidnapped you." Fatima pulled an expressive face at Gia. "Mom took him clothes shopping. Honestly, you'd think we were going to the dentist, from his reaction."

"That explains the loot," said Gia, looking at the two large shopping bags. "Bet your mom had a ball though."

"Any excuse to shop," said Fatima.

Gia had known Fatima and Ben since primary school. In fact, Ben was more like a brother than a friend, often spending more time in her or Fatima's homes than at his mother's tiny flat. It was only recently that Gia had figured out that, over the years, her parents and Fatima's had quietly done what Ben's mother could not. Feeding him when she was between jobs, making sure he had clothes and shoes, and even paying for his school fees, which must have added up to a considerable amount.

Ben's father was never mentioned.

Gia had the impression that his disappearance was somehow connected to magic, which was usually the case when grown-ups refused to discuss something.

"Come, let's go find a table," said Fatima.

They were greeted at the door by a girl dressed in a form-fitting, furry bodysuit. Large wolf ears were attached to her head and, as Gia saw when she turned to lead them to their table, a bushy wolf tail hung down behind her.

They took their seats, and the waitress handed them their menus.

"I'm Cindy, and I'm your were-tron. Welcome to —"

"A what-tron?" said Fatima, as she sidled between the table and the upholstered bench.

"Were-tron," said the girl, a touch defiantly. Then she suddenly deflated, and said in a normal voice, "Your menus are there on the table. Anyone want to order drinks?"

"Shame," said Fatima, when she was gone. "Imagine having to wear that!"

Gia instantly pictured the rather plump Fatima in a werewolf suit, and caught Ben's eye. It seemed they were sharing the same thought because he grinned and shook with silent laughter.

"Stop it," said Fatima, slapping at his shoulder, which only made him laugh harder.

Ignoring him, she turned to Gia. "So what's the problem with your mom?"

Gia shrugged. "Nothing new," she said. "Just the same old stuff. Are you eating?"

"You bet," said Fatima, pulling a menu closer.

Gia looked around the restaurant. It was dark, each table haloed with a single, low-hanging light. There were other lights here and there, decorative lights in the shape of the moons and stars. The walls were panelled with something that looked like wood, but sounded, under Gia's tapping finger, like plastic.

"I think I'll have a Blood-lust Burger" said Ben. "Or maybe a Bone Cracker. I wonder what that is?"

"Is this an American place?" asked Gia.

"You think?" said Ben.

"But they don't have any werewolves over there, do they?"

"Which is exactly why they can make places like this," said Ben. "Not having to actually deal with real werewolves—"

"Like you've had anything to do with them," scoffed Fatima. "I don't think you've even seen one. Outside of the news, that is. But it's true, they don't have any magicals in America."

"Yes they do!" protested Ben. "Just not any indigenous ones. And the rest are all in reserves. Or places like Disneyland. I think." He sounded uncertain for a moment. "No werewolves, anyway."

"What are you having, Gia?" asked Fatima.

Gia studied the menu. It had a decorative border featuring cute werewolf pups rolling on their backs, or chewing over-sized cartoon bones.

"Do you think they'll have anything vegetarian?" she asked.

Ben snorted, but Fatima said "Yep. On the right there. They call it a Half-Moon Burger."

To Gia's relief, their order came quickly. She was starving after her run. But before she could take the first bite, Fatima held up her hand.

"Hold on a sec."

She reached into the shopping bags, and took out a smaller bag.

"Happy birthday!" she said, holding it out to Gia.

"It's from both of us," said Ben.

"Sorry, it's not wrapped or anything," said Fatima as Gia opened the bag to find a glossy paperback book.

"Wow, thanks guys!" said Gia, flipping it over to read the back.

"You don't have that one do you?" asked Ben.

"No. But it looks fantastic."

"What did your parents give you?" asked Fatima. "Did you do anything special?"

"Well," said Gia, putting the book down. "It was right in the middle of the move, you know. So it kind of got postponed."

Fatima's eyebrows went up.

"You mean they forgot? About your *sixteenth birthday*? That's so typical of your mom."

Gia was surprised by a rush of protective loyalty towards her mother. "It's not a big deal, really," she said. Fatima seemed about to say something more, but to Gia's relief she thought better of it.

"Well then. Let's eat."

The food was good. There was something comforting about the dark and noisy restaurant. Gia ate slowly and with enjoyment, listening to Ben's account of the math camp, at which it seemed very little studying got done, and Fatima's stories about her older brother's latest escapades.

"Did I tell you my parents bought him a new car? A new truck, I should say. It's one of those ginormous four-wheel-drive things." She sighed. "And here's me, buzzing around on my little bike. I can't wait to be eighteen, so that I can get my licence."

"Assuming you even get your licence," said Ben. "The way you drive."

But Fatima was not listening to him. "Ben," she said, digging in her handbag. "Before I forget. I wanted to ask you. I got a pendant from a second-hand shop, and I wondered if you could do your trick with it?"

Ben looked at her.

"Please, Bennie? Just quickly. I just want to know more about it."

With a sigh, Ben took the pendant, a silver disk dangling from a ribbon of black silk. He sat, looking down at it, and for a moment Gia thought he was going to refuse. But then he closed his eyes, threw his head back, and held the pendant up in a shaking fist.

"I see a young lady," he proclaimed, and Fatima sat up, startled.

"A beautiful, young lady, though pale, pale as the moon and slim as a willow wand, with flowing golden hair and eyes as blue as the midnight sky. She has around her neck, this pendant, yes, this very pendant that I hold, here, today—"

"Oh, give it a rest," said Fatima in disgust, slumping back in her seat. But Ben was just getting into his stride.

"She has a brother— or no, it is her lover! Yes! I see him, approaching through the storm-torn night. Wait, it is fading— no— I can still see him. Oh, it is too horrible! He is strangling her with this very ribbon…"

Ben slumped forward, one fist extended dramatically in front of him. "Ah, the pain! No, I cannot stand it— Hey! Stop!" This last was in reaction to Fatima, who was upending a glass of water down his neck.

"Come on, Ben," she said. "I've not asked you for ages. Don't you see anything?"

Ben sighed and mopped at his collar with a serviette. "Okay, okay, I'll try again."

This time he simply held the pendant in one hand, and closed his eyes. After a moment he opened his eyes and gave the pendant back to Fatima.

"Well, did you see anything?"

Once again, Gia sensed his reluctance, and wondered if she should intervene. But she knew from past experience that once Fatima got fixed on an idea, nothing could divert her.

"It's quite old," said Ben at last. "And it's been in that shop, lying on a shelf for a very long time, but not on display. In some dark place, for many years. A drawer, maybe.

"And before that, I feel several people, all women, I think. Sisters, probably, or maybe a mother and her daughters. They all seem similar, somehow. Very quiet and proper, with a smell of lavender, you know, and Ceylon tea. But not much other than that. That enough?"

It seemed to be. Fatima tucked the pendant back into her handbag with a satisfied air. "I just like to *know*," she said comfortably.

"Would you like the bill?" It was the waitress, hovering anxiously. "I don't want to bug you guys, but there's a queue for tables—"

"Okay, I suppose we better go," said Fatima. "Do you need a lift, Gia? I'm meeting my mother and I'm sure she won't mind."

"No, it's okay," said Gia. "I better get home. I'll take a taxi."

৳০ঞ

For once, Gia flagged down a mini-bus taxi without any trouble. She was feeling a bit guilty about the way she'd run away. Once Mandy went home, Saraswati would not be able to work if there was nobody to keep an eye on Nico.

The sooner she got home, the better.

As always, spending time with Ben and Fatima had helped her forget her frustrations, and now she found it hard to remember why she'd got so upset. She looked dreamily out of the window at the landscape flashing by outside. The sky was a deep, midsummer blue, with little puffs and streaks of cloud. High in the blue drifted the moon. She frowned at it, pulled out of her thoughts.

The moon was fattening, and only a few days from full.

Her contentment chilled, and she shivered despite the sunny afternoon.

Maybe it will be different now, in this new house. Maybe I was just imagining things.

Then she had to pull her thoughts back to the present as the taxi slowed towards her stop.

৳০ঞ

It was only much later that evening that Gia finally got up to her room.

Things had not been as tense as she'd feared. She'd come home to find her father out, and her mother much calmer, having found a place that rented overlockers at a reasonable rate. Disaster was averted, for the moment at least, and with the pie Mandy had made for supper, things seemed almost normal.

Still, it was good to be by herself for a change.

She took a careful look around her room, checking for the telltale signs that Nico had been there. He always used to do that in her old room back in Plumstead. Getting into her art supplies, or just generally poking around.

But nothing was amiss.

With the trapdoor closed, her room felt like a tree house, quite independent from the house downstairs. She wished that there was a rope ladder, instead of the fixed stairs, something that could be pulled up behind her. Since that was not possible, she contented herself with bolting the trapdoor.

The first thing she'd done that morning after waking was to check if the envelope of things that had been in the newspaper nest was still there. She had not been surprised to find it missing.

The knowledge that something had got into and out of her room, despite the closed trapdoor and the wards on the window, was a little unsettling.

Still, she was not going to give up her room now. There was nothing she could do about her mysterious visitor. Best ignore it. After all, the most likely explanation was that the creature had moved out, now that its attic lair had been invaded.

Her shelving plan had worked out fairly well; a row of plastic milk-crates stacked on their sides. The move had meant a purge of possessions, but she had kept her core collection of books, and her favourite dolls.

These she now unpacked, and propped up on top of the shelf. Old dolls, faded and worn, with missing eyes and scraggly hair, still dressed in the clothes that Saraswati had made for them so many years ago.

Gia was just opening the first box of books when she heard a thump on the floor behind her, followed by a low yowl. She turned and saw Pouf crouching on the floor. Sure enough, the black cat had something trapped between his front paws. He backed away as she approached, giving another self-satisfied miaow.

"What have you got there, Pouf? Some poor bird?"

She knelt down, hoping that the bird was already safely dead and would not need to be euthanized.

For a moment her eyes refused to accept the unfamiliar shape and tried to turn it into a sparrow or a starling. Pale limbs, and dark, matted hair. Wings like plastic cling-wrap furled around the body. Gia drew back in shock, but as the thing did not move, leaned in for another look.

Dead. It must be dead.

But no, it had to be alive, or it would have crumbled into leaves and mud. *This must be one of the haarskeerders from that nest they broke.* She remembered the blurring shadow that had hovered just behind her, when she'd been looking at that gutted nest.

A survivor.

It lay face down on the floorboards, arms curled up underneath it, legs half bent. Its wings were long and thin, like those of a dragonfly, shot through with a web of black veins.

So human.

It twitched, and she started back. The movement was horribly like that of an insect.

Gia sat frozen with indecision.

What now?

It was undoubtedly alive, but it was hurt, too. Broken limbs, or internal injuries. She remembered her father breaking the neck of an unfortunate bird that Minou had caught, giving it the mercy death. But how would she go about killing this thing? It was too large to stomp like a bug, and she knew she could never bring herself to touch it, never mind wrap her fingers around its little neck.

Dump it in boiling water, like you killed a crayfish?

Pouf, who'd finished washing himself, dabbed at the thing with a paw, eyes bright with good-natured interest.

"Stoppit, Pouf!"

She grabbed him by his scruff and to Pouf's indignant surprise, carried him, dangling heavily, to the window, shoved him onto the roof outside, and slammed the window shut. She knelt on her bed, ignoring Pouf's outraged face staring in at her through the glass. Then, mind made up, she stepped carefully round the thing on the floor and opened the trapdoor. Luckily her parents were both in the studio, working late. Nico was sleeping, so there was no one to disturb her.

First, she ransacked the kitchen. An empty ice cream tub, several dishcloths, a wooden spoon, and, after a moment's consideration, the washing-up gloves. A quick trip to her mother's room for the hairdryer, and she was back up the stairs again.

The thing had not moved.

She plugged in the kettle, and waited impatiently for it to warm up.

Not boiling. Just to make the water warm.

She poured a little of the water into the ice cream tub, testing it with a careful finger. Then she put the tub down next to the thing, and hesitated.

What if it flew up suddenly?

She picked up the spoon and with infinite care, edged it under a shoulder, and lifted. The creature rolled over onto its back. She could see its face now, although indistinctly, through the straggle of long hair. It had a round face, with a curiously flattened and elongated nose. Its enormous eyes were closed, but she could see that it was alive. Its chest rose and fell as she watched.

Gia put on the gloves, and tried to pick the thing up, but this proved too difficult. It was slippery with mud and cat spit, and the gloves were too large for her and made her clumsy. In the end she had to pick the creature up with her bare hands. It felt cold to her shrinking fingers, but not as nasty as she'd feared.

Supporting the head with one hand, she lowered it into the ice cream tub. The water was still warm, and just deep enough to cover its legs and torso. There was an awkward moment when one wing got stuck to the side of the tub, clinging to it wetly, but she managed to get it settled at last.

She crouched over the tub, holding the creature's head out of the water.

Better get some of this mud off.

She sluiced some water over the tiny body.

It was female, and still quite young.

But who knew? Nothing says that these things develop in the same way people do.

Its body looked human, except for the hands that had only three long fingers and a thumb, or the feet, that had toes that were nearly as long as its fingers. Its skin was covered in a silvery down that reminded her of hairy leaves. To her relief there were no obvious wounds. Some scratches, and some marks that looked like old scars, but nothing new. And as far as she could tell none of the bones were broken either. The water was cooling down too quickly. She'd have to add some more.

The water in the kettle was still just warm enough. As she lifted it, she saw that the creature's eyes had opened, and it was watching her.

Gia froze, kettle held in the air.

The haarskeerder looked much less human now. Those eyes were far too large, and they were entirely black.

For the first time Gia thought about the danger of being caught in the thing's glamour. The last time she'd looked directly at a haarskeerder, she'd been instantly hypnotised. But nothing happened.

Tilting the kettle, she poured the water directly onto its body. It closed its eyes, and the chest rose and fell as it sighed. When she judged that it was warmed as much as she dared, she looked around for the dishcloths, and cursed under her breath when she saw that she'd left them on her bed, out of reach.

Nothing for it.

She slid her hands under the haarskeerder again, lifting it out of the water, holding it so that its head and shoulders rested on her wrist, while its legs dangled between her fingers. The matted hair clung to her skin and the wings hung down on either side of her hand. Its eyes were closed again.

Gia carried the creature to her bed and, working one-handed, wrapped it in a dishcloth so that only the head was visible.

What now?

Her plan had been to dry it with the hairdryer, but looking at it now she did not know if that would be such a good idea. It would be too loud and too harsh.

And besides, the hairdryer looked so very like a weapon.

Instead, she turned to the boxes of books she'd been about to unpack, and up-ended one of them, emptying the books onto the floor. She lined the box with the rest of the dishcloths, and placed the creature inside.

Then she sat back, thinking.

It's going to need to eat. What do they eat?

With sudden inspiration she dug in her schoolbag for her copy of *Brink and Moolman*.

The section on haarskeerders was long and not particularly helpful. It had a long list of the various names, and very little about their actual habits. Was it a water creature, an omnivore that lived on tadpoles and duckweed? Or was it a cattle-pricker that sucked the blood from cows?

In the end she decided on the oldest folk remedy, milk and honey.

Folding the top of the box closed, although it seemed unlikely that the thing would move, she once again went downstairs.

Milk and honey were easy to find, as was a saucer. But there was no hot-water bottle, or any other way to warm it.

The haarskeerder still lay as she'd put it, without moving.

She bundled the dishcloths around it in a nest, and placed the saucer of food next to it.

What now?

It was certainly not warm enough, even in its dishcloth nest. In fact, she could see it shivering, big, convulsive shivers that shook its whole body.

It will die if I leave it like that. Or should I just leave it alone? Maybe everything I do just harms it more.

Haarskeerder

With a deep sigh, Gia reached into the box and lifted the creature out again.

She pulled up her shirt and put the creature on the bare skin of her stomach, and after checking that it could still breathe, pulled her shirt back down over it.

It felt cold on her skin, and at first it lay, slack and unmoving except for the shivers that shook it.

Gia shifted around until she was leaning against her bed, trying to find a more comfortable position on the hard floorboards. Gradually, she felt the shivers subside. She was just nodding off herself when she felt it move. It crawled further up inside her shirt, and finally came to rest, snuggling against her chest.

She woke again some time later, uncomfortably cold.

I can't sleep with her like this. I'll roll over and squash her.

Gia extracted the sleeping creature from under her shirt, not without difficulty. Although she still seemed fast asleep, she was unwilling to leave the warmth of Gia's body and caught hold of a bra strap, refusing to let go. At last Gia got her free and placed her back in the box again.

The haarskeerder had lost that half-dead look. There was colour in her cheeks, and her body was warm to the touch. Gia covered her with a dishcloth, and folded the top of the box shut.

Then she crawled into her bed, glad of her own warm blankets.

ಬOಚ

THE CHANGELING

Gia woke with a start. Somebody was hammering on the trapdoor hard enough to lift it in its frame.

"Gia! Open this *at once!*"

She scrambled out of bed, slid on a pile of books, and nearly fell as she stumbled into a box in the middle of the floor. Still muzzy from sleep, she pulled back the bolt and the trapdoor opened to reveal her mother's face.

"Gia, you're late — *Gia,* did you sleep in your clothes again?"

Gia blinked sleepily, but Saraswati did not wait for a reply.

"You've missed the bus already. Get dressed and get your things. Karel can give you a lift. He's taking Nico this morning. And don't dawdle, he won't wait for you, and then you'll simply have to walk to school."

Before Gia could arrange her thoughts, her mother was already going back down the stairs.

She sat back and rubbed the sleep out of her eyes. An urgent thought was trying to get through to her.

Something about the books she'd stood on, and the box —

The box!

It had fallen over on its side, one cardboard flap hanging open. Her heart beating, she tipped it back upright with a foot, listening for movement from within, but nothing happened.

"Gia?" came her father's voice from below. "You better be dressing!"

"Yes Dad!" she called and started taking off her clothes, still staring at the box.

She turned her back on it for an instant to dig for clean underwear. Luckily her uniform was within easy reach, draped over the back of a chair. A sniff-check told her the shirt was clean enough.

Dressed, she prodded the box with one foot. Then she crouched next to it and peered inside. There was a jumble of towels, but no sign of any creature.

Was it dead after all?

Hesitantly at first, and then more boldly she reached inside, dreading what she might find. What if all that was left was a little heap of soil and leaves?

As she pulled out the towels the saucer that had held the milk and honey fell out and bounced on the floorboards. It had been licked quite clean.

"Gia!"

She looked around the room as she put on the rest of her clothes, but could see no sign of the creature.

It must have got out. But how – ?

The window was still firmly closed. And besides, it was warded. In fact, now that she thought about it, it was interesting that Pouf had managed to cross the wards with the creature in his mouth.

But there was no time to look any further. She pushed her copy of *Brink and Moolman* back in her school bag and with one last look around her room, climbed down through the trapdoor and slid it shut behind her.

Mandy intercepted her in the kitchen, gave her a lunch box and pointed out that her shirt was buttoned up wrong, and then she was downstairs, where her father waited in the car, the engine already running.

"Good," he said, and pulled off just as she had the door closed. "I'm hoping to miss the traffic."

Gia buckled herself in and turned round to check on Nico, who was bouncing on the back seat.

"Hi Nico. You going to Mrs Winterbach today?"

"Moses, Moses, Moses supposes!" chanted Nico. He rocked himself forward and backward as if listening to a marching band that only he could hear.

"Calm down, Nico," said Karel with a glance in the rear-view mirror.

"Why's Mom not taking him?" asked Gia.

"She's got a client coming for measurements. One of the dieting brides."

"That one with all the lace panels?"

Karel nodded and slowed the car to allow a group of schoolchildren to cross. Then he shot down a small side street.

"If that girl loses any more weight," he said, "we're going to have to use glue to keep the dress from falling off her. And she's probably going to cry all over Saraswati again. I swear, we should start charging extra for the therapy sessions."

"Moses, supposes, supposes, supposes!" chanted Nico.

"Oh, good," said Karel. They'd reached the on-ramp, and although the traffic was heavy, it was still moving. "Looks like we'll make your school on time."

He reached over and switched on the radio. "Find some music on there, won't you?" he said as he merged into the flow of the traffic. "Calm the boy down a bit. I hate dropping him off when he's like this."

Near the Good Hope Centre the traffic slowed to a complete stop, and her father grumbled his irritation, trying to see ahead. "What's the holdup?"

There was a noise up ahead, a noise like people chanting at a sports match. A moment later they saw them, a marching crowd, some holding up signs, others carrying large home-made banners.

"No, no, no!" they shouted, shaking their signs in time to their chant. "Grey List must go!"

Karel groaned. "A protest. These people could not just wait 'till the rush hour was over?"

"No, no, no!"

The traffic was moving again and Gia saw that there were policemen up ahead, directing the protesters away from the cars. The crowd moved back quite willingly, but they did not stop their chanting.

Sentient rights! said one sign, and *Impure and Proud of it!* said another.

Office workers and students, normal, everyday people. Gia saw a little girl with plastic fairy-wings riding on her father's shoulders, smiling and waving at passing motorists.

Not all of the protesters were as charming. Some way along, Gia saw a knot of people who stood, swaying, on the edge of the road. They had the air of sleepwalkers, and there was something disturbing in the way they held themselves, as if they were in pain, or cringing from some sound that only they could hear. Some of them had their hands over their faces, or their arms wrapped around themselves. One woman raked her fingers through her hair.

They too, chanted, but it was a slow chant, and softer than the other protesters.

"Oh, no, no," came their voices. Or was it *"Sorrow, sorrow, sorrow"*?

"Guilters," said Karel, seeing where Gia was looking. "Those are guilters. They've been in the news lately."

Gia noticed that Nico was staring as well, and moving his lips in time with the chant.

"Sorrow, sorrow, sorrow."

Then they were past, and the car accelerated away from the last of the crowd. Nico looked back at them for as long as they were in sight.

※O※

Gia made it to school on time. The bell rang as she came through the gate, and she joined the students gathering outside the school hall before any teachers appeared. Sonella caught her eye and beckoned, and Gia slipped into line behind her.

"Best not to stand right at the back," explained Sonella. "Then you could end up sitting in front of the standard-nine boys, and they're forever pulling at your hair or trying to stick chewing gum into it."

The teachers checked that the last stragglers had joined the lines, and at the signal, they started walking, line by line, into the school hall. There was an air of suppressed excitement. On a normal day, they'd all be moving to their first-period lesson, and the change in routine had stirred up the whole school. There was more than the usual amount of noise. Everyone either craned to see who was on the stage, or turned toward their neighbour to ask what was going on.

"Silence, please!" That was Mrs Kemp, standing at the back of the hall. "Settle down. Prefects, keep your classes in order, please!"

The noise gradually died down, but the atmosphere remained charged. Gia could see Mr Peterson, the headmaster, standing at the lectern and fussing with the microphone. On the chairs behind him sat two people she did not recognise— a middle-aged man and a young boy, both dressed in grey uniforms.

The man sat comfortably, taking in the crowd with an air of unconscious command, his booted legs stretched out in front of him. The boy sat tensely upright, eyes down.

When the last of the students were settled, Mr Peterson gave a nod to Miss Rademan, who sat ready at the piano, and the first chords of the school song crashed out.

Everyone got to their feet again. As she sang, Gia tried to get a better look at the visitors, but it was difficult to see around the row of boys in front of her. The chords changed, and they sang the national anthem. At last, the singing was over and everybody sat down again.

"Good morning, boys and girls!" said Mr Peterson, waking a squeal of feedback from his microphone.

"Today we have some very special visitors for you."

Gia had a better view now. The man was short but powerfully built. His companion, Gia realised, was not a boy. She was a girl— no, a young woman. It was her hands that gave her away: slim, delicate hands, one placed precisely on each knee. Otherwise she seemed almost sexless, her hair cropped close to her skull, no feminine curves visible under her shirt.

"And with no more delay, let me hand over to Captain Witbooi."

Captain Witbooi rose from his chair, nodding to acknowledge the applause. Ignoring Mr Peterson's attempt to herd him towards the lectern, he strode to the front of the stage. He lifted his arms, wrists crossed, and hands balled into fists. His sleeves drew back, revealing two wide silver bracelets, bright against his dark skin.

"Pure and true!" He settled back on his heels and looked out over the audience. Then he nodded in satisfaction. "Ladies. Gentlemen." His unamplified voice carried easily across the hall.

"It is easy to forget, these days, how lucky we are, all of us, here in South Africa. Here in this hall. I see you, young men and young women, black and white together under the same roof, and it's easy to forget that only a few years ago, this was not possible. Only a few years ago, this would have been an illegal gathering. Only a few years ago, we were fighting for our freedom."

He smiled out at them. "But I see what you are thinking. Another old fart droning on about the past."

The students giggled obediently.

"Who cares? Isn't that what you are thinking? That is all the past. We are safe now. We have our freedom."

He stopped and scanned them again, seeming to look at each of them in turn, one by one. Gia felt the magnetism of his look, found herself hoping to catch his eye.

"But you are wrong. We're not safe. We're not free. Or — let me rather say, our freedom is under threat."

He started pacing across the stage.

"Something you learn, when you are a soldier — and make no mistake, a Special Branch member may be called a policeman, but we are soldiers — is that *nothing* is guaranteed. The fight for freedom is never over. There is always someone who has to be out there, at night, in the dark, so that the rest of you can sleep safely in your warm beds. While you are dreaming, we're out there fighting the nightmares: the werewolves, the ghasts, the ghouls, creatures that would make your blood run cold."

Gia felt herself yearning to be out there with Captain Witbooi, facing unknown dangers, and scornful of those who curled up in the safety of those warm bedrooms.

"But what can you do, you ask me. You are young. Still at school."

A lone voice from somewhere in the audience yelled "First Exit!" causing a ripple of nervous conversation.

"True," said Captain Witbooi, holding up a hand for silence. "Those of you in standard eight are approaching that time now, I believe. You can leave school early, take First Exit and join the working world. Some of you may take that chance to join us in Special Branch! And I would be proud to welcome you. We can always use new recruits!

"But for most of you — what can you do? That is what I am here to tell you."

He looked out over the audience, once again holding their full attention. "There is something that each and every one of you can do to keep your country safe. To keep your *freedom*, safe."

He gave a signal and an image appeared on the screen at the back of the stage. It was a photograph of a boy's face. He had a strangely vacant expression, and Gia could immediately see that there was something wrong with him.

Captain Witbooi looked at it, and nodded to himself. He turned back to his audience. "I'm sure that all of you have heard of the term 'changeling'?"

The school murmured in agreement.

"Now in the past, the ignorant and superstitious believed that the Faery, the 'fair folk', as they called them, could steal human babies and replace them with their own. I've never understood why they'd want to do this, but that was what people believed.

"Any child who was a little— shall we say— *different*, was thought to be a changeling. Some of these children were killed. Some died of simple neglect. A terrible thing. Terrible." Captain Witbooi shook his head gravely. "These days, in these more *enlightened* times, we know better. We have terms for these children. We say they have Down's syndrome. We say they're *autistic*. We say they have 'special needs'. But our scientists are still unable to tell us what causes these—" He gestured at the image of the boy. "These children. Now, I'm here to tell you today of another reason for the changelings.

"As you may know, Special Branch has its own research division. We have our own scientists. Scientists who risk their lives every day, who get their hands dirty. They do not dabble with theory— they deal in fact. With rational, measurable *fact*."

The school hall was utterly silent now, everyone present focused on the speaker.

"I suppose it's possible that some of these children are autistic. That some of them have some syndrome, some neurological condition. But in case after case, we've found the *cause*." He paused, and when he spoke again, his voice was soft, intense. "The cause is magic."

The audience murmured, but fell instantly silent as he continued speaking.

"Changelings are magical beings. They have special abilities. Some of these are inherited. Some come from we don't know where. It doesn't really matter what the cause is. It's the result that matters. And here is where you come in— each and every one of you. It is important— no, it is essential that we identify these changelings."

He held up his hand, as though to stop an interruption.

"Not to arrest them. Not to hurt or frighten them. But to help them. With our help, with the help of our scientists, we can rescue these children from their mental prisons. We can free them. Not to become normal citizens, I won't lie to you; in most cases, that is impossible. But to become *better* than normal. To become warriors in the fight against evil."

Captain Witbooi nodded again, looking from student to student. "And now, I present you to somebody who can tell you better than anyone else, why we need your help."

He turned to face the girl, who had sat unmoving throughout his speech.

"Cadet."

The young woman rose, and took a step forward. She raised her arms in the crossed-fist salute, revealing the flash of twin silver bracelets. "Pure and true." Her voice was as clear as the captain's, but low, a beautiful, singer's voice, surprising from that spare, straight body.

"Cadet Lee is a changeling," said Captain Witbooi. A gasp swept through the hall, then all was silent again. "She will now tell you her story." He nodded to her. "Cadet."

Cadet Lee bowed slightly to her captain. "What the captain says, is true." She spoke as confidently as Captain Witbooi, but unlike him, she did not look at her audience. Instead, she kept her eyes unfocused, standing as stiffly as if she were on a parade ground.

The picture on the screen behind her changed. Now it showed a slightly blurred image of a woman and a little girl. The woman smiled at the camera, but the girl's face was expressionless, mouth slack, one eyelid drooping.

"Until the age of twelve, I could not speak. I could not write, or read. I was 'on the spectrum', diagnosed as autistic. My parents believed that I would spend my life a burden on society. I had no friends. I did not know how to feed myself, or dress myself."

The picture changed to show the girl, older now and painfully thin, face turned away from the camera.

"On my twelfth birthday, by chance, my mother enrolled me in a new program. She did not know that it was a Special Branch experiment, but so it was. The scientists of Special Branch did their tests, and discovered that I was not autistic, as my parents had always believed. I am a telepath."

Another gasp from the audience, and a rustle of murmured conversation. The cadet waited until it died away.

"My mind was wide open. I had no filters, no way of blocking out the thoughts of everyone around me. It was only with the help of Special Branch that I learnt to control the input. Because I no longer had to fight every second, waking and sleeping, to shut out the barrage of emotion, I could hear and see my world. For the first time, I could see."

A new picture. The girl, clutching a pencil, eyes focused on her drawing, tongue out in concentration.

"I became human."

A group photograph of many children with their hands up and waving. The girl, now finally recognisable as Cadet Lee, was in the middle, smiling directly at the camera, her eyes sparkling with excitement and intelligence.

The cadet's voice was without emotion, but Gia felt tears starting in her own eyes.

"Special Branch rescued me from hell. I beg you. If you know of anyone else who is like I used to be — help them. Let us know, so we can help them become — human."

She bowed again, and sat.

There was a moment of awed silence, then somebody started clapping. In a moment, the entire school was applauding. Gia saw girls weeping openly and felt a lump in her throat. Some of the boys were on their feet, giving the crossed-wrist salute. When the noise subsided, Captain Witbooi spoke again.

"Thank you, Cadet. So. Ladies and gentlemen, teachers— we rely on you. It is essential that we get to these children before it is too late, while they're still young. By the time they become teenagers, it is often too late for us to do anything.

"We have given leaflets to all your teachers, with a contact number for the Special Branch Children's Unit. If you know of such a child, help us help them. Thank you, Mr Peterson, for allowing us to speak today."

There was more applause. Then everyone sat, uncertain what to do, and the noise of conversation grew until one of the prefects shouted, "All rise! Everyone go back to your *second* period class. Your *second* period class."

The bell rang and then everyone was getting up, talking and laughing. A teacher tried to make an announcement, but was drowned out in the noise.

Gia sat where she was, letting the others in her row squeeze past her, hardly aware that they were leaving. Only when Sonella touched her shoulder did she come to herself and get up.

Captain Witbooi and the cadet were standing in the front near the doors, talking to one of the teachers. Gia hesitated near them, and then, hardly knowing what she was doing, she walked up to the cadet.

Up close, Cadet Lee was slighter than she had seemed on stage. Her face was pale, and she had a delicate scar that bisected one eyebrow, and cut down over her cheek. She stared coolly as Gia approached.

"Um," said Gia, her mouth dry. "I just wanted — I just wanted to say thank you. For telling us your story."

The cadet said nothing, but her expression was not unfriendly. Gia was peripherally aware that the teacher and Captain Witbooi were looking at her, but she felt driven to ask her question.

"I wondered — if you don't mind me asking — do you ever, I mean —" She stopped, and tried again. "Do you ever see your parents?"

The cadet blinked, and her eyebrows went up in surprise.

"I mean," said Gia, "now that you are, you know —"
She felt her voice dry up, but before she could try again, there was a hand on her arm.

"That's quite enough now. Come along."

Miss Huisman was frowning down on her. "You are going to be late for class. Go on!" she said when Gia did not respond. At a push from Miss Huisman, Gia moved away. As she went out the door she took one last look, and saw Captain Witbooi staring after her.

∞O∞

For the next few hours, Gia struggled to pay attention to her lessons.

The captain's words kept coming back to her. *"If you know of such a child, help us help them."*

What if it were possible, what if Nico —

Her mother would never let anyone take Nico away. *And they would take him away, wouldn't they?*

Even if they did not, she winced at the thought of telling Saraswati about the captain's speech. There had been too many doctors over the years, too many false hopes: too many miracle cures that worked only if you had faith in them. It had been a relief when her parents had at long last seemed to accept that Nico was just the way he was. *"No such thing as normal"* had become a mantra in their house.

But it was hard to ignore the words of the cadet, and those photographs.

What if there really was — not a cure, but a way to help Nico become what he was meant to be?

The last lesson of the day was supernatural studies. This time, Gia sat next to Sonella.

This turned out to be lucky, as Miss Huisman announced that the lesson would begin with a group-work exercise.

"We will be discussing today's Special Branch talk in a moment," she said in reply to a student's question.

"But first, we will complete the homework I set for you yesterday. You were supposed to identify two examples of a creature or entity that has been re-classified, or that has some controversy over its classification. Now you will each fill in a worksheet answering questions about the creatures you have chosen."

Miss Huisman made available a pile of books from the school library, to supplement their reading of *Brink and Moolman*.

Gia enjoyed paging through illustrated volumes such as *Tobert's Bestiary* or *Creatures of the Home and Hearth*. It was a relief to be distracted from her thoughts. Both she and Sonella selected dust bunnies as one of their creatures. Gia decided on the haarskeerder for her second creature, and Sonella chose something called a gombaardjie, a creature that lived in filing cabinets and desk drawers.

The class was buzzing with activity as the other groups made their way through the worksheet, with occasional flare-ups when there was a dispute over who would get the next look at one of the more popular books. Miss Huisman ignored most of these, quelling anyone who got too noisy with a chilly look and raised eyebrows.

This was just as well, as Gia and Sonella kept having to fight down fits of giggles as they read up about the gombaardjie, which apparently sucked the ink out of ballpoint pens, and had an unfortunate habit of sneaking out at night to pee on computer keyboards or telephones.

Haarskeerders also proved interesting. Gia learned that they were a kind of winged fae, indigenous to South Africa. The hypnotic trance that she'd experienced was triggered by the movement of their wings and was used to protect their nests from predators, particularly humans.

Apparently their habit of collecting things led people to raid their nests. Rural haarskeerders, Gia read, were relatively harmless, as long as you avoided being hypnotised too often, which could result in brain damage. But in urban areas, haarskeerders could be a menace and a danger. If a colony grew large enough, they started swarming, forming large, aggressive groups that attacked without warning.

At one point, while everyone still had their heads down over their worksheets, Gia glanced up just in time to see Miss Huisman fiddling with the grey intercom unit that was fixed partway up the wall at the front of the classroom. It looked as though she'd draped a handkerchief over it.

"Right, time's up!" said Miss Huisman, closing the classroom door. "Monitors, gather up the worksheets. Class, make sure that you have written your name, and the date, at the top of your sheet."

When everyone had settled down again, she continued. "Now, we had a most interesting visit from Special Branch this morning. As this is, after all, supernatural studies, and Special Branch is concerned primarily with supernatural phenomena, I thought we would put some time aside to discuss what we saw and heard."

A girl put up her hand. "Miss, why did they both say that thing?" She gestured with crossed wrists.

"Pure and true?" said Miss Huisman, giving the salute, her wooden bracelets clattering. "Can anyone answer the question?"

Several hands shot up.

"Yes, you there by the window."

"That's the Purist salute, Miss. They call it the Silver Cross."

The boy made the gesture, jaw jutting as he slammed his wrists together. "The Special Branch, they all do it."

"And who are the Purists?"

"A political party, Miss."

"The army."

"Special Branch!"

But Miss Huisman shook her head. "Any more attempts?"

A tall boy had his hand up.

"Your name?" asked Miss Huisman.

"Justin February, Miss."

They boy was skinny in that lanky, teenaged way, but he had a quiet self-confidence that Gia admired.

"So you can tell us all about the Purists, Mr February?" said Miss Huisman.

"They're part of the New Rational Party, Miss. The Realists."

"Very good." Miss Huisman nodded. "So does that mean that President Langa is a Purist?"

"No, Miss," said Justin seriously. "President Langa is a Realist in the old style. But some of his party are getting more extreme, and are forming their own group. Those are the Purists."

"That is correct," said Miss Huisman, turning back to the rest of the class.

"The Realists have recently developed a vocal subgroup that call themselves the Purists. They're not as yet a political party in their own right, but they're a significant force within the government. For example, the president's own son, Luxulo Langa, is one of their leaders. They also have an inordinate amount of influence in Special Branch, which is somewhat worrying. And what do these Purists believe?"

Justin had his hand up again. "They say all magicals are dangerous. Or only useful for fighting other magicals."

"Very good," said Miss Huisman. "Another interesting thing about the Purists, and by extension, Special Branch, is their attitude to science. They are very rational. They believe that magic can be studied like any other phenomenon. 'All will bend to reason' is one of their slogans, as you've probably seen on the posters. Yes, Charlie?"

"That's what they do at Valkenberg, isn't it, Miss?" said Charlie Wexton eagerly.

"Valkenberg is the Special Branch headquarters," acknowledged Miss Huisman. "It's where they conduct much of their research."

Gia could feel the frisson of interest in the classroom. Valkenberg was a name often said in jest, but always with a tinge of fear. *You'll end up at Valkenberg!* was a frequent playground insult.

All children in the Cape went to Valkenberg for a government-sponsored field trip during their first year of school. It was one of the most vivid memories of Gia's childhood. The first time she'd seen real, live, magicals.

As Miss Huisman explained about the Purists, Gia's attention wandered as she thought back on that visit.

There had been a bus trip. All the children had to hold hands, probably to prevent any of them from wandering off and getting lost. There had been a strong scent of formaldehyde, and everything had been lit with a hard, white, fluorescent light.

She could remember the creatures quite clearly. Most of them had been dead.

Rows and rows of glass vessels, with shapes floating inside them. A tiny mermaid, its lacy gills spread out behind disturbingly human ears. Things that looked just like monkeys, but the teacher had explained that they were something else, Gia could not remember what.

Then the live display.

Small creatures in brightly lit boxes. *Snaartjies*, tiny things almost like butterflies, with filmy, rainbow-coloured wings. They had fluttered up and down, up and down, always staying at the back of their cages. The teacher explained that the wire that fronted their cages was silver, and that the touch of silver burnt them "like an electric shock".

She tried to remember how she'd felt about it all, but could not call up her long-ago feelings.

"Gia! Attend." Miss Huisman frowned down at her.

"As I was saying," said Miss Huisman, turning away from Gia to address the rest of the class again, "we have yet to study the classification system used by the South African legal system, but shortly, it divides all magical beings into useful, neutral and harmful.

"The Purists, however, are challenging this system of classification. They believe that there is no such thing as a neutral creature, and while they are willing to make *use* of magicals, they refuse to acknowledge that such creatures can be useful in any way other than in fighting the battle against the more dangerous creatures. And that is, partly, what the coming referendum is about. The establishment of the Grey List.

"Now." Miss Huisman strode to the blackboard, where the words she had written the previous day were still visible.

"In a modern country such as ours, where magical beings, and people with magical abilities live together, it is necessary to have a more practical way to organise things than these categories." She wiped away the day before's headings.

"Instead, we have the lists. The Red List, and the White List." She wrote the words on the board as she spoke. "Red List is for dangerous creatures, that are to be destroyed on sight. A menace to society. White List is for useful creatures. They may be dangerous, but they're too valuable to destroy. Who can give me an example of a Red List creature?"

"Blistermen!"

"Vrekkers!"

"Marrow Maids!"

"Werewolves!"

Miss Huisman wrote these down under the "Red List" heading, all except for werewolf. This, she wrote under "White List".

"Why are werewolves not red-listed?" she asked as she wrote.

"They're useful, Miss," said a girl near the back of the class. "Special Branch use them. They neuter them with — arsenic or something, and tie them up all with muzzles and chains and stuff so they can't bite."

"Well," said Miss Huisman. "I'm not sure about the arsenic, but for the rest you are correct. Weres are used for their exceptional tracking abilities, especially for sniffing out other magical creatures. Here is another example."

She added the word "troll" to the White List.

"Trolls. Exceptionally dangerous, but widely used for their strength and endurance. So. We will continue to add examples to these lists as we go on. But what about this one?"

She wrote "Grey List" on the board.

There was a hum of conversation from the class, but no hands went up.

"The Grey List, or 'Luxulo's list' as it's also called, is different from the other lists. It is not just a list of types of creatures. It is an actual record of individual creatures, their names, if they have names, their descriptions, where they live, and their identity numbers, if any. Everything the government and Special Branch would need to keep track of each individual on the list."

Miss Huisman drew a circle around the word "Grey List".

"Unlike the Red or White lists, the Grey List will include *all* magical creatures, sentient or not, even creatures previously unlisted, such as all the neutral creatures. Including, by the way, humans with magical abilities."

"But that's a good thing, right, Miss? Then we'll know where we stand!" said the boy near the window.

Miss Huisman stared at him grimly, and he wilted a little under her gaze. "That's what they say," she said at last. "But what did you learn in your homework, and in the worksheet you just completed?"

Gia nodded to herself. It was true. The one thing that had emerged clearly from the reading she had done it was that categorising creatures according to their attributes was far from straightforward. Something that was considered useful to one person, was a menace to another. And if you tried to apply that reasoning to humans—

Miss Huisman was following a similar train of thought. "If the Purists had their way, the young lady we saw today, Cadet Lee, would be a Grey Lister. And something that I've not mentioned yet, and which in my opinion, is overlooked too often when we discuss these things, are the implications of being listed.

"A being on the proposed Grey List would no longer be a citizen. Did you know that?"

There was a general shaking of heads.

"They will not be able to vote. They won't have the right to own property, or to sign a contract. Yes, Sonella?"

"But, isn't that against the constitution, Miss Huisman?" asked Sonella. "To take somebody's vote away?"

"Precisely, Miss Pretorius." Miss Huisman nodded in approval. "But according to our laws, a listed being is by definition, not human. So human rights don't apply to them."

The buzz of conversation grew louder, then quietened down at Miss Huisman's raised eyebrows.

"Which brings me back to Captain Witbooi and his young friend. Both are Purists, as you saw. They believe that all magical beings, human or otherwise, must be listed. That they're either useful in the war against magicals— or they're harmful, and must be destroyed."

A boy sitting behind Gia had his hand up, and she nodded at him to speak.

"Why did Captain Witbooi say that a Special Brancher is more like a soldier than a cop?" he asked. "What's the difference?"

But the bell rang before Miss Huisman could respond.

"An excellent question," she said when the noise died down. "Remind me of it in tomorrow's class. And that brings us to the end of today's lesson. Your homework for tomorrow—" She raised her voice to drown out the protest. "Your homework for tomorrow is to find some item in the news that pertains to magic or magical beings. For classroom discussion."

"Well, that's easy, with all this stuff going on about the half-orcs in the rugby team," said the boy behind Gia.

"Save it for tomorrow," said Miss Huisman, smiling. "Class dismissed."

She caught Gia's eye. "Miss Grobbelaar, could you stay behind for a minute?"

Gia, surprised, stood by her desk. While the students trooped out, Miss Huisman started sorting through the stack of worksheets. As the last student left, she drew back her chair and sat down at her table. "Just close the door, please, Gia."

Gia closed the door, then walked over to Miss Huisman's table, unsure what was expected of her.

Miss Huisman was rapidly dividing the worksheets into several piles, counting under her breath. Looking up and seeing Gia standing in front of her, she gave a quick nod.

"Don't worry, girl, I'm not going to eat you. I just wanted a quick word." She took off her glasses and peered at Gia, her naked eyes looking unexpectedly tired. "You are Carlo Gotti's child, not so?"

Gia nodded.

"I've met your father. And your mother. At an art opening or two. Lovely people." She put her glasses back on, picked up a red pen, and drew one of the worksheets closer.

"Gia, a word of advice." She started marking, the pen darting rapidly over the sheet. "It may be a mistake to draw attention to yourself, particularly—" She paused to count through the marks she'd made, then jotted down the total. "Particularly when dealing with the *Special Branch*."

Miss Huisman picked up another worksheet, and shot Gia a glance over the top of her glasses. "Captain Witbooi is an admirable man, and, no doubt, excellent at his job. But his interests and yours may not, shall we say, coincide?"

Gia looked at her blankly.

Miss Huisman put down her pen, and sighed.

"Gia, I don't know why you went to speak to the cadet. But I've found that some things are easier to put into motion than to stop. We live in uncertain times. Also, I must warn you not to trust— " She turned to look at the door, as if a sound had attracted her attention, but Gia had heard nothing.

Miss Huisman pushed back her chair, then walked calmly over to the intercom unit. She reached up and snatched the handkerchief from it, folded it, and tucked it in her sleeve. There was a knock on the door, and before anyone had a chance to respond the door opened to reveal the headmaster.

"Ah, Mr Peterson," said Miss Huisman, quite unruffled. "We were just talking about you. A moment." She turned back to Gia.

"So, Gia," she said. "We have an understanding then? We will have no more of these excuses about homework being forgotten or lost, or whatever it was this time. Agreed?"

Gia met Miss Huisman's steady gaze, nodded, and looked down at her shoes.

"Yes, Miss. Sorry, Miss."

"Good girl," said Miss Huisman. "Well, run along then, child."

"Good afternoon, Miss, Sir," said Gia, and left as quickly as she dared. Outside, the corridors were rapidly emptying as students and teachers left for the day. She walked quickly to the exit, her mind whirling.

What had just happened? Miss Huisman was warning her against Special Branch – but why?

৩০০৪

It was only when she got home that Gia remembered about the missing haarskeerder. The events of the day had driven it clear out of her mind.

"Mandy!" she called, as she let the front door slam behind her. "Mandy, have you been up in my room?"

"No!" came the answer. "Why?"

Gia spotted Minou sunning herself on a windowsill and scooped her up, and tucked the cat under her arm before going through to the kitchen, where Mandy was folding laundry.

"No reason, just wondering," she said.

"I've got a question for you, Miss," said Mandy. "Have you been taking things out of that rat's cage?"

"What? No, why would I?"

"Nico's been going on about it since he got back. He put some biscuits in there yesterday, and is convinced that somebody stole them."

"Poepie probably ate them."

Mandy shrugged. "That's what I told him, but he just shakes his head. Anyway, your father said for you to go down to the studio. Meeting," she said, significantly. "You go get changed out of that uniform, and come right back down, you hear? I'm also going."

"Alright," said Gia. She'd have to be quick, then.

Minou allowed herself to be carried up the stairs to Gia's room, a slight twitch of her tail the only sign of protest.

A quick glance told Gia that the haarskeerder was nowhere in sight. She put the cat down in front of the box and stood back, watching.

The white cat looked about her with interest. Then she saw the box. She stiffened, and sniffed. Took a step closer, whiskers fanned out and ears forward. She lowered her nose to one of the dishcloths that lay on the floor near the box.

The hair rose on her back. She sniffed intently. Then she scanned the room with wide, round eyes, a low moan throbbing in her throat. Gia watched, holding her breath, but after a few seconds, Minou relaxed and dropped her nose to the floor and sniffed again. When she'd satisfied herself that there was nothing in the box, she jumped on Gia's bed and sniffed at the window. Once again, she scanned the room.

At last she jumped down and walked, slowly at first, then with increasing confidence straight to the milk-crate shelf, and disappeared behind it. Gia heard a peremptory "miaow" and looking behind the shelf, saw that Minou was crouched down and pawing at a gap between the wall and the floor.

Of course! thought Gia. *This room can't be the entire attic, it's far too small. There must be more space behind that partition. The thing must have gotten through there, somehow.*

"Gia!" came Mandy's voice from below. Gia pulled off her uniform and quickly got dressed in a t-shirt and jeans.

As she dressed, she saw that her paint-box had been moved and was standing wide open, and the jar that held her feather collection was on the floor, instead of on the shelf where she'd left it. A quick check told her that some of the smaller feathers were missing.

She sighed in exasperation.

Nico again.

Drat that boy. Always nosing around in her things. Or could it have been the haarskeerder?

She could imagine the haarskeerder taking feathers, but it could not be strong enough to have moved that paint-box. That had Nico written all over it.

She looked around the room again.

Was it still there, behind the wall in the rest of the attic? Or had it gotten completely away, outside?

She was disappointed that the creature was gone, but it was also a relief. It was just one more complication she did not have to worry about.

"Gia!"

"Coming!" She went to pick up Minou, but the cat had ideas of her own, and was already disappearing down the steps. Gia followed her down.

෨O෬

When she got to the studio, she found her father at the cutting table. The pattern he was working on had been cut out of fabric, and he was joining the pieces, basting them together by hand with quick, deft stitches. Saraswati sat at the other end of the table, with a pile of files and notebooks in front of her, and Nico on her lap.

He was squirming about a bit, and Saraswati smiled gratefully as Mandy took him from her.

"Come sit here next to me, on a chair like a big boy," said Mandy, fishing a pen and piece of paper from Saraswati's collection. "Why don't you draw something while we talk, then you won't get bored."

"Thank you, Mandy," said Saraswati. "Karel, shall we start?"

Karel stuck the needle into the fabric and spat pins into his palm. "Sure. Gia, get a chair."

He waited until Gia was seated. "Good. Gia. Mandy. Just a quick meeting, we're all busy so we won't waste time.

"Gia, we want to include you in our business meetings from now on. We're going to be relying on your help a good deal more in the next few months. And not just to do the odd little thing here and there, like you've been doing up to now. We need you to take on more responsibility. To do that, you need to know what's going on."

There goes my free time, thought Gia. But the thought was without bitterness. It was flattering to be treated like a full member of the team.

"Mandy will be helping us as always, of course." continued Karel. "But for the moment, we cannot afford to employ any of the part-time ladies — which means that some of the work will be repetitive and boring."

He waited for Gia's nod.

"Now in the past, Gia, you've worked very well with Mandy, but I want to say it here so there can be no misunderstanding. As far as you are concerned, Mandy is in charge, as much as me or Saraswati. There will be times when we'll need you to do more creative work, but for the moment, you are Mandy's assistant."

Gia nodded again.

"We'll make sure that the work does not interfere with your school work, of course," said Karel. "That is the most important thing. Now. Saraswati — ?"

"I'll start with a quick report-back of our financial situation." Saraswati pulled a file away from Nico's exploring hands. He seemed to have forgotten about his drawing, and she tapped at it. "Nico, you haven't put any armour on that dragon. Shouldn't it be protected from the knights?"

When Nico was safely drawing again, she continued. "We're better off than I'd feared, Karel. We've received the final payment from the sale of the house, and I've managed to get us out of having to pay another month's rent on our previous studio premises, despite our breaking the lease a month early."

"That's lucky," said Karel. "Or maybe not just luck. You could sweet-talk a cave-troll. That landlord did not stand a chance."

Saraswati smiled. "We've had a lot of luck, when it comes to that. The fact that we were able to buy this house so cheaply has made all the difference. But it all depends on the next few months, if we can hang on to our old clients, and attract new ones. Which brings me to the point of this meeting."

She looked seriously at her daughter. "Gia, what we're about to tell you is in strictest confidence. We can *not* afford for this news to be spread about."

"Sure, I understand," said Gia, wondering a little at her mother's intensity.

What on earth is this about?

"We're going to be designing and making Kavitha Pillay's wedding gown," said Karel.

Mandy gasped, and Gia laughed. Karel smiled back at them.

"Apparently Luxulo is set on turning the wedding into what he calls a 'showcase of South African talent' and we've been chosen for the fashion side of things."

"And Luxulo?" asked Saraswati. "Do you know yet if we're designing his suit, Karel?"

Karel pulled a face. "No. I tried to convince him, but he's got some other guy working on that. Would not say who it is, but I've got my suspicions."

"Hmm," said Saraswati. "Well, it's quite enough work to keep us busy as it is."

"It's a fantastic opportunity," said Karel. "There's the money of course, but this thing is really going to put us on the map. *La Femme International* will do a photo shoot of the wedding party. And the American media are interested too."

"And that's another reason why we have to be so careful about this news," said Saraswati. "Karel tells me that Kavitha's mother, and Luxulo Langa too, are both incredibly paranoid about publicity. They're convinced that there's some kind of media conspiracy against Kavitha, so they're keeping everything about the wedding preparations top secret. It's essential that none of this gets out. No one, Gia. Not even your friends."

"Yes, Mom, I do understand," said Gia, unable to keep the irritation out of her voice.

Then her parents turned to discussing the logistics of dates and timetables, and Gia stopped listening.

That'll be a challenge, she thought. *Fatima's going to kill me when she finds out I've been keeping this secret from her.*

Kavitha Pillay and Luxolo Langa were rapidly becoming the best-known couple in South Africa, and there was hardly a day when they were not featured on the cover of magazines and newspapers. President Langa was immensely popular both locally and overseas — especially in America — so his eldest son and future daughter-in-law were automatic celebrities. But Gia knew that Luxolo was famous in his own right, although she was fuzzy on what exactly it was that he did.

With the upcoming referendum there were posters of his face on every lamppost, and his voice was constantly on the radio or television news.

"Gia!" When she saw that she had Gia's attention, Saraswati continued. "I'm going to meet Kavitha and her mother tomorrow afternoon, so I need you to come along to help me. Apparently they won't be coming here like our usual clients because of all the secrecy. We're being picked up and taken there, so I need you to be here and ready to go at three tomorrow afternoon."

Saraswati was on her feet. "Mandy — I'm going to take Nico out to the park and I thought I'd do a grocery shop afterwards. Could you finish off the rest of that tailored jacket that's hanging up in the workroom? You'll see what needs to be done. And then the bodice of the lace dress needs to be unpicked again. Just the side-seams, on both sides from the bottom of the armhole to the waistline."

"Okay," said Mandy, getting up. "If you are doing a shop, you need to get some Handy Andy. And bags for the vacuum-cleaner."

Gia was off in her own thoughts again.

I'm going to meet Kavitha Pillay!

ಬO಄

When the door closed behind Saraswati, and Mandy had disappeared into the workroom, Karel turned to Gia. "Want to see how this one works?" He nodded at the pieces of dress that lay on the cutting table.

"Yes, please," said Gia.

Her father loved showing off his designs, and she was always happy to watch him work.

Karel spread each piece of the dress on the table, flicking the slippery fabric so that it lay without a wrinkle.

"This was a really tricky one," he said. "Wait, let me show you the map."

He opened the large envelope that Gia knew held all the pattern pieces, and slid out a sheet of paper. This was what her father called the "map", a scaled-down plan of the way the pattern pieces fitted onto the fabric. Fitting each piece on the cloth in such a way as to minimise wastage, and aligning each piece to the grain of the fabric was time-consuming work. The map made a useful record in case the pattern was ever used again.

"These two pieces are the front sleeves, right and left, you see, over here," he pointed at the relevant marking on the map, "And this long piece is this special waist panel that wraps all the way around and then folds over at the back in a pseudo-bustle effect."

The light suddenly dimmed, and there was a shout from the workroom.

"Power's out!" called Mandy.

Karel sighed, and went over to the door to look out. "Looks like it's just us," he said. "Gia, do me a favour and go see if the caretaker's in? It's probably a fuse or something but I don't dare touch the wiring in this place."

"The caretaker?"

"Oh, of course, you've not met him. Useful guy, kept helping me out when I was setting up the studio. He looks after this whole row of houses. If you go up the street to the left, you'll see his door at the end of the row. Down some steps. Number— I don't know the number, but you can't miss it."

It was easy to find after all, a door at the bottom of a short flight of steps, below the level of the pavement. It must be some kind of basement level.

There was no knocker, and no bell either, just a little plaque with the words "The Caretaker" painted in neat black letters. There were no wards either, Gia realised, or none visible. Feeling suddenly nervous, she knocked on the door and stepped back, unsure what to expect.

After a few seconds the doorknob rattled and the door opened.

"Yes?"

Gia found herself looking at the front of a white shirt, old and shabby but very clean. She had to look up to see the man's face.

His skin was so dark that only the whites of his eyes were visible in the shadow of the door. He opened the door a little wider, and she could see him more clearly.

He was an old man, so tall that he had to stoop slightly in the door. His build, and blue-black skin, made her think he might be from one of the northern countries, Ghana or Kenya, but his face had that high-cheekboned shape of a Bushman.

He looked down at her with calm amusement, and she realised she'd been staring.

"Um, our lights just went out," she said. "My father asked if you could come have a look?"

He gazed at her for a while. Then he gave a nod. "Number five."

"Yes!" said Gia with relief. "We're at number five. Can you help us?"

He inclined his head in seeming agreement, but then stepped back and closed the door gently in her face.

Gia blinked in surprise, and after a few moments, walked back to the studio, not sure if she was supposed to wait.

Her father looked up as she came in.

"You find him?" and seeing Gia's perplexed look, he laughed. "Odd sort of a guy. But just magic with anything mechanical. Been living down there forever, apparently."

A few minutes later the caretaker appeared, ducking his head a little as he came through the studio door. He lifted a hand in silent greeting, and walked through to the back where, Gia guessed, the fuse box must be. He'd pulled on a faded denim jacket over his shirt, and carried a toolbox like a small metal suitcase.

The lights came back on, and then the hum of Mandy's sewing machine.

The caretaker came back into the studio.

"Blown fuse?" asked Karel, but the caretaker just shook his head. He stood by the table, looking at the pieces of fabric spread there and after a moment, reached out and gently stroked one finger over the silky cloth.

Then, without another word he left, closing the studio door silently behind him.

"Strange guy," said Karel, watching him go.

"I wonder how old he is.

෨O෬

HAUNTED LIGHTS

"Gia Grobbelaar, you most certainly won't find the answer outside the window," said Mrs Kemp.

Gia sighed, picked up her pencil again, and tried to concentrate on the maths problem. Her mind was full of the appointment with Kavitha Pillay. Not only would she be meeting the bride-to-be of the president's son, but she would be going as her mother's assistant.

Up to now she'd often helped in her parents' business, but it had been small jobs, working when she had the time or inclination. The past few months she'd done more, helping her mother and Mandy at the old premises while her father set up the new studio. There had been some late-night sewing marathons, but mostly it had been odds and ends, and she never worked directly with the clients.

This was different.

She was part of the team now, thrilled and nervous at the thought. None of which helped her focus on her schoolwork.

Sonella, who shared Gia's desk, twisted a wisp of white-blond hair as she worked her way through the exercises. Gia wished that she could tell Sonella her news, but that, of course, was impossible.

Everything about Kavitha Pillay was top secret.

The murmur of conversation told her that the rest of the class were nearly finished. Mrs Kemp did not seem to mind, as long as the noise level stayed low.

What kind of dress would Kavitha want? Something traditional, or more modern? It would have a full skirt, maybe, cut on the bias so that it draped like this –

Gia's pencil left the columns of numbers and moved across the page, drawing a series of smooth, softly curved lines.

The bodice would have a modest neckline –

A few more lines, and the possibility of a dress glimmered among the sums.

"That's so pretty," said Sonella, and sighed. "I wish I could draw like that." She drew a finger along the swoop of the skirt.

"Could you make a dress like that?"

"Yes, I guess," said Gia. "But I've never done one completely on my own. Just helping my parents. They're both fashion designers."

"I know," whispered Sonella. "Carlo Gotti."

She smiled at Gia's surprise.

"All the girls know Carlo Gotti's your father. They're all dying of envy. And Saraswati is your mother. She made that beautiful peacock dress. I think I've got a picture here."

She opened her diary. Gia had noticed it before; it was covered in a collage of pictures from fashion magazines, and the pages were fat with clippings. Sonella paged to a picture that Gia knew well, of a heavily beaded and embroidered ball gown.

"That's right, isn't it? Your mom made that?"

Gia nodded. "It took her ages." She turned the page, and then another, looking through the clippings.

"I collect them," said Sonella a little self-consciously. "But I only get old magazines. The new ones are so expensive and my parents don't really approve. They don't say anything, but they think it's all just a waste of time. *Girly* stuff, you know."

Sonella's parents were academics, lecturers at the University of Cape Town. Gia thought they sounded hopelessly stern and intimidating.

"You know," said Gia, "we've got tons of magazines lying around. My parents get just about all the magazines you can possibly think of. Once my father's worked his way through them, he just piles them up in heaps. Drives Mom crazy. I could bring you some. Or maybe you should come for a visit, choose what you want yourself."

"Oh," said Sonella. "That would be *amazing*. Do you think—"

The intercom gave a preliminary crackle. *"Could Gianetta Grobbelaar please come immediately to Mr Peterson's office? Thank you."*

It took Gia a moment to realise that it was her name that had been announced. She sat staring at the little grey box.

"Well, Gia, up you get, and out you go," said Mrs Kemp. "You'd better finish those sums for homework."

"Oh," said Gia getting to her feet. She stared at her bag, wondering if she should take it.

"Don't worry, I'll look after your bag," said Sonella quickly. "If you're not back before the bell. Go on."

"Do you know where to go, Gia?" said Mrs Kemp.

"Yes, Miss," Gia stepped over her schoolbag and

sidled between the desks, aware that everyone was looking at her.

What on earth could this be about?

ഔOര

The headmaster's secretary gave her a cursory look.

"Gianetta Grobbelaar?"

She glanced at a door behind her. There were two lights above it, one of which was glowing red.

"Headmaster's still busy," said the secretary. "Sit there."

Gia sat where she indicated, her heart bouncing in her chest. She had to suppress the urge to jump up and pace.

Something's happened. To Dad. Or Mom. Or maybe Nico. Or have I done something?

The secretary tapped away at her keyboard, uninterested in Gia. At last there was a click. The red light switched off, and the green light came on.

"You can go in now," said the secretary, not lifting her eyes. "Just knock and go in."

Gia stopped at the door. There was somebody talking beyond it.

"Knock. And go in," said the secretary loudly and distinctly.

Gia knocked and turned the handle. She was so nervous by now that she did not take in anything about the room beyond the fact that there were two people in it.

Mr Peterson sat at a desk, and a woman stood facing him. They had clearly just finished some discussion.

"Ah!" said Mr Peterson. "Mrs Solomons, this is the girl I was telling you about. Gianetta, this is Mrs Solomons."

"Hello, Gianetta," said Mrs Solomons, holding out her hand. Gia shook it awkwardly, wondering a little. She'd never met a teacher who shook your hand before.

"Mrs Solomons is our social worker. Or should I say our school therapist?"

He seemed to think he'd made a joke, and Mrs Solomons smiled politely.

"Mrs Solomons is just going to ask you a few questions, Gianetta. Just routine."

"I'll need a room, Mr Peterson," said Mrs Solomons.

"Ah! Of course. Next door, next door. Sonya will show you."

"Well then. Afternoon, Mr Peterson."

Mrs Solomons put a hand on Gia's shoulder and steered her gently out of the office.

"We're just quickly going to use this room," she said to the secretary in passing. "Please don't let anyone disturb us."

Then they were in another office, a smaller one that seemed to be used mostly for storing files.

"Don't worry, Gianetta," said Mrs Solomons. "This really is just routine. There were a few things that should have been sorted when you joined the school, that seem to have been left out somehow. I'm going to ask you a few questions, just to check that we've got everything straight. I'll sit here, and why don't you draw up that chair and make yourself comfortable."

Gia did as she was told.

Mrs Solomons leaned over and touched her arm.

"Don't be nervous! You must have had a shock to be called out like that. Now you just relax while I get myself organised here." She opened a folder and paged through it briskly, stopping occasionally to lick a finger.

She was a small woman, with neat, glossy black hair. Her movements were quick and precise and for a moment Gia could picture her as a make-up compact, a polished little box that could snap open to reveal a perfect row of office-appropriate colours.

"Ah. There we are. So. You are Gianetta Rozalia Grobbelaar, sixteen years old."

"Yes, Ma'am."

"Your mother is Saraswati Grobbelaar, and your father is Karel. Or is it Carlo? We seem to have two names here."

"His real name is Karel Grobbelaar, but the business name is Carlo Gotti. Lots of people call him Carlo."

"Oh, I see." Mrs Solomons made a note. "Gianetta, it says here that you are adopted?"

"That's right, Ma'am."

"Do you know anything about your, um, birth parents?"

Gia hesitated. *Why is she asking about that?* "I'm sorry — I'm not sure I understand the question."

Mrs Solomons smiled. "Do you know who they were? When you were adopted and so on?"

"Oh. Their names were Jeanette and Benjamin de Koker. They died just after I was born. They were friends of my parents, so my parents adopted me."

Mrs Solomons nodded sympathetically. "That was a generous thing to do. Your parents are special people."

She made another note.

"You've been here at this school for more than a term now." She looked up at Gia. "How's that been, Gianetta? Are you settling in okay? Making friends?"

"Oh, yes," said Gia. "It was a bit strange at first but I'm getting used to things."

"That's good. And I see you have a brother." She pointed at the page. "Niccolo. Is he adopted too?"

"No, Ma'am."

"What school does he go to? Is he here?"

"Nico's just turned seven. But he does not go to school yet."

Mrs Solomons looked interested. "Oh? He should be, at that age."

"My parents are still trying to find a school that will work for him."

Mrs Solomon's eyebrows went up, and she looked at Gia expectantly.

"He does sort of go to school," said Gia. "He has a therapist he sees almost every day. I think she's working to get him ready so he can join a school. He — he doesn't easily get on with strangers."

Mrs Solomons nodded. "I see. He has special needs. And do you know this therapist's name?"

Again, Gia hesitated, suddenly uneasy. *Why is she asking this?* For some reason, Miss Huisman's warning came back to her.

"I must warn you not to trust — "

Mrs Solomons looked at her, pen poised.

"I, um, I don't know," said Gia at last. "My mom takes him there, I've never actually met his therapist or anything."

She felt a blush rise in her cheeks. *Why was she lying to this woman?*

But Mrs Solomons was smiling again. "I'm sorry, you must be wondering why I'm asking so much about your brother. I did my master's thesis about children with special needs, especially *autistic* children. Is he autistic, your brother? I'm still fascinated by that whole area."

"Oh, he's not autistic," said Gia. "The doctors thought so at first, but it turns out they don't really know what's going on with him."

"Well, each child is special in their own way," said Mrs Solomons. "I just wondered if I knew this therapist. Pity you can't remember the name."

She paused for a moment, as if waiting for Gia to answer. The silence stretched out between them, becoming awkward.

"Well then," said Mrs Solomons brightly, closing her file. "I think that's everything."

Then she laughed as the bell rang. "Saved by the bell," she said, getting up. She took out a card and handed it to Gia. "That's my number, if you ever need to chat. Thank you, Gianetta. You've been very helpful."

ಬOಲ

"And what's that great big frown for?"

Gia started. "Sorry Mandy. Just thinking."

She was in the kitchen, having a second lunch while Mandy ironed shirts. The room was full of the crisp scent of warm cotton. Soft, scratchy music played from Mandy's radio, where it was perched on top of the fridge.

"Huh," said Mandy. "Just thinking, are you? Anything worth sharing? And don't eat with your fingers. There's a fork there just right next to you."

Gia obediently picked up the fork. "Mandy, how long have you been working for my parents?"

Mandy placed the iron with a soft thump, and

manoeuvred it with expert care. "I don't know. Many years. Why do you ask?"

"I was wondering, were you working for them before they got me? Or only afterwards?"

The iron went into its bracket with a clatter, and Mandy pulled out a chair and sat down across from Gia.

"So what's brought this on?"

"Oh, it's nothing really. Somebody said something today and I started thinking about it. Mom and Dad met in Italy, right? When Dad was studying there. And they came back here soon afterwards. In the nineties some time."

"Ninety-eight," said Mandy.

"Right. So they must have adopted me just then as well. Just when they got back."

"Well, no." Mandy took off her headscarf and ran her hands through her hair so that it stood up in a scruffy grey cloud. "Your mom and dad brought you with them. From Italy. I started working for them just after they arrived, and you were already part of the picture. I'm sure I've told you this before?"

"I guess so. But that does not makes sense, Mandy. I mean, my birth parents were South African, weren't they? How could Mom and Dad have adopted me in Italy already?"

"Yes, they were South African. But your parents—I mean— your m*om* and *dad*—" Mandy snorted. "I mean Mr Karel and Madam Saraswati, they met your other parents when all of them were in Italy together."

"Oh."

Gia ate another mouthful.

"And you used to work for Ouma, before. Dad's Mom."

"That's right."

"And they all— I mean Dad's family— they disowned him, for marrying Mom?"

"That's right. I never understood that myself, but there you go."

"And Mom's family? Are they in Italy?"

Mandy frowned at her.

"That's the thing," said Gia. "I never thought about it before. Mom must have family *somewhere*. But she's never said anything— I don't think she's ever said anything about her own mom, or brothers and sisters, or anything like that."

"Your mother is a very private woman," said Mandy. She opened her headscarf on the table, absentmindedly smoothing it with both hands.

"I always thought," she said, "and I don't know why— but it always seemed to me that Madam had a very hard time growing up. Many people lost family at that time, in Europe, I mean."

"You mean the tronadas?" said Gia.

Mandy nodded. "That's right. That's why I've never really asked Madam about it. Seems like something best left alone."

Gia stared at her. She'd known about the tronadas all her life, the European anti-magic riots. But somehow she'd never thought of them as something that had really happened, something that could touch her own family.

"Of course," she said slowly. "That was all happening then, right? In the nineties."

It was not a comfortable thought.

"It's just so odd that I've never noticed before, that Mom never speaks about her own family." She tried to remember whether Saraswati had ever mentioned anything about her past, without success.

"When I was a little girl, I used to think that Mom was a princess. I even made up a story about a fairy-tale place where she'd grown up. A palace with lots of fountains and things."

"She does have that air," said Mandy.

They heard the front door close, then Nico came rushing into the kitchen. He scooted all around the room, making loud "vrooming" noises, and disappeared out the door again.

"What was that?" laughed Mandy.

Saraswati came in with Nico close behind. He made another lap, buzzing and hooting as he went.

"It is unbelievably windy out there," said Saraswati and brushed her hair back with both hands. "Gia, I'm just going to change quickly, then we have to go. Could you get the wedding book? And the drawing books too, just in case. You know where they are?"

"Yes," said Gia, getting up. "Thanks, Mandy." She dumped her dishes in the sink, and went to find what she needed, her mind racing ahead to the meeting with Kavitha Pillay.

෨O෬

All Gia could see of the driver was the back of his head and shoulders. That was enough to make her wonder if he was human. His too-flat head sat on a neck so thick it was hard to tell where neck ended and head began. He was silent, too— he'd hardly said a word since he'd picked them up in the parking lot of the Gardens Centre.

All this secrecy was rather nerve-wracking.

Gia was sure that nobody had noticed her mother and herself waiting in the parking lot, or watched as they got into the car. The car was certainly eye-catching. Long, low and black, with deeply tinted windows. The dark glass made the view outside slightly unreal, as if there was an eclipse, or an approaching storm.

Gia was reminded of the time there had been a fire on the mountain, and the smoke had cast a twenty-four hour twilight over the city. She kept expecting to smell that ashy scent of a mountain fire, but all she could smell was leather and plastic.

Her mother was in the back seat with her, sitting as upright as ever, hands folded over her handbag. She seemed calm, but the occasional tap of a finger or nod of her head told Gia that Saraswati was going over her mental list of everything that had to be dealt with, checking and rechecking that she was prepared for the meeting.

Gia's texter beeped and she automatically felt for her pocket, before she remembered that she was not wearing jeans. Saraswati had made her put on a blouse and skirt, and the skirt had no pockets.

She reached for the little shoulder bag her mother had lent her.

"Better switch that off," said Saraswati. "Makes a bad impression if it beeps in the middle of the meeting."

Gia nodded absently as she read the message. It was from Fatima.

coming out with me and B tonight? going jolling.

Gia responded, aware of her mother's cool attention.

Where? Time?

The answer came quickly.

the playground - pick you up at 9? on bike :)

Gia answered quickly.

Will check if I can go. Can't talk now.

The car slowed to turn into a driveway, then rolled to a stop at a pair of enormous wrought-iron gates. A guard spoke briefly to the driver, and the gates swung open to reveal yet more driveway.

This place must be enormous. Gia could see glimpses of the house through a screen of large trees and a tall clipped hedge.

"We're going round the back," said the driver. "Kitchen entrance." He hesitated, and glanced at Saraswati in his rear-view mirror.

"Uh— no disrespect intended, Ma'am. Just less conspicuous that way."

"Of course," said Saraswati. "I completely understand. It's kind of you to explain."

The driver nodded, but said no more. The car slowed to a stop and the doors clicked as they unlocked.

Gia got out, but hardly had time to take in her surroundings before two men in suits hustled them through a door, and she found herself in a large, busy kitchen.

There were people everywhere, all bustling about with trays or pots. They were cutting, cleaning, or cooking, but none of them so much as glanced up as the two men walked Gia and her mother through the room.

In the passage beyond they passed several other people, all servants, Gia guessed from their black-and-white outfits, but nobody met her eye. It was unsettling, as though she and her mother were invisible and inaudible.

A door closed behind them and they were in the main part of the house.

Everything here was muted. Soft white carpet underfoot, soft light filtering from recessed lamps. There was a faint scent of vanilla in the air.

Their escort opened a white panelled door and stood back, waiting for them to step inside.

The room was enormous, but seemed even larger than it was because the entire outside wall was made of glass. Through it was a view of a garden as perfect as a photograph in a magazine, with fountains, clipped hedges, and mossy borders. But Gia hardly noticed the view, her attention on the two people by the sofa.

One was a woman, in her fifties, Gia guessed. She stood as they entered, and made a welcoming gesture with her hands.

"Madame Saraswati. Welcome to my home."

This must be Mrs Pillay, Gia realised, and looked at her with interest. Karel had called her a "dragon lady" and Gia could see why. Mrs Pillay wore rose-patterned linen, but she held herself like a major general.

"Please, sit down. Will you have tea? Coffee?"

"No, thank you," said Saraswati. "We are fine. Good afternoon, Mrs Pillay. Miss Pillay."

The girl on the sofa bent her head. "Good afternoon," she said.

Kavitha Pillay was far more beautiful even than the flattering photographs Gia had seen.

This truly was a fairy-tale princess come to life. That pale golden skin, the perfect mouth, the enormous, coal-black eyes, hidden for the moment under lowered lashes. Kavitha sat on the edge of the sofa, her hands folded demurely in her lap, but she was far from relaxed.

Gia thought that she looked like a bird, listening for the approach of a hunting beast. For an instant Gia imagined her leaping, desperate, her cream-and-rose dress swirling around her as she flew up, up into the air and dashed herself against the plate-glass window that barred her escape, her perfect nails breaking as she scrabbled for purchase on the glass.

"Gia, could you hand me the wedding book? The first one, thank you."

Saraswati's voice pulled her back into reality, and Gia hurriedly handed her mother the book. Her eyes met Kavitha's, and Gia was startled to see a direct and calculating intelligence that nevertheless seemed coolly amused. Gia wondered uncomfortably what Kavitha guessed about her thoughts.

It was clear that Mrs Pillay was in charge, and that she did not expect any input from her daughter.

"I thought, for the gown— something *simple*," she said, nodding serenely. "Simple, but traditional. Feminine. Something, well, you know. *Romantic*."

Saraswati inclined her head in agreement. "I know exactly what you mean," she said. "I think you might like some of these designs here—" She flipped open the book open, and both women bowed over it, studying the pages.

The book was really a fat file, filled with photographs and drawings of all the wedding gowns Karel and Saraswati had created over the many years they'd worked together. Gia, who had spent many hours paging through it, knew it by heart.

There were the headings in Saraswati's neat handwriting, dividing it into categories: "Victorian", "Princess-line", "Modern," "Mature Brides," and many more. Some pages had fabric swatches and scraps of veiling, all of them had photographs of the brides modelling their finished gowns.

Gia could tell, from sections of the book that Mrs Pillay kept turning to, that she was set on what Karel called a "meringue", stiff, ultra-formal, wide-skirted, and swathed with lace and ribbons. Saraswati, while seeming to agree with every word, was gently steering her to consider some of the simpler gowns near the back of the book. Kavitha seemed completely detached from the process, eyes half closed as she looked into the mid-distance.

Gia felt a rush of sympathy, but also irritation. There was something so exasperating about the way the girl just sat there, as though she'd switched herself off. On an impulse, Gia took the rest of the books out of the bag.

"Would you like to see these?" she said, and plumped herself onto the couch next to Kavitha. She flipped open a book so that it lay across both their laps. Kavitha seemed surprised, but willing to look as Gia turned the pages.

Gia had chosen one of the many drawing books, a collection of ideas rather than a record of designs. These were impressions, sketches that hinted at shape and texture, dream dresses and possibilities. Some were just a few brush strokes. Others were more complete, but all were quick, vibrant, and colourful.

Many of the drawings were by Karel, some going as far back as his student days. Many were by her mother, but more and more these days, the books were filled with Gia's own work.

At first Kavitha just looked politely, but after a few pages Gia sensed her awakening interest. She touched Gia's hand to stop her turning a page. She tucked a strand of hair behind her ear, tilting her head as she studied the drawing. Then she started turning the pages herself. Gia noticed that although Kavitha's hands were elegant, her fingernails were bitten to the quick. Between turning pages she curled her fingers into her palms, hiding her nails from view.

Kavitha moved the book onto her own lap and paged rapidly forward, then back a few pages. She kept returning to the same page — one of Gia's drawings, done at a time she'd been fascinated by all things Japanese.

"Do you like that one?" Gia asked, careful to keep her voice low.

The drawing was in blood-red ink, more detailed than most of the sketches. The design was deceptively simple, saved from stark modernity by the sculpted, many-folded drapes that echoed the traditional dress of the geisha.

Kavitha touched the drawing, clearly fascinated. Then she looked up at her mother, who was still deep in consultation with Saraswati, and sighed. It was as if she had allowed some part of her to unfold, and was now pulling it back again.

Gia once again felt that mixture of irritation and compassion. "Mom," she said. "I think we've found it."

She pulled the book from Kavitha's unresisting grasp.

Saraswati looked up, startled, and then down at the drawing as Gia held it out to her. Mrs Pillay, caught mid-sentence, stared at Gia in open-mouthed surprise, then finished what she'd been saying. "Ivory lace. What — ?"

Saraswati, after a quick look at Gia, smiled at Kavitha. "Is this the one, Miss Pillay? An excellent choice. Possibly not in that colour — ?"

Kavitha blinked, then lost her blank look. "Oh, no, of course," she said. "Red would be absurd. Maybe something like that swatch that Mother has there."

Mrs Pillay looked at her daughter, then down at the slip of ivory silk she'd been fingering.

"I agree," said Saraswati. "Your mother has such excellent taste."

"And there's an outfit in there that would be perfect for you, Mother. You were just telling me that we should use the wedding as an opportunity to celebrate Indian culture."

Gia let her take the book and Kavitha paged quickly to another drawing. "It's like a sari, but more tailored. Isn't it elegant?"

Mrs Pillay's eyebrows went up. "I— well." She looked at the drawings, then up at her daughter again. "Oh. Well. I was not planning on having anything specially *made* for myself," said Mrs Pillay. "I was thinking to wear my Ci Hestler suit—"

"Oh, Mother, no," said Kavitha. "The press will have a field day with that. You wore that to Praveshni's wedding."

"These sari designs are very flattering," said Saraswati smoothly. "And you will certainly be very much in the public eye."

For a moment, Mrs Pillay sat silent, her lips pursed. Then she slowly nodded. "Very well. It is true, I should have an outfit made, what with all the publicity the wedding will receive." She paged back to the wedding gown. "And Kavitha would look lovely in this. Although it is very bold." "Excellent," said Saraswati. "Shall we do the measurements? Gia, could you get my notebook and measuring tape?"

ஓ௦ஐ

The drive back to the Gardens Centre was much more relaxed, although Saraswati did not say anything, clearly not willing to speak in the driver's hearing. It was only once the black car had pulled away, and they stood in the parking lot once again, that she threw back her head and laughed, then gathered Gia in for a fierce hug.

She stood back and stared at her daughter. "Gianetta Rosalia, you are more like your father than I ever realised. Poor Mrs Pillay never knew what hit her."

Gia grinned back at her. "I could not bear to see that poor girl being just—" She threw up her hands in exasperation. "Ignored like that. As if she weren't even in the room."

"Yes," said Saraswati. "That woman has a will of iron. But I think the daughter is not quite as soft as she looks." Saraswati got into the car and fastened her seatbelt. "That gown you chose will be murder to get right, but it *will* be a sensation. And Mrs Pillay's outfit will be a breeze. A sari dress!" She laughed again. "We can whip that together, no trouble. Your father is going to be pleased."

Gia waited a few minutes, until they were out of the parking lot. Then she said casually, "Fatima wants to know if I can go out with her tonight. Ben's going too. They'll lift me there and back."

The "they" was not strictly honest. Fatima would be fetching her on her bike, and of course, there was just room for one passenger. Gia knew Saraswati would never agree to her going with Fatima on her bike. It was better to make it sound as if Fatima's mother would be driving them all.

"Where are you going?" said Saraswati.

"Oh — to a movie, I think."

"You think?" Saraswati lifted an eyebrow. But then she smiled again.

"Oh, very well. You've earned it. Back by eleven, as always. And you'll have to ask your father first."

"Thanks Mom!" said Gia, her texter out, already tapping a message.

She knew what her father would say.

ೞOಬ

Fatima's red helmet nodded and Gia just had time to wrap her arms round Fatima's waist before the road whipped out from under her feet. Her own helmet prevented her from looking up to check if anyone had seen them leave.

Forget about all that now. I can deal with Mom when I get back.

Racing round the corners on Fatima's little bike was utterly different from being in a car. The cold night air blew inside her jacket and down the gap at the back of her jeans. Headlights glared, and the road seemed very close. Fatima's skirt fluttered back over Gia's legs, and she guessed from the various hoots and shouts that they must make quite a sight.

She grinned to herself, inside the helmet, and leaned with Fatima as they took another corner.

The trip to town was a lot shorter from Walmer Estate than it had been when she still lived in Plumstead. A few minutes later they were waiting at an intersection on Long street, the bike buzzing beneath them. There was a small crowd of people standing on the sidewalk, staring upwards.

Gia tried to see what they were looking at.

It's the lights. They've gone all weird.

Gia felt Fatima laugh. The traffic lights dimmed and glowed again, pulsing rhythmically. The pulse seemed to travel from light to light, like a signal, or as if the lights responded to something Gia could not sense. The colours were cycling too, from green to blue, through blue-white, to ice-white, warming to candlelight, sunlight, firelight and blood-orange.

Fatima said something, and Gia leaned forward to catch the words.

"They're *haunted*," said Fatima "I've heard they get like this sometimes, but I've never seen it. Isn't it cool?"

She laughed again, but Gia felt a chill travel down her spine.

Haunted? How could a traffic light be haunted?

The flow and throb of the colours seemed to be more than random. It was like a message, a code she could decipher if she just stared at them long enough.

But Fatima had leaned forward and they were off again.

A few minutes later Fatima was chaining up her bike in front of the club, and Ben waved at them from the entrance.

"Hi!" he said. "I hope you guys brought your IDs, there's a bouncer checking tonight."

Gia could hear the music already, a dull beat that came up through the soles of her feet. She felt a thrill of excitement. She'd heard a lot about The Playground, but she'd never been to it before.

"Is there a band?" she asked.

Ben nodded. "Automatic Dread."

A live band meant a higher cover charge. Gia hoped she had enough money on her.

"On me," said Fatima. "This is your birthday treat, girl."

She had her wallet out and walked up to the entrance, where the bouncer turned to face her. Gia felt her heart thump.

The bouncer was a troll. He filled the door, impossibly wide shoulders straining the black fabric of his suit. "Good evening, ladies," he rumbled, staring down at Fatima.

Gia found she had stopped dead. She took a few steps closer.

Why is he staring at Fatima like that?

"Three, please," said Fatima, holding out her money.

The troll took the notes and put them in a cash-box. His eyes glinted as he looked her slowly up and down.

"Nice jacket," he said.

Oh, God. She's wearing that troll-hunter jacket.

Gia cast Ben a horrified look, and saw from his expression that he'd realised what was going on. But Fatima was either unaware of the troll's reaction, or she simply did not care. She pulled back a red sleeve and smiled up at him. The troll blinked down at her bare arm. Then with a shrug that might have been a laugh, he pressed his thumb first in an inkpad, then on her arm, leaving a print on her skin.

"Thanks!" said Fatima. "Come on, guys!" and she was gone inside the club. They stepped forward to follow her, but the troll put out a big hand to stop Ben.

"ID, please."

Ben flipped open his wallet. "Why didn't you ask her?" he asked, jerking his head in the direction Fatima had gone.

Gia started taking out her identity document, but the troll shook his head. "Don't worry, darling."

And then seeing Ben's frown. "Ladies, dude. Ladies."

He gestured with his thumb, and Ben and Gia held out their arms for their thumbprint stamps.

ఎOఇ

They went down to a basement level.

The passage was plastered with band posters and signs. There was the usual list of banned cultural weapons, "pickpockets active, watch your bag", and a large red and yellow "No Ear Worms" sign that made Gia wonder if she should have brought earplugs.

You never knew what music might be played in a club like this.

Although it was early evening, there were already many people brushing past them on the stairs and crowding the dance floor. The music was loud and urgent, with a racing double beat that had Gia hopping. Ben would know what band it was, but all she cared about was getting out onto the dance floor.

The Playground had a reputation as a place where strange people hung out, and Gia looked curiously about her as she danced. The floor was a checker board of black-and-white tiles, and the walls and ceiling were black. It was hard to see anything else as the strobes kept glaring in her eyes. Fatima's teeth glowed in the black-light, and Gia saw that Fatima had already attracted a couple of admirers, two young men who stood nearby but never did anything so uncool as to look directly at her.

Ben was also on the dance floor, but it was hard to tell if he was dancing, or just standing there with his hands in his pockets, occasionally shifting his weight from one foot to the other.

There were all kinds of people on the dance floor.

Two girls gyrating in the middle of the floor were certainly not human, although Gia was not sure what they were. They were far too broad to be human, and they moved with a massive grace. Gia noticed that the other dancers kept well clear of them.

A man nearly bumped into Gia, and as he turned to apologise she saw that what she'd taken to be a furry jacket was actually a ruff of fur growing from his naked back— he wore no shirt.

Some distance away, a thin girl clad all in black whipped her long, white hair as she danced. The hair flowed through the air as if in slow motion, the ends trailing off into puffs of white vapour.

Soon enough, swept up by the music, Gia forgot the other dancers. Clouds of dry ice filled the room and for a while everything was a ghostly mist, with glimpses of other dancers silhouetted against the flashing lights.

"Come. Drinks," Fatima shouted in her ear, and dragged at her hand.

They found Ben and went up the stairs again, and then into a quieter room, where the music was a muffled beat in the distance. Gia's ears rang, and she felt a little disoriented. She kept tripping over people sitting on the ground, until Fatima found them a corner near the back, on a heap of cushions.

"Back soon," she said, and disappeared over to the bar.

"Wanna fairylight, Babe?" said someone, and she turned to find a bearded man grinning at her, holding a glowing vial. There was something inside it, something dark like a tiny body curled into itself.

"Fuck off, dude," said Ben, sitting forward so that the man had to back off.

"Hey, chill," he said, but he seemed oddly unaffected by Ben's aggression. To Gia's relief, the man disappeared back into the shadows.

Now that her eyes had grown used to the dark, she could see there were people huddled up against the walls, cupping little vials in their hands, their faces bathed in the soft glow.

"Sparkle-heads," said Ben. He swallowed as if he'd tasted something bad. "Wasters. Stay away from them, Gia, okay?"

"Sure," said Gia. Fatima returned with a beer for each of them, and Gia lay back against the pillows again.

A change in the flow of people moving into the chill room told them that the band had started playing, and they went back to the dance-floor.

Automatic Dread turned out to be not quite a band. The act consisted of a skinny white guy behind a pile of electronic equipment: multiple black boxes covered in knobs and sliders. The stage was a web of cables, among which Automatic Dread moved like an anxious spider, constantly adjusting, tweaking, plugging and unplugging.

But the musician soon became irrelevant as Gia was carried away by the sounds he created. She could almost see the music as it exploded around her, rusty blocks of sound, or huge chains that strained almost on the edge of breaking.

The first hint that something else was happening came from the lights.

The hectic white of the strobes slowed and softened, flickered and faded like candlelight. Tiny dots of luminescence drifted out over the dancers, who reached out to catch them. Gia, pulled back into herself, noticed that Automatic Dread was frowning at his equipment. He looked up, trying to see somebody at the back of the dance floor.

Something's wrong.

The music played on, but it seemed to slow and drag, pulsing in time to the fading lights. Gia stopped dancing, her attention on the person who now joined Automatic Dread on stage, a technician of some kind. The sound had lost all its brilliance and become a foggy booming moan, like huge waves. Gia felt it rolling through her, shaking her to the bone.

Once again, as she had with the haunted traffic lights, she felt everything around her respond to some secret signal. But this time she was on the cusp of receiving it herself, as though she was being tuned closer and closer to the right frequency.

Words began to form in the music, but they were too loud, or too slow to understand. The men on stage were frantically pulling on sliders and switches but their actions had no effect on the sound.

Gia closed her eyes and strained to catch the words.

The almost-voice rumbled in her chest, a long, groaning sigh.

"O – oh," it said, stretching out the word across the room from dancer to dancer.

"Ss – o – h – o – w".

Gia was only half aware that the movement of the dancers around her had changed. Everyone was moving together, swaying in response to the sound.

"Soh – oh – so – o – ow"

With a tingle of horror Gia realised that the voice was coming out of her own throat, and from the dancers that surrounded her. They were all sighing out the words that moved through the music. Her eyes flew open just in time to see Automatic Dread rip out cable after cable, and look desperately out at the room as nothing changed.

"*Sor – row.*"

Gia felt her tongue move in her mouth, forming the word.

"*Sorrow.*"

Then with painful abruptness, the music dropped away to total silence. An instant later the lights came on, not the dramatic lighting of the nightclub, but the everyday glare of fluorescent, flat and bright.

The dancers stood dazed, then the dream broke and they screwed up their eyes. Shouts of protest rose from the crowd but they seemed half-hearted. Then there was a stir near the entrance.

"Cops!" somebody shouted. "Raid!"

Somebody swore loudly, and Gia saw several people turning out their pockets, letting small objects fall on the ground to be trampled by the crowd.

"This way." It was Fatima, tugging her away from the entrance. With Ben close behind, Gia followed her as she ducked behind one of the curtains that draped the wall.

"Back way," explained Fatima.

They ran down a passage and then up some stairs.

"What just happened?" said Gia. "With the music. Did you hear –?"

"The cops cut the power or something," said Fatima.

"No, I meant –" but Gia let the question trail off. It was clear that Fatima had not noticed anything out of the ordinary. She looked at Ben, but he avoided her eyes.

Fatima led them round a corner to a door. She opened it carefully, just wide enough to see the street outside. Gia and Ben waited for what seemed a full minute. Then Fatima turned back with a nod.

"All clear," she said. "It looks like there are only a few cops out there, and they're just looking at IDs. I think it's safe to go out."

They stepped out into the blissfully cool night air.

"Wow," said Fatima, lifting her hair to cool her neck. "I think I'm deaf."

Gia nodded. Her ears were ringing.

There was a Special Branch vehicle pulled up outside the club's entrance. People were crowding out of the club, flipping their IDs at the policemen.

As they watched, two more policemen appeared, holding between them the hairy man Gia had noticed on the dance floor. They'd cuffed his hands behind him, and were steering him toward the back of the van.

"Crap," said Ben. "What's going to happen to him?"

Fatima shrugged. "Guess he's an illegal. Magical, at any rate. They'll take him to Valkenberg, I suppose."

"We'd better go," said Ben, his voice strained.

Then they all turned as someone emerged from the door behind them. Gia recognised another of the dancers— the skinny, white-haired girl. The girl's eyes widened as she saw them, but she did not stop, brushing past them to disappear down the street, covering her startling hair with a dark scarf as she went.

"I suppose we better go too," said Fatima. "Pity. Still so early, it can't even be midnight yet. And just look at the moon," he said, smiling up at the sky.

Gia looked up.

There was the moon, a perfect disk behind a wisp of cloud. She felt her warm mood drain away.

Full moon. "What's the time?" she said, feeling for her texter. "Oh, bugger."

There was a message there.

Where are you? 11:15.

That was her mother. And it was now fifteen minutes before midnight.

"Fatima, I'm sorry — but I've got to get home. Look, I can take a taxi—"

"No way," said Fatima. "Don't stress, I'll take you."

"How are you getting home?" Gia asked Ben.

"Don't worry, I'm walking." And then in response to her astonished expression, "It's not far. See you Sunday, Gia." And with a last glance at the policemen, he was gone.

"Well, he's in a hurry," said Fatima. "Come on, then."

ೞOಇ

To Gia's relief there was no more delay and soon she and Fatima were on the bike, pulling on their helmets.

Somehow the ride back was less thrilling. Gia kept wanting to look at her watch to check the time, but there was no way she could reach it safely, with the rate that Fatima was flying along.

At last they neared Gia's road. She squeezed Fatima to get her attention.

"Fatima, can we wait here on the corner, just for moment. I need to check something."

Fatima was clearly puzzled, but nodded and switched the engine off. Gia looked at her watch, then along the street to where she could just make out the front door to her house.

Ten minutes to midnight.

The door opened, and a figure stepped out into the street. It wore a long coat with the hood up, but Gia knew who it was.

Saraswati.

Gia watched as Saraswati walked along the street. Now it was too dark to see her, but she could hear the slam of a car door, and the engine starting.

"That was your mom, wasn't it?" said Fatima. "Where is she going? Looking for you?"

"No," said Gia, as she got off the bike.

"Okay," said Fatima when it became clear that Gia wasn't going to say anything else. "You don't want to speak about it. Want to meet again? Sometime later this weekend?"

Gia shook her head.

"My parents will probably ground me for being late."

Fatima grimaced. "Tough luck. Well, let me know if you can get out."

"Thanks for the night. It was great, really."

"You going to be okay now?"

"Yes, I'll be fine."

Gia gave her a quick hug, then turned and walked up the street. The sound of Fatima's bike receded behind her.

ಖOಆ

When had she first noticed her mother and the moon?

Gia sat in her window-seat bed, looking out over the view below her. It was dark except for the streetlights, and here and there a gleam from a window.

It seemed like she'd always known there was something special about the moon, something that must not be mentioned.

How had she known that?

One of her earliest memories was of being held in Saraswati's arms, while her mother looked up at the moon. Her face had turned away, as though something pulled at her from above.

These days, she had started noticing the change in her mother every month. As the moon rounded towards full, she grew quiet. Tense. Distracted. And there was the way Karel watched Saraswati at these times, as though she were a bird that might fly away if startled.

Lately, full-moon was the time that Gia was most likely to fight with her mother. Small things that would otherwise have been ignored, flamed up. And it was not the usual monthly thing that all women had to deal with. There was something more, Gia was sure of that.

Mandy had explained all that to her, the way a woman's body changed, the monthly rhythm. Mandy had made it all normal, had bought her the things she needed to deal with the cramps and blood, when her first time came.

Gia had never spoken to her mother about those things.

She pulled her blankets up around her and took a bite from the sandwich she'd made herself.

The past few years, she'd gotten into the habit of waiting up, on full-moon nights. Waiting until she heard her mother's footsteps, and the soft thud of the front door closing behind her.

Always just before midnight, on a full-moon night.

Where does she go?

Gia had thought of following, but how could she do so without being seen?

Maybe I don't want to know. I don't want to know where she goes. Or what she does when she gets there.

She put the half-eaten sandwich on her bedside table. Somehow she was no longer as hungry as she'd thought. But she did not feel sleepy either.

Too many thoughts.

If she tried to sleep, she was sure to have nightmares. Maybe she should do some work on the doll. That would help her relax.

She took out the doll, and unpacked her paints, the full moon still dominating her thoughts. No longer the small icy disk she'd seen that night, but a dreamy, blue-and-silver dream-moon, surrounded by stylised clouds.

Gia found her thin brushes, and the piece of glass she used as a palette. Soon the doll was laid out on a sheet of newspaper, and her paints were ready. She paused for a moment, licked her lips, then began.

Shades of blue. Like old tattoos...

The paint went onto the doll's skin smoothly. Spidery lines, as thin as the strokes of a pen. Half- and quarter-moons on her forearms, with clouds circling her wrists like bracelets. The full-moon on her forehead, surrounded by wisps of cloud in that curly, Oriental style. Maybe a single red teardrop, a bead of blood, poised between the eyebrows? As if the moon was bleeding? Or even a teardrop of red in the moon itself?

The night sounds filtered in from outside as she worked. The late-night traffic on the freeway, the fluting chirp of frogs from nearby gardens. A distant drumming made her pause.

Could it be?

The drumming repeated, a definite pattern.

Trompoppies. Gia had heard them described often enough to recognise the sound.

She waited, listening and soon enough, there was an answering rumble. Somewhere, on the surrounding roofs, a small creature must be crouched, ears fanned and fists drumming on the corrugated iron.

Gia sighed, a deep sigh that seemed to fill, then empty her whole body, and bent happily over her work.

ಸಿOಜ

THE WOLF AT THE DOOR

Gia woke to sunshine pouring in the window, and sat up with a start.

Overslept.

Then she remembered it was Saturday. She flopped back down on her pillow, only to start back up again a moment later, and frown at the plate on her bedside table. The sandwich had been opened up, and every bit of jam licked off. The cheese was still there, but no jam.

What?

She looked quickly around the room, but could see nothing out of place. As she dressed, she continued searching for any clue to the identity of the jam thief.

Down in the kitchen, Nico was mashing at his breakfast with a spoon, and Mandy was on her knees, head inside the cupboard under the sink.

"We're out of milk," she said. "Good morning, Gia. Go down to Granny's and get us some."

"What are you doing?" asked Gia.

"Mice," said Mandy from inside the cupboard.

Gia thought about the sandwich. *Would a mouse open a sandwich, lick off all the jam, but leave the cheese?*

"Where are Mom and Dad?"

Mandy edged herself backward until she could look up at Gia.

"Madam has gone out to get some supplies, and your father is working downstairs. Milk!"

"All right," said Gia. "What's up with Nico?"

He was frowning ferociously at his porridge, and had that wincing look again.

"Mister Nico is in a mood this morning," said Mandy. "Apparently somebody moved the rat's food bowl last night, and he's been in a sulk about it all morning. I ask you." Mandy sighed. "If it's not one thing, it's another."

"Thief!" said Nico, thumping the table with the handle of his knife.

"Want to come with me to the shop, Nico?" said Gia.

Nico stared up at her, his frown gone.

"Come," she said holding out her hand. "We'll march there."

She began marching on the spot, declaiming the old marching rhyme she'd used with him since he started walking.

"Lik, lak, lik, lak—"

"Lik, lak, ley!" answered Nico.

She took his hand and headed him, still marching, out the door.

"You got money?" Mandy called after her.

"Lik, lak, lik, lak, lik lak, yes, I, do!" said Gia.

They marched down the corridor and out the front door. Down the stairs and out onto the street.

"Lik, lak, lik, lak, lik, lak, ley!" said Nico in his too-loud voice, slamming down his feet.

"Lik, lak, lik, lak, lik, lak, ley!"

Gia ignored the stares and smiles, and marched along with Nico. They marched all the way down the block and across the street, stepping in place whenever they had to wait.

"Lik, lak!" Nico's voice sounded louder than ever as they entered the shop.

"Okay, Nico, we're in the shop now, so we're going to stop marching," said Gia.

"Lik, lak, lik, lak, lik, lak, *ley!*" shouted Nico, louder than ever. "Lik, lak —" Then he stopped, mouth open, staring around the shop, his wondering gaze coming to rest on Granny.

"Morning," said Granny. "You like my shop?"

Nico did not respond. His eyes moved up to the strings of beads, umbrellas, and garden tools that hung from the ceiling.

"You go on, get what you need," Granny said to Gia. "I'll look after him."

"Here," she said to Nico as she got down from her chair. "Here, I've got something to show you."

Nico blinked at her.

Granny, standing on the floor, was about as the same height as he was, although the extravagantly wrapped scarves made her seem taller. She clinked as she moved, bangles, earrings and necklaces swinging as she bent down to drag a box out from under a shelf.

"Shells," she said, dusting her hands with a clash of bangles. "Forgot I had them. Found them the other day."

She pried open the cardboard flaps and rummaged inside the box as Nico looked on with obvious interest.

"Look."

A shell in her hand, a smooth egg fringed with lacy whorls.

Nico squatted next to Granny, totally absorbed.

Gia got the milk out of the fridge. Seeing Nico still happily occupied, she took the chance to look around the shop.

There was the usual selection of tinned food, toiletries, and cleaning products, but among them were more intriguing things.

A box full of painted paper fans was tucked in next to the detergents. Tubs of Vaseline shared shelf space with tarot cards.

Among all these, Gia noticed a row of rat- and mousetraps.

Those could be useful, she thought, remembering Mandy's complaint.

She picked up a mouse-trap and was puzzling out how it worked, when a voice spoke behind her.

"No need for that."

Her heart bumped, and she turned to find the caretaker looming over her. He took the mousetrap from her and put it back on the shelf.

"No mice at number five."

Gia found her voice had dried up.

"No mice," the caretaker repeated with finality.

"And you might catch something you'd regret," said Granny, appearing at his elbow.

The caretaker stared down at her. "That's true," he said. "Might catch some bad luck, setting a trap in number five, Lever Road."

Gia looked from the one to the other, trying to understand the joke they clearly shared.

"Okay," she said. "I'll just take this then." She patted the milk bottle.

Nico, still on the floor, stared up at the caretaker, a shell forgotten in his hand.

The caretaker put his hands on his knees, and sank down into a crouch.

"Well. Hello," he said.

There was a tinkle of bells from the door, and Granny turned to see who had come in.

"Hi, Granny," said the new arrival. "I've come to pick up our order. Is it ready yet?"

The voice was familiar.

"Sonella!" said Gia.

"Oh! Hi, Gia," said Sonella. She looked quite different out of her school uniform. "I thought I might run into you. Just came to pick up our lunch order. You live just round the corner, don't you?"

"That's right," said Gia. "But I thought you lived in Woodstock."

"I do," said Sonella, accepting a bag full of paper parcels from Granny. "But that's not far from here. Just on the other side of Eastern Boulevard."

"Oh," said Gia, embarrassed. "I don't really know the area yet."

"That's your brother?"

Gia looked over her shoulder to where the caretaker still knelt in front of Nico. If she had not known better, she'd have thought they were deep in conversation. Nico was showing something to the caretaker. From the various bolts, springs and bits of plastic in the caretaker's open hand, it looked like Nico was emptying his pockets.

Gia stared in astonishment.

Nico *never* interacted with strangers.

Sonella stirred, and Gia realised that she must be wondering what was going on. She tore her gaze away from the strange interaction. For a moment the two girls looked at one another. Then Sonella shifted the bag in her hand and glanced awkwardly behind her.

"I better get going," she said. "Nice seeing you."

"Okay," said Gia. Then, at a sudden thought: "Sonella, wait—why don't you come and visit? Maybe not today," she said, seeing Sonella's hesitation. "But tomorrow? We're at number five, Lever Road. You can come for lunch or something."

Sonella smiled and Gia saw that she was going to agree. "Your mom won't mind?"

"No! It'll be cool. Wait— I don't have your number."

As they exchanged texter numbers, Nico came up next to Gia. "Lik lak!" he demanded.

Gia saw Sonella's startled glance, and waited for the veiled, polite look that people got when they first saw Nico. But Sonella just said, "Hi, Nico," with a touch of shyness.

Nico, as usual, did not respond.

"So you'll come then," said Gia. "I'll just check with my mom, and I'll send you a text later today."

Sonella nodded, and with a wave to Granny, was out the door.

"You girls friends?"

Gia realised that Granny had been watching them.

"Yes," she said. "We're at school together."

Granny nodded. "Good girl, that one. You can trust her."

The caretaker, now leaning against the counter, nodded in agreement.

Nico tugged at Gia's hand again.

"Yes, Nico, we're going now," said Gia.

She paid for the milk, and left the shop, aware of their amused scrutiny.

ෂ O ଔ

As Gia unlocked the burglar gate, she heard the studio door open. Nico pulled at her hand, straining toward Saraswati.

"Good morning, Gia."

Here it comes.

She considered pretending that she'd not seen Saraswati, but Nico made that impossible. She let him go, and he ran to wrap his arms around his mother.

"So what time did you get back last night?"

I could ask you the same question. But Gia she knew that she did not dare. Instead she kept her eyes on her mother's hands as she stroked Nico's hair, noticing again the particular way she had of running strands of it through thumb and finger, as though she were smoothing each separate lock.

"I thought we had an understanding."

Maybe if she just kept quiet, Saraswati would give up and they would not have to have another fight.

Another dreary, boring, fight.

"Gia, look at me when I'm speaking to you."

The touch of irritation in her mother's voice sparked Gia's anger.

"*You* had an understanding, Mom. Why can't I go out with my friends? Why do you have to be so—" She clenched her fists in frustration. She hated the sound of her own voice when things got like this. She hated fighting. Her face got hot and words came out, and she did not even know if she meant them.

"*I came home before midnight,*" was what she wanted to say, but that was dangerously close to the forbidden topic.

Midnight. Full moon. Where were you last night, Mom? Where do you go?

Saraswati hitched the strap of her handbag higher on her shoulder.

"I don't have time for this now—"

"Then why did you start it?" flashed Gia.

They stood there, staring at one another. Gia could almost see the unspoken words that gathered round them. She waited, flinching, for Saraswati to snatch them and fling them at her like knives. But Saraswati just shook her head, and her voice was soft, and tired.

"Please don't talk like that, Gia. As if I am your enemy."

A small part of Gia wanted to rush to her mother, bury her face in her hair, as she'd so recently been able to do. She wanted to say— She did not know what she wanted to say, but all she could do was wrap her arms around herself, look away, and keep her expression stony.

After a pause, Saraswati spoke again.

"I'm taking Nico to Mrs Winterbach's. If you could help Mandy?"

Gia nodded and turned back to the gate.

Great, she thought as she stomped up the stairs.

Now it's my fault. I'm the horrible one. Why can't she just leave me alone? All I did was get back a bit late. It's not like I was getting drunk or taking drugs, or whatever it is she thinks I'm doing.

She slammed the front door behind her.

၈၀O၀၃

Gia sat at the kitchen table, helping Mandy sort through dress patterns that had been mixed up in the move. Each envelope had to be opened and the contents checked, and then marked off on a list. It was boring work but Gia did not complain. Fighting with her mother was one thing, but Mandy was not to be trifled with.

They had just finished one pile when there was a knock on the front door, followed by somebody trying the doorknob.

"Special Branch, open up!"

Mandy's eyes went wide. She opened her mouth to say something, when the knock came again. "Open up, Mr, uh, Grobbelaar. This is Special Branch!"

Seeing Mandy frozen, Gia ran for the shaking door. She must have forgotten to lock the burglar gate again.

Mom's going to kill me.

"Okay, just give me a chance!"

She pulled out her keys, then hesitated. Shouldn't she call her father up from the studio?

But how?

He never answered the phone, and there was no time — The door was shaking again.

She got the key in the lock and opened the door on the chain.

"Who — ?"

"Special Branch Sniffer Unit 332. I'm Constable Brand, and this is Controller Mba."

A big man with a tired face held out a piece of paper. There was somebody else, two people, Gia thought, but it was difficult to see.

"What's this?" came her father's voice from the stairs behind them.

Gia breathed in relief.

Constable Brand stepped back, and now Gia could see his companions; a black woman in the Special Branch uniform, her broad build emphasised by her bulletproof vest, and a man whose face was hidden under a hood.

"Routine search," Constable Brand was saying. "We have a warrant to—"

"Why are you here?" said Karel. "By what right do you come barging in here?"

A chill of unease touched Gia's spine.

He is afraid.

Constable Brand held out the paper patiently. "Sir, we have a warrant—"

But the female officer did not wait for him to finish. With no change to her placid expression, she rammed the door with her shoulder. Gia jumped back as the chain snapped and the door slammed back against the wall.

"Come," the policewoman said to the hooded man, and tugged him after her. She had him on some kind of leash.

Gia glimpsed an impossible face under the hood, and nearly choked at the stench of rancid cat pee that trailed in his wake. Seeing them heading for the kitchen, she ran after them.

In the kitchen, Mandy stood behind the table. The policewoman faced her impassively.

"Controller Mba, just a minute," said Constable Brand. "Stay where you are, Mamma," he said to Mandy. "And you, miss, go and stand there by her."

"This is unacceptable," said Karel. "Who is your superior—"

"Sir, could you stand there by the table."

Karel stepped abruptly closer to Constable Brand, and Controller Mba put a hand on her holster.

"What is going on here?"

Saraswati stood in the kitchen door. She had spoken softly, but there was a chill in her voice that drew everyone's attention.

Constable Brand was the first to react.

"Just a routine inspection, Madam," he said. "Looking for traces of illegal magicals and magical activity."

Before Saraswati could respond, he turned to the controller.

"Free his hands," he said. "But watch he doesn't mess anything. I've had enough trouble with that one."

The controller jerked on the leash and the man held up his bound hands.

Gia was trembling with tension. She forced herself to look at the man's hands, not knowing what it was she feared to see. He had large, pale hands with a light dusting of ginger hair; the fingers of his left hand were stained yellow with nicotine. The controller released the straps from around his wrists, and led the man out of the kitchen.

Constable Brand looked at his clipboard.

"Now. Let's get this done. Mr Karel Grobbelaar—"

As the constable asked them their names and identity numbers, they could hear the controller and her companion moving around the house. There were sounds of drawers opening, and furniture moving. Gia, who stood close beside her father, felt him flinch at each new bang and scrape. The constable seemed oblivious to the noise.

"And that is everyone who lives here?" he asked tiredly. "What about— " He glanced at his file. "Niccolo Grobbelaar. He is not here?"

Constable Brand looked questioningly at Saraswati, but she stared back at him and did not reply. "Is there a Niccolo Grobbelaar at this address?"

Gia wanted to answer, but the look on her mother's face silenced her.

The constable's gaze shifted to Karel. When he did not get a reaction, he sighed.

"Sir, Madam, you are just making things difficult here. Is there a Niccolo Grobbelaar at this address?"

Once again, there was no response, and Gia had to bite back the urge to fill the awkward silence.

There was thud from the living room, a crash of something falling and then a sound that Gia could not at first identify — a delicate pattering sound, like a trickle of rainwater on leaves. It was only when she saw the look on her mother's face that she realised what it was.

Beads. All those little bottles of beads, spilling out onto the floor.

Then the controller and her companion came back into the kitchen. She shook her head at the constable's enquiring look.

"Low level, old stuff," she said. "No traces of recent magical activity so far."

"Check through there," the constable indicated the pantry behind the kitchen. "And then you can come and do this lot."

He sighed, dug his fingers into his neck, and rolled his shoulders. Cupboards opened and closed in the pantry. Gia felt her father's arm go round her, and turned to bury her face in his shoulder, breathing in his comforting smell.

Would they see her trapdoor?

She shuddered as she imagined those pale, hairy hands pawing through her clothes.

And what about the haarskeerder? Surely they would pick up traces –

"Sir!"

"Controller?"

"We've found some items, sir."

Mandy stirred, attracting the constable's attention. She tried to speak, then had to stop to clear her throat.

"Those things," she managed at last. "Those things in the cupboards, they're not ours. We just moved here. The woman who used to live here, it's all hers."

The controller put a box on the table. It was clear from the dust and cobwebs that the box had not been opened for some time.

"Back of the cupboard, Sir. Good readings."

"Recent?"

She shrugged. "Hard to tell." In response to the constable's raised eyebrows, she continued, reluctantly. "Not recent. Old."

"Hmm." The constable flipped open one flap of the box with his pen and peered inside, then shook his head.

"Nothing worth noting. This thing has not been opened for years. Well, let's finish here then. We don't want any trouble now, so let's get this over with. One at a time, each of you come and stand here."

He pointed at Mandy. "We'll begin with you, Mamma."

Gia felt her father stir, and saw that Saraswati gripped his arm. Mandy made a small noise in her throat, then stepped forward.

The controller tugged the hooded man toward her. "Hold your arms out to the sides, Mamma," she said to Mandy.

Gia watched in fascinated horror as the man slid back his hood.

He had the face of a fighting dog, broad in the jaw as a pit-bull. His muzzle was criss-crossed with many scars, and he had two large wolf ears, notched and torn. A wide leather strap bound his jaw and passed round the back of his head. The leash, Gia saw, was attached to this muzzle in such a way that the controller's tugs twisted his head with little chance of resistance.

Gia could not see Mandy's face, but she could see the fear in the lift of her shoulders and her trembling hands. She wanted to go to her, but felt her father holding her back.

The man— *the werewolf*— bent toward Mandy and sniffed, first at her hands, then at her face, then a quick pass over her body. He snorted and stood back.

"Next."

With a start, Gia saw that the controller was looking at her. Her heart hammered as she stepped forward, aware of a sudden pressure in her bladder. She had to fight down the urge to giggle.

Please God, let me not wet myself.

"Hold your arms out."

The werewolf moved closer and she stared at it, transfixed. Russet fur curled over his collar, and the muzzle had rubbed raw patches under his eyes. He had something in his mouth, a piece of metal like the bit of a bridle that passed under his tongue. The straps that bound his jaw were stained with saliva.

Unable to help herself, she looked into his eyes.

Human eyes.

He blinked, and his eyes rolled slowly, as though he were drunk or dazed.

Chemically neutered.

Then he focused on her, and lowered his head to sniff.

This close, she could smell his stench. Musky urine, and something like wet dog and old cigarettes. She flinched as his whiskers brushed across her cheek. She could feel his breath on her skin. His nose touched her stomach, and then her hands. She was about to step back when he gripped her wrist and wrenched it upward.

A word-like growl came from the muzzled jaws, and the werewolf rolled his eyes toward the controller.

Gia stared at her arm, unable for a moment, to understand what the werewolf had found.

Then she understood.

The troll-bouncer's thumb-print.

The controller peered at her arm. "What's this?"

"Uh," Gia had to swallow to get her voice back. "It's just— ink. A stamp from a nightclub I went to."

She licked her lips, aware of her parents listening.

"What nightclub?" said Constable Brand. "And why would their stamp have magical residue?"

"The Playground." She wanted to turn to see her mother's reaction. "They have a— um. A troll for a bouncer. That's his mark. It's just ink."

At a sign from the controller, the werewolf released her arm and she stood back, rubbing at the thumbprint.

"That place was raided last night," said Constable Brand. "What were you doing there? That's not a place for a young girl."

"Just dancing. With my friends."

"Hmm."

With relief, she saw that he was not going to ask any more questions.

"You next, sir."

Karel held out his arms and the werewolf sniffed him over quickly.

"Nothing there," said the controller.

"Next."

Saraswati moved forward, and for a moment Gia thought that her father would intervene. But he did nothing.

Gia could see her mother's face as she looked up at the werewolf, who was much taller than she was. The creature lowered its head in a grotesque parody of a lover seeking a kiss, but only sniffed at her face. Then the heavy muzzle moved along her arm, down toward her hand where it snorted and jerked back, stung.

"Hold," said the controller.

Saraswati stood without moving as the policewoman reached out and gingerly pulled back her sleeve to reveal the ornate silver bracelet around Saraswati's wrist.

"Silver," said the controller in some disgust. "Nothing there. All clean."

ೞOಋ

As soon as the police had left, Saraswati walked swiftly to the living room.

Gia followed and found her mother on her knees, surrounded by beads.

"It's not as bad as I thought," she said, looking up. "They didn't touch the dress. Just the bead containers got knocked over. Careful! Don't step on them."

This last was to Karel, who'd pushed past Gia.

"It could be worse," he said, stepping back reluctantly. "At least they did not go into the studio. Or at least they better not—"

"They've left" said Mandy from the door. "I saw them drive away."

"Well." Karel sighed with obvious relief. "That's all right then."

"We can sort the beads later, Madam," said Mandy. "Let's just pick them up for now."

Leaving her mother and Mandy sweeping up beads, Gia went to lock the burglar gate at the street entrance. She felt shaky, but somehow excited, and wanted badly to tell somebody what had happened.

I wonder what Fatima and Ben are up to.

She found Mandy and Saraswati still hunting for beads under the furniture.

"Mom, can I go and—"

"No." Saraswati did not even look at Gia. She sounded tired, her voice flat. "No going out tonight. And no visits from friends today."

Gia opened her mouth to argue, then thought better of it.

Oh well. I'll ask again later, when she's calmed down.

As she watched, Saraswati picked up something from the floor and looked down at it for a moment— a tear-shaped bead, blood-red in her white palm.

ஐOஐ

Gia spent the rest of the day helping Saraswati.

The concept drawing of Kavitha's wedding gown had to be redrawn. At the moment it was just an idea sketch. It had to be turned into a design for a real, three-dimensional garment. The work seemed to calm Saraswati, and she recovered some of her vitality. Soon they were sitting amid a pile of reference books and magazines, working out the best way to achieve the look suggested by the sketch. Because of the complexity of the design, Saraswati planned to create a toile: a test gown made out of an inexpensive fabric. This toile would be used to test the dress before creating the final version in silk.

Saraswati was an expert at modelling draping fabric directly on the dressmaker's dummy, an art that required skill as well as patience.

It was a new experience for Gia to work with her mother. She helped her father often. Karel was an excellent teacher, but he could be impatient, and learning from him was often a case of watching what he did and trying to keep up. Gia found her mother's method very different.

They were partners, fellow explorers rather than teacher and pupil. Where Karel decided on the design first, and then planned out the pattern to fit it, Saraswati worked directly with the fabric; pinching, lifting and folding it. Searching for the potential garment in the way the fabric draped and fell from her hands. She was as interested in Gia's ideas as in her own.

Right now, however, she used some of Karel's techniques, drawing a tentative mock-up of the design before she started draping the toile.

As she watched her mother draw, Gia wished that it could always be like this. These days, every interaction seemed to turn into a fight, and every situation a misunderstanding. If only she could stop herself from getting so irritated with Saraswati, or at least from showing her irritation.

Her thoughts went back to the events of that morning.

It's a good thing Nico wasn't home.

Her parents clearly did not want Nico involved in the search, or why else would they refuse to tell the police where he was?

Because he is a – changeling?

But that was absurd. Whatever that Special Branch captain had said at school, Nico was just Nico. Why would the police be interested in a seven-year-old boy?

She remembered Mrs Solomons, the social worker who had questioned her. That woman had seemed particularly interested in Nico, too. For a moment Gia hesitated on the brink of telling her mother about the Special Branch talk and the social worker's questions.

But she'll ask me why I've not told her before. She will get angry, and we'll be fighting again. Rather leave it.

"Gia, what do you think of this one?" Saraswati pushed a drawing towards her. "The waist is a bit bulky," she said. "The back of the bodice extends down into this folded bit here, and then drapes down into the skirt."

"Is it one continuous piece?" asked Gia. "That's pretty much how I pictured it. Would that be possible?"

She reached for the pencil, forgetting her doubts as she was drawn into the challenge of turning pen and ink into three dimensions of sculpted cloth.

༂Oൽ

The rest of the afternoon was without drama, although everyone still felt the reverberations of the invasion. Karel went to fetch Nico, and Mandy, who was still rattled by the search, burned supper. Saraswati insisted that they could not afford to buy takeaways, so their evening meal was an unpleasant affair. Gia, who would normally have complained or refused to eat, ate quietly enough, not wanting to disturb the fragile peace. She comforted herself with the thought of the cardboard box the police had found in the pantry cupboards.

Mandy had refused to touch it after the police left, and no one else seemed particularly interested, so Gia had smuggled it upstairs to her room, planning to have a close look at it after supper.

There must be something interesting about it, to make that werewolf think it's magical.

It was only much later that evening, when everyone else had gone to bed, that she got her chance.

After double-checking that the trapdoor was bolted, she opened the box. It was filled with small boxes and bottles, all very old and covered in dust. Some of the things she recognised, such as the Sky Blue brand laundry bluing, which she knew from Mandy was often used in purification rituals. Other things were not so familiar.

A spice-bottle with a handwritten label that said "Rattlesnake Salt".

Another full of black powder that was unexpectedly heavy for its size.

So far, not very exciting.

She lifted out one of the small cardboard boxes. It had once been brightly coloured, and even now, faded with years, it was pretty under its coat of dust.

Curly writing in what she supposed was Arabic script, surrounded a calligraphic painting of a rose and several rose-hips. There was a label stuck on this one too, with the same handwriting.

Rose-hip tea, it said. *Small pinch in water just off the boil. A talkative tea, lazy, but without guile. Partial to honey. Very particular about its china. Use a quality cup.*

Gia's eyebrows went up.

Now that sounds interesting.

She carried the box over to the tea corner where she'd set up the kettle and mugs.

Might as well try some of this.

She went downstairs to fill the kettle and get some honey. After some hesitation, she went to the living room and opened the glass-fronted cabinet where the good china was kept. She took one of the cups, a delicate rose-pink china so thin it was nearly transparent.

Better not break this.

"Gia."

Her heart bumped, and she nearly dropped the cup.

"Nico," she whispered. "What are you doing up? Go back to bed."

Nico stood in the door, blinking sleepily at her.

"Tea," he said, looking at the cup in her hands.

"Nico. You're supposed to be in bed."

She expected to hear her parents' bed creaking, and her mother's voice asking what was going on.

Nico opened his mouth to say something else.

"No," Gia hissed. "Shh! Don't speak."

He closed his mouth, and stood there, staring up at her. Something stirred at the breast of his pyjamas, and Poepie's head emerged, whiskers twitching.

"And you're not supposed to have that rat out at night, anyway."

Nico shrugged. Gia saw that she was not going to get him back into his bed without a fuss.

"Okay, then," she said. "Come along with me. But you've got to promise to be quiet. And don't touch anything. Okay?"

He followed her up the stairs to her room, where he looked about with interest.

"No, you don't," said Gia. "Don't touch anything. Sit there." She indicated the bed. "And don't let Poepie run around."

Nico sat obediently. Now that he had his way, he was perfectly willing to do as he was told. He watched with interest as Gia switched on the kettle and dropped a pinch of the rose-hip tea into the cup.

When the water finally boiled, Gia let it cool for a few seconds, then carefully poured a little onto the tealeaves.

The air filled with the fragrance of a sunny rose garden. Curls of steam rose from the tealeaves, then more, and more and for a moment Gia wondered if the water had been too hot.

Nico sat forward, peering at the steaming cup, as fascinated as she was. Even Poepie was staring, ears forward, eyes bright, whiskers stiff as bristles.

Instead of drifting away, the steam gathered over the cup, forming a small cloud. It curled around itself in a curious way. Was it her imagination, or was it shaping itself into —

"*Salaam aleikum!*" said a voice. "Some more hot water, if you would be so kind, my mistress."

Gia nearly dropped the kettle in her surprise, but quickly added a bit more water to the teacup, careful to keep her hand well away from the steam which was now taking a definite shape.

Nico's eyes were wide, but he did not seem to be

frightened. He slipped off the bed, rat cupped in both hands.

"Nico!" whispered Gia, but he ignored her, squatting down next to her and staring at the steaming cup.

"Ah," sighed the voice. "That's better. Gives me more puff, you know."

Gia could see the speaker now. The steam had shaped itself into a tiny figure that drifted over the teacup.

He had a plump face topped by a neat white turban. His head and shoulders were distinctly visible, but lower down his body became transparent and faded out into curls of steam.

"Mrs Moses is no longer with us, I presume?" he said.

For a moment Gia was at a loss. Then she remembered that the caretaker had referred to Mrs Moses, too.

"Is that the woman who used to live here?"

The tea genie nodded gravely. "Indeed, Mrs Moses was resident in this house— if this is number five, Lever Road? I've not been in *this* room before, my mistress used to receive me in her sitting room."

He looked about the attic, and Gia wished she'd taken the time to tidy it before experimenting with the tea.

"Nico!" said Gia. Nico had slipped the rat into the collar of his pyjamas, and was about to poke a finger into the steam.

"Get back. Now!"

He shot her a measuring look and apparently decided that she was in earnest, as he returned to his seat on the bed.

The genie took no notice of this exchange. He was peering at the cup below him.

"I cannot fault your taste in china. A most becoming cup. What is its mark?"

"I don't know," said Gia.

"Oh well. Never mind. But I am forgetting myself. Introductions are in order."

He drew himself up, then bowed deeply and declaimed: "Salaam Aleikum, young mistress. I am Maarouf Asghar, genie of the rose-hip tea. Your wish is my command."

"Salaam," said Gia, hoping this was the appropriate greeting. "Um. I'm Gia. And this is my brother Nico."

Then she bit her lip. *Weren't you supposed to keep your name secret from magical beings? Oh well, too late now.*

Remembering the stories she'd heard about genies, she decided to be careful.

"What exactly do you mean by *your wish is my command?*" she asked. "Is there a limit to the number of wishes?"

"Not at all. Although I cannot promise that I will be able to grant them all. Is that a rat?"

He looked at Poepie with distaste.

"Yes," said Gia. "His name is Poepie. He's Nico's pet."

Nico held Poepie out for inspection and for a moment the genie and the rat studied one another.

"So," said Gia. "What can you do?"

The genie bobbed around on his column of steam to look at her. "You do like to get to the point, don't you," he said. "Very well. I am a genie of the cup. The cup, not lamp or drum, so my powers are, shall we say, circumscribed. But I am by no means a weak tea. Not at all. I prefer to refer to my abilities as *subtle*." He adjusted his robe. "Not everybody needs to go around building castles, or creating entire armies out of thin air. Obvious, and crude."

"Of course," said Gia, seeing that this was a sore point. "I would never ask for anything like that."

The genie seemed mollified. "My expertise lies in finer skills. I can provide small items of clothing and food, unlock doors, find items you have mislaid, sort, count, weigh, and measure. I can also answer questions, although of course, only on topics of which I have knowledge.

"For example, I can spy on your lover— provided he is not warded— but I cannot tell you what he is thinking, or what he might do. I cannot foretell the future or read minds. And my strength is limited at all times by my tea. When that has drawn past a certain point, I will fade, and only wake again if you add another pinch to the cup."

"I see," said Gia and opened her mouth to say something more, but Nico had his own ideas.

"Supper!" he said, and before Gia could say anything, the genie drew himself up again and flourished both hands.

"Your wish is my command!"

There was a pop of displaced air and a plate appeared next to the genie's teacup. Then with three more pops, a knife, fork, and serviette. The plate was blue and white china, and it held a piece of pie and a baked potato, split open and topped with a pat of butter.

Nico gave a squeak— a similar plate and cutlery had appeared on the bed next to him.

"Wow! Thanks!" said Gia, and reached for the fork, breathing in the delicious scent of chicken pie and melting butter. Then she paused.

A piece of the pie was missing. And on closer inspection, both the knife and fork had clearly just been used.

She put the fork down.

"Don't touch it, Nico," she said sharply. Nico gave her a startled look and put the plate down again.

"This is somebody's supper, isn't it?" said Gia to the genie.

The genie shrugged. "Of course. The food has to come from somewhere. You surely don't expect me to make it from scratch."

Gia was horrified. "You just took somebody's food out from in front of them? You've got to put it back!"

The genie looked mulish.

"At once!"

"If you insist." With a sulky look he made a gesture and the plates disappeared again.

"Oh!" said Nico.

Poepie jumped off his arm and sniffed at the spot where the plate had been. Gia was not sure which of them looked the most baffled.

"I only follow your orders," said the genie huffily. "Do make up your mind. Do you want food, or not?"

"I didn't know you were going to do it like that." Gia frowned. "What if I gave you some money? Then you could get me some food, and leave some money in exchange. But it's got to be something that's already for sale. From a shop, or a restaurant."

"Very particular, you are."

Gia found her wallet and dug out a few rands.

"I'd like another pie. And one for Nico too." The words were hardly spoken when the money disappeared from between her fingers, and a moment later two paper-wrapped parcels plopped down: one on the table, and one on the bed.

"Happy now?" said the genie.

"Yes, thank you," said Gia. The parcel bore the label "Mamma's Pies" and the pie inside was quite cold. Nico bit into his, sending a cloud of dry pastry flakes drifting onto her bed.

Gia thought with regret of the golden pastry of the vanished supper.

"Don't you want something too?" said Gia, remembering the instructions on the tea box. "Some honey, maybe?"

"Honey? Well now," said the genie, swaying on his column of steam. "I would not say no to a drop or two." He watched avidly as she opened the jar, and added a teaspoon of honey into the cup.

"Ah," he closed his eyes. "No, don't stir. Just leave the spoon in, don't want to waste any."

Gia ate her pie, watching with amusement.

The genie seemed to enjoy honey as though it were a scented bath oil, breathing in the fragrance that rose from the cup below him. He glowed with pleasure, the wisps of steam that made up his not-quite-solid body changing hue from pink to purple, or glowing in little honey-coloured spangles.

It almost made up for the dryness of the pie, which was mostly crust.

Nico gave Poepie a lump of pastry to nibble on, and happily ate the rest of his pie.

"If you can find lost things," said Gia quickly, while Nico's mouth was still too full to speak, "can you tell me what happened to the haarskeerder that disappeared from here the other day?"

"Hey?" The genie seemed to have some trouble focusing. "You've lost a haarskeerder?" He yawned. "How very careless."

"My cat caught it and brought it in," said Gia. "So I helped it get clean, but then it just went missing. I think it's still around." There was no answer. Gia found that the genie's sleepiness was infectious. Her own eyes were closing and she suddenly felt very tired.

Nico's head was nodding too, and in a moment he had curled up on top of her blankets, with Poepie nestled up against his chin. Still, she shouldn't sleep yet. It was a waste, not to get the genie to do more things for her.

His words swam into her memory.

"… *find items you have mislaid, sort, count…*"

She jerked awake.

"Wait," she said. "You can sort things? And find lost things?"

"Yes," said the genie sleepily.

"Do you have to be able to see the things to sort them?"

"Ideally, yes. And be in the same room as the lost things, to find them. Why?"

Gia unbolted the trapdoor and looked down into the house below, listening. All was dark and quiet. Nico was fast asleep.

"Come," she said, picking up the genie's cup with both hands. She carried him over to the trapdoor.

"Where are we going?" said the genie, looking down the ladder. "Surely not—"

"Shush," whispered Gia. "We don't want to wake anyone. No more speaking."

She climbed down the ladder, careful not to jar the genie or tilt the cup.

He bobbed gently as she climbed, glancing nervously at the drop below, but to Gia's relief he kept quiet.

The house was dark, but the genie's glow was just strong enough for her to make her way to the living room without bumping into anything.

She knelt down and put the cup on the floor.

"Now," she breathed. "See that box over there?"

The genie peered, then nodded.

"It's full of beads. All mixed up. Can you sort them? There's a whole bunch of little bottles and tubes in there as well. Put each kind in its own container. Do I have to open the box?"

"It would be easier."

Gia opened the box and took out the large jar that contained all the beads. Then she unpacked the little containers, popping open their lids.

"There's probably some beads on the floor still," she whispered. "Under the furniture, or in the cracks between the floorboards. Find those, and sort them too."

"Your wish is my command." The genie bowed deeply, and came out of his bow with his hands flourishing.

Gia had expected him to be a little sulky at being asked to perform another task so soon, but it was clear that he was enjoying himself.

At first, nothing happened. Then, like a miniature earthquake, the beads in the jar started to shift about.

"Hmm," said the genie. "By colour, and by shape. And size too, I presume."

She could hear the beads moving now, rasping against the side of the jar.

Then without warning the jar leaped, and Gia had to jump forward to stop it from falling over as a fountain of beads rushed up into the air. She ducked, expecting to hear the crash as they hit the floor but instead, the beads separated into multiple strands of colour, like searching tendrils. Soon each strand earthed itself in a small container and pattered neatly down inside.

Gia had hardly recovered from her surprise before the last bead tinkled into place and it was all over.

"Wow!" she breathed. "How did you do that! That was amazing!"

The genie beamed with pleasure.

"Ah, that was nothing. A few beads, a few colours—" He shrugged modestly. "But we're not done yet. There are still beads on the floor?"

He closed his eyes.

"Ah. Yes indeed."

Gia felt a light breeze, and with a series of clinks and plinks, a few more beads dropped into various containers.

"And that," said the genie, brushing off his hands with a satisfied air, "is that. Your wish, my mistress, has been granted."

৫০O৫

Back in her attic bedroom, Gia gave the genie another teaspoon of honey.

"You deserve it," she said, which made the genie glow anew with pleasure.

"If you could just put me over there by the window, my dear, then I could look out at the view as I fade. I do so love seeing the lights at night." He sighed deeply. "Candlelight, it used to be. Or lamplight. Or when I was with the soldiers, hundreds of campfires glowing away into the distance…"

Gia fitted his cup into the space between the edge of her mattress and the window. She packed the tea back into the box.

Nico was still fast asleep. She doubted she could wake him, and he was too heavy to carry all the way down to his bedroom. She moved him to the side of the bed and pulled the blankets over him, checking that the rat was safely in his pocket. Then she switched off the light, and crawled in next to him, propping up her pillow so that she could share the genie's view.

His glow reminded her of the night-light she'd had when she was very little and too afraid to sleep in the dark.

"Good night," she said.

"Good night." The genie yawned.

శాOœ

THE SILVER WEB

The next morning, Gia got a very sleepy Nico down and into his own bed before her parents woke. Then she went out for a run. Sunday mornings were always best for running.

She still had to figure out the routes in this new neighbourhood. Walmer Estate streets were steep and narrow. Rows of parked cars forced her to run along the middle of the road, which was just as well, as the sidewalks were dangerous even for walking. It seemed as if every second drain cover was missing, and no one picked up after their dogs.

The streets in Plumstead had been wide and clean. Gia wondered if the street-cleaning trucks ever reached these narrow roads. Or did they only go to the richer suburbs? It had been part of her old life, the sharp stink of the stuff they sprayed against snaartjies and vrekkers, and other small magicals.

That was one thing that Saraswati would appreciate about this neighbourhood, thought Gia. Her mother hated the smell of the street-cleaners. She always stayed indoors when they were anywhere near, and never allowed Nico outside either.

The Plumstead streets might be easier, but there was something exhilarating about running up a street as steep as a staircase, finding that perfect rhythm of step and breath.

She paused on a corner, gasping. *Not as fit as I thought!* She laughed at herself.

The view was spectacular. She could see all the way over the harbour, over the bay, beyond Bloubergstrand and Table View to the mountains beyond. Behind her rose the slopes of Devil's Peak, orange in the early morning light. Gia eyed it speculatively.

Now that would be a great place to run.

Getting up to the mountain proved more difficult that she'd guessed. De Waal Drive cut off all easy access and even on a Sunday morning there was enough traffic to make the crossing difficult. Cars came speeding round the bends, and there was no stretch straight enough to give her a long view of approaching traffic. At last she took a gap, and was across the freeway. The mountain surrounded her, the crunch of its soil under her feet, the scent of fynbos, the sounds of small life stirring.

Running was tricky.

It would be easy to twist an ankle amid the stones, but this was worlds better than tar and cars. She could stay up here all day. Run all the way around to Newlands, maybe. But not today. Gia slowed to a walk and let herself think about the events of the past week.

School was not so bad these days. She was getting on with the other students, and she'd found a new friend in Sonella. Working for her parents cut into her time, but the work was interesting, she couldn't deny that.

So much had happened since the move. There was her encounter with the haarskeerder. That had been pretty strange. She wondered where it was. And the tea genie had been even stranger.

She found a smooth rock and sat, looking down the slope to the city below. There was something about being high up above everything that made her troubles shrink back to manageable size. Even the inspection yesterday no longer seemed quite as portentous. Yet, it had been frightening. A sniffer unit search was not something she'd ever experienced before.

And what about Nico? He would have been frightened if he'd been there, but her mother's reaction had suggested something more. As if there was something about Nico that she'd wanted to hide.

Why was everyone suddenly so interested in Nico?

She though back to the Special Branch presentation. Then there had been Mrs Solomons, who'd asked so many odd questions about him. And now this sniffer unit.

Was Nico a "changeling"? Had the sniffer unit been sent specially to find him? But that was absurd.

In any case, according to Captain Witbooi, the Special Branch Children's Unit was the perfect place to *help* Nico. They would see his potential. Maybe he would be another one like that girl, the cadet. She'd spoken as though Special Branch had rescued her. Was it right to deny Nico the chance?

Gia sighed in frustration.

Maybe she was allowing other people's fears to cloud her own. Mrs Huisman had warned her against Special Branch. She'd made Gia feel as if the few words she'd spoken to the cadet had been a dangerous mistake. As though by attracting their attention to her, she'd exposed herself somehow.

The memory of the werewolf rose again, but she found it difficult now to understand why she'd been so frightened of it. It was just a poor, misshapen creature. It must have been her mother's reaction that had influenced her own fears.

It was understandable that Saraswati had seen the search as a terrifying experience. Saraswati, who had fled from Europe when she was only a little older than Gia.

Gia got up. Already the roar of traffic was increasing, and pretty soon it would be impossible to get back across De Waal Drive safely. She stretched and shook her hands to warm them. The sun had not burned away the morning chill yet, and the rock she'd been sitting on was cold. She walked quickly back down to the road, not wanting to risk a fall by running downhill.

Crossing the freeway was decidedly more difficult on the way back. She had to stand on the central island for a long time, getting the courage up for the last dash to safety. A blare of hooters sent adrenaline rushing, but she made it across at last.

Then she was back among the steep roads of Walmer Estate. Running downhill was never as comfortable as uphill and Gia came around a corner just a little too fast. She had to jump into the road to avoid a large man who stooped over some rubbish bags. He reared up, scattering bits of rubbish and cursing at her.

"Sorry!" said Gia, and then she had a proper look at him.

Grey skin, and eyes like raisins sunk deeply into unbaked dough. Teeth like dried chickpeas. The stench of rotten eggs breathed off him, and Gia had fight the urge to gag.

The walg swayed where he stood, looking her up and down, as if he considered adding her to his bag of scraps. Gia took another step backward, and was about to run the way she'd come when a car braked next to her.

"Hey! You! Get back to your business!"

It was a Special Branch patrol car, with two officers in bulletproof vests. The one in the driver's seat gestured at the walg. "Get back to your rubbish. Or do you want trouble?"

The walg turned its tiny eyes to the car, then back to Gia.

"*Voetsek!*" said the policeman, and the walg shrugged, picked up its rubbish bags and shuffled off down the road.

"Sorry about that, miss," said the policeman. "You by yourself?"

Gia nodded.

He looked her up and down in a way that was not entirely friendly.

"You better watch it," he said. "Get into trouble running about alone around here. That thing there, he'd like a nice snack, if you give him the chance."

Before Gia could think of an answer, the car revved its engine, and accelerated off down the street.

Gia gave up on running and walked the last few blocks home.

ೞO೦ಽ

There was a knock on the bathroom door. Gia heard her mother's voice, but could not make out the words.

"I'm just getting out!" she said, pulling out the bath plug.

"Gia, is Ben coming, do you know?"

"He said so." She wrapped a towel round herself. A look in the living room showed what had prompted her mother's question.

Nico had cleared everything off the table, and was setting up the game he and Ben played.

It was a simple card-game called "Mystic Forest", but Ben and Nico between them had modified it almost beyond recognition, adding new cards and changing the rules until Gia had only a vague idea of how it worked. Nico had laid out all the starting cards, and was now carefully straightening them so that the rows were exactly aligned.

No wonder Saraswati seemed a little anxious. There would be a major melt-down if Ben did not show up.

Up in her room, dressing, Gia saw that Ben had sent a message to her texter.

"He's coming, Mom," she shouted down the hatch. "He says he'll be here at nine."

The other message was from Sonella, asking whether it was still fine for her to come round.

Gia briefly considered asking her mother's permission, then discarded that idea. If Saraswati was happy for Ben to visit, she'd couldn't have a problem with Sonella.

"Come any time," she replied, and pocketed the texter.

Mandy had Sundays off, so Gia had to do the breakfast dishes. The doorbell rang just as she rinsed the last bowl. Saraswati pushed the button that released the lower gate just as Gia got to the front door.

"Ben!" said Nico, jumping on the spot.

"I hope so, my darling," said Saraswati as she opened the front door. "But let's just see..."

A hand appeared around the edge of the door.

"Beware," said a voice from outside. "I am the boy-snatcher!"

Nico gasped with excitement and grabbed Gia round the waist, half hiding behind her.

"Benbenben!"

The door swung all the way open, and Ben stood there, grinning at them. He clapped both hands to his hips like a cartoon cowboy, and with a flick, drew two cards and held them out.

"Made two new ones," he drawled. "Manticore and Mandragyn. Read them and weep!"

"Salt! Salt!" shouted Nico, and rushed into the living room to fetch the appropriate card.

"Morning, Tannie," said Ben to Saraswati in his normal voice. "Hi, Gia. What a cool place!"

He admired the entrance hall which Gia had to admit looked much better now that all the boxes were cleared out, and Saraswati had put up the wall hangings.

"I'm so glad you could come, Ben; you are an angel," said Saraswati, leaning in to give him a quick kiss. "How is your mother?"

"Oh, she's fine. Her turn to entertain the church ladies again, so she's in her element."

Gia privately suspected that Ben's Sunday visits were as much to get away from his mother's social events, as visiting her or Nico.

"Salt, salt, salt!" chanted Nico from the living room.

"I'd better get in there," said Ben.

Gia was about to follow him, when she heard a voice echoing up the stairwell.

"Hello? Hi, Gia?"

"Sonella!" she called. "Come on up!"

She pressed the gate button and heard the clang as the lock released. "Mom," she said as Sonella came into view. "This is Sonella, my new friend from school. I told you about her, remember?"

"Oh?" said Saraswati. "Good morning, Sonella."

She smiled at Sonella, who stood in the door looking a little stunned.

"Good morning, Saras— I mean, Mrs Gotti-Grobbelaar?" She blushed furiously.

"I'm Mrs Grobbelaar, really," said Saraswati calmly, ignoring the girl's confusion. "Gotti is really just a name for stuff related to the business. But you can call me Saraswati."

Sonella swallowed and smiled nervously but seemed to relax a little. "It's such an honour to meet you. I've been collecting pictures of your dresses all my life. Especially the bird dresses. Those are so lovely. I saw the Peacock Dress at the National Gallery but I could not get close to it as there were so many other people…" Sonella stumbled to a halt and blushed again.

"I'm busy on a new one," said Saraswati. "Would you like to see it? It's only just started, so there's not much to see."

"Oh, could I? I'd love to."

"In here." Saraswati led the way into the living room.

"Ben, have you met Gia's friend Sonella?" she said.

"Hi there." Ben raised the cup he was holding in greeting, then rattled it and rolled the dice.

"Seven! Basted!" declared Nico and flipped over several of the cards.

"Basted and battered!" said Ben pointing at the last card.

"No use talking to them when they're playing," said Saraswati. She pulled away the cloth that covered her work table.

"I've not really unpacked these yet," she said, opening one of the boxes. "I keep meaning to work at them but something always gets in the way. These are some of the pieces I've made so far."

Sonella stared in admiration as Saraswati drew out the lengths of embroidered fabric.

Gia felt a stir of pride in her mother's work. Sunlight from the window fell directly on the embroidery, waking glints of deepest purple and emerald amid the glossy black of the thread.

"What is it this time? A crow?" asked Sonella.

"It might be," said Saraswati, and seeing Sonella's puzzled look, laughed.

"I don't always know what they are. This one started out being a gull. But it's turning out far too grand."

"Yes," agreed Sonella. "It could be a crow. One of those with the white breasts. *Witbors kraai.*"

Gia eyed the box that contained the beads.

Had she dreamed about the genie, and sorting them after all?

Saraswati reached for it now, and she got her answer in her mother's startled reaction. "Oh!" Saraswati looked up. "Gia? Did you?"

Gia felt herself blushing.

"Gia, was it you? Did you sort these beads for me?"

But Gia only shook her head. She could see that

her mother was moved almost to tears, and for some reason she felt hugely embarrassed.

"Well." Saraswati looked down at the box again, then with a visible effort, pulled herself together.

"These are the beads I've been collecting, Sonella," she said. "Some of these are older than I am." She reached into the box to extract one of the tubes, and the awkward moment passed.

As Sonella exclaimed over the beads, Gia got her mother's attention.

"Mom, can I give Sonella some of Dad's old magazines? The ones he's finished with?"

"Of course you may. There's a whole pile there behind the sofa. I keep meaning to throw them out. In fact, you girls would be doing me a big favour by sorting through them, and packing the ones you don't want into boxes. Let me go get some."

ಞО೧

Soon, Gia and Sonella were settled on the sofa surrounded by stacks of magazines. Sonella, once she was sure that she really was allowed to, paged until she saw something that caught her eye, removed the page with an expert tug and added it to the growing pile at her feet. Gia divided her attention between finding interesting pictures for Sonella, and watching Ben and Nico play.

She'd played the original, unmodified game of Mystic Forest herself, many years ago. Ben and Nico had been adding cards and making up new rules for more than a year now, and Gia could not decide if the modified game was just so baroque that an outsider could not make sense of it, or if there were no real rules at all, and Ben and Nico were making the game up as they went along.

Right now, they were going through a sequence where they would each roll the dice, play a slow hand-clapping game while they muttered a series of numbers, and then both would dart at the table and turn a card over and slap it down shouting "dead on!" or "salt!"

Saraswati sat at her worktable, embroidering her bird dress. With a sting of what felt almost like guilt, Gia realised that it had been a very long time since she'd seen her mother working on anything but client work.

She hardly ever gets a chance to work on her own stuff. It's always something for Dad, some wedding gown or matric dance dress.

"Grub's up!" Karel stood in the door, hands full of paper parcels.

"No, don't get up," he said to Sonella, handing her a parcel. "Have one of these— I think that's a beans bunny. Hi, you must be Sonella. Sari warned me we had visitors, so I made a quick run to Granny's for some food. Hello, Ben!"

"Gia," said Saraswati. "There are some paper plates in the cupboard next to the fridge. And some serviettes. And a damp cloth for wiping up."

Soon they were all sitting around the room eating.

Nico reluctantly left the game, and sat on the floor next to Ben, allowing his mother to dissect his bunny-chow into manageable pieces. Saraswati had introduced Nico to Sonella, but the boy hardly seemed to register her, his unfocused gaze sliding over her, then back to the food. To Gia's relief, Sonella was not at all startled or worried by her brother's obvious strangeness.

Karel perched on the arm of the sofa and ate his portion quickly, trading jokes with Ben. "Well," he said at last, sucking some sauce off a finger. "That was nice, but I've got to get back to work." He looked across at Saraswati. "Need your help, sweetheart. The lace gown. Bodice is just not sitting right. Can you come?"

Saraswati nodded. "I'll be right down." She cleaned her hands with the damp cloth, then folded the fabric she'd been working on and packed it away. She was still fitting the lid back on the box when the doorbell rang.

"Who on earth?" She frowned and went for the door. Gia heard her greet somebody, the surprise clear in her voice, and a moment later she was back.

"Nico," she said. "Here's a visitor for you."

She stood back, and the caretaker stepped into the room. He held his toolbox in one hand, and another box under his arm.

"Mr— um— Caretaker, this is Gia's friend Sonella. And this is Ben, an old friend of the family," said Saraswati.

The caretaker bowed his head briefly, but his attention was focused on Nico.

"Good afternoon, Nico," he said. "I brought you some things."

"Toy," said Nico.

"That's right," said the caretaker, and turned to Saraswati. "Just some old things I found. Might amuse him."

"That's very kind of you," said Saraswati and hesitated.

"Sari!" came Karel's voice from below.

"Just coming," called Saraswati, looking uncertainly at the caretaker. "I'll be right back. Gia, please make sure Nico does not make a nuisance of himself."

"It's okay, Mom," said Gia. "I'll look after things."

ಸO಼

When Saraswati was gone, the caretaker put down his boxes, and lowered himself to sit on the floor in front of Nico. Gia noticed that although he seemed to be an old man, he sat cross-legged with the ease of a child.

Nico watched as he opened the box to reveal an ancient tape recorder, the size and shape of a shoebox.

"Go ahead," said the caretaker.

Nico took the tape recorder with both hands.

He turned it over.

He opened the battery compartment.

Slid the handle in and out.

Pressed each of the chunky buttons in turn, and then, hearing the mechanism move, peered inside the cassette compartment. He struggled with the record button, which refused to go down.

The caretaker sat and watched, never saying a word.

"Would you like something to drink?" asked Gia. "Tea? Or coffee?" But the caretaker shook his head.

Nico grumbled to himself, and then gave a little hoot of pleasure as he discovered that the play and record buttons could be pressed down together. Then he started prying at the panelling. The caretaker touched him on the arm to get his attention, and Gia thought he was going to tell Nico to be more careful. But instead he opened the toolbox and handed Nico a small screwdriver.

Gia heard the front door close and her mother was back at the door, her arms full of fabric.

"Thought I might as well come and work up here," she said, her eyes on the two on the floor. Then she noticed Sonella, who was picking up the empty food containers. "Oh, thank you my dear, you are a sweetheart. You'll find a bin in the kitchen, down there at the end of the corridor."

Saraswati sat at her little work table, and started setting out the pieces of lace and white satin. Sonella came back from the kitchen, and stood uncertainly at the door. Gia noticed that Ben also seemed at a loss for what to do, now that Nico was distracted by this new toy.

"Hey," she said. "Do you guys want to see my new room?"

Ben jumped up.

"Cool!" he said. "Let's go."

ಸಿOಯ

"Wow, this is so much better than your old room," said Ben as he came through the trapdoor.

"Oh, you're so lucky," said Sonella, following on his heels. "It's really cosy. And such a great view!"

"The roof rattles a bit at night, when the wind blows," said Gia. "But I kind of like that."

Sonella was inspecting the bookshelf. "You've got such great books. I've not read this one," she said, pulling out a volume. "Is it any good?"

"It's okay," said Ben. "But it's not the first in the series. I've got the first one. You can borrow it, if you like."

Gia watched as they looked through her books, amused. Ben had dropped his usual joking manner and treated Sonella with a gentle attentiveness that he never showed to Gia or Fatima. Soon they were all three sitting on the floor, chatting.

Gia showed Sonella her doll, which was suitably admired, and the conversation turned towards what each of them planned to do once they finished school.

"My mom expects me to go and study to be a dominee," said Ben with a snort. "Like that's ever going to happen. I don't even go to church with her any more, but she still hopes that I'll have some kind of conversion experience and realise that I'm destined for a religious life."

Sonella was still looking at the doll. "I'm a good girl, I'm afraid," she said. "I wish I had a fantastic talent like this, and could go to art school, or study drama or something. But it looks like I'll be doing just exactly what my parents expect. University."

"You still planning on taking First Exit, Gia?" asked Ben.

Gia nodded.

"Parents know about it yet?"

Gia shook her head, and Ben laughed.

"You know," said Sonella suddenly. "I could swear I saw something sitting on the windowsill just now. But every time I look directly at it, there's nothing there."

They all turned to look.

"Must be one of the cats," said Ben.

"No," said Gia. "I think I know what you mean. It feels as though something's watching me, sometimes."

"I bet this house has some uncanny things about it," said Ben. "Maybe this is your own little ghost."

Sonella seemed excited by the idea. "I bet that's right. You should get somebody in to do some tests for you. Although, it's more likely a brownie than a ghost."

"Well, actually," said Gia. "We had a visit from a Special Branch sniffer unit yesterday."

This got their attention.

"You're joking," said Ben, eyes wide.

"It was horrible, actually," said Gia. "They came banging in here yesterday morning. Just shoved right through the front door before I could stop them."

"But that's illegal!" said Sonella. "They need a warrant. They can't just barge in?"

"I think they had a warrant. They had some bit of paper anyway."

"But why did they come?" Ben wanted to know. "They don't just do random searches do they?"

"I don't know," said Gia. "They had a werewolf with them and everything. Damn thing sniffed all through the house. It was seriously creepy."

Sonella looked even more worried. "That doesn't make sense, Gia. Sniffer units, I know, well— my parents know about these things. Getting permission to search civilians is a long process. Or at least, it is at the moment. All that will change if the referendum goes the way it seems like it will, and all this Grey List stuff happens."

"Well, I don't know," said Gia. "But nothing really happened. They just left when they were done. But check this out."

She reached over and pulled the box out from next to the shelf. "There was one thing that the werewolf found, that did have traces of magic on it."

She was gratified by their reaction. Both Ben and Sonella stared at the box as though they expected it to levitate.

"This is a box from one of the pantry cupboards," she explained. "Left over from the woman who used to live here." She paused and widened her eyes at them. "Seems she was a bit of a witch."

"No ways," said Ben. "Well, go on, open it!"

They both craned forward as she opened the box. "Oh," said Ben, disappointment clear in his voice. "It's just a bunch of old stuff."

But now Sonella took over.

"She really must have been a witch," she said. "Look. That's the stuff you sprinkle around before a cleansing ceremony. And these are smudge sticks."

"You know a lot about it," said Ben.

"My mother's a historian," said Sonella. "She's always telling me about things like this."

"What's Rattlesnake Salt for?" asked Gia.

"I think it's just a tonic," said Sonella. "It's supposed to make you strong. But it looks old, it will be all worked out by now."

"These are the really interesting ones," said Gia, lifting out one of the tea boxes.

"Isn't it just tea?" said Sonella.

"But read the label."

"*Brennernissel*" read Sonella. "That's nettle tea."

"Go on, read the rest."

"*Brennernissel. Steep gently, and do not stir. Opinionated and rather sour, but very well read. Use earthenware cup, the plainer the better.*"

Sonella looked up at Gia, puzzled. "What does that mean?"

"It's a tea genie," said Gia. "I called one up last night. It looks like— Like a little man, but all made of steam. And it's a proper genie and everything. It brought me food."

"Now *that's* more like it," said Ben. "What are we waiting for!"

"A *tea* genie?" said Sonella. "I've never knew there was any such thing. That's amazing, Gia. And they still work? I mean, this tea looks pretty old."

"I put some in boiling water and it just appeared. Poof! Like in the stories."

"Do you think— Do you think we can try—?"

But just at that moment, first Gia and then Ben's texters beeped.

They looked at one another.

"Fatima," said Gia, digging hers out of her pocket. "She must be coming over."

"Yep," said Ben, reading his. "Fatima. She's here already."

"I better go let her in," said Gia, but a voice from below forestalled her.

"Hello, up there!"

Feet sounded on the steps and a moment later Fatima's head appeared through the trapdoor.

"Hi, Gia! Your mom let me in. Hey, Ben, you here too."

"Fatima," said Gia. "This is Sonella, my friend from school. Sonella, Fatima."

For a moment Fatima seemed to Gia like a cat— a plump, pretty, domestic cat, eyeing an intruder and deciding whether it was worth unsheathing her claws.

But all she did was smile, and say, "Hi there."

Her glance fell on the box and its contents.

"What's all this then?"

"Some stuff I found," said Gia. "Magical stuff. Looks like the previous owner here was a witch."

Fatima shuddered dramatically. "Ugh," she said, and sat on the bed. "Magic stuff. Ben, don't touch, that's disgusting."

Ben was rummaging through the box, lifting out bottles and boxes to read their labels. "Most of these seem to be stomach medicines. And these are somebody's reading glasses."

He reached for them, a spindly pair with round lenses and wire frames. Then he dropped them again as if he'd been shocked.

"Damn," he said, grimacing. "Damn."

"There, see," said Fatima. "Told you to leave it alone."

"What's wrong?" said Sonella, but he shook his head at her.

"Give me— a moment. Damn. It's okay."

Gia, who'd seen this happen before, watched as Ben tried to recover his equilibrium.

"That was a bad one," she said. "Did you get a feeling off the glasses?"

Ben nodded, then glanced at Sonella, and Gia realised that he was acutely embarrassed.

Sonella just looked mystified.

"Ben can know about things, sometimes, by touching them," said Fatima. "Like, he can tell who used to wear something, what they were like, where they lived, and so on. But it doesn't work with everything."

"But that's psychometry!" said Sonella, clearly impressed.

They all stared at her.

"Being able to divine the history of an object by touching it?" she said. "That's called psychometry. That's amazing Ben. Can you really do that?"

"Yep," said Ben wryly. "Never heard it called that. My mom calls it my 'weakness'. When she ever mentions it."

"It's just Ben's knack," said Fatima, dismissively.

"But—" Sonella seemed at a loss for words. "That's more than a knack. Psychometry is really rare. Especially if you get it strongly. Have you had any training on how to use it?"

Ben shook his head. "It's really not something we talk about in my family."

"Oh. I'm sorry," said Sonella, seeing his discomfort. "I'm being rude. It's just that in my family, there are lots of people with, well, knacks. Talents, you know."

She was talking quickly and smiling at Ben, clearly trying to set him at ease.

"Like, my aunts for example, Tannie Hessie and Tannie Amanda who are living with us at the moment. Tannie Hessie is a medium. She speaks to ghosts and things, and Tannie Amanda is a green witch. She's really good with plants. They can't stand each other."

"That must be awkward," said Fatima, and Gia saw that the cat was back.

Sonella did not notice her tone.

"It is!" she said eagerly. "Just yesterday, Tannie Hessie wanted to watch *Days of our Lives* and Tannie Amanda wouldn't let her. She says the television signals interfere with her plants. So then Tannie Hessie said that a cake that Tannie Amanda had just baked was haunted. She called it the 'cake of doom' and wouldn't let any of us touch it."

Sonella laughed.

"Tannie Amanda said it was all nonsense, but she didn't eat any of the cake either."

"Sounds like they both belong in Valkenberg," said Fatima. "They can join the rest of the freakshow."

There was an awkward silence.

Sonella went red in the face and seemed about to say something, but clearly thought better of it.

Ben was the first to speak again. "I better get going. It's getting late."

"Need a lift?" said Fatima quickly.

"Um—"

"Course you do. Gia, you coming out with us tonight?"

Gia shook her head, and Fatima shrugged. "Oh well. Next time then."

"Bye," said Ben to Sonella. "Nice meeting you. I'll give that book to Gia, she can give it to you. Or maybe you can come out with us some time?"

"That sounds good." said Sonella. "Bye, then."

ഖOര

"I don't think your friend likes me," said Sonella as they climbed down the stairs a few minutes later.

"Fatima?" said Gia. "I don't know what was wrong with her today. She's really nice, most of the time."

"Um."

Sonella stood for a moment, staring down at her feet.

"Is there something wrong with Ben and his mom?"

"I don't really know his mom that well," said Gia. "She's super-religious and uptight. And I think, well, you know how it is, nobody ever says anything out loud, but I always got the impression that his father left because of some magical thing."

"What do you mean?" said Sonella, intrigued.

"I don't know. Maybe I got it wrong. He never speaks about his dad, and I just got the impression that he was a magical. And that's why he left. Sounds dumb now that I say it out loud."

She shrugged helplessly. "But I think that's why Ben's a bit touchy about his knack."

"Oh."

Sonella walked slowly, then turned to face Gia. "I hope I didn't go and say something to upset him?"

"No!" said Gia. "Ben's cool. You saw him. He's not upset."

"Okay."

"Let's go get your magazine clippings."

They found the living room floor covered with small machine parts. At some point, somebody had fetched the dismantled overlocker, and Nico was setting out all the pieces in an organised explosion all over the carpet. He held up one piece at a time, and the caretaker told him what it was, and what it did, and then Nico decided where on the carpet it belonged.

"Is he fixing it?" Gia mouthed at her mother, who was putting the final touches to the lace bodice.

"Who can tell?" Saraswati said.

It had been a long time since Gia had seen her mother looking so happy, and so relaxed.

Gia walked Sonella partway home, helping her carry the magazine cuttings.

"You're sure you'll be fine the rest of the way?" she said as they parted before the footbridge over the Eastern Boulevard.

"Sure. My house is over there, you can just about see it from here. See you Monday."

"See you!"

That night, Gia lay awake in the dark, thinking over the day's events.

She was drifting off when there was a knock on the trapdoor.

"It's open," she said. "Come in."

She heard the trapdoor slide aside, and reached for the light switch.

"Don't switch on the light."

Saraswati appeared, holding a small, glowing object that lit her face and arms. A small, round cake with three tiny candles burning on top of it.

Gia sat up, pushing her hair out of her eyes.

"Happy Birthday," said Saraswati. "A little late, but not forgotten."

She sat on the bed and held out the cake.

"Go ahead. Blow them out."

Gia blew, and the candles flickered and went out, leaving only the hot scent of wax.

"Your father and I have been waiting for an evening when we're both home, but it doesn't look like that's going to happen for a while," said Saraswati in the candle-scented dark. "So we'll just have to have our delayed celebration, just the two of us."

"Thanks, Mom."

"I know the move has been hard on you, Gia. And you've been very good about your birthday getting lost in all of the fuss. But birthdays are important." Saraswati gave a little laugh. "Sixteen! It's so hard to believe. The little babe that I held in my arms has become a young woman."

She plucked the candles one by one. Then she brought out a flat parcel wrapped in tissue paper.

"Happy birthday, Gia."

The parcel was soft under its wrapping, and surprisingly heavy for its size.

"Thanks, Mom."

"That's from both me and your father. He really wanted to be here when you opened it. But there was another client to entertain tonight. Oh, don't worry about the paper. Just tear it open."

Gia tore the tissue wrapping. The light from the window was enough to reveal what she held, but she could tell what it was even without that. Her hands moved over the soft folds of fabric.

"Oh, Mom, it's beautiful."

"Let's get some more light on it."

Saraswati switched on the bedside lamp. "Go ahead, try it on."

The dress was dark, almost black, but shone with hints of deepest marine, shades of blue and green. The fabric had a subtle pattern, long, flowing shapes like undulating ferns. It was a simple cut, all the lines gentle curves, from the scooped neckline to the graceful fall of the full skirt. Gia spun where she stood, delighting in the swirl of the heavy fabric around her.

"Let me see." Saraswati, one hand on Gia's shoulder, looked her over with a professional eye.

She ran a hand down a side seam, then tugged the sleeves.

"I was worried it would be too tight— it's not too tight, is it?"

"It's perfect, Mom."

Gia buried her hands in the skirt, which felt as soft as rose petals. "I guess I better take it off now."

Saraswati laughed. "You'll have plenty of chances to wear it soon enough. Give it here, I'll hang it up for you."

Gia drew the dress off, holding it up to her face for a moment. It smelt so new.

"Why don't you cut that cake for us so long," said Saraswati as she looked around the little attic room for a place to hang the dress. "I'll get you a cover for it, to keep it safe."

She joined Gia on the bed and accepted her half of the little cake.

"Mind if I switch the light off again?" she said. "It's so peaceful up here in the dark."

She leaned against the window frame as she ate, looking down at the stream of late-night traffic on the freeway below.

Gia finished her piece of cake, and after brushing the crumbs off the sheets, crawled back under her blanket and lay there, looking at the lines of light and shadow on her mother's face.

"Mom?"

"Yes?"

"Could you tell me my birthday story again?"

Saraswati looked at her. "You've not asked for that story for years."

Gia snuggled into her pillow and looked expectantly at her mother.

"It was many years ago," Saraswati said after a long pause. "I was only eighteen. Only a little older than you are now, Gia, when I married your father. And at that time, we'd been told that we could never have a baby. And we both wanted a child so badly. I dreamed of you, Gia, did I tell you that?"

"Yes," said Gia sleepily.

"I dreamed that I found an egg, just lying by itself on a riverbank. And the egg rocked and rocked, but it was clear that the little chick inside could not come out. So I helped— I remember being terrified of doing the wrong thing, and hurting the little baby inside the egg.

"But at last the shell cracked, and there was the baby. And then I woke, of course. It was at that time that your parents told us that they could not keep you. You were just two days old, and the smallest baby I'd ever seen. Your mother was devastated, and so was your father, but they had to go somewhere far away, where it was dangerous to take little babies."

Gia stirred. She knew that her parents had died in a car accident, and that this was just Saraswati's poetic way of working that horrible event into the story suitable for a small child. But somehow, it sounded different to her now.

She felt too sleepy to work it out. "Did this happen in Italy, Mom? I only figured out recently that you must have been in Italy when you got me."

Saraswati nodded. "That's right. Anyway, your mother and father could no longer look after you, and they asked me and Karel to take you. They said that they were giving you to us, forever and ever."

Saraswati sighed a deep sigh. "It was a terrible time, and a wonderful time. Terrible, because I loved your parents. They were our friends, and I was sad to lose them. And wonderful, because you became ours."

Gia had heard this story many times over the years. When she was little, she'd just accepted it, as she accepted all the strange and confusing things that happened in stories. Now, she had questions— but she did not want to interrupt her mother's gentle voice to break the calm mood.

"I remember the very first time I held you in my arms. Your eyes were so big! And you were *you* already, even then, Gia. I was a silly girl, and I thought babies were— I don't know. Like eggs, all blank and clean. But you were already *Gia,* looking out at the big world and deciding what you thought of it."

Saraswati leaned forward and stroked Gia's hair. "And now here you are, my big girl. Old enough to have her own going-out dress." She sighed again.

"I remember when I was still longing for my first party dress. I used to watch my sisters get ready to go out, and I couldn't wait to be old enough to put up my hair and wear a beautiful long dress and pretty shoes…"

Gia held her breath, wondering if her mother would go on. She'd never spoken about her family before. Carefully, hoping she would not break she spell, she said, "Were you the youngest, then?"

Saraswati nodded. She was staring into the dark, but Gia did not think she saw the shadowed attic room. "That's right. I was the seventh. Seven sisters…"

There was a long silence, and at last she seemed to come back to herself.

"We never saw your parents again, Gia. I don't know if they're still alive. But I promised your father that I would take care of you and keep you safe, and I promised your mother that I would tell you all the time, that she loved you very much, and that her love would always, always be with you."

Gia closed her eyes. She always felt so strange when Saraswati told this story. Happy, and sad, lost and comforted, all at the same time. Softly, Saraswati started to sing the song that she always sang after Gia's birthday story.

It was a strange song, in a language Gia did not understand. The melody made unexpected lifts and twirls.

When the song was finished, Gia woke enough to ask another question.

"Mom, those words. Do you know what they mean?"

Saraswati was silent long enough for Gia to open her eyes, but she spoke at last.

"I can translate it for you, I think. But I don't think the English words will rhyme. Let me see."

After a pause, she spoke again.

"Winter is coming
So we will spread our wings
You and me, my love,
You and me
And we'll ride the wind
Over the sea to summer."

Gia felt for her mother's hand and found it, and allowed herself to slip down into sleep. She could feel the bond between her mother and herself. She could almost see it, fine silver threads, delicate but strong as steel, binding them one to the other. The image became clearer, and there were more threads, an intricate network that joined her mother to them all — to her, and to Nico, and to her father.

And as she drifted deeper into sleep, she wondered if her mother ever longed to free herself, to cast off that silver web that wrapped so tightly around and around her.

SARIS AND CIGARETTES

Gia was coming out of the school gates when she saw her father waving from his car. She said goodbye to Sonella, and ran over.

"Get in, sweetheart," he said. "Had a good day? Listen, get in, we're running late."

"Where are we going?"

She got in, and her father pushed his way into the after-school traffic.

"The Pillays want another meeting. Nothing's ready to show them yet, but Mrs Pillay is getting antsy already. Don't worry, it's just showing her the drawings and reassuring her that it's all on track. She particularly asked for you. Apparently you made quite a hit with her and Kavitha."

Her father grinned at her. "We're doing the cloak and dagger thing again, meeting the chauffeur in a mall parking lot. But we were supposed to be there ten minutes ago."

"Sorry — I was chatting with Sonella. I didn't know."

"No problem. It's not far. Did you like your present? I'm sorry I couldn't be there when you opened it. Your mother says it fits like a glove."

"It does. It's beautiful, thanks Dad."

"I picked out the fabric, but your mother did most of the work. Here we are."

He swung into the parking lot, a different one than the previous meeting, and Gia could see that the long black car was already there, waiting for them.

It was the same driver behind the wheel, and although he did not say a word, Gia thought he seemed disappointed to be picking up her father, and not Saraswati.

Once again, they went round the back and entered via the kitchen.

This time, Mrs Pillay met them in a small cream-and-gold sitting room filled with ferns and antique furniture. Kavitha was there too, wearing a moss-green sari. She looked just as beautiful as before, her hair bound back in a simple plait, and two coral-pink eardrops that matched her perfect lipstick.

Gia sat on the edge of her chair.

Mrs Pillay and Karel were soon deep in conversation, with Karel showing the drawings and explaining the various stages that the garments would go through. There did not seem to be anything for Gia to do.

A touch on her arm drew her attention. It was Kavitha, glancing significantly toward the door.

"Where are you going, my dear?" said Mrs Pillay without looking up.

"I thought Gia would like to see the gardens, Mother," said Kavitha.

"Very well. But don't be too long." Mrs Pillay looked up and frowned at her daughter. "And please be careful not to set off any alarms while you are out there. Let the gardeners know where you want to go."

"Yes, Mother."

But the place Kavitha took her was no garden.

It was a small courtyard that, as far as Gia could guess, backed onto a kitchen. One wall was covered in silver ducting, and there was a strong smell of cooked food.

"Only place they don't put smoke alarms," said Kavitha.

She took a box of cigarettes and a lighter from the folds of her sari.

"Want one? No?" She lit the cigarette and drew deeply at it, holding it between thumb and forefinger. "Aah," she breathed, allowing the smoke to curl slowly through her lips. "Wow. I needed that. Listen."

She shot a sharp look at Gia. "I like you. And I like your mom. Your dad looks okay too. So I thought I'd warn you."

She took another drag of the cigarette, so hard that Gia could hear it sizzling. Then she let out two streams of smoke from her nostrils, looking, Gia thought, like an unusually pretty dragon.

"Your work on the dresses. It's coming along okay? No delays?"

Gia nodded. "It's going really fast, actually."

"That's great. And none of you have— let slip anything?" She stared at Gia.

"You mean, have we told anyone that we're doing your dress? No!"

Kavitha laid a hand on Gia's arm. "No offence. Just getting information."

She took a last drag at the cigarette, then stubbed it out and put the extinguished butt back into the cigarette box. "The servants tell on me when they find butts," she said, seeing Gia's puzzled look. "Thing is, I don't know how much you know about Luxulo.

But he's a total control freak. If any of the wedding plans get out, or if anything runs late, he's going to be looking for somebody to blame. And Luxulo— well." Kavitha twisted her lips. "Let's just say you don't want to get on his bad side. I've seen him destroy people for smaller things than messing with his wedding plans."

She tucked the cigarette box back under her sari. "People like me, we look out for number one. If we help somebody, it's because they have pull."

She looked at Gia. "You don't know what I mean, do you? That's why I'm warning you. I like you. You don't play the game. You're for real, you and your parents. I've seen it too many times now, little people like you with no connections; you just get ground underfoot when Luxulo starts stomping around. You know what his nickname is?"

Gia shook her head.

"*uBhuldhoza*. That's what they call him. He never loses his cool, but that doesn't mean he doesn't do damage."

She gave a little laugh at Gia's expression. "I know what you're thinking. This is the man I'm about to marry, right? What do the newspapers call it, the 'fairy-tale wedding'. Well, I can tell you, Luxulo's no fairy-tale prince."

"But don't you want to marry him? They can't force you?"

Kavitha lost her smile, and looked down at her hands. For a moment Gia felt that she was being allowed a glimpse behind the mask of hard words and pretty make-up.

"No, nobody's forcing me," said Kavitha. "I'm going into this with my eyes wide open, don't worry."

"You don't, um, you don't love him, then?" asked Gia, and then blushed, and wondered at her own daring. But Kavitha took the question in her stride.

"Love? No. Thank God for that. Imagine if I loved him." She shuddered. "No. But it's sweet of you to care. Which is why I'm warning you now. Watch your back. I'm sorry, I know this is not much help, but I thought that I could at least warn you, so you know what you are getting into. Don't give Luxulo any excuse to go after you. Just keep everything on track and on time and you should be fine."

"Thanks," said Gia, seriously. "I will tell my parents."

"You do that," said Kavitha. "And now we better get back before Mother starts sending out servants to look for us."

ಸಿಂಅ

When they were back in their own car again, Gia told her father of Kavitha's warning.

He blew out a breath. "Well. That's something."

For a while he drove without speaking.

"It's not as if I've not heard the rumours. But it's something to hear it confirmed. Can't say I'm surprised though. Luxulo Langa did not get to where he is by being Mr Nice Guy." He hooted at a taxi that was blocking the lane ahead. "After all, he's going places these days. He's at the head of that new bunch of fanatics in Parliament. The Purists. And I've heard people are making him out to be the next big man after his father steps down as president."

"Is there anything we can do?"

Her father looked over at her.

"Not really, sweetheart, nothing that we're not doing already. But don't you go worrying about it. As long as we stay on time with the work, I can't see how he can have a problem."

He laughed. "Seems you got on the right side of his future wife. That must count for something."

∞O∞

Gia realised something was wrong as soon as they got home.

Mandy met them at the door wearing her worried face, and her mother's voice came from the living room, talking a little too loudly. Saraswati stood hunched over the phone, looking at some sheets of paper.

"But it only arrived today, and the date— yes. I understand that, but—"

Karel went up to give her a kiss but she turned her face away.

"All I'm asking— No. All I'm asking is if there is a way to reschedule this appointment."

Karel looked at Mandy. "Do you know what's going on?"

But before Mandy could answer, Saraswati waved a silencing hand at them, and cradled the phone closer.

"I'm sorry? I missed— oh. I see."

After a moment, she slowly put the phone back in its cradle, and stood staring down at it.

"Sweetheart," said Karel. "Something wrong?"

Saraswati stood abruptly back from the phone and shoved the pages at him. "There. That's what's wrong. This came just now."

Gia tried to see, but all she could make out was that it was some kind of official-looking document. Karel frowned and turned to the second page. "But that's crazy. Why on earth—?"

Gia was thoroughly nervous by now. "What is it, Dad?"

He stared at her, then looked back down at the letter.

"It's from Special Branch. They want you and Nico for some kind of test. 'Deep testing at the Valkenberg Annex.'"

Gia felt her stomach lurch.

Valkenberg.

"Why?"

"I have no idea."

"I do," snapped Saraswati. "And you do too, Karel, but you just don't want to see it. They're testing for magical potential. That's how it starts. Next, they'll come painting red letters on our door—"

"Saraswati, this is South Africa, not Italy," said Karel. "Let's not instantly jump to the worst possible—"

"Karel, I'm not going to wait until they—"

Karel spread his hands in a calming gesture. "Right. Okay. Let's just back up a bit here." He looked at the letter again. "The testing is supposed to happen—"

"Tomorrow morning!"

"Right."

"That doesn't give us any time!"

"Sweetheart, can I just read this thing through?"

Gia went and stood next to Mandy, who gave her a quick hug. They both stood watching Saraswati pace as Karel read carefully through the letter.

"Right," he said at last. "I'm guessing you tried to get the test postponed?"

"I tried," said Saraswati. She sat on the sofa, almost as if her knees gave way.

"There doesn't seem to be any way to get it extended. It has to be tomorrow. And the horrible woman even hinted that as I'm not a citizen, they could take the children away."

Gia felt another surge of fear. But her father stayed quite calm.

"That's just them trying to scare you, Saraswati," he said. "They could never do that. Now, let's look at this in a logical way."

"Can I see the letter?" said Gia. Her parents looked at her, and Gia realised that they'd forgotten she was there.

"Can I see it?" she asked again.

Karel held it out to her.

"Is this because of the sniffer visit?" she asked as she took it.

Saraswati nodded. "That's the only explanation," she said, and Gia was glad to hear her sounding much calmer. "It would be just too much of a coincidence, otherwise."

Gia sat on the arm of the sofa, and read through the letter. Most of it was printed, but there were gaps where somebody had written in her and Nico's names, and the date that the test would be.

Deep testing at the Valkenberg Annex.

Once again, the name sent a chill through her.

She read through it to the block of fine print at the end, half her attention with her parents, who were talking again.

"I could take the children somewhere until all this blows over," Saraswati was saying. "There must be somewhere we can go."

"Sari, we can't do that. Apart from the fact that

we simply don't have the money, what about the business? You can't just—"

"Oh, bedamned be the business, Karel! Is it always about the business? *You* don't have to do anything. I can go—"

Saraswati was on her feet again, and Karel put out a placating hand.

"I can't do it all by myself, Sari," he said. "If you go, it will all fall apart."

There was a moment's silence as Karel and Saraswati stared at one another.

"And Sari, there's something else," said her father, still in his calm-and-reasonable voice. "When we were with the Pillays just now, Kavitha specially took Gia aside to— you tell her, Gia."

Gia licked her lips nervously. She hated it when her parents fought, and now she was right in the middle of it with no way out.

"It's true, Mom," she said. "Kavitha warned me. She said that Luxulo would take any excuse to blame us, if anything went wrong. Like if we fell behind with anything. And that he could destroy us, if he wanted to."

"And he could do it," said Karel, his voice now urgent with his need to persuade Saraswati. "Luxulo Langa is one of the most powerful men in South Africa, Sari. We cannot afford—"

Saraswati turned away, rubbing her hands along her silver bracelets. "So Karel, tell me, what are we to do?"

Gia hesitated, and put her finger on one of the paragraphs of fine print.

"Um— It says here, that if there is more than one test scheduled, the first test must happen by the date they specify. So, maybe, if *I* went for tomorrow's test, they would let you postpone Nico's test to later?"

"But that's just putting off the inevitable," said Karel.

"No, Gia, I'm not having you go to that place—" said Saraswati.

Gia shook her head. "Mom, it doesn't matter about me. This is all about Nico, isn't it?"

Saraswati seemed about to say something. Then she just nodded.

"If they allow you to postpone Nico's test," said Gia, "then at least it gives you a little more time to make a plan, get him out of it somehow."

There was another tense silence, and Gia held her breath.

What am I doing?

The thought of her mother going away, disappearing somewhere, and taking Nico with her was almost impossible to think about. It would be like a gash right through the heart of her family. It would be the end.

Why was she helping her mother to do that?

At least, this way, we'd have a little more time. Maybe everything will come right.

Saraswati gave a great shuddering sigh, and turned to look at Karel, who was nodding.

"If that's possible, that gives us a little more time," he said. "No need to go off half-cocked."

Then, as Saraswati stepped towards the phone, he laid a hand on her arm.

"Sweetheart, maybe it's better if I do the phoning. You're a little overwrought."

For a moment, Gia thought her mother would explode again, but then her shoulders dropped and she nodded in agreement.

꽁○꽃

Gia realised that Mandy had retreated to the kitchen, and went to join her.

She found her rinsing the teapot, and the kettle just coming to boil.

"What's going on now?" asked Mandy. "Sounds like things have calmed down?"

Gia explained quickly. "And Dad's phoning now, to find out if it's possible to postpone Nico's appointment if I go in to be tested at the right time," she finished.

Mandy blew out a breath. "Well," she said, measuring tea into the pot. "Rather you than me, is all I say. Going to Valkenberg." She shuddered dramatically.

"Get the cups, will you Gia? One for everyone."

"Is it really that bad, Mandy?"

Mandy shrugged. "I guess I'm being silly. Valkenberg has a bad name, but it's probably just a place like any other." She poured the steaming water into the teapot.

"It used to be a mental hospital, many years ago. I've heard that it's become some kind of experimental—prison, or something, for the people who get caught by Special Branch."

Gia felt a chill flow down her spine. "A prison?"

Mandy gave her shoulder a reassuring squeeze.

"Oh, I've probably got it all wrong. But anyway, you've already been there, don't you remember? Hand me that tea cozy, over there by the sink."

"You mean the school trip? When I was little? But I don't really remember anything much. Just the creatures."

"Well, it can't be that bad a place if they let little children go there on school trips, can it?" said Mandy reasonably.

She was pouring the tea, when Karel came in.

"Ah, Mandy, you are an angel," he said, accepting a cup. "Just what I need now." He took a deep swallow. "It's all arranged, Gia," he said in answer to her questioning look. "You're going tomorrow morning at nine, and Nico is going Friday."

"What about school?"

"Don't worry, I've arranged that already. You're going to miss a few classes, but we should have you back there before lunch. Got to run now, fetch Nico home. Gia, I think your mother needs your help. She's started piecing together the toile of Kavitha's gown."

ଈO୧

Gia tried to speak to her mother as she helped her, but Saraswati was withdrawn.

When Karel arrived with Nico, she asked Gia to take the boy upstairs and keep him occupied, saying that she could manage her work better on her own.

"Could you put Minou's lotion on her?" said Saraswati as Gia went out the door. "That cat's been baking herself in the sun, and her ears are looking a bit pink."

Nico got the box of overlocker parts from his bedroom, and started unpacking them on the living room table.

"Hold on a minute," said Gia. She found an old newspaper and spread it out for him. "Work on that," she said. "You'll scratch the table."

Nico had several rolls of wire, a pair of wire-cutters, and some long-nosed pliers that she did not recognise.

"Where did you get those?"

"Caretaker," he said.

She watched him for a while, fascinated. She'd assumed that he was reassembling the overlocker, but instead he seemed to be making a structure of some kind, stringing the parts together onto a wire frame. He was doing a good job too. The bits of machine went together so neatly that they looked as if they'd been designed to fit that way.

"Oh," she said as she recognised a shape. "That's an arm!"

"Leg," said Nico, picking the limb up and bending it at the knee to demonstrate. "Foot." He showed her, pointing at another group of objects that had been neatly wired together to shape a long-toed foot.

"These aren't all overlocker pieces, are they?" asked Gia, fingering the delicate metal rods that made up the toes. "This is all kinds of stuff. Where did you get them?"

"Caretaker."

Then Nico looked up from his work, staring towards the door. At first Gia did not know what had attracted his attention, then she heard it too. A scuffling and squeaking, from Nico's bedroom. There was a clang that could only be the rat's cage.

Nico was up and off.

"Hey, wait!" said Gia, but he was too fast for her. By the time she was out the door he was already in his room. She heard him shout, then there was another clang, much louder this time.

"Nico!"

The rat's cage was on its side, sawdust and torn up newspaper spilling out.

Nico was down on the floor, grappling something.

Something small, and cat-sized. It flickered in and out of view like a badly projected image, a little shadow blurring on the edge of sight.

"Thief!" shouted Nico. "Thief!"

The cat-thing was moving too fast for Gia to see it properly. She dived in and grabbed hold of what turned out to be an arm and a leg.

"Smash!" shouted Nico through gritted teeth and lunged at the thing, his head connecting painfully with Gia's chin.

"Nico! Stoppit!"

She backed away, dragging the thing out of his hands. The creature, fully visible now, turned its head and lunged at her, trying to bite.

"No you don't!" She shifted her grip so that she had it by the nape of its neck, and caught a kicking foot with her other hand.

Nico was still shouting.

"Nico, stop. Stop. Calm down."

They both stood staring at one another, panting.

"Hurt Poepie!" he gasped. "Hurt! Eat!"

"Well, it's not going to hurt Poepie now," said Gia. She struggled to keep her grip on the twisting thing. "Anyway, it was probably just trying to steal his food."

"Thief!" said Nico.

The thing squirmed again, but then Nico was there wrapping a towel around it, pinning the flailing limbs.

"Good boy!" said Gia. "Got it!"

The thing glared at them, only its head sticking out from the bundled towel. It struggled hard, jerking its head around, and Gia had to pull the towel tighter to prevent it escaping.

"Thief," said Nico furiously. "Thief!"

Gia could feel it trembling inside the towel.

It had large, cat-like ears and round, green eyes. It was covered with gingery fur and its cheeks and eyebrows sprouted a cloud of quivering whiskers that reminded Gia more of a rat than a cat.

"Calm down, Nico," she said. "Where's Poepie? Was he in the cage when it fell?"

This distracted Nico, who started looking round the room for his rat.

"You," said Gia to the thing. "Stop that." It was stretching its head around, trying to bite her arm.

"What are you doing here? Was it you who's been stealing the rat's food?"

The thing glared up at her. The look in its clever, skinny little face was more human than animal.

"*Steal* from a *rat*?" it said in a tone of withering scorn.

Hearing it speak was a nasty surprise.

"You can talk?" she said, but it just stared up at her.

Nico was trying to coax Poepie out from under the bed with a fragment of biscuit.

"Let go!" spat the thing, giving another wriggle.

"Well. If you can talk, you can understand," said Gia. "I want to let you go, but I'm not going to until you promise not to harm either me or Nico," she caught Nico's eye. "Or the rat. And stop stealing the rat food."

It pulled its mouth this way and that, blinking furiously. Gia watched it, ready for it to start struggling again.

"I don't want to hurt you," she said. "Promise, and I'll let you go."

"Oh, alright," said the thing.

"Not good enough. What do you promise?"

"I promise," it said, looking at her sideways through

gingery lashes, "no harm to you or him, or *rat*, and no stealing rat's food."

Gia tried to think, but she could not spot a trick. Her arms were getting tired. She'd have to let it go soon anyway.

"Good," she said. "I'm going to put you down now." She lowered the creature to the floor, and then let go, stepping back quickly.

Nico hopped onto his bed.

The thing pulled the towel off with ruffled dignity, and then shook itself, exactly like a dog. It wore a miniature olive-green safari suit, but no shoes. Before Gia could get a better look, it vanished.

"What—" said Gia, and Nico let out a squeak.

The creature had not run away, it had simply faded.

For a minute or so Gia hardly dared move. She and Nico looked around the room, but there was no sign of the creature.

"Gone," said Nico at last, and went to tidy up Poepie's cage.

Gia stayed with him for a while, half expecting the creature to come back, or to do mischief of one kind or another, but there was no sign of it.

After a while, seeing that Nico was going to be occupied for quite some time in calming the rat, and settling it back into its cage, she decided to leave him to it.

Saraswati had asked her to put some sunblock on Minou's ears, so she went looking for the cat. Minou was in her current favourite spot, on the balcony railing. She allowed Gia to pick her up and carry her to the sofa. The white cat loved the sun, but her sensitive skin burned easily. The vet had warned about cancer, and given them sunblock to apply to her ears and nose.

Gia settled the cat on her lap, and took out a comb. Minou loved to be combed, and hated the lotion, so Gia always tried to put her into a receptive mood by combing her for a few minutes first.

"No, Pouf! Not now."

As usual, Pouf was trying to muscle in on the action. He shoved his head under her hand, and being rebuffed once again, lay down on the sofa next to her, purring loudly, kneading her thigh and drooling slightly.

Minou purred too, a silent vibration as Gia pulled the comb through her fur. But after a minute or so, the purring stopped, and her tail twitched. At first Gia thought that she'd combed too hard, but then she noticed that Pouf, too had fallen silent, and that both cats stared at the same spot. The shadows on top of a tall display-cabinet that stood next to the door.

Gia felt the hair stir on her neck, but she forced herself not to look.

Once again, she had the feeling that she was being watched. She turned her head slightly, so that the cabinet was in her peripheral vision. Was there something there? It was impossible to see anything in the shadows.

Minou and Pouf both moved their heads, their eyes refocusing as they tracked something. Gia drew her hands over Minou, feeling the tension in the little cat's body.

"You're up there, aren't you," she said, feeling a little foolish. "Are you invisible, or just good at hiding?"

There was no response.

"Don't worry about Nico," said Gia. "He's too busy with his things to take any more notice of you. As long as you stay away from his rat, that is."

There was more silence, but Gia no longer felt that she was talking to empty air, although a quick glance told her that there was still nothing visible on top of the cabinet.

She tried to make her voice as normal and everyday as possible. "How do you make yourself invisible like that? I wish I could do that."

More silence. Then, just as she was sure nothing more was going to happen, something spoke.

"Mostly," said the voice. "Mostly people don't *want* to see. So I just let them. Not see me."

Gia started combing the cat again. "It sounds very useful."

"It is," came the answer. "But it's not something a straight can do. Hope not."

"What's a *straight*?" asked Gia.

The voice gave a rough little laugh. "Crooks and straights," it said. "I'm a crook. You're a straight. Simple."

Gia shot another glance. She could almost see it now, something perching on the very edge of the cabinet.

"You mean— magicals? And, um, non-magicals?" She'd been about to say "Magicals and humans," but somehow that seemed rude.

This time the voice gave a snort. "Typical straight thinking. Dividing things. Ca-te-go-rise things. But magic's everywhere. That's what the caretaker says."

Going by the direction of the cats' gaze, whatever it was, was climbing down one side of the cabinet.

"You know the caretaker?"

"Everyone knows the caretaker. He's been here since the beginning."

"He's a— a crook, then?"

"Yup." The voice had reached floor-level, and she could see the thing again. As she suspected, it was the same creature that she and Nico had caught in her bedroom.

"I like your outfit," she said. "The safari suit. Did somebody make it for you?"

The creature looked down at itself. "Oh. Yes. Mrs Moses," he said. "Very useful. Lots of pockets."

It glanced over its shoulder towards Nico's room. "I came back," it said, "to ask what you want." It pushed its hands deep into two of the trouser pockets and hunched its shoulders.

"What do you mean?" asked Gia.

"Well," it said reluctantly, wriggling around a little. "I'm down one. To you. You did me a good deed."

"Oh, you mean stopping Nico from hurting you? Oh, don't worry about that! I don't think he would really have hurt you anyway."

The thing looked far from convinced.

"Yeah, right. Gentle as a kitten, that's what he is. I must pay my debt. Don't like owing." It shifted from one foot to the other, then stared at the floor.

"Okay," said Gia. "I'll think about it, okay? I don't have to ask for anything right away, do I?"

"Guess not."

Gia reached for the bottle of lotion, and placed a dab of it in her palm.

"What are you doing with the cat?" He craned his head, clearly fascinated.

"I'm putting this stuff on her ears. She gets sunburn. Because she's so white."

"She does?" It moved closer. "Does it help?"

Gia noticed that the pale skin visible under the gingery fur was distinctly pink in places.

"Would you like some? You look like you've had a touch too much sun yourself."

He ran a self-conscious hand over an ear. "Will it help?"

Gia put a little more lotion in her hand. "Here you go."

He edged closer, dipped one long finger in the puddle in Gia's palm and sniffed at it suspiciously. "Pongs," he said.

Gia suppressed a laugh at the look on his face. "It does have a bit of a smell. I think that's chamomile."

"You just rub it on?"

"That's right." She watched as the creature smoothed the drop of lotion onto the back of one hand.

"Feels good!" it said. "Nice and cool. But pongy."

"Would you like some more?"

"Yes!"

The next moment, Minou went scampering off her lap as the creature hopped up to take her place. He perched on her knee, perfectly balanced and trembling a little. Gia could sense the thrumming energy of his skinny body. She could smell him too. He smelled of tobacco smoke.

Gia put some more lotion in her palm, and the creature dipped his fingers in the puddle and rubbed the lotion over his hands and face.

"You're quite burnt on the back of your neck," she said. "Your ears too. Wait, let me give you some more."

She watched as it smoothed lotion onto its large ears, and around its neck.

Paddavis

"Feels good," he said. "Will this keep the sun off?"

"It should, but not forever. Just for an hour or so. And you should be wearing a hat, really."

"That's what Mrs Moses said," he said, climbing down from her lap. "Hate hats. Squash my ears."

He was smoothing down his fur, then sniffing at his fingers. "Well," he said. "I owe you then. You need something, just call my name."

Then he shot Gia an amused look. "Paddavis. That's what I'm called." He gave a nod, and vanished.

৪০○ত্থ

VALKENBERG

There was a guard post at the entrance to Valkenberg, and a boom blocked their way.

"So. How do we get in?"

Karel slowed the car to a stop, and craned to see if there was anyone in the guard post.

More delay. Gia felt her stomach knot with nerves.

She'd be okay, if only she could get this over with quickly. But everything was going wrong this morning.

Nico had flatly refused to cooperate with anything Mandy had asked him to do. It was as though he sensed something was wrong. Gia had not felt hungry either, and had looked on in sympathy as he turned his head away from his porridge. He had boiled over into a silent tantrum just as they were about to leave, which meant that Saraswati, tense and pale herself, was too distracted to say goodbye properly.

Now he sat, stiff and silent in the back of the car.

Karel beeped the hooter, which made Gia jump.

"Well, there we go," he said. "Here comes somebody. Not having a good day, by the looks of him!"

Gia looked anxiously at the approaching guard. It was true, he did have a sour expression.

"Papers."

"Hold on a mo," said Karel. "We've come for testing. Here."

The guard looked over the letter, then peered into the car. "Who's being tested?"

"I am," said Gia.

"Not the boy?"

"Not this time," said Karel.

"Then you'll have to turn round here, sir. Only children under twelve are allowed a parent or guardian."

Karel opened his mouth, but Gia forestalled him. The argument would take precious time, and she wanted to get this over with.

"It's okay, Dad," she said. "You're going to be late getting to Mrs Winterbach's as it is."

"Yes, but—"

"Please, Dad."

He frowned at her, the worry and concern so clear that for a moment she wavered.

But she was no longer a child.

"I'll be okay now," she said. "It can't be worse than the dentist, can it?"

This got a reluctant smile. "You sure, Gia?"

She nodded. It was a lie, but a lie that made her feel stronger.

"Well, you give me a call as soon as you're done and I'll come and pick you up."

She made herself smile, and gave her father a quick kiss. Nico turned his head away, so she gave his hand a squeeze.

She got out before she could change her mind.

"Bye, Nico. Bye, Dad."

With a crunch of gravel, the car turned and she was alone.

"You're going to the annex," said the guard. "Not the main building. I'll call somebody to escort you."

Another guard appeared and gestured for her to follow.

They walked along a road that wound through a rather shabby, old-fashioned garden. Various buildings stood back from the road among the trees. Gia could see the largest of them some way off. A large, Victorian place with a tall tower. At first she thought this was their destination, but the guard turned down a side-road to a long, modern building with large glass doors.

He tapped at a keypad, and the doors slid open.

Inside was a metal detector and another guard.

"Come for testing," said Gia's escort to this guard. Then without even a glance at Gia, he went back the way they had come.

"Keys, texters?" the door-guard said in a bored voice.

"I'm sorry?"

"Keys, texters?"

Seeing that Gia still did not understand, he sighed and came alive enough to explain.

"Don't want to set off the metal detector. Do you have any keys on you, or a texter, anything like that?"

"Yes. I've got a bunch of keys, and a texter in my pocket."

"Right. Put them in this tray."

Gia did as she was told, then stepped through the metal detector.

The doors slid shut behind her.

The receptionist glanced over her letter, then nodded towards the row of plastic chairs. "Take a seat, please. I'll let them know you're here."

There was no one else in the reception area, and nothing to look at but a few plants in pots. Gia spent some time trying to decide if the plants were real or plastic, and then, for want of anything better to do, read through the letter again.

Deep testing.

What did that actually mean?

She realised that the receptionist had called out her name.

"You're to go to B-21," she said, writing the number on the letter. "Through that door, all the way to the end, up one flight of stairs and then to the right. You'll see the numbers on the doors. And better leave that bag with me. Security won't like you taking anything inside."

Feeling a bit lost without the familiar weight of her bag swinging from her shoulder, she approached the door where a security guard stood waiting.

"Letter," he said, and she showed him the document.

"Do you have any weapons on you? A camera?"

"No."

He looked her over, and for a moment she thought he was going to search her. Instead, he nodded. "You are aware that the taking of any photographs, or any recordings, of any kind, is strictly prohibited. Also the removal of anything from these premises without permission."

This was rattled off almost too fast for Gia to follow.

"Yes," she said. "I mean, I understand."

He waved her through.

Beyond the door was a long corridor, lit by humming fluorescent striplights. Every few metres there was a small black glass dome, fixed to the ceiling. These puzzled Gia until she realised they must be security cameras.

She was relieved to see that all the doors had numbers on them. It should be easy enough to find B-21.

A man in a lab-coat stepped into the corridor ahead of her. A door shut behind him with a soft but solid thump, like the door of a safe. He walked past, his glance sliding over her.

At the top of the stairs she stood for a moment in rising panic, having forgotten the way. But the door numbers helped her and soon enough she stood outside number B-21, which was slightly open.

A voice responded to her knock. "Come in! Just push it open and come in. It's a bit stiff — that's right."

A small woman sat behind a desk, scribbling on a notepad. "Hello," she said. "Sit right there. I'll be right with you."

She wore a pastel blue outfit that reminded Gia of a nurse's uniform, and her hair was pinned neatly into a cap of the same colour. She had blue eyes, and soft, white skin, and Gia found herself wondering if she burned as easily as Paddavis.

"Right," said the nurse, closing her notepad. "Have you got your letter? Good."

She took the letter and copied something from it into her pad.

"I'm Nurse Lily," she said, sitting back. "And you are Gianetta Grobbelaar? Excellent. Gianetta, I'm going to ask you a few quick questions, and then we'll go back there—" She nodded to a curtained area behind her. "And do a few little tests. Right? Good. Now. How old are you, Gianetta?"

She went on to ask a list of questions, about Gia's weight and medical history. These everyday questions, in this peculiar place, made Gia feel almost dizzy with strangeness.

In this air-conditioned box of a room she felt further from her own world than she'd ever been before.

There were not even any windows to let in some air or sun. There was nothing to connect her to the world in which, only a few minutes before, she'd been saying goodbye to her father.

A knock made them both look round. A young woman stood in the door. She wore a grey uniform, but had none of nurse Lily's easy confidence.

"Ah, Cadet Dunson," said Nurse Lily. "We're just about ready to start. If you could pull up the charts?"

Cadet Dunson nodded, and went to the curtained area where a small computer was set up. She switched it on, and started tapping at the keyboard, without once looking at Gia.

"Now, Gianetta," said Nurse Lily. "If you go have a look behind that curtain you'll find a gown folded on the bed. Just slip out of your clothes and put on the gown for me, while I get a few things ready."

Gia felt a stab of nerves. She got up reluctantly and walked over to the curtain. Behind it was a narrow bed, and a counter that held several medical-looking machines. The curtain did not give her much privacy, but a quick glance told her that Cadet Dunson was completely absorbed in whatever she was doing. Gia spotted the security camera up in one corner of the ceiling, but there was nothing she could do about that.

She undressed, and drew the gown on quickly, shivering a little in the chilled air. Unsure what to do with her clothes, she folded them as neatly as she could on a nearby chair, hiding her underwear under the pile.

Thank God that I'm not having my period, she thought, then wondered whether that would have affected the test results.

The gown was very short, and hardly closed in front. As she was still trying to tie it shut, Nurse Lily came pushing through the curtain, a stethoscope round her neck.

"Ready? Good," she said. "Hold your arms out to the side for me — that's right."

She flipped open the gown, and cast a brisk eye over Gia's body. "Turn round."

Gia felt the gown lift, then drop back.

"Good. Good. Now, sit on the bed. No, more to the left. That's right."

She drew a thermometer out of her breast pocket, gave it an expert flick, and popped it in Gia's mouth. "Just hold that under your tongue, dear."

Gia felt herself shivering, more with nerves than with cold, and flinched as the nurse put the chilly stethoscope on her skin.

"Take a deep breath — and let it out. Another. And let it out. Good."

Nurse Lily tucked Gia's gown around her, and slipped the thermometer out of her mouth.

"Cadet Dunson, are you ready?"

"Yes, nurse."

"Good. Record a temperature of thirty-seven degrees, chest clear, heart normal.

"I'm going to draw a little blood now," she said to Gia.

Gia watched as she primed the syringe, but looked away as the needle went in. It was not as bad as she'd feared, a dull pain in the crook of her arm.

"Hold this for me."

Gia held the little patch of gauze on the puncture wound while the nurse secured it with a scrap of tape.

"Cadet."

Cadet Dunson took the syringe to one of the machines, standing in such a way that Gia could not see what she did. There was a click and a clunk, and then a hum that rose in pitch and then settled at a steady note.

While Gia was still wondering what was happening to the blood sample, Nurse Lily reached and folded something down from the wall behind her.

"Just lift your arms, dear, and place them— that's right."

Two armrests dropped into place on either side of her, and Gia found herself leaning back against a padded board. Before she realised what was happening, Nurse Lily had snapped two broad, black straps around each of her arms, one around the wrist, the other just below the elbow. She tried to lift her arms, but they were securely fastened. Then a strap was pulled around her chest, forcing her against the backrest.

Nurse Lily leaned forward and did something out of her sight.

Gia felt her head trapped between two soft but solid barriers.

"Sit quietly now, my dear," said the nurse. "That's

just there so you don't move by accident. The equipment is so sensitive..."

Her voice died out as she leaned to one side, then with a rattle, she pulled something down from overhead. It looked like the machine that optometrists use, a complicated collection of lenses and disks in glistening chrome.

Nurse Lily swung it down and towards her, fitting the lower half over Gia's neck and shoulders, with a curved section cupping her chin. "There. Can you move your head, dear?"

Gia tried. "No."

"Not too tight?"

Yes, too tight, take it off! was what she wanted to say, but did not want to seem impolite.

"No, it's fine." It was hard to talk, as she could not really move her jaw.

"Good." The nurse twisted something down that slotted in place over Gia's left ear. Her vision was blocked on that side, and she felt, rather than saw, as Nurse Lily made more adjustments. She felt the nurse's breath on her cheek, smelt the faint lavender scent of her perfume. There was a series of clicks, then a soft whoosh of compressed air. There was pressure in her ear, building until just below the edge of pain.

Then the nurse drew back, apparently satisfied.

The same procedure was repeated, this time with her right ear.

"What are you doing?" Gia asked, trying to move her head but failing once again.

"Now, you just relax, my dear," said the nurse.

Her hands came into view, and she tightened a band around Gia's forehead.

"Close your eyes for a moment— that's a good girl."

Gia felt something move in front of her face, and when the nurse told her to open her eyes she found that a new part of the machine had been lowered, this one to fit over her eyes and forehead.

There was another click, and she had to screw her eyes shut against the light.

"A bit bright, isn't it?"

Another click or two, and the light dropped to a more bearable level, although it was still glaring in Gia's eyes.

Gia was starting to find it hard to breathe.

What's happening to me? said a small voice deep in her mind but she suppressed it. If she allowed herself to be frightened now, she'd be in a screaming panic, and losing control was the worst thing she could do.

At least my legs are still free.

But when she surreptitiously tried to swing her feet, she found that they, too had been fastened somehow, and she could not move at all.

Her heart thumped in her chest and she tried to relax, taking breaths as deep as the chest strap allowed.

Nurse Lily turned away and Gia heard her speaking to the cadet. A moment later, she was back, holding something. There was the sound of a latch clicking and Gia guessed that it was a box of some kind. The nurse looked down at whatever it was, and back at her eyes again, comparing.

"Hmm. Yes. Number fifty-six, I think."

She lifted something out of the box — something the size of a small egg, but round — and inserted it into the part of the machine that framed Gia's eyes. Gia heard it drop into place with a clunk, and was suddenly sure she knew what it was.

A glass eye.

"No," mused the nurse. "Too dark. Maybe a fifty-four."

She released the thing, catching it in her palm, and replaced it with another.

"Much better. Now just a little finesse on the lighting…"

She adjusted the angle of the light.

"Now, Gianetta, I'm going to put a liquid in your eyes. It's completely harmless, in fact, it will feel just like your natural tears. Just look to the left for me— to the left, dear. That's right."

Gia tried not to see the nurse's hands so unbearably close, then blinked uncontrollably as something dripped into one of her eyes.

"One more time."

The second time was not so bad.

"No, don't blink it out. Just keep your eyes open. That's right. Open your mouth. This has got to go under your tongue."

She slipped a thin object between Gia's lips. It tasted metallic, with a sour tang that reminded her of licking a battery. She could feel a line of spittle drip down her chin, but could do nothing about it.

"Now, Gianetta, I'm going to show you some pictures. All you have to do is look at them. You don't have to say anything, or do anything. Just try to focus on them. Don't worry about what they are. Some of them may be a little upsetting, but remember, they're just pictures."

Gia felt herself tensing again, and once again, tried to force herself to relax.

"Can you see here?" The nurse was holding up a card, with a big black "X" on it.

Gia tried to nod, but of course, her head could not move at all.

"Yes," she said instead.

"Cadet Dunson, are you ready? We are on stage five now."

She held up another picture. It was hard to see what it was, with the light glaring in her eyes, but after a moment Gia made out that it was a photograph of a cat.

A new picture took its place, this one of a squirrel.

Each time she held up a new picture, Nurse Lily looked at Gia's eyes, then to the side, at what Gia guessed was the glass eye, and called out a number. Gia could hear the keyboard clicking as Cadet Dunson typed it in.

The next picture was of a squirrel as well, but this one was dead. Recently dead, and probably run over by a car.

Then, an open hand.

A hand, holding a feather.

The feather by itself.

Then a series of abstract patterns. Lines, and crosses, and dots.

The probe in her mouth made her salivate, spit pooled in her mouth, and her neck was beginning to ache.

Another picture — a hammer on a white-tiled floor.

Then the empty hand again.

A naked woman, clutching her upper arm, blood trickling from between her fingers.

A glass of milk.

A fish, split open to the spine.

A tooth.

A cracked teacup.

An egg.

The images repeated, each time in a different sequence.

At last, Nurse Lily nodded.

"Good. That's the lot," she said, snapping off the lights.

She released the forehead strap, then drew the contraption away from Gia's head and folded it back out of sight.

"All done. Now, that wasn't so bad, was it?"

When her hands and arms were free, Gia rubbed her face, then hugged herself, shivering.

She saw that she'd been right about the glass eye. There was a flat, leather-bound box open on the bed beside her, holding row upon row of very lifelike eyeballs, each with a small number engraved on the white.

"You can get dressed now," said Nurse Lily. "And then Cadet Dunson will show you to the waiting room. Cadet, stay with her, please."

ಸOಽ

Once Gia was dressed, Cadet Dunson showed her to a room further down the passage.

There were some people already there, mostly young men, all dressed in the same grey uniform as Cadet Dunson. Some of them sat around a table, playing a game with coins. Others simply lounged back in their chairs, chatting.

At one of the tables, sitting by herself, was a pale young woman with short-cropped hair and a faint scar that ran from eyebrow to cheek.

Cadet Lee.

Gia saw the flicker of recognition in the cadet's eyes.

"Can anyone watch this one?" said Cadet Dunson. "I've got to get back to Section C."

Cadet Lee nodded, and gestured for Gia to take the chair next to her.

"You just been for testing?" she asked.

Gia nodded.

"You want some tea? Coffee?"

"Yes, please. Tea, thanks."

The cadet got up and went to a table against the far wall that held an urn and a row of cups. Gia tried to ignore the stares from the rest of the room. The sound of voices drew her eyes back to the door, and she glimpsed two people as they walked past. One was a man in a white coat, but the other—

What was *she* doing here?

Surely that had been Mrs Solomons, the school social worker?

At Valkenberg?

"Here you go. Sorry, it's not very hot— that urn never really boils."

It was the cadet, holding out a cup of tea. She wore gloves, Gia noticed, thin, white gloves of some flexible, leathery material.

"Thanks."

The tea was warm, and unexpectedly sweet.

"Put some sugar in for you," said Cadet Lee. "Need something sweet, after being tested."

She watched as Gia took another swallow. This close, Gia could see the delicate veil of freckles that covered her face. Her eyelashes were so pale they were nearly invisible.

"I freaked out when they did me," said the cadet. "Screamed so much I was hoarse for weeks." Her voice was perfectly level and without emotion, as if she were commenting on the weather.

"That's horrible."

"It was."

The thought Gia had been suppressing since the test began, finally surfaced.

Nico.

Nico, strapped down, lights shining in his eyes...

She felt herself beginning to shiver again and wrapped her hands round the comforting warmth of the teacup.

"I've seen you before," said the cadet. "You're the girl who came to speak to me after that school presentation."

"That's right."

Gia remembered the question she'd asked.

"Do you ever see your parents?"

She wanted to ask it again, but did not quite dare.

"Do you know how long I have to wait here?" she asked instead.

Cadet Lee's pale eyebrows rose. "Didn't Dunson explain? Well. Dunson is a cold fish. It should just take a few minutes for the initial results. Then, if those are positive, you'll have to go for more tests."

Gia felt her heart sink.

More tests.

How long would she have to be here?

"Don't worry," said Cadet Lee. "Doubt you'll get a positive. You seem pretty straight to me."

With an involuntary start, Gia remembered that the cadet's special talent was telepathy.

Can she tell what I'm – ?

Cadet Lee laughed. "No need to look like that," she said. "I can't read people these days unless I'm touching them. Anyway, I don't need to be a telepath to figure out what you're thinking. You need to learn to hide your feelings a bit more."

A bell rang somewhere down the corridor.

"Hey-up," said one of the other cadets. "There goes another one."

"Freaking freaks," replied one of his companions.

There was a sound of hurrying feet in the corridor outside, and Gia glimpsed several blue-clad nurses striding by the door.

The bell rang again, but this time it mingled with another sound, a thin, tearing wail.

Was that a voice? Somebody screaming?

It was clearly not a mechanical noise, but before Gia could decide if it was human or animal, it stopped abruptly.

Could that have been a child?

Gia shook the thought from her. The cadet seemed completely unmoved by the sound. *It must just have been some kind of alarm.*

To distract herself, she looked at the posters that lined the walls. They were Special Branch recruiting posters, each with brightly coloured photographs of cadets in various poses and situations. A cadet holding a billowing South African flag against a bright summer sky. A cadet striding out of a burning building, a baby cradled in his arms. A cadet with a determined look on his face, holding the leash of a snarling dog. All of them had the same message printed in large, bold letters.

Make A Difference. Special Branch Youth Brigade Has A Place for You.

"Thinking of joining?" There was a glint of irony in Cadet Lee's smile.

"Um, not really."

"University then?"

"Well, no. I'm hoping to take First Exit and go to art school."

The cadet's eyebrows rose again. "Art school?"

Gia started answering, but was interrupted by a movement at the door.

"Gianetta?" It was Nurse Lily.

"Good news, Gianetta. No need for more tests," she said. "All negative. You can go."

"Negative?" asked Gia, getting to her feet. She was surprised by the stab of disappointment.

"No magic," said the nurse. "You have unusually high empath score, and your realisation range is particularly strong, but all readings are still within the normal, human range. Here, you'll want this — your certificate of purity."

Gia took it from her — a creamy piece of paper with several official-looking stamps.

So I'm a straight after all.

She tried to convince herself that she was relieved.

"You can fold it, and tuck it into your ID book," said the nurse. "Cadet, can you take Gianetta down to reception?"

And before Gia could reply, Nurse Lily turned on her heel and left.

"See," said Cadet Lee. "Told you you were straight. And now you've got a certificate to prove it."

She got to her feet.

"Well. Let's go then."

ഇOര

Sonella held down the certificate as the wind caught at it.

"I didn't know you could get these already," she said. "I thought it would only be if the Purists got the referendum." The two of them were sitting in a sunny spot in the school courtyard. It was second break, and a group of boys were playing a lively game of lunchbox soccer.

"The nurse told me to put it in my ID book," said Gia. "As if she thought people would be checking for it."

Sonella shook her head. "I don't like the sound of that. That's how it is all over Europe now, people having to have papers proving they're human. And things are getting bad again. Did you see the news last night?"

"No. What happened?"

"There's been more riots in Greece, and a man got set on fire in the middle of the street. They say the crowd thought he was a moldyman, but he was probably just some poor homeless guy. And my mother told me, a lot of the refugees that are running away from that kind of thing, if they don't have the right kind of papers proving they are—" Sonella tapped the certificate, "— non-magical, they get put into trucks, and nobody knows what happens to them then. They get *disappeared*."

Gia felt a chill, as though the sun had gone behind a cloud.

That was what had happened in Italy, at the time her parents had returned to South Africa. Riots and burnings. Religious zealots whipping up crowds in the after shock of the stock market crash. The government passing laws that made it impossible for anyone with magical abilities to get work, or even to move around without continual harassment. Whole families had been taken into custody and never seen again.

They got disappeared.

With an effort, she pulled herself back to the present.

All that was long ago. And it could never happen here.

"Were the tests horrible?" asked Sonella.

"I guess they weren't that bad," said Gia. "I mean, it was pretty freaky. But what I'm worried about, Nico's *never* going to cope. We're just going to have to find a way to get him off."

"Why? Do you think they'll — ?"

Gia, startled by the strength of her feelings now that she was finally voicing them, spoke slowly, figuring out what it was that was frightening her. "It's not just the tests. I mean, *I'm* fine with them, just a bit shaken, but Nico…"

She wondered if Sonella would think she was exaggerating.

"I think if he had to go through what I went through, he'd just— snap."

She shook her head helplessly, trying to convey her sense of horror. "But that's not all. I think, well, I'm pretty sure that Nico won't test negative."

Sonella nodded. "I think you're right about that."

They both stared down at the gravel for few moments, busy with their own thoughts.

"Sonella," said Gia at last. "There's something I've been meaning to ask you but I keep forgetting. You know the school social worker? Mrs Solomons?"

Sonella looked puzzled. "I didn't know there *was* a school social worker. There's a school nurse—"

"No, not her. Wait, I'll show you."

Gia took took out the card that Mrs Solomons had given her.

"No. I've never heard of her."

Gia put the card away again, and felt her worries stirred up again like mud at the bottom of a pool.

"You remember when Mr Peterson called me in, on Friday? It was to see this woman. She said she was the school's social worker. I thought it was a bit odd, because she asked the strangest questions. Mostly about Nico."

"Oh?" said Sonella. "That's odd."

"Yes. I thought so too. But the thing is, I saw her today. Or at least, I think I saw her. At the Valkenberg Annex."

"So what are you saying?"

"It just seems strange to me that all this stuff is happening now. The sniffer unit, and this testing thing. After Mrs Solomons was asking all those questions about Nico. And now it turns out she's got something to do with Valkenberg."

Sonella was looking worried. "You think all this is about Nico? That they want him for some reason? But why?"

"I don't know," said Gia.

After a moment or so, Sonella spoke again. "What do you think they'll do, if Nico tests positive?"

Gia had to shake her head. "I have no idea. They couldn't just keep him there, could they?"

"I don't know," said Sonella. "Your parents can't do anything?"

"My father doesn't seem to think we *should* do anything. I think he's scared of drawing the wrong kind of attention. Mom just wants to go into hiding, and—" Gia hesitated. She'd promised not to tell anyone about the Pillay job, but the urge to share her worries was too strong.

"Thing is, if Mom goes away, we're in the dwang anyway. Sonella, you can't tell anyone this, okay? But we're working on Kavitha Pillay's wedding dress—"

Sonella's eyes widened in surprise and she grabbed Gia's hand. "But that's wonderful, Gia!"

"Yes. It is," said Gia, and she couldn't help smiling at Sonella's reaction.

"But the thing is, apparently Luxulo Langa has a reputation for being extremely nasty to anyone who gets on his wrong side. And without Mom, we'll never get the gown finished in time."

Sonella lost her smile. "Oh," she said. "Luxulo. I forgot about him." She stared at Gia. "It's true. Gia, can't your parents get out of that? I've heard some dreadful stories about that man. I mean, you know he's the *head* of the Purists. And Valkenberg is like his special project."

"It's too late to get out of that now. But if we can find a way to keep Nico from having to be tested…"

"Well, I can ask my parents, I guess," said Sonella. "They might know of some way. But really, what you want is to get in touch with the Belle Gente."

Gia wondered if she'd heard right.

"The Belle— but, aren't they like— terrorists?" She faltered, embarrassed at her own ignorance.

"No, not at all, that's just Purist propaganda," said Sonella. "Most of them are just normal magicals, people who were hounded out of their own countries by fanatics like the Purists. They just want to be left alone, just like anyone else." She looked earnestly at Gia.

"I know some of them are extreme — there's some of them that believe in an eye for an eye, and that they should fight fire with fire. But the leadership is all for a peaceful solution."

"Well, anyway, how on earth am I going to get hold of them?" said Gia. "It's not like I can just look them up in the phone directory?"

Sonella laughed. "No. But you know the caretaker?"

The bell rang for the end of break, and they got to their feet.

"Yes," said Gia. "But you're not going to tell me *he's* a member of the Belle Gente!"

"No, he's not. But he'll know who you should speak to."

"You think so?"

"Definitely. Everyone knows the caretaker, and he knows everyone. Tell your parents to speak to him. I'm sure he can suggest something."

಄O಼

When Gia got home, Mandy was in the studio. She came out to give Gia a hug.

"You okay?" she said. "The tests weren't too bad? I was so worried. Listen, your lunch is on the kitchen table. I'm still going to be busy here for a while. But I'm looking for your dirty clothes, I want to do a wash."

Since Nico was still at Mrs Winterbach's, Gia had the house to herself. She added her clothes to the laundry, then tried to settle down to her homework.

She could not concentrate.

Sonella's suggestion to contact the Belle Gente now seemed absurd. But what other plan was there? She kept thinking of that scream she'd heard at the Valkenberg Annex, and the other cadets' reactions.

Freaking freaks.

What would they think of Nico?

Even if Nico got through the tests, he might test positive. Surely they would not just let him go with — what? A certificate of impurity?

Sonella assumed that Gia would tell her parents about the caretaker, and contacting the Belle Gente. But Gia knew what her father would say. He'd laugh, and tell her not to worry. Her mother, she was not so sure of. As a rule, Saraswati avoided discussing anything to do with magic.

Why was that?

No. She could figure that out later.

If anyone was going to speak to the caretaker, she'd have to do it herself.

ഗO‍ଌ

BRAKMAN

The caretaker took so long to answer her knock that Gia nearly gave up and went away. When he did open the door, he looked exactly the same as the first time she had seen him. Far too tall, and with a calm question in his eyes.

"Hello," she said, and swallowed nervously. "I've got to ask you something. Can I come in?"

He looked down at her for a moment longer, then stepped aside.

It was dark in the caretaker's place. The only light came in through some narrow windows near the ceiling. Gia realised that the room was almost entirely below ground, and that the windows must be at pavement level outside.

The room was crowded with objects, but the light was so dim she could not see much. It smelt very like a garage, of oil and dust and ancient cardboard, and the floor was bare concrete.

As she followed the caretaker, her eyes became used to the dark, and she started to make out what was around her.

The space looked like a cross between a mechanic's workshop and a junk heap. The walls were invisible behind cupboards and shelves. Tools of every description hung in uneven rows.

And everywhere were *things*.

Radios. Telephones. A washing machine. A stack of typewriters. A pile of alarm clocks. Boxes full of broken toys. Things she did not recognise, with dials and knobs and handles. Engine parts. Bicycles. Things sprouting wires, and things with cogs and springs.

Bits of machines spilled out of drums, hung from the ceiling, and were stacked against the walls.

There was so much stuff, that Gia had to thread her way through a path between them, and it was difficult not to knock into anything.

Nico would love this.

As she moved deeper, she could see that it was not as chaotic as she'd first thought. There was a sense of order about it all. The room was larger than she'd guessed, and Gia realised that it probably ran under several, if not all, of the houses in the row.

The caretaker reached an open space in the forest of machine parts. It was lit by a bare light bulb that hung from the ceiling. There was a workbench there, with even more shelves and great number of tools ready for use. In front of this stood an ancient office chair, sagging on its wheels. On the chair, curled up into a tiny ball, lay Paddavis, apparently fast asleep.

"Shoo," said the caretaker, poking at him with a long finger.

Paddavis made a show of stretching and yawning.

"Hmm," he said to Gia, and hopped onto the workbench. "Come to visit?"

He began grooming and preening his whiskers. The caretaker lowered himself into the chair, and gestured to another, smaller chair.

"Sit."

Gia sat.

"So. You have something to ask?"

Gia swallowed. She'd rehearsed what she would say, but the unexpected presence of Paddavis threw her off.

"I— that is, we— we need your help."

"Your parents know you are here?"

She shook her head. "No."

The caretaker stared at her with no change of expression.

Where should she start?

"It's about my brother. Nico."

"Ah."

"Special Branch are after him," said Paddavis smugly. "Told you."

Gia turned quickly to him. "How do you know?"

Paddavis shrugged. "Been listening. Been watching." He curled his tail around himself, and examined his nails. "Saw the sniffers banging about." He gave a delicate shudder. "No good ever comes of sniffers."

Gia turned back to the caretaker. "It's true," she said. "I think Special Branch are after Nico. They sent a letter. He's got to go in for testing at Valkenberg."

The caretaker went very still.

"Somebody," said Gia, "a, um, a friend, suggested that you might be able to help."

"I cannot help you with Valkenberg," said the caretaker softly. "That is a place of endings."

Gia felt an uncontrollable shudder go through her.

A place of endings.

She pulled herself together and plunged on. "My friend thought, that maybe, you might, you know — be able to tell me who could help me?"

There was an uncomfortable silence.

"I think I should speak to the, um Belle Gente," said Gia. "They could help, couldn't they?"

She ignored Paddavis's smirk.

"They could, if it suited them," said the caretaker. "But they'll ask a price."

Gia was not sure how to answer, and in fact, was not sure if he expected an answer. So she just sat and watched him. The light bulb made a small cave of light around them, casting everything else in deep shadow. A flutter caught her eye, and she looked up, expecting to see a moth attracted to the light.

A very large moth.

It took her a moment to realise what she was looking at. It was the haarskeerder, hovering in the dusty air just at the edge of the circle of light.

"Oh!" she said, half rising. "There she is!"

The caretaker lifted his hand, and the haarskeerder swooped in and perched on it.

Gia stared in wonder. The creature was just as strange and marvellous as she'd remembered — more so now, as she looked in perfect health. Her wings, which had been pale wisps, glittered now with refracted colour.

"She's been staying here with you?"

The caretaker nodded. "She's too young to go off on her own yet."

The haarskeerder jumped off his hand and, wings spread, glided down to his knee.

"Paddavis tells me you rescued her," said the caretaker. "But after all, it was your cat that caught her. And your kind that destroyed her nest."

Once again, Gia was not sure how to answer.

What did he mean 'your kind'?

"I've been putting out food for her," said Gia. "I didn't think she could survive, away from her nest." She glanced at Paddavis. "But I don't think she got much of that food. It was you, wasn't it, cleaning the dishes."

Paddavis grinned at her.

Her gaze was drawn back to the haarskeerder. "Is it safe to look at her?"

"She won't dazzle you," said the caretaker. "They only do that if you threaten their nest." He held out a knuckle, and the haarskeerder rubbed her cheek on it. "And this little one doesn't have a nest. All by herself."

The creature started to gnaw on his finger. Her teeth looked sharp, but the caretaker seemed unperturbed.

"So," he said. "Young Nico."

Paddavis, who'd been scratching behind one ear, looked up.

"Those silvers won't let him go, once they got him," he said. "And he's crook, all right."

The caretaker gave him a quelling glance, but Paddavis did not seem to notice. "They won't even need to test him, they'll see as soon as they look."

"Silvers?" said Gia. "That's— Special Branch?"

"Yep," said Paddavis. "Or anyway, the Pure ones. Thought your Mom was one at first, what with that silver on her arms. But I soon see she's not one of *them.*"

Gia frowned. She'd never thought about her mother's silver jewellery in that way. The Purists, with their silver salute, were a relatively new thing, and Saraswati had worn her bracelets for as long as Gia could remember.

"But what can I do, then?" she asked. "If you can't help me contact the Belle Gente?"

The caretaker looked up. "I did not say that I would not help you."

Gia, whose heart had been sinking, felt a surge of hope. "So you'll tell me what to do?"

The caretaker was looking at Paddavis now.

"Brakman," he said. "You should take her to see Brakman, Paddavis. He's the man for this kind of job."

Paddavis looked irritated. "I should, should I? And why is that?"

"Don't you owe the girl a favour?"

Paddavis pulled at one ear. "Hmm," he muttered. "Right."

"Can't you just tell me where to go?" asked Gia.

Both of them shook their heads.

"Brakman will not see you without me there," said Paddavis. "Suspicious old dog, is Brakman. Paranoid."

He grinned at Gia. "Don't worry, I don't mind going to see him. See how the old fart's getting on."

಺O಼

All Paddavis would say about Brakman was, "You'll see when we get there."

Gia knew he lived in Rosebank, but Paddavis refused to take a taxi, so they would have to walk all the way there. She considered asking Fatima for a lift, but then she pictured Fatima's most likely reaction to Paddavis. With the exception of Ben's talent, Fatima tended to treat anything to do with magic with disgusted scorn. And maybe it was better not to involve too many people in this meeting.

Paddavis was excited by the prospect of the walk down to Rosebank.

"Not far," he said. "Through Salt River, then down next to Liesbeek. Haven't been that way for years."

Saraswati was still out, so Gia left a note that she'd gone for a run.

"I'll go on your shoulder," said Paddavis, and that is what he did, one hand resting on her head. Gia supposed that he was doing his invisibility trick, because nobody so much as glanced at them.

The streets below Eastern Boulevard were new to Gia.

As they crossed Woodstock Main Road, Gia began to feel a little uneasy. This part of town was much the same as Walmer Estate, a poor neighbourhood. There was a lot of rubbish lying around, and the sidewalks were greasy with ancient filth.

Most of the people seemed harmless though. Just normal people going about their daily business. But not everyone seemed equally approachable.

As she drew near Salt River Circle, she saw a group of young men lounging on a street corner. They had not noticed her yet, but they would soon enough, and she wondered if she should backtrack and choose another route. There was something about the way they stood, all attitude and arrogance, that made her very nervous.

"Paddavis," she muttered. "Can you include me in your invisibility thing? Make them not notice me, or something?"

"I can," said Paddavis. "As long as you don't bump into people. That makes them notice."

There was no sign that he'd done anything until she was quite close to the group. Then it was their lack of reaction that convinced her Paddavis's trick was working.

It was uncanny. Usually, they would be eyeing her up and down. There would be remarks, whistles and catcalls. Even attempts to block her from walking by. She'd have to play that frustrating old game of ignoring them, while they did, and said, whatever they pleased. Now they simply acted as if she was not there.

It was the strangest feeling. She found herself slowing down to enjoy it, staring at the young men without being seen in return.

"Don't push it," muttered Paddavis, and she picked up her stride and left them behind.

Now that she felt safe from notice, Gia found that she enjoyed the walk much more. She admired the hand-painted signs outside the hair salons, boasting of the variety of styles they could achieve. There were tailors displaying brightly patterned men's shirts, grubby little stalls where you could recharge your texter, and a martial arts club named *The Moroccan Royal Panther Society*.

Scents wafted from every door she passed. The pungent smell of offal and cabbage cooking. The chemical sting of hair straighteners and hairspray mixed with incense and boxer cigarettes. The wet, dark green pong of marijuana. The shops here had visible wards up above their doors, horseshoes and wreaths of rosemary.

A splash drew her attention to a row of plastic buckets filled with live snoek, their black backs gleaming in the sun as they struggled, drowning slowly in water not even deep enough to cover their bodies.

Paddavis pointed out things she might have missed, and explained them to her.

The streamers that fluttered from some of the

lampposts were coded messages, a system used by the local magicals. The tiny glass vials that rolled under her feet, crunching into glass-dust, were the cast-offs of the spore-junkies and sparkle-heads.

They crossed a bridge and the landscape changed. The path ran along a grassy bank next to a broad, shallow river.

"Liesbeek River," said Paddavis. "All kinds of people live here. But you won't tend to see them in daytime."

Despite that rather unsettling idea, it was pleasant walking next to the river.

"Tell me about the Belle Gente," she asked.

Paddavis had moved to the crook of her arm, which made it easier to talk to him.

"Pah," said Paddavis, and pulled a face. "They're mostly *uitlanders.* Foreigners. Don't know anything about how things work here."

"Aren't you an uitlander yourself? Don't you come from Britain or somewhere like that?"

Paddavis shot her a disgusted look. "I come from *Ireland,* thank you very much."

"So doesn't that make you a foreigner too?"

"Not any more than *you* are a foreigner."

"Okay. So I was born in Italy. But my parents were born here, and their parents too."

"And I've been living here since before your grandparents' grandparents were born."

"Oh."

They reached a place where the grassy bank widened. There were people here, walking their dogs or sunning themselves on benches.

"So, the Belle Gente are foreigners, then," said Gia. "But who are they?"

"That's the question," said Paddavis. "Nobody really knows. There are rumours. About the leaders. The old ones. *They* haven't been here long. Things were getting too hot for them over there, so they come here. From China, Russia, Germany, all those places."

"So the leaders are all foreigners? Aren't there any South African, um, old ones?"

"Don't know. Don't think so. Too easy here in South Africa. No need to get organised." He gave a snort of disgust. "During the struggle, it was all 'crooks and straights together' and 'sentient rights for all'. And after we overthrew the old regime, the straights seemed to keep their promises. I mean, some people squeaked that there weren't enough crooks in parliament, but there was all this talk about the 'new South Africa' and the new constitution, everything bright and shiny. So most of us didn't really pay attention.

"Things were pretty good. Who cared what was happening overseas? I didn't. And then, of course, they all started coming *here.* All these refugees. No wonder the straights started getting antsy, what with sniplisters and bonecrunchers and whatever-all slipping over the borders."

Gia listened, fascinated. This was a completely different perspective on the history she'd learnt at school.

"We never learnt about magicals helping during the struggle," she said.

"Exactly," said Paddavis. "I'm not surprised to hear that."

"What is a bonecruncher?"

"Ghoul. Looks like a human, but you can tell him by his big jaw. And the smell. Poof! They do stink."

"Are any of the, um, crooks that I'm likely to meet South African? I mean, indigenous South African?"

"Indigenous? Not many anymore. Some little ones. Snaartjies, vlêrremeisies, roos-dorinkies, streepies, that kind of thing; you see them if you look. Haven't seen any others for years. Used to be, you could count on seeing a vrekker or a slaap-suster even just walking down Main Road. I remember there was a takman living down in Roodebloem 'till just a few years ago. Maybe if you went out into the country, you'd still find them. Kurk-trekkers, seepmeide, krapsoeitjies, suurklokkies..." He sighed and fell silent.

"And this Brakman we're going to see. He's one of the high ups in the Belle Gente?"

This made Paddavis laugh. "What, Brakman? No, he's just a cypher."

And more than that, she could not get out of him.

ಸಿ O ಲ

Gia was beginning to wonder just how long the walk would be, when Paddavis told her to cross one of the bridges that spanned the river into Rosebank.

This part of Rosebank looked old and unchanged. Most of the houses were behind high walls or screened from view by their lush gardens. The houses were large and luxurious, but many showed signs of neglect, and one or two were clearly abandoned.

Paddavis directed her into a road that ended at a block of flats, three storeys high. The fence was rusty and patched in places with rolls of barbed wire, and weeds sprouted in the cracked concrete. There was a gate with a bank of buttons and nameplates, and it was some time before Paddavis spotted the right one.

"There," he said, pointing. The button number was twenty-seven, and the label had "B. B." written on it in faded pencil.

"That's him," said Paddavis.

Gia hesitated, suddenly unsure.

"Go ahead — push it."

She did. Nothing happened.

"Hold it longer."

Gia obeyed. Still nothing.

"Try another one."

"Which one?"

"Doesn't matter."

Gia pushed a bell at random, and after a few seconds the speaker crackled.

"Um, Hi!" said Gia. A voice spoke, lost in static.

"Hi, I've — I've lost my key," said Gia. "Can you let me in?"

To Gia's surprise, the gate clanged and the lock released.

They took the stairs to the second floor, and found number twenty-seven. This time Gia pushed the doorbell without being prompted. A curtain stirred in one of the windows.

"He's home," she said.

"Of course he's home," said Paddavis. "Where else would he be? Put me down." He scaled the burglar bars and hammered on the door. "Brakman!" he shouted. "It's me, Paddavis. Stop messing about and let us in."

After a long pause, a key turned in the lock.

By now Gia was thoroughly nervous, and ready for any strange creature, but the face that appeared around the door was that of an old man, with pale, watery eyes.

"You're not Paddavis," he said looking up at her grumpily.

He wore a woollen cap with long flaps that fell down on either side of his face, which struck Gia as odd in the late-summer heat.

"No, she's not, but I am!" said Paddavis. "Come on, Brakkie, let us in."

"Oh. There you are." The old man wrinkled his nose at Paddavis. "What do you want?"

"Caretaker sent me."

"Caretaker?" Brakman peered at them for a few more suspicious moments. "Oh. Very well then."

The door closed and Gia thought he'd gone away again, but then she heard the chain release and the door opened all the way.

"Wait a moment, wait a moment."

Brakman sorted through his keys and unlocked the burglar gate.

The rest of him was just as odd as the glimpse Gia had already seen. He was twitchy in a way that made Gia think of a small dog, one of those that limped for no reason. His clothes were clean but faded, and he wore a pair of gloves that matched his woollen cap. She felt the drag of disappointment. How on earth could this ridiculous little man help Nico?

"Come in, come in," said Brakman impatiently.

He led Gia down a short passage and showed her into a room, with Paddavis following close behind. There was nothing much to see. Only a filing cabinet, a trestle table with a computer on it, a chair, and a sofa.

"So what do you want?" said Brakman. "The caretaker sent you?"

"That's right," said Paddavis, who'd already made himself at home on the sofa. "We need some records wiped."

Brakman frowned. "Wiped? I can't help you with that."

"Of course you can," said Paddavis.

"Um," said Gia quickly, as the little man drew himself up in irritation. "We're sorry to barge in on you like this, Mr Brakman. But we don't have much time. The caretaker told me that you are the only one who can help me, so I'm sure you are very busy. I hope we did not interrupt anything important?"

Brakman stared at her for a moment in surprise. "Oh, no, not really. Just routine stuff." He sniffed and peered at her. "Caretaker said I was the one, hey? Always like that. Jump when things get ugly, and forget about you the rest of the time."

Gia did not know how to respond to that, so she said nothing.

"Oh, sit, sit," he said, waving a hand at the sofa. "Might as well get it over with."

There was a nest of blankets on the sofa, and Gia felt sure that this was where Brakman spent his nights. One corner of the room was piled high with pizza boxes. The air was stale, and she wished she could open a window. Brakman pulled up a chair for himself and sat there, glancing from Gia to Paddavis, who was bouncing, grinning at some private joke.

"So, what's this about then?" said Brakman.

Seeing that Paddavis was not going to help her, Gia took the plunge. "I need help to get my little brother out of testing by Special Branch."

Brakman's eyebrows went up. "Why do they want to test him?"

"They think he's crook," said Paddavis while Gia was still looking for words. "And he probably is. A bit like you. A useful crook. Useful to them. So we need to wipe his records, as soon as he's got any."

"What does that mean?" said Gia, frowning at Paddavis. "Wipe his records?"

Paddavis twinkled at her, clearly enjoying himself immensely.

"Brakman here, he's a hacker."

"A *cypher*," corrected Brakman testily.

"Whatever," continued Paddavis. "He works on the Special Branch computers. That machine over there speaks through the phone lines, or something, to their machines, where they keep all their records. Soon as little Nico is tested, Brakman can change their records to whatever we want it to be."

"Really?" said Gia.

"No," said Brakman. "It's nothing so simple as that."

He nibbled at the knuckle of a glove.

"The caretaker sent you, you say?"

Gia nodded.

"You owe him, don't you?" said Paddavis.

Brakman shot him an angry glance, but Paddavis was unimpressed.

"You want me to tell him you're not helping?"

"Okay, yes, okay. Give me a chance," said Brakman. He worked his jaw about, as if chewing something distasteful.

"Well, some of it is true," he said reluctantly. "I can access the Special Branch servers remotely from my machine here, and do what is necessary to change the results of a test."

"But how's that possible?" said Gia. "Surely they

notice? And have some— I don't know, some security thing to stop that from happening?"

"Indeed, they do," said Brakman. "But I'm very good."

"Oh," said Gia.

"He works for Special Branch. Computer mechanic," said Paddavis. "In and out of Valkenberg all the time, no problem."

"Not any more, I'm not," grumbled Brakman. "Or anyway, not for long. Those Purists are getting rid of all the crook staff, haven't you heard? Or anyway, all the magicals except for their pet sniffer-weres and such, and those kids they've got trained up in their Youth League or whatever the hell they call themselves. I'll not be able to get in to bypass the new security codes, once those are set again."

"Really?" said Paddavis, for once at a loss.

"I'm sorry," said Gia. "I don't understand. I thought that you were part of the Belle Gente. So how is it that you also work for Special Branch? Don't they check up on that kind of thing?"

Nobody said anything. Brakman picked nervously at his gloves, avoiding her gaze. Clearly she'd said something wrong. She tried again.

"If Special Branch are getting rid of all magical staff, does that mean you'll lose your job? You are, um, a magical, aren't you?"

"Good question," said Paddavis.

This brought another glare from Brakman.

"Well, I'm magical enough for the Belle Gente to keep their hooks in me," he said. "And I'm magical enough for Special Branch to treat me like dirt."

He turned back to Gia. "You want to know if I'm a magical?"

He pulled off his gloves and held up his hands to her, palms inward. Each finger ended in a flat pink scar where the nail should have been.

"And this!" He took off the knitted cap and turned his face away, pushing the side of his head toward Gia, who could not suppress a gasp at the scarred stubs of his ears.

"Oh! What happened?"

"They cured me, that's what happened." said Brakman. "Special Branch. Cured me."

"What do you mean?"

Brakman met her eyes for a moment, then looked down at his scarred hands. His shoulders slumped.

"Can't you guess?" he said in a softer tone. "I used to be a were. Changed every month. Lucky they got me early, when I just hit puberty so they could stop the changes taking hold. So I'm not really fish, nor flesh, as your friend here will tell you. Neither crook nor straight."

All the anger had gone out of him, and he seemed greyer than ever. Gia wanted to apologise, but he was still talking.

"Not the worst fate, for a were. Got proper training. Information technology, network management, all those are the coming thing, you know. I'm a qualified security expert." His back straightened a fraction. "Good enough that the old ones at the Belle Gente pay me a pretty penny. Get them the data they need. Change a file here and there. Needs a subtle touch, that."

"But you said you can't do that anymore?" asked Gia.

"It all depends," said Brakman. "When is the test happening?"

"On Friday."

Brakman sniffed.

"Hmm. That's still before they'll be doing their next reboot and changing the passwords."

"What does that mean?"

"It means you are lucky. I still have access to the system on Friday. Special Branch change their passcodes soon after, and after that, I'm out. If you can tell me the exact time, and all goes well, I should be able to intercept and adjust the test data. Put stuff in there, do you see? Make it so they won't be interested in doing any further tests. He'd end up with a certificate of purity too, which comes in pretty useful."

"Really? You can do that?" said Gia, hope flaming up again.

Brakman shrugged. "If you can afford it."

Gia blinked at him. "I'm sorry?"

The old man got up and went over to the filing cabinet.

"It's been a while since I've done one of these," he said, riffling through a drawer. "Let me get the contract…no, that's not it. Ah."

He pulled out a cardboard folder, and came back to his chair. "Here you go." He gave Gia a printed page from the folder.

"That's the contract. You'll have to sign that, before I can go any further. Agree to the fee."

"The fee," said Gia. She felt knocked off balance. "What— fee?"

"There's always a charge," said Brakman. "I do the work so I get the cut, but the contract is with the Belle Gente. That's who you'll be paying. Look, you'll see, it's all written down there."

Of course there would be a fee.

Gia felt a blush sting her cheeks. It made her feel like a foolish child, to have been taken by surprise. She tried to read, but the words seemed to make no sense. "Where does it say the amount?"

Brakman leaned over to show her. "There. See?"

Gia read. "But this says in *gold*."

Brakman gave her a wintery smile. "The old ones are *old*. They still do things the old way. You'll just have to convert it into rands, that's all."

"And how much does that come to?"

"About five thousand."

Gia stared down at the contract again. Five thousand rand was a lot of money, but it was not impossible.

"By when?" She ran a finger along the lines of print. "Says here, twenty-four hours before the 'procedure'. So that must mean we have to pay by Thursday?"

"That's correct," said Brakman.

"And— how do we pay? I mean, who do we give the money to? You?"

Brakman opened the folder again.

"No. They would never trust *me* with that much money. Here."

He handed her a plastic card. Gia turned it over in her hand. It was perfectly white, with a magnetic strip along one side.

"What's this?"

"That's what you'll pay with. Take it to any bank machine that has a deposit facility. Punch in the number that's on that form— the one that's stamped on the top there. That's your procedure number. Punch that into the teller. Then you'll get instructions on how to go on from there."

Gia looked at the contract again. There was something baffling about its bland normality. It looked like a utilities bill, or a demand letter from the municipal library.

What am I getting into?

But what choice did she have? Nico would still have to go for the tests, and that was bad. But it would be only the one set of tests, and then he'd have a certificate of purity. The way things seemed to be going, having a piece of paper that certified you as 'non-magical' might turn out to be very useful indeed for Nico.

She turned to Paddavis. "You have a look at it. I'm not sure I understand it all."

"Sure!" Paddavis took the contract and looked it over in a most business-like way, nodding, and tapping his finger on the paper.

"Looks all square to me," he said, handing it back to Gia.

"Well then," said Gia. "Okay. Let's do it. What do I have to do?"

"Just sign it," said Brakman. "Come over here by the table so you've got something to press on."

He took out another copy of the contract. When Gia had signed and dated both of them, he handed her a pin. Gia took it, unsure what he meant her to do.

"Give your thumb a prick with that, and press it top of your signature," said Brakman. "That seals it."

She ran the pin into her thumb. It went deeper than she'd meant, and the bloody fingerprint made the ink of her signatures blur a little.

Brakman signed too, and took off one glove to prick his thumb and seal both his signatures in blood. "There," he said, blowing on the paper to dry it. "One more now, so you have a copy."

She repeated the procedure, and Brakman put her copy of the form in an envelope.

Now that she'd made her decision, Gia was in a hurry to get back home. She'd been away much too long already, and her mother would be wondering where she was.

"Thanks," she said, and took the envelope from Brakman. "I've really got to go now. Thanks so much for agreeing to help."

She hesitated. "You're sure it will work? We just take Nico in to the test — we don't have to do anything?"

"It will work," said Brakman. "Done this many times before. Nothing for you to do. Just go in and have the tests done, just as normal."

ಸಿ೦ಡಿ

On the walk back, Gia was so preoccupied that she hardly took in her surroundings.

Paddavis lay in the curve of her arm, and at times seemed to be dozing. It was getting late, and she did not feel at all safe walking by herself, even if Paddavis was still making her invisible.

When she got home, she found Saraswati in the studio, working on the toile of Kavitha's wedding gown. For a moment, Gia forgot about her own concerns. Even in this unfinished state, and made from cheap fabric, she could see that the final version was going to be glorious.

"It's looking great, Mom!"

Saraswati was on her knees, pulling out the skirts to see how they would fall.

"It's turning out rather well," she said. "Can't really know until she's tried it on."

Her hands moved over the garment, touching here, moving a seam there.

"The true test is how it looks with a moving body inside it."

"Has she bought the fabric yet?"

"Not yet."

Gia watched her mother for a few moments longer. She'd spent most of the walk trying out explanations of where she'd been, but now that it came to the point, she did not know how to start. At last she just held out the contract.

"Mom, I think I've found a way to get Nico out of having to take that test. Or — at least, he'll still have to go to the test, but that will be it, they won't…"

Her voice trailed off as her mother took the envelope. "What do you mean, Gia?" she said as she opened it. "What's this?"

Saraswati's brows gathered in a frown as she read through the contract.

"Gia, what's this? Where did you get this?"

"It's a contract. The caretaker told me where to go. To contact the Belle Gente. They've agreed — well, actually, just this man called Brakman, he can get into the Special Branch's computer system and…"

Saraswati felt behind her for a chair, and sat down, still reading.

"Gia." Saraswati spoke quietly, but Gia felt her whole body tensing as if she expected a blow. Her mother's face was very pale.

"Where did you get this? Who did you speak to?"

"I was just telling you," said Gia, trying to keep her voice light. "That contract is with the old ones of the Belle Gente. I met with this, um, representative of theirs called Brakman. He's the one who can help us. I know it's expensive —"

"You went somewhere, to speak to— a 'representative' of the Belle Gente?" Saraswati's voice had lost some of its calm now. "Gia, what— I don't even know—"

She got up from her chair.

"How did you contact this, this—" she gestured wordlessly. "You went off somewhere, with a strange man, Gia, have you lost your mind? And then you actually *signed* a *contract,* and in blood too, without even thinking to—"

Her voice ran out and she shook her head in disbelief. But her silence was only for a moment.

"You shared our private family matters with some— some stranger. It's bad enough that you put yourself in danger. But to drag our private troubles through the muck in public, and with these— " She seemed unable to find a word that was bad enough to express her distaste.

By now she was up and pacing, and Gia had to back away. Anger came off her like heat from an oven.

"Have you ever stopped, just for a minute, have you ever stopped to think *why* it is that I never have anything to do with the magicals? The Belle Gente? That there might be a *reason*, Gia, a reason that you know nothing about? That these people are not to be trusted? Haven't you seen the news? Haven't you seen their slogans? These are people who will sacrifice *anything*, Gia, they will do anything to further their cause. I saw it happen, in Italy. I saw—"

But by now, Gia's blood was up too. "How am I supposed to know anything, if you won't tell me anything? There's nothing but secrets with you! No, I don't know what happened in Italy because nobody ever wants to talk about it!"

They stood, breathing hard, glaring at each other.

Saraswati was the first to recover. She put a hand over her eyes, took a deep breath, and let it out. "Well, most likely this person you spoke to is nothing but a confidence trickster and has nothing to do with the Belle Gente. You did not give him any money, did you?"

Gia shook her head. She held her breath, waiting for her mother to reach out to her, to do anything that would make it possible for her to apologise and end the fight. But although the heat of her anger had died down, Saraswati was still pale and grim, and as tense as ever.

"Mom," said Gia, trying to speak calmly. "The caretaker himself said that Brakman worked for the Belle Gente. And it's like a standard procedure. I mean, he's done this before. He can get into their computer system. If you pay them, Brakman will make sure that Nico only has to do the first set of tests and he'll get a certificate of purity. That's what you want, isn't it? Some way to make sure that Nico will be safe?"

Surely, once Saraswati understood that she'd only been acting with the best intentions, she'd understand?

But Saraswati kept her eyes on the contract, smoothing it out on the table. Her face was rigid, and her lips thin and her hands were trembling.

"It's very unlikely, Gia, that this person you met is anything but a conman. That's how it works, I'm afraid. When times are bad people like that gather like vultures. It's not surprising you were taken in."

She rubbed her hands over her face, and raked her fingers through her hair. "I'll speak to the caretaker. I want to know what on earth he thinks he's doing, getting you involved in this mess."

Brakman

෩О෬

Saraswati would not allow Gia to go with her to the caretaker.

"Go upstairs and stay there until your father gets home and we can discuss this matter." She came back a few minutes later, frustrated. The caretaker was nowhere to be found.

Gia wanted to go on arguing, but she could see that her mother was still too worked up for there to be any point in it. The more she thought about it, the more she doubted. Had it all just been an elaborate trick?

In any case, all her efforts were wasted. If Saraswati did not believe in the contract, she would not pay. And if the money was not paid on time, Brakman would not do whatever it was he did, and— what would happen then?

Nico would be tested, and life would go on, just as it had before.

Had she worked herself up over nothing?

When Karel came home, the situation was discussed again, this time more calmly.

Nico had been put to bed, and Gia and her parents sat around the kitchen table. Although her father spoke to her more sternly that he usually did, Gia found his words easier to take than her mother's anger. Even being grounded for a week did not seem to matter much.

"No visits from friends, and no hour-long phone-calls either," said Karel, winding down at last. "This is serious, Gia. You acted without thinking, and could have been involved in a serious situation, going alone into a stranger's house."

Not alone, she thought, but did not speak her thoughts out loud. Somehow, she'd not got around to explaining about Paddavis, and doubted that it would make much difference.

Saraswati, who'd been reading through the contract again, reached out and touched Karel's sleeve.

"Karel," she said with a slight frown. "Have you read this thing?"

"No," he said. "Why?"

"Just have a look at this clause."

He read the paragraph she pointed to. Then he read it again.

"What is it?" asked Gia, feeling once again that stir of unease.

"Well, it doesn't really matter," said Karel, folding the paper away. "It's not as if it's a real contract, after all. I mean, we know this guy must be a conman, right? He was just hoping we'd pay the money, and then we'd never have heard from him again."

But Gia could see that whatever he'd read had worried him.

"What is it, Dad?" said Gia.

Karel glanced at Saraswati. "If I understand it right— and that language is hideously old fashioned, so I might have it wrong—"

He unfolded the contract again and pointed to a paragraph just under the place that stated the fee. "It says here, that if the fee is not paid by the stated time, the Belle Gente reserve the right to claim the test subject in lieu of payment."

Gia looked at him blankly. "What does that mean?"

"It means that in theory— if this thing were real— and we did not pay them on time, they can take Nico."

The shock of it flowed like ice-water through Gia's veins. "They can't do that, surely?" she said faintly.

Karel pushed himself away from the table. "That's why you must never sign anything you don't fully understand, Gia. We're lucky this thing is not real. Otherwise, we could be in some nasty trouble here."

"But you are sure it's not real?" Gia stared up at him.

"Of course. Now, I've got to get back to work. Good night, Gia."

ಸO಼

After Karel left, Saraswati still sat staring down at the table.

"Gia," she said at last. "I'm thinking, if I could have a word with this— what was his name?"

"Brakman?"

"Yes. If I can see him and speak to him, then I'd know for sure. And if there is any chance he really is what he says he is, maybe he'll be open to renegotiation."

"But I thought you said—"

Saraswati looked up. "I don't really know quite what to think right now."

They looked into the studio on their way out. Saraswati spoke to Karel, but she let him think they were just going out to get some bread.

Somehow, that was more frightening that anything else that had happened that day.

Gia thought of a glass vase, pure and solid, but with the thinnest of cracks running through its base.

Invisible, but inevitable.

It was much harder to find Brakman's flat than she'd anticipated. Driving was different from walking, and none of the landmarks looked quite as she'd remembered them. It was quite dark by the time they turned into the right road and she pointed out the block to her mother.

Saraswati pushed the bell, but as before, there was no response. Luckily an old woman, loaded down with shopping bags, stumped up the steps, and did not even noticed when they slipped in behind her.

Gia led the way to number twenty-seven, but they found it dark and quiet. There was nobody home. Nobody responded to their knocks and calls, and at last they were forced to leave, as a grumpy neighbour threatened to call the police.

Saraswati said nothing on the drive home.

ಸOಇ

ASKING GRANNY

The next few days were tense and uncomfortable.

Neither Karel nor Saraswati mentioned the contract, but Gia could tell it was still on their minds. She herself could not stop thinking about it.

One moment she was convinced that it was a fake, and that all she had to worry about was how Nico would deal with the testing. The next moment she was horribly sure that the contract was real, and that by signing it, she'd committed her family to who-knew-what dreadful agreement.

She realised now that she'd been a fool to ask Paddavis to look over the contract, or to rely on him for any kind of advice. Thinking back about it, she doubted if he could even read. She'd tried calling his name a few times, but he never appeared. Her stomach hurt, and she had trouble sleeping.

If her parents did not pay, did that mean that the contract was broken and not worth worrying about? Or could the Belle Gente still claim Nico, just come and take him away?

Nico tried her patience too.

He refused to accept that her room was off limits. Saraswati was unsympathetic, even when Nico took a bottle of cowrie shells and several feathers from her collection. There was no mystery what he wanted them for — it was for the sculpture he was making out of the overlocker pieces.

He worked on it whenever he could.

Despite her irritation, Gia had to admit that it was an impressive piece. It had a head and body now, articulated legs ending in two large, splayed feet. The cowrie-shells did duty as teeth, and it had a feathered crest all the way down its neck.

Gia tried to find the caretaker, but while she saw him in the distance once or twice, she never got close enough to draw his attention. She desperately wanted to speak to him, particularly about the contract.

At least she could share her thoughts with Sonella, but that was also a small comfort. Sonella was concerned and attentive, but did not seem to understand Gia's horror at the idea of the Belle Gente.

"They're not terrorists, Gia," she said. "I mean, I know you don't want *anyone* to take Nico away. But I'm sure they don't mean to do *that*. And even if they did, at least they're not Special Branch."

Because of being grounded, the only contact she had with Fatima and Ben was via texter, and texters were not any good for anything longer than a few words.

Then there was the approaching deadline for First Exit.

Soon, she'd have to make her final decision.

Stay at school, or defy her parents and apply for a place at the art school. The doll was ready, and that made it worse, as she had nothing to occupy herself. All she could do was think, and worry.

Miss Huisman took her aside after class one day to ask about the testing at Valkenberg. Gia was tempted to ask her for advice, but her mother's words about "sharing our private family matters" still weighed on her conscience.

Late one night, Gia went down to the kitchen for a drink of water and found her parents there. She paused at the door, and after she'd heard a few words, stepped back out of view.

"For the last time, Sari," her father was saying. "I can't let you go into hiding with Nico. I understand that you are concerned. From what Gia's said, Nico's not going to deal well with those tests. But we'll get through this, as long as we stand together—"

"If we have that choice!" Saraswati's voice was ragged with fatigue, and Gia guessed this conversation had been going on for a long time.

"Karel, I'm not letting those fascist pseudo-scientists anywhere near my son. Yes. I don't yet know where I can go, but if you will only let me have access to the money—"

"Sari, be reasonable. You don't know for a fact that there is any danger to Nico. Even if there was somewhere for you to go to, if you disappear now it will only attract the wrong kind of attention. The best thing would be for us to play by the rules—"

Saraswati gave a kind of sob.

Gia wanted to put her hands over her ears. She'd never heard her mother like this before.

"That is exactly what my father, when my sisters—"

"Yes, I know, and I'm sorry, but this really is not the same. You are not being rational here, Sari. Please try to be calm. As long as we stay together and trust one another we can get through this, but you're pulling away from me all the time. I'm not going to give you any money, and that's flat. Not if you are going to use it to take my son into danger."

Gia had had enough.

She turned and went back up to her bedroom, crawled into her bed, and curled around the hurt in her stomach.

༄O༅

Gia had trouble concentrating on her schoolwork the next day. The conversation she'd overheard kept repeating over and over in her head, and every time it woke more questions.

Why could Saraswati not get the money from the bank herself? Had it always been like that— that her father controlled the money, and her mother relied on him to give her what she needed?

Now that she thought about it, while Saraswati was always planning and managing the family's finances, Gia could not remember her ever actually withdrawing any money herself.

Maybe it was something to do with the fact that her mother was not a South African citizen? But that seemed unlikely.

She dragged herself away from these thoughts, uneasy at what they might reveal about her parents.

Saraswati wanted to go away, to try to hide, to escape somehow, both from the Special Branch and the Belle Gente, and that was why she needed money.

Could she do it anyway, even without money? Was there anywhere she could go?

She had no family of her own, or none that Gia knew about.

She had no friends either.

For the first time, Gia thought about this, and found it strange.

Her mother was well known, and well liked. But she had no special friends— the kind of friends she could turn to in times of trouble.

Why was that?

There was Mandy. But Gia found it hard to imagine Saraswati confiding in Mandy, even though Gia thought of Mandy as one of the family.

Was it simply because Saraswati was foreign? That could not be the only reason. After nearly sixteen years, she could have made some connections by now.

Gia wondered what it must have been like for her mother, coming to a strange country. Saraswati had been about eighteen years old. And there had been her, Gia, a new baby to care for.

That could not have been easy.

Gia was so deep in her thoughts that she was barely aware of what went on around her. The only incident that drew her attention happened during English, when Mrs Kemp knocked on the door and said she had an announcement to make.

"You all know that it's only two days before First Exit."

Her words made Gia sit up.

"On Friday, those of you who wish to take First Exit will be given the opportunity to visit the First Exit displays in the school hall. If you have portfolios, curriculum vitae, or anything else to submit for consideration, those must be brought to the hall the first thing in the morning.

"Ensure that everything is clearly labelled with your name, as well as the name of the person who will be judging your work.

"Some advice. It is always a good idea to visit several of the stands, and speak to more than one of the representatives. You may think you know who you wish to go with, but you can keep your options open until the moment you sign up with them.

"Anyone who needs advice, or more information about any of the exhibitors, make an appointment with me. You will find the list of exhibitors up on the noticeboards, as well as many pamphlets."

ಸಂOಣ

When Gia got home, she found that both her parents had gone out. Mandy was in the tiny backyard, taking down laundry. Karel had told her all about Gia's trip to see Brakman.

"You're always rushing into things, Gia," she said. "But no use crying over spilt milk."

She picked up the laundry basket and started making her way back up the stairs. "Madam's been worrying herself sick all morning. She went out to Granny's to get some milk and bread, and came back as white as a sheet."

"Do you think Granny told her something?"

"I wouldn't be surprised."

Being grounded meant that Gia was not allowed to leave the house without her parents' permission. Things were still tense with Saraswati, and she hesitated to do anything to worsen that situation, but in the end, she decided that she would risk visiting Granny's shop while her parents were still away.

Granny was sitting at the counter. "Good afternoon," she said as Gia came in. "What can I do for you today, sweetheart?"

She had a row of jars and bottles lined up in front of her and was wiping one of them with a soft cloth.

"My mother was in earlier, wasn't she?" said Gia.

"She was," said Granny.

Gia tried to imagine what Saraswati would have said. Surely she would not talk about their troubles to a relative stranger. But she would still need information.

"Did she ask you anything about a man called Brakman?"

Granny's eyebrows rose, but she went on polishing the bottle, working with slow care. "She did, at that."

"So you know him? Brakman?"

The old woman turned the bottle upside down and worked the cloth carefully inside. "I might."

Gia hesitated. She did not know quite how to phrase her next question. "Brakman told me he worked for the Belle Gente."

"Hmm," said Granny. She gave the bottle a last wipe, then put it down and selected another one.

"Is it true? Does he?" asked Gia, but before Granny could answer, two women came in, and Gia had to wait while they had a leisurely chat with Granny about the weather, the new umbrellas that Granny was going to order, and the fact that tomatoes just did not taste the way they used to. When they'd finally bought their cigarettes and left, Gia spoke again.

"Is it true? About Brakman?"

Granny scratched at a spot on the bottle with a long, yellow fingernail. "Why are you asking?"

"You told my mother what you knew about Brakman, didn't you?"

Granny shrugged. "I might have."

"And I bet you did not make *her* explain why she needed to know."

Granny seemed to find this amusing. She held the bottle to the light and squinted at it critically.

"You're right about that," she said. "Your mother knows how to get what she wants."

Gia clenched her fists. She did not have time for this. Her parents would be back soon, and she wanted to be home before them. But before she could say anything, Granny spoke again.

"Maybe I can tell *you* why you are asking me all these questions."

She rubbed the cloth over the bottle in a meditative way.

"Saturday, you had Special Branch sniffing around. Interesting, that. Special Branch don't do that without a reason. Maybe it's got something to do with that brother of yours. Don't look so surprised. Special Branch has been after the young ones for a while now. What got their attention on your brother, I don't know."

She shot Gia a gleaming look. "Any road, when your mother comes in here and asks, ever so casual, about Brakman, well. I can put two and two together. Special Branch have got their hooks in you, and they want to test that little boy."

Granny's mouth twisted up and for a moment Gia thought she was going to spit. "Test him at Valkenberg. And who would you turn to, but Brakman?"

"So he wasn't just trying to trick me? He really can help — he does work for the Belle Gente like he said?"

Granny nodded. "That's right. He does. And he can."

Gia was not sure whether to feel relieved or alarmed. She had not been fooled after all. She'd been right to trust the caretaker. But that also meant that the contract was real, and that the Belle Gente might act on their claim.

"Some advice, sweetie." Granny put down her cloth, and focused her full attention on Gia. "It seems you've been getting mixed up with us crooks. And maybe you've found that interesting. Having an adventure like a girl in a story.

"Thing is, the old ones— the Belle Gente— they're not like me, or the caretaker, or any other little ones you might have run into here and there. *We're* just regular people, even if we might seem a bit odd to you.

"The Belle Gente, they're the lords and the ladies. Most of them aren't even from around here. Some of them are very old, and they've have been fighting for a very long time. Crooks and straights, that's all they see."

"I don't understand," said Gia. "What are you telling me?"

"The old ones are *old*," said Granny. "They saw slavery, and wars, and worse, and survived. They are willing to do anything, to sacrifice anything. They have no doubt, you see. They *know* they're right. They set their mill grinding, and don't care that the small ones break their bones between the mill-stones."

A shudder prickled down Gia's spine.

"Now, I would guess that if you've been dealing with Brakman, you got yourself into an agreement with the Belle Gente. Signed a contract, maybe. You may find that paying their fee is not quite as straightforward as you'd like."

"What do you mean?"

"Let me put it this way. What the old ones want is not gold. Gold they have in plenty. But if they can get a soldier, even a small one, that may be worth more than gold to them. And a soldier that's been certified as a straight— certificate of purity, don't they call it that? That would be very convenient."

"They'll try to take Nico?"

Granny looked at her for a long moment. "Not try," she said at last. "Take. What's to stop them, after all?"

She picked up her cloth again. "Unless, of course, you can make them a counteroffer."

෩O෫

As she'd feared, Gia's parents returned home just as she reached the front door. But neither of them noticed that she'd been out without permission. They seemed preoccupied, and asked her to join them in the studio.

"Gia," said Saraswati. "Did the man you talked to, that Brakman, explain how to make this payment?"

"He gave me a sort of bank card. He said you could use it on any bank machine."

"Do you still have it?"

Gia got her wallet and fished out the card. "Have you decided to pay then?"

Saraswati frowned at the card. "How does it work?"

"He said there's a number on the contract. Apparently you just punch it into the bank machine, then there will be instructions on how to pay."

Saraswati took the contract out of her handbag and Gia showed her the stamped number.

"Any bank machine?"

"That's what he said."

Gia noticed a shopping bag of fabric on the cutting table. The little bit she could see was a dusky ivory, and had the sheen of silk.

"Is that Kavitha's fabric?"

"Yes," said Karel. "Shantung silk. We went there this morning to do a fitting with the toile, and it's pretty much there. They're insisting on us finishing the dress as soon as we can, so we're going to be busy next week."

He glanced at his watch.

"Sari, if we go now, we can do this payment and pick up Nico on our way back."

Then they were gone. Gia stared after them thoughtfully.

Whatever Granny had said to Saraswati, it was enough to convince them to pay Brakman.

೫‌O೦౩

Gia did her homework while Mandy ironed, then she helped fold and put away the laundry. Neither of them spoke much, but Gia kept glancing at the clock.

Something must have gone wrong.

It could not take this long simply to deposit some money into a bank machine.

Mandy got out the Brasso and polishing cloths, which told Gia that she, too was feeling anxious. Mandy loved polishing copper- and brassware, and tended to bring out the polishing things whenever she was unhappy.

Gia went up to her room and took out the doll. She knew there was nothing more to do to her, but it was comforting to touch the braided hair, and run her fingers over her painted skin.

Was she good enough? In less than twenty-four hours, she would know.

She put the doll back into the box, and tucked the folds of tissue-paper in around her. Then her gaze fell on the stacks of sketchpads in her milk crate shelf.

Maybe she should take some of those too. She took a few at random, and put them on top of the doll's box.

She'd waited for this so long, and had expected to be unbearably nervous, but all she felt was hollow. It seemed so unreal. What would Karel, what would Saraswati say when she told them that she'd committed herself to leaving school?

She told herself that by the time she really had to leave, thing would have worked out somehow.

Nico was having his test tomorrow. Once that was done, the worst would be over.

൞O൛

Mandy had gone home by the time her parents returned with a very tired and hungry Nico in tow.

Gia met them at the front door.

Her father shook his head at her. "Didn't work."

Then he went into the kitchen, Nico on his hip.

"What happened?" she asked Saraswati.

"It just flashed a message," said Saraswati. "We went to four different bank machines, had to queue at every single one."

"What message?"

Saraswati shook her head. "I don't remember the exact words. But they didn't want our money. Listen, please help your father with Nico. I'm going to have a quick shower."

൞O൛

FIRST EXIT

Their English teacher was late, and everyone was chatting. Their voices were louder than usual, and there was a sting of excitement in the air.

It was First Exit day, after all.

"So, are you going to do it?" asked Sonella.

Gia nodded, but she felt far from sure.

Part of her kept jumping with little shocks, as she remembered, and remembered again, that today was the day of Nico's test. She couldn't help imagining what he must be going through.

She told herself that they would have gentler testing methods for a child, especially a child with Nico's needs. But Cadet Lee's words kept intruding.

I freaked out something dreadful. Screamed so much I lost my voice for weeks.

Cadet Lee had been older than Nico was now, when she was tested. Surely they'd make allowances for a seven-year-old?

And if he got through the tests, and Brakman delivered on his promises, what then? Why had the Belle Gente not accepted the fee? If she understood Granny, they would prefer Nico himself as payment.

How would that work? Would they just take him away?

She simply could not picture it.

Then there was First Exit to worry about.

For months now, she'd obsessed about how she'd get the doll and the rest of her portfolio to school without awkward questions from her parents. As it turned out, they were so focused on Nico that they'd not even noticed the unusually large bag.

She'd expected to be nervous now, worrying whether the lecturers from the art school would think her work was good enough. Instead, she was second-guessing the whole idea.

Was she really going to go off on her own, now, after all that had happened?

And under it all, a thought was growing, like a mole pushing at the soil. What was it that Granny had said?

Unless, of course, you can make them a counter-offer.

The more Gia thought about those words, the more certain she became that Granny was hinting at a plan. She wanted Gia to do something.

The subterranean thought stirred again, nudging nearly at the surface, but Gia was too scared to brush the soil away, to see what it might be.

Sonella put an arm around her and gave her a hug. "Don't worry. It's going to be fine."

Gia did not know if she was referring to Nico's test, or to First Exit, but it was comforting all the same.

The bell went.

"Well," said Sonella. "That's it!"

ೲOೲ

The school hall was transformed. All the chairs were stacked up against the walls, and various display stands and tables had been set up throughout the space. Some were undecorated, with only a neat stack of pamphlets. Others were covered in banners and posters.

Gia quickly spotted the Special Branch stand. It was one of the most popular in the hall, particularly with the boys.

Sonella pulled at her sleeve and pointed.

Gia felt her heart bump at the sight of the art school stand. Somebody had made a small exhibition out of the various portfolio submissions. A group of students crowded around, admiring the work.

Miss Huisman stood there, chatting with a bearded man.

"Is that yours, Gia, the doll?" said one of the girls. "Wow. She's so lovely!"

The bearded man smiled at Gia. He was a thin man, with long, greying hair.

"Are you the girl with the doll? You are signing up with us? Are you on the list yet?" He looked at Gia with sharp interest.

"Um, I— I guess—" said Gia. Her gaze was drawn back to the Special Branch stand.

"You are—" The man checked the label on the doll, "Gianetta, aren't you? This is your work?"

He indicated her sketchbooks, several of which had been propped open to display the drawings inside.

Gia felt herself blush. "Yes," she managed.

"That's great," he said. "So good to see something different for a change. You have real talent, Gianetta. I'm thinking— are you related to Saraswati? Isn't her real name Grobbelaar too?"

"She's my mother."

"Well, that explains it. It's in the blood," he said, grinning at her. "Your mother is a very talented woman, and I'm not surprised her daughter has inherited that talent."

But I'm adopted, was what Gia wanted to say, but she managed to bite the words back.

She saw that Miss Huisman was smiling at her, a kind and encouraging smile.

"I didn't know you were planning to go for art school, Gia," she said. "But I can see why! That doll is quite something."

"So, you'll be wanting to sign up with us then," said the man. "Let's get the paperwork out of the way."

"Actually," said Gia. "I— um. Well, I need to look at some of the other tables first."

She could feel Sonella's astonished reaction even without looking at her.

"Just to be sure, you know."

The man put the forms down again.

"Good idea," he said. "You go right ahead. Have a good look around. You know where to find me once you've made up your mind."

The hall was quite crowded now. Officially, only standard eights were supposed to attend the First Exit exhibit, but inevitably other students sneaked in too.

There was a lot to look at. There was a stand for paramedics, and one that showed beautiful samples of woodwork and furniture design. Another stand had something to do with the care of animals— that one had a particularly large crowd of students around it.

As she made her way towards the Special Branch stand, Granny's words kept repeating.

Let me put it this way. What the old ones want, is not gold.

Sonella touched her arm. "Where are you going, Gia?"

There was a group of boys around the Special Branch stand, listening to a man in uniform. Gia recognised him.

It was Captain Witbooi.

"No, by joining the Youth Division, you are not joining the police force," he was saying. "The police have a selection procedure, and then there's two years of training before you even get started.

"The Youth Division is a separate thing; it's support for Special Branch. You will get training, of course, some of it tough. We need recruits of all kinds, who can work with their heads as well as with their hands."

"So what will we be doing?" asked a tall boy.

"You'll be helping Special Branch. Keeping our community safe from all threats. You'll be trained to deal with this stuff. This is not just theory! This is going out and getting your hands dirty, doing something real."

"Do we get paid?" asked another boy, which drew much elbowing from his friends.

Captain Witbooi flashed a smile.

"You are paid a small amount per week, but your bed, board and clothing, and any equipment is provided by Special Branch. If you have a talent, such as, for example an aptitude for medicine or science, you will receive specialised training by Special Branch experts.

"Cadet Thompson here." He put his hand on the shoulder of a tall and skinny cadet. "He's turning out to be an expert in all kinds of weapons. A real sharpshooter, too. And Cadet Mantjies over there, he's got a knack for chemistry. Especially the kind that explodes. Don't let him mix you a drink!"

The boys laughed dutifully.

"Will we be in danger?" asked another boy.

The captain gave a considering nod. "You will be exposed to a greater amount of physical and psychic danger than the average citizen. That is inevitable. However, that is what your training is for. To equip you to be able to face, and handle, any threat that you may come across."

Cadet Mantjies raised a hand, and got a nod from the captain. "The great thing is, you're never alone. You're part of the team, and we all got each other's backs. It's tough! Not for sissies, if you know what I mean."

This drew a laugh from the boys, and when it was clear that Captain Witbooi had finished his talk, they gathered around the table, chatting to the cadets and fingering the pamphlets.

Gia pushed through and took a pamphlet.

"Are you interested in joining?" asked the captain.

"If I do — it's for two years?"

"That's right."

"And I've got to go live there in Valkenberg? Do all the cadets live there?"

"Yes. We do allow cadets to visit their families sometimes, but as training is intense, it works best if everyone lives together under one roof."

"Can anyone join? I mean, is there some kind of test, or portfolio or something — ?"

"Some candidates are rejected, mostly on mental health grounds. But that rarely happens. We are looking for a wide skillset, not just strong-men."

"Till when do I have to decide?"

"Till the end of the day. If you need to speak to your parents or anything like that. Although really, by the time candidates come here they generally know what they want already."

She wondered if he recognised her, and remembered the question she'd asked Cadet Lee, but his attention was already elsewhere, as he turned to chat to one of the other boys.

Gia turned away from the stand and started to leave the hall. She expected Sonella to demand an explanation, but Sonella just walked quietly next to her.

They sat in their usual place, and shared one another's lunches while Gia looked through the Special Branch pamphlet. She found she was trembling as she sat, as if she were cold despite the sun. The pamphlet shook in her hands.

What was it her father had said?

You must never sign anything you don't fully understand.

But how did you ever fully understand the consequences of any big choice? Sometimes you just had to choose, and none of your choices were right.

If they can get a soldier, even a small one, that may be worth more than gold to them.

Those had been Granny's words.

What had she been trying to tell Gia? What value would the Belle Gente find in a small boy?

In a children's story, they'd throw him in a pot, or change him into a raven. In the real world, there must be another reason why the old ones would want to claim a seven-year-old boy.

There was only one way she could think to stop them.

You can make them a counter-offer.

Once the decision was made, she no longer felt afraid. She turned to Sonella, about to explain, then paused. If this was going to work, she'd have to keep it secret even from Sonella.

The thought sank to her stomach like a stone and lay there, cold and hard. It would be so easy, and so infinitely comforting, to explain, to ask for reassurance, to check that she was not making an awful mistake. But she had to keep it secret. This was the first step on a tightrope, and she had to focus all her attention on getting it right.

Brakman had said it himself. Special Branch was getting rid of all magicals, except for people like Cadet Lee, or the weres they used as sniffers. Soon, he would be useless as a spy, and they would need somebody, somebody on the inside. Who better than her, with her certificate of purity?

Sonella was watching her with concern.

She should just get up now, and walk into the hall. Just keep her expression blank, and pretend not to understand. Nobody, not even Sonella, should have even a hint at her real purpose. But she couldn't do it.

"Sonella," she said in a rush. "I'm going to do something now. Please don't ask me why, okay? It won't make sense to you, but I've got to do it."

Sonella nodded. "Okay," she said, wide-eyed. "It's got something to do with saving Nico—?"

They stared at one another for a moment. Suddenly Sonella flung her arms around Gia, so unexpectedly that her forehead bumped Gia's nose. They clung to one another wordlessly for a moment, then let go.

"You don't need to tell me," she said. "Do what you've got to do."

Gia got to her feet and took a deep breath.
"Okay. Let's go."

☙ O ❧

Captain Witbooi inspected the fingerprints critically.

"That will do," he said, and handed Gia a tissue to wipe her fingers.

To Gia's surprise, she was the only one who signed up with Special Branch. The boys had hung around, joking with the cadets, but in the end they had drifted away to other stands, or out into the sunshine of the courtyard.

Charlie Wexton, immensely impressed at Gia's signing up, had thumped her on the back and shaken her hand.

"Wish I could join you," he'd said. "But my dad would *kill* me."

She felt calm, but it was that numb after a slip of a sharp knife, when you still wondered how much blood there would be. Everything seemed fragmented, a little unreal.

Mr Peterson smiled benevolently as he added his signature to the relevant forms. Miss Huisman looked at her in uncomprehending surprise and disappointment.

Now, all Gia had to do was get through the day. Get home, and make sure that Nico was okay. The test would be over by now, and he'd be home, working on his overlocker sculpture.

What if it had all been for nothing, and the Belle Gente never intended to claim Nico at all? Had she made it all up, a big cloud of dust whipped up out of her own fears?

Sonella, sensing her confusion, kept the conversation light. She reminded Gia to collect the doll and the sketchbooks, and helped pack it all back in her box. She diverted the curious questions of the other girls, which Gia, deep in her worries, did not even hear.

At last it was time to go home.

"Oh, Gia," said Sonella, just as they parted at the school gates. "I keep forgetting to ask you. Could you give me Fatima's number? And, um, Ben's? I'd like to invite you guys over some time. When you're no longer grounded, of course."

ഌOൽ

When Gia got home, she found that her parents and Nico were not back yet. Mandy was downstairs in the studio pressing a jacket her father had finished the previous evening.

"Nothing," she said. "I've not heard anything from them."

As Gia climbed the stairs to the front door, she could not think how she was going to bear the next few hours. She badly wanted to tell Saraswati what she'd done, to see her face change as she realised that there was hope, after all. She would be angry at first, but surely she would understand that this was the only way?

Her father had to know too, of course, but it was her mother who realised the danger all along; her mother that needed comfort. In the days since the fight over the contract, things had been strained between them. In the past, their fights had blown over quickly, dissolving in hugs or forgiving words.

Not this time.

Saraswati's first anger had been replaced by a despairing energy, like a trapped animal pacing, or gnawing at its bonds. She did not have the strength even to be angry at Gia anymore, but the fight was not resolved. It hung in the air like the stench of burnt food.

Gia wandered around the house, not able to settle to anything. She opened the door that led to the balcony, and stood there, watching the street. Mandy came upstairs and started vacuuming.

At last there was the sound of car doors slamming and feet on the stairs. Gia was at the door, opening it as they came inside.

"Mom—" she started, but saw instantly that something was wrong. Saraswati had Nico in her arms, her face set and pale. Karel was right behind them.

There was a long, wet stain down Saraswati's skirt and Gia realised with a shock that Nico must have wet himself. She smelled the tang of urine as Saraswati brushed past her.

"Dad—?"

Saraswati carried Nico through into the bathroom. There was the squeak of the shower curtain opening, and then the loud hiss of water hitting tiles.

Ignoring her father's attempt to stop her, Gia followed her mother into the bathroom. There she was, standing in the shower stall, fully-clothed, still holding Nico. The shower was open, hot water streaming over mother and child. Saraswati's long hair was loose and hung round both of them in wet black tendrils. The room was already steaming up. As Gia backed out, she heard her mother begin to sing, softly, under the rush of water.

It was an old song, and one that she'd heard many times in the long nights when Nico would not go to sleep.

The north wind does blow,
And we shall have snow,
And what will the robin do then?
Poor thing!

He will sit in a barn,
And to keep himself warm,
Will hide his head under this wing.
Poor thing!

ಸಲΟಲ

"What happened, Dad?"

Karel was in the kitchen, looking lost. Mandy bustled around him, making tea.

"Dad, what happened?"

He shook his head. "I don't know. They took him away, and we just had to wait there. Nobody told us anything. For hours." He shuddered. "And then when they were done they brought him out all curled up. I thought your mother was going to attack that nurse."

"Is he going to be okay?"

Karel licked his lips. "I think so, Gia. Now that he's home and safe. He just had a horrible time there."

"The monsters," muttered Mandy, thumping down the kettle. "To treat a little child like that—!"

"It's all over now, thank God," said Karel. "We can get back to our lives. That's what Nico needs now. Normality."

"And the certificate? Did they give you the certificate of purity?"

"Yes, yes, that was all fine. Everything is settled now, and we can put it all behind us."

Gia looked at him doubtfully. Surely he did not really think it was going to be that simple?

"But Dad, what about the Belle Gente? They didn't accept your payment, did they? You don't think they'll—"

"Really, Gia, I thought we'd gone over all of that. Yes, your mother insisted on paying that con-artist, but luckily for us his payment system didn't work. And as it turns out, we did not need the man in any case. Nico tested negative, so all the worrying was for nothing."

Gia gaped at her father. Surely he could not really believe that? But he seemed so calm in his certainty.

The noise of the shower ceased, and a few moments later, Saraswati called from the bathroom.

"Karel? Can you come here a moment?"

Her father came back just as Mandy poured the tea. "She wants us to go get some things from the health shop," he said, taking his cup and blowing on it. "I'll just finish this, then we can run. Can you go to her, Mandy? The boy is calm now, but I think she needs a hand undressing him and getting him to bed."

᠍ஓOଔ

From the moment she got in the car, Gia knew something was wrong.

It seemed strange for Saraswati to send them both away, at a time like this. The things they were getting were none of them urgent.

She turned as they drove off, and saw nothing alarming. Only Granny and the caretaker walking slowly toward them, deep in conversation.

Karel found a parking spot, and they went first to the health shop, then to the pharmacy. By the time they got back to the car Gia had to stop herself from telling her father to hurry. As soon as she opened the front door, she knew it was too late.

Her parents' bedroom door stood open.

One of Nico's socks lay in the corridor.

Saraswati and Nico were gone.

ೞOಚ

GONE

"But I don't understand. Why did she go?"

Karel stood in the bedroom he shared with Saraswati, staring at the open cupboards.

"We got through all that Special Branch stuff. It's over now. And he's got his certificate. Why would she go *now*?"

"Dad—" Gia felt at a loss. Did he really not know? "Dad, it's the Belle Gente."

Her father turned to her, his look more dazed than angry.

"You think she's running away from the Belle Gente, because of that contract? But that's just— just crazy stuff. Why would those people want a little boy? What could they possibly want with a seven-year-old—?" He shook his head in frustration. "Anyway, that contract cannot be legal. I mean, maybe if me or Sari signed it. But you are his sister. You don't have the authority to agree to that contract."

Gia wished she could share his certainty.

"I don't think they operate according to the law," she said. "Or anyway, not laws as in courts and judges and that. It's more like a bargain. Like in the old stories."

Her father was not listening to her.

"Where's Mandy? She must know—" He was on his feet again and pushed past Gia, calling out Mandy's name. Gia heard him checking the backyard, then come back through the kitchen.

"She's gone too." He glanced at his watch. "They must have gone together. Listen, Gia, you stay here, in case they come back. I'm going to go to Mandy's. Maybe—"

The front door slammed behind him.

ഩO ൫

The house felt very empty, once her father was gone.

Empty, and silent.

Gia went back into her parents' bedroom, searching for clues among the scattered clothes and open drawers. Where had Saraswati gone? How long did she plan to stay away?

Everywhere in the house she found signs of desperate haste. Suitcases had been pulled out of the top shelf of the linen cupboard, and somebody had gone through the sheets and blankets. The toothpaste was missing from the cup in the bathroom, and so were Nico and Saraswati's toothbrushes. Nico's shoes lay scattered all over the floor of his room, and there was a stack of his t-shirts and underpants piled on his bed.

The box with his overlocker monster and materials was missing from his cupboard.

At first Gia hoped to find a note, but she soon gave up on that.

As she searched, her anger grew. To be sent on a fool's errand, while her mother made her getaway. Saraswati could have trusted her, allowed her to help. Even if she did not want to say where she was going, anything was better than just going, without even leaving a note.

Maybe Paddavis would know.

She called his name, quietly at first, then with rising irritation. No answer. Useless creature. She should never have trusted him.

Had Saraswati really gone off with Mandy? That seemed unlikely, and Gia could not shake the image of Granny and the caretaker that she'd seen from the car. She was out the door and down the stairs into the street, dodging pedestrians and dogs.

The caretaker's door was closed, but then, it always was, so she knocked hard and waited, trying to hear past the noise of her breathing and the pounding of her heart. After a minute or so she knocked again, but she knew it was no use. No one was home.

Once again she ran, this time down the street to Granny's shop. But she slowed to a walk, and then to a stop. She could already see that the shop was locked up, dark and quiet.

She'd never seen it closed before. That, more than anything, made her certain that Granny, at least, had some knowledge of where Saraswati had gone.

Gia turned and walked back up the hill.

What now? Why, and when, and where, and how long, and what could I have done –

Over and over until she wanted to smash her fist into a wall so that the pain would distract her. She stamped up the stairs to the front door, and slammed it so hard that the knocker rattled.

Saraswati must have asked Granny and the caretaker for help. How long had she been planning this? Why had she not asked Gia for help, or even hinted at her plans?

That thought smoldered, hot as a cramp in her belly.

She tried to imagine Karel returning with Saraswati and Nico, but her mind kept slipping away, unable to focus on the picture of how it would be. Being alone became suddenly unbearable and she took out her texter and sent a message to Fatima.

Can you come over?

She stared at the little screen, willing the letters to appear, and sure enough, less than a minute later the texter buzzed.

Sorry! Stuck helping mom. Tomorrow?

Gia closed her eyes and waited until the disappointment passed.

Sure! Message me when you can come.

After another moment, the reply arrived.

Will do. Anything wrong?

After several false starts, Gia gave up in even trying to explain.

Tell you when I see you.

Okay, take care then, hugs!

A car door slammed, and a moment later the burglar gate clanged. Gia ran to the front door just as her father came in.

"Did you find them?" But she already knew the answer even before he spoke.

"No."

"Was Mandy home? Did she know anything?"

Karel went through to the living room, heading for the phone.

"No. She wasn't home yet. Her daughter thought she was still on her way. Promised to phone."

He had the phone cradled against his chin and started dialling.

"Hello. Hello? I'd like to report— Hello? Yes. I'd like to report a missing person. Two. Missing persons."

ಸ⊙ಡ

"So— wait. What?" Fatima took a big bite of scone, then licked the cream off her fingers.

"Your mom took off because she thinks the Belle Gente are going to kidnap Nico?"

Gia tried not to be irritated at Fatima's obvious disbelief. She took a bite of scone herself, finding that she was hungrier than she'd realised. There had hardly been any supper last night, and she'd skipped breakfast, feeling too tense to eat.

So strange to wake up in a house with no mother, and no Nico.

It was a relief to be away from home, but the story of why Saraswati had left seemed unreal here in the bustle and buzz of the mall. Fatima's mother had swung by to pick Gia up that morning, and dropped the two of them off at Cavendish Square while she did some serious shopping. Gia and Fatima had headed for Café Rosa, a favourite meeting place.

"I know, it sounds nuts," said Gia.

"And aren't you supposed to be grounded anyway?"

Gia shrugged. "Dad's forgotten all about that."

"You're sure there isn't some other reason she went away?" asked Fatima.

"Like what?"

"Well," Fatima drank some of her hot chocolate. "Have your parents been fighting more than usual?"

"I don't think so," said Gia, but even she could hear the doubt in her voice.

Fatima shrugged. "Parents are like that. They don't tell you stuff."

Gia wanted to argue, to explain again about the contract, the test and her mother's fears, but somehow she did not have the strength. Fatima had listened to her story patiently enough, but Gia sensed that the more she told, the more uncomfortable her friend became. In the end she'd only explained the bare outline, and not even told Fatima that she'd joined the Special Branch Youth Division.

Even thinking about *that* gave her a little shock, like a pinch of static. It was much easier to eat her scones and cream, and allow Fatima to convince her that things were not as weird as she'd thought.

"Your dad must be going spare."

"He is. He's convinced that Mandy knows something, but Mandy says that Mom didn't tell her anything about where she was going."

"Mandy was there when she left?"

Gia nodded. "She was. I don't think she knows anything. And Dad's freaking out about the business too. There's a lot of work to do on the wedding—"

She stopped, realising that she'd not told Fatima that they were making Kavitha Pillay's wedding gown.

Fatima looked at her, clearly curious.

"Listen, Fatima, I'm not really allowed to tell you this. And if anyone finds out, and I mean *anyone* then we can be in serious trouble."

"Wow." Fatima's eyes were gleaming, and she sat forward. "Give! What's going on?"

Gia opened her mouth, but at that moment the waiter leaned in between them to clear their plates.

She waited while he piled up their cups and plates. Only when he was well out of earshot did she speak.

"We're doing Kavitha Pillay's wedding gown."

"Oh. My. God!" Fatima's hand went over her mouth. "You're kidding me, right? Oh my God, Gia, Kavitha Pillay?"

"Fatima, please!" Gia glanced around to see if anyone was watching. "Keep your voice down, okay?"

"You've met her?"

"Yes. She's pretty cool, actually."

"Wow." Fatima sat and stared at her, eyes wide. "That's so amazing."

"Thing is, it's supposed to be this big secret. Luxulo is super paranoid. He wants to keep it all a secret, nobody must know who is doing the dress until the wedding day. Things can get seriously sticky if this gets out."

"Okay, no, wow. I won't tell anybody, promise, Gia. Luxulo Langa's no joke."

"That's what Kavitha said."

"Really?"

Fatima was clearly bubbling over with curiosity. To her own surprise, Gia felt reluctant to gossip about Kavitha. "She warned me that we better not fall behind or mess up this job, apparently Luxulo Langa's not very forgiving."

"Oh. And with your mom gone—"

"That's right," said Gia. "She's finished the toile— or pretty much finished, but there's still more than a week's work on that gown."

Fatima gave her arm a squeeze. "I'm sure she'll be back soon."

∽O∾

Gia got home just as her father came out looking for her.

"Gia! Good. Listen, we need to go. Kavitha needs one last fitting with that toile. Can you come? Good."

Once again they met the driver in a mall parking lot, and soon they were in the air-conditioned, vanilla-scented rooms of the Pillay home.

Gia helped Kavitha put on the toile under Mrs Pillay's sharp eyes.

"Such a pity that your mother could not come, Gia," said Mrs Pillay, walking around Kavitha and looking her up and down. "I hope she feels better soon. To have the flu on such a lovely day!"

Gia smiled and nodded, but did not trust herself to speak. Instead, she concentrated on making sure that the toile was positioned correctly. She adjusted the fit of a shoulder, then checked that the skirt draped as it should.

"Not bad," said Mrs Pillay. "I thought it would be too stark, but it's really rather lovely. Your mother is a talented woman, Gianetta."

"Is it comfortable?" Gia asked Kavitha. "Try walking a bit."

Kavitha took a few steps, then lifted her arms.

"It's much better now," she said. "It caught me across the shoulders before, but now it feels fine. It's not too loose?"

"It looks perfect to me," said Gia. "Can we go out into the other room? I'd like my father to see."

"Of course."

Kavitha moved through to where Karel was waiting. Gia watched her walk, checking the length of the skirt, and watching for any awkward pulling of the fabric. The dress, even in this dull cotton incarnation, looked even better than she'd imagined. The sculpted folds framed Kavitha's graceful figure without dominating her.

"Oh yes!" said Karel as Kavitha entered. "That's the way. Turn around, will you my dear? Lovely."

He took one of Kavitha's hands, holding it up as if he were dancing with her. "Comfortable? Is it tight anywhere?"

"Perfectly comfortable."

"Sit down. Stand up. Move around. Remember, you'll be dancing in this dress."

Kavitha followed his instructions, and Karel nodded in approval. "I think we've got it fitting now."

"We need the final dress by the end of next week," said Mrs Pillay. She held up a hand, as though silencing Karel, although he'd made no move to speak.

"I know, I know, the wedding is still weeks away. But Luxulo is anxious to have this settled. There's no arguing with that man!" She smiled indulgently, a smile that did not reach her eyes.

"Of course," said Karel. "Of course. It will be our pleasure."

ೞOೞ

Gia watched her father on the drive back.

He looked exhausted. Now that he was away from the Pillays, his shoulders slumped and she could see the sleepless night in his face.

"Are we going to make it, Dad?" she asked.

"What?" Karel looked startled. "Oh, you mean finish the dress in time? It's possible. But it's going to be tough without your mother to help."

"Can I do anything?"

He glanced at her. "I'm afraid you'll have to. Between the two of us, we should be able to get it done. Problem is, I've got another big deadline on Monday that I've moved already. That's the one that will be paying all our bills. So I'm going to be relying on you a bit more than usual, sweetheart."

"Okay, Dad. Just tell me what to do."

He nodded, but she could see his thoughts were already pulled away from her, as he stared ahead into the traffic.

The song that had been playing on the radio came to an end, and the news came on. Gia did not really listen to it, until a phrase caught her attention, and she turned it up.

...strange phenomena. These are often electrical in nature, but seem to affect humans too, inducing a trance-like, hypnotic state. Mr Khwete says that there have been a rising number of incidents of strange crowd behaviour in public places. There are also increasing numbers of the so-called "Guilters", individuals who leave home and family to wander the streets, chanting meaningless phrases.

The leader of the Purists, new splinter group within the New Rational Party, Mr Luxulo Langa, has called on the government to act. He says, and I quote:

"These are terrorist actions of the Belle Gente. We have tolerated these radical elements in our country for long enough. The time for talking is over. We must act."

And now for the weather...

Gia turned the volume down again, frowning.

Strange phenomena that affected crowds as well as technology? That sounded very like what she'd experienced at The Playground. That strange, hypnotic state, and the way both the lights and the music had seemed to be infected by something.

Was that the Belle Gente's doing? But what would that achieve?

ꜱOʀ

Unpick the toile.

That's what Karel had told her to do, before he went off again.

Gia looked at the cotton gown, which she had put back on the dressmaker's dummy.

Well, that's easier said than done.

It was not that she'd never done it before. It was tedious work, but easy enough. The picked-apart toile would become the pattern, according to which the silk of the finished gown would be cut.

But she'd never worked on anything this complicated before. The gown was like a piece of origami, many sections folded multiple times to create that deceptively simple, sculpted look. If she took it apart, it would become a collection of flat, white pieces.

How would anyone know how they should be put back together again?

There was no one to help her. Mandy had gone by the time she and her father got home, and Karel left again almost immediately, as soon as he was sure that neither Saraswati nor Nico had come back during their absence.

Gia collected all the tools she needed, and spent more time than was necessary arranging the gown on the dressmaker's dummy.

She'd not been ready for the shock of the empty house. Apparently some part of her still could not believe that her mother and Nico were gone.

She took the unpicking tool and put it down again. The dress, even made from dull cotton, was beautiful.

Gia was unsure if she could bear to undo her mother's careful, precise work.

What if they never came back?
Where were they now?
Were they safe?

Gia scrubbed her hands over her face, then back through her hair. She had to do this. Her father was counting on her. She closed her eyes and leaned her forehead against the dummy's hard shoulder. The cotton had a comforting scent. It even had a trace of her mother's perfume. With that scent came the memory of her mother's voice.

Take it slow. Solve one problem at a time.

She would mark the fabric as she unpicked it, noting on each piece where it went, which way was up, where the folds were. If she worked slowly and methodically, she could keep control of it all. A fabric pen was all she needed.

After that, it was easier. The toile became an interesting puzzle, flat sections of cloth fitted together to create a three-dimensional shape. Each piece had a name. It joined like this, had darts *here* and *here*, was folded *here* and *here*. Each fold was marked with the fabric pen, each edge named, right, left, back, front, up, down. Each seam undone, each dart unpicked.

Gia kept stopping and going back, refolding, pinning edges back together, checking, and double-checking, and triple-checking that she understood how the puzzle worked.

As she worked, the tangle in her mind started unravelling, and she began drawing certain threads loose from the knot. *How long had Saraswati been planning to leave? Why had she not left earlier? Why put*

Nico through the trauma of the test? Why leave after the test and not before?

Because she wanted the certificate of purity.

Was it worth it? Would that certificate keep Nico safe?

From Special Branch, maybe. But what about the Belle Gente?

Gia unpicked the last few stitches, and smoothed the fabric. She became aware of the ache in her back and neck. A glance at the window showed that it was getting dark.

She got to her feet and stretched. Then she placed the last piece on the cutting table. The toile had become a pattern now, abstract shapes scribbled over with letters, numbers, arrows, and dotted lines. Almost impossible to picture it coming together into a graceful gown.

Time to go.

ஐOஐ

Gia locked up the studio, very aware how vulnerable she was, out alone on the street after dark. Luckily it was only a few steps to the gate. She made sure that she had the key ready. It was darker than it should be. The nearby streetlights were out.

She felt a tingle of alarm even before she saw the figure standing just next to the burglar gate. It was a man, but too short to be Karel.

Not Ben either, Ben would have waved or spoken by now.

She was about to turn back to the studio, when a passing car threw its headlights over the man's face.

Gia relaxed instantly, and stepped forward with a smile. "Sorry to keep you waiting!"

Lucky she had the key ready. How rude of her to be so suspicious! She unlocked the gate.

"Come upstairs," she said, and heard his footsteps behind her as she climbed toward the front door. Afterwards, she wondered what made her reach for the knocker. She had the front door key ready. All she had to do was fit it and turn, but instead she reached out and placed her hand on the doorknocker, the ward in the shape of a hand with two thumbs and an eye embedded in its palm. The ward that protected that door from magical intruders.

A small, submerged part of her must have been aware that something was wrong, and had reached for the only protection available. The moment her fingers touched metal the glamour dropped away. She knew where she was, and what she was doing.

There was a stranger behind her on the stairs, and she'd been within a hair of inviting him into her home.

Keeping her hand on the ward, she turned to face him.

"Ah. Well," said the man.

All the light in the stairwell came from the entrance below so it was hard to see him clearly.

"Are you going to open that door?" He had an accent, and he chewed at something as he spoke.

"No," she said, proud of how calm her voice sounded while her heart was fluttering in her chest like a bird. "Who are you? What do you want?"

For a few seconds he just looked at her, and Gia could hear him chew.

"I've come for the child," he said.

It was like a dream, that unavoidable moment that came at you with no escape.

"For Nico."

"That is correct. Are you going to let me in?"

She swallowed. Even with her hand on the door ward, she could feel the glamour tugging at her, soft, insistent, like an undertow dragging her down. "No."

"How inconvenient."

Gia struggled against the persuasion. She knew that he could not enter her home without being invited, but that was a small comfort when she was trapped here against the front door. Would opening the door count as an invitation? She did not know, and could not risk it.

"He's not here. My mother took him and went away."

"Well." More chewing. "If that were true, it would be unfortunate. Is it true?"

"It is," said Gia. She was finding it a little easier to think clearly. "They left yesterday. I have no idea where she took him. But that doesn't really matter. I want to make a, um, a counter offer."

He tilted his head.

"Really?"

"Yes. You need spies in Special Branch, don't you?" He said nothing, but she could tell she had his attention. "They're getting rid of all the magicals who work there, so you no longer have any, um, inside source. Isn't that true?"

The man shrugged slightly, his face giving nothing away.

Gia felt her certainty wavering. She'd been so sure of this part of her plan.

"I've just got a certificate of purity. I'm not magical at all," she said.

"Admirable. But by itself, having the certificate is not of much use to us, I'm afraid. The child has one. That was the whole point of the deal."

"I've enrolled in the Special Branch Youth Division."

A long, considering silence.

Gia took a breath, and forced herself to focus. "I'll be more use to you. I'll be in there, in Special Branch. They won't suspect me at all. Nico is just a little boy. What use can he be?"

Another silence.

"Well. An interesting proposal."

She could feel him studying her. What was it he saw? A scared teenage girl, clutching at a doorknocker?

At last he spoke again. "Let me see what they say."

He took something out of a pocket. It lit up, a small, soft glow that barely reached his face. As his fingers moved over it, Gia realised it must be a texter. How odd, that the Belle Gente would use something so ordinary.

"You can let go that ward now," he said without looking at her. "I've stopped the pushing."

Gia stayed as she was, although her arm was starting to get uncomfortable.

The texter beeped, and the man typed a response. A car drove by outside, its headlights flashing on the walls and stairs.

Gia changed her position, relieving the strain on her arm.

What if Dad shows up?

She found herself hoping he would not.

The man seemed to be waiting for something. He stood, unmoving, staring down at the texter.

At last, it beeped again and he gave a little grunt.

"Hmm. That's as I thought."

He put the texter away and looked up at Gia. "They want to see you. Come with me."

He turned and walked down the stairs. When Gia did not follow, he looked back up at her. "You can come now, and discuss this counteroffer, or we can stay with the original agreement. It is entirely up to you."

Gia still had the key ready in her hand. She could go in and slam the door shut before he reached the top of the steps. Then she'd be safe.

Or would she?

And what about Nico, and her mother?

How long would it take this man, or his friends, to find them?

She released the doorknocker, and followed him down the stairs.

He was waiting for her outside.

Despite the better light, it was hard to see what he looked like. Each time she blinked or shifted her focus, he had a different face. The features did not change shape, but she kept finding she was mistaken in what she saw.

He has a boxer's nose, but no – his nose is straight. Hooked. Broken. His face is as blunt as a boot, framed by dark curls – no, short cropped hair – no, look again, he has a fine-boned face as delicate as a cat's. His eyes are small, dark, wide, narrow, round as a marbles –

She looked away, nauseated, and heard him chuckle.

"Come along, then."

She followed him toward a car, her misgivings stronger with every step. "Where are we going?"

He unlocked the car and held the door open for her. *She could still turn back.*

She got into the car, and he closed the door on her. It was a sports car, lower than she was used to. It was old, too, the interior worn and cracked. The man got

The Door Knocker

in on the driver side. Gia did not look at him. The shifting features were too disconcerting.

He reached across in front of her and took something out of the glove compartment. "Put this on."

She took it from him, a piece of stretchy black cloth.

"Over your head. Go on. Can't have you seeing where we go."

The cloth was like a cap, except it fitted completely over her head and face. She felt his fingers at her neck, fastening something, and the blindfold tightened round her throat.

"See if you can get it off."

She pulled at the edge, but it was too tight, almost tight enough to restrict her breathing. She tried to think of something that would distract her from the rising panic.

"Why don't you just glamour me not to see?"

He started the engine, an unexpectedly low rumble. "Too much effort. Uses up energy."

She felt the car pull away.

"Makes me hungry. Much easier this way."

"Oh."

The thought of hunger, or food of any kind in relation to her companion made her distinctly uneasy. She could not hear him above the engine noise, but she was sure he was still chewing. Her breath made the inside of the cloth uncomfortably warm.

The car slowed down.

This must be a stop street, or an intersection.

She sat there with her eyes closed, trying to stop herself from scrabbling at the passenger door and flinging herself out of the car.

Keep talking, she told herself.

"Do you do that thing with your face all the time?"

He laughed. "No. That would attract too much attention. I try to pick one face and stick to it."

"But why not just show your own face?"

He did not answer, and she began to wonder if she'd made him angry. The car rocked, and turned, slowed down, then accelerated again.

"An interesting question," he said at last. "My own face."

She waited for more, but no more came.

"What is your name?" she asked.

"Why do you want to know?"

"Just curious."

"Some people call me Ochre."

"Oak—?"

"No, Ochre. As in the colour."

"Oh. Like oil paint? Sienna, ochre, burnt umber?"

"That's right."

A strand of hair on her neck was caught in the clip, or catch, or whatever it was that held the blindfold tight behind her head. It stung every time she moved.

Calm. Just stay calm.

Talking helped. *Keep him talking,* she found herself thinking. *Then he's less likely to think of you as food.*

She took as deep a breath as the constricting cloth allowed and tried to think of another question.

"Where do you come from?"

"What do you mean?"

"You have an accent. You're not South African, are you?"

"No."

Another long silence. She had given up on an answer when he spoke again.

"I used to live in Morocco. Before that, Spain. For many years."

"You were born there? In Spain?"

"Yes."

By now she was just wishing for the journey to be over. She'd long ago given up trying to figure out where they were driving. It was difficult to know even how much time had passed. In any case, he was probably driving some circuitous route so it was no use trying to guess where they were.

At last, the car slowed down and stopped, and she heard the creak of the handbrake

"Just stay where you are," said Ochre, and she felt the car rock as he got out.

A door opened.

"Come along then."

As she got out of the car, Gia tried her best to sense what kind of place she was in.

The ground was hard. Tar, or concrete. Somewhere in the city, then, as there were no insect noises, and no sound of wind in foliage. She guessed it was some small side road that did not get much traffic. She could hear the dull thumping of music not too far away, and somebody laughing in the distance.

"What's this then?" said a woman right next to her.

Gia jerked with fright. She'd not heard anyone approach, and was not even sure where Ochre was.

"Visitor," said Ochre. "Got an appointment. Can you take her down?"

"Sure. Why isn't she tied up?"

"Not necessary."

Somebody took her by the arm.

"Come," said the woman.

Gia allowed herself to be steered. She could hear somebody following behind. Not Ochre. Somebody large.

"Step up here."

From the sound, they'd moved into an enclosed space of some kind. Not indoors, from the sounds and the feeling of the night air. Possibly the space between two buildings?

"Stand."

The woman moved away from her, and the other person put a hand on her shoulder. A large, and unusually heavy hand. She heard the woman give a little grunt, then there was a metallic grinding. Like somebody opening a manhole cover.

Gia tried to swallow but her mouth was dry. The woman was back at her side.

"Okay," she said in Gia's ear. "We're going down a ladder. It's inside a manhole, so watch your step. I'm going first, and my friend will help you down. Try anything stupid and you'll regret it, right?"

Gia heard the ringing of feet on metal, and guessed the woman had started down the ladder.

Her guard nudged her forward.

"Better sit, and slide yourself in," came the woman's voice from below, booming a little with echo.

Gia did as she was told, sitting on the ground and sliding herself toward the place she guessed the manhole was. One foot went over the edge, and she felt the guard behind her take hold of her shoulders, steadying her. She felt around with her foot until she found the ladder.

This was terrible. She could not possibly go down like this, with her back to the ladder. Using the silent guard's hands to steady her, she slowly turned around. She was glad of his presence now. He held her hands firmly, guiding her down the ladder.

He had a scent, something like an overheated stove plate, or sun-warmed rock.

She could feel the drop below sucking at her, and wondered how far she would fall, if her feet slipped now.

Don't think about it.

She lost her balance and snatched at his arm. A part of her mind registered that the sleeve under her fingers was made of leather, and had many buttons at the cuff. One of them must have been loose. It came away in her hand. Without thinking, she closed her fingers around it. Hoping that it was dark enough to conceal her actions, she slipped the button into a pocket.

She had hold of the ladder now with both hands, and climbed down. It was not as far as she'd feared.

"Stand just here," said the woman. "You're standing on a stepping stone. There's water all round it so don't lose your balance."

Gia moved where she was guided. *Water?*

She must be in some kind of underground tunnel. The place stank, — a dank, old smell, tinged with the sour stink of garbage. The water must be still, as she could not hear anything but a low gurgle.

She heard the other guard, the big one, climbing down the ladder.

"The ceiling's very low. You may have to duck down. Step carefully, or you'll go into the water."

Someone pulled at her and she stepped forward, feeling for the ceiling.

Bricks, she thought as her hand brushed over it. At least the stepping-stones were steady, and not too far apart. At one point she stepped short and her foot went down into the water, causing her to stumble and graze her knee, but her companion pulled her up.

She'd stepped into the water, but it was not as deep as she'd feared.

Knee-deep, she thought as the stench of it welled up around her. But the water was very cold, and her jeans were wet through now.

At last, her companion stopped. There was a hollow, wooden sound.

Knocking? On a door?

The rattle of a latch, and somebody speaking. Then the hand on her arm again, and she was pulled through the door into what must be a room.

"There's a seat just behind you," said the woman. "Sit."

Gia lowered herself with shaking knees onto what felt like a perfectly ordinary sofa. She leaned back and closed her eyes.

How much longer was this going to go on?

Gradually she became aware of more sounds. An airconditioner humming. An occasional rattle that might be a door stirring in a draft. Soft voices murmuring somewhere, probably in the next room. Her companions had either left, or were standing perfectly still. Gia could not even hear them breathe.

It would be easy to start imagining things.

There might be somebody sitting next to her. Or a whole room full of people all staring at her. She tried not to think what might happen next. The blindfold was getting more and more uncomfortable. She could breathe, but her breath got trapped inside the fabric, hot and unpleasant.

At last she heard a door open, and somebody said something in a language Gia did not understand. The woman replied, and Gia felt a hand on her shoulder.

"Come."

Once again, someone guided her forward. She guessed she must be walking through a door into another room. There was the noise of a chair scraping on the ground, and a door closed behind her.

"Blindfold off." An old woman's voice.

Gia guessed the speaker was sitting down, by the direction of the sound.

Somebody — Gia thought it must be the woman who'd been leading her — did something to the back of her neck, and then pulled the cloth away, pinching the hair at her neck.

Gia blinked at the scene before her.

The room was small and badly lit. A table lamp stood on a desk piled high with stacks of paper. A man and a woman sat on either side of the table, their faces glowing in the light of the lamp.

It was the woman that caught Gia's attention.

For an instant, she was reminded of her mother. The black eyes, the dead-straight, ink-black hair. The long, white neck, the way she held herself. But then the impression faded. Saraswati was warm and alive. This woman looked as if she'd been carved out of ivory, all her edges sharp as bones.

The man was utterly unremarkable. He wore a suit and tie, and the light gleamed off his glasses so that his eyes were hidden.

Gia glanced aside at the woman who'd brought her in, and found, to her surprise, that she recognised her.

This was the white-haired girl she'd seen at The Playground, that evening she'd been out dancing with Ben and Fatima. For some reason, she found this fact gave her courage and she was able to turn back and meet the ivory woman's gaze without flinching.

"Gianetta Grobbelaar," said the man. "Sister of Niccolo Grobbelaar, who is our lawful property, according to agreement."

He tapped a piece of paper on the table in front of him.

"According to this contract, signed by you in ink and blood. Why are you here, and not your brother?"

Gia swallowed. She could feel her legs beginning to shake with nerves. "I have a counter offer."

The woman's eyebrows rose in mock surprise. "And what can this be?"

"Take me instead. I will be much more use to you than Nico."

"How so?"

Gia had to take a deep breath before she could answer. "Nico is just a little boy. He cannot— he has problems. He can't really speak properly, and—"

The woman's voice cut across hers. "Of course. He is Saraswati's son, is he not? That is what happens, when blood is mixed."

Gia stared at her. "I'm sorry?"

"Saraswati is his mother, so? Your mother too. The only surprise, is that you are so—" The woman's eyes measured her. "So remarkably normal."

Seeing Gia's surprise, the woman continued. "Our blood does not mix well with the humans." Her lips curled. "*Crooks* and *straights* as they say. Their children don't often come out so uncomplicated."

Gia stared into the cold, black eyes. Her heart drummed in her ears. "I'm adopted."

"Ah." The woman inclined her head. "That explains. You are quite *straight* then. What use for us? The boy would be of interest. He has his mother's blood."

This was her chance. Gia spoke quickly. "That's exactly the thing. You can no longer have your people working in Special Branch, can you? Special Branch are getting rid of all the crooks. And you need spies, especially now that the Purists are getting so strong."

The man turned his head toward her, his glasses flashing, and Gia felt the woman's eyes were boring into her.

"I have a certificate of purity. And I've just signed up for the Special Branch Youth Brigade."

She stopped for breath, looking from one of them to the other. Neither moved, or gave any sign.

"I can work for you."

Was it her imagination, or had the woman's expression changed, ever so slightly?

"An interesting offer," the woman said and glanced at the man.

"What are your skills?" he said.

"I'm sorry?"

"What can you do? What are you good at?"

Gia felt blank. *What could she do?*

"I can draw," she blurted, then felt instantly mortified. *What use was that?*

Then it came to her.

"Can I have some paper, and a pen or pencil?"

The man drew a pen out of his pocket and held it out to her.

Gia stepped forward to take it. "Thanks. Can I use this?" She pointed at a notepad that lay between them.

He nodded, so she pulled it closer to her.

"These are some of the people I saw while I was there, at Special Branch," she said, drawing quickly.

She'd always been good at this, capturing the rough likeness of anyone that had caught her interest. First,

Nurse Lucy appeared in a few quick lines. Then she drew Cadet Lee, spending a bit more time on her. Cadet Lee had a fascinating face, and deserved a little more care. As she drew, she could feel their attention on her.

Her confidence grew, and she drew a quick sketch of Captain Witbooi, head and shoulders, and then Mrs Solomon's face.

There, she told herself. *That's enough.*

She straightened, then had to stop herself from flinching as the woman reached out to take the paper.

The eyebrows went up again. "You saw these people only once?"

"Well, no," admitted Gia. "Most of those I saw more than once. But that doesn't really matter. I can remember faces quite well, if I need to."

Drawing had calmed her, and she was pleased at how confident she sounded.

The woman put the drawing on the table and tapped it with a long finger. She glanced at the man.

"Give me your hand," said the man. He held out his hand. His fingers closed around hers.

"Look here." He was taking off his glasses. Gia braced herself for whatever would be revealed, but found herself looking into a perfectly ordinary face. He was not young or particularly handsome. His eyes, now revealed, were mild.

Gia was just starting to wonder what she was supposed to do, when she became aware that she could no longer look away. She could not turn her head, nor even blink.

She could still see, but somehow she did not know what she was seeing.

His attention became a searchlight, blasting her vision into a blind white haze.

Her thoughts shrank, then steamed away like ants under the focused beam of a magnifying glass. Their little deaths left scorch marks on the white sheet of her mind, and these were considered with slow care. There was nowhere to hide from the unrelenting focus of his gaze.

Abruptly, the sensation ceased and Gia found that she was on her knees, retching. She gasped, and fought down the urge to vomit, desperately swallowing the saliva pooling in her mouth. Her head ached and she put her hands up to her face, half expecting to find some terrible wound or absence.

Nothing was wrong. Or at least, nothing she could feel with her fingers.

"What—" She struggled to control her voice. "What did you do?"

"Just checking," said the man. He had his glasses on again, and Gia got to her feet, backing away almost to the door.

"Straight as a die," he said to the woman.

"Good. As I thought, then," she replied.

She looked at Gia. "We accept your offer."

ಸಂOಡ

SILK

The headache woke her.

She struggled up through the tangle of dreams, relieved to find herself safe, in her own bed.

The night had been full of nightmares, of running, and hiding, dodging from shadow to shadow in an effort to evade the unrelenting searchlight of the hunter.

She blinked in the bright sunlight pouring through the window.

The events of the previous night were confused in her memory and at first she was not sure what had been a dream, and what had been real. But the envelope under her pillow was evidence that some of it at least, had really happened.

The revised contract, resigned, and resealed.

Proof.

That thought brought her upright, to stare out the window then relaxed as she saw that it was still early. She had not overslept after all.

The first part of her plan had gone better than she'd expected, but her mother was still not home. Saraswati would not come home until she knew the danger was past, and Nico was safe. Getting her back was all that mattered. Then things could return to the way they should be.

Her mind skittered away from the thought that it might already be too late for that. She'd made her bargain, after all.

Soon enough, she'd be leaving for Special Branch and nothing would ever be the same again.

That doesn't matter, she told herself. *It won't be forever. As long as everyone here at home is together, nothing else really matters.*

There was no one in the kitchen, apart from Pouf, who sat waiting hopefully in front of the fridge. He followed her to Nico's room.

Nico's shoes were still lying all over the floor. They looked like dead things. Gia picked them up and put them back into his cupboard. As she moved around the room, she heard a rustle of bedding from Poepie's cage and saw him watching her, his little pointed rat face emerging from between the bars.

Pouf, seeing the movement, jumped onto the bed and started ducking his head up and down, preparing to jump.

"No, Pouf!"

Pouf looked up at her with huge, innocent eyes, then ducked to wash his shoulder.

Gia checked to see that the rat's water bottle was full, and put some new pellets into the empty food tray. He sniffed at them and picked one up, rotating it in his paws.

There was a rattle from the lid of the fish tank. Something was stuck under there.

Looking closer, she saw that the skeekers had grown considerably since she'd last checked. All of them had developed legs, and quite a few were clinging to the plants or the side of the tank, just above water level, their long, frilly tails spreading out behind them. Some even had wings and she knew now what was causing the scratchy, ticking sounds from under the lid. Some of them must have completed the metamorphosis from skeekers into crimpers. How long had they been stuck under the lid, trying to fly? She'd have to let them out, otherwise they'd fall back into the water and drown.

She leaned back as far as she could, and lifted the lid.

Nothing happened.

Expecting to feel the tickle of crimper feet on her hands and arm, she fought back the urge to drop the lid, and lifted it higher. For a moment she saw them clinging there, their newly dry wings gleaming, and then with a buzzing hum they lifted, one after the other and flew up into the room.

Damn! The window!

Gia put the lid back and rushed to open the window, where several of the crimpers were already flinging themselves at the glass with loud tocks. Before she could get there, Pouf was on the windowsill, tail lashing. He jumped up, batting a crimper down onto the sill.

"Leave it, Pouf!"

Gia swept him off the windowsill.

The crimper was up and against the glass again, scrabbling with its thorny legs.

"No, stop! You'll hurt yourself. Wait—"

The window was stiff, but she got it open at last and then watched with relief as the little rainbow-coloured creatures flitted out into the early morning air, tails fluttering. Pouf gave a disgusted miaow and stalked out of the room, his tail lashing.

"Gia? Is that you?"

"Yes, Dad." She closed the window, thinking that she'd better check on the tank again tomorrow.

Her father was in the kitchen. He had been asleep when she got back late last night, and as far as she could tell, had not noticed that she'd been gone.

"Morning, Gia." He stood, leaning against the kitchen table. She studied his face but although he looked tired and sad, there was no sign that he'd been aware of her absence last night.

"Morning, Dad."

"Up early," he said. "Going for a run?"

"Maybe." She'd already decided that she would not tell him anything yet. There were too many uncertainties. What if she could not find a way to get a message to Saraswati? What if Saraswati did not return after all?

Better not to raise any false hope.

"I finished unpicking the toile last night," she said.

"Really? That's great. You can lay it out on the fabric today. Mandy can help you."

"It's Sunday, Dad. Mandy's not coming in today."

He rubbed his forehead. "Oh, yes. Well, then I'll have to give you a hand. Just to start you off. I have to go out again. I want to go round to the hospitals this morning."

She blinked at him a moment before she understood. "I'm sure nothing like that's happened, Dad."

"Then why hasn't she sent a message?" His voice cracked with anger and frustration. Then he looked away. "Sorry." He took a shaky breath, and let it out.

"It's just so hard not knowing."

ೞOಜ

Gia left her father in the kitchen, having persuaded him to eat some breakfast. Outside, the neighbourhood was just starting to wake. It was still very early, and Gia wondered if she was wasting her time, but to her relief she saw Granny rolling up the grid that protected her shop at night.

"Good morning," she said when she saw Gia. "Help me pull."

Gia helped her tug the grid all the way up, then watched as Granny secured it with a chain.

"Granny, could you give a message to Mom?"

The old woman finished tying up the end of the chain, then got a bunch of keys out of her pocket and unlocked the shop door.

"You don't have to tell me where she is or anything like that. It's just that—"

"Shush," said Granny. "Ears out here. Tell me inside."

Gia fell silent and waited while Granny propped open the door.

"Take this, and put it right against the door so it doesn't swing closed."

Granny pointed at a bucket of garish plastic flowers. Gia did as she was told, then followed Granny into the shop.

"Right," said Granny, levering herself up into her chair behind the counter. "Talk now."

Gia got the envelope out of her pocket and gave it to Granny.

"What's this?" said Granny, fishing a pair of reading glasses from among the strings of beads around her neck. When she had the glasses balanced on her nose, she took the contract out of the envelope and squinted down at it.

Her face remained expressionless as she read it through.

Then she looked at Gia over her glasses.

"You did this — when?"

"Last night."

Granny gave a nod as she folded the contract.

"You did right to show me this," she said, handing it back to Gia. "But don't show it to anybody else. Nobody, you hear?"

"Don't you want to keep it? I thought you'd need to show Mom—"

Granny was shaking her head. "No, I don't need that. I'll take the message."

"Are they — are they all right?"

"They're fine. Don't worry."

Granny took off her glasses and looked at Gia again, her eyes intent. "You did well, girl."

ʂɔOʋʁ

Gia paced the studio.

She was not sure what to do. She was supposed to lay out the pattern of Kavitha's wedding gown on the silk, ready to be cut. Her father had promised to help her with this, but he was still out.

At first, she'd decided that she'd wait for him.

She tidied away the pieces of the toile, and swept up all the little scraps and threads left behind from the unpicking. The cutting table looked clean enough, but she cleaned it all the same, wiping it with a clean, dry cloth. As she worked, she wondered how long it would be before her mother and Nico came back. Granny had promised to pass on the message, but how long would that take? Her body ached with the lack of sleep. At last there was no more tidying to be done, and she realised that she would have to start without Karel's help.

The silk was still folded in the bag, along with another piece that had to be the lining fabric. That gave her pause. She'd forgotten all about the lining. Usually, the lining would have its own pattern, simpler than the outer gown. Had Saraswati made one?

She set the lining aside, and took the silk out of the bag.

After a last look to see if the cutting table was spotless, she spread the silk over the table. Tired as she was, she could not help responding to the beauty of the fabric. She thought of white feathers, pearls, shells, polished ivory. A scent like newly cut grass breathed up from the folds.

It was also longer than the cutting table. Should she fold it in half? The dress was symmetrical, after all. She could lay out half the pattern— or should she spread the silk flat and place each piece of the toile separately?

More doubts assailed her. How would she secure the pattern to the silk? Should she use pins? Wouldn't pins make holes? Was the pattern supposed to lie with the grain of the silk, or on the bias? She'd have to check the toile to see. The longer she stood there, the less sure she became.

Was this even the right fabric? It was Shantung silk, and the colour seemed right, but what if she'd misunderstood somehow? Even if it was the right fabric, what if her father stayed away? What if she had to do all of it herself?

She pictured herself cutting into the silk, and shrank from the thought. Surely her mother would be home before it came to that.

Gia leaned on the table, eyes closed. What she needed was a snack and maybe a shower. She folded the silk again, careful to get it as neat as possible, and put it back in the bag.

ಸಂOಳ

Eating helped to wake her up, but the shower did not calm her as much as she hoped. It reminded her too much of her mother. Thinking of her mother reminded her of the way the ivory woman had spoken about Saraswati.

As Gia turned her face up into the stream of hot water, she tried to remember exactly what the woman had said. She had spoken as if she knew Saraswati. Before she'd realised that Gia was adopted, she'd said that she was surprised that Gia was so normal.

Normal.

She'd said that word with an ironic twist, the way she'd used the words "crooks and straights."

Blood.

That was another word that kept coming up. She'd said that Nico was the way he was because he was Saraswati and Karel's son.

Our blood does not mix well with humans.

Did she mean that Karel was human, and Saraswati was— not?

What is she then, if she's not human?

Again she remembered Saraswati looking up at the full moon.

All at once, it became unbearable. There was so much she did not know. So many secrets, so many things that she'd always just known she should not ask about.

No more. I want to know.

She dried herself and dressed quickly. This was her chance, now, before anyone came back.

In her parents' bedroom, she hesitated, looking around. If there was anything to be found, it would be here. She opened one of the small drawers in the dressing table.

Jewellery. Makeup.

It felt wrong, scratching through her mother's private things, but she pushed aside her doubt.

I want to know.

Other drawers revealed photographs, but they were all pictures Gia had seen many times. Her mother holding a baby Nico. Herself in her first school uniform. Her father's brother, whom she'd never met. A wedding photograph, Karel and Saraswati, young and smiling. There was nothing else worth looking at. No secret drawer, no diary, no cache of letters.

As she closed the last drawer, a memory that had been niggling at her for some time finally came to the surface. That day when the furniture had arrived, there had been a chest. A metal trunk that she'd not seen before the move, and had certainly not seen since.

A locked metal trunk.

She remembered Saraswati's reaction when she'd asked about it. The startled glance, the way her face had closed, and she'd turned from it. A thing that large would not be easy to hide.

She looked in all the obvious places. Under her parents' bed. In the cupboards. On top of the cupboards. She searched the living room, the kitchen, Nico's room, everywhere that anything that size could possibly be hidden. Then she went down to the studio and looked everywhere she could think of.

At last she was back in her parents' room, looking in the cupboards, and under the bed again.

"Lost something?"

Gia knocked her head on the bottom of the bed, and sat back with a hand to her forehead. Paddavis was on the headboard, his little legs dangling down.

"Where did you come from?"

"Me?" He shrugged. "I'm always here. What are you looking for?"

Gia thought about asking him why he'd not come when she called him, but thought better of it. She did not want to antagonise the little creature now.

"It's a metal box. Like a trunk. About this big." She gestured with her hands.

"Why do you want it?"

She shrugged. "I need to look inside it. Don't you know where it is, then?"

Paddavis scratched himself. "I might. What's in it?"

"I don't know."

That caught his interest. "Really? I thought it must be important, for your father to hide it like that."

"You saw him hide it?"

Paddavis slid down the headboard and bounced on the bed. "Want to see?" Then he gave another bounce and scampered out the door.

"Wait!" Gia was just in time to see him disappear into the kitchen.

"Hey! Wait up!"

She caught up with him in the pantry. He was hopping up and down in front of one of the lower cupboards.

"I've already looked in there. It's empty. Look."

"False back," said Paddavis.

"What?" But Gia had already seen what he meant. The cupboard was far too shallow. Why had she not noticed that before?

She got down on her knees and reached inside, running her fingers along the back panel's edges. It fit too tightly to get her fingernails in there.

"Get me a knife," she said, still head and shoulders inside the cupboard.

She heard a clatter of cutlery from the kitchen, and Paddavis was back, holding out a table knife.

"Thanks."

The knife slid easily between the panel and the cupboard wall. She moved it up and down, working carefully so as not to leave any marks. She could already feel the panel moving under her hands. A moment later, it was loose and she pulled it free.

There it was. The metal trunk, just as she'd remembered it. A little dented here and there, with some of its paint flaked off. She grabbed the handle and pulled. It was lighter than she'd expected, and it rumbled as it came.

"Open it!" said Paddavis.

Gia jiggled the lid, wondering if she could force it. But she did not want to leave any marks on the trunk. No one must know she'd opened it. "In a moment," she said.

Ignoring Paddavis's impatience, she first put the panel back in the cupboard so that it looked as it had before. Then she picked up the trunk.

"Out of the way, Paddavis," she said. And then, "Can you open that trapdoor for me?"

Paddavis scampered up the stairs and slid open the trapdoor to Gia's room. Getting the trunk up the stairs was trickier than she'd thought, but at last she dumped it next to her bed and stood there, rubbing her hands. The edges had dug cruelly into her fingers.

"You going to open it now?" Paddavis was almost dancing with impatience.

"It's locked." Gia jiggled the lid to show him.

"Oh. Don't you have the key?"

"Of course I don't. But I've got a plan. Here." She gave him the kettle. "Go put some water in this. Don't fill it up, just a cup or two."

He frowned, but took the kettle and was off down the stairs. He was back faster than she'd have thought possible, with the right amount of water.

She plugged the kettle in and switched it on. Then she dragged the cardboard box out from next to the shelf. Paddavis clearly recognised it at once, and understood its significance too.

"Oh!" he said, grinning. "Clever, clever. Which one are you going to use?"

She lifted out the box of rosehip tea.

"This is the only one I've tried so far," she said.

"That's a good one," said Paddavis. "Some of the others are useless, really. They just want somebody to complain at. But Maarouf's not bad."

The fancy teacup was still among the more ordinary mugs. She took a pinch of tea, and once the water boiled, poured it into the cup, closely watched by Paddavis.

Would it work?

She was just beginning to wonder if she'd done something wrong, when the steam started rising from the cup and forming the plump little figure.

"Good afternoon," said the genie. "It is afternoon, is it not? So hard to keep track of time."

Then he noticed Paddavis and his expression tightened. "Oh. You."

Paddavis smirked at the genie.

"I've got some honey here," said Gia, reaching for the pot she kept with her other tea things.

"Oh?" The genie lost his frosty tone. "How delightful. Could you by any chance —?"

"Of course," said Gia. "But I do have a favour to ask of you."

"Indeed," said the genie. "How can I be of service?"

Gia tapped the trunk. It boomed hollowly under her finger. "Can you open this for me?"

He closed his eyes and frowned. Then he gave a nod. "Old locks. Stiff. But not outside my range."

"Fantastic. Here." She scooped a fat teaspoon of honey into his cup. "Is that enough?"

"Marvellous. Marvellous."

"Don't give him too much. It just makes him giggly," said Paddavis.

The genie shot him a cold look. "I'm quite capable of controlling myself. Unlike some people I might mention. Now. The locks."

Flushed with colour from the honey, he clasped his hands and closed his eyes.

Gia held her breath. She sat with her hands on the trunk, not sure what to expect.

The genie frowned and bowed forward on his plume of steam. Just as Gia thought nothing was going to happen, there was a double click and she felt the trunk vibrate as if somebody had given it a slap.

"There!" said the genie. "A little stiffer than I'd anticipated."

Gia looked down at the trunk. It looked just as it had before.

"Aren't you going to open it?" said Paddavis. His whiskers nearly brushed the trunk in his eagerness to see inside. The genie, too, was craning curiously.

Now that it came to it, Gia felt reluctant.

Probably nothing important. She shook off her nerves, took hold of the lid, and lifted.

It was stiff, and at first it opened only a little way, enough to slide a hand inside, but not enough to reveal the contents. She could smell something. A scent poured out of the trunk. A resiny perfume, frankincense and jasmine, far too strong to be anything but magical. She shifted her grip and pulled the lid all the way up, ignoring the creaking groan.

Then she sat staring down at its contents.

Feathers. The trunk was full of white feathers.

"Don't touch!" said Paddavis, just as the genie's "No!" stopped her from reaching inside.

It wasn't just feathers. She could see the outline of a wing, the long, crisp pinion feathers arranged one overlapping the other like the scales of a fish. It must be a skin, with the feathers still attached. There was not enough space in the trunk for an entire bird.

"Gia!"

For a moment longer she looked at the open trunk, trying to make sense of what she saw. Then the new sounds registered. There were steps down below, and somebody had called her name.

"Gia?"

Her father. As quietly as she could, she shut the trunk, then pushed it back far from the trapdoor, wincing at the noise. She'd have to hide it properly later.

She noticed that Paddavis was already gone. The genie floated on top of its little cloud of steam, looking quite astonished.

"Coming, Dad!"

There had been something in his voice. He had sounded almost—

"Gia?"

"Mom?"

She nearly fell down the stairs. A moment later she was in the kitchen, and there was Saraswati, and there was her father, holding Nico.

"Mom!"

Saraswati turned and gathered Gia into her arms.

ಸOಐ

FEATHERS

That afternoon and the evening that followed had an unreal quality. Saraswati and Nico were home again, but nothing was said about where they'd been or why they had left.

Karel had spent the day searching from hospital to morgue, and returned home to find them coming down the street, hand in hand. Gia expected him to interrogate her mother, to demand answers, but he said nothing.

It was as though everyone were holding their breath, avoiding the thin ice.

The closest Gia came to breaking the spell was at Nico's bedtime. The last time she'd seen him was wet and bedraggled in Saraswati's arms. Now he was back to normal, and demanding his bedtime story.

Gia and Saraswati stood in the door watching as Karel read to him.

"How has Nico been?" Gia asked softly. "It must have been difficult with him."

Saraswati shook her head. She'd just had a shower, and was combing out her hair in long slow strokes.

"No," she said. "The caretaker was there all the time. Keeping him working on that sculpture of his. That man is amazing."

She swept her hair back over her shoulders and took a deep, calm breath.

"When Nico's with him, it's like he's a different boy."

༄O༅

Later, up in her room, Gia looked at the trunk. She no longer wanted to know its secrets. She'd wait until everyone was out of the house, and then she'd put it back where she'd found it. In the meantime she pushed it against the wall furthest from the trapdoor, where it was half hidden by her milk crate bookshelf.

There was no sign of Paddavis, and the genie had drifted away, leaving behind a cup of cold tea.

༄O༅

The next day, Monday, was a normal school day, and Gia kept remembering that it was one of her last. No more school, soon.

A few more days and she'd be leaving for Valkenberg. Sonella got some of the story out of her, about her mother's disappearance and return, but she told no one about the bargain she'd struck with the old ones. The closest she'd come to thinking about it was when she found the button that she'd pulled off her guard's sleeve, still in her pocket.

It did not give away any secrets.

A plain button, rather scratched, made of some kind of brassy metal with a black stone set into it. Unusual, but there was nothing about it that told her who its owner was, or where he might be found.

That afternoon Saraswati unpacked the toile, and smiled at Gia's over-precise notes.

"It's good to be careful," she'd said. "Now, you show me how to lay it out."

It was quite different, throwing the silk out over the cutting table under her mother's watchful eye. Whenever she was uncertain of the next step, Saraswati was there — never telling her what to do, but guiding her to find the right question.

"You have to have confidence," Saraswati told her at one point. "If you keep telling yourself 'this is difficult' or 'I'm going to do this wrong' then you will never get things right. You must *pretend* you know what you're doing, and your hands will know what to do."

Karel did not speak much. He and Saraswati kept touching one another. Karel would take Saraswati's hand as he was explaining something about a client, and she'd stroke his arm. Then Saraswati would turn aside from what she was doing to bury her face in Karel's shoulder. Just for a moment, and then they would go on with their work.

The calm spell lasted until that evening over supper, when Saraswati at last turned to her and said, "Gia, does Karel know?"

Gia put down her fork.

In her mind's eye, she saw the glass vase again. The fracture lines spreading, but the glass was not yet broken. The pieces still held together for a few moments more.

She avoided her mother's eyes, aware that her father, too, had stopped eating.

"Gia?" said her mother.

Gia shook her head, then swallowed. Her throat had gone very tight.

"Do you mean about the— about the bargain? With—" She could not get the words out.

"That's right."

There was a silence.

"Gia?" said Karel.

When she did not answer, he turned to Saraswati. "Sari? What's this?"

"I think it's better if Gia tells you."

"It's about the Belle Gente," said Gia. It came out as a whisper. "I made a bargain with them. So they would not take Nico."

She looked up at her father. "That's why Mom came back."

From then on, things came apart.

She made a mess of explaining, telling things in the wrong order. Ochre's arrival to fetch Nico. Her signing up for First Exit with Special Branch. The late-night trip, the blindfold, the conversation with the ivory woman and the man who'd looked inside her head. By the time half of it was told her father was up and pacing.

He refused to believe it at first, and she had to fetch the paperwork, the documents she'd signed with Special Branch, and the new revised contract with the Belle Gente. Then he tried to find a way out.

He'd phone Special Branch. He would speak to the headmaster of the school. He'd take the contract to a lawyer. He'd contact Captain Witbooi.

Gia watched him pace, and tried to answer his increasingly angry questions. It was like a horrible dream that would not stop. At last Saraswati, who'd been silent, spoke again. "Karel. It's done."

He turned on her and for a moment Gia thought that he would shout, but all he said was, "So you knew about this. And you let it happen."

He looked tired and defeated, but Saraswati shook her head.

"No. I would have stopped her if I could. But I was not here to stop her."

Mother and daughter looked at one another.

"Gia is no longer a child, Karel. She made this bargain, and she has to stand by it. I don't like it any more than you do. But this is what she did, and she did it to save Nico."

Saraswati reached across the table and took Gia's hand. "It was bravely done. And it's too late to stop it now."

ஐОಛ

Although Karel let the subject drop, Gia soon saw that he was far from accepting Saraswati's words. He was convinced that there must be some way to reverse the First Exit commitment she'd made.

Over the next few days, to Gia's embarrassment, he phoned the headmaster, and went so far as to arrange a meeting with him, that Gia had to attend. It soon became clear that there was no way to back out of joining Special Branch, not without Gia's consent. Mr Peterson made that perfectly clear.

According to the law, as long as the First Exit criteria were met, Gia was of age to make that decision for herself and there was nothing her father could do to stop her.

While she was relieved to hear this confirmed, Gia hated the patronising way Mr Peterson spoke to her father. The headmaster was all concerned sympathy, nodding earnestly as he listened to Karel, but he had the manner of an adult patiently listening to an unreasonable and sulky child.

For a while Gia worried that Karel would try to contact Special Branch directly, but Saraswati must have put a stop to that.

She did not understand what he hoped to achieve. After all, if she did not join Special Branch, that would break the bargain with the Belle Gente. Did he simply refuse to think about that?

One good thing was that her parents had forgotten that she was supposed to be grounded. She met Fatima and Ben several times, and went to visit Sonella more than once. Gia always found some excuse why they could not meet at her home. The trunk was still in her room. She'd not had a chance to put it back where she'd found it, and she could not think of a way of explaining it to her friends.

She did not tell Fatima or Ben the whole story. They did not know about her bargain with the Belle Gente. She told them that Saraswati had gone into hiding to escape from the attentions of the Belle Gente, and made some deal with them so that she could return home safely. Fatima seemed perfectly happy to accept this, and if Ben had his doubts, he did not say anything.

Sonella was less easy to sidestep. Gently but relentlessly, she pulled the full story out of Gia as soon as they were alone together. It was a relief to have somebody to talk to, and Sonella made a good audience. She listened with total attention, and some awe, as Gia told her about meeting Ochre, and her trip to the secret room. The description of the ivory woman interested her in particular.

"I think I know who she might be," she said. "My mother's been researching that stuff. The history of the resistance all over the world. One of the important leaders in China is a woman called The White Crane. You know there have been dreadful crackdowns over there, and many people have disappeared. There have been lots of rumours that she's here in South Africa. I wonder if it could be her. She's one of the most powerful magic users in the world now."

She was fascinated with every aspect of the story, and even the button interested her.

"You know," she said, turning it over in her hand. "You could give this to Ben to hold. Maybe he could use his psychometry to figure out where that meeting place is."

But Gia shook her head. "I don't think I want to know," she said. "I think it might be dangerous to know that. If they went to so much trouble to keep it secret." Then she looked at her friend. "Sonella, you know that this is all dreadfully secret, right? If anyone hears that I'm involved with those people, I don't know what might happen. Special Branch is not a joke, and neither are the old ones."

But Sonella was nodding earnestly. "Don't worry Gia. I won't tell anyone." She gave a wry smile. "Not even Miss Huisman."

Gia gave an unhappy laugh.

Miss Huisman had not said anything, but she clearly had strong opinions about Gia joining Special Branch. She was perfectly polite, but her manner toward Gia had definitely cooled.

It stung. Gia hated disappointing a teacher she respected. But it was too late for regrets now. Miss Huisman was part of the life she was leaving behind.

FLIGHT

Now that Saraswati was back, Gia's days took on a new rhythm.

She ran every morning, and after school, as soon as she'd finished her homework, she helped Saraswati with the wedding gown.

It was now less than a week before she'd have to leave home and go and live at Valkenberg, but she tried not to think of that fact.

The caretaker came every day and spent most of the afternoon with Nico. Between them they worked on the overlocker sculpture. They seemed to spend as much time building it as taking it apart. Gia loved watching them work. When Nico was with the caretaker, he lost many of the nervous twitches that had marked him out as not-quite normal before.

Karel was as busy as ever. He'd taken on all the other work, in order to free Saraswati and Gia to focus on the wedding gown. He was often out, meeting new clients, or sourcing fabric.

There was a lot to do on the wedding gown, and they were kept very busy. It was exhausting work, but it also meant that there was not much time to think, and that suited Gia.

One afternoon the caretaker had left earlier than he usually did, just as Mandy started reorganising the kitchen cupboards. This was something she'd been threatening to do for days.

"There's something living in there," she'd said. "And it's not mice, for all that I keep finding droppings."

Organising cupboards and looking after Nico were two things that did not go well together, so Gia and Saraswati took a break from sewing to keep an eye on him. They were working together so well now that neither wanted to carry on without the other, and as Saraswati said, they both needed a rest.

Saraswati sat on the couch, eyes closed, face turned into the sun. The only sign that she was not asleep was her hand slowly stroking a purring Minou, who was stretched across her lap.

Nico worked on his overlocker monster. It was quite a magnificent beast by now. Each limb could bend at the joints, and if Nico turned a little crank near the tail, the head swung from side to side, jaws opening and shutting.

Gia felt her own eyelids drooping. It was a lovely day, one of those rare, windless, late-summer days that deny the existence of winter. A pigeon cooed outside the window, a warm pulse of sound.

She came awake to Nico pulling on her hand.

"Feathers," he said. "Feathers?"

She blinked at him. "What?"

He gestured at the monster.

Well, at least he's asking for permission now.

"Oh, yes." She yawned, and felt a tremendous reluctance to get up.

"Well, you know where they are on my shelf. Why don't you just bring the whole jar."

Nico nodded and scampered off.

For a while she sat, nodding in the warm sunshine.

"Where's Nico?"

Saraswati's sleepy voice brought her awake, and she realised that Nico had not come back yet. It should not have taken him long to go up to her room and fetch the jar of feathers. Then she relaxed at the sound of footsteps in the passage outside.

"There he is," said Saraswati and then— "What have you got there, my boy?"

Something in her mother's voice made Gia turn her head to look.

Nico walked slowly, his arms full of something white. It draped down to the ground and dragged behind him. Gia froze, the shock of it prickling up her spine and stopping her breath.

Nico's arms were full of white feathers.

She'd forgotten all about the trunk, shoved back as it was against the wall. Nico must have seen, and opened it.

Saraswati eased Minou gently off her lap, and rose to her feet.

"What have you got there, sweetheart?"

Gia felt as if a hand was clasped over her mouth, stopping her breath. She wanted to shout, to pull her mother's attention toward her, away from the thing that Nico held.

Saraswati brushed her hair out of her face, and smiled down at Nico, her eyes intent, interested, but still calm. She reached down, and took the feathered skin from her son. Eyes closed, she lifted it to her face and breathed in the smell of it. The feathers rustled like silk, and the scent filled the room, a resiny scent that hung in the quiet, sunlit air.

Saraswati swung the skin over her shoulders so that it hung around her body like a cloak. She stroked her hands down the length of it, luxuriating in its touch, like a young girl in her first party dress.

Everything slowed, moved with an underwater speed.

Gia could see every detail with unnatural clarity, but her ears were deafened by a rushing roar.

Saraswati looked down at Nico and took both his hands in hers. The feathered cloak clung to her body, wrapping down her arms until it almost seemed as if the white feathers were sprouting out of her skin. The little frown, the waking flicker of anxiety in her eyes.

Then her arms rose, dragged up and back. Her hands slipped from Nico's grasp. With an effort, Saraswati brought her arms back down, her face white, all calm gone now. She stared down at her wrists, at the silver bracelets that circled each arm. Her mouth opened in a soundless scream and she pulled at the silver, curling her body around the unbearable pain of it.

Gia at last found the strength to move and threw herself forward. All she could hear was Saraswati's heavy breathing, seeming to form one harsh word over and over:

"Off. Off. Off."

She grabbed Saraswati's arm ignoring the feathers that were pushing out between her fingers, out of her mother's skin. She hooked her fingers under the silver bracelet and dragged it off, then grabbed for the other arm. There were more feathers now, but she could still see the red marks on Saraswati's white skin where the silver burnt her like acid.

"Off. Get it off."

For a horrible moment the bracelet stuck. Then it was off, sliding clumsily over her mother's hand.

Gia looked into Saraswati's face, so close to hers and for one last moment saw her there, warm, living, a woman's eyes. Her mother's eyes closed, and opened as the eyes of a stranger. The bird-woman opened her arms and brought them down again and again, each rushing beat shaking out more feathers, shaping her arms into wings.

Gia's hair blew back at the wind of it, and she grabbed hold of Nico who was standing, blank-faced, staring.

"Open the door!"

Somebody pushed past Gia. Mandy was struggling with the door to the balcony.

"Help me open it, or she'll go through the glass!" screamed Mandy.

Gia sprang to help her. The winged creature snaked her impossibly long neck and threw herself at the now open door. For a moment Gia thought she was going to crash down onto the road outside but the great wings stretched and caught the air, and with a rush of feathers and a keening scream, the swan launched herself over the balcony rail and was gone, flying beat after beat up into the blue, late-summer sky.

ಸ⊙ಇ

"Better come back inside."

Mandy stood in the door, her headscarf askew, breathing heavily. Then she held up her hands.

"No!"

Nico, who'd been standing white-faced and staring, was heading for the open balcony door. Mandy caught him clumsily and they both fell onto the floor. Gia tried to help Mandy, but Nico was almost too strong for them, struggling desperately toward the balcony. He screamed as they dragged him back into the room. A thin, inhuman, thread-like scream that went on and on.

The front door slammed and a moment later Karel was there.

"Nico!" he roared, and the surprise of it stopped the screaming, and Nico stared up at him, mouth still open. Then he reached for his father, and Mandy and Gia let him go.

Silent again, he flung himself into Karel's arms. They sat there on the floor, man and boy. Karel rocked a little, back and forth, his arms wrapped around his son.

"You okay?" said Mandy, and Gia nodded. Her throat was sore. She must have been screaming. Something crunched under her foot.

"Careful," said Mandy. "There's glass everywhere."

One of the panes of the balcony door had shattered.

Karel looked around the room, taking in the shards of glass, and the white feathers that drifted down through the still air. His gaze fell on the silver bracelets that lay discarded on the floor.

"Sari?" he said softly.

He looked up at Gia and Mandy, shaking his head. His lips moved, but he seemed unable to speak. At last his voice came.

"So she found it. But how — ?"

Then he stood up, awkwardly hoisting Nico onto his hip, the boy's face still buried in his shoulder. "I'll take him to bed."

Gia stared at her father. "Aren't you going to go look for her?"

Karel did not answer, just turned and walked out of the room, carrying Nico.

ಸಿOಜ

Gia ran out the front door and down the stairs.

Too late, too late, drummed in her head in rhythm with her steps.

Out on the street, there was no sign that anything unusual had happened. Cars drove by, and a few pedestrians strolled unhurriedly on their way.

Hadn't anyone seen anything?

A woman stood in her door across the road, smoking. Gia caught her eye, but as she approached the woman turned and shut the door behind her.

Maybe they did not want to see.

She craned her neck, looking up at the roofs, or up into the sky, hoping to see some sign of the swan. As she searched she walked, faster and faster until she was running. Her school shoes hurt her feet and sounded loud on the pavement, but she hardly noticed. All she cared about now was driving out the memories.

Too late, too late.

The dark, hard, uncaring eyes of the swan in her mother's face.

The bruising blows of its wings as she pulled at the bracelets.

The angry wheals on Saraswati's white skin where the silver had burnt her.

The bird, beautiful, powerful and utterly alien, snaking its neck, hurling itself desperately at the door like a trapped thing. As if nothing mattered as much as getting free. As if it were willing to die rather than be trapped any longer.

The desperate beauty of the scramble and falling flight, picking up, winging up into the sun.

Gia ran.

Her breath raced and her heart pounded as she drove herself on and on up toward the mountain. She was no longer looking for the swan.

The angry blare of a horn shocked her back into herself and she found that she was on the edge of the freeway, a stream of cars roaring by in front of her. There was no way across De Waal Drive at this time of day. She stepped back onto the kerb, disoriented, and stood there gasping, feeling the wind of the passing cars tug at her.

ஐOஐ

When she got back to the house, all was quiet.

Karel and Mandy sat at the kitchen table, facing one another. Mandy's headscarf was off, her hair standing on end as though she'd been running her hands through it. Karel stared down at the silver bracelets that lay on the table in front of him.

It's as if somebody's died.

They looked up as she came in.

"Oh, good," said Mandy. She reached out and took Gia's hand. "Come, sit down. I'll make you some tea. Would you like some tea?"

Gia nodded, although she did not really. She sat in the chair that Mandy pulled out for her.

"Nico?" Gia asked.

"He's sleeping," said Karel, not lifting his gaze from the bracelets.

For a while they sat there, as Mandy moved about, filling the kettle, opening and closing cupboards.

"What happened, then?" said Karel at last. "Did you see?"

"Yes," said Gia

Karel looked up at her, his face bleak. "How did it happen?"

"It was me."

He frowned, puzzled, so she continued. "I found the trunk. I found it a few days ago, when— when Mom was still gone."

She did not dare look at him now. "I opened it. I did not know what it was. Just a lot of feathers."

She glanced up and saw he was watching her. His eyes were grave, but there was no sign of anger.

"I did not know what it meant." Then she shook her head. "No, that's not right. I did not let myself think about what it meant."

It was easier to talk now.

"I was going to put it back, but I never got a chance. And then Nico went up to my room—"

Karel closed his eyes as if in pain.

"He brought it to her," she ended in a whisper. "That thing. That feather cloak."

The kettle bubbled to a boil, then turned itself off with a loud plastic click.

"Do you know where she's gone, Dad?"

Karel shook his head. He rubbed his thumb over the whorls in the bracelet.

"Where has she gone? Who knows? I guess I always knew it would happen one day," he said, as if to himself. "But I let myself believe that she'd choose to stay."

I don't think it was a choice, thought Gia, but she kept that to herself. How could she guess what had gone through her mother's mind when she saw that swan-skin cloak?

Mandy put the teapot and the cups on the table, and sank back into her chair. "It just needs to steep a bit," she said. "And you'll have to have honey. We're out of sugar."

"How did it happen?" asked Gia.

Karel looked at her. "What do you mean?"

"I mean," said Gia, "how did it all begin? With Mom? How did it happen?"

He shook his head. "Gia, it was so long ago—"

"No!" The vehemence of that word startled even her, and she took a breath to calm herself. "No," she said again, but more quietly. "Enough secrets. I deserve to know. We deserve to know."

She turned to Mandy. "You didn't know, did you? This about Mom?"

Mandy shook her head. "I knew Madam had her secrets," she said. "But it was not my place to pry them out."

Karel did not move. His eyes were back on the bracelets, but he stared at them blindly, as if he did not see what was in front of him.

"The first time I saw your mother, she was with her sisters. There were seven of them. Seven sisters." A ghost of a smile touched his lips.

"They were something else. Like royalty. Everyone would stare at them, but they did not care. Nothing could touch them.

"I was a student then, in Italy. We used to go to lots of parties. A whole group of us. Jennie and Ben too."

Gia started at the mention of her birth parents, but her father did not notice.

"Jennie was already pregnant with you at that time, but she never let that stop her going out with the rest of us...thank you, Mandy." He accepted a cup of tea from Mandy, and blew on it.

"Sari was different from her sisters. The older ones were a wild lot. They'd dance you off your feet, drink you under the table. Sari was always more reserved. Her sisters were very protective of her. She was the youngest, you know. It was a job getting close enough even to speak to her. But I managed it in the end."

He nodded slowly.

Gia wondered if he remembered who he was speaking to, he seemed so lost in his memories.

"Once I persuaded her to get away from her sisters more, we used to meet quite often, the group of us. Your parents were always there, some others too. We used to talk all the night through."

He smiled sadly. "We solved all the problems of the world. Nothing was impossible to us. Sari was pretty quiet mostly, but when she spoke, everyone would listen. She was so different from the rest of us. And she seemed to enjoy those meetings. At any rate, she kept coming.

"Of course, by that time I knew what she was. I'd followed her and her sisters out one night and saw them change themselves back into swans, putting on their swan skins. I never said anything about it. I thought that if she knew that I knew, she'd stop coming. And by that time, I was so in love—" He sighed. "It sounds terrible now. But things were so different then. It was like being in a war. Things were happening. Nobody cared about the past or the future. All that mattered was getting the most out of every moment. I didn't think about what I was doing, I just knew that I could not bear to lose her." For a long moment he sat, staring down at the cup in his hands.

"Then everything changed. It really happened overnight. First it was just talk, and things in the news about attacks on magicals, people being denounced, show trials, that kind of thing. Then suddenly it was real. There were riots. I saw a man being— no. No need to talk about that.

"I knew by then that Sari's sisters were involved in the resistance. They were in danger all the time. They wanted to take Sari away somewhere, for her to be safe but their father refused to go, and they could not leave him behind. Every time I said goodbye to her, I thought it might be the last time.

"We were a couple by then, and I did not want her to go. Every time she went to join her family, she was going into danger. We argued about it endlessly. I wanted her to come away with me, back here to South Africa. We were going to start a business together. Me, your mother, and your parents, Gia.

"I'd even bought the tickets. It was all organised. It was clear we had to leave. Italy was no longer safe. We were just waiting for you to be born, and as soon as Jennie was strong enough, we'd go. It was the only thing to do. But Sari would not agree."

"She did not want to leave her family," said Mandy.

Karel looked up, almost as if he'd forgotten there was anyone there and was surprised to hear Mandy's voice. "That's right," he said.

"At last I could bear it no longer. I found out where she hid her swan skin, and hid it away so that she couldn't leave. She didn't know it was me, at first. I let her think that some random stranger had stolen it. That was wrong of me, I know.

"There wasn't really much time to think about anything by then. You were born, Gia, and then everything started happening. Somebody— I never found out who it was— denounced your parents to the authorities. They were supposedly spies for the resistance, or some such thing. It did not make sense, but then it did not have to. Being accused was proof of guilt.

"Sari and I were sharing rooms with your parents by then, and one night we came home to find the doors broken down. Your father, Benjamin, he was gone. Jennie was hiding in a cupboard with you in her arms. She told us that the police had come to take them away. I'm pretty sure they killed your father that night. There was a lot of blood—"

Karel must have seen Gia's expression, as he stopped, and put his hand on hers.

"I'm sorry, Gia."

She shook her head, and managed, "It's okay. Go on."

He nodded. "I haven't spoken about that night to anyone for so many years, it seems like a dream, now. I remember thinking that Jennie was unusually calm. She was so logical about it. She said that we were to look after you, that she had to go looking for Benjamin.

"I think she knew that he was dead. In any case, she had to go. She made us promise to leave as soon as we could, even if she did not come back. All she cared about was that you were safe, to get you safely back to South Africa. Then she left. We never saw her again."

For long time they sat without speaking.

At last, Gia said, "And then you came here? With Mom?"

Karel nodded.

"That's right. Sari figured out by then that it was me who took her swan skin. I mean, it would have been impossible for me to conceal it from her. I'd packed it in a trunk, and had to bring it with us. I'd have got rid of it if I could, but I did not dare. I think something would have happened to her, if any harm came to her skin.

"She knew I had it. But I think she stayed mostly because of you, Gia. Because she was looking after you by then. After all, it was just locked in a trunk. If she'd wanted to go so badly, she could have found a way to get it open."

"I've always heard," said Mandy quietly "that a bird-woman cannot take her skin, once it's been locked away like that. Somebody has to give it to her."

Karel looked at her bleakly. "I did not know that," he said at last. He touched the bracelets.

"I bought these for her. As a disguise. We had to get out of Italy somehow. It took some pretty heavy bribes too. But everyone believed that only full humans could bear the touch of silver, so nobody ever suspected she was more than she seemed, once they saw the bracelets."

Gia wanted him to stop speaking. Each new revelation fitted into place, but brought with it a new and unexpected pain. It was as if somebody had taken her life and turned it inside out. Still, she had to know.

"Do you think my parents might still be alive?" she said.

Karel shook his head. "Once we were back here, I did my best to find out. I even paid a man I knew over there to investigate. But we never found anything. I used to look up anyone I knew who came from Italy, or any part of Europe, and ask them for news. They told us the most terrible stories and I lost hope.

"Then the years went by and there was no word from them even after things settled down. There would be no reason for them not to contact us, at least. But we never heard anything. I'm sorry, Gia. I'm as sure as I can be that neither of them survived that night."

Gia nodded, feeling strangely calm.

There was something else she needed to know. "Dad, why did Mom go out every full-moon night? Was it something to do with her being— well, something to do with being a swan-woman?"

"You knew about that? Oh. Well. I followed her a few times, to see where she went. Actually I think she knew perfectly well that I was checking up on her. I was terrified that she was going to leave, but when she kept coming back I stopped following her.

"It was to meet her sisters. They did not always show up. In fact I think they hardly ever came. But every now and then, on a full-moon night they came to meet her. Always down there by the Liesbeek River. I only saw them once. There were just two of them. Two of her sisters. The other times she just stood there, waiting for them, until she had to go home again."

Suddenly he pushed the chair back and got up from the table. "Listen, I'm— I'm going out for a bit."

Mandy put a hand out to stop him. "Mr Grobbelaar, do you want me to stay here the night? With the boy?"

He stared down at her, then nodded. "Can you do that, Mandy? I think that would be good." Then he left abruptly.

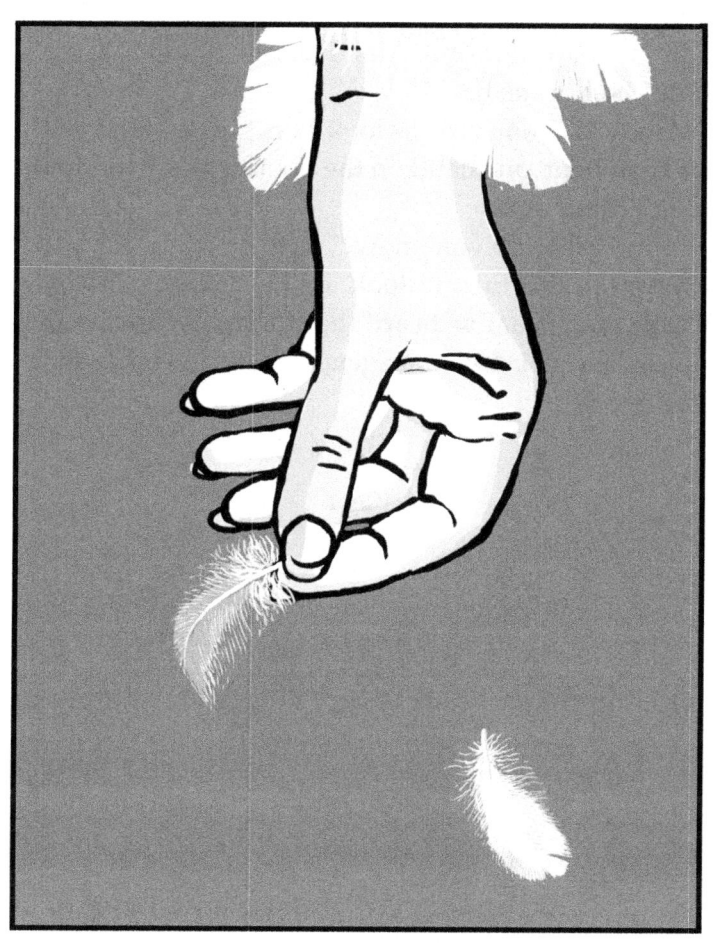

"Well then," said Mandy, getting up. "I'll just give them a call at home, to say I'll be spending the night here."

As Mandy reached the door, Gia could no longer hold in the question. "Mandy," she said. "Do you think she'll come back?"

Mandy did not turn to look at her. She stood with her head bent, one hand on the doorframe. "No, child. I don't think that."

"Why? How do you know?"

Now she did turn to look at Gia. "Your mother is not the first, Gia. I've heard the stories. It's always the same. Once a bird-woman gets her feathers back, she's gone forever."

ಸಿOಇ

NEIGHBOURS

The next day Gia stayed home from school. She slept late into the morning and even when she was up and dressed, she still felt groggy and half asleep.

Mandy was in Nico's room, sitting on his bed and talking to him. He lay curled up into a little ball, sucking his thumb, Poepie in the crook of his arm.

"How's he doing?" Gia asked softly, once she caught Mandy's eye.

Mandy shook her head. "Little boy is far inside his own head," she said, stroking Nico's hair.

"Did he sleep okay?"

"He did. But there were some dreams, poor boy." She looked significantly at a bundle in the laundry basket that stood by the foot of the bed. "If you could just go put that sheet there in the machine. I don't want to leave him like this."

"Okay. Where's Dad?"

"Working downstairs."

Gia picked up the basket and carried it to the kitchen. She bundled the sheet into the washing machine, put some soap in the dispenser and turned it on.

Not a good sign. It was years since Nico had wet his bed.

She stood for a while watching the sheet tumbling round and round in its soapy suds. The doorbell brought her back to reality.

"I'll get it," she called to Mandy.

The man standing outside the burglar gate was vaguely familiar. He was old, but stood upright, and held something covered with a very clean dishcloth.

"Good morning," he said as soon as he saw Gia coming down the stairs.

"I'm sorry to disturb— *ahem*." He cleared his throat. "I'm Mr Joubert, your neighbour." He indicated with his chin. "Number three. I should have come to introduce myself before. Rude of me. *Ahem.*"

He nodded to himself. "And now I come at a time like this. Terrible thing. Terrible thing. Private and all that, I know, don't mean to pry but I could not help hearing."

He stared at Gia, brows bristling. "I don't pay mind to the, ahem, neighbourhood gossip as a rule, but I know that your family has been through the wars lately, what with Special Branch sniffing about. And now this thing with your mother." He shook his head. "I'm so terribly sorry."

"Well, uh, thanks," said Gia. Her gaze went to the bundle in his hands again, and he gave a start.

"Oh! Ah. I happened to be baking this morning, so I made an extra pie for your family. I know you won't feel like cooking at a time like this."

"Thanks," said Gia, unlocking the gate. "That's very kind of you." She took the pie dish from him.

"Don't put it in your fridge yet," he said. "It's still

too hot. But it keeps quite well, if, *ahem*, you don't want to eat it right away."

Gia could see that he was not ready to go yet, so she waited there, holding the warm pie dish. Mr Joubert looked at his shoes, nodding to himself. After a few more nods and throat clearings, he straightened himself up.

"Don't want to keep you. Give my regards to your father."

And he turned on his heel and walked back to his own front door.

౸O౷

Not all the neighbours were as understanding as Mr Joubert.

When Gia went to get some milk and bread, a group of women gossiping on the corner fell silent as she went by, and their looks were far from friendly. One of them drew her toddler back as if she thought Gia might snatch her up.

"*Birdy-girl,*" somebody hissed.

Gia walked on, her face burning, biting her lip to keep tears back.

Why cry about something stupid like that?

A tall young woman with a far-too-short skirt and glossy waist-length hair, caught her eye and grinned. "Don't mind them," she said, in an unexpectedly deep voice. "Old bitches." She flicked her cigarette derisively.

"We'll chew them up and spit them up, hey, darling." She straightened up from the wall that she'd been leaning against, her eyes suddenly serious. "Your mother was a lady, doll— " She grimaced "Is a lady, I mean. Always used to compliment me on my style."

She smiled and flicked her hair back. "Don't let those old bitches get you down."

Gia gave her an uncertain smile. "Thanks," she said.

In Granny's shop the conversation died down as she entered, then started up again in a too-loud, too-cheerful way.

Gia waited until the other customers left before she approached the counter.

Granny took both her hands. "Oh sweetie, I'm so sorry," she said, and suddenly Gia felt like crying all over again.

"Does everybody know?"

Granny laughed a little. "Sweetie, a swan comes crashing out of a window and flies down the road like an angel from heaven, yes, everybody knows."

Gia frowned, struggling to keep the tears back. "Did you know, I mean, before? That my mother was—?"

"I had a guess, my sweetheart. But Granny's been around, you know. I spot the signs. You're sore because nobody told you what your mom really was?"

Gia nodded dumbly. It was ridiculous, she knew, she was acting like a little child but Granny had gone to the heart of it. The hurt of feeling like a fool for not knowing, for never guessing.

"How's the little one taking it?" asked Granny, releasing Gia's hands. "Wait, don't use your sleeve. Here's a tissue."

"He's not so good," said Gia, wiping her face and then blowing her nose.

"Poor little thing. The caretaker not been round yet this morning?"

"No, I've not seen him."

"But I hear Mr Joubert came with one of his pies." She laughed at Gia's surprise. "Told you Granny knows everything. He's a good man, Mr Joubert. Had his own trouble with Special Branch messing him about. They don't like his kind, if you know what I mean."

Gia did not know, but she nodded anyway.

"Well, I'll let you go back then," said Granny.

"Granny," said Gia. "Will she— is she really gone? I mean, she might come back—?"

But Granny was shaking her head. "No." Her eyes were dark with unbearable knowledge. "No. Once they fly away like that, they don't come back, my girl. They never come back."

ஓOஒ

A little later, Granny knocked at the door. She had a box of odds and ends from her shop. Gia showed her in to Nico's room.

"Thought you could make a jungle gym for that rat of yours," she said to Nico. She plumped down on his bed, and started taking things out of the box.

"I've got lots of these tubes," she said, "and I think these connectors will fit. You could make a whole maze for him to crawl around in. And then there's this thing, it could be a little window…"

Nico lay watching her for a few seconds, and then, intrigued, reached for some of the objects.

"Look, they fit together like this," said Granny, demonstrating. Nico sat up. Soon he was absorbed in the possibilities of the various bits and pieces from the box. He did not speak, but at least he wasn't just curled up with his thumb in his mouth.

"Gia, can you come down?" said Mandy from the door. "Your father is calling a meeting."

"What about Nico?"

"Leave him with Granny."

Down in the studio, Karel asked Gia and Mandy to join him at the cutting table.

"I'm calling a meeting," he said when they were both seated. "There are some difficult decisions to be made. I know that the business is probably the last thing you want to be thinking about now. But we have some serious commitments we have to honour, and deadlines to meet."

He paused for a moment, lips moving as he searched for words. Then he got up so abruptly that Gia had to catch his chair to prevent it from falling over. He walked a few steps away, then stood there, rubbing his forehead. When he spoke again it was so softly that Gia had to strain to hear.

"If it were just me, I would just drop everything and go looking." He shook his head. "But it's not just me involved here. If I let it all go to hell, we will lose—" He gestured to indicate the studio, the house upstairs. "I can't, do you see?"

He looked from Gia to Mandy, trying to convince them.

"Of course not, Mr Grobbelaar," said Mandy. "And we're here to help, aren't we? Gia's been doing the gown, and I'm to put in the linings into all those jackets. What else needs to be done?"

Mandy's words seemed to calm him, and Karel returned to the table and sat down once more.

"That's what we need to figure out. Gia, I've had a look at the gown. You've done a lot, but it's far from finished. If your— if your mother was working on it I would say we're well within the deadline. How do you feel about it? Can you finish it by yourself?"

Gia licked her lips. "I don't think so Dad," she said. "I mean, Mom was pretty much holding my hand all the way. If you could—"

Karel was shaking his head. "I can do it, of course," he said. "But that means leaving all the other work, and if we don't make our other deadlines we're in serious trouble."

"I guess I can take on a bit more," said Mandy but even Gia could hear the doubt in her voice.

"No, Mandy, you are already overstretched. Also, there's Nico to look after."

"Well, he's only really here in the afternoons—"

"Can't you hire somebody to help Mandy?" asked Gia.

Karel looked unhappy. "That would be a solution but we simply don't have the money for that right now."

"And there's not many who would agree to work for us as things are," said Mandy heavily. "I'm sorry, Mr Grobbelaar, to have to bring it up, but the stories that are flying around about Madam...well. Also it's difficult to find anyone worth having, who wouldn't be worse than useless. We need an experienced seamstress."

"Taking on help is not an option right now," said Karel. "Gia, I'll be busy, but I can keep an eye on what you're doing."

"But Dad," said Gia. "I'm not going to be around for that much longer. I'm leaving for Special Branch the day after tomorrow. There's no way I'm going to finish Kavitha's dress in that time."

There was a silence.

Gia forced herself to look steadily at her father,

tensing, ready for him to shout, or slam his hands on the table in frustration. But all he did was sigh.

"Gia, that's all over now. You must see that. You can't possibly still mean to be going through with this crazy scheme?"

"Dad—" Mandy put out a warning hand.

"Dad," she said in a quieter tone. "I made an agreement. I can't go back on that."

"You have a commitment to this family, Gia. That should be your first priority."

Gia tried to stay calm.

"That's right," she said. "It's because of family. To keep Nico safe from the Belle Gente. If I break my bargain we'll be in an even worse mess than we are now."

෩O෬

Gia sat on the front stairs, watching the street through the burglar gate.

The meeting had ended in stalemate. Her father would not concede that she had to honour her agreement with both Special Branch and the Belle Gente. She knew he was right about the work that had to be done. Even if Kavitha's dress was finished on time, there would be other jobs after that. Without Saraswati's help, how could the business continue?

I can't finish that dress even with him to help me, in the time that's left, she thought bitterly. *How does he expect me to do it all by myself?*

"Hey!"

She looked up with a jerk, and had to shade her eyes. "Fatima!"

There was somebody else behind Fatima, and a moment later Ben was hanging on the bars of the gate, with Sonella smiling past him.

"Aren't you going to let us in?"

"Okay, okay — just hang on a mo—"

She unlocked the gate, and Fatima smothered anything else she'd been going to say in a hug.

"Sonella called us," she said. "Said you'd not been to school and she's sure something's wrong. Is it?" She held Gia at arm's length, and nodded. "Come, let's go upstairs and you can tell Auntie Fatima all about it."

She tugged Gia up the stairs, Sonella and Ben following close behind.

There was music coming from Nico's bedroom. Granny must have put on a record for him.

They went through to the living room. "You sit here," said Fatima as she pulled out a chair, "and tell us what's going on."

Gia looked at Sonella.

"Sonella hasn't told us anything," said Fatima. "So. Spill."

Gia opened her mouth and closed it again. She should be irritated at Fatima's bossy manner, but in fact it was an incredible relief to see her friends.

"I don't know—"

"None of that," said Fatima. "I know there's been a lot of weird stuff going on and that you've been keeping it mostly to yourself. But this has gone far enough, Gia. Tell."

"But— Okay! Okay. Don't look like that."

Hesitantly at first, and then with more confidence, Gia told them the events of the past few days.

It took a while to tell it all. At first Fatima kept interrupting, but Ben put a stop to that, which made the telling easier.

She told the whole story, leaving nothing out this time. When she came to explaining about her mother, what she was, and how she'd left, Gia found herself holding on to the edge of the table as though that would steady her. When she was finished, she looked up to find them all watching her.

"So that's why Nico is the way he is?" said Ben.

Gia nodded, then gave a sigh that was almost a sob.

"That's right. And everyone tells me that Mom's not going to come back. And that's another thing. We are seriously in the dwang. Dad's up to his neck with client work. We need to finish Kavitha's dress, but without Mom, I just don't know how we're going to manage that."

"Damn," said Fatima softly. She'd been very quiet throughout the last part of the story, and Gia was far from sure what she was thinking.

Sonella reached out to touch Gia's hand.

"Gia, you're going to have to contact the people you spoke to in the Belle Gente. You'll have to renegotiate."

"What?"

"I'm serious. They need you. Things have changed with this thing with your mom. You'll have to let them know."

Gia shook her head, sitting back. "There's no way they're going to let me off—"

"No, I don't think so either," said Sonella. "But there might be something they can do to help."

"Like what?"

"I don't know."

Ben frowned at Sonella. "Why would they want to help?" he said. "Seems like they're pretty much just getting what they can out of the situation. It's not like they care what happens to Gia."

"I know," said Sonella. "But they need her. If she can't go, they don't have a spy. You have something to negotiate with, Gia."

"But even if I wanted to," said Gia, "how do I contact them?"

Sonella shrugged. "The way you did before? Go to the guy who did your contract for you? Brakman?"

"No," said Gia. The idea that had seemed so impossible a moment ago was starting to take root. "That would seem so weak. I need to surprise them — show them I'm a step ahead. If I go back to Brakman that just puts them in charge again."

"So what's your plan?" said Ben.

"It's something Sonella said.:" Gia took the button out of her pocket and put it on the table.

"What's that?"

"It's a button that I found at that place they took me to when I was blindfolded. If I can figure out where it is despite everything they did to prevent me knowing —"

Sonella already knew what she meant. "That's right," she said nodding eagerly. "You must take them off guard."

"Um, I don't know," said Ben. "If you mean what I think you mean."

"You can do it, can't you, Ben?" said Gia. "I won't ask you to if you don't want to."

"Of course I'll do it," said Ben, sounding almost angry. "But what happens if they can feel me doing it? They've probably got some serious security going. What if I trip some — psychic alarm or something?"

Gia stared at him, unable to think of anything to say.

"Can they do that?" said Sonella.

"I don't know," said Ben. "But those people are not a joke. Ah, what the hell—" Before Gia could stop him, he picked up the button.

Gia wished now that she'd never said anything, but it was too late. Ben held the button cupped in both hands in front of his face, eyes closed, frowning with concentration.

"Um," he said at last. "I don't think the person who wore this was human. Smells like— soil. Stone. And stale beer. Cigarette smoke."

Gia nodded, torn between wanting to stop him, and fascinated by his words.

"Not a daytime kind of guy. Night, mostly. Lots of people. Strobes—"

He rocked slightly from side to side, as if to a beat no one else could hear. Then he sighed and put the button down on the table. "It's at a club. The Playground, I'd say. Could be a troll."

Gia saw him in her mind's eye. The troll bouncer at the Playground.

"You're sure?" said Sonella.

"It's a guess. But I'm sure."

"Thanks, Ben," said Gia. "I shouldn't have asked. I didn't think."

"No, it's okay. Nothing happened anyway."

We hope.

"But what now?" said Sonella. "Are you going to go there, Gia?"

"We're all going," said Ben.

"No, no ways," said Gia, half getting up. "There's no ways you guys are coming too."

"Hold on," said Ben, and Sonella was also speaking. "Gia," she said "We can't possibly let you go—"

But Gia shook her head. "You don't understand," she said. "I should never have told any of you any of this. Don't you get it? I'm a spy."

She gave a wry laugh. "I know it sounds ridiculous. But this is real. If anyone finds out what I'm doing, I'm— I don't know what will happen to me. Or to Nico. They wouldn't have gone through all that trouble blindfolding me unless it mattered to them who knows about where they are. Sonella," Gia looked at her desperately. "You said it yourself. They need me. They can't do anything to me. But you guys will just be—" Words failed her.

"Don't you understand? These are people who will do worse that kill you, if they think you know their secrets." She found she was trembling, remembering her few seconds trapped in the gaze of that terrible, quiet man.

"The girl is right."

They all looked round, startled, to see Granny standing at the door, holding Nico by the hand. "You can't just go blundering in there like a bunch of bumblebees on a summer's day.

"Gia must go," she nodded at Sonella. "That is right. You're a girl with sense. But the rest of you..." She shook her head grimly.

"But Gia can't go by herself," said Sonella.

"Who said anything about her going by herself?" said Granny.

Gia felt a rush of hope. "Oh, Granny, you'll go with me?"

"Yes, I will," said Granny. "Oh don't look so happy about it girl. It's no picnic."

"When?"

"Tonight. Best see them at night. We'll walk together, you and me."

"You're going to walk all the way there?" said Ben. "Don't you have a car?"

Granny shook her head. "You think I can drive? It's a bit further than I'm used to, but a bit of exercise would do me good."

"I'll take you," said Fatima suddenly. She'd been unusually quiet, but now she seemed to have regained her old confidence.

"What, on your bike?" said Ben. "I'd like to see that!"

"Don't be a *doos*," said Fatima. "I'll borrow my brother's car."

"But that just brings us back to where we were before," protested Gia. "They'll see that you know where they are —"

"I'll drop you off in town and you can walk the last bit," said Fatima.

"But will your brother let you use his car?"

"Don't worry. He won't even know," said Fatima.

ഏOര

PLUM AND BAMBOO

Gia grabbed the safety belt as Fatima stomped on the brake.

"Sorry!" said Fatima. "Didn't realise how fast we were going."

"Lucky I put my belt on," muttered Granny from the back seat. "I'd be all over the windscreen by now. I thought you said you knew how to drive."

"I do! I can drive alright. It's just this thing is such a monster." The lights changed and she wrestled with the gear lever, engine revving. This time, Gia was ready for the jerk as they pulled off.

"I've not hit anything yet, and that's all that counts."

"If that's your definition of driving then I suppose — watch it!"

This time Gia did close her eyes as they careened round a corner then passed far too close to a line of parked cars.

"Sorry, sorry. Why do they park there, anyway?"

"Maybe drive a little more slowly?" said Gia. "The engine sounds way too loud."

"It does," said Fatima. "Oh." She released the handbrake and the note of the engine dropped abruptly. "That's better."

After that, things calmed down a bit.

They were driving down Main Road, as no one had wanted to risk the freeway with Fatima at the wheel. When Fatima had offered to "borrow" her brother's car, Gia had not asked what kind of car it was. It had been quite a shock to see the enormous four-by-four roaring down their narrow street with Fatima barely visible above the wheel.

Granny insisted that they could not start before eleven, so it was thoroughly dark by that time.

Ben and Sonella had gone home hours ago. They had tried to find reasons to go along, but in the end Granny had prevailed.

"There's no reason for you two to tag along, and you'd be safer in your beds. Less chance of things going wrong. I'll have enough on my hands as it is."

Granny had also insisted that Gia wear "proper clothes."

"The people you are going to speak to, they care about that kind of thing. Don't give them an excuse to ignore you. And if you go as you are now, they'll not let you in the door."

So Gia had washed her hair and put on her birthday dress. She'd also borrowed a pair of Saraswati's shoes that fit her well enough but were far from comfortable.

"Okay, nearly there now," said Fatima, turning into Bree Street. "Hey! This time I even remembered to put on the indicator."

She laughed at Gia's horrified expression. "Oh, chill. No lives lost yet. And not a scratch on the car either, which is what really matters. If Manny figures out I drove his car, he'll have my guts for garters. There." She slowed and stopped, mostly in a vacant parking space.

"Ah, what the hell, good enough."

She pulled up the handbrake and switched off the engine. "You sure you don't want me to come along?"

"No, really, Fatima. Let's stick to the plan," said Gia.

They had decided that Fatima would wait at a nearby restaurant, rather than sitting in the car where she might attract the wrong kind of attention.

Gia opened the door and looked doubtfully down to the pavement, which seemed an unusually long way down. She jumped down and stumbled in her unfamiliar shoes.

Granny had no problem getting out of the enormous car.

"Let's go," she said, and Gia had just enough time for a hug and a "Good luck" from Fatima before she had to hurry to catch up with the old woman.

Granny walked sturdily along, staring about her. "Haven't been in town for too long," she said. "Things do change."

It was strange and a little awkward walking down Bree Street with Granny. Gia was uncomfortably aware that they must make a odd couple. Granny barely came up to her elbow, but she more than made up for it with her brightly striped headscarf and multiple strings of beads that clattered as she walked. There were quite a few people hanging about on the street, smoking or waiting to go into restaurants and clubs, but Granny seemed completely unaware of the stares they attracted.

"Now, before we get there," she said. "You got to act like you know what you're doing. Be a little bit arrogant. The old ones like to treat the rest of us like we're not worth scraping off their shoes. They still think things will go back the way they used to be, when everyone was pretty much their servants."

She laughed grimly. "That's the way it used to be, but that's not the way it is now, no sir. But no use reminding them of *that*. So if you behave as if you are the aristocracy, you'll have a better chance of being listened to."

Gia felt far from sure about this advice, but she did not argue.

"The two you spoke to, I've heard about them," continued Granny. "The woman is an old one indeed. She has many names, but I've heard her spoken about as The White Crane so that might be a safe name to use. The man, I think he's a recent arrival. Bad lot, that one. If he's the one I'm thinking of, they call him the Blind Man. But don't make the mistake of thinking he's actually blind. No such thing."

"I know," said Gia with a shudder. "Do you think I'll have to speak to him?"

"I don't know," said Granny. "Let's take things as they come. Just be respectful and you should not come to any harm."

"I thought you said I had to be arrogant."

"You do! But that doesn't mean you have to be rude."

Gia had to laugh at this. They turned down a side street and she could see Long Street up ahead.

"Pretend to be your mother. That should do it," said Granny. "In fact it's in your favour that Saraswati is your mother. They know that, don't they?"

"They do."

She could see the entrance to the club now, with the troll bouncer standing outside. As they approached, Granny tugged at her sleeve.

"One more thing," she said. "Don't eat or drink anything they give you. You know that, right?"

"Okay. But aren't you going to be with me?"

Granny did not answer. There was a crowd outside the club, lining up to go inside. Gia realised that there must be some act or other, and a popular one at that.

She headed for the back of the queue, but Granny grabbed her arm and propelled her toward the bouncer. It was the same troll who had been at the door the last time Gia had been to the club.

He wore the same leather jacket, and Gia saw that each sleeve had a row of decorative buttons. Brass buttons, inset with black stone.

He did not look around at their approach and to Gia's horror Granny tugged at his sleeve and shouted "Excuse me!" over the thump of the music coming from inside the club. Gia took a step back as the troll turned.

"Young lady here needs to speak to you," said Granny.

For a moment Gia and the troll eyed one another. Then Gia got her words in line.

"I wanted to thank you for helping me the other night," she said. "I would have fallen without your help."

The troll's eyes narrowed, and he thrust out his jaw. "What?"

Gia had to fight the urge to step back. "You helped me. At the ladder? Down the—?"

He gave a warning snort. "What do you want?"

Several of the people in the queue had noticed them now, and were watching.

"I need to speak to— the woman."

The troll blinked. "Hmm," he rumbled. "But does she want to speak to you?"

"She will, when she hears what I have to tell her," said Gia. Then she jerked her chin at the growing audience. "But I can't say any more out here."

"Hmm," said the troll.

He turned and spoke to someone behind him, then gestured that Gia and Granny should step aside. "You wait here," he said when Granny made as if to protest.

Gia wished she'd brought a jacket. It was not cold, but she felt exposed wearing just the dress. Everyone was staring at her now, and it seemed a long time before a man stepped out from behind the troll and beckoned for them to come inside.

"Not you," he said as Granny made to follow, and the troll put out one of his arms to bar her way.

Gia opened her mouth to argue, but caught Granny's eye, and shut it again.

"Go ahead, girl," said Granny. "Go on. I can't help you anyway past this. Remember what I said."

Gia wanted to say something, but the man was already disappearing back into the club, and she had to hurry to catch him up. She tried to see more of him, but he walked quickly down the stairs so all she could tell was that he was young and had long brown hair. Instead of going down the main stairs to the club, he pulled aside a part of the fabric that draped the walls, and opened a door.

"Are we going in that...tunnel again?" she called out.

Granny might say what she like about good impressions, but it would not be fun negotiating manholes and underground tunnels in these clothes.

"No," the man said over his shoulder. "You're lucky. The Lady is upstairs tonight. Wouldn't let you go to the tunnel anyway, not without a blindfold."

The man unlocked another door, and this time they were outside, going up an exposed staircase. Gia climbed, wincing as the metal stairs rang under her heels.

At the top of the stairs was a door protected by a rusty metal grid. It did not look like much, an unimportant back-entrance, except for the fact that there was a troll standing in the shadows on each side of it.

"Stop here", said the man who'd been guiding them, and knocked on the door.

Gia tried not to shiver as she waited. Her heart was pounding, and not just from the climb.

Somebody opened the door.

It was the white-haired girl who had been Gia's guide when she'd been blindfolded. She met Gia's eye for a moment, but showed no sign of recognition or greeting.

"You can go back," she said to the man, and "come," to Gia.

ಌO೩

The corridor beyond the door was quite empty. The floor was tiled with red, white and black tiles, but they were broken, with large stretches missing. The windows had been painted over, so very little light came in from outside. There were several doors, but only one of them had slivers of light shining round its edges.

The girl went to this door and knocked softly. A voice said something from inside, and the girl opened the door, blocking Gia's view.

"My lady," she said.

Once again a voice spoke, and the girl nodded, then turned and beckoned to Gia.

By now, Gia felt ill. Her shoes clattered on the tiles and she wished she'd thought to wear something more sensible. Remembering Granny's words, she drew in a breath and straightened her spine.

Pretend to be your mother.

It was a different room, but just as dark as the previous one had been. It was lit by two white-shaded paper lanterns that glowed on the face and hair of the ivory woman.

The White Crane, Gia told herself, and made herself meet the woman's regal stare.

"You can go now. I will call you when I need you."

The white-haired girl bowed and backed out the door, closing it behind her.

The woman said nothing, and Gia felt herself starting to lose what self-confidence she had.

Better say something.

"Thank you for agreeing to see me," she said, and bowed slightly. She was relieved to find that there was no one else in the room. The ivory woman was bad enough, but she was not sure if she could have faced the Blind Man as well tonight.

"Why have you come?" said the woman. "And how did you know to find me here?"

Gia's eyes were adjusting to the lack of light, and she could make out that the woman was sitting perfectly still, her bony hands folded in her lap.

Gia swallowed. "I have a request." She was proud of how calm her voice sounded. *What had that girl called her?* "My lady," she added belatedly.

The woman did not nod, or blink, or stir a finger and Gia felt the silence sucking at her, tempting her to fall into nervous chatter. Instead she closed her mouth, and waited.

At last the woman spoke. "You have a request. Why should I listen to you?"

"If you don't," said Gia, "then I won't be able to help you."

She dared to look at the woman's face and saw her eyebrows twitch into a frown.

"You mean, you won't be able to spy for me. Is this blackmail?"

"Oh, no!" said Gia. "No, it's nothing like that. If you would allow me to explain?"

Again Gia felt her ignorance about the polite way to speak to such a person, but the woman did not seem to take offence. The white face nodded once.

"You know about my mother, Saraswati? I think you know what she is?"

The woman nodded again.

"You probably know what has happened. That she's— that she's gone?"

"I have heard. And I've heard of the manner of her leaving."

"Then you know that she's not coming back."

Again, that single nod.

"The thing is, without my mother, my father cannot run his business. If I was staying at home I could help but now I'm leaving to, well, to spy for you. At Special Branch."

The black eyes blinked twice, slowly, and Gia

wondered what thoughts or emotions lived behind them. It would be easy to think of this woman as a lifeless carving, an automaton incapable of emotion.

"I cannot leave my family like that, my lady," she said. "And I cannot break my word to you. How can I resolve my dilemma?"

The eyes closed briefly as The White Crane nodded. "You speak well. I acknowledge your right to ask my help in this. As you are my spy, you are under my protection, at least for as long as you remain useful."

The cold black eyes were staring at her again. "Some would say that you are presumptuous to demand this from me before you've even proved your worth. But then again, some would say that the very presumption is proof of your worth. I have no use for blind obedience. What is the nature of the help your father requires?"

Gia hardly dared hope.

"He needs a skilled seamstress, my lady. Somebody who can put together garments, and not just doing the seams or pressing things, somebody who can work creatively, under his guidance."

"I see."

For a few moments the woman looked down at her hands. Then she rose, and took up one of the lanterns. She moved deeper into the room and by its light Gia could see tall shelves of books and many boxes piled on top of one another. She had an impression of haste, as if these things had been moved into the room in a hurry, and would be moved out again soon.

White Crane bent and pulled something from a shelf, then returned to the table with it. It was a narrow black box, made, as far as Gia could tell, from black leather.

"Come."

Gia hesitated, then stepped closer as White Crane unfastened the metal studs that closed the leather box.

"Do you know what this is?"

The box was filled with row upon row of small white objects, ivory rectangles, each with a tiny picture or symbol carved into its surface. They clicked softly against one another as The White Crane drew her hand over them.

"You don't?" she said, and Gia was surprised to see a smile touch her thin lips.

"This is a game. Mah jong. Maybe you've heard of it? No? No matter."

Her fingers were moving over the pieces, first picking out one, then another. "Some powerful magic here," she said. "You cannot read the writing."

It was a statement, not a question. The letters were not in the Western alphabet. The looked like Chinese characters.

"This is the East Wind," the woman said, pointing at a piece. "This is the West Wind. The South, and North. We will not release these, not yet."

Her finger continued down the row of pieces. "Red Dragon, Green Dragon, and White. Their time has not yet come."

She picked out two pieces, cradling them in her palm. They clicked together softly as she caressed them. "Plum and Bamboo," she said, speaking down to them.

"Yes. These will do."

৪০০৫৪

"So, after I point blank *forbade* you to have anything to do with these people, you went out anyway, in the middle of the night, and let Fatima, who is too young to have a driver's licence, drive you there? Gia—" Karel shook his head in disbelief. "What is the good of my talking to you at all? You do what you want."

Gia looked unhappily down at the two mah jong pieces that lay on the table between them. They were in the studio's workroom, she, her father and Mandy.

"Don't you have anything to say for yourself?"

"Dad, I had to go. I'm leaving! Today is my last day here—"

"There is no—"

"Dad!" Gia stopped. "Dad," she said again, more softly. "I'm going. There is no way you can stop me. I don't want to go, Dad. Do you think I want—"

She had to stop again, as her voice was starting to wobble. After a few breaths, during which no one said anything, she continued. "I have to go. If I don't go, they'll come for Nico. It's as simple as that. Now I can't leave you and Mandy in the lurch like this, which is why," she gestured at the mah jong pieces, "I got those."

Karel took in a breath to respond, but Mandy spoke first.

"Gia is right, Mr Grobbelaar. It's too late to go back now. That contract is signed and there's no two ways about it. We've got to make the best of it."

Karel let his breath out in an exasperated puff. "So you're against me too, Mandy?" But he sounded more defeated than angry, and Gia hoped that this was the end of the argument.

"So," he said, poking at one of the pieces. "How are these supposed to work?"

"We summon them," said Gia, relieved at the change of subject. "Or actually, you summon them."

"Won't people think it's funny that I suddenly have two assistants helping me? How do I explain that?" said Karel.

"The Crane said they're not visible. I'm not sure I completely understand, but they're not people, really."

"But they can sew?"

"That's what she said."

"You realise that that's exactly the kind of thing that can get us into endless trouble? Invisible magical help? If any rumours of this get out, that's the end of our good name." Karel sighed and poked at the pieces again. "I suppose I have to try. What do I do?"

"Take them in your hand, and breathe on them. Then you call them by their names. This one is Plum." She pointed. "And this one is Bamboo."

Karel squeezed his eyes shut. "I don't believe I'm doing this."

He picked up a piece and, holding it up to his face, blew on it. Then he replaced it on the table. "Um. Bamboo?"

There was a swirl of air, as if somebody had opened the door on a windy day, and the room was filled with a fresh, watery, marshy scent. Gia found herself thinking of mud, and frogs, and dragonflies. She was aware of a presence next to the table, although there was nothing visible there.

"You called," said a quiet voice. "I come."

"Ah. Yes," said Karel, and swallowed. "Thank you. Welcome. I am Karel."

"I am Bamboo. I see Plum's stone on the table. Are you calling her too?"

"Yes, I am."

"That is good."

The scent had faded, but not completely, and there was still the sense of outdoor spaces.

Karel picked up the other stone and blew on it. "Plum," he said, more confidently.

The next arrival was gentler. There was a scent of sun-warmed stones, and warm grass. Gia thought she could hear the murmur of bees buzzing.

Plum, when she spoke, had a softer voice than Bamboo.

"You called," she said. "I come."

"Thank you, Plum," said Karel. "I am Karel. Thank you for coming."

There was the impression of someone bowing, although how she knew this Gia could not say.

"We are here to help," said Bamboo's voice. "What are we to do?"

"You can sew?" asked Karel.

Both voices laughed. Then, "Yes, we can sew," said Plum. "Although I've never used machines like these ones here. These are sew machines?"

"Sewing machines," said Karel and glanced at Mandy, who was watching him with wide eyes. "Don't you like working with machines?"

"I don't know," said Bamboo.

"I've never tried," said Plum. "We both sew very well, very quick. But we're willing to learn."

"I can show you how," said Mandy, her voice a little shrill. "It's not difficult."

A movement attracted her attention and Gia saw that Minou was at the open door. The cat stared at the spot the voices came from, eyes wide, first at one place, then the other. For a moment she puffed out her fur, then shuddered it flat again. She walked slowly across the floor and extended her pink nose for a sniff.

Then she gave a little "brrrp" of greeting and jumped up on Gia's lap where she sat smoothing down the fur on her flank with deft licks.

Karel snorted a small laugh, and visibly relaxed. "Well, it seems her ladyship approves at any rate," he said. "Let's get to work."

☙O☙

THE LIESBEEK

Gia looked from the Special Branch pamphlet to the suitcase on her bed. The list of things she was allowed to pack was short. In fact, it was more of a list of things she was not allowed to pack.

No toiletries, perfumes or cosmetics. No books or writing materials. No electronic devices, e.g. cameras, texters.

Nico sat on her bed, watching her. She was not sure he understood that she was leaving. And as far as she knew, nobody had spoken to him about Saraswati's transformation.

What do you say?

What sense had he made of what he'd seen? It was no wonder he was traumatised. At least he was up and about now, and had even eaten some breakfast.

Still no speaking, though.

She looked at her half-full sketchpad, and reluctantly decided that it must fall under "books or writing materials" and set it aside. She'd packed what she could. Underwear, socks, and some t-shirts and jeans, but according to the pamphlet she would be wearing a uniform most of the time.

What about pyjamas?

That thought led to another.

Where will I be sleeping? Will I have to share a room?

It was the uncertainty that woke the butterflies in her stomach. By this time tomorrow, she'd be there. But where would that be? Her imagination drew blank, and that frightened her.

What else should I pack? Running shoes?

How long will it be before I can come home again?

She sat on her bed next to her brother and put her head on her knees, feeling overwhelmed. It was not just that she was going to join Special Branch. She was going as a spy. And that, too, was unknown. What would she be asked to do?

She felt Nico's hand on her shoulder, a light touch that made her sit up and look at him.

"You go look?" he said. "Mom?"

Surprise drained her ability to speak.

His gaze was intent, frowning a little with concentration to find the right words.

"You— go find Mom?"

"I— I don't know where she is, Nico."

He shrugged, as if she'd said the obvious, and looked suddenly so like his mother that Gia felt a lump in her throat.

"You know I'm going away, right, Nico?"

He nodded.

"And I won't be back for a long time."

Another nod.

The sound of her father's footsteps made her sit up. He climbed up into her room.

"You finished packing?" said Karel.

"I think so."

"That suitcase big enough? You can borrow—"

"I think it's okay, thanks, Dad."

There was an awkward pause. Gia cast around for something safe to talk about.

"So I'm giving you a lift then, tomorrow morning?" said Karel.

"Would you, Dad? I've got to be there before six."

"Of course I'll take you. How else were you going to get there?"

"Thanks, Dad."

"Good."

And then, "Gia, I was thinking. I know it's not full moon tonight, but I was thinking of all of us going down to the Liesbeek."

Gia looked at him. "You mean, go to the place where Mom used to go when the moon was full? To wait for— ?"

"That's right," said Karel.

ಸಿOಜ

There was very little traffic along Liesbeek Parkway, so late at night.

Gia could not help looking up the turn-off to Valkenberg as they drove past. There was a guard on duty, silhouetted against the light from the guard-post.

That's where I'm going tomorrow, she told herself, and shivered.

Not much farther along, her father turned the car into a side street that led to a bridge. He pulled off onto the grassy bank. It was very quiet after the sound of the engine and for a while they just sat in the car, listening. Then Karel unbuckled his seatbelt.

"Let's go."

It was not nearly as dark as Gia had expected.

The streetlights all along Liesbeek Parkway lit a wide area of grass and reed between the road and the river, and there was the occasional sweep of headlights from a passing car. Frogs cheeped, and she could hear the rushing of the river, quite low this late in the summer.

She held Nico's hand and the two of them followed Karel down a path that led in between the reed beds, until they were quite hidden from the road.

For a while she could not see the river, as it was behind a screen of tall bamboo, but all at once they came out from the reeds to a wider grassy space, where they could look out onto the river.

Karel stopped where he was.

"This is where she used to wait," he said. "Just down there on the bank."

Gia looked up at the sky then along the river on either side.

All she could see were the silhouettes of the trees, stirring slowly in the night breeze. She could hear the breeze as well, rustling in the stand of bamboo behind her. Other sounds came to her ears.

A soft cheep-cheep of a bird nesting in the grass. The all-pervasive creaking of crimpers, such a constant sound that one almost stopped hearing it. Frogs peeped, and maanbesies sang their silvery sounds. Every now and then there was wavering whistle-cry of a mousekink.

Nico stood close against her, shivering slightly in the chill night air. She put an arm around him, drawing comfort from his warmth.

All three of them started at the alarm cry of a disturbed paddawagter some way up the bank. For a few minutes Gia stood tensely waiting, not sure what she expected to hear, but gradually, as nothing happened, she relaxed again.

So this is where she came. Every month.

She could almost see it. Her mother, still as a shadow, waiting on the bank below. The moon would be full, so the shadows would be sharp edged, distinct. Which direction would they come from, the swan sisters? Maybe they came drifting quietly along the river itself. Or they might glide in on wide wings to settle on the bank.

Graceful women, as dark-haired as her mother.

"Hey."

Her father's voice started her out of sleep. She'd been nodding where she stood, deep in her dream of swan wings and moonlight. Nico was sitting on the grass at her feet, leaning against her legs. She could hear by his breathing that he was asleep.

"Dad?"

"Yes?"

"Have you been coming here every night?"

"Yes."

"Since Mom left?"

"That's right."

She saw her father's shoulders rise and fall in a sigh. "Well, we better get going, Gia. It's getting late and you've got an early start."

"Dad?"

"Yes, Gia?"

"You know I don't want to go, right?"

"I know, Gia."

He picked up the sleeping Nico, and they turned to go back to the car.

Gia woke to find Mandy bending over her with a cup of tea.

"Mandy?" She tried to see her alarm clock. "What time is it?"

"Don't worry, you're not late. I came in a bit earlier today. Can't have you leaving without saying goodbye now, could I?"

Gia rubbed her face in an effort to wake, then took the tea from Mandy.

"Better get up," said Mandy. "Your father's getting breakfast ready."

When she got down to the kitchen, she found her father busy at the stove.

"Pancakes!" he said. "Send you off in style."

She put her suitcase down, and returned his smile. There was a dull ache in her stomach, and she was far from sure she'd be able to eat anything. "Thanks, Dad."

Despite the nerves that knotted in her stomach, she managed to eat a few pancakes. At last, Mandy glanced at her watch. "Better go.".

Gia put her plates in the sink. "Dad, I meant to ask you. Would it be possible — Could I — ?"

"Spit it out, Gia."

Gia took a breath. "I was wondering, if I might take Mom's silver bracelets with?"

Karel did not react.

"I thought, you know, most of the other cadets are Purists. If I'm wearing bracelets they'll assume I'm one too."

He nodded. "Good idea. I'll go get them."

A moment later he was back. Gia made as if to open her suitcase.

"Better put them on," said her father.

The bracelets were stiff, and at first she thought that they would not fit, but with some pressure they slid onto her arm. They felt strange. Cold, and heavier than she'd guessed they would be.

"Better get going," said Mandy again.

"Nico still asleep?" asked Gia.

Mandy nodded.

"I'll just look in on him."

Nico was curled up with the blankets pulled up over his head, his skinny legs sticking out the bottom. Gia smiled down at him.

"Bye, Nico," she whispered. "Look after Dad, will you?"

She waved a finger at Poepie, who peeped out from his cage.

Then it was Mandy, in the hallway. She put her suitcase down for the hug.

"You're coming back soon, aren't you?" said Mandy into her ear, then holding her at arm's length. "When are you coming back?"

"I don't know, Mandy. Maybe not for a while."

Mandy pulled her in for another hug. "You be careful, girl."

When she was free again, Gia said, "Will you say goodbye to Fatima and Ben and Sonella? I never got a chance to say proper goodbye to them."

"Well, it's not like you're going to the other side of the world, is it?" said Mandy. "You'll soon be seeing them yourself."

A car hooted.

"Oh, that's Dad. You'll tell them?"

"I will. Off you go."

Gia ran down the stairs and out onto the street, where her father was waiting for her.

ଛOଓ

About the Author

Masha du Toit is an artist and writer. She reads far too much, draws pictures that tell stories and writes stories about every-day magic. She lives with her musician husband Brendon and dogs Anna and Pippin in a sunny house in Woodstock, Cape Town, South Africa.

A message from Masha:

I hope you enjoyed this story at least as much as I enjoyed writing it. Why not review it and help others find it?

Want to be notified when the sequel is launched?
Sign up for the e-mail list at: http://eepurl.com/jNuxj
I won't share your address with anybody, I send mails very infrequently — and you can unsubscribe at any time.

See Masha's other books at masha.co.za

Printed in Great Britain
by Amazon